TRIBES, GOVER[...]
HISTORY I[...]

R

Tribes, Government, and History in Yemen

PAUL DRESCH

CLARENDON PRESS · OXFORD
1993

reet, Oxford OX2 6DP
'oronto
adras Karachi
ng Kong Tokyo
Cape Town
Madrid
mies in
Berlin Ibadan

Oxford is a trade mark of Oxford University Press

Published in the United States
by Oxford University Press Inc., New York

First published 1989
First issued in Clarendon Paperbacks 1993

British Library Cataloguing in Publication Data
Dresch, Paul
Tribes, government, and history in Yemen.
1. Yemen, history
I. Title
953.'3
ISBN 0-19-827790-3

Library of Congress Cataloging in Publication Data
Dresch, Paul.
Tribes, government, and history in Yemen / Paul Dresch.
Bibliography: p. Includes index.
1. Yemen—Social life and customs. 2. Tribes—Yemen.
3. Yemen—History. I. Title.
DS247.Y44D74 1989 953.3'2—dc20 89-9368
ISBN 0-19-827790-3

1 3 5 7 9 10 8 6 4 2

Printed in Great Britain
on acid-free paper by
Bookcraft (Bath) Ltd.,
Midsomer Norton, Avon

To my Mother and Father

Preface and Acknowledgements

It has come to be expected (and rightly so) that ethnographers give some account of their experience, of where they obtained their information, and of where they stand within anthropology. The last of these is important primarily to other anthropologists, and will take up most of the preface; but it is also much the most difficult to deal with satisfactorily. There are few things more irritating for the reader than larding one's text with what Stephen Potter would have called 'OK anthropology names' or bracketing what one has to say between portentous discussions of 'theory' as if the latter had some life of its own apart from ethnography. Perhaps, unhappily, it does. But the ethnography is what matters. We seem to be divided into those who argue theory with ethnography as illustration and those who identify theoretical sophistication with avoiding the asking of faulty questions. My sympathies lie all with the latter group, and more trust, I think, should be placed in readers than is now conventional.

Again, the genuine problems of ethnographic writing cannot be finessed by an appeal to personal experience, by an account of presumed agonies and ecstasies in field-work. My own field-work, I should say at once, was generally enjoyable. But even had it been miserable, this would be of only prurient interest. The stories are told somewhere else entirely, for specific reasons that attach to the place of telling, and few ethnographers have the literary skill to make such stories shed light on what in fact they did. One cannot, for example, pretend afterwards to a cultivated naïveté in the face of other cultures so as to enliven one's own account of them—not, at any rate, if one has read much ethnography or, better, many novels, biographies, and collected letters. One must expect life to be different here from there or then from now. Field-work itself is less a revelation than, as Weber says of politics, 'a strong and slow boring of hard boards. It takes both passion and perspective.'

Perspective is the more difficult of these to maintain, and with it a necessary sobriety and care in one's writing. I have fallen a long way short of what I would have liked. But the problems one is dealing with are, in essence, fairly plain.

> It is by recognizing that he is engaged in a dialogue of three—himself, the society studied and his fellow sociologists—that the objectivity peculiar to [the ethnographer] is preserved. . . . It is clear that if he eliminates any one of the partners . . . the dialogue is broken and he falls back into the collective representations of his own or the other society. (Pocock 1971: 105)

How far I have fallen back into one or the other will not be clear for some time: anthropology is certainly cumulative in the sense that as a profession we rethink what we do and decide in retrospect what it was that we left unthought. It is only in retrospect that one can do so. But I have tried to provide sufficient material for readers (particularly Yemenists) to disagree with me in the shorter term and decide, if they wish, on some other analysis than the one I give. There are other interpretations that come even to my mind, and if there are not the means for others to arrive at their own interpretations, then the fault is mine. Two points are at issue in saying this: that the analysis of any culture should be open-ended, and that anthropology itself, despite passing appearances, is in fact a collective effort.

Pocock felt himself to be writing within a specific tradition. A generation later it is this same tradition, however much developed or attenuated, that I am writing in here, not so much through some conscious choice as through trying all sorts of things and finding in the end that this was what made most sense to me. One must simply own up to it. The tradition in question gives an important place to the *Année sociologique*—to such writers as Mauss and Hertz; much less, be it said, to their teacher Durkheim—and after them to Evans-Pritchard, who promoted a certain reading of their work among a British audience and also a taste for certain other authors from Fustel de Coulanges to Van Gennep and Hocart. Those interested in what this list implies and yet not comfortable with it are referred to Pocock's short book, which remains one of the best available statements on the subject. Much has happened since his book was written, but rather little, I think, has been discarded.

Evans-Pritchard himself characterized anthropology's business as 'the translation of culture', and in his first major work gave a gnomic account of how one does this: 'I have tried to explain a fact by citing other facts from the same culture and noting interdependencies between facts. Explanations, therefore, will be found embedded in my descriptive account and are not set forth independently of it' (Evans-Pritchard 1937; 5). Towards the end of his life he put it in rather similar terms:

> Can it be said too often that in science empirical observations to be of value must be guided and inspired by some general view of the nature of the phenomena being studied. The theoretical conclusions will then be found to be implicit in an exact and detailed description. (Evans Pritchard 1973: 3)

The twist is in the last line. There are in some sense ethnographic facts, the things one works away at in field notes (and one can argue endlessly about what these comprise), but they have no sense until set in order; and their arrangement is itself the analysis. The corollary, of course, though less often discussed explicitly, is that no innocent or neutral presentation is possible, and topping and tailing one's account with long mentions of other anthropologists, if not mischievous, is usually superfluous: the damage has been done or the benefit reaped already.

To employ the method with complete consistency would require a very lengthy book. One has no option but to summarize, précis, and at points impose order all too brusquely if one is not to produce a long, nineteenth-century novel; and I have felt free to intrude my own explanations bluntly, particularly where there seems to me a risk of readers misidentifying Yemeni facts with facts from a Western background.

None the less, the declaration of method does impose obligations on any writer who takes it seriously. One always has to add something to what local people say and do if this is to be made intelligible to non-local readers. But rather than 'interpreting' actions, utterances, and supposedly 'key' terms one by one (on the model perhaps of Freud before the Pietà), or setting them in order by some formal analysis in terms quite foreign to the local system, one is trying to reproduce the ordering of items to each other that one found in the field and thus guess at the ordering principles. The test, I suppose, would be economy: how much has the writer added that could be struck out and leave the 'observations' intelligible? I have probably been clumsy and added far more than I should or is warranted, but the test of economy is one I have tried to meet.

Apart from the ancestral line which passes through Evans-Pritchard, there are later figures who in different ways attach to the same tradition and whose works provide certain bench-marks.

Louis Dumont is certainly one, David Pocock is another, and the Africanist, Thomas Beidelman, has for a long time seemed to me to exemplify in his work most of the virtues one should aim for. I suspect what I find attractive about all of them is that their ordering of material is rather sparsely done: one can tell nearly always when they are speaking and when the people with whom they lived, so one is free to disagree with the author's own arrangement. Godfrey Lienhardt is another author I should mention in the same connection, and his work more than any shows what 'translation' might involve ideally.

It is a common experience in translating prose to find the block coming not so much from the foreign language—one can see pretty much what is being said; one might even respond to it fairly well—but from one's inadequate grasp of English: one cannot think quite how to put it. The same is true, but more so, of translating culture. The difficulty is often not to 'know' what is happening, or even to acquire some practical competence in taking part (though one should not delude oneself that this is ever all that great); the difficulty is much more usually to find a form of words in English and a set of reference points from one's own culture to evoke what was evoked in the first place by one's reading or by what one experienced elsewhere. It is here I find my own greatest weaknesses. I do not know enough of my own world to do justice to the small parts I grasped of another, and unfair demands are made of readers that they share with me a home world that probably they do not. The only solution is to try to keep things clear and simple. But a form of words is always the answer to what seems an analytical problem.

Further afield, I have felt myself influenced by the Marxist theoretician, Louis Althusser, although neither his style nor his method, I hope, intrude much on what I write. Behind my reading of him lies reading Lévi-Strauss, though there is nothing formally 'structuralist' about what I do. But at least an equal influence on my own thought by now is the philosopher of history, R. G. Collingwood. What draws these disparate writers and many others together in my imagination is that all of them have considered seriously the relation between analysts and their material, and the implications of misrepresenting this. Their influence therefore shows primarily in the avoidance of certain types of statement, and in an attempt, at least, to avoid what Marxists call 'theoreticism'.

The book tries throughout to follow a method of particularities. There should not be one simple message at the end of it, though I hope there is a clear enough narrative line. The recurrent themes which I myself find interesting are those of autonomy in the tribal world, of continuity in tribal forms, of different concepts of time, and of relations between tribal practice and Islamic learning or nationalist ideals. There are others which readers may find more central than I do myself. But there is no simple relation proposed between 'us' and 'them', the 'West' and the 'East' or, worst of all, the 'self' and the 'Other'. I cannot say I ever met anyone or anything that might correspond to the last of these capitalized figments (I doubt anyone but an advanced paranoiac ever has or could), but what I met were a great many 'others', much as one might do anywhere. The relation between them and the impersonal patterns one has to construct to make sense of what they said and did is the stuff of writing ethnography.

A considerable debt is owed first to Shaykh 'Abdullāh b. Ḥusayn al-Aḥmar of Ḥāshid. I arrived to do field-work late in 1977, just after the President of the time had been murdered, and the bureaucracy was at a stand-still. I arrived in Khamir, unannounced and unsought, where I met Shaykh 'Abdullāh almost immediately through his son, Ṣādiq. At this distance in time one can decently confess that my first encounter with this famous person shook me almost witless. A certain distance was needed also before I could see how difficult a period this was in Yemeni politics, when it would have been far easier for any shaykh to send an anomalous foreigner straight back to Ṣan'ā'; but Shaykh 'Abdullāh made me welcome and, as I realized later, explained to many less trusting people roughly what I was. Over the years he was much more than kind.

Shaykh Mujāhid Abū Shawārib was in those days 'Abdullāh's right-hand man at Khamir and is now deputy prime minister for internal affairs. I met him almost as soon. He installed me with what were in effect his bodyguard, about thirty of us in a squalid barracks built in the Imam's day, which I took to be a slice of ethnographic life. Only much later did some of the men I had been living with point out that they went home every so often and had been wondering all along what unhappy circumstance kept me living there for so long at once. In retrospect I can only concede that it was good for my spoken Arabic. Mujāhid allowed me to go along with the rest of them when he went elsewhere to deal with local problems, which was often; and, whenever he could, he found someone to explain to me what was going on. A number of us who have worked in Yemen (Robert Wilson, Sheila Carapico, and myself, at least) have known Mujāhid at different places, at different times in his career. All of us have reason to be grateful for his ability to put one at ease in what would otherwise be difficult settings.

It was being 'Mujāhid's *naṣrānī*' (his tame 'Christian', an ascribed identity if there ever was) that gave me easy introductions to a wide range of tribal contacts. Even people on 'the other side' in a serious tribal battle proved extremely hospitable later on; they had heard of me already, and my association with Mujāhid was enough to suggest to them that I was not a menace. There were tougher social nuts to crack at some points, but these lucky associations early on stood me in good stead with most of them.

Six months based in Khamir also determined what it was I wrote on. At that time many of the major shaykhs were still estranged from Ṣan'ā', as they had been under the lately dead President, and Khamir was a lively centre of tribal affairs. People were constantly coming and going between there and tribes throughout the north. It became obvious that a 'village study' would leave one in the position of the wise men with the elephant: one might get a trunk or a leg, but not the shape of the whole beast. It is the shape of the whole beast that I have tried to sketch. Other views must be postponed for other publications. But a constant concern in writing has been to prevent the tribes appearing as a sealed society that entirely defines itself: they are not, and most probably they never were.

In that first brief period of field-work I got to know people from Banī Ṣuraym, Khārif, al-'Uṣaymāt, 'Iyāl Surayḥ, and Dhū Muḥammad, a very few from Sufyān also. But Arḥab, most of Sufyān, 'Iyāl Yazīd, and Dhū Ḥusayn seemed inaccessible at the time, when political troubles were at their height. On a couple of occasions I was told I should visit the 'Cubans' in northern Arḥab (who they really were, God knows), but it seemed on balance better not to.

When I returned to Yemen after several months off in California, things had changed. Many of my initial contacts were now in Ṣan'ā', the Khamir axis, as it were, having joined the government, which was informative in itself. But I was now able to visit more of

Sufyān, I got to know Jabal Baraṭ and al-Ahnūm, and I travelled extensively in the areas I had known before. I was in Yemen from December 1978 to June 1980, and thanks are due to the United Kingdom SSRC (now the ESRC) for support during much of this. My work was delayed by rather severe illness in early 1979, and by a bout of hepatitis in early 1980. My money ran out and I took a job with the German (GTZ) clinic at ʻAmrān which kept me closely involved with tribesmen's families in the area around Qāʻ al-Bawn. I returned in the summer of 1980 to write up my thesis at Oxford, which occupied me until early 1982.

A junior research fellowship at St John's College, Oxford, allowed me to do a further year's field-work in 1983. Thanks are due not only to St John's, but again to the SSRC for funding the project. By this time things in Yemen were much easier. I was able to 'fill in the gaps' by visiting much of Sufyān, parts of Arḥab, Murhibah, Jabal Baraṭ quite frequently, and even some of the areas beyond Baraṭ at the edge of the sands. The ethnographic present, when I use it, refers to the end of 1983. By that time I feel I knew Khārif, Banī Ṣuraym, Sufyān, the upper parts of al-ʻUṣaymāt, and the parts of Dhū Muḥammad and Dhū Ḥusayn around Baraṭ fairly well, the other areas less so. It is cause for regret that I never went to Nihm and know little of Khawlān al-ʻĀliyah.

My geographical coverage was better than I had hoped. My coverage of different kinds and conditions of men was not all that uneven. Although I had begun in 1977 with major shaykhs, by the end of even the first bout of field-work I had made friends with all sorts and degrees of tribesmen, with various 'weak' market people, some sayyids, and some of the few Jews who live in the area. In the following years this range of contacts broadened considerably, and I cannot say I felt limited in which men I could or could not talk with in what settings. The book is unashamedly about subjects which in some sense concern men more than women. I did not find it the case that I could not talk to women (indeed, some became friends), but most of what I know of women's lives in Yemen comes from my wife and from female colleagues. To try writing about it at second hand would be foolish. Readers interested in the subject are referred to Dorsky 1986.

The people I got to know best were usually tribesmen of about my own age, so we were all *shabāb* or 'young men' to start with and supposedly a bit more solidly enmeshed in our responsibilities by the end. My closest friends tended to be literate, though not all were by any means. There were several older men I got to know well. Overall, there is a certain 'shaykh's eye view' in what I have written, I suspect, because major shaykhs and the ethnographer alike, though plainly for different reasons, are usually trying to work with a broader picture than most people and discounting a great deal of detail: the corollary is that, having generalized of necessity, they are more likely than other people to be caught out by events. But this is a society of a kind that in any case demands one avoid too firm a narrative closure, which also should be borne in mind as a point of method.

The book has largely been written at the University of Michigan: the anthropology department granted a term's leave from teaching, the Rackham graduate school a faculty fellowship one summer, and the Faculty Fund gave financial help in preparing illustrations and indices. The maps and most of the figures are by Jaye Schlesinger, who did the work privately, and to her I should like to say a word of thanks.

Considerable thanks are due also to all those who helped me in Yemen. I owe a debt, as do all foreign researchers who were in Yemen in the late 1970s, to Etienne Renaud of the White Fathers. The Yemeni Studies Centre (variously retitled before and since) granted permission for the work throughout. Sheila Carapico and Rick Tutwiler were a great source of encouragement. So too were Dr Yūsuf 'Abdullāh of Ṣan'ā' University and Dr 'Abduh 'Alī 'Uthmān. Several other Yemenis in Ṣan'ā' were extremely helpful, most particularly Dr Ḥusayn al-'Amrī (at various times foreign minister, minister of education, and minister of agriculture). At the eleventh hour, in Michigan, Dr 'Alī Muḥammad Zayd al-Khalaysī provided a Yemeni check on a great many points of detail.

The number of Yemenis in the countryside who deserve my thanks is unmanageably large. 'Abdullāh Dhaybān (Sufyān) and 'Alī Shawīṭ (Banī Ṣuraym) I remember with particular fondness, a pair of wise and decent men whose kindness had stood up to a lifetime of rather fearsome politics. Yaḥyā al-Qudaymī was as good a friend as one could wish throughout my different bouts of fieldwork, also 'Azīz al-Qudaymī and Shaykh Aḥmad Shāyif al-Qudaymī, Ṣāliḥ Muḥsin and Khālid al-Raḍī (Khārif); Shaykh 'Abdullāh Fayshī, and 'Abdullāh Muḥammad and Aḥmad Muḥammad al-Aḥmar (al-'Uṣaymāt); Muḥammad Nāṣir al-Shāyif

(Dhū Ḥusayn); Nājī and Manṣūr Radmān (Arḥab); Sayyid Ibrāhīm Luṭf 'Ushaysh, Sayyid Muḥsin Sārī, and 'Alī Muḥammad Zayd (Ḥūth); Ṣāliḥ Nāṣir Shawīṭ and Shūkhī Muḥsin Shūkhī (Banī Ṣuraym); Muḥammad Ḥasan Dāris, Ḥamūd Muḥammad Abū Ra's, and Ṣāliḥ Muqbil Juzaylān (Dhū Muḥammad); Shaykh 'Abdullāh 'Ā'iḍ Ya'qūb (al-Ma'āṭirah); Shaykh 'Alī Zāyid (Murhibah); Shaykh Yaḥyā Muḥsin al-Ghūlī ('Iyāl Surayḥ); Sayyid Sharaf al-Mutawakkil (Khamir); and Shaykh Aḥmad 'Alī al-Maṭarī (Banī Maṭar). Many others deserve mention. But a word of caution should be added. We all disagreed about a great many things, and much of the fun of working in tribal Yemen was constant argument. One should not assume one can tell who said what or who gave me what information. Even documents concerning one tribe I very often got on to initially through someone from another. I carefully checked and rechecked what were the facts for whom, but the views expressed and even the data gathered, unless explicitly stated otherwise, are very much my own.

The mention of these friends and helpers prompts a small note on method. It is surprising when one looks over recent monographs how often anthropologists still seem to have (whether at the forefront or back in the shadows) research assistants, interpreters, porters, even cooks and such domestic retainers, as if set to take up again the white man's burden. This was not possible in Yemen. My comparative poverty was often a joke; most tribesmen had more cash at hand than I ever did, and those few who were literate had usually more urgent demands on their skills than writing out texts for a field-worker. The kind of inset verbatim texts from skilled informants that have added a dimension to monographs from at least *The Azande* onwards proved impossible to collect.

The modern supplement to such texts, the tape-recorder, was scarcely more practicable. Tribesmen tape-record songs and poems, but conversation is an evanescent matter between the persons present at the time: to tape it would raise suspicions of spying where it did not simply pin a man to some permanent statement and thus violate the care for specific circumstance which informs all that people say. Personal reminiscences of the past (set pieces, almost) one certainly could record. Engaged as I was in more general enquiries, I could seldom arrange the 'bracketing' that would set reminiscence aside as a separate and recordable genre. There is a whole project to be done on reminiscence and story-telling, but it would not have mixed well with general field-work.

Usually notes were made after the event (the responsibility for doing so was mine, as too was that for copying documents); likewise, notes jotted down in company about the kinds of things people thought sensible matter for a book (technical terms, names of places or plants), were later reworked with the help of friends, in an attempt to get the spelling and the turns of phrase right. There are now several Yemeni researchers doing much the same thing. The people I worked with, however, were not Western-trained academics and would have had no reason to write the sort of book I have: everything over which I labour would be obvious to them and vice versa.

The point at which we could most closely check our assumptions (so I found what they left unthought and they found what I did) was the endless discussion of cases and documents, going round and around until we could at last skip the explanations and just argue about the content. Such elisions of interest and practicality must, I suppose, inform most ethnographies. In the case at hand, the presentation of material in the book coincides with certain interests of those whose culture is the book's subject; and the shadow of what they said and did is apparent (to me at least) even in semi-conscious matters such as ordering the paragraphs. But documents, in particular, are not dead. They were a trace of something very like power when they were written, and that trace re-emerges as one reads them in company; the experience was valuable, and one began to see for once what Collingwood meant by 'reliving' past events by rethinking them.

How much my interest in history stems from the ethnography (which I have felt to be the case throughout) and how much in fact from currents within anthropology is impossible for me to say. A very noticeable development in the anthropology of the last two decades has been an emphasis on local versions of the past: Wendy James (1979) and Renato Rosaldo (1980) are two names one might quote to show that something important has been stirring on both sides of the Atlantic. A great deal of interesting work has been done on societies with no written record of their own. Another impressive body of work has been done on societies with literate traditions that have markedly non-linear constructions of the past (e.g. Errington 1979; Siegel 1979). Much less has been done on societies that use dates and writing, roughly as we do ourselves, and have a long documented record.

In expressing what seems to me to be at issue I have used some of Braudel's terms: the *longue durée*, in which patterns or structures outlast events; the much shorter term 'conjuncture'; and *histoire evénementielle*, the 'history of events' which deals with what appear as discrete occurrences (see e.g. Braudel 1972). Having started doing so, I found that colleagues dealing with the rather similar ethnography of Oman, from very different view-points, had found use for the same terms (Eickelman 1987; Wilkinson 1983). To go on and criticize the basis of Braudel's own distinctions ('conjuncture' is the weak link) would take us far beyond the scope of the present book, but all of us who have used his terms would probably agree also with the late Emrys Peters (1977: 81): 'Before social anthropologists . . . rush to history . . . they should at least know what sort of history they are treating.' I hope that something of the Yemeni sort comes across in what follows.

The relevant distinctions apply, however, not only to those chapters of the book that deal explicitly with the past, but also to those that use the ethnographic present or discuss the events of only the past few years. The image that has come to mind in writing (not so much in the course of field-work, be it said) is of 'layering', whereby one order overlaps another, the distinction between them being sometimes apparent in space and sometimes more readily in time. In any case, one moment at least of the anthropology I find sympathetic is itself more like history than like 'the sciences of observation and experiment'.

> In the organization of meteorology, the ulterior value of what has been observed about one cyclone is conditioned by its relation to what has been observed about other cyclones. In the organization of history, the ulterior value of what is known about the Hundred Years War is conditioned, not by its relation to what is known about other wars, but by its relation to what is known about other things that people did in the Middle Ages. (Collingwood 1961: 250)

One of the concomitants, as Collingwood goes on to say, is that the two types of venture have different starting points: the exact sciences begin with assumptions, often stated as propositions, while history begins with facts which must then be resolutely questioned and rearranged until they make sense. Anthropology is usually in this latter position.

Indeed, an earlier image Collingwood used of philosophical writing often comes to mind also, that of lens-grinding (Collingwood 1933: 214): one may well have a 'fact' in the first months of field-work, but only endless reworking of what one first wrote down produces anything useful. A book then reproduces the process. One starts with something obvious, as near a 'given' as ethnography gets, and by the end should be able, as it were, to see through it. But the course of this process should be determined always by the specific ethnography, not by arguments elsewhere.

This is not to rule out generalization, wider discussion, or even cross-cultural comparison (in the footnotes I have indicated where some of my own interests lie). It is, though, to suggest that such things might best be handled separately. Most of the arguments that might arise from the present work, if others happened to find them interesting, would be better had out, I think, in separate articles. Certainly they should not constrain or determine the ethnography, or the tail would end up wagging the dog.

This much therefore falls to the reader: that one take any work of anthropology, at first reading, on its own terms. One may decide that, in those terms, it fails. But by accident or design the form of the exposition will usually in fact connect with the subject matter. As I know from experience with published articles, there will be those who read the present book and, despite what they read, will believe it is all to do with 'lineages'; there are others who will think it structuralist, others who will think it functionalist, others still who will label it part of some other -ist or -ism with which they think they disagree. It is contrived, in fact, to be none of these. The style and content, for better or for worse, are less dissoluble than they would be were one writing on meteorology.

There remains the other half of Evans-Pritchard's prescription: one must approach the material in the first place with some general view, or one sees nothing at all. To list any more of the works contributing to my own views, at the outset or later, would be of little interest. But the decisions on what to do with other people's ideas (indeed, one's noticing the ideas at all, or failing to) are the author's sole responsibility. There is much more than convention, therefore, to the line that the faults are the author's and what is good in a book is owed to one's friends and teachers. It could not be otherwise, and correspondingly there is more than a long-postponed pleasure in acknowledging one's debt to others.

My supervisor in anthropology at Oxford was Edwin Ardener, who unfortunately died in the summer of 1987 before the draft of this book was finished. His students owe him a great deal. Most of us, I suspect, pay him the compliment paid to really fine teachers, which is to have him always at the front of that imaginary audience one needs when writing. Just how large my own debt to him is I have no way of knowing, but it must be enormous. As my other supervisor for the D.Phil. out of which this book has finally grown, I had the great good fortune to have Albert Hourani. Since then he has been kindness itself, always ready with help and with suggestions on yet another draft. In a long academic career he earned the reputation of never letting down a student; and the obligation imposed is probably not one to be repaid directly, by thanking him for his enormous help, but a debt to be discharged in Maussian fashion by passing it on to the next group and the one after. For the moment, my sincere thanks must serve at least as acknowledgement.

On Yemeni matters Professor R. B. Serjeant has been extremely helpful. We have rather different biases toward the material (his toward the sayyids perhaps, mine toward tribesmen), but I have often felt I am not doing much more than writing long footnotes to what he worked out in the first place. My frequent citations of his work point to only a small part of what I owe him. As great a debt is owed to Robert Wilson, first for getting me to medical help in Yemen when I could no longer move myself, then for passing on so much of what he knows about Yemen, and most of all for drumming into me over several years now some sense of how Arabic works. Were my eye for Arabic as good as his for anthropology, I should rest content.

Michael Gilsenan and John Wilkinson examined my thesis many years ago and since then have passed on parts of their different visions of the Middle East. Michael's work will be well known to anthropologists already, and to most people concerned with Middle Eastern topics. John's perhaps less so as yet; but his weightily impressive *Imamate Tradition of Oman* (1987) I'm afraid leaves my own work as a dwarf relative of his. Someone else will have to restore Yemen to its proper eminence. The Oman connection is strengthened by Dale Eickelman, whose academic acquaintance I made fairly late in the project. His energy as a correspondent is matched only by his energy as a bibliographer, and a long correspondence with him has done much to clarify my thinking as well as broaden my knowledge. Dale Eickelman, Michael Gilsenan, Albert Hourani, Michael Meeker, Bill Miller, and Robert Wilson were all kind enough to read the whole manuscript through in draft. Their suggestions and corrections have been invaluable.

Particular thanks are due to three students and friends of mine at Michigan: Walter Armbrust, Michael Fahy, and Andrew Shryock. They have all read large parts of the book in draft and supplied a good deal of criticism, but my thinking about the Middle East generally has also benefited enormously from their ideas. Their own books, when the time comes, will be better than mine, but mine is far better for their help than it otherwise would have been.

By far the largest debt of all is owed to Melinda Babcock, who was with me during much of the field-work from early 1979 onward and has lived with the writing of this book ever since. Throughout the whole venture she has been a model of courage, perception, and calm good sense I only wish I could better imitate. Definitely she was someone to 'go into the jungle with', or in this case the mountains; and her critical eye has been invaluable in the writing up. Whenever she came to a passage I thought particularly fine, she struck it out; for which my other readers should be thankful also. The index is hers. So too, I feel, is much of the book, but no thanks can express the worth of her help and friendship. Lastly, a word of apology to our son Patrick, who has had to put up with all this since he was born; in Britain, Yemen, and now America he has spent the first six years of his life oppressed by a monograph, which somehow seems too early to have that happen.

Ann Arbor P.D.
1988

Contents

List of Plates

(Between pages 226 and 227)

List of Figures

List of Tables

Transliteration

I CANNOT claim to be an Arabist. Those who are Arabists will soon spot that my knowledge of the language is essentially practical; although I was taught when I started what a diptote is, for instance, I would not always recognize one now (but then neither would tribesmen). However, anthropologists who do not know Arabic should be aware that the language is remarkably regular and its different varieties are often closely connected—with the result that an Arabist can, in practice, often play Mauss to the anthropologist's Malinowski and spot, without ever going there, that one has misunderstood what one heard. I have therefore tried to reproduce what I heard and read as carefully as I can. Very probably I have missed possible meanings (certainly I will have missed associations) which I hope the experts might be able to recover.

I do not have a trained ear. When in doubt, therefore, I have reverted to classical vowelling. Sometimes one really cannot tell what written vowel would correspond best to the spoken: for example there is a type of bean called *tujrah* or *tijrah*, and I have no way of deciding which, if either, is the better rendering. Consonants, on the other hand, are usually distinguished quite clearly (so, in the areas where I heard the word it was certainly *tujrah/tijrah*, though it may well be *dujrah* elsewhere), and the Arabic spoken in the areas north of Ṣan'ā' is, in any case, rather close to the classical language. My simplified and classicizing versions probably do not obscure all that much. But one should certainly not use them for any fine-grained linguistic purpose.

I have usually not inflected nouns and adjectives any more than tribesmen themselves do. Verbs are given in the usual colloquial forms. The transliteration employed is a simplified version of that in Cowan's translation of Hans Wehr's dictionary, and should, I hope, be fairly easy to follow: *th* for ṯ, *kh* for ḵ, *dh* for ḏ, *sh* for š, *gh* for ḡ, and *iyy* for *īy*. Initial *hamzah* is not marked. Some Arabic words I have treated as English words (e.g. Zaydi, qadi, sayyid), with explanations given in the text. The other terms, names, and phrases I have tried to transliterate sufficiently fully that one could write them accurately in Arabic. The Arabic *bin* or *ibn* ('son of') where it comes between two names has been given as simply b. throughout. Translations from Arabic works and documents are my own unless stated otherwise. Where I quote from other people's translations I have modified their transliteration to conform with the scheme used here.

1 Introductory

The people of Yemen are the most tender, gentle hearted of men. Faith and wisdom are both of them Yemeni.

The Prophet Muḥammad

Non gloriabantur antiquitus Arabes, nisi gladio, hospite et eloquentia.

Sephadius, quoted by Gibbon after Pocock

Yemen is the mountainous region at the southern tip of Arabia. The present book is intended primarily as a contribution to the area's ethnography, and particularly to that of a large bloc of tribes there named Ḥāshid and Bakīl. These tribes are important nowadays, when Yemen itself receives quite frequent mention in the Western press, both as the site of a large oil find (1984) and as supposedly a strategic point on the straits which link the Red Sea with the Indian Ocean. In such connections the tribes are usually mentioned also. But their ethnographic interest runs far deeper than current affairs. They have been much where they now are since at least the beginning of the Islamic era (indeed, they were prominent in the rise of Islam itself, which scattered Yemeni names from Spain to Central Asia), and tribesmen have always since then been prominent in Yemen's history. The aim of this book is to combine the history with ethnography so as to show not only what sort of identity the tribes themselves comprise over such long periods, but what their place is in the contemporary world. The country remains so little known, however, that a preliminary sketch of people and places is worth providing.

A SKETCH OF PHYSICAL AND CONCEPTUAL GEOGRAPHY

Until recently, Yemen was distinguished from the rest of the peninsula by mountain ranges and by its place in Arabic tradition, not by the boundaries of nation-states. Such boundaries are a product of the present century. 'Natural Yemen', for many

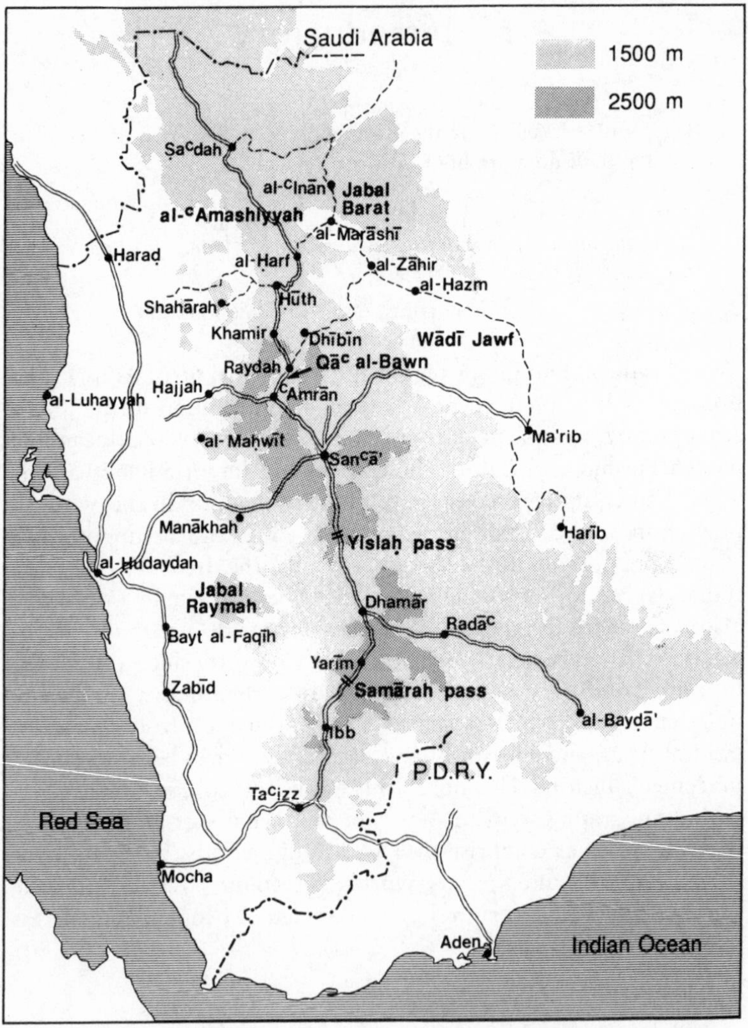

FIG. 1.1 The Yemen Arab Republic

Yemenis, would include areas now within Saudi Arabia (particularly Najrān and ʿAsīr) and perhaps even parts of Oman.[1] But two states now have the name in their titles, and between them occupy most of what traditionally was ever part of Yemen. The Yemen Arab Republic (North Yemen) has its capital at Ṣanʿāʾ. The tribes who form the subject of the present work are found within its borders, and most of the events with which we shall be concerned took place in what is now North Yemen's territory. The republic was declared in 1962 as the successor to the Mutawakkilite Kingdom of Yemen (the kingdom of the last Zaydi Imams), whose northern border with Saudi Arabia was drawn after the Saudi–Yemeni war of 1934, while the border with South Yemen (now the People's Democratic Republic of Yemen, capital at Aden) was drawn by an Anglo-Turkish commission before the First World War. From 1839 to 1967, South Yemen was in varying degrees occupied by the British. We shall occasionally have cause to touch on events there in the period before that.

North Yemen's eastern border with Saudi Arabia remains undemarcated, and the exact area of the country is therefore moot; but the figure would lie between 135,000 and 200,000 square kilometres.[2] The country is some 450 kilometres from north to south and 300 kilometres or more from west to east, from the Red Sea coast through the mountains and plateaux to the desert. (A map is provided as Fig. 1.1). The major tribes of Ḥāshid and Bakīl occupy the north-east quadrant, from south of Ṣan'ā' to the Saudi border and from the edge of the plateau eastward to the desert (see Fig. 1.2). The terrain on which they lie is mostly semi-arid plateau and mountain country at an altitude of about 2,000 metres.

The divisions between tribes in the north are territorial, and the vast majority of tribesmen and their families are farmers. Tribes in Arabia are often assumed by Westerners to be all nomadic, and we shall see in a moment that the same assumption haunts Arab intellectuals also; but these Yemeni tribes have been predominantly farmers since tribes were first recognized in the area in late pre-Islamic times (Robin 1977: 154–5), just as many tribes to their north, in what is now Saudi Arabia, have always wandered with their tents and flocks.

Arab historians, in Islam's early centuries, divided their forebears into two separate lines, the Northern Arabs (sons of 'Adnān) and the Southern Arabs (sons of Qaḥṭān), and 'learned genealogists do not differ in considering Qaḥṭān the father of Yemen' (al-Jirāfī 1951: 18). Qaḥṭān's descendants include Saba', and Saba' in turn had two sons named Ḥimyar and Kahlān. The first of these names is associated with the southern parts of Yemen (Kay 1892: 215). Most of the tribes from Ṣan'ā' northward are derived, by contrast,

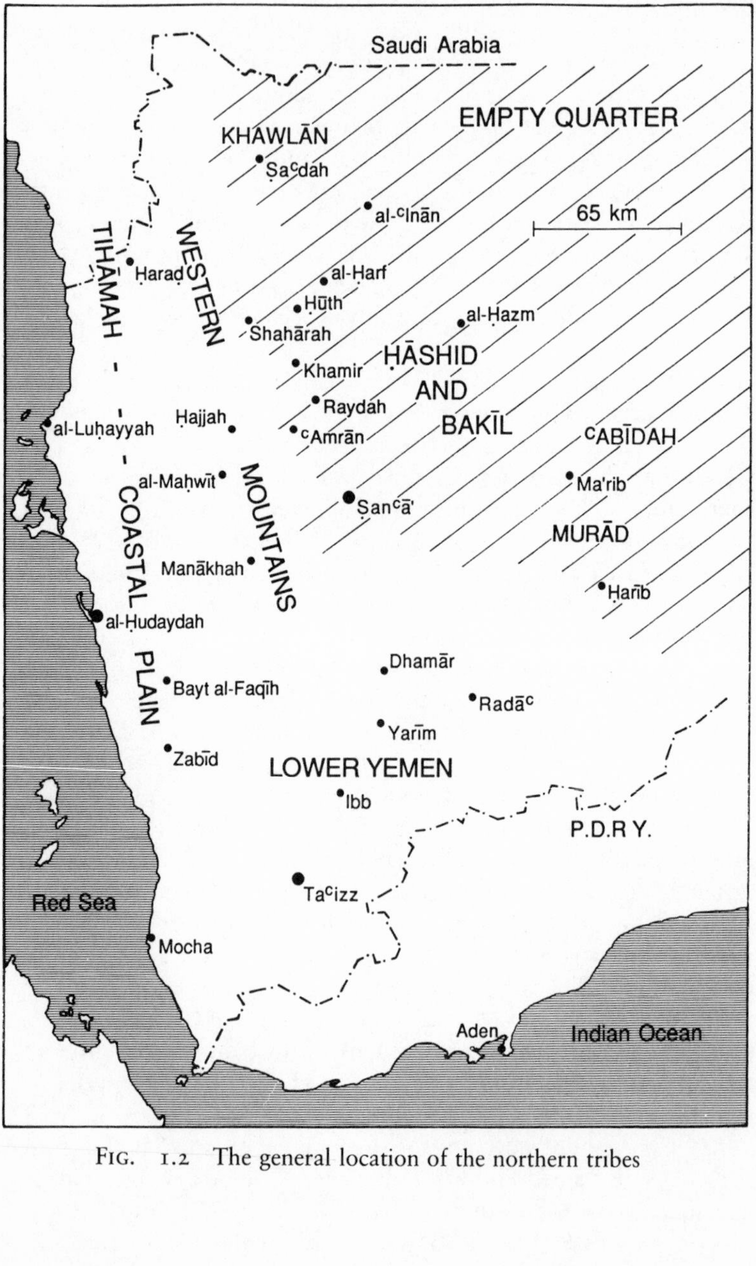

FIG. 1.2 The general location of the northern tribes

from the other branch of the genealogy: Kahlān begat Zayd and 'Arīb; Zayd begat Mālik, whose sons were Nabt and Awsalah; Awsalah begat Hamdān, 'and from Hamdān came the two tribes which are considered the most famous and the most courageous in Yemen; Ḥāshid and Bakīl, the two sons of Jusham b. Ḥubrān b. Nawf b. Hamdān' (al-Jirāfī 1951: 19). The genealogy is shown in Fig. 1.3. Ḥāshid and Bakīl can claim clear title to their place on the northern plateau, and it transpires that their names are indeed pre-Islamic.[3]

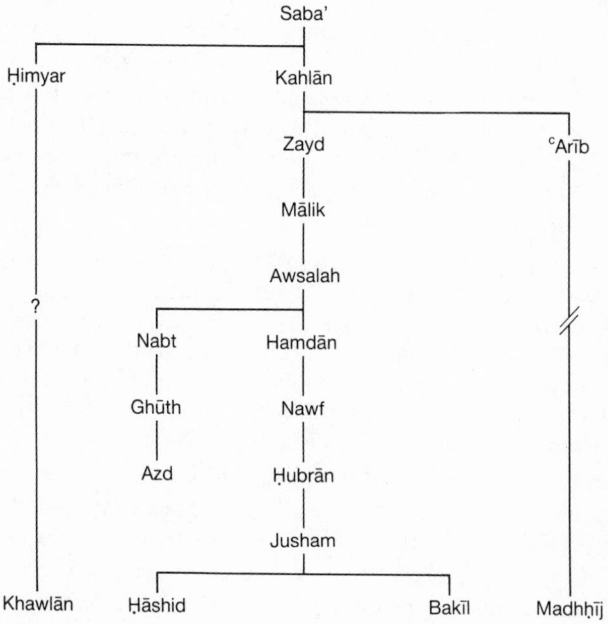

FIG. 1.3 Genealogy of Ḥāshid and Bakīl

Their more distant ancester, Saba', is identified with the biblical Sheba, and Ḥimyar can be equated with the Homeritae of certain classical authors; both names, in fact, refer one to the succession of major states that ruled much of South Arabia before Islam and built cities in what was later to be desert at the east of Yemen. 'The days of Saba' and Ḥimyar' is a phrase one hears often. The ruins of these civilizations and the inscriptions carved by them in stone are still to be seen, and there is scarcely a Yemeni author who does not devote part of his work to their antique glory. But, even in the highlands, the sites of what were evidently major towns are now set about with only small villages. The golden age was over even before Islam. The collapse of the Ma'rib dam (Qur'ān 34: 16) is the mythical moment of Yemen's own collapse, when many of the famous tribes migrated, and the tribes who remain are the inheritors of a fallen world. Indeed, the east, which was the centre of this 'high' culture, was ever afterwards a byword for disorder and supposed ignorance.

Tribesmen themselves are prone to contrast at least their prevalent disputes with the unity they assume was enjoyed by Yemen in the distant past, and the old Qur'ānic tale of the collapse of the Ma'rib dam is now reworked by others in modern form. An article in a collection called 'Toward an Arab Ideology', for example, argues that the interaction of the ancient states, in their decline, with tribalism from elsewhere has produced the present state of affairs.

> The loss of the state and the lack of political authority, or at least its weakness, led to a loss of security and a lack of order. From that point on, raiding became a means of life, revenge a sacred duty, force a means of self-defence and a sign of manliness. . . . From this came the badu's contempt for the peaceful, settled person who fears for his profits, who submits to sociability and who will endure any humiliation to bring his simple produce to market and safeguard his interests. (Ṣabrah 1972: 112)

The opposition proposed between badu (tribesmen, who presumably are nomads) and settled folk (*ḥaḍar*) suggests that settled tribes such as these must be the product of some freakish circumstance, which they are not. The author goes on to say that the image of the wild badu is more appropriate to the Northern Arabs, and he suggests the agricultural Yemenis fell under their influence to become tribal themselves. The natural development of society, he says (ibid. 115), would be from collective ownership to feudalism and then to 'more developed relations'—but tribalism has somehow blocked the process. The theory of society and history in evidence here is distinctive of our own time. Facts are readily sorted within a scheme of 'stages' that owes much to Marx and nineteenth-century anthropology, and by these lights, which are those of many *shabāb* or educated young men, the tribes and tribalism have a curious value.

By 'tribe' I simply translate *qabīlah* and by 'tribesman' *qabīlī* (*qabā'il*, one might note, may be the plural of either). But the Arabic terms have, for many, now gathered the same associations of the archaic that their equivalents have in English, as if they should properly refer to another age in history. Yet, at the time of writing (1987–8), the northern tribes are as powerful as they have ever been, the influence of their leaders in national government is immense, and the President of the republic is himself from a tribal background (from Sanḥān, in fact, a Ḥāshid tribe near Ṣan'ā').

An interview with the President in 1986 (*al-Majallah* 347, 1–7 October) posed what to many intellectuals was an obvious question: 'To what extent has Yemen succeeded in moving from the stage of tribalism to that of the state?' 'The state is part of the tribes', said the President, 'and our Yemeni people is a collection of tribes.' In fact there are distinctions to be drawn here: there is a sense in which 'tribesman' (*qabīlī*) for a townsman means almost any sort of country bumpkin, and not all rural people by any means belong to major tribes such as those dealt with here. The dominant theme in the western and southern parts of Yemen is of landlords and peasants, and these areas are in effect non-tribal. But the surprise occasioned by the President's answer is apparent in the article's layout: four pages of conventional political interview, of a kind one sees from most Arab countries, is headlined in large type, 'Yes . . . we are all tribesmen.' The assumption is made quite readily by intellectuals, and by others also, that tribes and states must be somehow opposites, whether the difference in practice is a matter of spatial separation or of 'advanced' and 'backward' elements in the same society.

The widespread modern imagery of 'stages', and of cultural evolution perhaps thwarted by the tribes' existence, is plainly different from the older image of genealogy. Yet the newer version reworks, and thus retains, most of what the older scheme offers. Again, the evolutionary image has an obvious affinity with recent ideas of development; but one of the government's most conspicuous development projects has been the 'rebuilding' of the Ma'rib dam. The venture has been funded largely by the ruler of Abu Dhabi, whose family is supposed, in the older tradition of the genealogies, to have migrated from Yemen in the distant past and thus to be in some sense Yemeni. Two versions of the past are brought together by a civil engineering project.

History and geography are themselves conceived in terms that can only be explained ethnographically (they are never neutral), and within such conceptions the tribes always have a place. Different views of what tribes might count for at present in fact draw on much older relations of physical and conceptual geography. Briefly, the tribes occupy the poorer, semi-arid part of the country toward the north and east, while the areas outside tribal territory, to the west and south, are agriculturally richer. The relation between the country's two poles is conceived as an opposition between north and south, between Upper and Lower Yemen.

In the desert areas of the east there was once extensive agriculture based on runoff from the mountains, and it was here the great kingdoms were based in pre-Islamic times. But throughout the Islamic period, Ma'rib and the area around it have been parched and poor. In the Tihāmah, the lowland coastal plain at the west of the country, runoff from the mountains was also used for farming, and still is nowadays; but the Tihāmah never matched the power and prosperity of the ancient east. The dominant area of Yemeni history for the last millennium and more has been the rain-fed plateau and mountain country running north to south. (A transect through the northern part is provided in Fig. 1.4.)

Yemen's agriculture, whether rain-fed or spate-fed, has always depended on the monsoon rains. Local details vary, but from October to March or April the winds come mainly from the north-east and for the rest of the year from the south-west, so that in the

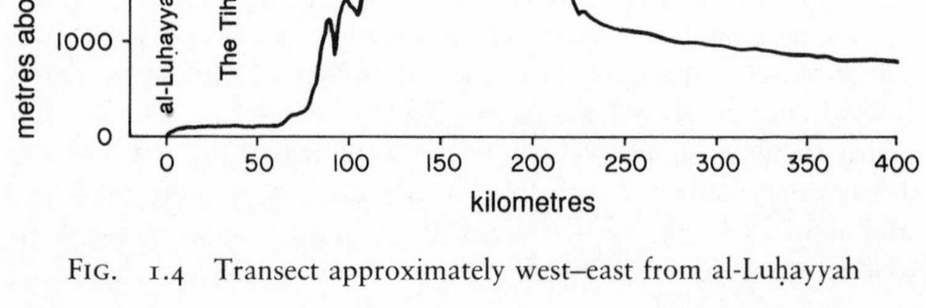

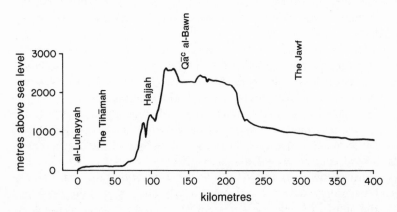

FIG. 1.4 Transect approximately west–east from al-Luḥayyah

highlands two periods of rain are expected: one in the spring, around April or May, and one in late summer, around August. The timing is crucial. As the proverbial tag says, 'God, don't send us the east wind before summer, or the west wind before autumn.'[4] The backing of the major winds at the right time is all that makes what rain there is useful, and the history of Yemen is dotted with frequent poor harvests, with drought, and with major famines. The mountains, of course, receive the bulk of precipitation. Rainfall in the southern mountains, in the area around Ibb, can be 1,000 millimetres or more per year, and Ibb itself is rightly known as 'the green province'. The western mountains, around Ḥajjah for instance, would expect 600 to 800 millimetres per year. But the average rainfall per annum falls off as one moves north and east into tribal territory (see Fig. 1.5) so Ṣan'ā' itself can hope for about 300 millimetres and Ṣa'dah for perhaps 200 millimetres.

Average rainfall of about 250 millimetres per annum is often quoted as the minimum required for effective 'dry' (rain-fed) farming (see e.g. Bates and Rassam 1983: 8). Yet the tribal areas of the north and east, where average rainfall is no greater than this, depend largely on dry farming for subsistence. The staple crops are sorghum, wheat, and barley. Within these areas north and east of Ṣan'ā' a wide range of techniques is used to exploit what rain there is: spates are tapped, wide areas of runoff are kept clear (often several times the area of the fields), and rain is channelled over rocky, bare terrain to the fields themselves along ducts or ridges *(masāqī)* built of stones or dirt.[5] In the more arid eastern regions, there is a greater reliance on herding sheep and goats; indeed, in parts of the east (and in a few parts of tribal territory elsewhere) one finds nomads, though not in large numbers. But the comparative poverty of the north must always be borne in mind. It is not surprising that its people have often been drawn to depend on subsidies from elsewhere (as in part they do nowadays), or to raid other parts of Yemen.

There is no reason to suppose that ecology has changed significantly in the last millennium or so (Gochenour 1984: 29). It would seem, from what we know at present, to provide a fairly constant basis for cultural and political history. However, cultural and political fixity cannot in any simple way be derived from it, and the comparative constancy of human affairs (over, let us say, a millennium) deserves noting as a fact in its own right.

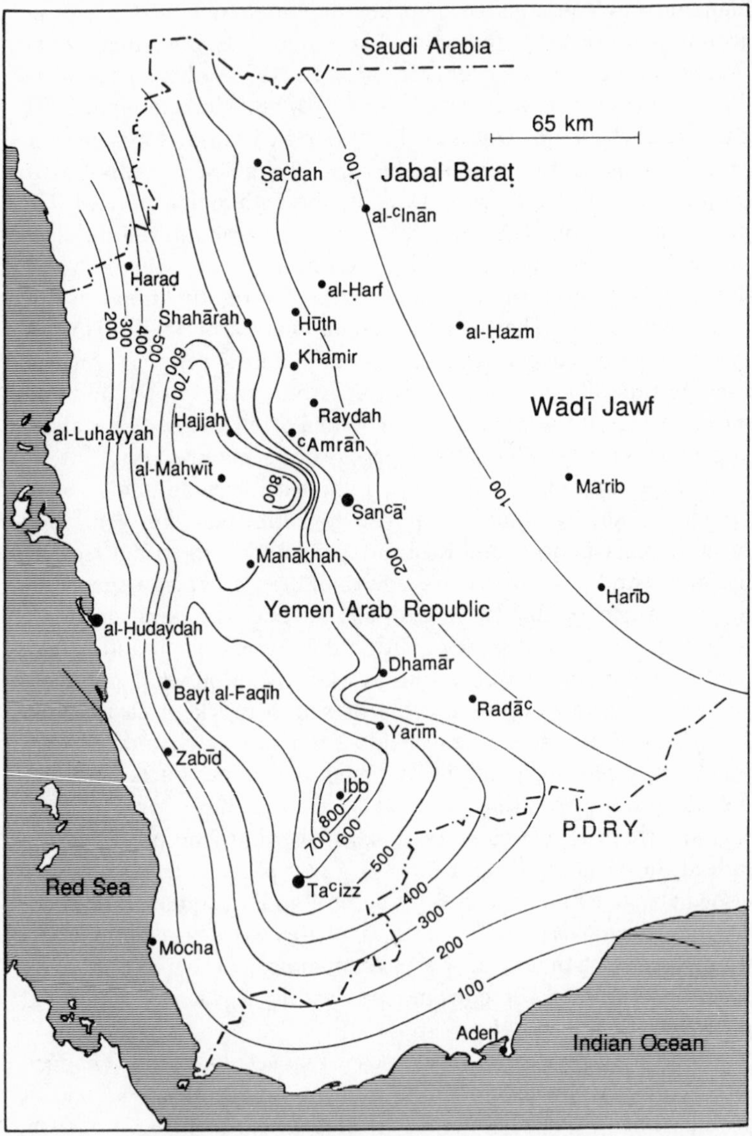

FIG. 1.5 Distribution of annual rainfall

The northern tribes have been much where they now are throughout the period, and from the end of the ninth century AD to 1962 were associated with a succession of Zaydi (Shiʿite) Imams drawn from the descendants of the Prophet.[6] Zaydism developed early in Islamic history and has little in common with later developments of Shiʿite ideas in such countries as Iran. Zaydi scholars were usually hostile to undisciplined ecstasy, the veneration of saints, or millenarian longings, and they promoted instead a rather sober religious style which is still that of most tribesmen today. The Imam was ideally both a scholar and warrior who could 'order what is right and prohibit what is reprehensible'. The Imamate's political fortunes varied greatly, but the association of Zaydism with the tribes is of long standing.

The southern mountains and the Tihāmah have been predominantly Shāfiʿī (Sunni) for almost as long,[7] being ruled by a succession of more or less powerful states and sometimes raided or dominated by the northerners. The Shāfiʿīs have much more tolerance for such practices as venerating saints, and they recognize less close an association than did Zaydis between religious doctrine and temporal power. The Imamate was the major difference between the two schools. Apart from this, the doctrinal differences between Zaydis and Shāfiʿīs are not very marked, and it is only at a few points in their history that either group attempted to suppress practices approved by learned men of the other. But the northerners, with or without the Imams' encouragement, often dominated or even occupied Lower Yemen. At several periods the Imamate controlled both ends of the country, and southerners today show a marked distrust of northern tribesmen.

Yemen has twice been occupied by the Turks, once in the late sixteenth century and again from 1871 to 1918. The two episodes are surprisingly similar. The history of the Zaydi Imamate in the north is itself highly repetitive, as we shall see, and certain of the Zaydis' enmities also repeat. For example, the Ismāʿīlīs in the western mountains were among the Imamate's earliest foes; they were attacked at several points in the medieval period (see e.g. Yaḥyā b. al-Ḥusayn 1968: 511); they were enemies of the Imam after the Turkish withdrawal of 1918; there are still Ismāʿīlīs in the areas around Manākhah now. Odder still, the Ismāʿīlīs received intermittent support over almost as long a period from their cosectarians in Yām, a tribe of Najrān, miles away to the north-east and now within Saudi Arabia.

Several features of Yemeni affairs thus outlast by a long way the events of history, at least from the tenth century to the early twentieth. In several connections we shall have to distinguish 'rules that outlive all events',[8] before we can understand the events themselves or changes in the more immediate patterns from which they arise. On the largest scale, there are distinctions and oppositions which between them organize a conceptual map of the country and have done for a long time.

Upper Yemen (*al-yaman al-a'lā*) stands opposed to Lower Yemen (*al-yaman al-asfal*), very often as Zaydis stand opposed to Shāfi'īs and tribesmen to peasants. A Lower Yemeni politician of our own time has worked this into a thesis explaining the disorders of political history.

> The escape of the fertile areas [of the west and south] from the Imams' control, or more properly from harsh and unjust exploitation by the mountain people, at certain historical periods provided the motive for persistent new attempts [at independence]. These took the form of constant struggles, which on many occasions tore Yemen into petty states each trying to gain control over parts of the country, to the point where the country as a whole has been unable to unify under a central government more than three times in the last eleven centuries. (Nu'mān 1965: 25–6)

Unity under a central government is as little questioned a value in Yemeni political rhetoric as in that of most modern Arab countries. The accusation that 'the mountain people' spoiled it is serious. The thesis is not in fact easy to sustain (whatever value one puts on it), and few educated Yemenis would miss the point that Nu'mān is arguing a political case of his own, feeling at the time he wrote that his fellow Shāfi'īs in central government were outweighed by the Zaydi northerners. But his argument only sustains an opposition of much greater antiquity: that between Upper and Lower Yemen, between tribesmen and peasants. 'Naturally the division between badu and farmers *(fallāḥīn)* was not a matter of choice. . . . It is a product of the land itself; the sterile earth which produced baduism and the green [fertile] land which afforded the opportunity for agriculture, (ibid. 21). We shall come back in a moment to this equation of the northern tribesmen with 'badu', the same equation ventured by Ṣabrah. What it obscures in such descriptions as

Nu'mān's, apart from the dominance of indigenous Lower Yemeni landlords over their own people, is that the northerners themselves are farmers.

The argument develops in ecological terms that find considerable support in the histories. 'When the area for grạzing [in the north and east] was reduced by scarce rainfall and its extent was not commensurate with the number of inhabitants, who multiply year after year, there was a temporary migration from their arid homelands to the fertile plains of the west and south' (ibid. 22). In fact not all migrations were temporary. One of the striking characteristics of Yemen's history is the way in which the northern tribes consistently lose population; and when the northerners move permanently to the west or south they usually cease to be tribesmen and become instead landlords or peasants like the people around them.[9] The 'temporary migrations', often in the form of raids, are none the less striking. Often they were indeed provoked by drought. But it is farmland that is most vulnerable.[10] Nu'mān's mention of 'grazing' again refers one to the 'badu', who bring to mind not only tribesmen, but tribesmen who may well be nomads: the polar opposite of the settled and peaceful peasantry. In these terms Nu'mān feels able to condemn 'the northern tribes who want to live without working in the fields because agriculture in their view is not honourable work the way killing is in accordance with the badu understanding of what honour means' (ibid. 29). In fact farming is reckoned perfectly honourable, and a man who did not farm would in most areas be reckoned no tribesman.[11] But that aspect of the tribal world is readily obscured in the language of political history. The imagery of violence and disorder comes always to the fore.

I have felt it worth quoting Nu'mān at length. He is a perceptive writer whose views, well known to educated Yemenis, strike a chord with his readers. But they involve a stereotype (a set of assumptions from which all judgements start) which is of very long standing: Upper Yemen is opposed to Lower Yemen as tribesmen to peasants, which is to say as warlike to peaceful, and in the end as uncivilized to those who might form part of an ordered state.

Such oppositions can be traced back also to Ibn Khaldūn.[12] The 'badu' for him were those outside the city and marginal to the order of city-based government: most were plainly settled (he mentions bee-keepers and even breeders of silkworms; Ibn Khaldūn 1967: iii.

249), but occupational categories are not the primary concern. All else is informed by the opposition between *ḥaḍārah* (civilized life), of which the most developed form is that of the city, and *badāwah* (less civilized life, the life of the countryside), of which the extreme example is that of nomads, the people Ibn Khaldūn calls 'Arabs'. This same use of 'Arab' to mean people marginal to civilized order is typical of the Imams and sayyids (the Prophet's descendants) at most periods of Zaydi historiography: for them the tribesmen are 'Arabs', though they themselves usually lived among the tribes and under tribal protection. Nomads are simply the extreme example. Pastoral nomads are rather scarce in Yemen,[13] but from the civilized, town-based viewpoint, or that of the learned, the settled tribesmen of the north are assimilated to them: they are all of them badu and as such are civilization's lack and at the same time its antithesis.[14] What is distinctive of the Yemeni case is that such oppositions are readily aligned with that between the northern and southern parts of the country.

There is, of course, no line on the ground. The areas directly south of Ṣan'ā' toward Dhamār, which interestingly are said to have switched from being Shāfi'ī to Zaydi in the seventeenth century (Zabārah 1956: i. 1/58), are readily assimilated to Upper Yemen by southerners and to Lower Yemen by northerners. The line between Upper and Lower could as well (or as arbitrarily) be drawn 125 kilometres south of Ṣan'ā' at the Samārah pass, or only 40 kilometres south of Ṣan'ā' at the Yislaḥ pass. In the last few years political rhetoric has given prominence to the phrase 'the central areas'—the points of reference here are North Yemen (Ṣan'ā') and South Yemen (Aden)—but again this is a conceptual location not firmly pinned to topography, and it in no way displaces the older opposition.

More generally *yaman* means simply 'south' of wherever one is, a synonym for *janūb* or, more commonly, *'adanī* (toward Aden). Its usual opposite is *qiblī* (toward Mecca). The terms for east and west are the standard Arabic ones of *sharq* and *gharb*. Their associations come out clearly only in the rhetoric of the tribesmen themselves.

Being a tribesman is as much a work of the imagination as a simple fact to be borne with. Many of the values to which tribesmen claim adherence are best exemplified in stories of wonders and heroic deeds, which themselves usually occurred at some earlier date or in some place other than where one is—and most often somewhere east of where one hears the story. The Jawf is the favoured location (the vast, barren wadi leading out toward Ma'rib), closely followed by Jabal Baraṭ in the far north-east of Yemen. It is there, others often suggest, that one will find the authentic (*aṣlī*, 'original') customs and the 'real' tribesmen, both in the sense of the fiercest, least manageable, or most contrary, and in the sense of the most generous, honourable, and fearless. The east, toward the empty desert, is the home of those furthest removed from the values of cities and government; and in a wadi further eastward still, beyond the next sand-hills or outcrops of rock, are the 'badu' who, predictably, 'speak the best Arabic'.[15] The west, by contrast, is where men or families go when they cease to be tribesmen: a land of comparative prosperity, but also of hierarchy and of order imposed by others. Further westward still is the Tihāmah, a hot, humid place, very much under the government's control, and populated by African-looking people whom tribesmen are inclined to talk of as being *'abīd* (slaves, or at least sons of slaves), which in fact rather few of them are.

In the views of both tribesmen and non-tribesmen, west is readily assimilated to south, and east to north. We shall see more of this in later chapters. However the details may be worked out in particular cases, the effect is always to cast the tribes as marginal to the ordered affairs of the state and of civilization. The recent addition of a time-line, whereby the tribes are reckoned not only 'ignorant' or 'marginal' but 'backward' also, or at best archaic, simply develops ideas already present. Time and space are now elided, as so often in national cosmologies, in the concept of a 'backward area', a concept to which most tribesmen themselves subscribe.

Ṣan'ā' remains for most people the centre of the conceptual as of the physical map. The tribes of the north and east remain contrasted with the southern peasantry in much the way we have sketched. Not only do tribes occupy what for others is marginal land, but, despite their undoubted power, they remain oddly marginal to the rhetoric of national government. The current President is from a tribal family, though he rose to influence through the national army. The short-lived President before him, who was murdered in 1978 as his own predecessor had been in the year before, was from a family of tribal leaders; indeed, he was brother of a paramount shaykh from a tribe near Ṣan'ā'. Yet in the years around 1980 it was often said, jokingly, but in some ways quiet accurately, that the government's 'territory' (*bilād*) stopped just north of the Ṣan'ā' ring-road. In the terms now natural to many young, educated people, there is an element almost of paradox in the tribes' position.

RECENT ECONOMIC CHANGES

Some of the conceptual features just sketched have remained fixed over long periods. But Yemen in recent years has experienced immense short-term changes, not least demographically and economically. Under the last Zaydi Imams (that is, from 1918 to 1962), little was done to develop the country. From 1962 until about 1970 most of North Yemen was embroiled in a civil war between republicans and royalists, respectively backed for much of that time by Egypt and Saudi Arabia. It was only in 1970 that development efforts gathered pace. With the boom in neighbouring oil-based economies after 1973, Yemen then became flooded with money from its emigrant labourers, a flood which started to ebb only in 1983; and in 1984 it was announced that Yemen had a major oil find of its own.

My field-work was done in the period between 1978 and the end of 1983. The corrected 1975 census (see Steffen 1978: i. 73, 92) estimated the total population at 5.3 million, of whom 630,000 were outside the country. A census in 1981 put the total population at more than 8.5 million, of whom almost 1.4 million were emigrants (CPO 1983: 25).[16] The population of Ṣan'ā' is estimated to have risen from 135,000 in 1975 (if anything, one would suspect an overestimate) to over 211,000 by 1981 (an underestimate, if anything).

Yemen has usually been a poor country. It had the unhappy distinction to be on the UN's list of 'least developed countries', and many of its demographic parameters bear comparison with the worst the Third World has to offer.[17] But by the late 1970s many people were financially well off, and foreign analysts in the country spoke (albeit off the record) of the economy as being simply 'a big party'. This disorderly prosperity was fuelled almost entirely by Yemenis working abroad (largely in Saudi Arabia and the Gulf), whose remittances grew exponentially until about 1977 (see Fig. 1.6).[18] The government at the time was often teetering at the edge

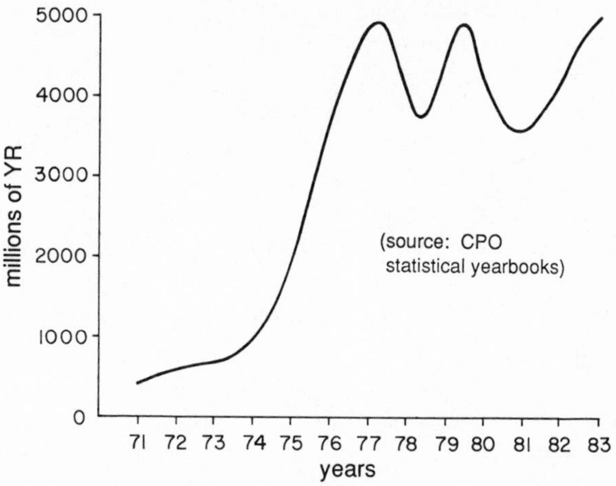

FIG. 1.6 Net private transfers (millions of YR)

of insolvency. With the flood of remittances came a flood of imported goods (see Fig. 1.7). Inflation was quite marked,[19] but the cheerful atmosphere of free spending went on into the 1980s: not only were consumer goods snapped up, foreign grain accepted as a normal staple, and shops filled with tinned food and cigarettes, but innumerable people bettered their lives with electric generators, water pumps, and trucks. It was a prosperous time.

The flow of cash to the country through private hands can now be seen to have peaked as early as 1977. The system was too decentralized for this to be felt collectively at the time. From 1978 to 1983 the boom was felt by most people in the countryside to be continuing, albeit at perhaps a slower pace. There had always been an element of competition and patronage in getting visas and jobs abroad, and if this sharpened slightly, then it was a matter of each individual's experience (and very hard to be sure of) rather than of mass awareness. Government efforts to fix grain prices, to ban the import of fruit, and in general to encourage Yemen's own agricultural production were felt by most people as arbitrary, disconnected events. The facts were brought home only in 1983. In the late 1970s the Yemeni riyal (YR) had been pinned (no doubt via the Saudi riyal) at 4.5 to the US dollar, but in 1983 this quite suddenly slipped: well within a year the exchange rate had doubled to YR 9 or YR 10 per US dollar. The curve of net private transfers shown in Yemeni riyals in Fig. 1.6 would plunge steeply after 1983 were it to be redrawn in dollar values.

Where so much is imported, this matters greatly. However, rural Yemenis in particular seem almost to have been expecting a set-back, and what discontents there may have been remained fragmented. The discovery of oil in eastern Yemen during 1984 may yet produce considerable effects. It would be a wholly new thing if central government could pay for itself and accumulate capital; but whether such capital can be usefully fed into agriculture and manufacture or whether it will be lost to the

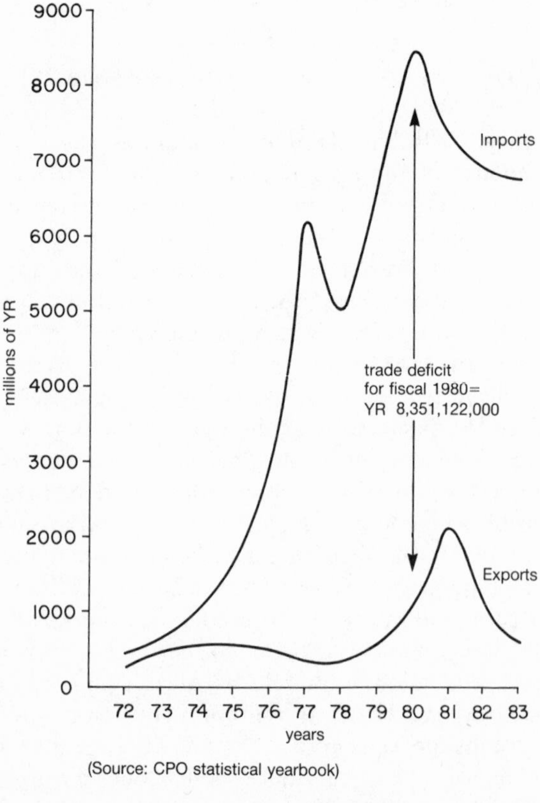

FIG. 1.7 Balance of trade (millions of YR)

military and to building follies one must still wait and see. Certainly oil will not be a panacea for the country's ills.[20]

The national economy and the government's expenditure are very hard to assess. The huge statistical literature rests on often insecure bases,[21] but of making economic models there is no end. In the late 1970s and early 1980s most money was outside the banking system, and in the north of the country Saudi currency was as freely used as Yemeni, so that the amount of money could not accurately be estimated, far less its rate of circulation. Silver Maria Theresa thalers are still widely used, and no one knows how many there are. To approach the matter through individual cases only increases the outsider's feeling that no sense can be made of it.[22]

In the northern tribal areas not all the money comes from migrants' remittances. Large political subventions, which appear on no one's accounts, are made sometimes by outside powers and sometimes by the Ṣan'ā' government, which in turn has acquired outside funds. In recent years North Yemen's neighbours, Saudi Arabia and the PDRY (South Yemen), have often been at odds. North Yemen has been caught between them, and for much of the period of my own field-work, in the years around 1980, the South promoted a National Democratic Front to pursue guerrilla warfare against the Ṣan'ā' government. The tribes were involved on both sides, and both sides wooed them with guns and money. This position bedevilled the country's politics and confused its finances, the latter being almost impossible to untangle. One can only note local cases. In 1983 (a quiet time by comparison with a few years earlier), certain shaykhs in the north-east, who were men of good standing but certainly not of the first rank, were getting some YR 15,000 or YR 20,000 a month from Ṣan'ā' and as much from Saudi Arabia. Such sums are not trivial. Again, some months after the murder of President al-Ḥamdī in 1977, a delegation of tribal leaders went to Ṣan'ā' and pledged their support to the new President, al-Ghashmī; when they returned to Khamir it was as if it had snowed, there were so many new YR 100 notes around.

Whatever the sources, money was being spent very freely in Upper Yemen in the years either side of 1980 and imported goods were a commonplace. In fact, imports were nothing new. A sketch of the position just before the First World War is worth quoting.

Hudaydah imports chiefly food-stuffs from India . . . a long way behind this most important item come sheetings, cotton piece-goods and yarn from the United States and Manchester. Petroleum, which penetrates further into Arabia every year, comes from the United States and Russia. Iron and steel for smithy forges, comes from Germany. . . . Finally, if a reader will try and imagine all that can be found at a general store in a rural district and label it Austria or Italy, the rest of Yemen's imports will be roughly represented. (Wyman-Bury 1915: 119)

Since then Japan and China have taken more than the share which fell to Austria and Italy; the pattern of petroleum trade has changed rather drastically; Manchester is not the power it was; and America, not India, now provides grain. But, if the detail and scale of the phenomenon have changed, Yemen seems to have been importing many of its requirements for a long time.

Wyman-Bury also mentions the rural Yemenis having a taste for elastic-sided boots; but unlikely footwear is now complemented by foreign cigarettes, elaborate lighters, tape recorders, television sets, and video recorders. Cars and trucks are everywhere, the most isolated country markets have imported fruit, biscuits, and fizzy drinks, small towns have shops which sell a wide range of cassette recordings, and winking fairy lights adorn trucks and tea shops. There is evidence everywhere of the recent building boom and every town has rows of welding shops making water tanks, decorative grilles for trucks, and extravagant gates for houses.

Among the things on which money was, and still is, being spent is *qāt*. This is a mildly stimulant shrub whose leaves are chewed usually at gatherings in the afternoon, where general conversation goes on until a torpid quiet sets in around sundown.[23] It is a pleasantly sociable habit. The Yemenis are no doubt tired of foreigners harping on it, and foreign writers have produced a tradition of mildly pompous condemnation, of which Hugh Scott provides a typical example: 'Altogether it is sad to see so much of the best land, above all land that might yield first rate coffee, devoted to this baneful little tree' (Scott 1942: 95). Except that coffee has an accepted place—and a price on the exchanges—in London, it is hard to see what sense underlies this. The leaves produce no more desperate effect on the user than does coffee or strong tobacco, and the institution of the *maqīl* or 'conversational gathering' where one chews *qāt* is a thoroughly civilized one: it is here that, according to company, crops are discussed, disputes mediated, poems composed and exchanged, or the fate of the country pondered.

The increase in *qāt*-chewing, the influx of consumer goods, the availability of transport by truck affected all of Yemen. So too did the spread of opportunities to work for cash as a welder or driver, or be a trader or entrepreneur. But a great many people were affected by this without altogether losing their earlier place in society. The 1981 census estimated that about 73 per cent of the labour force was still rural and directly engaged in agriculture (CPO 1983: 6). The 1975 census had documented the extent to which Yemen is a village society (see Table 1.1). Despite the growth of Ṣan'ā' and the comparable growth of many smaller towns, this picture remained broadly valid for the early 1980s. The emigration rates are startling (20 per cent of the male population is not unusual, and in some areas it was much higher at the height of the boom), but most emigrants return, after a spell abroad, to the villages where they started. Those who move into the cities usually retain links with their rural relatives and return to the village quite frequently. Most of these villages, as one can see from Table 1.1,

TABLE 1.1 *Population Distribution, by Size of Settlement*

Settlement size (no. of inhabitants)	% of settlements	% of total population		
0–50	53.1	14.5	34.1 (0–100)	
50–100	24.7	19.6		
100–250	17.1	29.6		86.6 (0–1,000)
250–500	3.8	14.3	52.5 (100–1,000)	
500–1,000	1.0	8.6		
1,000–5,000	0.3	4.4	7.0 (1,000–50,000)	
5,000–50,000	small	2.6		
Over 50,000	small	6.4		

Source: Steffen 1978: ii. 149.

are small. They are dotted fairly evenly across the mountains and plateaux of each area, though the density varies between one area and the next with the availability of land and water. The country is divided also into larger blocs by governmental divisions, and in Upper Yemen by the territories of different tribes.

GOVERNMENTAL DIVISIONS AND THE MAJOR TRIBES

Central government is based in Ṣan'ā'. Its presence elsewhere is organized by governorates, of which there were ten in the late 1970s and are now eleven (see Fig. 1.8).[24] Each provincial governor is assisted by such functionaries as judges, security officers, and military commanders. The precise divisions of responsibility are seldom clear. Local functionaries will often refer their differences to their respective superiors in Ṣan'ā', rather than resolving them on the spot, and much depends upon the personal abilities of the governors themselves.

The government, by the standards of most Arab states, allows considerable autonomy to local organizations. For example, three-quarters of the *zakāt* or canonical tax on agriculture was allotted to the rural co-operatives (*ta'āwuniyyāt*, usually known in the Western literature as Local Development Associations, or LDAs). A 'confederation' of these organizations, with its offices in Ṣan'ā', was greatly strengthened in the early 1980s, but the co-operatives themselves remain locally staffed, elected, and run.[25] Were one to write a micro-political account, then in many areas of Yemen the co-operative would be the main *mise en scène*. A broadly parallel organization of local 'committees' was set up in 1982 to provide a unified system of political involvement culminating in a General Popular Congress (*al mu'tamar al-sha'bī al-'āmm*).[26] This was received with a surprising degree of enthusiasm. Again it has not reduced local autonomy. What becomes of the hope that it will provide a workable form of national unity remains to be seen.

These extensions of government to the countryside are in formal terms the same throughout Yemen. Their powers are exercised very differently, however, in different parts of the country. A purely anecdotal version, proffered by several Yemenis, makes the point well enough: if a man from Lower Yemen deserts from the army, he is retrieved by force and his village is fined if they took him in; if the man is from the western mountains he is retrieved just the same, but what fines are imposed are probably allotted to local projects, not lost outright by his village; if he is from the north or east, then he just goes home, and probably takes his rifle with him. The story is an overstatement but is not without substance. Certainly in the areas north of Ṣan'ā' and east of the plateau edge, the divisions

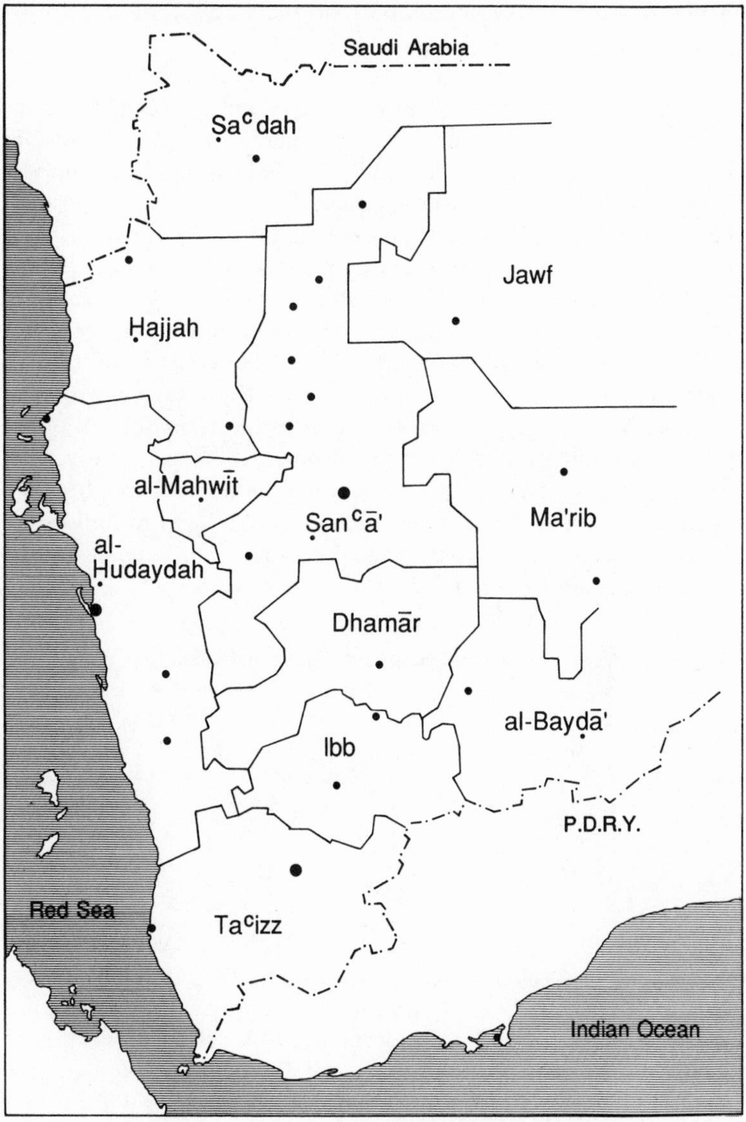

FIG. 1.8 Distribution of governorates or provinces

between tribes are more important than any lines drawn by government.

The north-east quadrant of Yemen was described by the tenth-century author, al-Hamdānī, as *balad* (the land of) Hamdān. In the modern period it is more usually referred to as the land of Hamdān's two major divisions, *bilād ḥāshid wa-bakīl*, or simply as 'the land of the tribes' (*bilād al-qabā'il*). This implied opposition between Ḥāshid and Bakīl dominates much of tribal rhetoric. These two major units are themselves simply 'tribes' (*qabā'il* or *qubul*), but for convenience, and without wishing to imply anything about their nature, I shall refer to them on occasion as confederations, which makes the exposition a little clearer. The constituent tribes of each are quite numerous and an exhaustive list of them is probably not possible, but the most important are as shown in Table 1.2. The population and territorial extent of these tribes vary greatly from one to the next, but the median population lies probably between 20,000 and 30,000. The whole mass of people with whom we are concerned here numbers upwards of 500,000. The locations of the major tribes are shown in Fig. 1.9.

TABLE 1.2 *Important Constituent Tribes of Ḥāshid and Bakīl*

	Ḥāshid	
al-'Uṣaymāt	Sanḥān	
'Idhar	Bilād al-Rūs	
Khārif	Hamdān Ṣan'ā'	
Banī Ṣuraym		
	Bakīl	
Arḥab	'Iyāl Yazīd	Āl 'Ammār
Sufyān	'Iyāl Surayḥ	Āl Sālim
Dhū Muḥammad	al-Ahnūm	Āl Sulaymān
Dhū Ḥusayn	Murhibah	al-'Amālisah
Nihm	Banī Maṭar	
Wā'ilah	Banī Ḥushaysh	
Banī Nawf	Khawlān al-'Āliyah	

The tribes of Hamdān are not the only tribes in Yemen. The Khawlān b. 'Āmir tribes around Ṣa'dah are neither Ḥāshidī nor Bakīlī. Such eastern tribes as 'Abīdah and Murād are not either.

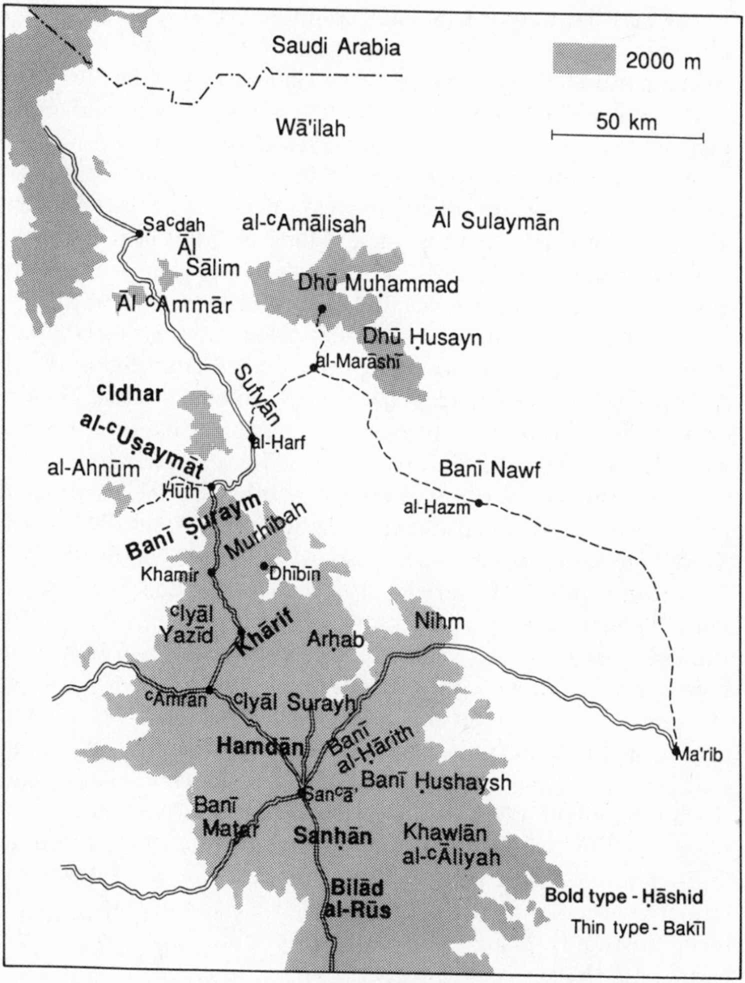

FIG. 1.9 Distribution of the major tribes

Even Khawlān al-ʿĀliyah, just east of Ṣanʿāʾ, which is unequivocally part of Bakīl, will be given only rather passing attention here (for a full account and admirable analysis see Caton 1984). The focus of the present study is to be thought of as falling on the plateau to the north of Ṣanʿāʾ at about the latitude of Ḥūth, although the information drawn on comes from a wide area and I shall try always to keep clear the geographical provenance of details.

The classification of tribes as Ḥāshidī or Bakīlī extends, in fact, into the western mountains. Al-Hamdānī listed such areas as al-Ashmūr and Ḥajūr (north of modern Ḥajjah) as Ḥāshidī. They still reckon themselves so today. From the point of view of one on the plateau, however, there is little arbitrary about where one draws a line in the west: the tribes shown in Table 1.2 are constantly involved in each other's affairs, whereas the people of such places as al-Ashmūr or Ḥajūr are simply not.[27] Indeed, in this instance, a line is almost visible to the eye. To the east of it, in the areas that concern us directly, mosques are usually simple cubes, often attached to people's houses; to the west of it they are usually more elaborate, domed structures reminiscent of Lower Yemen or indeed of North Africa. To the west of the line one is involved with a world of more explicit hierarchy, of tax-gathering, share-cropping, and precedence: a world quite different from that of, say, Arḥab and Khārif.

Even within the territory of the major tribes, on the plateau and in the east, there is considerable variation of terrain. The steep, densely terraced mountainsides so often shown in pictures of Yemen are more a feature of the west and south. The land of Ḥāshid and Bakīl is by comparison *ṣāfī*: clear, pure, less cluttered to the eye. Just north of Ṣan'ā' the main road runs across a plain dotted with volcanic cones, the territory of Hamdān Ṣan'ā' or Hamdān al-Yaman, and the landscape is broken by houses and field-walls predominantly of dark, volcanic rock. The road then crosses a broad ridge of lava before dropping down to 'Amrān and the intermontane plain of Qā' al-Bawn. On the west side of al-Bawn is Jabal 'Iyāl Yazīd, a steeply scarped, flat slab of sandstone thinly pocketed with sandy soil. On the east side of al-Bawn are lava-strewn mountains, largely held by Khārif, and east again of them are sandy plains, dotted with volcanic cones, which are largely Arḥab's territory.

The road through al-Bawn again climbs at Ghūlat 'Ajīb, coming out on the sandstone plateau where Khamir stands in the territory of Banī Ṣuraym. At first glance there is little to be seen but flat, windswept rock to the horizon, but hidden in the hollows of the rock terrain there are extensive fields arranged in shallow flights of terraces. Beside these stacked lines of fields are stone watch-towers. The houses of the area, mostly clustered in quite large villages and often four stories high, are also constructed of pale dry-stone, with the villages usually some distance from one another.

Ḥūth, the next town along the main asphalt road and thus roughly on the major watershed, is a little lower. The landscape and the housing are quite similar to those near Khamir. The track westward, however, from Ḥūth to Shahārah, drops steeply from the plateau across crumbling, weathered strata that give the impression of a world decayed; and at the bottom, in the lowlands of al-Baṭanah, one is in a quite different landscape. The temperature and humidity are higher than on the plateau, agriculture is far richer (exploiting spates from the mountains), and the insect life in summer makes the fizzing crackle of a broken insulator on some massive power cable. The dense fields of sorghum are interspersed with houses that are often no more than shanties. A few watch-towers stand out on rock elevations. It is here that al-ʻUṣaymāt and ʻIdhar are found. On the western side of al-Baṭanah is the rugged, terraced mountain massif, about 2,500 metres high, where Shahārah stands and where al-Ahnūm have their territory.

The main road on the plateau north of Ḥūth crosses Jabal Aswad to Ḥarf Sufyān. From there northward through the rest of Sufyān the terrain is largely flat and sandy. In season the sorghum stands out clearly, but seems only to emphasize the lengthy space between one village and the next. Here one sees more flocks than further south, and the architecture changes from stone to mud. In the north of Sufyān, extending west from the road, is the barren rockscape of al-ʻAmashiyyah, and north again is the sandy plateau near Ṣaʻdah where the landscape is dotted with walled grape gardens.

East from Sufyān, across a mountain ridge, is Wādī Madhāb, where there seems always to be flowing water: at several places it is flanked by reeds and frequented by wading birds, but the river makes a very thin ribbon through the arid landscape. From near al-Marāshī the track then climbs up Wādī Nīl. In the lower reaches there are fields of sorghum which depend on seasonal spates, but higher up is very dry. Acacias dot the bed of the wadi. There are always little family groups of herders with their sheep and goats. On either side as one slogs up the wadi are sheer cliffs that have always made the area something of a natural fortress.

At the top one is at Jabal Baraṭ (about 2,100 metres), a separate plateau of basalt outcrops and sandy wadis along which are strung the villages and little fields. Rain sometimes fails to come at all here. The sky is clear and a very deep blue. The horizon is very close, as though it were the top of the world. The architecture is all of packed mud and is distinctively handsome, the houses being often more than five stories high and very cleanly shaped; and the local aesthetic has distinctive traits, such as the placing of flowers and aromatic herbs in public rooms. It is here that the tribes of Dhū Muḥammad and Dhū Ḥusayn are centred, whom a learned author of the early nineteenth century calls 'the firebrand of the Yemeni Arabs and those of them who have [most] courage or vigour'.[28] These are the tribes whom the same author describes as swarming toward Ṣan'ā', 'like locusts' (al-Shawkānī 1929: i. 460).

East and north of Baraṭ are wadis such as Amlaḥ and Silbah, which for Ṣan'ānīs were once expressions for the end of the world. Along some there are wells and villages with date palms and sorghum. Along others there is only sand, some thorn trees, and wandering groups with their goats and camels. These wadis connect with the Empty Quarter and the world of Central Arabia, which has always been distinguished from that of Yemen for all that people came and went freely between them. The major traffic in recent years has been of migrants from Yemen seeking work elsewhere and of smugglers bringing in consumer goods. All of this was new. But there has never been a time when the tribes were wholly isolated from the world around them.

Tradition has it that the Prophet himself sent 'Alī b. Abī Ṭālib to Yemen, and 'all of Hamdān became Muslim in a single day' (al-Ṭabarī 1968: iii. 120). Certainly, since then, tribesmen have usually had among them religious specialists, who in turn have often condemned much that tribesmen do and had their message listened to. Nowadays there are school teachers throughout the north, promoting not only literacy but visions of nationalism, of progress, and of Islam, whether more or less radically conceived. Tribalism itself is not conceived as self-sufficient. Men throughout the north are attached, as they have always been, to ideas and institutions that they distinguish from their own and consider to be in some way necessary; and these other ideas usually give to the tribes a subordinate or marginal place.

The acceptance by many tribesmen that their society is of its nature somehow incomplete deserves noting clearly. We are used enough to areas at the periphery of Europe, for example, being culturally 'half-worlds';[29] but their dependence is imposed, often quite directly, by powers at the centre. The twist to the Yemeni case, as to those in many parts of the Middle East, is that the tribes themselves are the basis of what power most governments have ever held. Not only have many prominent figures in recent national politics been of tribal background, but the tribes themselves remain important, and one cannot follow the events of the last few decades, any more than those of preceding centuries, without some grasp of what the tribes amount to. In the midst of which the assumption is widespread that they will all one day disappear.

For others, as we have said, the tribes appear as an undifferentiated bloc, marginal to the ordered affairs of proper government. Trucks and televisions have done little to change this, and it remains a rare author who attributes two sides to the place of the tribes in the country's history.

> The hand which grasps the plough and turns the land into a carpet of green is the very hand which grasps the firing-piece of a rifle and turns the land into a fiery torch. The awesome human energy apparent in dividing up the mountainsides and establishing on them extraordinary terraces for agriculture is the same energy that sweeps the fertile plots away or defends them. . . . The armour which has protected Yemen from every aggressor is the sword which has sometimes pierced the body of the community. (al-Wazīr 1971: 149)

It would be easy to find descriptions that stress only the violence. The view of the tribes which Nuʿmān (1965: 32–3) ascribes to the Ṣanʿānīs and the Imam's officials, 'the fang of a cur in a cur's head', is not dead by any means. In less apprehensive moods the townsfolk still see the tribesmen as bumpkins, which is often to say almost by definition as irreligious dolts: 'the tribesman never blesses the Prophet except when he bumps his head'.[30] And the conceptual order suggested by the detail of tribal names and locations is a blank to most other Yemenis, for whom 'the land of the tribes' remains land beyond the pale of sociability.

AN OUTLINE OF THE CHAPTERS WHICH FOLLOW

The chapters which follow are grouped for convenience into three blocks. Chapters 2, 3, and 4 rest mainly on field-work and are written in the ethnographic present, although some of the material involves reference to the past and historical parallels are often cited in endnotes. Chapters 5, 6, and 7 concentrate on history. Yemeni sources from different periods have been read very much in the light of ethnography, but readers who wish to know what happened when will find most of the material here laid out in roughly chronological sequence. Chapters 8, 9, and 10 deal again with the present, and the past is touched on primarily as a matter of present concern. Within this, and particularly in the last chapter, an attempt is made to pick out those considerations that are distinctively of our own time, not least of which is a certain conception of time itself. The early ethnographic chapters will then be in context, and a context, I hope, which may situate the history also. An effort has been made at all points to group material in such a way that readers can skim what least interests them and not lose touch with the book's development.

In Chapters 2 and 3 we shall discuss some of the salient ideas by which the tribesmen's own world is organized. Chapter 2 deals primarily with the language of honour as applied to individual persons, Chapter 3 with the same language as applied to tribes. We should not assume that one derives from the other. Indeed, one of the interesting aspects of the moral system is the parallel conception of persons and collectivities within it. This involves not only certain concepts of the person and of how persons combine, but also of timeless identities attached to territory and of the position of shaykhs (the tribal notables) as guarantors between men or groups. In Chapter 4 we shall look at places and groups which are found within tribal territory but which by the tribes' usual terms are 'exceptions to the rule', being protected by tribesmen and set aside from disputes. It is here that tribalism produces points of insertion for views of the world that are sometimes quite different from its own.

The descendants of the Prophet often occupied such points, and around them was organized the set of values that gave rise to Zaydi history and historiography. These are the subject of Chapter 5. The history is a long one (from 896 to 1962), but I have attempted to pick out the features which are common to all of it: that is, the structure of ideas which constitutes what was done and written as a Zaydi history and not as something else.

Tribalism and Zaydism were always intertwined, though each can be roughly circumscribed for analytical purposes. One or other often was drawn clear of its fellow for purposes of rhetoric (Gochenour 1984 rightly sees each as a *da'wā*, or summons to action), and when this happens we are faced with a collective representation that tempts one to think of it as an 'indigenous model'. The first thing to be said is that there are at least two. Each lays stress upon features that the other's protagonists accept (in at least some circumstances) but which they underplay more or less consciously. An unexceptionable feature of one scheme may (on occasion) be picked up by the other and denounced or praised. I have tried to keep track of some of these possibilities through the endnotes in most chapters: where the text participates in one representation, the notes often provide a counterpoint.

Chapter 6 follows the history through from post-medieval times to the 1950s to show what place the tribes have had in the affairs of the country generally. The rise and fall of governments and of tribal leaders would be scarcely intelligible without reference to Lower Yemen (well outside tribal territory), to tax-farming, and to foreign invasion. Chapter 7 deals with the eventual overthrow of the Imamate and with the tribes' involvement in the long civil war of the 1960s, when outside powers and rival ideas of monarchy and republicanism were pitted against each other in tribal territory.

The stretches of time dealt with here are unequal. The first (Chapter 6) runs from the seventeenth to the twentieth century, while the second (Chapter 7) covers only the few decades of anti-Imamic or 'modernist', 'progressive' rhetoric. Both chapters, of course, include discussion of the ground of events and of events themselves. As throughout the book, each has the mandatory two aspects which have often been apportioned to separate subjects: 'the historian is concerned with the relations between individuals (individual people, groups or events) that produce change: the social anthropologist has been concerned so far more with the atemporal patterns by which a society can be seen as a meaningful whole' (Pocock 1971: 96–7). The professional division of labour is not so marked as when that passage was written,[31] but the analytical division, whether made within one subject or the other, remains hard to avoid. What needs to be born in mind is that sequence, whether built into change or stasis, is a product of social forms just as much as the social forms are to be seen as 'coping with duration' (ibid. 111).[32] Neither Zaydism nor tribalism is ordered to a concept of change. Each can pick out a *principium individuationis* (ibid. 98) from the other as part of its own generalizable scheme; but neither turns in on itself to revalue its own products and make the past alien. The older opposition of history to anthropology as change is opposed to atemporal pattern, or statistical to mechanical models, seldom readily applies here.

Not only was the history of the Zaydi Imamate highly repetitive, but the tribes themselves are immensely long-lasting. The subject is touched on at several points in the book so as to keep it before the reader's mind; but the common idea, so readily carried over from older African ethnography to that of the tribal Middle East (Evans-Pritchard 1940; Peters 1967, 1977), that tribal views of the past are determined primarily by present concerns and are thus not 'historical' turns out to be misleading here. When tribesmen say that 'our tribe has been here for ever', they are often more nearly right than one at first supposes. The sheer longevity of tribal divisions is a prime ethnographic fact.

Chapter 8 looks at the villages, which underpin tribal life and outlast most of its events. The village represents not only the greatest geographical continuity in the tribal system but also the locus where the most immediate economic changes are played out. Chapter 9 summarizes what sort of entity the tribes are, both from the point of view of atemporal patterns and from that of temporal sequence: it tries to see, in other words, what type of history tribalism itself can produce and register.[33] From this perspective the recent events touched on in Chapters 7 (the civil war) and 10 (the contemporary world) take a different sense than they might otherwise; and the 'individual' features of the present can be set against those of general value. Chapter 10 considers the place of the tribes and of tribalism in what is now a world of nation states, of development, and ideas of 'progress': a world, in short, in which the idea arises that tribes are archaic or the remnant of another age. This last chapter also offers some conclusions that try to pick out the possibilities, if not the probabilities, of change.

'Social change' has been the dominant interest of much recent work on Yemen: changes since the early 1970s in employment, cropping patterns, income, and the like which can be measured in statistical patterns. I have tried to turn the other way. Upper Yemen has a long documented history. From it emerge principles without which the present and its reams of figures can be given no useful values: the forms of change would remain obscure, the tribes would artificially be severed from their surroundings, and one could not in all honesty say even what tribes or tribesmen are. Ḥāshid and Bakīl still occupy at least a quarter of the country. They have done so for a very long time. They cannot be dismissed as an archaic remnant except in terms of indigenous schemes which themselves form part of the same ethnography.

NOTES

1. See Stookey 1978: 1; Peterson 1982: 10; and al-Thawr 1968: 7, 8, 25, 499 ff.
2. The lower figure is taken from the Swiss demographic team (Steffen 1978: 60), the higher from the CPO, or Central Planning Organization of the Prime Minister's office (1983: 6). A map issued by the Swiss in 1977 showed an approximate eastern border as a dotted line, which then had to be diligently obscured with sticky tape before the map could be distributed.
3. For the way in which Ḥāshid and Bakīl in pre-Islamic times came to form two halves of an entity named Hamdān see Robin 1978.
4. *Allāhummā lā taj'al al-sharqī quddām ṣayf-nā / wa-lā al-gharbī li-nā bi-kharīf* (heard in Banī Ṣuraym).
5. For sketches of Yemeni agricultural technique see al-Mujāhid 1980; Varisco 1982*a*; 1982*b*: 109–144; and 1985; Serjeant 1974; Tutwiler and Carapico 1981; Kopp 1981: 106 ff. Some details specific to the tribal north will be given in ch. 8.
6. Zaydism traced the righteous descent of authority from Zayd b. 'Alī b. Ḥusayn b. 'Alī b. Abī Ṭālib, who in 740 was slaughtered, like so many of his kin, by the Umayyads. In early times the movement was a serious contender for control of the Islamic heartlands. Questions of doctrine are largely beyond my competence, but see the brief overview by Sharaf al-Dīn 1968: 105 ff.; Ṣubḥī 1980 (particularly pt. 3); the very detailed discussion in Madelung 1965; and Van Arendonk 1960: 1–106. Madelung 1971 is a more general article on the concept of the Imamate and is extremely useful as an outline of the main Zaydi positions on the subject and their relation to Sunni theories.
7. Yaḥyā b. al-Ḥusayn 1968: 203 dates the first appearance of the Shāfi'īs in Lower Yemen to AD 912–13. The history of Lower Yemen is largely beyond the scope of this study, but for potted histories of the whole country see Playfair 1859, Stookey 1978, Sharaf al-Dīn 1964, and al-Jirāfī 1951.
8. The phrase is from Saussure, quoted in Ardener 1971*a*: xxxviii. This latter reading of 'Saussure's relevance to anthropology has been borne in mind when formulating many of the problems dealt with here. See also Ardener 1971*b*. Saussure himself (1986: 94) maintained that panchronic rules were to be found only in phonetics and were of no use at all in dealing with 'specific facts of language structure'. In part this guarantees his own analytic distinction between synchrony and diachrony, the former being the semantic element and the latter related to it by a peculiar imagery of violent contingencies (see ibid. 93, 149,

151, 197). The same view of time appears in much of Lévi-Strauss's work (e.g. 1966). As we shall see, this assumption of something like entropy is highly problematic in the ethnography at hand, at least as the linguistic metaphor is applied to the higher order features of politics and cultural self-definition.

9. The other areas of Yemen can only be given passing attention here. Fortunately, there are surveys or ethnographies of many. For Lower Yemen see particularly the brilliant ethnography of Ibb in Messick 1978; for the western mountains see Tutwiler 1977, 1987, and Weir 1984. For a highly sympathetic account of the problems now faced by the Tihāmah see Mundy 1985. See also Carapico 1979.

   In the present context one should note particularly that the area immediately north-west of Ṣan'ā' has been the subject of two very useful works dealing directly with 'tribalism': Varisco 1982*b* (see pp. 156, 179, 384), and, particularly, Adra 1982. From the point of view of the major plateau tribes it is not fully tribal at all. The problems of comparison, which would need separate consideration, are broadly those of caste at the edge of Hindu India (see Dumont 1970: ch. 10), in so far as the language of the two areas is similar but in one of them the organizing principle is absent, in this case, that of formal equality of territorial neighbours.

10. At Baraṭ, for example, 1983 was the fifth successive year when there was insufficient rain for field crops. The wells still held water, though not enough to maintain all the flocks. The grazing was quite intact. In conditions like these a hundred years ago it would have been the shortage of grain that, by a long way, bit first.

11. Tribesmen often draw a line between themselves and Central Arabia by saying all 'Yemeni' tribesmen till land, even if it is only a little. 'Nejdis' they think of as having only flocks. This is quite inaccurate, empirically speaking, but none the less noteworthy.

12. Ibn Khaldūn is, of course, in no way representative of Arabic historiography. The *Muqaddimah* is an oddity. It is relevant here because it was widely read by progressive Yemeni thinkers in the middle years of the present century, and such works as Nu'mān's probably rest on it quite directly.

13. Steffen 1978: i. 127 estimated tent-dwellers to make up 0.8 per cent of Yemen's population in 1975. In some areas of the east they formed as much as 25 per cent of the total (ibid. ii. 124), but these areas are rather few.

14. 'For instance, they need stones to set them up as supports for their cooking pots. So they take them from buildings, which they tear down to get the stones. . . . The very nature of their existence is the negation of building which is the basis of civilization' (Ibn Khaldūn 1967: i. 303–4).

15. Equally predictably, when one does meet these nomads their Arabic is often only semi-intelligible. The Arabic of the major plateau tribes, by contrast, is quite close to the classical language, and the consonants are nearly all distinguished. The particular usage of the north and east

seems to share several features with that of Nejd. For an introduction to Yemeni material see Rossi 1939, Diem 1973, Behnstedt 1985. For the purpose at hand, the reader need only note that ẓ and ḍ are often assimilated, and that *qāf* in Upper Yemen is pronounced /g/, not /q/.

16. The corrected 1975 figure seems itself to have crept up over the years from about 5.3 million to almost 6.5 million (CPO 1977: 52; Steffen 1978: i. 73, 92; CPO 1980: 39). The major area of disagreement is the number of emigrants. Overall, the corrected figures for the 1975 census (see Steffen 1978) correspond fairly well to what I found in the areas I knew at all thoroughly. Yemeni friends involved in the later (1981) census have every confidence in its findings. The recent vast increase in population seems not to be in much doubt.
17. The infant mortality rate in the 1970s was of the order of 160 or 170 per thousand (ibid. i. 88; CPO 1983: 67). By comparison the rates in India and Britain were about 140 and 19 respectively.
18. The diagram shows net private transfers from all sources, which is, of course, not the same as gross remittances from labour; but the two are almost certainly parallel. The figures are consistent in successive CPO yearbooks, except that the 1982 and 1983 editions give differing amounts for 1982 (CPO 1982: 186–7 and 1983: 200–1).
19. Where 1977/8 = 100, the retail price index for food in Ṣan'ā' in 1983 was 159, and for housing 154. Where 1975/6 = 100, the corresponding figures for 1983 are 230 and 239 (CPO 1983: 151–6).
20. *The Middle East* (London, May 1986) quotes what seems to me a very likely estimate by a US embassy official in Ṣan'ā': 100,000 barrels/day would not compensate for the loss of income from other sources; 200,000 b/d would probably do so; 400,000 b/d (the projected maximum capacity) would change the economic situation noticeably but not dramatically, because of the country's relatively high population density. The political effects are likely to be more marked. Until now, Yemeni governments have rarely been able to pay for themselves without either squeezing the southern peasantry, which is what the Imams did, or taking subventions from the Saudis, which is what has often happened since.

    The period of transition will not be easy. The Yemeni government has carefully counselled caution to its own people and directed its efforts to encouraging agriculture, but aid from other Arab countries has been falling off: from $440 million in 1982 to $160 million in 1983 by *The Economist*'s reckoning (12 Oct. 1985). *Mid-East Report* (1 Nov. 1985) gave the same figures and suggested Saudi Arabia was paying a further stipend to the President and some $70 million a year to the northern tribes. The latter figure is probably about right.
21. Anyone working with the 'grey literature', largely foreign-produced, soon comes to recognize the same figures, inverted, summed, squared, and logarithmed in one publication after another despite their utter unreliability to start with. 'Development' has become an industry. Large numbers of foreigners have done handsomely out of producing reports such as that touching on the sudden increase in the number of

cars and trucks: 'This jump reflects several aspects about (*sic*) rural Yemen, such as—the financial propensity to own and operate vehicles has widely existed latently for some time.' It would require an Evelyn Waugh to do the subject justice.

22. For example, a pair of men whom I knew fairly well, and whose only visible means of support was a tea stall, bought a bulldozer worth about $100,000 at 1980 prices. I never did find out how this was done. Lancaster's experiences with the Rwala (Lancaster 1981: 97–9) were similar.
23. Weir 1985 provides an elegant account of *qāt*. Her bibliography makes any detailed account of it on my part superfluous. See also Varisco 1986.
24. Provinces then subdivide in *qaḍā*'s, and these each comprise several *nāḥiyahs*. As of 1983 there were 168 *nāḥiyahs* in Yemen (CPO 1983: 11).
25. The Confederation of Yemeni Development Associations (CYDA) was set up in 1973. For an account of the co-operative movement see Swanson 1985: 133.
26. See Markaz 1983 for details of the system.
27. Even al-Hamdānī's account of this western area 'suggest(s) strongly it never truly belonged to . . . Ḥāshid' (Wilson 1981: 100). Rather, the plateau tribes seem already to have dominated people to their west. Tribal families on the plateau have often owned land in the west. But the western mountains are also full of families who came originally from the plateau and have left the major tribal system. See particularly Tutwiler 1987.
28. *Jamrat ʿarab al-yaman wa-ahl al-shawkah min-hum* (al-Shawkānī 1929: i. 459). Both Serjeant 1983: 86 n. 161 and al-ʿAmrī 1985: 20 read this as 'a gathering' or 'assembly' of the Arabs of Yemen, but see also Zabārah 1958: 15.
29. 'Half-worlds' is from Chapman 1978 on the Scottish Gaidhealtachd. For a large-scale example of cultural dependency of this sort see Herzfeld 1984. Some of the analytical problems that arise in the Yemeni case are touched on in Dresch forthcoming *d*.
30. *Al-qabīlī mā yuṣallī ʿalā l-nabī illā baʿd-mā yadkum raʾs-hu* (al-Akwaʿ 1984: ii. 790–1).
31. For an indication of more recent positions adopted by historians toward anthropology and by anthropologists toward history see the special issue of *Journal of Interdisciplinary History*, 12 (1981). I shall only add that in practical terms there remains a real division: anthropologists wanted certain sections of the present book greatly expanded, for instance, and historians wanted to expand quite different sections. In fact the historical sections have had to be somewhat cut, and neither party will be wholly satisfied with the compromise adopted. But the 'type' of history at issue dictates how one sets about dealing with it. See the thoughtful Prolegomena to Wilkinson 1987.
32. See also Pocock 1971: 112: 'Social anthropology . . . must devise a language which enables us to conceive of society in duration. It is

the play of society maintaining itself, modifying itself to meet, the steady flow of new individuals—whether people or events—which constitutes the object of our study: not that in society which makes for stability and communication only.' This identifies duration with time as something prior to social life. One can as well see duration itself as something constructed (see Collingwood 1926; Barnes 1971) which is what I try to do here. For some of the major ethnographic issues involved see Pocock 1967 and Eickelman 1977, and for the problems of writing on these see the papers collected in Fardon 1985.

33. The approach here and throughout is thus 'possibilist', if one may put it that way, and not determinist or probabilistic. It is rather different, and perhaps less ambitious, than the fashionable approach which reifies structure so as to contrast it with practice (e.g. Bourdieu 1977; Sahlins 1981). The latter approach, one fears, poses imaginary problems for its authors to solve, much as with the older 'problem' of individuals in history: 'here again we are dealing with a short-circuit between crossed terms which it is illegitimate to compare: for to do so is to compare the knowledge of one definite object with the empirical existence of another!' (Althusser and Balibar 1979: 111–12). A very similar point is made by Collingwood 1926: 135 about time and events. The present work, by contrast, tries to err on the cautious side by recognizing the modelling or rethinking of the past and present for the constructive process it inevitably is. There is nothing out there one can simply 'report on'. The distinction between structure and event is of the analyst's making, and one must not pretend otherwise.

2 The Language of Honour

> C'est donc grâce aux éléments de l'honneur que les Arabes communaient dans les mêmes idées et fraternisaient dans les mêmes pratiques pour constituer ce qu'on appelle une société.
>
> Bichr Farès, *L'Honneur chez les Arabes avant l'Islam*

FIRST APPEARANCES

The most noticeable thing about tribesmen at first glance is that they are armed. Every tribesman but the poorest owns a rifle (many have more than one), and in public each carries his rifle with him. Antique Turkish pieces and old service rifles are supplemented rather than replaced by modern self-loading and automatic weapons, some of which are all but the latest of their kind; and downstairs in many houses, among the grain and goats, are heavy weapons such as mortars, machine guns, and even light artillery. Weapons are a mark of tribesmen's standing.[1] 'Weak', non-tribal people who live scattered about in tribal territory are not permitted to carry rifles, although many now own less ostentatious pistols, and men of learning, although they are permitted to carry rifles, seldom do so (these non-tribal people will be described in Chapter 4).

These other estates of society are also distinguished from tribesmen by the way that daggers are worn obliquely, whether to the right or left. A tribesman wears his dagger (*janbiyyah* pl. *janābī*) upright in a curved sheath at the front of his belt. The sheath is often decorated with horizontal bands of green leather strings called *maḥābis*, or with a worked silver front-plate called *ṣadr*, and sometimes with a pointed cover on the sheath tip called *tūzā* or *tūzī*. The whole assemblage *(al-jihāz)*, which measures about 35 centimetres high, is conspicuous. The daggers can be very expensive. The 'head' or haft of a good dagger is of rhinoceros horn or giraffe bone, often decorated with a pair of gold sovereigns and a pattern of silver nail-heads,[2] and there is great connoisseurship in knowing the worth of a dagger by the shades and striations of its haft. A good one, which is necessarily thought to be old, may cost the equivalent of $30,000, and quite ordinary tribesmen are often the owners of daggers worth more than $1,000. Rifles too can be expensive.

As we shall see, rifles and daggers figure prominently in many contexts: there is, for example, a veritable language in which they are proffered and exchanged to form pledges (Mauss 1970: 60). The dagger in particular is also, like the Nuer spear (Evans-Pritchard 1956: 238), 'the point at which two complex social representations meet': that of the tribesman and that of the named group to which he belongs, whether the family or tribe. In an argument or in declamation a man may slap his dagger sheath and identify himself with his tribe by a conventional phrase, as a man from Khārif, for example, might shout *ibn al-khurūf min khārif.*[3] This is rarely heard in earnest. When it is, then the import is serious: the man and his tribe are identified with each other and the honour of both is put at stake explicitly. Again, in desperate circumstances a man may break his dagger sheath in front of his fellows, the implication being that his honour is 'broken' and so is that of his tribe if they fail to help him. In less dramatic settings, where a man is perhaps being made fun of by others, he may finger his dagger haft to denote that things are going too far: his honour is being toyed with too lightly and they should desist.

This quality of honour, which is marked by weapons and often seems focused in them, is referred to as *sharaf*. The term has associations with ideas of distinctness and of distinction: each man is set apart from those like him,[4] while all tribesmen are in some sense aristocrats and the term can often be translated 'nobility'. Honour is an eminently public matter and as such is also publicly at risk.

> A tribesman's *sharaf* is 'broken' as they say, by *'ayb*—the word cannot adequately be translated, but perhaps 'disgrace' is the nearest approximation. A tribesman can commit an *'ayb* by acting in a way demeaning to himself—for example, by killing a woman or person of inferior standing to his own, or, on the contrary, he can have an *'ayb* inflicted upon him. (Serjeant 1977: 228)

He can also inflict an *'ayb* on others. The transitive verb *yu'ayyib* may variously be translated as 'to demean', 'to disgrace', or 'to insult'; so an *'ayb* is a blameworthy action whether done or suffered. This lexical equivalence between active and passive is distinctive, denoting, as it does, a moral symmetry that pervades the whole ethnography. Just as distinctive is the lack of any such equation between wrong-doing and a capacity to monitor faults in one's self: such private capacities are never marked by a term in public discourse. '*Ayb* is always purely external.[5] The term '*ayb*, as we shall see, is also used of the amends by which an insult or disgrace is repaired.

The word is constantly used to control, or try to control, small children, and all the time one hears '*ayb yā wasikh* ('shame, you dirty beast') yelled at toddlers by mothers or older sisters. Here, if one can talk about meaning at all, it means something more like the English 'bad' or 'don't' than like, let us say, 'naughty': it applies far more to the momentary fault than to the little person who committed it. Children do not blush at being caught out, or brood and weep over their own wickedness. They are yelled at and swatted, they run away if they can or fight back, but there is little of the worried flirtation ('Am I good?', 'Was I bad?') that accompanies these things in our own culture. Nor do adults caught out, perhaps with a hand in the till, seem disgraced to themselves. A man may be discomforted by chastisement, but he too will yell back and, if cornered, fight. What rankles afterwards is the insult, the attack on his public standing, not the wound to his self-respect.

'*Ayb* is thus very much part of the public domain. As such it is rather foreign to our own representations of the person, with their stress on presumed internal states. One can suffer an '*ayb* or commit an '*ayb*, but one cannot 'have' an '*ayb* as one has a guilty conscience or a feeling of shame. There is certainly an idea that something may be '*ayb* to do whether or not a serious rebuke is likely. One might, for instance, hear two tribesmen in a Ṣan'ā' alley late at night, not sure if they have found the right house and wondering if they might wake the wrong people: 'Go on, knock, it's their house.' / 'It's '*ayb*.' / 'No, knock.' / "*ayb*, brother, we don't know it's them.' / 'What's with you? Knock.' Just as *sharaf* is in some sense '*ayb*'s opposite, so is *adab*, 'good manners', a central value in all Middle Eastern societies and one ethnographers tend to leave out.[6] But the overt suggestion that one's manners are not good necessarily touches honour: there are few other terms to address faults in the first or the second persons.

'*Ayb* is what damages *sharaf*, or honour as presented to others. Both terms have a wide range of application, but both have associations with the more dramatic end of that range, as Serjeant's explanation of *'ayb* by reference to murder rather than to lesser crimes suggests. Honour as presented to outsiders is bound up with hyperbole. Tribesmen are not personally boastful (they are not modest either, let it be said), but they are willing to credit themselves and others with an heroic style of conduct. A poem which, from its content, must date from the end of the last century, but is still widely known, illustrates at least something of their interest.

> [My tribe] all answer me, old men and young men,
> Don't trust who committed disgrace,
> The worthless man whose conduct's no use to me.
> We take only [rifles] with smooth-moving parts,
> The 'Mart' [the Martini-Henry rifle] with the quiet loading-lever,
> And death lying snug in its place [i.e. a round in the breech].[7]

The period flavour given by the name of the rifle (a one-shot breech-loader the British used against the Zulus) is not seen in quite that way by tribesmen, armed though they now are with more modern guns. For them the continuity is more immediate: our fathers were warriors and their fathers before them, and we are a race of warriors in our turn; our honour and theirs is one and the same.

This assimilation of ancestral *sharaf* to present concerns forms part of a distinctive view of history (cf. Meeker 1976) which we shall see signs of at several points later. It is worth noting at once that threats to honour do not endure in the same way. Just as one cannot 'have' an *'ayb,* so a tribe does not carry in the eyes of others any burden of specific faults to complement the noteworthy deeds people grant it. The faults of persons and groups have no hold on them until someone else brings them up, at which point one is dealing again with a specific *'ayb*, an insult that is here and now. Honour is certainly vulnerable but, in all but the most extreme cases, it is a social given and not reduced to specific criteria, while *'ayb* is by contrast contingent and specific. Most public encounters thus seem to start much where the last did.

It is only in drama that the outlines of honour show up clearly in black and white. The patterns which emerge are apparent in all public life, however, and terms such as *sharaf* and *'ayb* are used explicitly at the first sign that honour is being slighted. A man who feels that his rights and his dignity are in some way infringed, whether by an equal or by someone more powerful than he, will at least say resentfully, 'I have my *sharaf* too'; or 'Everyone has his honour, be he ever so small' (*wa-law huw ṣaghīr*). Often he will be stung to do something about it. The dramatic can emerge from the downright mundane with scant warning. What the outsider might wish to distinguish as real and imaginary therefore cannot be separated without losing the significance of much that tribesmen do, and the reality they make for themselves is itself highly colourful.[8]

For example, the daggers that tribesmen wear have about them a dramatic charge. They are often spoken of rather poetically as the 'white weapon', a phrase with much the same associations of romantic bloodshed as the *arme blanche* of European cavalry. As associated with their owners they are treated with great respect, although there is nothing sacred about daggers as such (they are used to fix plugs and dig processed cheese out of tins), and they are always said to be 'for killing men'. Certainly one does not see them used to slaughter beasts, and men are sometimes killed with them, but daggers are in fact rarely sharp enough to cut string; even so, one hears endlessly about the man who returned his dagger to the sheath without looking and by accident disembowelled himself. We are in a world of romance and tall tales.

It is part of this image they have of their world and of their own kind that tribesmen are feckless and disorderly—men not quite in control of their destiny or even of their own actions. A tribesman should be *khafīf al-dam*, 'light-blooded'. Used of an educated man the phrase might simply mean witty or a good conversationalist, but in the tribal context perhaps 'mercurial' is the best general gloss; someone not sluggish (*thaqīl al-dam*, 'heavy-blooded') but quick to respond to affronts and to take up arms in defence of honour. Again, 'red-eyed' (*aḥmar al-'ayn*) is a rather poetic description most often heard in formal rhetoric, but it is a quality which tribesmen in general attribute to their kind; fearless and fierce like leopards.

There is a corresponding lack of restraint that pervades much of tribal life. Tribesmen are not in fact particularly violent but there are few of them who would not at times identify with the protagonist of Muḥammad Ghālib's poem:

> I am the brave warrior . . .
> I am excellent at firing bullets . . .

My bullet never yet missed its mark . . .
For me war is work . . . (quoted Nu'mān 1965: 78)

Honour is exemplified to good advantage in heroic action, and sober reportage is not of the essence. Two men may squabble over what to the outsider seems minor (a strayed goat, for instance, or a plot of land where little could grow) and settle down to sniping at each other from house to house. The *sharaf* of each is at stake. For the same reason their dispute may be spoken of by others as 'war', just as may a battle involving hundreds (Dresch 1986: 316).

The men who indulge in heroic rhetoric and fine gestures of weaponry are farmers. Some now also drive trucks for wages, buy and sell imported goods, or draw government stipends, but farmland is important to all of them. Most claim to work their own land, as appears from Steffen's inquiries in 'Iyāl Yazīd (Steffen 1978: ii. 55) and my own on the other side of al-Bawn in Khārif (see Table 2.1). The appearance of equality is somewhat misleading: on the one hand, there are men who own property elsewhere (we shall return to this in later chapters); on the other hand, when a man says that he works only his own land he may mean family land, and within family groups there are often great inequities. Still, most men own land. Nearly all of them are farmers (*fallāḥīn*, *muzāri'īn*) or from farming families, but one could scarcely call them peasants. The idea of honour gives a specific value even to fields and land, just as it colours relations between men. The tribesmen in their own estimation are both cultivators and nobles, like so many 'bonnet lairds'.

They are also members of families, and in their own way are family men. *Sharaf* depends in part on ancestry. Although one might feel that honour is acquired by living persons and projected

TABLE 2.1 *Land Ownership and Use in 'Iyāl Yazīd and Khārif*

	'Iyāl Yazīd		Khārif	
	No.	%	No.	%
cultivate only their own land	71	92	44	88
cultivate theirs and others'	3	4	5	10
cultivate only rented land	1	1	1	2
land labourers	2	3	0	—

on their forebears, the assumption in rhetoric is that these forebears pass on honour to us, and *mā l-abūk* ('What's with your father?') is thus an insult. The sons of a father or grandsons of a grandfather have *sharaf* in common (see Fig. 2.1): B and C, and their sons 1 to 5, are together known as 'the sons of A' (the sons of Muḥammad, as it might be), and their common honour is precisely that of A, their shared eponym; 1 to 3 have shared honour of their own (that of B), distinct from and opposed to that of the sons of C; and the *sharaf* of each individual man (of B or C or any of 1 to 5) is similarly distinct from and opposed to that of all other men. The importance of these relations in practice varies greatly. It is by no means always the case that the sons of B close ranks against the sons of C in the event of trouble between one of each. However, the public reckoning of relations between men usually starts from, and invariably takes note of, these relations of shared descent. Men are named and considered as 'son of so-and-so'. You are known first of all as your father's son.

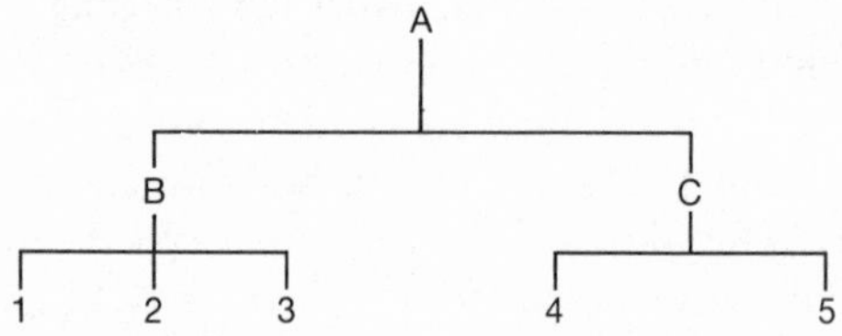

FIG. 2.1 Descent and honour

The idiom of shared honour through shared male descent is the starting point for most social accountancy; the map, if you like, on which bearings of all sorts are laid. By itself it says nothing about females. A man's honour, though, depends on his mother as much as on his father, and it depends in due course on his wives and daughters. Nor can a father dissociate himself from his daughter as he will often do from a son. A daughter's misbehaviour, and particularly her sexual misbehaviour once she is more than a small girl, can break a man's honour whether he is personally much interested in her or not. Sisters and daughters must therefore be 'controlled' and 'defended'. Their particular sexual honour, or *nāmūs*, cannot be infringed without breaking their menfolk's more general honour, and *yā maksūr al-nāmūs* ('you whose sexual honour is broken',[9] or whose women's honour is in doubt) is as much an insult as 'What's with your father?', though more often used jokingly. A tribesman's conspicuous weaponry is a statement of his ability to defend, among other things, the inviolability of his women. It is not that they are in imminent danger of attack (far from it), but to dispense with the imagery of defence would be to suggest a lack of care for their honour and hence for one's own.

The men of a family defend their daughters. Their daggers and rifles declare their ability to do this, and weddings, particularly where the bride is from outside the village, often include a specific gesture involving them.[10] When the bride's party arrived at the groom's house (usually that of his father) and are greeted at the door, the groom's father hands his wife or his daughter his dagger. She then holds this below the door so that the bride steps across it as she enters the house. Sometimes a rifle is laid down instead. There is always the danger that this gesture will be one day reversed, and the men on each side will take up in earnest the weapons which the women laid down and stepped over.

Marriage expresses or forms a relation between two families. It also forms a potential danger in that each now exposes its honour in part to the other's conduct, and a pattern of marriage which in other types of society might reasonably be spoken of in terms of cohesion or order will here lead often to insoluble problems. In one of 'Iyāl Surayḥ's villages, for instance, three men married, and so three 'houses' (*bayt*, pl. *buyūt*) were aligned in a circle. A married B's sister, B married C's sister, and C married A's (Fig. 2.2). B returned from a long spell working in Saudi Arabia and found, or thought he found, that his wife had been carrying on with A. The honour of a husband is besmirched by his wife's misbehaviour but, as Meeker puts it (1976: 390), he is not the one who must 'respond'. The indissoluble link of honour is between her and her paternal kin. B divorced his supposedly errant wife; that is, he divorced C's sister. C was enraged by this affront to his sister's honour and hence to his own. He held A responsible for the insult to his sister's good name, and therefore divorced his own wife, who was A's sister. One cannot, after all, have one's honour intimately linked with a man who gives others reason to believe he debauched one's kinswoman. Whether or not he was initially in the wrong, A was now at odds with both B and C. He divorced his wife, B's sister. Had he not done so (and his dispute with B was sufficient reason), she might have absconded to her paternal home and besmirched A's honour by leaving him. B and C could hardly combine against A, since the supposedly erring woman was the sister of one and the wife of the other, and her divorce had set them at odds.

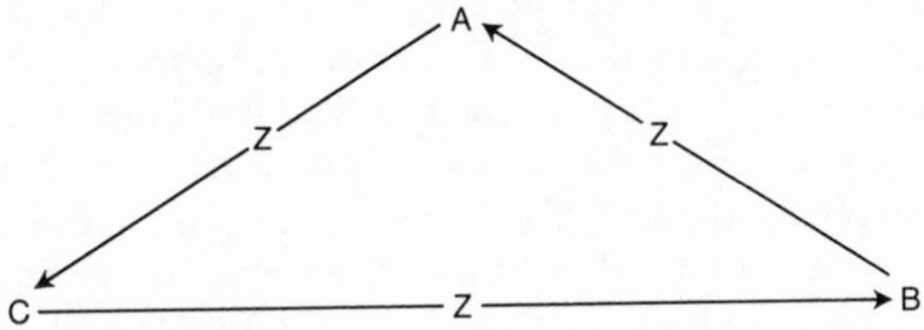

FIG. 2.2 Marriage in a circle

After all three women had been divorced, one might have thought the matter ended. But C had a claim against B for the insult to his sister, which B blamed on her and A; B had a claim against A for a number of reasons, and A against C.[11] This peculiar three-cornered squabble broke out early in 1979. It was pursued with particular vigour throughout most of 1980 and was still not resolved (how could it be?) by the end of 1983. The protagonists and their respective kinsmen were variously, successively, and repeatedly, put in jail, let out, and put back again. There was much talk of government officials taking 'hostages' as they had in the bad old days of the Imam. To the outsider it seemed more a matter of preventive custody. Every time two of the protagonists or their main supporters were let out they fell to shooting at each other's houses, and there was no one who could force them to accept parity and stop. 'He who marries . . . gives hostages to fortune'; but, in Upper Yemen at least, fortune operates on tribesmen very largely through other tribesmen, and he who marries outside his family makes vulnerable his honour and that of his agnates.

The potential problems of ties by marriage only illustrate something more general: a propensity of families or groups to face inwards; a necessity to sever what ties have been made and to defend one's particular honour at short notice. This is worth underlining briefly. Many societies familiar to anthropologists represent the identities of both persons and collectivities as dependent on standing 'relations', without which they have no value. Here, by contrast, 'cutting off relations' (*qaṭāʿ al-ʿalāʾiq*) is represented as the prime necessity; the phrase is used, in fact, of severing blood-debts and the like at arbitration (we shall come on to this in Chapter 3). Autonomy is the unmarked state, a lack of connection with others being what men take to be safe and in some sense normal. Links that cannot be severed are dangerous. Men can find themselves entangled with antagonists, like cats tied by their tails, and the results can be viciously bloody or only farcical. It is hard to predict which.

MORAL EQUILIBRIUM AND COMPENSATION

> If a man slays another, he shall pay as compensation [to the kindred] the ordinary wergeld of 100s . . .
>
> *Dooms of Aethelberht*, trans. C. Stephenson and F. G. Marcham.

An infringement of honour requires amends. Certain offences are themselves *ʿayb* (an attack on a woman, for instance), but even where this is not so (where one man is wounded by another, say) a debt is produced, and non-payment of compensation is in turn *ʿayb*, a disgrace by the culprit/debtor and an insult to the victim/creditor. 'Balance' (*mīzān*) must be maintained or restored if one man is not to have a claim on the other. The balance may be restored by payment of cash or, in case of 'blood-debt' (*dayn al-dam*), by the taking of blood revenge. The former is more common.

What counts as *ʿayb* will be specified more fully as we go on, but a few obvious and extreme cases deserve mention here. It is *ʿayb* or 'disgrace' to kill a man from behind, or from ambush if hostilities have not been announced, to take a dead man's weapons, to mutilate the corpse once one has killed him, or to leave the corpse 'out in the sun' (*bayn al-shams*), which means to leave one's victim as carrion. It is *ʿayb* to kill a man who is bound to one as a guest or a travelling companion, to kill a man at market or during a truce. In cases like these, multiple amends are required. In theory each offence is fined the equivalent of the blood-debt. So, if one killed a man from behind and took his weapons, one would owe three times the usual blood-money; one for the killing and one for each specific offence. In practice amends are scarcely so bound by fixed principles, but the principles themselves are clear. To pursue these is not to deal with rules and exceptions but with assumptions connecting them that inform both practice and local accounts of practice: in short, to specify the grounds on which men's actions or statements are intelligible to themselves and others.

To kill another tribesman in a fair fight, as it were, is not *'ayb*. Either the victim's people attempt revenge or they accept payment of the 'blood-money' (*diyah*). The amount of the *diyah* was traditionally 800 silver riyals or Maria Theresa thalers,[12] but tribesmen now accept the rate which the Ministry of Justice periodically sets for Islamic law courts: in the late 1970s this was some YR 60,000, which later doubled to YR 120,000. In practice, settlements can vary considerably. In one extreme case I followed, the victim of murder was from a tribal family of no very great standing and the killer from a family of newly rich shaykhs, who were not much esteemed on most counts but were certainly wealthy. The victim's people dropped their insistence on blood-revenge only after an agreement had been squeezed from the killer's family to pay more than ten times the usual blood-money. In general, however, it is agreed that a deliberate killing without aggravating circumstances of the kind mentioned above is to be paid for by the full blood-money (if revenge is not sought), and an accidental killing is to be paid for by some fraction of this. Negotiations begin with this shared understanding, whether admitted to or not, and most settlements are not widely removed from the rules' prescriptions.

In the case of wounding, 'wound-money' (*arsh*, pl. *urūsh*) is calculated in great detail.[13] The amount to be paid depends on the wound's extent. Revenge on the lines of 'an eye for an eye' is rarely pursued on the plateau, though it was once in the east and may perhaps still be in some areas. Material damage to property is paid for in cash. If the damage is done in some shameful circumstance (during a truce, for example), then amends for the insult are demanded too. Sometimes these are of the same amount as the value of the damage (Dresch 1987*a*, forthcoming *c*). Sometimes a standard *'ayb* is paid instead, which in the eastern Bakīl tribes is usually reckoned at 110 thalers and a bull, in Ḥāshid and the more westerly parts of Bakīl at a bull and 88 thalers (often referred to as 'the bull and his feed', *thawr wa-'alaf-hu*). Such fines may also be applied where an offence is committed but no material damage done: for example, where a man fires at another without good reason but misses. A 'half-'*ayb*' is reckoned at 44 thalers and 'half-bull', by which is meant a calf (*tabīʿ*) or a ram (*kabsh*). This is sometimes applied in such cases as taking a man's weapons from him (Dresch 1987a: 84–5).

The state of neither owing amends nor being owed is called *naqāʾ*. The dictionaries give 'purity', but in an anthropological context this might mislead (there is little emphasis on ritual cleanliness) and 'good-name' will serve better as a conventional gloss. The word is also used of the means by which good-name is restored. Sometimes it is applied to amends in cash or kind, but more usually it means wiping out an insult or disgrace specifically by murder or revenge. It is said, for example (I have never encountered an authenticated case), that a girl who committed a flagrant sexual indiscretion would be killed by her kin. This would be *naqāʾ*. Again, if a man is murdered, his kin are said to have a choice *bayn ghadāʾ wa-naqāʾ*; that is, between 'lunch' (or cash compensation) and 'good-name' (or killing in revenge). The implication is that revenge is the more honourable course. If one asks, one is often told that revenge is an absolute imperative; that, whatever other tribes do, 'we always kill' (i.e., we do not 'eat' the blood) and any tribesman worth the name would accept only blood in return for that of his brother.[14] In practice, cash compensation is far more common, or the claim is waived altogether. To understand how this is possible we must remember that what breaks *sharaf* is the disgrace or insult, not material damage.

In any society with a stress on honour, insult and injury will be linked (indeed, every injury will itself be an insult to some degree) and to settle a dispute or avoid one the two must be disentangled. The simplest case might be that of an offence between children. Children are reckoned *juhhāl* or 'ignorant' and are not responsible for their actions. If 'Alī's small son hits Muḥammad's small son and draws blood, there is nothing to be done about it (no one in his right mind would talk of revenge or even, if the wound were minor, of compensation), but an injury none the less exists and with it, perhaps, the implication of insult. The implication must be denied. Particularly if relations were already strained between the two families, an apology would be in order. 'Alī might, therefore, go to Muḥammad and remove and hold out his own head-cloth towards the victim's father: he is said to *yaṭraḥ al-jāh* or 'take off his honour'. No more need be said. If, however, relations were already strained and the gesture of apology were not forthcoming, the injury inflicted by a child (no notion of malice or intention is applicable) might be taken as an insult by his kin—'look what Bayt 'Alī have done now. Dirty troublemakers . . .' (here the women are speaking)—and violence might easily ensue. Antagonism (*khuṣmah*) can sprout like weeds.

In more serious cases, where the injury is greater or the presumption of malice more likely, greater gestures are needed to deny the insult. A slaughter-beast (*'aqīrah*, *maqṣad*) may be given; a sheep, a calf, or a bull, according to how serious the case is.[15] It is worth noting at once that all of the gestures employed in appeasement or apology are also employed in requesting help, and the ideas of apology and imposition are as clearly linked in tribal Yemen as in our own society ('I'm sorry to trouble you, but . . .'). In Yemen the link is provided by more explicit conceptions of honour whereby *noblesse oblige*, and as in all such systems it depends upon a tacit, powerful assumption of moral equality: the strongest claim on others is thus one's own claim of temporary subordination.

To apologize for missing an appointment one might hold out one's head-cloth or skirt hem. To bring pressure on a man in some small matter (let us say persuading him to come to lunch) one might hold out to him one's skirt hem, saying *hādhīh bayḍatī 'alayk* (literally, 'this is my whiteness on you'). The same gesture and phrase are appropriate to asking support in a dispute from a kinsman or from one's fellow tribesman. To demand help from those less bound to give it, or to demand help in more serious circumstances, a beast might be slaughtered. One often sees bulls slaughtered not only in front of great men's houses but outside, for example, the prime minister's office or military headquarters in Ṣan'ā'. To know whether this is a request for help or a gesture of appeasement one would have to ask. For the moment, though, let us concentrate on the aspect of appeasement.

If a man from one group kills a man from another, the killer's people should immediately offer the dead man's people a 'bull for the error' (*thawr al-hajīn*).[16] If this is accepted, which it may not be (we are dealing with a language, not a causal system), then the way is open for negotiations; but if the bull is not promptly offered, then the dead man's people can be expected to take up arms, if they have not already done so, and gather support for an attack in revenge. If you wound a man, then you should offer his people a rifle, called *bunduq al-ṣawāb* (a rifle of 'justice' or 'judgment') or *bunduq al-ṣabr* ('a rifle of patience'). This implies that you accept responsibility and offer the offended party right of judgment in the first instance (Dresch 1986: 314–15). When judgment is made or the temporary state of truce revoked then the rifle is handed back. If the wound is very serious, then the same rifle may be called *bunduq al-ḥayy wa-l-mayt* ('a rifle of life and death'), implying that you are willing to accept their judgment whatever the outcome. If the rifle is accepted (again, it may not be), then the victim's people agree in principle to negotiation and they undertake not to pre-empt by violence an attempt at settlement. Sometimes, whether for wounding or killing, these gestures are combined. A bull is hocked and the rifles 'for justice' laid on its corpse with the plaintiff's headcloth, the whole sequence of gestures being *ṭarḥ al-jāh* ('throwing down one's honour').

In the case of a killing, the first bull (the one 'for the error') may be followed, perhaps when the first instalment of compensation is paid, by a bull 'for accepting the blood-money' (*li-qublān al-diyah*) or 'to placate people' (*li-muṭāyabat al-nufūs*). At the last stage of settlement a final, third, bull may be given 'for the burial' (*thawr al-dafn*). This last bull, sometimes slaughtered at the grave, is also referred to as *thawr al-ṭayy*, the *ṭayy* being the circle of stones around the grave itself. It is said (and it sometimes happens) that neither these nor the single upright stone on top of the grave (called *naṣab* or *naṣīb)* will be put in place until the blood-money has been paid in full, the claim to it waived by the dead man's kin, or revenge taken (hence *tanṣīb* means 'revenge'). At this last stage of settlement, among some tribes of the east the murder weapon (*miqwād*) is handed over with whatever beasts and cash are agreed. At any point the negotiations may break down. However, the various protocols of appeasement offer a means to deny the insult to honour that a killing implies and so to settle the matter not by blood but by cash compensation. Often the cash is waived. The slaughter-beasts never are.

Let us give first a minor example. A man from Wāda'ah bought some land by the road in Khayār (both these are sections of Banī Ṣuraym in Ḥāshid) at the site of a new market. The seller died. When the buyer came to mark out the land for building, the seller's kinsmen arrived and claimed that it was still theirs: everyone knew it was not, but such try-ons are common and are to be expected. In the course of the ensuing squabble the buyer from Wāda'ah profferred his dagger to a group from Khayār, giving them right of judgment and thus (since *noblesse oblige*) all but guaranteeing himself a fair hearing. Despite this, one of the more excitable of the Khayārīs slashed at the man from Wāda'ah with his own dagger and wounded him slightly. He may have mistaken the gesture of appeasement for aggression, but, whatever the case, this was a serious matter and wound-money was certainly owed.

On the advice of one of their shaykhs, Khayār gave a rifle to Wāda'ah, implying right of judgment, and said they would come to the wounded man's house on a given day with slaughter-beasts. They brought a bull and two rams, but these were not actually hocked. The Wāda'ī had already slaughtered beasts of his own, which provided lunch for everyone, and he immediately waived his claim (*sāmiḥ-kum*, 'I allow you'). Compensation was owed but it was the creditor's prerogative to say that he did not wish it. Of the converse possibilities, accepting cash payment for wounds but actually refusing the beasts is self-contradictory.

The same sequence often occurs with a killing; a bull 'for the error' is given, and the dead man's people publicly waive their claim 'on account of the honour done them' (*li-muqābilat al-jāh*). The rhetoric sometimes refers to third parties. One might say that one waives one's claim, or perhaps reduces it, 'to honour those present' (*min shān wajīh al-ḥāḍirah*); in other words, out of respect for third parties who have come to help settle matters. In all cases, though, it is honour at issue. Damage may require payment, and blood certainly has its price, but compensation for injury can only honourably be claimed once the insult is denied.

In theory it is widely agreed that an accidental killing should be settled by compensation and that revenge is not called for. Men do not, however, wait soberly for 'balance' to be negotiated. The protocols of appeasement should be applied at once. During 1979, for instance, a repair crew was working on the main road in Sufyān when one of them from Āl 'Ammār was run over and killed by a truck driver from Banī Maṭar. The dead man's people threatened to attack the road crew and block the road against Banī Maṭar to extract compensation or revenge as the chance might be. The victim's relatives wanted revenge. A qadi (of a family of 'judges') from one of the Ḥāshid tribes, who was with the crew, and a shaykh from the part of Sufyān where the accident happened intervened and were given fifteen days by the dead man's tribe to settle matters. Although the accepted blood-money at the time was YR 60,000, the dead man's people demanded YR 64,000.

A delegation from Banī Maṭar arrived three days later, bringing with them a bull, two rams, and YR 2,000 worth of *qāt*. The threat of violence lapsed. In the course of the first day the blood-money demanded was halved 'on account of receiving the bull' (*li-muqābilat al-thawr*), and on the second day YR 8,000 was dropped 'to honour those present', intermediaries (*mutawāsiṭīn*) who had gathered from elsewhere. A further YR 8,000 was deducted the next day 'to honour Āl 'Ammār': in other words, to honour the victim's own fellow tribesmen who by now were pressing his immediate kin to settle. The sum finally demanded and agreed to was thus YR 16,000, or a quarter of that first demanded.[17] This was eminently reasonable, since the killing was plainly an accident, but it would be wrong to see Āl 'Ammār's initial bellicose stance as bluster or as a negotiating ploy. Were one a tribesman, it would be dangerous to do so. Had the protocols not been forthcoming promptly, the Maṭarīs would have seemed intransigent, insult would have been added to injury, and, accident or not, blood might well have led to blood.

This appeasement of affronted honour can be a delicate business, and the involvement of third parties who are themselves somehow honoured by those at odds can be almost mandatory. The performance of settlement can be complex. Tempo is as crucial here as in any case of exchange (see also Bourdieu 1977: 5–7 and, *pace* Bourdieu, Mauss 1970: 34–5), so that the room for error is large. But the conceptual building blocks out of which a particular case must be made are clear enough. Honour once breached must be recuperated. An audience must be assembled to approve the recuperation and to confirm that 'balance' has indeed been reached.

PROTECTING WHAT IS VULNERABLE

Whether in dramatic circumstances of death and wounding or in more ordinary parts of life, there is more to honour than this formal exchange and balance of courtesies. The publicity of the events described so far presupposes its complement, a privacy to be guarded against other men. The English law notion of trespass often comes to mind, and the importance of protocol points up what emerges from any discussion in the abstract of customary law (Dresch 1981: 84 n. 11): that there is, as it were, *injuria sine damno* (a breach of right where no damage is done) but no *damnum sine injuria* (no damage without breach of right). This right extends beyond one's physical self to constitute instead one's person, the social representation of the male individual that allows his relation to chattels, dependants, kin, and others.

The literature on inter-sexual relations in Middle Eastern societies, enormous as it is, brings this out clearly in one aspect. The rhetoric of honour, in this connection as in others, is not of random aggression so much as of defence: but the ethos of proprietary interest in fact also applies to much else, and the 'position of women' is an instance of something more general, whether or not one cares to take women as the paradigm case. Tribesmen show a certain *pudeur* about most things. In tribal Yemen, as throughout the Middle East, iron bars are set in the windows of houses with flimsy doors, and great padlocks are fixed on canvas saddlebags one could open with any penknife. Again, a marked unwillingness to reveal information to strangers is not only a worry about actual secrecy. The very fear of others 'spying out the land', which is common enough in tribal Yemen, is itself symptomatic of a proprietary stance. You can transcribe a document (the contents are not secret, although a journalistic discretion about sources might be asked for) but you cannot photograph it: the Bakīlī says 'Ḥāshid might see it', and the Ḥāshidī fears that Bakīl might. There is a private space to be maintained, of whatever size, that others should not peer into.

The tribesman, strung about with weapons, depicts himself as one capable of defending his own. The complement of the self-presentation is *'arḍ,* a term applied always in contexts of vulnerability. The term itself is associated in many Middle Eastern societies with the honour of women, and in Yemen, as elsewhere, can be all but synonymous with *nāmūs* or 'sexual honour'. In Yemen, as in parts of Palestine (Cohen 1965: 156 n. 3; Granquist 1931: 119), it is also explicitly linked with land: *al-arḍ 'arḍ*, 'land is honour', or again, *man aqdam li-arḍ-uk aqdam li-'arḍ-uk*, 'whoever transgresses against your land transgresses against your honour'. In fact it occurs in a wide range of cases. In general it is *sharaf*'s complement. The terms *sharaf* and *'arḍ* sometimes bear resemblance to what Pitt-Rivers dubbed 'honour=precedence' and 'honour=virtue' (Pitt-Rivers 1977: 9, 10, 15; Meeker 1976: 261), but the characteristic of *'arḍ* in the tribal Yemeni case is that this virtue must be defended.[18]

It would be an imposition to speak of two types of honour (men often say the words are synonymous), but the associations of the terms are in practice distinct. What breaks *sharaf*, apart from a specific disgrace, is said to be calumny or gossip (*al-ḥadīth bayn al-nās*): the quality is tantamount to reputation or good standing. What damages *'arḍ*, by contrast, is assault (whether against a tribesman himself or, for example, against his women-folk) and offences which make one unable to resist such assault; for example, taking away a tribesman's weapons (cf. Bourdieu 1965: 219).

The two aspects cannot be separated. One might clumsily say that *sharaf* depends upon *'arḍ* or contains *'arḍ*, and this spatial imagery accords moderately well with local usage. A man who is not of honourable standing (for example, because he fails to 'control' or 'defend' his women) is said to be 'deficient' in *sharaf* and 'wide' of *'arḍ*: the basis of his honour is, as it were, exposed to view and exposed to potential depredation by others. A man whose weapons are taken is, for the moment, similarly 'wide' of *'arḍ*, his vulnerability is laid open to others, whether or not these others exploit their chance or even think of doing so. Again, the difference between honour's two aspects is apparent in the verbs employed with them: *sharaf* can be 'broken' (the verb one hears is *kasara*), but with *'arḍ* it is always *hataka*, 'to ravage', 'violate', or 'expose' as in ripping aside a veil. The appearance of strength implies a corresponding vulnerability, a space that one has to defend; and one's moral vulnerability can only increase with one's prestige.[19] What the space contains is perhaps not crucial, but the opposition of such spaces to each other informs much of tribal life.

Again, let us start with women. An assault by a man on a woman in any circumstance is *'ayb*, a disgrace which must be repaired by particular amends. In a serious case, such as wounding or killing, the blood-money or wound-money might be paid over 'four-fold'. In less serious cases amends for an offence against a woman commonly comprise three parts. If, for example, a stranger strikes a man's wife but inflicts on her no serious wound, he might be required to pay 110 silver thalers, a bull, and a *kiswah* (set of clothes). The last of these goes to the woman herself, the bull is slaughtered at the door of her husband's house, and the money is paid to him. If a husband struck his wife inside the house, he might pay perhaps YR 200 to her father and brothers, and she might well go home to them for a time. If he struck her in public, he might be required to pay perhaps half the fine demanded of a stranger; a set of clothes for the woman, and perhaps a ram and fifty silver thalers to her paternal kin.[20] Four-fold compensation for a wound inflicted by an outsider is commonly divided between the woman herself and her husband or her father and brothers.

The double aspect of a wrong deserves noting clearly. For a man to offend against a woman is *'ayb* or 'disgrace' (a breach of the morality which tribesmen share generally), but that *'ayb* is at the same time an 'insult' to the particular men whose honour is bound up with hers. A breach of right is nearly always a breach of someone's rights.[21] Moreover, a woman threatened with wrong resorts to her husband or, if he is the wrongdoer, to her father's and brother's house, not to society at large or some public authority.[22] In general, the tribal world is made up of separate moral spaces, defined in opposition to one another, within each of which one might take refuge against violence or defamation. Right and wrong are in general agreed on. But the right is upheld only in the space coincident with a given man's *sharaf*, and that space is what one refers to as *'arḍ*. It may contain a man's dependants, his property, and much else besides.

Offences against a woman and the amends for such offences are both referred to as *tashwīf* (from *shawfah*, 'a woman', syn. *ḥurmah*, among other terms). That the same word is applied by men to offences against children is perhaps not surprising; the word is also applied, however, to offences against land, the house, and chattels. In the course of a protracted dispute between two families in Dhū Muḥammad, for example, a pile of firewood was ignited by tracer bullets. The owners of the wood claimed amends for *tashwīf*. During a dispute between parts of Sufyān and Arḥab a stand of cane was more deliberately set fire to. Again the claim was for *tashwīf*. The same term is heard used of killing livestock, harming trees, and even breaking windows.

A similar semantic field attaches to *bāyis*, a term used particularly of offences against women and children but also of those against livestock and crops. Wars in which the rules of decent conduct went by the board were referred to as *ḥarb jāzī wa-bāyis*, the *jāzī*, or *jāyiz*, being the arms-bearing men of the tribe, who may honourably be attacked, and the *bāyis* being in effect everyone and everything else, which may not (Dresch 1987*a*: 80 n. 28). Again, men may pledge to defend their *mu'awwarāt* in common. The word is related to *'ār*, which means serious 'disgrace' and is a common polite circumlocution for a man's womenfolk. *Mu'awwarāt*, then, are 'things which might shame or disgrace us'. The term can refer, though, not only to women but to crops, the house, and livestock; in the context of tribes, to borders, roads, and markets; indeed, in the end to anything which may be attacked and on which one's honour depends. In personal contexts it refers most often to a man's house and land.

The house provides a refuge from the constant disturbance of public life. The workaday phrase 'at home' (*fi l-bayt*) has about it a weight of meaning and is said with a forceful contentment well stressed by the accompanying gesture: the head tips a bit to one side, and the hands, palms down, come from chest height to waist height, as if patting in place the bedding, the cushions one sits on, the tea things, and all of life's cares. *Fi l-bayt, murtāh!* ('At home and comfortable') *al-ḥamdu li-llāh* ('God be praised'). A man at home and the house itself are *āmin fī amān allāh* ('safe in God's peace'), and are supposed to be *āmin ḍāmin* ('secure and guaranteed'). Few chances were taken. Until recently houses were built for defence (some still are) and, whether round towers or square-cornered structures, had no windows on the lower floors but only loopholes or slits. To fire on a house without good reason is a disgrace. Even with a good reason not all of the house exterior is a legitimate target. At Jabal Baraṭ, where imposing mud buildings stand four or five stories high at least, near the top of the house there is often a distinct level called *tajwāb*. Although this is usually at about the level of the kitchen (where the women might normally be), in time of trouble it provides a kind of 'fighting top' from which the defence is conducted. If you fire on the house lower down, you owe a bull and 110 silver thalers.

The status of the house is not limited to those occasions where it serves as a fort. Theft from the house also demands certain amends. A document from Baraṭ which purports to have been drawn up in the eighteenth century but may well have altered in the subsequent copying, specifies this as follows:

If one of the tribesmen should enter the building *(zabn)* of his fellow and steal something from it, he shall have no brother and no fellow [i.e. he can call on no one in the tribe for help] unless he pays the cost (*naqīsah*, i.e. of the thing stolen) and the cost of the house (*ghālī al-bayt*) according to the tribesmen's judgment/laws.[23]

The 'cost of the house' is a set fine for violating what we can call the house-peace. It is paid in cattle and sheep. At Baraṭ it was traditionally, it seems, (and still is) reckoned at a bull or camel for each door the culprit forces and a sheep for each floor he enters, plus four times the value of whatever he steals. In Arḥab a century ago the stolen goods were returned, a fine was paid of the same amount as the goods' value, and a beast hocked at the door (Glaser 1884: 176). The details still differ from tribe to tribe, but specific amends are everywhere recognized for what in English law would be breaking and entering. Taking things from a man by force elsewhere is not 'theft' *(saraqah)* but simply 'plunder' *(nahb)*. No specific amends are due. The Baraṭ document goes on to specify other offences, such as burning a house or part of its contents, or entering a man's house and firing on him from it. For all such offences amends are due, made up of slaughter-beasts and cash payment.

Amends for a breach of the house-peace, whether by firing at the home from outside or stealing something from within it, are commonly referred to as *hajar al-bayt* or *tahjīr al-bayt*. The root *h-j-r* suggests primarily that the house here is 'set aside' (we shall encounter related terms in other contexts later). That amends of some sort are due for an attack on the house might perhaps be expected, since the house is associated with women and with the private domain they control, and the term *ḥarīm* (the plural, in Yemen, of *ḥurmah*) itself means, in essence, a sacrosanct space and the persons who fall within it. However, amends may be due for a breach of the house-peace in circumstances quite unrelated to this. For instance, two guests in the public room of the house (the *dīwān* or *mafraj*) might quarrel and come to blows. If they did, they would owe the householder *hajar al-bayt*; a sheep to be slaughtered at the door of the house, or a bull in more serious cases. The householder suffers no harm himself, nor do his dependants, but he is still insulted: his 'face', as the tribesmen say, is 'blackened'.

THE IDEA OF A PERSONAL PEACE

> If anyone entertains, as a guest in his own house, a trader or some other man from beyond the border . . . and if he then does wrong to some one, the man [of the house] shall bring him to justice or satisfy justice in his place.
>
> *Dooms of Hlothaere and Eadric*
>
> If a man coming from afar . . . leave the highway and then neither calls out nor blows a horn, he shall be considered a thief, to be slain or to be redeemed . . .
>
> *Dooms of Wihtread* trans. C. Stephenson and F. G. Marcham

The face is a metaphor for a man's honour. What 'breaks' a man's *sharaf* is said to 'blacken' his face; not only insults from others, but cowardice on his part, miserliness, and disgraceful actions of all sorts. By contrast, the face is 'whitened' by courage, generosity, and honourable conduct. 'God blacken his face' is an expression of strong disapproval, perhaps even a curse, while 'God whiten your face' is an expression of thanks and approval used where one might equally say 'God strengthen you' or 'God bless you' (Dresch 1987*b*). A tribesman who wishes to promise you something emphatically will say 'my face' and draw a finger down his cheek to make the point. A gloss such as 'on my honour' would be reasonable here. If a man 'gives his face' to another, one can sometimes translate this simply as 'gives his word'.[24] However the same phrase can mean that he takes the other man 'under his protection', and in most contexts, 'in his face' *(fī wajh-hu)* has a sense only roughly bracketed by these quite separate English glosses.

Two guests in another's house are 'in the face of' the householder. If they fight, they insult him; but he is also disgraced or insulted (*muʿayyab*) if someone else does them harm, if they do him harm, or, most of all, if he harms them himself. The relation of host to guest (*muḍayyif* and *ḍayf*) is in part paralleled by that of escort to traveller (*muraffiq* and *rafīq*) and by certain others which may all be assimilated to the couple *jār* and *mujawwir*; 'protégé' (or 'neighbour') and 'protector'.[25] The principle is accepted by all tribesmen everywhere that *al-jār fī wajh mujawwir-hu*: the protégé is 'on the honour' of his protector, or in his charge, or must be defended by him. This responsibility for protecting one's neighbour or protégé is conceived of in the simple terms of honour described already—'my *jār*'s '*arḍ* is my '*arḍ*, and his *sharaf* is mine'—but a consideration of customary law relating to these responsibilities sketches out a structure which takes us some way beyond the terms themselves and is of general importance (Dresch 1981).

One should not harm one's own protégé. It would be '*ayb*, a disgrace for which heavy amends are due, such as four times or even eleven times the value of what was stolen. If the offence were serious, and particularly if the host killed his guest or the escort his fellow-traveller, it would be '*ayb aswad* ('black shame'), for which, in the case of murder, at least eleven times the blood-money would be due to the victim's kin if amends were accepted at all. The culprit's own kin might well drive him out. They might even, so it is said (Rossi 1948: 31), kill him themselves to wipe out the disgrace that his action brought on them. Quite what happens in practice when the unthinkable occurs is hard to assess (it would not be a thing people talked of),[26] but what matters for the moment is that it is the unthinkable: to murder one's guest or one's travelling companion is as black a crime as can be imagined.

If someone else offends against his protégé, the tribesman should extract compensation for his protégé from the culprit or take revenge. If, for example, a guest is robbed, the host is honour-bound to retrieve what was stolen or to make amends to the guest from his own pocket (it is '*ayb* if he fails to). If an escort or host failed to extract one's amends from the culprit or to pay from his own pocket, one could summons him publicly, but here in any case practice often confirms what the rule prescribes. A host will pursue a claim on his guest's behalf, or an escort on behalf of his travelling companion, though not always with the willing alacrity that honour demands in the ideal version.

The protector is himself also due amends from the culprit. If his protégé is killed, he must not only avenge him (or extract blood-money if the dead man's kin prefer payment), but must somehow wipe out the disgrace to himself. Numerous stories are told of escorts who gave over years of their lives to extracting from the family or tribe of the man who killed their travelling companion seven deaths in return for the one that besmirched their honour. Such tales are, of course, apocryphal. They are part of the heroic image the tribesmen have of themselves. Again, though, there is no doubt about how seriously the matter is taken, and cases of revenge in practice (though not seven-fold that I am aware of) are supplemented by cases of multiple compensation, where the tribesman whose protégé has been killed demands four times the blood-money or more.

If a protégé is the victim of outside assault, no one else but his protector can take up his case to extract from the culprit revenge or compensation. If a guest is robbed, it is for the host to make amends. Not even the guest can seek out the thief and extract compensation for himself without insulting his host (in other words, it would be *'ayb*), and if he did so, the host might claim amends from him. Nor may third parties intervene unless explicitly asked by the host to do so, they would presume on his rights and owe him amends themselves. The case is comparable (and considered so) to one man presuming to right some wrong against another's dependants or womenfolk. He violates the protected space on which a tribesman's honour itself depends. If one has a claim on a tribesman's protégé, one must therefore go to the tribesman, the corollary being that the protector is answerable for his protégé and the latter is answerable to him.

The status of protector and protégé can be given by specific relations. Those of hospitality and of escort have already been mentioned. One can add to these the case of formal 'refuge' (*qaṭār* or *rubā'*), whereby one man is granted another's protection for a specific length of time; of 'companionship' (*rafaq*, a more general link than that to the 'travelling companion' or *rafīq al-janb*) whereby a man is responsible for another in some stated circumstance; and 'guaranty' (*ḍamān*), which we shall say more of in the following chapter. In all of these cases the tie is between one tribesman and another. Certain other people are protected at all times on account of their birth: the Jews, for example, are all *jīrān* ('neighbours' or 'protégés', the pl. of *jār*). Ḥayyim Habshūsh (see Goitein 1941: 40) relates a late nineteenth-century case where a Jew was killed by a tribesman, and an assembly of shaykhs from Ḥāshid and Bakīl judged that the killer's people should pay four times the blood-money. The possibility that the killer himself be killed was waived on the grounds that he was mad, which may or may not have been so, and the compensation was divided: half to the dead Jew's kin and half to the tribesmen 'on whose honour' he had lived. Such payment four-fold is commonly prescribed for a wide range of offences against non-tribal, 'weak' people in addition to the Jews.

They too are *jīrān*. As was mentioned earlier, offences against women may require payment four-fold. Again, these amends were divided between the victim and those 'on whose honour' she was.

The cases just listed are each spoken of in terms simply of *sharaf* and *'arḍ* (of 'honour'), and they form a list of instances where honour is at stake. The terminology used, though, does not by itself express the idea that the defence of dependants is not only a responsibility, but a right and a prerogative to be upheld against others. Something like personal sovereignty or jurisdiction is at issue. The cases listed rough out a moral structure of great importance, but no case by itself describes that structure and no one Arabic term denotes it. Let us call it a personal 'peace'. Each tribesman by dint of his honour/nobility has a peace not unlike the Old English *mund* (see Jolliffe 1961: 11, 46; Dresch 1981), and the breach of that peace, from within or without, requires amends like the *mundbryce*. Such amends are paid in addition to (or more properly before) any compensation for material damage. As we have already seen, amends may be due where no damage is done at all. We are not here concerned with a straightforward guide to action (the degree to which rules are upheld varies greatly), but the structure the rules comprise, and which itself makes sense of them, is of general applicability. It is this which underpins the social representation of the tribesman's person.

The boundary of the peace works a complete reversal of what is appropriate toward others, a point admirably discussed by Pitt-Rivers (1977: 101, 110) and apparent in a great deal of anecdotal material: outside my peace you are potentially my rival and your honour is opposed to mine, while inside my peace your honour and mine coincide in that mine now depends upon my care for yours. Crossing the boundary is, as one might expect (ibid. 119), carefully marked. When one comes in the door to a group of men, who already are in the peace of the householder, the formal exchange of courtesies is elaborate.[27] Among the eastern tribes (those of Baraṭ, for instance, but particularly Murād) the courtesies are much as they were in Glaser's day (see Glaser 1903: 37):

kayf int? (How are you?)
salimt. (I am well=quite safe.)
kayf ḥālak. (How are things?)
sallim ḥālak! ([God] make things good for you.)

ṭayyib? (All right?)
ṭāb allāh fīk! (God make things all right for you.)
quwwīt! wa-'ilm-ak?: ([God] strengthen you. Your news?)
'afākum allāh, ma bi-h 'ilm! (God spare you. No news.)
'ilm wa-lā khabar? (No news at all?)
kull 'ilm zayn. (Only good news.)
ḥayyā 'llāh man jā'. (God grant life to the one who comes here.)
ḥayyākum allāh . . . (And God grant you life . . .)

In Murād and to the east of Baraṭ even the long string of courtesies Glaser gives would be a minimum. The exchange of *aysh ḥālakum? / sallim allāh ḥālakum. aysh ḥālakum? / allāh yusallim ḥālakum, aysh ḥālakum?* can be easily repeated six or eight times with the principal man in the room. An exchange or two is also required with every other man present. One is gradually tied to what in effect is a formal truce. One is made a guest, or a fellow guest or a fellow traveller, where before one was a stranger and potentially hostile.

The combination of persons in these terms makes up much of the course of public life. Among certain of the eastern tribes, much of conflict and settlement turned on a recognition of the individual's peace in a discrete, legalistic sense. Only men of good standing could take others in or escort them, and for certain offences this standing (*malzam*) was suspended until due amends were made (Dresch 1987*b*). A man in fear of revenge could take refuge as a *qaṭīr* with another for a stated length of time (the length of a crop season were he settled; four months and ten days were he a nomad) but only in some circumstances, not in others, and while he had this status he could not be attacked. The *qaṭīr al-dukhkhān* (so called from the 'smoke' of the kitchen fire) came and stayed with his protector, but the *qaṭīr al-ujrah* (who 'paid' two silver riyals or Maria Theresa thalers) could still enjoy protection though he stayed where he was in his own village.[28] Again, various categories of escort were recognized (*sāyir* or *rafīq al-janb*), whose protection a man could claim for a time under some circumstances but not others. The man who offered protection was to be respected by his protégé's antagonist, and in the course of a dispute one would seem to have moved from one man's peace to another's, and then to another still, according to the options prescribed in the wake of one's particular offence, for given times under given conditions, as if in an elaborate board game. Nowadays the provisions are not so complex on the plateau. However, who is in whose peace at a given time, and whether they are so by 'refuge' or 'escort', 'companionship', 'guaranty', 'arbitration', and so on, is important. The alignment of such relations is the stuff of small-scale politics, and, as we shall see in later chapters, provides the outlines of larger alignments too.

It is important to note that a tribesman may enter another's peace without demeaning himself. The asymmetry of the relation is possible because it is not given but contracted and temporary. The protected person has a peace of his own and one day the man now giving protection may be in it (Pitt-Rivers 1977: 104, 108). A man who has no peace of his own (a person born 'weak', or a subject share-cropper) is demeaned by always being under another's protection, and where a relation is in other terms asymmetric but honour needs to be maintained (as, for instance, where a powerful man has tribesmen attached to his household), the position is defined with due care: a shaykh's close adherents are his *khubrah* 'companions'). But in the classical relations of protection (host to guest, escort to traveller, etc.) the personal asymmetry is vital: one man is clearly he whose honour is at stake, and who is answerable to his fellows.

There can also be discerned in some circumstances an impersonal peace; a moral space, if one likes, on the inviolability of which depends the honour of several men but which is not itself coincident with any one man's honour. A case in point is the 'bond of bread and salt', linking men who eat together. The law in eastern Yemen is said to be that 'eating meat and bread [together] gives eight days obligation (*thamāniyah wujāb*), grapes and raisins, dates and milk give four days, and coffee just that day, according to the custom of our fathers and forefathers'.[29] For any of those who have eaten together to offend against another during the specified period is '*ayb*, or 'disgrace', and to kill him is 'black shame'. Moreover, if an outsider attacks one of these men during the specified period, those he ate with are honour-bound to defend him. In a case like this, we might say that it is the obligation which is 'on the honour' (*fī wajh*) of each man, rather than one man being the protégé of another. A comparable instance is found where, instead of one acting as escort, a group of men agree to travel together (*yatasāyarū*).

These combinations of men in symmetrical relations are often fragile. A man of generous disposition will aid another with or without such bonds, while the churl is seldom constrained by them to act otherwise than he would anyway. To kill a fellow traveller would be 'black shame': very heavy amends would be required if amends were accepted at all, and public opinion would be outraged. However, simply to lose interest in a fellow traveller and leave him to his own devices would excite rather little comment: the impersonal peace can so readily collapse into the defence of each individual's honour. If the first man claims the second is at fault in abandoning some common or mutual commitment, the second can claim the fault lies with the first, and nothing will result but some pointless shouting back and forth between them, which may even lead to fighting but will certainly do nothing to restore relations.

To maintain particular ties, therefore, an asymmetric relation is looked for that is necessarily personal: one man must clearly commit his honour to upholding the peace between other men. There is no notion of symmetrical contracts such as in practice would give rise to a corporation, whether sole or aggregate. This is plainly important, and we shall see what results it has when we turn to consider groups in the following chapter. For the moment let us stop short with the formal distinction between a personal and impersonal peace: two types of protected space within which rights should be upheld, and outside which these rights can only be fought for.

A CASE OF VIOLENT ANTAGONISM

Something of the conceptual order involved in the language of individual honour has now been laid out. It does not always correspond to political order even in the sense of events following a set pattern, far less in the sense of a lack of violence. None of what has been explained so far corresponds to a set of causal rules, nor do tribesmen suppose it does. There is seldom agreement in a given case whether or not a man's action is really honourable; the common position is that 'Everyone is at fault but me'. The notion of 'balance' *(mīzān)* is recognized generally, but life being what it is, and tribesmen being what they are in their own view, balance is seldom unequivocally reached. Disorder, in the baldest, most violent sense, is a constant threat.

Let us look briefly at a case where blood simply led to blood.[30] In the late 1970s, 'Alī Muṭlaq, a shaykh from a certain Bakīl tribe, was deeply involved with the National Democratic Front in opposition to the Ṣan'ā' government of the time. His son Aḥmad 'Alī and his son's friend, Muḥammad Sa'd, were both with the Front as well, but they somehow fell out with each other over dividing a shipment of arms. When Aḥmad 'Alī's petrol station was fired on one night, he held Muḥammad Sa'd to be the culprit. Whether he was or not, God knows. Aḥmad 'Alī went to the truck repair shop in the tribe's market town where Muḥammad Sa'd worked, and in the course of a violent quarrel shot Muḥammad Sa'd and wounded him badly. Muḥammad shot Aḥmad back, killing him, then lurched out of the shop and ran towards the main road. He was shot again by one of Aḥmad's companions and was picked up in the road by other men from the tribe, who took him under their protection. They sent him to Ṣan'ā'. When he came out of hospital there, he moved into a house not far from that of Ḥāshid's paramount shaykh. When he recovered fully he joined the (para-) Military Police in Ṣan'ā', whose chief of staff at the time was a Ḥāshidī.

'Alī Muṭlaq and his friends saw the hands of the Ḥāshid shaykhs in all this. For years they had been at odds. He had now lost his eldest son, and the killer, as he saw it, was protected by the government, whom in any case he saw as under Ḥāshid's influence. Another of his sons, Ḥusayn b. 'Alī Muṭlaq, had been killed in Ḥūth a year earlier, in Ḥāshid's territory. A group from one of the Ḥāshid tribes had, some years before that, killed a man from a section of 'Alī Muṭlaq's tribe, and that section had killed in revenge a man who happened to be a minor shaykh. The particular group from Ḥāshid involved in this refused to accept parity. They demanded 'a shaykh for a shaykh', although no sanction exists for such things in custom, and it was Ḥusayn 'Alī Muṭlaq, then some fourteen years old, whom they ambushed and killed in return. A particular viciousness on the part of those involved was perhaps behind this (men from their own tribe certainly thought so), and the whole case was anyway poisoned by a deep disagreement on national politics between the leading shaykhs on each side.

When a truce was eventually made between the Front and the government, 'Alī Muṭlaq went into Ṣan'ā'. Some say he demanded that his eldest son's killer, Muḥammad Sa'd, be removed from Ṣan'ā' and from the government's protection. Whatever the case,

Muḥammad reappeared in the tribe. His pay was now issued not from Ṣan'ā' but from a town much nearer the tribe, where his antagonists might more easily trap him. Some say he arrived laden with arms and money given him by shaykhs from Ḥāshid, others that he hid in his house not knowing what to do. Some saw in events a plot whereby 'Alī Muṭlaq's antagonists in Ḥāshid and their supposed government allies now intended to wipe out Bayt Muṭlaq totally. In fact, the timing of events makes this not just unlikely but almost impossible. No motive, though, was too dark to be plausible. Antagonism draws all things to it and is not itself bound by strict logic.

Muḥammad Sa'd's pay was now administered from a certain town. 'Alī Muṭlaq rented a house overlooking the road to (para-) Military Police headquarters there, and he and his friends then waited their chance to murder Muḥammad. The latter, though, got his blow in first. He ambushed 'Alī Muṭlaq's party on the road, killed yet another of 'Alī's sons, Fāris, wounded 'Alī Muṭlaq himself, and wounded one Yaḥyā Shāfī who was with them. This Yaḥyā Shāfī was a friend of Muḥammad Sa'd, as Aḥmad b. 'Alī Muṭlaq had once been. Muḥammad now sent him gifts at the hospital by way of Yaḥyā's uncle. The uncle then seems to have done a deal with 'Alī Muṭlaq's family, for a party of them moved into the uncle's house, next door to the house where Muḥammad Sa'd was hiding in fear of his life. Not suspecting anything, Muḥammad came up on the roof. From the roof of the next door house 'Alī Muṭlaq's men shot him in the stomach.

A battle began from house to house. Muḥammad Sa'd's mother went in search of a doctor, and when she returned was shot dead by a stray round through the window. According to most accounts she fell across the body of her son, who had died in her absence. According to many accounts she was deliberately killed by the enemy when they stormed the house (which they never did); others claimed she killed herself in her misery at finding her son dead (which is not what happened either). Neither of these stories was confined to those far away and unlikely to know what happened: they were believed by anyone with some sympathy for Bayt Sa'd. That a woman was killed was quite shocking enough, but for her to be murdered intentionally would be a hideous breach of honour, a breach of the sort that cannot be repaired. Antagonism makes all things seem credible, and most of those close at hand were willing to commit at least their feelings to one side of the breach or other.

A cease-fire was forced by another section of the tribe, who came under white flags and slaughtered bulls. Muḥammad Sa'd's mother was carried out by her own people (from another tribe altogether), and the truce soon ended. The shooting began again from house to house. The next morning 'Alī Muṭlaq's relatives fired shots over the grave of Aḥmad Alī to show he had been avenged (Muḥammad Sa'd's death paid for his), but when, some days later, one of Muḥammad Sa'd's cousins was shot dead too, no shots were fired over Fāris's grave. Bayt Muṭlaq did not accept that balance had been restored. In another village Aḥmad b. 'Alī's mother had by now been wounded by an unknown sniper one night. In a third village a group of Bayt Muṭlaq's relatives, who had been seen moving into a house near that of Bayt Sa'd's relatives, were sent to ground by bazooka fire. A little later one of Bayt Sa'd's women, who was carrying a sack of flour into her house, was shot and badly paralysed.

The rest of the tribe at last managed to force a truce, but it should by now be clear that the imagery of weapons and the rhetoric of honour, which most often have a playful aspect, can be part of fearful events. Heroic rhetoric perhaps fits well enough the excitement of shooting and being shot at. The fear that builds up as the firing goes on and on, though, is no less for the tribesman than for anyone else. The suspense of waiting makes his palms sweaty, just like anyone else's. Certainly the wounds are as ghastly to him as to any man, and some of those wounded are not even combatants. It can all be horribly real. Too much can be made of these possibilities, and it is not the case that great fear is felt all the time, which then bends the whole way tribesmen see the world; but the wearing of daggers and the chanting of boastful ditties are one thing, and being left on the ground with a broken thigh or one's belly ripped open is quite another.

Tribesmen are not violent people. They are quite well aware of what can happen in a society armed as theirs is, and they do what they can do to restrain their fellows. If two men quarrel, others intervene unasked. Any man can 'call a halt' (*yudarrik*, classical *yudārik*; Zabārah 1956: i. 2/252) between two others by raising his head cloth and coming between them, but it would often need to be a brave man who did so. A first intervention is seldom successful

Intermediaries build up gradually and impose on the people at odds, first throwing down head cloths then slaughtering bulls, but the conflict may already have taken hold, and once men are killed their fellows may want revenge. Persuading them otherwise can be a long, complex business.

'Alī Muṭlaq's position as of late 1983 was that the death of Muḥammad Sa'd's cousin did not pay for the death of Fāris b. 'Alī Muṭlaq, but only for the insult to the latter's escort. The stones had still not been placed on Fāris's grave. A death was still owing. It seemed, though, that the matter would prove negotiable and a settlement would be reached.[31] If it was, we should remember the much earlier death of Ḥusayn b. 'Alī at Ḥūth, who was murdered in return for a shaykh who himself was killed in return for a man from Bin Muṭlaq's tribe. One side said that the balance had been restored. The other side said it had not. Straddling as it does the divide between Ḥāshid and Bakīl, and thus being entangled with 'Alī Muṭlaq's dislike of certain Ḥāshid shaykhs, which in turn involves all manner of political history, the outstanding blood-debt for Ḥusayn b. 'Alī has an ominous look of longevity. He was still young when killed, which undoubtedly rankles. He was killed without warning on a main road where he should have been safe. In his kinsmen's view he was killed for no good reason, since balance had by then been reached. There is some doubt as to whether he was even armed. For a number of reasons his murder was widely reckoned a particularly vicious business, and although whether the matter resurfaces in the immediate future depends on imponderable tangles of personal, tribal, and national questions, it may well be remembered for years yet. It may form in due course a part of some quite new conflict. Not only can 'antagonism' (*khuṣmah*) spring up with alarming speed, but it spreads and then clings so it is hard to root out completely.

Nor does antagonism affect only personal rivals. In the case at hand, for instance, other men from Bin Muṭlaq's tribe who had links with Ḥāshid felt themselves in danger. They stayed in their homes with their shutters closed and no lights shown at night for fear of snipers, although they themselves had no part in the killings and no wish to take part. Squads of government troops came and went without resolving anything, and life in the immediate area was repeatedly brought to a stand still as the dispute sputtered on. More generally, men are involved in events that they did not start and now cannot control. One can only stay 'home' (*fi l-bayt*) and wait for events to subside. There is no community to appeal to, seldom someone in charge, usually only the 'light-blooded' tribesmen. As a problem expands, it involves not just those first at odds, but their kin and their tribes and, potentially, tribes at a greater distance.

NOTES

1. One can scarcely avoid Doughty's experience with the Badu of 100 years ago: 'Some put in my hands their long guns; and when any inscriptions were upon their arms they desired that I should read them.' The provenance and naming of fire-arms is discussed endlessly and deserves a paper to itself.
2. The decoration of dagger hafts with gold has often been condemned by reformers as un-Islamic (see e.g. Zabārah 1929: i. 111; al-Shawkānī 1929: i. 421), but Imam Yaḥyā himself seems on occasion to have sported a golden sheath (Zabārah 1956: ii. 212). The present paramount shaykh of Ḥāshid and his son wear splendid gold dagger sheaths, the orthodoxy of which is seldom questioned by anyone but a few fundamentalists.
3. Such nonce plurals as *khurūf* (the same word as that for 'sheep'; or perhaps *kharūf*, 'a small sheep') are not accorded any referential meaning. I have never heard any puns based on them. Nor have I heard meanings ascribed to tribal names in the way that, for example, al-Ḥimyarī 1916: 32 derives Khārif from 'one who guards date palms and vines'.
4. It might be relevant to note that *yushrif* means to strip the leaves from sorghum so that the stem stands out clearly (see al-Ḥibshī 1980: 472).
5. If I use the word 'shame' in passing, it is only as a synonym for disgrace. The classical couple of 'honour and shame', worked out by anthropologists primarily for southern Europe, would apply poorly here because the relation of individual persons to society is rather differently conceived. Where in Greece, for example, one could politely say *dropi* (shame), appealing in one word to communal values and a presumed respect for them, in Upper Yemen one could only say *iḥtaram nafs-ak* (respect yourself), which could well start a fight.
6. For excellent material on *adab* among the learned in South Asian Islam see Metcalf 1984.
7. *Labbatī shaybah wa-shāyibi* (sic) / *lā tu'amminū man kāna 'āyibi* / *wa-l-fasl mā 'adlī bi-sīrat-hi* / *mā naksab illā ḥāli l-dawālibi* / *al-mart allī jarr-hu mughayyabi* / *wa-l-mawt sākin fī madīnat-hi* (transcribed in Upper al-'Uṣaymāt). Rossi, translating a rather similar poem to the one transcribed here gives *labbatī* as '*Suvvia, venite in mio aiuto . . .*' (1939: 113). Informants explained it as 'answering the 'summons' of the tribal name'. The word *mughayyab*, which would usually mean 'invisible' (as if far away) was consistently explained as 'inaudible' and

thus useful for ambushes. The 'Mart' was first introduced to Yemen in 1892 and made a great impression with its lengthy range (Zabārah 1956: i. 2/71). It was reckoned worth five 'Arabi' muzzle-loaders (al-Ḥibshī 1980: 515), and when the tribes captured their first bolt-action Mausers they wanted to swap them for 'Marts' (Zabārah 1956: ii. 18). There are still a few around today.

8. For all the stimulating points of discussion, Black-Michaud's distinction (1980: 161, 187–9) between realistic and non-realistic conflict has to be rejected. In practice it can be sustained only by privileging our own society's metaphors of economic necessity over what local people say, a problem that also vitiates much of Bourdieu's discussion of exchange (Bourdieu 1977: 6–8, 163, 171–3, 181).
9. *Nāmūs* is not only a man's sexual honour as put at stake by his women-folk, but also that of the woman herself. The word can mean the hymen. So *maksūr (at) al-nāmūs* can have the more precise physical reference of 'deflowered'. Whether the phrase as applied to men has any homosexual connotation I am not at all sure. In apostrophizing the 'control' and 'defence' of women I follow Meeker 1976, with the general line of whose writing on honour I agree strongly although we phrase several problems differently. The present brief discussion of male/female relations turns on appearances, propriety, and meaning, not always on power.
10. For an account of Yemeni weddings see Chelhod 1973.
11. The reader may wonder how much bride-wealth was at issue: between each woman's husband and her paternal family some YR 70,000–80,000 had changed hands. However, all the women had been married for more than three years, after which no claim to reimbursement is usually recognized in custom. In fact it is the question of honour that gives bride-wealth its meaning, rather than a dispute over bride-wealth being merely glossed in terms of honour. Rather similar cases might be cited even from Dhū Muḥammad, where marriages within the tribe involved no *sharṭ* at all (no bride-price between families) but only *mahr* (paid to the bride herself) of about YR 5,000.
12. This sum of 800 MT is agreed on by most informants, supported by what little documentation I have seen from the turn of the century, and parallel to practice in the Hejaz at that time (Robertson-Smith 1885: 64 n. 1). Alternative computations arrive at 770 MT (Goitein 1941: 39; Rossi 1948: 5, 7), 300 gold thalers (Glaser 1884: 176), or 787 ½ silver riyals (Zabārah 1956: i. 1/66). In Sufyān and Suḥār of Khawlān b. 'Āmir (but nowhere else) I have been told several times that 800 thalers was paid and then 12 ½ thalers of it returned, the latter sum being called *milqāṭ* ('tweezers', 'pincers'). No rationale was offered.
13. For the details of calculating wound-money see Zabārah 1956: i. 1/66; al-Murtaḍā 1973: iv. 441 ff.; al-Ghazzālī 1979; Dresch forthcoming *a*, forthcoming *c*. The calculations are common to Islamic law and tribal custom, although the resulting quantities are sometimes applied in multiples by custom, which Islamic law disapproves.

14. Such statements are very common. Black-Michaud 1980: 42, for example, cites Hanoteau and Letourneux's assertion that 'La dia n'est pas *Kabyle*' but probably borrowed from the Arabs. One can almost bet that their Arab neighbours see compensation as 'not Arab' but originally *kabyle*. It is not a matter of exceptions to the rule, perhaps imported from elsewhere, but of defining whether or not an insult is retracted and thus of which rule to apply.
15. I use the term 'slaughter-beast' precisely because this is not a 'sacrifice' as usually understood either by religion or by anthropology. The option exists of depicting it as such. This option has often been taken up by those wishing to convict tribesmen of ignorance or incipient polytheism, and we shall return to it briefly in ch. 5.
16. Chelhod 1976: 74 n. 14 gives *thawr al-hajīm*. In ordinary usage /n/ and /m/ are often swapped (e.g. *janbiyyah*, *jambiyyah*), and it is quite possible that both versions are correct. The meaning, though, would surely be 'a bull for the offence', rather than *'le taureau qui attaque'*, as Chelhod has it.
17. The value of the livestock and *qāt* brought by Banī Maṭar at the outset was some YR 8,000–9,000. This was not referred to at any point in the negotiations.
18. The comparison of different rhetorics of honour requires separate treatment, but a single structure recurs throughout the tribal Middle East; a quite different structure is found in village societies of the area (e.g. Tunisia, northern Turkey); and both are quite different from the southern European scheme. The key point of difference for the present purpose is hinted at by vocabulary. In southern Europe a single term covers roughly shame as disgrace, shame as decency, and shame as a sense of modesty (e.g. Spanish *verguenza*, Italian *vergogna*, Greek *dropi*, cf. Pitt-Rivers 1977: 20–1). In Upper Yemen there is no such equivalence. Indeed, no term or set of terms corresponds even roughly to the range of English 'shame'. In Tunisia, by contrast, we find a 'sense of modesty' term (*ḥishmah*) related to that for disgrace (*ḥashm* = *'ayb*), though not to that for decency or vulnerable honour, and it is complimentary to say a man is *ḥashshām* (Abu Zahra 1982: 96), which one could not say in Upper Yemen. Typically, in the former setting *'arḍ* refers, among other things, to one's sociability and one's care for communal values (ibid. 97, 101, 120, 140), in this resembling the Turkish *nāmūs* (Meeker 1976: 261, 265). In Upper Yemen the stress is all on the defence of *'arḍ*, never explicitly upon one's care for an approving community or one's adherence to its shared ideas of decency. Herzfeld's point (1980) is well taken that honour and shame as English-language glosses are inadequate and often misleading. There remain, though, distinctive structurings of experience that we must find some way to deal with, and the subject is very far from exhausted.
19. Meeker 1976: 263, 266 makes the point that the greater one's projection of honour as prestige, the greater must one's care be for protecting one's virtue or decency. Pitt-Rivers's Spanish grandees, by contrast, could flaunt their prestige by counting virtue unimportant.

No man in the Yemeni scheme is free from the moral danger of 'exposure' or 'violation' (*hatk*). It is probably this latter term, though in a curious form, which appears in a passage I found obscure when I first translated it in 1982 (see Dresch 1987*a*: 57 n. 37).

20. The formal amends for *tashwīf* are remarkably regular. The great variations of payment come, instead, under the rubric of 'wound-money' (*arsh*). For example, an unpleasant (and, one should add, unusual) case of wife-beating in one of the more northerly tribes resulted in the husband paying *tashwīf* of a bull, 110 MT, and a *kiswah* worth SR 300; but the wound-money was reckoned at YR 3,600, which, since the woman was assaulted rather than badly battered, must have involved counting separately each discernible mark and bruise.
21. The English usage here very roughly parallels the Arabic. The Arabic term *sinnah* can mean that which is right because accepted as custom (cf. classical *sunnah* for the 'usage' of the Prophet). It can also mean a man's personal rights (a synonym often for *ḥaqq*, *ḥuqūq*) or his particular right, such as that to take in protégés, which derives from his tribal standing (here it is a synonym for *malzam*). A man who commits a serious offence for which no amends are recognized may also 'have no *sinnah*': it is so far removed from what is right that no settlement is possible. Lastly, a culprit may ask his victims for *sinnah* (Rossi 1948: 7 n. 2), meaning that they should specify, and show willing to accept, the amends which would satisfy them and so absolve the culprit.
22. If the marital and natal male relatives agree with each other at the woman's expense, she can take refuge with the structurally neutral figure of an Islamic judge (Mundy 1979: 179).
23. This is from the Baraṭ *qawā'id* which I first collected in 1979 and which I hope still to publish in full with Gerd Puin. The Arabic text is now available in Abū Ghānim 1985 and al-'Ulaymī 1986, though their explanatory notes should be treated cautiously.
24. The metaphor is sometimes deadened to the point where one says 'he has the face in his hand' (e.g. Ḥibshī 1980: 404, 435), meaning he has received a solemn promise.
25. For a list of these otherwise disparate instances see Rossi 1948: 3–4. For the rationale of treating them together, as here, see the preliminary attempt in Dresch 1981.
26. In the one case of this kind for which I got much detail the traitorous escort and his people paid eleven times the blood-money, and eleven '*ayb*s of a bull and 88 thalers. This occurred in the 1940s. The victim's children were minors, and this may well have influenced the decision to press for cash on their behalf rather than for blood revenge.
27. When tribesmen wish to acknowledge fellow tribesmen as such in these circumstances, or to distinguish themselves from men of learning, then, as Caton 1986 points out, the details of the exchange are specific.
28. The latter status has been done away with. Not only might the *qaṭīr*

al-dukhhkhān move in with you because he was afraid, but he might also move in because you were. You would be in his peace, although he had moved into your village. For further details of this elaborate system see the Baraṭ *qawāʿid* in Abū Ghānim 1985 or al-ʿUlaymī 1986.

29. The quotation is taken from a variant of the Baraṭ *qawāʿid* which was shown me by Ḥamūd Abū Ra's. The same passage occurs in a text shown me some years before by Muḥammad al-Ruʿaynī, who copied it from a document shown him in the Jawf. The specific provisions listed here seem to be recognized throughout the eastern areas of Yemen.
30. For obvious reasons the names in the following account have all been changed. They now bear no relation to the originals.
31. The matter of the murdered women might appear a stumbling block. In fact it seemed likely that their deaths would be redefined as unintentional (*bi-ghayr ʿamd*), which is done by soliciting oaths from the culprits. Although such definitional shifts are not always easy to produce, they are common and of obvious importance.

3 Tribes and Collective Action

> Everyone is . . . so far independent, as he is able to repel all violence, and avenge to his heart's content all damage done to him, and in general to live after his own mind. . . . If two come together and unite their strength, they have jointly more power . . .
>
> Spinoza, *Political Treatise*

Tribesmen all belong to particular tribes. This gives them 'authenticity' of descent (*aṣl*) and hence the quality of honour which they consider distinguishes them from non-tribal, weak people. The tribes themselves are territorial entities. Usually the territory of each is contiguous, each has known borders with its neighbours, and there are very few points within 'the land of the tribes' which do not belong clearly to one tribe or another.[1] The now rather worn image of the Saussurean chess-board is therefore appealing (Ardener 1971*a*; xxxvi; Dresch forthcoming *b*): one is always in a space whose value derives from its position among others like it, and what one does then takes its meaning in large part from where one is. Within this general system are the tribesmen themselves, their shaykhs, and the collective identities coincident with tribes and sections.

TRIBES AS ELEMENTS IN THE LANGUAGE OF HONOUR

The size and internal structure of tribes both vary from case to case. Banī Ṣuraym, for example, comprises nine 'ninths' (*atsā*'), which are not arranged in higher-order units such as pairs or triplets, and each ninth has a discrete territory of its own within that of Banī Ṣuraym as a whole (see Fig. 3.1). The number of tribesmen mustered by each ninth varies greatly from one to the next; so if Banī Mālik and al-Ghuthaymah numbered only about 500 each as of 1983, Banī Qays stood at about 2,000 and Wāda'ah probably at more than that. The ninths are themselves subdivided. Khayār, for example, contains six 'sixths' (*asdās*): al-Qubbah (about 150 men),

Banī Shawīṭ (about 100), Banī Nāshir (100), al-Ḥablah (200), al-Mahāṣir (150), and al-Qadārīn (150). Each of these comprises a geographically rather scattered village cluster which none the less has clear borders with its neighbours. Each recognizes a single shaykhly family as having some prominence in its affairs, and indeed two of the names, Nāshir and Shawīṭ, are those of shaykhs.

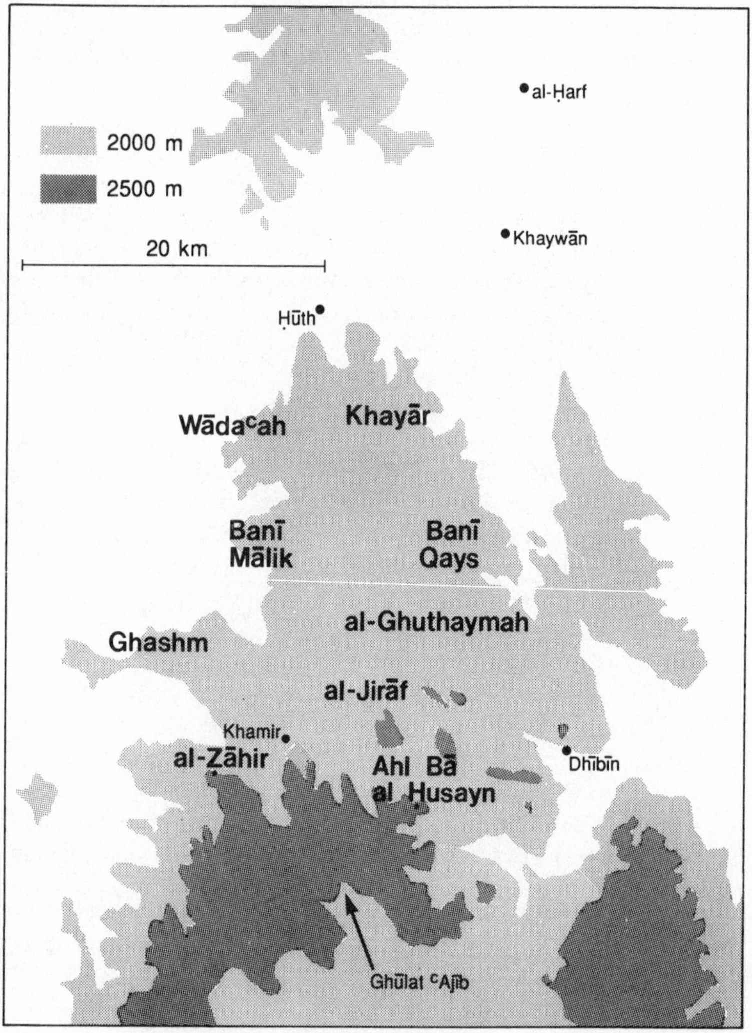

FIG. 3.1 Geography of Banī Ṣuraym

Al-ʿUṣaymāt has a more elaborate internal structure. The tribe is said by its members to derive from four siblings (Jabrah, Qīsah, Faḍlah, Ghanāyah) and a more distant relative of theirs (al-Muʿammar). Dhū Qīsah now comprises only seven heads of families and their dependants, but Dhū Jabrah (at the same level in the organizational scheme) subdivides extensively, as shown in Fig. 3.2. Some of these sections subdivide further still: Dhū Mashar and Dhū Jābir b. Jallah between them compromise twenty-four named units. Some ideas of the numbers involved is given by noting that Jawādī as a whole musters about 600 arms-bearing men and al-Ḥumrān about 150 (more will be said about al-Ḥumrān below; they are the section from which Ḥāshid's paramount shaykh comes), while Sallābī musters probably between 1,000 and 2,000.

The classification of tribal divisions sometimes involves ambiguities that neat diagrams like these disguise,[2] but the two examples just given show at least the scale of the units we are dealing with. Each tribe is loosely spoken of as descended from either Ḥāshid or Bakīl, or as simply 'going back to' (*tarjaʿ ilā*) one or the other, which need not mean much more than 'belong to': one can say, for example, that London 'goes back to' England.

For most purposes such identities are taken as given (the forms of change in fact are rather specific, as we shall see in later chapters), and analytically it is as well to distinguish between the tribe and the people who at any one time make it up. Tribes outlive by a long way their individual members. More important, perhaps, the tribes are taken to be geographically fixed (there is no rhetoric of

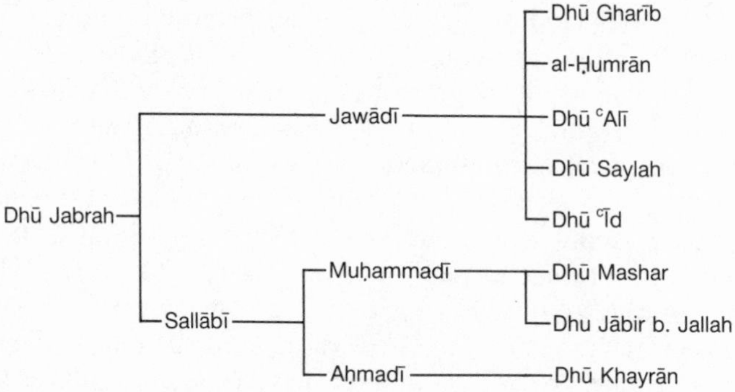

FIG. 3.2 Divisions of Dhū Jabrah, al-ʿUṣaymāt

conquest or displacement), while men and families need not be. A glance at any detailed map is enough to reveal place-names in one tribe that refer to another, such as Bayt al-Wāda'ī, Bayt al-'Ammārī, and Bayt al-Ḥāshidī in 'Iyāl Yazīd (Steffen 1978: ii. 53), and the assumption is usually made that the village founder was from the other tribe. When one comes to look at individual families the effect is still more marked. Even when the family name is not that of a place or tribe other than their present one, people often have traditions that their ancestors at some point were *naqā'il* (pl. of *naqīlah*), people who moved in from elsewhere. The tribes themselves, by contrast, are usually taken 'always' to have been where they now are, as also are most smaller collective identities at anything above family level.

The men of a tribe speak of themselves as 'from one forebear' *(min jadd wāḥid)* and thus as 'brothers' to each other. The sections of the tribe are also reckoned 'sons' of the tribal eponym, and the tribesmen are sons of their particular section (and brothers within that section) as well as sons of the whole tribe—so a segmentary classification is described in an idiom of shared ancestry.

Men do not, on the whole, take this idiom to describe personal descent. Tribes may be derived by their more learned members from two unrelated sources and still be spoken of as 'from one forebear',[3] while men or sections who are known to have joined the tribe only recently are as much 'from one forebear' as those who have shared the tribe's eponym for as long as anyone knows. The idiom of shared ancestry is not elaborated with detailed descent lines, and it is unusual to meet a tribesman who can, without consulting old land-deeds and the like, name any more distant forebear than his great-grandfather.[4]

The vocabulary denoting sections and subsections varies from place to place, but there is no privileged level of organization that stands out in all circumstances, nor any standard distinction of terminology between one level and the next.[5] One could not, for instance, pick out Dhū Gharīb from Dhū Jabrah in al-'Uṣaymāt (above) by phrasing a question around a specific word. Which element of the classificatory structure is at issue is usually given by context, somewhat as in the classical case of the Nuer *cieng* (cf. Evans-Pritchard 1940: 135–6). Nor do sections, at whatever level of the scheme, coincide with any bounded system of exchange or responsibility. Like persons and like tribes, they take their value from their contradistinction to elements of the same kind as themselves, and their relevance is therefore given by structural relations in particular settings (ibid.). However, the explicit conception of value is very different from that in Nilotic societies.

The name of the tribe (that of the 'ancestor') is the *dāʿī* or *daʿwah*, the 'summons' to collective action by the tribe's members. As is to be expected from what was said in Chapter 2, the idiom of shared male ancestry expresses the occurrence of shared 'honour' or *sharaf*. Just as the sons of a father have honour in common and may be called on to uphold it, so the men of a tribe may be called on to uphold their common honour, which is that of their shared eponym. Where there is *sharaf* there is also necessarily *ʿarḍ*, or 'honour defended'. Again, just as an individual man has *naqāʾ* or 'good-name', so too does a tribe, and the term is also used of restoring good-name by payment or, more usually, by blood revenge.[6] The honour of a tribe, like that of a man, is broken by *ʿayb* or 'disgrace'. The one term in this set which is used of individuals but not of tribes is *wajh* ('face', or honour as committed in specific instances). The significance of this will be touched on later.

Just as the instances of individual honour may be summarized as denoting a 'personal peace', or moral space attaching to a tribesman, so the instances of honour relating to collectivities may be summarized in terms of a 'tribal peace', the defence of which constitutes a responsibility, a right, and a prerogative. If a man is killed in the territory of Banī Ṣuraym, for example, and the killer is unknown, then responsibility devolves upon Banī Ṣuraym. If Banī Ṣuraym suspect that the killer was from the victim's own tribe (let us say Sufyān), they can demand oaths from Sufyān to the effect that no one there knows anything of the case.[7] If the oaths are received, then responsibility reverts to Banī Ṣuraym, who must pay the blood-money (*diyah*) to the murdered man's kin. Banī Ṣuraym, may demand oaths from other tribes, but they themselves must first pay Sufyān the *diyah*, or at least agree to. If the murderer then turns out to be from Nihm, for instance, it is for Banī Ṣuraym, not Sufyān, to bring pressure on Nihm and extract compensation or revenge. The killer and his tribe would not only owe compensation to the dead man's kin in Sufyān, which must be paid to Banī Ṣuraym and passed on, but would also owe amends to Banī Ṣuraym for the insult involved in a murder in their territory.

Amends for an offence committed in the 'territory' (*bilād*) of one tribe by someone from another are called *tahjīr al-bilād*. A parallel phrase, *tahjīr al-bayt*, it will be remembered, is used of amends for a breach of the house-peace. Just as the house-peace may be breached and so amends owed, even though the householder himself suffers no actual harm, so the tribe's peace may be breached though no assault is suffered by the tribesmen themselves or their dependants. The honour of the tribe or section depends on maintaining the 'inviolability' of its territory (*ḥurmat al-waṭan*, see Rossi 1948: 19), a concept which includes rather more than simple defence of the border line.

Borders and ancestral names are frequently mentioned together in the quasi-heroic poetry for which tribesmen show such a taste, where the rhetoric of shared territory complements that of shared descent in a particular way. For example, a widely known poem, said to be indefinitely old, runs as follows:

> How sweet it is when the rifle barrels go down [on the parapets]
> On the day that the noise [of battle] is raised
> On the day when our forefathers' names are called out
> On the day when [the enemy's] breast-works are thrown down.
> The war is won by trickery/strategy and our young men guard the borders.[8]

The shouting out of 'our forefathers' names' *(ibn al-khurūf min khārif*, for instance) marks the projection of collective honour associated with the term *sharaf*. Its complement, *'arḍ* or 'honour defended', is associated with territory and with borders, so that 'defence of the borders' (*zabn al-ḥudūd*) is an expression of care for the tribe's good name, much as defence of their womenfolk is for men of a family.[9]

This parallel is drawn by the tribesmen themselves: *man shall ḥadd-uk mithla-mā rakab marat-uk*, 'whoever seizes your border, it's as if he mounted your woman', or *man falat ḥadd-uh mithla-mā falat marat-uh wa-'ār-hu man jā' rakab*, 'whoever lets slip his border, it's as if he let slip his woman and was disgraced by whomever came and mounted her'. The cases are indeed broadly comparable: women are not in fact likely to be abducted or done harm, but they must nonetheless be 'defended', and were they to be violated, the response would be serious indeed. Similarly, borders are not often likely to be overrun (tribes never explicitly win territory from others), but it is on the borders that battles are fought, and the demonstration is made of defending honour.[10] The same considerations usually also apply to sections.

Within the borders of a tribe or section falls grazing land ('wasteland', *faysh*, pl. *fuyūsh*) and arable land ('wealth', *māl*, pl. *amwāl*). The arable land is privately owned. It is unusual to find it held even by the grandsons of a grandfather, and none is held in common by sections or whole tribes, but the possession of arable land is essential to one's standing as a tribesman and one is often told that 'brothers' in a tribe have rights of pre-emption: 'A private land-holder who wishes to sell one of his fields is constrained by *juwārah* [neighbour-right] to offer it first to the members of his settlement group and secondly to his fellow tribesmen (*ya'ruḍ 'alā l-mujāwirīn*)' (Dostal 1974: 10). In practice this idea is assimilated to the Islamic-law concept of pre-emption (*shuf'ah*), and the Islamic-law term is more commonly used. Moreover, pre-emption on grounds of kinship or spatial propinquity does not in fact always match the lines of shared tribal membership:[11] arable land from two tribes may abut in such a way that men from one tribe claim first choice of land sold by men in the other; and on the plateau, members of one tribe often own land in another tribe's territory (these points will be examined in Chapters 8 and 9). However, Dostal is right to draw attention to the rhetoric of 'neighbour-right'. Men feel strongly about arable land. Who is permitted to buy it where is a matter of common concern. It is certainly the case that a man who joins a tribe from elsewhere and is in such straits that he cannot buy land will be given land by those he joins, which makes him not only a 'brother' (one who shares the ancestral name) but a 'neighbour' (*jār*), and thus one who shares in territory.

Land is one of the first things mentioned in any list one elicits of *mu'awwarāt*: things on the inviolability of which honour depends, and hence things in defence of which one's 'brothers' should offer support against outsiders. The term is often virtually synonymous with *'arḍ*. It is said (and sometimes happens in practice) that a blood-debt between two families whose arable land abuts will be settled by a transfer of land from the killer's people to the victim's, rather than by cash payment; that the loss of a man will be recuperated by the extension of his family's holding. Sometimes one finds a killing between sections or tribes settled by a change of their common border, so that the victim's tribe acquires some of the other tribe's *faysh* or non-arable land; this is one of the few exceptions to the rule of borders' explicit fixity. The rationale in all such cases is that land or territory restores the *'arḍ* of the victim's people.

The classical term for honour (or honour defended) is *'irḍ*, but in Yemeni pronunciation this distinctive vowelling is seldom given. The term *'arḍ*, to which it is partly assimilated, has an enormous range of meanings. The resolution of these meanings is perhaps work for the philologist (nor am I claiming that there are not 'two words', or three or four), but from an anthropological point of view we should certainly note that ambiguities exist and that they often turn on a strong association of ideas between honour and territory. *Ahl al-'arḍ*, for example, is a phrase used of men, such as those of a particular section, who are held jointly responsible in some circumstance. The phrase will be explained by some as referring to shared honour, by others as referring to shared territory (*'arḍ* can mean 'width', 'extent'), or by others still as meaning those to whom one offers first sale of one's land (*'arḍ* can mean 'offer', as in *ya'ruḍ 'alā l-mujāwirīn,* above). Again, *rijāl ḥāshid al-'arīḍ* plainly means 'the men of all Ḥāshid', but the term *'arīḍ* is variously explained in terms of honour and of territory ('the men of broad Ḥāshid'). The two ideas at the least overlap, and often they cannot be clearly separated.[12] One shares honour, which must then be defended and kept inviolate, primarily because one shares borders, which define the tribe's or section's territory.

A rather different meaning of the term, and one that relates directly to what was said in Chapter 2, also deserves noting: the ability to 'intervene' in affairs among tribesmen, which one has by virtue of being a tribesman oneself, and particularly the ability to 'take on' such commitments as escorting a traveller or protecting a refugee. A tribesman in another tribe's territory will usually 'have no *'arḍ*'. He cannot, for example, escort travellers as he could in his own tribe's territory, or at least no right is granted him to do so.[13] Within a tribe it may be that *al-'arḍ wāḥid* ('it's one'), meaning that any one of the tribe's 'sons' can, for example, escort a traveller anywhere in the tribe's territory and a breach of that right should, in theory, be countered by all the tribe's members. In other tribes it may be that *al-'arḍ māḍī* (this right is 'recognized' or 'effective') only within a man's section; at the borders of his section he would need to hand the traveller on to another escort, and a breach of his own right would be the concern only of his own section's members.

The rules differ from case to case.[14] The ability to act as a tribesman, though, derives from membership in a tribe and shows precisely the spatial alternation and complementarity one expects in the language of honour (Pitt-Rivers 1977: 108–9): I can offer you escort in my territory, and you can escort me in yours.

COLLECTIVE ACTION AND RESPONSIBILITY

Within a tribe rules may be recognized which purport to describe how men act in concert: for example, how they gather or divide collective payments. Dhū Muḥammad, for instance, comprises five 'fifths' (*akhmās*), and practice confirms what one is told in theory, that levies for a common purpose are made equally on each. During a long confrontation with Dhū Ḥusayn during 1983, Dhū Muḥammad maintained a force in the field for some weeks (this is very unusual), and ammunition and stores for them were paid for equally by each fifth, although one of these (Dhū Zayd) counted perhaps as many as seven hundred men, and another (Dhū Mūsā) counted perhaps only two hundred. These arrangements were made quite efficiently. Dhū Ḥusayn, on the other hand, disagreed endlessly among themselves, and their opposing force all but melted away. Both acted typically. One can almost talk of tribes having different characters.

Arrangements are seldom as clear-cut as with Dhū Muḥammad. Khārif, for example, comprises three main divisions: Banī Jubar, al-Kalbiyyīn, and al-Ṣayad (Dresch 1984*a*: 35). It is generally agreed that a mulct on the whole tribe should be divided as half from al-Ṣayad and half from the other two together. Within al-Ṣayad are five 'fifths'. One is sometimes told that a levy would be raised equally from each fifth, but there also exists a division by thirds, as follows:

Khamīs Abū Dhaybah	400 men approx.	⅓
Khamīs Harāsh	1,500 men approx.	
Khamīs Ḥurmal	600 men approx.	⅓
Khamīs al-Qāyifī	500 men approx.	
Khamīs al-Qudaymī	1,800 men approx.	⅓

Neither scheme takes very accurate account of the number of men in each fifth, and there seems no general agreement on which scheme should be applied in a given circumstance. Within Khamīs al-Qudaymī in turn are nine or ten villages, and again there is no general agreement on whether each should contribute equally or whether the division should be made as follows:

al-ʻAraqah, al-Ẓubr, al-Lajān	1/4
al-Maḥam, Banī Muḥammad	1/4
al-Manjidah	1/4
al-Ḥadar, Nāʻiṭ (including al-Jifrah)	1/4

Again, neither scheme spreads the load equally by the number of men per division.[15] Very probably such arrangments show the trace in many tribes of state intervention at one time or another: an Imam or his deputy may have demanded troops, or a fine, or taxes, according to such schemes, and the scheme may then have remained in partial use thereafter. There is often no pristine version to be found that one could claim is the 'right' one or even the original.

In fact Khārif, like Dhū Muḥammad, generally contrive to organize themselves when the need arises, while Sufyān, for example, like Dhū Ḥusayn, generally do not. It should be noted, however, that these alternative schemes exist. They do not necessarily reflect alignments of any other sort. For example, for no other purpose than levying collective payments (*aghrām*) is al-ʻAraqah more closely aligned with al-Ẓubr than with al-Maḥam. For no other purpose is Khamīs Abū Dhaybah reckoned closer to Khamīs Harāsh than to Khamīs Ḥurmal. In the event of a dispute between fifths, the structural distance is to be reckoned the same between all of them.

An important area of indeterminacy lies in which unit as a whole is to be mulcted. If a man from a village in Khamīs Abū Dhaybah of Khārif kills someone from Arḥab (another tribe altogether), a debt exists between the two tribes, but who is to pay it: the killer's family, his village, the fifth, or the whole tribe? Informants in many tribes argue that if the man kills an outsider inadvertently, the blood-money would be raised by his section (a unit of the order of Khamīs Abū Dhaybah, or al-Ḥumrān in al-ʻUṣaymāt); if he kills in defending his honour (his *ʻarḍ*), then the whole tribe should contribute: but if he kills deliberately and gratuitously (*ʻuṭlah*), he should be left to pay by himself with whatever help he can muster from his kin and neighbours. Quite which of these rough categories a case falls in is plainly open to argument.

This same indeterminacy extends to vengeance, to the question of who is bound to kill in revenge and who is liable to be killed. A man's immediate kin are involved (those whom Islamic law recognizes as *awliyā al-dam*), but men much further from the particular antagonist may also be drawn in. If a man from section A of our tribe kills someone from another tribe, that other tribe might perhaps kill someone in a quite different section of our's, section B. Between the two tribes balance has been restored, and the two sections within our tribe cannot in a circumstance like this claim blood-money (*diyah*) from each other. Section B might, though, claim from A payment called *thawb al-īṣāl*. The amount varies. In Upper al-'Uṣaymāt, for example, it was traditionally reckoned at only 40 silver thalers (the full blood-money was 800), and in Lower al-'Uṣaymāt at 120.

Within a small section (such as al-Ḥumrān) at odds with more distant antagonists, such internal settlements are not usually recognized: *qad waṣal* (syn. *qad ḥaṣal*, 'it's happened')—balance with outsiders has been reached and that is an end of it.[16] Between two larger sections, on the other hand, the *thawb al-īṣāl* may be accepted or may equally well not. If A killed an outsider, and someone in B were killed in revenge, B might not recognize parity but insist on payment or blood-revenge against the outsiders to wipe out the specific affront to themselves. The balance between the two tribes may not carry weight with them, as in the succession of murders described in Chapter 2.

A whole tribe may therefore try explicitly to constitute itself a vengeance group. They agree in writing that *man ḥayy ramā wa-man qutil quḍā* (*sic*), 'whoever still lives will shoot, and whoever was killed was judged' (i.e. we will fight to avenge any one of us killed, and if someone is killed by outsiders in return for a killing by our brother in the tribe, then parity will be recognized);[17] or we shall henceforth be *'aḍud wa-sa'd* 'like the upper arm and lower arm', the parts always working together. Such agreements are comparatively rare and are often fragile. Only in a set battle between tribes (*yawm abyaḍ*, a 'white day') is it usually clear which units as wholes have between them a balance or debt of blood, and the ambiguities (still immense) are limited to collection or distribution of mulcts within each.

Despite such ambiguity, a tribe may at any point in hostilities be invoked as a bounded entity. Normally men are constantly crossing and recrossing tribal borders, which was always the case but is now conspicuous on the largest scale because of trucking and the like, in which tribesmen are heavily involved. Tribesmen also have personal commitments to people elsewhere. A man may, for instance, have a sworn personal ally or *ḥalīf* in another tribe (see e.g. Glaser 1884: 177; Dresch 1987*b*), and, of course, a man who has married from elsewhere has obligations to his affines in whichever tribe they live. In the event of serious conflict all this may be declared suspended. All ties with the other tribe may be severed ('cutting off', *qaṭā'*) and the borders closed to the other tribe's members. For example, in the dispute between Dhū Muḥammad and Dhū Ḥusayn mentioned at the start of this section, Dhū Ḥusayn closed their borders to the Muḥammadīs, specifically denying them access to a new market in the Upper Jawf, and at a meeting of the tribe they announced that they *ibtarū min al-ḥilf wa-l-man'*, they 'declared themselves quit' of personal alliances with any Muḥammadī and of personal obligations to Muḥammadī affines.[18] Such declarations, if made in the midst of conflict, can be compelling. Whether in practice they will stick for any length of time is a separate question.

In the course of disputes, groups form and align in various ways (not always those suggested by tribal classification), and these alignments are often explicitly denoted (Dresch 1986: 316 ff.). A given axis of conflict may, for example, be converted into the axis along which settlement of the dispute is arranged. If a man from Arḥab has a claim against someone from Khārif, he may pass rifles called *banādiq al-'arḍ* to members of Khārif. If the Khārifīs accept these, they thereby accept that their man is in the wrong, and they undertake to bring pressure on him to make due amends. Again, if a claim is made against members of Khārif, or against Khārif as a whole, men from there may themselves give the claimants 'rifles of good faith' (*banādiq al-wifā'*) as a pledge that they are willing to settle the claim but perhaps require time to collect the demanded sum or to negotiate with others.

Similarly, an implication of involvement in a dispute between two whole tribes can be denied by a particular section within one of them. At the outset a section may pass the opposing tribe 'rifles which clear them' (*banādiq al-ṣafw*). These may even be passed to the other tribe by a section they specifically accuse, in which case the rifles deny knowledge of the offence or deny support for one of the section's own members if he should be the culprit. They say in effect to the outsiders that they can pursue their claim against the culprit without involving themselves in a dispute with us.[19] Such rifles are more usually given as a dispute expands. Section A of Khārif, for example, is at odds with some section of Arḥab, and the two tribes involve themselves as wholes: men from Arḥab act not only against A, but against B, C, and D as well. Section B may pass 'rifles which clear them' to Arḥab, denying any part in the matter and denying that they will support their own brothers against Arḥab in this particular dispute. They can, in effect, opt out.

Rifles exchanged in this way are held as tokens of obligation until the obligation is discharged. They are then handed back to those who gave them. So long as they are held they denote a commitment quite different in kind from the layered, indeterminate (and, most important, deniable) obligations that derive from formal classification. A section or tribe which attempts to constitute itself a cohesive group will often refer to its members as *mutaḥāzimīn mutalāzimīn*. The latter term means simply that they 'stick together', or that they accept responsibilities in common. The former refers to them 'making bundles' of rifles to impose or accept an obligation together. They undertake not to enter separately into such commitments with outsiders.

Some such agreements are impressively long-lasting, others one knows to be worthless on the day they are made. These immediate features of the political scene (expressions, if you like, of different tribes' 'characters' at different times) are important in the short term and are soon learned from experience; but the basis on which they are formed is that of definitional sets that by a long way outlast them. The tribal classification provides a set of possibilities that remains fairly constant. These possibilities are not, however, 'realized' in the form of unthinking cohesion, and solidary groups do not materialize like the pictures in a pop-up children's book.

Those particularly at odds with outsiders cannot immediately demand help from their tribe by such compelling means as breaking their own dagger sheaths and thus declaring themselves 'weak like women': unless they were truly in desperate straits, they would be thought mad.[20] Killing a bull in the tribe's market is as dramatic an appeal for support as one often sees. Much more usually, support is demanded by giving rifles to sections whose support one wants, called 'rifles of obligation' (*banādiq al-talzīm*) or 'rifles of brotherhood' (*banādiq al-ikhā'*). If such rifles are accepted, then those who take them recognize an obligation (based on brotherhood in the tribe) to support one against antagonists from elsewhere. They may even confirm the pledge by passing back other rifles, also of 'brotherhood' or perhaps of 'good faith'. Even this does not mean that the sections are now bound together just for common offensive action. An obligation has been accepted, but it may be discharged in the end by intervention as guarantors or arbitrators, rather than by taking up arms.

Tribal divisions are not, however, simply neutral points of reference like the grid-lines on a map made by someone else, and the values of collective honour touched on earlier are often compelling. Particularly if recent events have already led to antagonism between elements of two tribes, and then men from one commit a fresh offence against men from the other, the two tribes as wholes may immediately be involved. Not everyone will answer the 'summons' on each side. Not every grown man will snatch up his rifle and head for the road or border. Enough men, though, will perceive the whole other tribe as enemy for everyone from each tribe to be set at risk in the other's territory, road blocks will be thrown up to trap trucks from anywhere in the other tribe, or fighting may start on the border. There is no convention of solidarity, however, no permanent coercive structure, and no standing authority coincident with a section or tribe; so the relation is problematic between the sets of men defined by shared 'ancestors' and the groups of men who actually form on a given occasion. Part of a section or tribe may do one thing and another part do something else.

SHAYKHS AS GUARANTORS

> In every tribe, superstition, or gratitude, or fortune, has exalted a particular family above the heads of their equals . . . and the most worthy or aged of the noble kinsmen are preferred to the simple, though important, office of composing disputes by their advice, and guiding valour by their example.
>
> Gibbon, *Decline and Fall*

A section or tribe has no 'face' as a man does, no ability to make undertakings or to commit its honour in a specific instance. It has, if you like, no legal personality. For all that tokens such as rifles may in practice align tribes or sections (or groups acting in these units' names), they must be exchanged by individual men who act in an individual capacity. The men who do this are commonly shaykhs, who thus 'give their faces' on behalf of tribesmen.

A shaykh (pl. *mashāyikh*) usually comes from an established family of shaykhs. Often the shaykhly family is referred to as the 'original' family or house of its section *(al-bayt al-aṣlī),* and sometimes the names of the section and family are the same (Dresch 1984*a*: 36). They are not generally accorded 'authority' (*sulṭah*) over others, nor do they have rights, for example, over others' land in the section, although they sometimes control funds from elsewhere. Within the family (a loose conglomeration of one man's descendants, which can number scores of men) 'the order of succession is', in Gibbon's phrase, 'loose and precarious'; and although a particular line may monopolize the position of shaykh for some generations, there is no rule that they should. Anyone of the shaykhly family may usually, in practice as well as theory, be chosen shaykh.

These families are very numerous. Khayār, in Banī Ṣuraym, recognizes six separate shaykhly families (one in each subdivision), as was mentioned above, and the other eight sections of Banī Ṣuraym are comparable; for example, 'the single fraction of al-Ẓāhir is commanded by eight shaykhs, who act independently of one another' (Chelhod 1970: 71). Again, Dhū Muḥammad comprises five 'fifths' (*akhmās*), and in each fifth a particular shaykhly house is prominent (Fig. 3.3). There are other shaykhly families too, but the five particularly prominent families (one for each fifth) are distinguishjed from the others as shaykhs of 'guaranty' (*ḍamān*), a term which will be explained below. It should be noticed that not every element in the tribal structure has a single family of shaykhs identified with it. There is no shaykh of Āl Aḥmad b. Swaydān, or al-Maḥlaf, for instance, or of Dhū Muḥammad as a whole.[21]

Arḥab provides a more complex case of broadly the same type. The tribe comprises two major divisions, Zuhayr and Dhaybān, which subdivide as shown in Fig. 3.4. Bayt Sinān, it will be noticed, are shaykhs of two named sections, Zindān and al-Khamīs. Bayt Suwa' of Shākir are shaykhs of 'guaranty' for Shākir and Marrān as a whole, having a certain precedence over the other two shaykhly

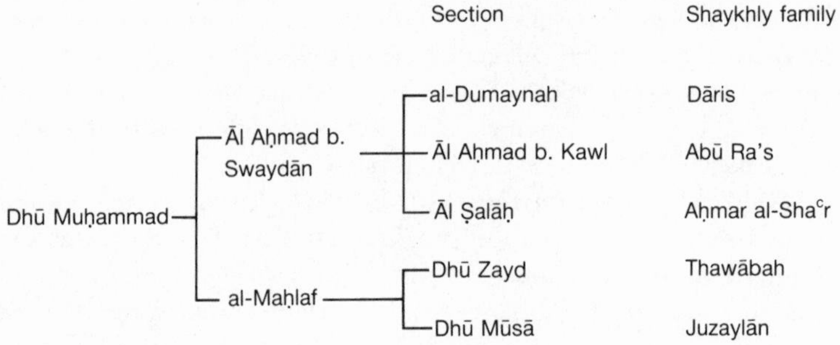

FIG. 3.3 Sections and shaykhly families of Dhū Muḥammad

families (al-Qasīr and al-Marrānī), both of whom are from Marrān. The shaykhs listed as attaching to the three sections of Ḥisān are each shaykh of 'guaranty' for their particular section, but Sha'b also contains another shaykhly family, Bayt al-'Idharī, who, although they are not accorded this title, are in fact rather prominent and in the mid-nineteenth century were conspicuous as leaders of the Bakīl tribes round Ṣan'ā' (al-Ḥibshī 1980: 113). Bayt Maraḥ of 'Iyāl bi-l-Khayr in Banī Murrah are 'shaykhs of guaranty' of Banī Murrah and al-Manṣūr together (note that Ḥisān, at the same classificatory level, has no one family identified with it in this way); and Bayt al-Ḥabbārī are 'shaykhs of guaranty' for al-thalāth al-laḥām as a whole. There is no shaykh of Zuhayr as a whole, of Dhaybān, or of all Arḥab.

At lower levels of organization than those in the diagram there are numerous shaykhs: for example, Banī 'Alī in Zuhayr comprises eight 'eighths', each of which has a shaykhly house of its own. One of these houses, Bayt Radmān, are also shaykhs of guaranty for all eight divisions together. Bayt Radmān will be mentioned again later (particularly in Chapter 6), but it should be pointed out at once that, as with arrangements for collective payment, the position of families as shaykhs of guaranty often shows the trace of state intervention: they stood guaranty for their men at one time or another to Imams or the Turks or republican governments, as well as to other tribes. As a result of such involvement with government, 'Alī Muḥammad Radmān in the eighteenth century became in fact rather wealthy (Zabārah 1958: 273).

The term 'shaykh of guaranty' (*shaykh al-ḍamān*) may be used as a title and almost as a rank, but it refers first of all to a function.

This was explained to Serjeant by informants in western Yemen as follows: 'the Shaykh al-Ḍamān pays for what has perished, i.e. blood-money, damages of all sorts, etc. He then goes to the shaykh of the guilty man . . . and recovers the blood-money, or damages if it be some different type of offence, from the shaykh of the murderer's group' (Serjeant 1977: 229). This description applies, in essence, to the plateau tribes as well; and it applies not only to compensation but to all group transactions and collective levies, whether from tribe to tribe or from tribe to state in the form of taxes. However, the phrase 'shaykh of guaranty' is far less a description of fixed rank on the plateau than in the west. For example, Bayt Radmān are shaykhs of guaranty for all Banī 'Alī, but the other seven shaykhs of the section each play the same part for their particular 'eighth', and the lesser shaykhs do not necessarily act through the section shaykh or as the section shaykh would wish. If, let us say, a man in one of the eighths suffers an

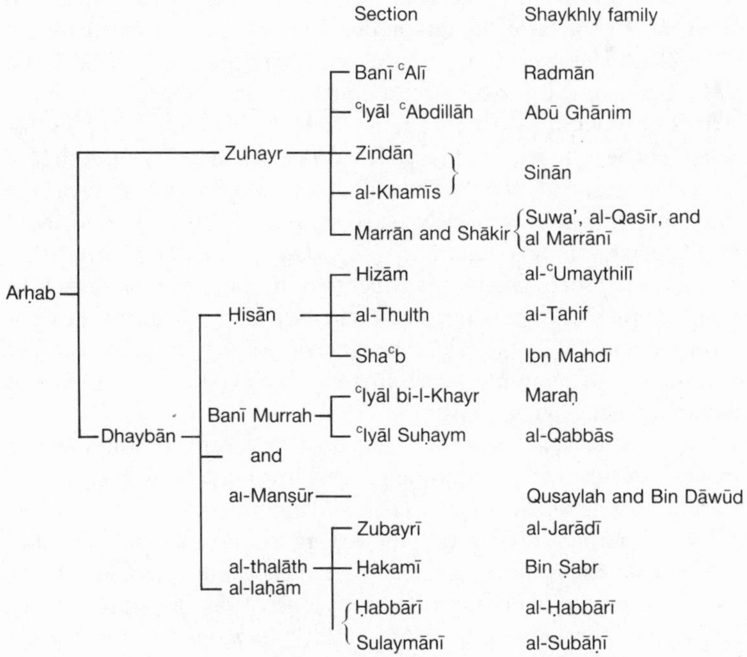

FIG. 3.4 Sections and shaykhly families of Arḥab

offence by someone from elsewhere in Arḥab, the shaykh of the eighth may 'pay for what has perished' and recover the damages, rather than the shaykh of all Banī 'Alī doing so.

The culprit's shaykh (at whatever level of collective identity) extracts amends from him and passes them to the victim's shaykh, who then passes them to the victim. The antagonists themselves are thus kept apart, the first step in 'severing relations' (cf. Zabārah 1956: iii. 268) and thus in settling the dispute. The shaykhs on each side cannot act in this way merely by being shaykhs, but must form specific ties of the sort already touched on. Perhaps one shaykh, or set of shaykhs, passes a 'rifle of '*arḍ*' to his opposite number, or a 'rifle of right' to signify right of judgment, and within each of the sections or tribes similarly specific ties are formed; so in any but the simplest case, the shaykh from each side would take from the particular antagonists in his section a rifle, a dagger, or a sum of money as 'surety' ('*adl*, lit. 'equity').[22] If the specific tie denoted by surety is breached (if, for example, the man who gives it attacks his antagonist in the other section), this is a 'disgrace' and an 'insult' to the shaykh; the latter would be due amends and the surety would be forfeit. The specific ties within and between sections make up what one can call a structure of containment.

It is only within such a structure that the process of 'paying for what has perished' takes place. The process is identical with that of 'severing relations' (*qaṭā' al-'alā'iq*, pl. of '*alāqah*), thus severing the unwanted connection of debt between antagonists and replacing it with a personal 'tie' of guaranty (not '*alāqah*, but '*alqah*). On either side of this process, tribes or tribesmen are prescriptively equal to their opposite numbers but separate from each other and thus not in fact commensurable. Guaranty provides the temporary context within which common measurement can be recognized and 'balance' thereby restored.

Similarly, a shaykh who is called on to arbitrate takes surety from the *ghuramā'* or disputing parties. In a minor case they simply lay their daggers before him to demand an opinion,[23] but in a more complex matter he will retain these daggers, or much more usually a rifle from each, until he can resolve their claims; and so long as these tokens are held, any offence by one of the disputing parties against the other or against the 'arbitrator' (*muqawwil* or *muḥakkam*) is '*ayb*. It is the function he takes on, not the fact he is shaykh, that entitles him to amends.

In all but the simplest case, the arbitrator will require 'guarantors' for each party (*ḍumanā'* or *kufalā'*, pl. of *kafīl*). Each party can choose the other's guarantors, who are then responsible for the other party's conduct and debts alike, whether such debts arise in the course of arbitration or are specified by arbitration as settlement of the claim. Party A chooses B's guarantor: *al-kafīl li-A 'alā B*, responsible to A for B's conduct. Party B chooses A's guarantor. If it is decided that B should pay A compensation, then B's guarantor collects it from B and pays it to A's guarantor who then pays it to A. The position of guarantor in arbitration is thus similar to that of a shaykh of guaranty in the settlement of a debt between members of different sections. The 'disputing parties' (*ghuramā'*, pl. of *gharīm*) are kept apart. Each guarantor is answerable to the other guarantor, to the other party, and to the shaykh who is arbitrating (see Fig. 3.5).

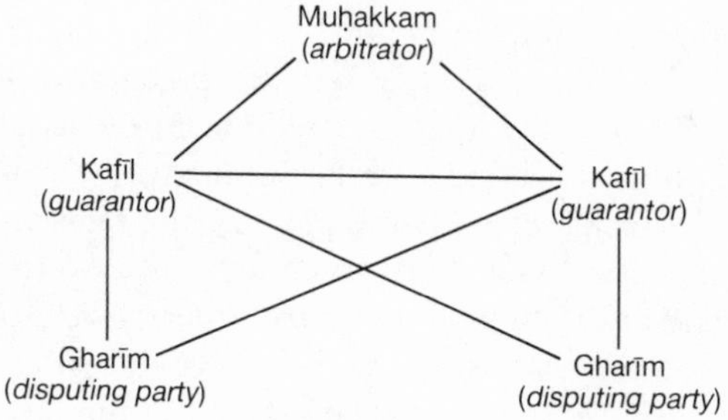

FIG. 3.5 The structure of containment

The guarantors must simply 'give' their faces, but the arbitrator at the centre of this web can take payment from those who seek his judgment.[24] Some take very little or nothing at all, but others make enormous demands; and tribesmen will often feel forced to pay heavily, for lack of any other way to settle their problems. Indeed, a noted arbitrator (and we shall see in later sections why there should be such men) can often increase his demands by stages, knowing that those at odds will in the end be driven to accept him. On the other hand, one of the parties to the dispute may himself 'up the ante' to oppress the other party, raising not only the amount to be paid to an arbitrator but the costs (*gharāmah*) to be incurred by convening guarantors, supporters, and intermediaries;[25] but in one or other of these capacities, whether more or less central or peripheral, a great many men are involved in such cases much of the time. A shaykh who contrives repeatedly to play a central part in such proceedings can acquire not only wealth but influence; and men at odds can go to any shaykh they wish for arbitration, whether inside or outside their tribe.

Among all the tribes, arbitration in practice lapses as often as it concludes with a verdict, and even fairly simple cases will commonly go to two, three, or four arbitrators in turn, each of whom adds his opinion to a lengthening scroll of paper. But the structure of containment holds so long as each attempt is pursued. Any breach of the peace by one of those at odds is an insult to his guarantor, who is usually due amends of the same amount as the damage done: *al-qirsh bi-qirshayn,* 'every riyal's worth of damage to be paid for by two riyals', half of which goes to the guarantor and half to the victim of the offence. Amends can be agreed in advance, when arbitration begins, at a much higher level; for instance, eleven-fold. If the person under guaranty murders his antagonist while the structure of containment exists, then his own guarantor is honour-bound to take what action against him the victim's people demand and has in any case the right of *kharāb wa-turāb,* 'laying waste' the transgressor's house and property. The guarantor may be called on to kill the murderer, which the victim's people cannot themselves do without insulting the guarantors together. In a less extreme case he may place the offender's own fields off-limits to him, which is done by setting up a thorn bush on the plots in question. If the guarantor fails to act against one who breaches the peace, he is answerable to the other party at arbitration and to the arbitrator, both of whom may claim amends for the *'ayb* they suffer.

The link between arbitrator and claimant, or guarantor and the man guaranteed, is accorded a value not much less than that of the tie between host and guest or traveller and escort. A defaulting guarantor, for example, may be publicly shamed. The claimant conventionally states his demands of the guarantor in the market on market day and if the claim is not met, a black flag and a white flag are raised, to be left for two weeks (see Dresch 1987*b*). If the claim is still not met, the white flag comes down and the black is left flying, which is a serious *malām* or 'blame'. The defaulter's face is 'blackened' and his honour besmirched before all the tribes. If the claim is not met even now, then in some of the northern and eastern tribes a *jidhn* may be placed, a blackened stump of wood, sometimes dressed in women's clothes, which is named for the defaulter. An insult of this magnitude is immensely serious (Glaser 1903: 76; Dresch 1987*b*). It is more than cause for whole tribes to go to war and, not surprisingly, is very rare; but a breach of guaranty is a plausible reason for a *jidhn* to be placed, while to plant such a 'blame' because the ordinary ties of brotherhood had been ignored would be nonsense.

The ties of guaranty, then, are a serious matter. They are temporary, and in the case of arbitration they last only as long as the arbitration itself, at the end of which the rifles denoting these ties are returned. They are formed when a truce is made. A truce lasts a specified time, seldom more than a year, and the 'rifles of truce' *(banādiq al-ṣulḥ)* are returned to their owners just as they are when the truce ends which accompanies the payment of agreed compensation.[26] Only in one case is guaranty permanent. If a blood-debt (a killing) is settled by payment, then the victim's kin, it is said, may still wish for revenge and may take revenge if the chance arises; so guarantors are sometimes appointed for both parties to the debt, and this guaranty lasts until the death of the dead man's brothers.[27]

Guaranty, however, is not limited to the process of settling claims between sections. It is also the means by which tribes form alliances and truces or commit themselves to the protection of places and events (we shall consider examples of such commitments in Chapter 4). In most such undertakings it is not only a few shaykhs who 'give their faces'. On an agreement affecting a whole tribe one might find the names of fifty or sixty shaykhs, if not more. Each signs 'on his own behalf and on behalf of his men' (*'an-hu wa-'an aṣḥāb-hu*). He is 'responsible for his followers' (*multazim bi-man ilay-h*), or 'every one is responsible for his fellow' (*kull wāḥid multazim bi-ṣāḥib-hu*). The shaykhs make the agreement together and will usually not oppose each other if a man attached to one of them breaks the general commitment. Nevertheless, agreements often contain lengthy clauses whereby not only does each shaykh sign for his men but each shaykh stands guaranty for others, locking all of them into a complex web of specific commitments. At the centre of this the resulting truce is the more compelling for the fact it depends on no single man or group. None can secede without others demanding amends from him for the slight to their personal honour. Even then they will often look further afield, to other sections or tribes, for *rudamā'* who act as 'guarantors of the guarantors' and thus 'cover' these initial commitments (Dresch 1987*a*: 76 n. 9).

Long lists of signatories are typical of all tribal agreements. Very rarely can one man, or a small group of men, sign on behalf of a tribe or even of all but the smallest section. A 'shaykh of guaranty' may be recognized. He will not usually be left by himself to provide guaranty for others' conduct. He may, however, be forced to do so by a ruler or state, and a 'shaykh of guaranty' may even be found where there was none before, as Khayār in Banī Ṣuraym, for example, seem not to have had a single *shaykh al-ḍamān* until Imam Yaḥyā demanded they have one in the early part of this century. The shaykh was then responsible to the Imam for maintaining order and collecting taxes.

In the west *ḍamān* and *iltizām* both have the meaning of responsibility to superiors in a hierarchy (particularly, responsibility for taxation), and such stable hierarchies are common in the west, which they are not among the plateau tribes. However, it should be noted that the *iltizām* ('answerability') of a shaykh is much the same, whether to another tribe or to the state. He may be held responsible at all times, where before he undertook this function only in specific instances, and he may always be the one to answer for his men, where before other shaykhs as well might have claimed to, but his position is not wholly dissimilar in the two cases. The function of guaranty forms a pivot around which very different systems of politics can turn.

Whatever the political context, the function of guaranty is deemed necessary because sections or tribes are not corporations. One deals with men as individuals, whether one at a time or serially in groups.[28] If a section or tribe is involved, individuals must be answerable for them. The person is not a privileged locus of moral values in quite the Western sense, nor the point at which conflicting values might be somehow resolved, but instead, in the tribal system, is a kind of irreducible element (Dresch 1987*b*): a man cannot opt out of his own commitment, as men or groups can from those affecting a larger set, and a particular man alone can therefore 'give his face'.[29] The distinction at issue is not that between 'spokesmen', let us say, and 'constituency' (far less between 'leaders' and 'followers'), but precisely that touched on in Chapter 2, between symmetrical and asymmetrical relations.

In the system at hand, all collective relations show symmetry, whether between 'ancestral' sets or within one set, and a symmetrical relation, it will be remembered, can dissolve quite readily, with no moral contradiction, into mutual antagonism between two parties: whether between sets or within sets again makes no difference. An asymmetric relation cannot. The shaykh who 'gives his face' for his fellows claims that those for whom he stands guaranty are within his care, much as guests with a host, and on that basis commits his own honour and theirs: without such a figure, regardless of considerations of 'rank', there is no assurance that ties between equals will be any more than episodes in mutual contradiction. Such episodes in any case recur constantly, and often they involve the shaykhs themselves.

'GATHERING' THE TRIBES

An important shaykh from Ḥāshid was inspecting land that he owned on the border with Sufyān and, as befitted his standing among the tribes and with the government, he was accompanied by a retinue of armed men from his tribe. These spread out to guard the area while he talked with visitors. A Sufyānī (a man of fractious temperament, who had been in endless trouble elsewhere) strolled down to the site and encountered the Ḥāshid guards. They asked or demanded that he put the catch on his rifle to 'safe'. He refused, saying they had no right to order him around and he would go where he liked as he liked and that this was his territory anyhow. A squabble broke out. He fired at them and they shot him dead.

The shaykh promptly appealed to all the Bakīl tribes in the area to slaughter bulls for the dead man's kin and prevail on them to settle the blood-debt peacefully. A delegation of Bakīl shaykhs and their followers, from Sufyān and from elsewhere, gathered at the dead man's village. The bulls were accepted. The dead man's father accepted the plea that the murder was an accident and agreed to the Ḥāshid shaykh's offer of four times the blood-money as amends. Some of his sons, though, refused. Guarantors were provided from all the Bakīl tribes to prevent them attempting revenge, and, with that done, a meeting was held between all concerned. The sons, however, fired on Ḥāshid at the meeting, a breach of the peace that insulted the guarantors and all those present: a meeting is always sacrosanct, as we shall see in Chapter 4. The shaykhs of Sufyān, themselves insulted by the breach of the peace, slaughtered a pair of bulls for the shaykhs from elsewhere in Bakīl as a gesture of apology, and marched with their men to the Ḥāshidīs present, chanting this *zāmil*:

> A million salāms ('peace be on you').
> The whole tribe is split over what we have done.
> We ask from you, be placated.
> The four-fold judgment has produced the split,
> And did what it did to courtesy.
> The man owed the bull desists,
> Saying, be welcome on our heads.[30]

With guarantors from throughout Bakīl again made responsible for the behaviour of the dead man's kin, the peace was upheld and the settlement concluded. The tension was pronounced, though. In securing Bakīl's intervention in the first place, the Ḥāshid shaykh at the centre of the dispute had distributed rifles and gifts throughout Sufyān and elsewhere. Everyone had in mind that a few years earlier a confrontation between Sufyān and Ḥāshid had led to war. That could easily have occurred again and numerous tribes been drawn into a fight that no one could easily break up.

A little after this, road-blocks were set up in the pass at Ghūlat 'Ajīb between Khamir and Raydah. A dispute over the organization of long-distance trucking was in progress between 'Iyāl Surayḥ and Banī Ṣuraym, where the villages of al-Ghūlah in the first and al-Sinnatayn in the second are heavily involved in commercial transport. Somewhere in the pass a man was shot dead whose family was originally from the Ḥāshid tribe of Khārif. The security forces at 'Amrān sent two gun-trucks and arrested seven or eight men from al-Ghūlah, including the shaykh. He was released that night on orders from Ṣan'ā' which also told the commander at 'Amrān to imprison two dozen men from each of al-Ghūlah and al-Sinnatayn.[31] Both villages denied any part in the killing.

The shaykh of al-Ghūlah then went to the Ḥāshid shaykh who had recently been involved in the incident with Sufyān. He offered him rifles, denoting that the Ḥāshid shaykh should judge the case, and asked him to use his influence to have the men from al-Ghūlah released. Al-Sinnatayn had refused to give up their two dozen men. The Ḥāshid shaykh refused to accept the rifles, and the shaykh of al-Ghūlah then wrote to shaykhs throughout Bakīl, who duly assembled at Raydah and agreed to give al-Ghūlah support, declaring publicly that any Bakīlī who refused to do so deserved to dress as a woman. The Ḥāshid shaykh who had previously refused to intervene now sent a delegation of his fellows to al-Ghūlah. The shaykh of al-Ghūlah refused to see them. Instead he wrote to the paramount shaykh of Ḥāshid, who accepted ten rifles from him as surety and ten from al-Sinnatayn, thus taking on the task of arbitration.

The threat of wider involvement from Bakīl was eminently plausible. Between al-Ghūlah's tribe, 'Iyāl Surayḥ, and the Ḥāshid tribe of Khārif there was already a debt of blood from a year or so earlier when a Surayḥī had been shot dead in a squabble over a truck blocking the road at Raydah. Before that there had been killings between the same two tribes for reasons deriving from national politics. 'Iyāl Surayḥ's claim against Khārif could readily have been assimilated to their new claim against Banī Ṣuraym (both Khārif and Banī Ṣuraym are Ḥāshidī), and a general antagonism between them and Ḥāshid might have been the result.

The sequence of events set out here covered only a few weeks (admittedly in a fairly tense period during 1980) and is typical of the kind of thing that happens, or is thought likely to happen, at most times. Nor is there any need laboriously to unpack what is going on. Readers can see for themselves where the points of advantage and disadvantage lie, where one shaykh or another has some grip on events and where events have escaped him. However, one can reasonably stress the shaykhs' prominence, because all of the indefinitely many minor shaykhs in their sections and villages are similarly prominent in events on their own scale. Someone must proffer the rifles or bulls, someone must call the tribesmen together, someone must speak for them as one group calls on another for support against a third or for mediation. There is no settled sense to what is occurring until someone steps forward and puts into words who is related how to whom. There is only an indefinite range of possible violence until someone 'gives his face', whether to the government or to the neighbouring tribe.

This external relation of a definite set of men to others requires a corresponding image of internal coherence. Someone must, as the saying goes, 'gather everyone's word' (*yajma' kalimat al-jamī'*). Without this, groups of tribesmen are oddly liable in public settings to disclaim any sense to their own actions. At about the same time as the events sketched above, for instance, a group of men from Banī Ṣuraym attacked an army post at Raydah: being heavily out-numbered and out-gunned, they were severely dealt with and lost two trucks, but they then simply said, 'We are tribesmen, there were no shaykhs with us.' Each individual had a story to tell but a group, of its nature, does not. The problem posed by the threat of other collectivities is to find an unequivocal statement of one's own position, a problem which subsumes the more particular one of political cohesion. The same applies to internal conflict. An arbitrator is a *muqawwil*, one who 'speaks' or 'announces' the truth of the matter; and arbitration itself is referred to often as *qawl*, a 'speaking' or 'declaration'.

A shaykh should be able to find the form of words that allows talks to move forward, and in general he should be discerning. His 'belly' should be 'full of politics', and among light-blooded men he should have 'weight' (*wazn* here means almost *gravitas*, as well as influence). Very few in fact have these qualities, but what all shaykhs of influence are ascribed, whether they project themselves grandly or not and however they distribute their funds, is the ability to solve problems. Men will follow such a shaykh even if he 'eats' their money. But there is nothing to ensure the following except the leader's success, and nothing to prevent endless fragmentation. The Jawf, for instance, is a byword for disorder, and a local there simply echoes a wider Yemeni belief when he says: 'The Jawf could be called the area of the two hundred shaykhs . . . and the five hundred families' (Steffen 1978: ii. 168).

When there is no strong figure to constrain men, they complain that 'everyone rules himself'[32] and 'there's a shaykh in every house'. The latter phrase by itself is enough to suggest a certain popular view of what shaykhs might do, although in practice they are not given the means, or if they acquire the means, then men promptly complain of 'tyranny'. But the former phrase, 'everyone rules himself' (*kull wāḥid yaḥkum 'alā nafs-hu*), is so frequently heard that one accepts it without due caution. Were a middle-class Englishman (or indeed a Greek villager) to complain of disorder, it would surely be to say just the opposite: that everyone fails to rule himself, that self-restraint was lacking and the common good therefore threatened.

It is a matter of emphasis, no more than that. But features of shared morality are genuinely little stressed in contexts other than contradistinction (cf. Bourdieu 1965: 228), and political order, or indeed its mere possibility, is a contingent good that groups have from outside. This is often conceived geographically: for example, the 'original family' of shaykhs may be thought to have come first and other families settled round them, or most families of a village may claim to have been there first and the shaykhs came from elsewhere, but very commonly the shaykhs and their people are ascribed different origins.[33]

Cohesion is not thought of as deriving, of its nature, from tribal identity. Order is the result of an active involvement in men's affairs. A shaykh who aspires to influence (and thus to a monopoly of such functions as guaranty) must identify his personal standing and honour with that of his tribe or section. Prowess and success in warfare are an obvious means of doing so. Mujāhid Abū Shawārib of Khārif, for example, acquired a tremendous reputation in the civil war battles of the late 1960s, and in a tribal battle in 1978 he showed very much his old form: having been hit in the shoulder (presumably by a ricochet, though *allāhu aʿlam*, God only knows), he continued leading an attack, rested for a while with a cigarette, a cup of coffee, and an intravenous glucose drip, led numerous attacks over the next two days, then spent the best part of a week negotiating the truce with his usual wit and poise before finding time to have the bullet out. One can quite see why men put up with him lambasting them as useless old women. Plainly there is honour to be had from association with a man who has such conspicuous *sharaf* himself. Nor is there much temptation to compete. Arbitrarily the man has *haybah* ('prestige'; he strikes other men with 'awe'), and one might follow his lead.

Such conduct will attract a following but it will not maintain one, and in the longer run patronage is at least as important: *karīm* or 'generous' (*mabsūṭ al-yadayn*, 'open-handed') is virtually a synonym at times for *sharīf* or 'honourable', and there is nothing dishonourable in demanding largesse from a powerful shaykh in the form of rifles or cash or perhaps a new truck. However, there is little idea one owes much in return. It is his own good fortune to be able to distribute *khayrāt* or 'bounty' ('the bounty of God', in the last analysis), and there are a great many patrons at most levels of organization. A tribesman will switch from one to another.

Constancy is not really hoped for. A man may take payment from a powerful shaykh, then fail to support him, or may even oppose him, and then come back for more without either he or the shaykh finding this uncomfortable; but, as so often with Middle Eastern tribes, the means for largesse come from outside the immediate moral system.

Great shaykhly families such as Bayt al-Aḥmar of Ḥāshid, Bayt Abū Ra's of Dhū Muḥammad, or Bayt al-Shāyif of Dhū Ḥusayn, have sometimes been extremely powerful, and their power has often been bound up with their owning land. But those wealthy families of shaykhs who had great semi-feudal estates had them in Lower Yemen and in the west (this will be discussed in Chapter 6), not among the tribes themselves. Wealth nowadays comes often from political patronage. A shaykh's dominance over his men, if he establishes any dominance at all, is therefore not 'riveted into the land by the material interests of tenure' (the phrase is Jolliffe's, 1961: 136), nor is it fixed by any consideration other than his own ability. One must always remember, also, the enormous number of minor shaykhs who are as indigent and powerless as the men around them. The few great shaykhs are exceptional.

The influence of such men can rise and fall freely without changes in the tribes' formal structure and without major changes in group alignments (Dresch 1984*a*), while their own position is made more difficult by the fact that in all but the smallest unit there are numerous shaykhs, not arranged in a hierarchy or even in order of precedence. Indeed, the number of shaykhly families is indeterminately large.[34] At any given time, the extent of the unit with which each is identified seems arbitrary, and as we have already seen, it is not the rule for a higher-order section or for a tribe to recognize a single shaykh. Where one is recognized he is referred to as 'the shaykh of shaykhs' (*shaykh al-mashāyikh*), a title which for convenience we can gloss as paramount shaykh. His position is expressed in a document which his brother shaykhs in the tribe all sign.

The most striking example of such paramountcy is provided by Bayt al-Aḥmar, who have been shaykhs of all Ḥāshid for generations. Their particular section, al-Ḥumrān, forms part of al-'Uṣaymāt, and al-Ḥumrān itself comprises eight subsections (*laḥām*), of which four make up Bayt al-Aḥmar (see Figs. 3.6, 3.7). The numbers in the diagrams refer to grown men living in Wādī

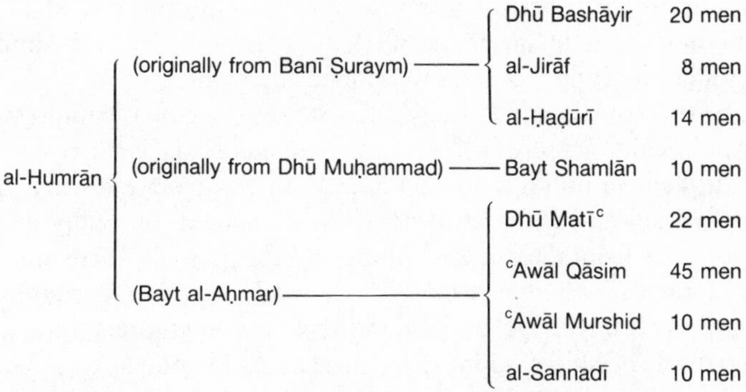

FIG. 3.6 Divisions of al-Ḥumrān, al-'Uṣaymāt

Ḥumrān and al-Khamrī, the family's 'original territory' just north of Ḥūth. There are others elsewhere in Yemen. Three of the subsections of Bayt al-Aḥmar descend from one 'Alī Qāsim, whom we know died in 1727 (al-Jirāfī 1951: 182), and al-Sannadī claim descent from a shared ancestor further back. 'Alī Qāsim the elder was head of all Ḥāshid in his day. The present shaykh's father and grandfather were both paramount shaykhs of Ḥāshid, but in about Ṣāliḥ b. Muṣliḥ's time the paramountcy was held by one 'Alī Nāṣir al-Aḥmar, a descendant of Yaḥyā b. Qāsim b. 'Alī Qāsim. The shaykhdom since 'Alī Qāsim's day seems always to have been held by descendants of Qāsim b. 'Alī, rather than any other of the family's branches.

The paramount shaykh is *hijrah* or *muhajjar* from Ḥāshid as a whole, which is to say that he is 'set aside' from the run of tribal conflict and protected. The term is from the same root as those already mentioned in connection with breach of the house's inviolability or that of tribal territory. Any offence against the shaykh is *'ayb* or 'disgrace' for which large amends are due (perhaps payment eleven-fold), and the responsibility for extracting such amends devolves upon Ḥāshid. It is also mentioned 'that Bin Aḥmar has a *dā'ī mujāb 'ind Bakīl* i.e., his summons to war would be responded to by Bakīl. The Bin Aḥmar would say to Bakīl that they were *dā'īn la-kum bi-ḥaqq al-hijrah tuḥāribū ma'ā-nā*, summoning you by the right/duty of *hijrah* (protection, etc.) to fight alongside us' (Serjeant 1977: 228–9). Quite what this link with Bakīl amounts to in practical terms is open to question (we shall see something of it in later chapters), but certainly Bayt al-Aḥmar's standing and influence is not confined to Ḥāshid.

The present shaykh, 'Abdullāh, is not only personally impressive, but politically is a power to reckon with: indeed, he is the one figure on the Yemeni political scene who, for all that his prominence may have varied at different times, has remained of really major importance from the 1962 revolution to the present. There are very few contexts, whether tribal or national, where one could not simply say 'Shaykh 'Abdullāh' and have it known one meant him. Moreover, Ḥāshid's supposed coherence and influence is widely attributed to him. Ḥāshid here in practice means only al-'Uṣaymāt, Khārif, and Banī Ṣuraym (Dresch 1984*b*: 170), but certainly there is no comparable group in Bakīl, and the classificatory equivalence of Ḥāshid and Bakīl as 'brothers' is often belied quite mundanely: for instance, identity cards and army pay-books used to have a space to record the man's tribe (*qabīlah*) and, while Bakīlīs would usually put Arḥab or Nihm or whatever was apt, men

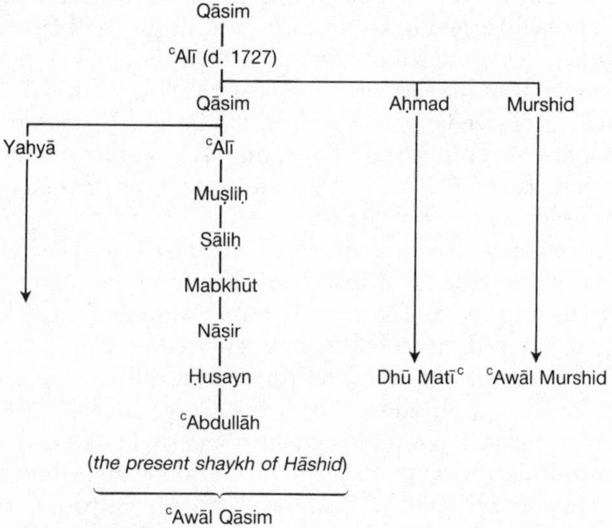

FIG. 3.7 Descent line of Bayt al-Aḥmar

from at least the three Ḥāshid tribes mentioned would almost always put simply Ḥāshid. Sociologically there is no warrant to divide cause and effect between the shaykhly house and the moderately coherent tribes; but it is important to note that what cohesion tribesmen think there is they attribute to a shaykh, not to shared 'ancestry' or their own decisions.

The comparative lack of coherence among certain Bakīl tribes (at least as some tribesmen on both sides see it) is taken for granted: lack of shaykhly influence is the unmarked state. Although men may criticize an uninfluential shaykh, they do not attribute to him personally the lack of 'one word' among his men. Paramount shaykhs of Bakīl, when there have been any (see Dresch 1984*a*: 37–8), have not for a long time matched those of Ḥāshid for influence or esteem, and the present paramount shaykh of Bakīl, Nājī b. 'Abd al-'Azīz al-Shāyif of Dhū Ḥusayn, who was elected in 1981, cannot claim much influence over his own tribe, let alone over others; but he too is in theory set aside from the run of ordinary conflict and protected by the signatories who made him shaykh.

This protected or elevated status (*hijrah*) is not accorded to all shaykhs, and its distribution is quite irregular: in Dhū Muḥammad, for instance, whose organization we sketched earlier, Bayt Abū Ra's are reckoned *hijrah* from the whole tribe, as are Bayt Aḥmar al-Sha'r; Bayt Thawābah are *hijrah* from Dhū Zayd, and Bayt Dammāj are *hijrah* only from al-'Utalāt, a minor section of one of the tribe's fifths, Āl Aḥmad b. Kawl. The others, even those who are shaykhs of guaranty, do not have this status, nor do the vast majority of shaykhs among the tribes, whatever the organizational level of the unit with which they are identified.

When shaykhs are reckoned *hijrah* it is because they are now respected personally or because their families were powerful at some stage in the past two centuries (the distribution of the term shows the trace of purely local histories), yet the status of *hijrah* is no simple reflection on either power or prestige: indeed, it resolves in part the contradiction power tends to imply in that men who are moral equals may not be admittedly subordinate to others and yet recognize leaders. The contradiction is avoided by producing difference. We shall consider the term *hijrah* at some length in Chapter 4, but this theme of difference can properly be stressed at once: among the root's several meanings, to do with movement, refuge, and protection, is also that of shunning, spurning, or 'setting aside'. A bridegroom at his wedding, for instance, is said to be *hijrah yawm-hu*, he has the status for that day; and he sits by himself, unspeaking, uninvolved, passed his food and his cigarettes by a taciturn pair of friends—he is honoured, but precisely by being so he is, as one might say, 'out of it', isolated from the stream of events.

The particular image, as it stands, is too extreme to be used of major shaykhs, but the principle would seem to be not dissimilar in their case and that of the bridegroom. A shaykh of prestige and power is 'set aside' by and for a tribe. They attach him to themselves, they make him available to lead them and to judge their disputes, and they do this by insisting that he is not quite like them: he does not pay their mulcts as they do, he receives no share of the blood-wealth they take, and he has no place in the field of potential hostility which defines all his tribesmen as equals; at the same time he does not explicitly rule them, although the hope is he will 'gather' them (*shaml*) as a body against outsiders and allow them to act as a unit in so far as he 'gathers the word of all'.

LIABILITY AND REFUGE

> In short, a change of social categories involves a change of residence, and this fact is expressed by the rite of passage . . .
>
> Van Gennep, *The Rites of Passage*

Relations of inclusion or hierarchy (of tribe to section, or section to village) are little stressed by themselves. Correspondingly, there is no fixed moral locus at which to pin down definitively who exactly is answerable on which occasion. A claim made against a tribe may be met with a denial of responsibility by one of the tribe's sections; a claim against a section may be met with similar denials from villages; and even villages may fragment into families and particular persons. Moreover, not all the abstract relations presented by the classification will be reckoned relevant (this section may have opted out, that one may have pledged support), and specific ties between individuals or short-lived groups usually pre-empt certain options that at first sight might seem available. The course of events is therefore complex. But to say this is only to register those events empirically and to complain that no model by itself predicts what will happen next. The principles, by contrast, carry through consistently. The types of events are remarkably constant, regardless of variation in the units or groups involved. One is dealing with claims and denials made on the basis of collective identities, none of which is ever fixed except temporarily by the acceptance of certain shaykhs as guarantors or as arbitrators for specified times and for limited purposes.

This has practical concomitants, not least the extraordinary open-endedness of tribal politics. Where there is no fixed level of moral reference, no bounded community that can judge its members in all circumstances, there is little chance of definitive problems or definitive answers: so, for example, people are very seldom expelled from the system and made socially dead. Nor is any one unit definitively at stake. At no point whatever, except that of an isolated family, is the definition of a unit fixed in such a way that appeals and rejections give place to simple conflict; that is, to a conflict that could only end with the removal of one or the other party. Instead there is an endless layering of dispute, arbitration, and (perhaps most important) mutual avoidance.

In this connection it is worth noting the lack of such things as physical defence lines. Fortified watch-towers often stand by lines of fields, but on the plateau one does not find lines of towers or breastworks along tribal borders.[35] Houses were always built for defence, and often they cluster together to form almost forts, but in strong contrast to certain other, non-tribal, parts of Yemen one does not come across walled villages, or walls along a tribal border: the fixed moral unit such walls might denote is rarely in evidence. No village, section, or tribe by itself can properly be said to be a moral 'community'—none has sense without its opposite numbers; but the tribes none the less form together a society, in that all are encompassed by the same values.

What is right and wrong is agreed on in general by all the tribes. Claims made by one on another are in supposedly a common language—that of *'urf al-qabā'il* or 'tribal custom'. But it is a principle of tribal law itself that where custom differs in detail between tribes or areas, then settlement is made in accordance with 'the custom of the side' (*'urf al-jihah*) from which the plaintiff comes. In other words, the plaintiff's right to demand those detailed amends that would satisfy him is often assimilated to the assumption that there are rules from which those details derive.

There is usually no occasion to produce the 'rules' and compare them. Men who are regarded as experts in arbitration are often presumed to have books or documents in their possession which show the 'real' tribal custom, but these are not available to other people.[36] A general statement of uniformity is therefore complemented by a practical fragmentation such that claims between equals are not always strictly commensurable and knowledge is particularized in the same way as enforcing justice. Truth is not attached to any hierarchy of persons or offices. Instead it is apparent in the existence of equals, whose precise definition itself shifts with changing circumstance. And when definitions do become fixed, to one's disadvantage, one appeals to or moves to a unit just like one's own.

If an individual tribesman feels he is badly wronged *(maẓlūm*, 'oppressed'), and neither appeals nor violent action have restored his rights, he can leave his own tribe and go to another. He will generally offer a bull to the tribe he goes to. The tribe he goes to (let us say, Sufyān) is honour-bound to take him in as a refugee *(qaṭīr* or *rabīʿ*, 'protégé') unless he is so plainly in the wrong that his face is already blackened among all the tribes. The shaykhs of the accepting tribe (Sufyān) should then write to the tribe he left (that of Banī Ṣuraym, for instance), setting out the man's claims and requiring an explanation. If no satisfactory explanation is received, they may accept the bull the man offers. With the spilling of the slaughter-beast's blood, the refugee from Banī Ṣuraym becomes Sufyānī. He becomes a 'brother' to the other members of Sufyān and a 'son' of the tribe's eponym. He is as much a member of the tribe as are those who have always been members. His rights and obligations are precisely theirs. He and his children after him may perhaps acquire the name al-Ṣuraymī if they have no distinctive family name already, but they are otherwise indistinguishable from their fellows.[37]

Men do not lightly go to another tribe for support against their own, and actually becoming a member of another tribe is a rare occurrence: it requires severing ties not only with men one has known all one's life, but also with one's land, to which tribesmen are strongly attached. Men will change tribes only as a result of duress, and usually matters will not go so far. Banī Ṣuraym's honour is broken by one of them leaving their protection for that of another tribe (it is rather as if a traveller declared his escort worthless, or a guest walked out on his host); they are honour-bound to retrieve him, and the custom among all the tribes is that they should go after their man within 'fifteen days' (two weeks, as we count them) and give rifles to the shaykhs of the accepting tribe. These are variously referred to as *banādiq al-naza'āt* ('rifles of removal') or *banādiq al-ikhā'* ('rifles of brotherhood'). They express Banī Ṣuraym's assertion that the refugee is one of them, but they are held by the shaykhs of Sufyān to express also that the refugee remains 'on their honour' or 'under their protection' (that is, 'in their faces').

The refugee may, if adequate assurances are forthcoming, return to Banī Ṣuraym before his claims are settled. If so, he remains the protégé of Sufyān, and any offence against him is thus an insult to Sufyān for which they will demand heavy amends. The insult would, in the first instance, be to the shaykhs who hold the rifles and who have thus 'given their faces' (that is, made the commitment personally). They would then call on their men, since the honour of the tribe as such is at issue too. The rifles are only handed back when the man's claims are resolved satisfactorily. Arbitration of the man's claim involves shaykhs from both tribes.

Temporary refuge with another tribe 'covers' a man from harm or injustice: indeed, a verb quite commonly used of this process among the eastern tribes is *taḥajjaba*, from the same root as the standard Arabic term for a veil or indeed for an amulet that 'covers' one from envious eyes. A man's moral status as the formal equal of others is preserved by the identification of his honour with that of a tribe; and where revenge or compensation are not acquired with collective backing, he may change his identification from one tribe to another, the tribes in turn being moral equals. No man by himself can cover his vulnerable honour (*'arḍ*) or that of his dependants. He must decide in the end on the collective identity to accept, on the tribe to which he already 'is brother' or now will 'become brother' (*yukhāwī* can mean both or either).

If the bulls are accepted and, for example, Banī Ṣuraym still wish to retrieve their man (as for their honour's sake they should) then they must give Sufyān a bull, or a number of bulls, themselves. These would be slaughtered at a meeting of both tribes or in Sufyān's market on market-day. With the spilling of blood the refugee who had become a Sufyānī reverts to being one of Banī Ṣuraym. His original tribe are said to have 'lifted the blood with blood' (*rafa'ū al-dam bi-dam*). There are thus rituals of incorporation and severance involved in changes of tribal membership. One is made clearly part of one tribe or another. The imagery of blood, in turn, is associated by the tribesmen with the image of shared descent, the 'ancestry' which defines their common honour, and with the obligations of blood-revenge in defence of this.

In practice these obligations may not be discharged reliably, as we have seen, and the move between tribes is an exchange of one negotiable set of claims for another. The possibility of such exchange, however, is characteristic of this type of system. There is no position within the system from which one tribe can be definitively judged against another, or the particular tribesman judged right or wrong. The tribes are opposed just as black squares to white squares, so that a man who loses his position in one is almost sure to regain it in the next, moving from one set to another which is opposed to the first and entirely discrete from it, yet in the relevant terms identical. It is this serial quality of the tribes that, ethnographically, is in the end most striking. They are all of them equal and opposite, not in numbers or size, but as they divide up a moral world, the terms of which all tribes share.

NOTES

1. Apart from the city of Ṣan'ā', the only point I can think of that is clearly 'extra-tribal' is Ẓafār Dhībīn, protected by, but not part of, Khārif, Murhibah, Arḥab, and certain other tribes (see Puin 1984; Dresch forthcoming *a*). Al-Sawād, a very barren area in the far north-west, contains small settlements from at least three sections of Sufyān, from Āl Sālim, and from part of Dhū Muḥammad, none of which tribes is identified with the area as a whole; but this can properly be said to be outside the 'land of the tribes'. The territorial system must, of course, give way to the very different Central Arabian mode at some point in the extreme east; but quite where and how this transition occurs is not known yet in much detail. A sketch of the territorial system at these eastern fringes of the area is given in ch. 9.
2. Al-'Uṣaymāt provide a case in point, where a group called Ahl al-Wādī is not definitively Jawādī or Sallābī. Sallāb say they would not support them against Jawād, while Jawād say they would support them against Sallāb, but the expense would fall on Ahl al-Wādī.
3. Banī Maṭar, for example, are said by many of their members nowadays to derive in part from Khawlān al-Ṭiyāl and in part from Dhū Maḥram the Ḥimyarite. They are still *min jadd wāḥid*, in this case Maṭar.

4. The rhetoric of shared 'ancestry' is a simple statement of identity. It takes only intermittent note of history and produces no history of its own in the form of structural time or depth (Evans-Pritchard 1940), but simply follows the general Semitic practice in speaking of groups as kin (Robertson Smith 1885: 14–16; Beeston 1972: 257). There is no reason why the same 'ancestor' should not recur at different levels of the classification or why an isolated claim to descent should always denote inclusion. So, the five Khawlān b. 'Āmir tribes of Ṣa'dah are said to be Munabbih, Suḥār, Rāziḥ, Jamā'ah, and Khawlān (Chelhod 1976: 74 n. 15). Many informants assert that the eponym of the tribe and of the confederation are the same Khawlān. Again, Sufyān is reckoned 'son of Arḥab', and has been since at least the tenth century AD, but Sufyān and Arḥab are quite separate tribes.
5. To document this negative proposition at all fully would take more space than can be spared here, but a few points deserve noting. First, the term 'tribe' (*qabīlah*) may itself be used of very small units (see e.g. Dresch 1987*a*: 81 n. 32), but this is highly unusual in all but a very few areas of the north-west. Second, most sections are referred to as 'quarters', 'thirds', 'fifths', and so forth, rather than by generic terms such as *fakhdh* or *ḥabl*. There is in any case rarely a need to talk about the system in abstract terms: the outsider's attempts to do so easily produce confusion and false classifications that are artefacts of one's questions. Lastly, such attempts as Dostal's (1974: 3) to equate '*amārah* with a 'maximal lineage', *fakhdh* with a 'major segment', and so forth are to be treated with the utmost caution even if one can decide what is meant by the European term of each proposed pair: I saw nothing in Upper Yemen that looked at all like an African 'maximal lineage'.
6. The *naqā'* of a tribe is often referred to in verse and decked about with poetic imagery: 'like the throne of Bilqīs', 'like the pillars of Ma'rib', and so on. The untainted good name *(naqā' ṣāfī)* is very much what we mean by a spotless escutcheon.
7. Conventionally, forty-four oaths are required in cases of murder (often twenty-two for lesser crimes), and those demanding sworn testimony can nominate the particular people they wish to provide oaths. For the forms of oath see app. 3/1.
8. *Yā mā ḥalā ṭaraḥ al-ma'āniqah / fī yawm shabb al-ṣawt*
fī yawm nusab al-jadūd / fī yawm duhak al-matāris
wa-l-ḥarb li-layāt / wa-aghmār-nā zabn al-ḥudūd
(transcribed in Khārif).
9. For an historical use of 'reciting the forefathers', meaning simply to fight bravely and not give up, see al-Ḥibshī 1980: 549. One might note in passing that the projection of *sharaf* is associated in the poem with elders, and the defence of '*arḍ* with young men, much as with fathers and brothers in the case of families.
10. Tribes do not invade other tribes' territory, nor do tribes carry off other tribesmen's womenfolk. But when one unthinkable act is done, so others follow. When al-Thamthamī of Sufyān carried off the

daughters of al-Ziyādī of Ḥāshid, late in the nineteenth century, Ḥāshid invaded Sufyān, occupied part of their territory for almost two months, and laid the area waste before withdrawing to their own border (Glaser 1884: 170). In the normal way of things even penetrations of a kilometre or so to outflank positions on the border line in a battle are made very tentatively, and the idea of permanently wresting territory from one's neighbours is foreign to tribal rhetoric in most areas: the one exception would seem to be the Upper Jawf and the extreme north-east, where nomads are quite numerous.

11. Unfortunately some authors (e.g. Kopp 1985: 44) are now generalizing Dostal's comments and writing of a 'law of *juwārah*' in areas other than where Dostal worked. This needs to be treated very carefully. The rules vary greatly between different ecological zones (see chs. 8 and 9, below), and where rules of exclusion do exist they are local expressions of *juwārah*, not the whole of *juwārah*'s substance.

12. A similar ambiguity is found in the otherwise very different ethnography of village Tunisia (see Abu Zahra 1982: 97, 113), although '*arḍ* in the Yemeni case is what one must 'cover' and in the Tunisian case seems almost itself to be the covering God provides decent people.

13. For example, al-Ma'āṭirah are a tribe or section very closely associated with Dhū Muḥammad. I have heard a shaykh of the latter tribe say *yā ma'āṭirī mā la-k 'arḍ 'alā l-muḥammadī*, meaning you have no right to give one Muḥammadī refuge from another or to claim from us recognition of your protecting outsiders; we are not bound to support your action as we would each other's.

14. For variations in collective responsibility between one tribe and another 100 years ago see Glaser 1884: 176. The differences are still very much as they were.

15. In this particular case there was also a choice between what exactly to count: in matters of blood-money and the like, only grown men were counted; in common projects, such as to install a shared water-system, women and children were counted too; in raising fines it used to be that land and livestock were counted along with each man, assessing contributions by 'persons and property' (*ḥāl wa-māl*).

There will not be space to pursue the matter fully in later chapters, so let us note here that the same mismatch of general classification with mulct-raising groups that one finds in tribes recurs also at village level: the groups who raise or divide *ghurm wa-jurm* in a village are not necessarily coincident with patronymic sets, although the patronymic sets in a village are defined by actual, traceable genealogy.

16. The distribution of blood-money within a tribe or section, if compensation is accepted, varies from tribe to tribe. Khārif, for example, claim that the whole sum goes to the victim's immediate kin. The same is true of Upper al-'Uṣaymāt. In Lower al-'Uṣaymāt the usual claim is that half goes to the immediate kin and half to the remainder of the victim's section (e.g. Dhū Ghānim, one-twelfth of Dhū Muḥammad

'Alī), unless the whole tribe has been involved in the dispute, in which case the half would be divided among all of them; but no one was able to cite a case where this had happened. In Sufyān it seems the immediate kin received only 110 MTs, the rest being divided up among the immediate section (e.g. Dhū Ja'rān, about 250 men).

17. Alternatively, *man qutil waṣal wa-man qatal aṣṣal,* which is a version I have heard both in al-Uṣaymāt and Sufyān.

18. This use of the term *man'* (pl. *manū'*) to mean an affine (synonym *nasīb*) is found not only in the extreme east but also, for example, in al-'Uṣaymāt. The word may also mean protection or a protected person. Among Dhū Muḥammad it is used of tribesmen of subordinate status who do not share the Muḥammadīs' capacity to act as escorts, etc., the same people whom Dhū Ḥusayn called *qabā'il al-wasaṭ*. There is no such subordinate stratum on the plateau. That *man'* in the present case referred specifically to affines was carefully checked.

19. The meaning of the rifles is often equivocal. 'Rifles which clear you' where your tribe as a whole is at odds with outsiders and you wish to opt out might equally be 'rifles of patience' (*banādiq al-ṣabr* or *banādiq al-tarzīh*) that give the outsiders right of judgment, win for you a truce, and leave open the matter of who the culprits in your own tribe are and who will make amends. The ties denoted by rifles are all of equal worth. But the precise nature of each tie is usually negotiable, the negotiations being pursued by proffering and taking further rifles in turn.

20. Where it is appropriate, breaking the dagger sheath is a powerful gesture. A Sufyānī shaykh did this to claim support against Ḥāshid in 1978 and the effect produced on both sides was comparable to that produced in our own tradition by a declaration of war, say, or by the news that an army has crossed the border. We shall touch on the case that occasioned this in ch. 10.

21. Some of the other shaykhly families of Dhū Muḥammad are Bayt Fāḍil and Bayt 'Awfān (al-Dumaynah; the latter were shaykhs of guaranty before Dāris); Dammāj and Sa'dān (Aḥmad b. Kawl); Ja'dar and al-Baḥr (Dhū Mūsā). Amīn Abū Ra's was recognized as shaykh of the whole tribe in the 1960s and early 1970s. Now no one is, not even 'Abdullāh Dāris, who acquired considerable national prominence as leader of the 'popular army' (the government's tribal levy) in 1982/83.

Āl Aḥmad b. Swaydān and al-Maḥlaf seem generally not to be thought of as likely 'summonses' against each other, group against group; but rather similar divisions in neighbouring Dhū Ḥusayn were spoken of in just those terms. For a discussion of the significance of shaykhly domains not corresponding with all the levels of tribal classification see Dresch 1984*a*.

22. The more classical form, *'adāl*, is certainly used for surety; but, unless my ear deceives me, the form *'adl* (or perhaps *'idl*) is the more common among tribesmen.

23. Laying down one's dagger obviously imposes an obligation in the manner discussed in ch. 2, and one occasionally hears it called *'aqīrah*

(in other words, a parallel is drawn with 'slaughter-beasts'). At the same time, for the shaykh to hold the dagger (sometimes he physically holds it; often he lets it lie before him) is to hold in pawn the autonomy of the man who gives it. Very rarely is a dagger actually taken away. A rifle may be, or money. The pattern is extremely widespread. Educated young men in Ṣan'ā', if they have no weapons about them, will lay their watches before a stranger to have him arbitrate small disagreements over literature, geography, or Western politics.

24. Black-Michaud (1980: 97–8) thinks the Rwala (Musil 1928: 493) are an exception to a general rule of arbitrators taking payment. In fact, on closer inspection, the Rwala material seems to support precisely the distinction one finds in Yemen: arbitrators take payment, guarantors do not.

25. Some indication should be given of these 'costs'. In 1979 a Jew from Arḥab built a second story on his house in Raydah, next door to the house of a Kharīf shaykh, and decorated his efforts with a six-pointed star. A squabble then started over whether this was a star of David or a seal of Solomon or what it was, and should it be there? The stone was replaced at Arḥab's expense and an agreement made that any harassment of a Jew be fined 'eleven-fold'. But to reach this rather minor decision, each tribe brought about 70 men to Khamir for a week and ran up 'costs' of about YR 70,000.

26. It is very common to spread a given payment over three separate, yearly instalments. I have found no evidence of the system Glaser was told of in Arḥab whereby 'The surplus of killed must be paid for, to the tribe with more dead, at 22 thalers per head in the first year, 5 or 7 thalers in the second year . . .' (Glaser 1884: 177). If this were done, it was surely not as Glaser suggests because the full blood-money could not be raised, but to maintain the relations of guaranty and thus the truce.

27. Although the logic of disputes is in most respects parallel to that of feuding societies (see Peters 1967; Meeker 1976: i. 255; Dresch 1986: 316), feud as such is not a feature of the Yemeni system anywhere than perhaps parts of the Jawf. Long-standing links of guaranty and truce usually take its place.

28. Groups are recognized, liability derives often from membership of some collective set, yet there are no corporations or councils and there is always an individual person looked for. Serjeant 1977: 235 cites the extreme case of Ḥaḍramī sultans dealing with their own slave soldiers through the latter's headmen. Since Middle Eastern tribes are so often aligned with certain African societies on the grounds of formal segmentation, it may be worth pointing out the immense contrast between them in this other connection. As Strathern says, the identity of persons with offices, and the place of collective ritual in confirming this, all of which is salient in older African ethnography, provides 'a fascinating indigenous commentary on the nature of agency' (Strathern 1985: 65). No such identity of individual and legal persons is prominent among Yemeni tribes. They are nearer, in fact, to certain

New Guinea societies where men do not so much have power 'over' others as the power to 'do' things: successful headmen or shaykhs 'are able to exert influence . . . because evidence of control is fixed in them' (ibid. 73), not in any group identity.

29. In classical Arabic, *wujūh*, *wajīh*, *wujahā'* are 'leaders' or 'notables', perhaps an indication of this same distinctive relation of group and persons. To mention the individual as a privileged locus of value is, of course, to place ourselves on ground that Louis Dumont has made his own, but we cannot look to borrow ideas from him directly: as Yalman 1969 points out, Islamic material fits very uneasily in the contrast between hierarchy and individualism as originally set out in *Homo Hierarchicus*.

The reference to resolving a conflict of values is specifically to 'Politics as a vocation' (Weber [1919] 1970), perhaps the most interesting of Weber's essays and an almost exact complement to the earlier part of Dumont's work. Having cited classical Hindu theory as an enviable moral escape not available to the protestant West, Weber portrays the politician as a romantic, indeed tragic, figure in whom the ethic of ultimate ends and the ethic of responsibility are fused when he says, 'Here I stand; I can do no other'. Middle Eastern Islamic material, of course, offers a potential opposite to Dumont's India: it is full of 'individuals in relation to God' who are not at all 'world renouncers'. Yet it also offers an opposite to Weber's West: it is full of exemplary figures, yet none resolves in himself conflicting claims in the manner of the tragic politician.

Dumont's later generalization (1986) of hierarchy and individualism to the level of principles allows us to see the shape of the problem better. This question will be touched on again in the context of Islamic historiography in ch. 5, but the problem is to work out 'the historical forms of existence of individuality' (Althusser and Balibar 1970: 112) in each culture, not to place the cultures on a single scale.

30. *Salām bi-l-milyūn yatfarraq jamī' al-qabīlah*
fī mā jarā min-nā wa-nabghā min-kum ṭayyab al-nufūs
al-ḥukm bi-l-marbū' dhī farraq wa-athara mā rafaq
wa-ṣāḥib al-dam qad 'afā qāl irḥabū fawq al-ru'ūs.

These ditties, by the way, are made up on the spur of the moment and then chanted to set 'tunes': probably few of them can be crammed into proper verse metres.

31. If the government's action in arresting men from suspect villages seems high-handed, one should remember that it simply follows the tribes' own rule that a tribe or section is answerable for what happens in its territory.

32. This expression is by no means limited to tribesmen. See, for example, al-Sayāghī 1978: 50: *wa-kulli wāḥid ḥakim nafs-hu muṭlaq al-'inān wa-lā dhikr li-l-maṣlaḥat al-'āmmah bi-l-marrah*; 'everyone ruled himself on a completely free rein, giving no thought at all to the general welfare'.

33. To place one's affairs in the hands of a man like oneself, except where

the logic of reciprocity and alternation holds (as with hospitality; Pitt-Rivers 1977: 104), is to admit a principle that tribal rhetoric makes no room for. To place one's affairs temporarily, or repeatedly, in the hands of a man unlike oneself is another matter, and the attribution to shaykhs of a separate origin seems to be a minimal condition of doing this. Some very prominent shaykhly families, such as Āl al-Shāyif of Dhū Ḥusayn, are thus accorded an origin quite outside Yemen, in 'Asīr, though I have never seen any evidence to support this historically.

Shaykhs are sometimes chosen from non-shaykhly families ('Alī al-Julaydān, for example, became a shaykh in Banī Qays of Banī Ṣuraym in the civil war), but this is unusual. Prominence is often rationalized by a 'must have been' story. After 'Alī 'Abdullāh Ṣāliḥ, a man of very ordinary tribal background, became President of the republic, many tribesmen argued that his family 'of course' had long ago been shaykhs of Ḥāshid. In fact there is no connection at all but the name of his village.

34. The number of shaykhly families is indeterminate because there can be local disagreement over whether a man should be called a shaykh or an '*āqil* (Dresch 1984*a*: 36). For details on terminology see app. 3/2.

35. There is a half-collapsed stone wall across Wādī Dhībīn on the border between Khārif and Bakīl, but no one can remember when or why it was put there. Apart from this, the only constructions I have seen that looked specifically like border defences are to the east of Baraṭ: even these could be old cairns (I could not examine them because fighting was in progress), but from their position they might well be elaborate breast-works; if so, they were in an area frequented only by nomads until about five years ago.

36. The place of documents in customary law requires a paper in itself. Briefly, codes of customary law do exist (see e.g. those discussed by Rossi, 1948; R. B. Serjeant has copies of some of these and additional material of his own) but they are not readily accessible. Much more accessible are records of particular cases, copies of which are given to the disputing parties. There is not, however, any formal doctrine of precedent, nor can there be without instituting a hierarchy of knowledge quite foreign to the tribes' self-definition.

37. The possibility of movement without subordination is widespread in Middle Eastern tribal societies, just as is that of temporary refuge (see e.g. Musil 1928). Indeed it is characteristic. Somewhat contrary to Black-Michaud's thesis (1980), the nomadic tribes and the sedentary tribes of the area are in this respect more like each other than either is like the settled village societies where such reciprocal movement is missing and events are then sometimes pushed to very bloody conclusions.

4 Estates of Society within the Tribal Peace

If we approach the study . . . with ready made divisions of life into trade and religion and politics and war, we shall never understand why the *agora* is at once a market place, a place for ritual and for political assembly.

Hocart, *Kings and Councillors*

[He who breaks] the peace of the church [shall pay] double compensation; the peace of a public assembly, double compensation.

Dooms of Aethelberht, trans. C. Stephenson and F. G. Marcham

There are few geographical spaces between tribes. But within tribes there are frequent moral spaces where the logic of opposition is drastically modified, and it is these we shall look at next. In particular, two broad estates of non-tribesmen are recognized as having rights and obligations within tribal territory. The first such estate are the 'weak' people (*ḍu'afā'*, pl. of *ḍa'īf*), whom the tribesmen consider beneath them; they either carry no weapons at all or traditionally wore their daggers obliquely to the left, where the tribesmen and shaykhs wear their daggers upright at the centre of the belt. The second broad estate of non-tribesmen are the men of religious learning (*'ulamā'*): the sayyids, who claim descent from the Prophet, and the qadis, or 'judges'. Both of these have often considered themselves somewhat above the tribesmen, on account of their claim to knowledge, and traditionally they wore their daggers obliquely to the right.

As Glaser discerned (1885: 202; cf. Gerholm 1977: 107–8), it is not easy or productive to rank these estates and their components on a single scale; which is why I use the term 'estate' here rather than 'status group'.[1] Each is associated in part with a particular viewpoint, and each might equally serve as the centre of its own ethnography. Here it is the tribes which are our main concern, and the other estates of society are of importance as they have a place in the tribal world. The place of these other estates among the tribes is related to the way in which tribesmen themselves set apart certain events and places from what they conceive of as ordinary tribal life.

'WEAK' PEOPLE SUCH AS BARBERS AND TRADERS

'Weak' people have no *'arḍ*. They do not have the tribesman's ability to intervene in affairs between other tribesmen by taking someone into their peace and providing protection. In the game of tribal honour and standing they are not recognized as players. For a tribesman to offend against a weak person is a disgrace, although in practice the offence must be recognized as such by other tribesmen; that is, by men who themselves have honour and are capable of demanding and exacting amends. And the offence is at the same time an insult to the particular set of tribesmen under whose protection the weak person lives. Amends are often demanded four-fold, to be divided between the victim and his tribal protectors.

A case of this kind was touched on in Chapter 2, in which in the late nineteenth century four times the blood-money was prescribed as amends for a Jew who was murdered. There are few Jews now remaining in Upper Yemen, but those who do remain are still reckoned *jīrān*, or tribal 'protégés', and they refer to themselves (though perhaps not among themselves) as 'Yahūd Banī Fulān', the Jews of the particular tribe to which they are attached. Usually they were forbidden to carry arms at all. In the countryside many farmed as the tribesmen did, and indeed some had part of their land worked by tribesmen for cash or for a share of the crop. Others, both in rural villages and in towns, were associated with crafts such as leather-working and silver-working.[2] Where the Jews in a village practised such crafts to the exclusion of agriculture they were supported by a contribution in kind from the tribesmen at harvest time called *māḥibah*. Some large villages were populated almost entirely by Jews (for example, al-Mahāṣir, from which the subsection of Khayār in Banī Ṣuraym takes its name), and most villages in tribal territory would seem to have had a small Jewish presence, but since 1948 there remain only a few scattered families to suggest what their place once was.

Those who are weak but Muslim are nowadays far more numerous than the Jews and in most places are a more conspicuous part of society. In the tribesmen's view the ideal type of such weak people, to whom other categories are often assimilated, are the *mazāyinah* (pl. of *muzayyin*). The *mazāyinah* act as barbers and butchers, perform circumcisions, and are the drummers at feasts or when the tribesmen march in a body to a meeting or to war. They are found both in the tribal villages and in the towns. They are also conspicuous in the houses of great men, where they see to the comfort of guests at *qāt* chews, bringing cold water to drink, tending the water-pipes, and sweeping up debris afterwards. Their servile status is considered hereditary. The *mazāyinah* are referred to by tribesmen as *nuqqāṣ* or *nāqiṣ al-aṣl*, 'lacking' or 'deficient in' the authenticity and standing provided by tribal ancestry and so lacking honour of the kind tribesmen claim for themselves.[3] Until the 1962 revolution the *mazāyinah* all wore their daggers to the left. Some now wear them to the right, which was once largely the prerogative of men of religion, and a few wear them at the centre as tribesmen do. It is still the case that few tribesmen would intermarry with *mazāyinah*, and in the countryside the taint of servile ancestry is not lost easily (see Chelhod 1970: 80; Serjeant 1977: 231).

As people who lack tribal honour, the *mazāyinah* do not 'count' in some circumstances. For example, they are admitted to the tribesman's *ḥarīm* (that is, among his womenfolk), where other tribesmen apart from close kin would not be; and the tribesmen themselves sometimes flirt (quite harmlessly, be it said) with *muzayyin* women in a way that would be thought extremely ill mannered were the women tribesmen's daughters. It is not simply that the *muzayyin* does not or cannot object (some do, and their objections should be respected), but that the tribesmen themselves consider such joking harmless. There is nothing at stake. The *mazāyinah* lack tribal standing and are neither potential enemies nor potential partners in marriage. A *muzayyin* should also be able to cross the lines between warring tribes in safety, and in practice weak people are often used to carry messages where a tribesman could not safely do so. Something of this protected status is also perhaps apparent in the way that a *muzayyin* usually accompanies a bridal party, especially in cases of marriage between tribal families from separate, and thus opposed, villages (Chelhod 1970: 76 and 1973: 23).

Apart from the *muzayyin* in the strict sense (that is, one who acts as a barber and butcher and performs circumcisions, among other things), there are other hereditary occupations which form part of the same low, non-tribal estate: for example, the *muqawwit* who buys and sells *qāt* on a small scale, the *muqahwī*, who runs a coffee shop or lodging house in the small towns, and the *qashshām* (or *ghashshām*; the word is from that for a white onion), who runs a small vegetable garden and sells the produce himself at market.[4] For a tribesman to sell his own produce at market was, until perhaps the end of the 1960s, reckoned *'ayb* or disgrace. Grain was sold by the tribesmen, where they sold it at all, through 'weak' intermediaries, and according to many informants even to grow green vegetables, let alone to sell them, was thought disgraceful. The tribesmen, living mainly on parched, rain-fed land, may have been making a virtue of necessity in this last case, but disdain for the market was part of the tribesman's own self-esteem, and in many areas it still is.[5] The market and commercial transactions were viewed in much the same terms as the servile and unclean work of the *mazāyinah* (the barbers and butchers).

The weak people drew their own distinctions, which we shall say something of later, but the tribesmen even now often use the term *bayyā'* (which means 'trader') as a synonym for *jīrān*, in the sense of weak and protected people, and they tend to gloss both terms as simply *mazāyinah*. The whole, weak, non-tribal estate is tagged with the name of its lowest part. The tribesmen themselves have now taken, in many areas, to the commerce and petty manufacture which was once the preserve of the 'traders', but they have not let drop the hereditary distinctions which once went more strictly with occupations.[6] There are still very clearly tribesmen and weak non-tribesmen.

One further set of non-tribesmen deserve noting briefly. The *dawāshīn* (pl. of *dawshān*), whose status is also hereditary, are conspicuous as 'heralds'. They are something of an anomaly in that they are weak and are under tribal protection but wear their daggers upright at the front of the belt in the same way as tribesmen do. No tribesman, and few weak people, would consider intermarriage with them. Until recently most of the *dawāshīn* who lived in areas where the tribesmen are settled farmers were themselves semi-nomadic,[7] and each family of *dawāshīn* still has its own 'pitch' of tribal territory where it has the right to claim gifts in kind from the tribesmen for services or at harvest time.

In formal settings the *dawāshīn* often serve in effect to insulate tribesmen from other tribesmen. If, for example, one tribesman has a claim on another and wishes to press his claim publicly, he may appear at the market on market day and fire shots in the air to draw a crowd, but a *dawshān* will then stand up beside him and bellow out what he wants to say, adding an embellishment of established and formal phrases. We shall have occasion later to mention the place of such 'heralds' at tribal meetings. At weddings and at other feasts it is customary to have a *dawshān* eulogize one's guests. All sorts of public announcements are made by the *dawshān*, and a letter between shaykhs of two tribes at odds is delivered most formally by a *dawshān* rather than by any other type of weak person or by a tribesman.

All of the weak people (the Jews, the butchers and barbers, the traders, and heralds) are under tribal protection. The precise distribution of responsibility varies. In Dhū Muḥammad, for example, each family of weak people is attached only to a particular family or minor section of the tribe, with the exception of two *bayyā'* ('trader') families who attach to Dhū Muḥammad as a whole.[8] However, the *jīrān*, or 'weak' protégés, even if they attach formally only to particular sections, come high on the list of the whole tribe's *mu'awwarāt*; things on which honour depends and in defence of which each part of the tribe should support each other against outsiders. The idea of noble protection is, of course, very old. Al-Hamdānī, (d. AD 945), for example, flatters a tribe of Jabal Baraṭ with the following tag: 'Its people are the bravest of Hamdān, protectors of women [or 'shame' or the 'weak'], and defenders of the protected person', *wa-ahl-hu anjad hamdān wa-ḥamāh al-'awrah wa-man'ah al-jār* (quoted Rossi 1948: 9).[9] How well the system worked from the weak people's point of view would be hard to assess. Personal relations between tribesmen and protégés, on which the chance of prompt action often rests, vary greatly and cannot safely be the subject of generalization. The structural relations between tribesmen and protégés acquire unequivocal value only when 'our' protected people are explicitly set on by outsiders, and even then action may or may not be taken to right the wrong. By comparison with the weak people, however, the tribes form a sort of 'arms-bearing aristocracy' (Serjeant 1977: 227), and one tribe may in part claim its honourable standing as against other tribes in the defence of people who are not themselves tribesmen. The parallel with individual men's claim to defend their women and children requires no stressing.

At the same time, the presumed separation of 'weak' people aligns them with the problem of equality and contradiction often evident in transactions between tribes or tribesmen.

It seems to me almost a characteristic of the society to turn to a third party to mediate in even quite trifling transactions, and so the tribes will resort on the one hand to the religious aristocracy, or to the non-arms bearing group inferior to them. To communicate with one another they will use the *muzayyin* or the *dallāl* or broker who entertains them when they are in town and buys and sells for them on commission. (ibid. 240)

Similarly, Stevenson (1985: 101) writes of 'middlemen' (*maṣlaḥīn*) who brokered specific goods and were of low status. Again, the 'measurer' or *kayyāl* weighed out grain at market, providing a supposedly impartial service for tribesmen and himself being 'weak' (ibid. 102). Indeed, 'in most transactions the notions of buyer and seller tend to be dissolved in the network of middlemen and guarantors . . .' (Bourdieu 1977: 174), and the same principle extends in fact far beyond the market-place to characterize, as Serjeant says, the society itself.

It is not, I think, that this works 'to transform the purely economic relationship between supply and demand into a genealogically based . . . relationship' (ibid.); rather, to weigh one's own grain, to broker one's own goods, to negotiate directly with one's opposite number on any issue was to surrender autonomy on one side and grant definitional power to the other in a meeting of conceptual equals. So the only circumstance in which the measurer of grain was not 'weak', for example, was where the measuring was for the Imam's taxes (Stevenson 1985: 102)—autonomy had been surrendered already. Otherwise insulation was needed, or separation. And if direct exchange threatened moral equality, so too did the possession of common valuables. If the *dawāshīn* often mediate the exchange of words between tribesmen, they are also *ma'mūnīn*, 'trusted' not to pass information unasked; and documents concerning a whole tribe, for example, are lodged, not with the shaykh, but usually with the *dawshān*. He may be the lowest in society but is surely also the most different from the tribesmen, any one of whom might otherwise identify a common undertaking as his own at the expense of his equals. Again, a *muzayyin* lacks honour (and on precisely that basis is employed as a broker), yet when a tribe or a village rather than a particular household, wishes to honour a guest, it is with the *muzayyin* that the guest is lodged (Serjeant 1977: 231).[10] This goes a long way beyond 'economics' in any normal sense of that term, and beyond the idea of 'self-interest' made popular by Bourdieu.

Economic relations between tribesmen and weak people are in fact not by any means constant, though some of the protected people who practised crafts no doubt filled specific niches. Political relations between tribes may involve the weak people as at least a *casus belli* and in extreme cases as a compelling point of honour which must be defended.[11] Outside the few towns, however, the weak people are not numerous (two or three families in a village of thirty tribal families is not unusual), and nowhere do they have the standing to serve by themselves as a constant focus of tribal identity or to alter the course of events between tribes by their own views. Some of the places with which weak people are associated may, by contrast, be given considerable importance by the tribes; most notably, markets.

MARKETS UNDER TRIBAL GUARANTY

There are weekly markets throughout the north. Some are held in towns, others at sites which are named only for the market held there and where on the other days of the week there is nothing to show but, at most, a few stone booths. Even at very small markets, imported goods such as cigarettes, fizzy drinks, tea, and fruit were usually available in the early 1980s. Imported grain was commonplace, but local grain was also sold, together with fodder, local vegetables, and coffee husks (*qishr*) from western Yemen. The butchers, who are nearly all *mazāyinah*, set up their tripods of sticks or scaffold poles to slaughter and cut up meat. The tribesmen now generally arrive by truck. News is exchanged. By midday the crowd of market-goers is usually breaking up, and by mid-afternoon there is nothing to see of a small market but waste-paper wrappers from the imported goods and puddles of drying blood where the butchers were. At a few larger markets (Sūq al-Ṭalḥ near Ṣaʿdah is the best known case) the proceedings go on for three days and one can buy almost anything: cloth, tinned foods, televisions, washing machines, new cars, and all sorts of weapons.

The large markets are plainly a recent phenomenon, dependent on cash and imports. However, all weekly markets, of whatever size, are under tribal protection, and the form that protection takes is of long standing. A market is *hijrah* or *muhajjar*: it is set aside from the run of tribal conflict and all violence there is forbidden. The singular status of the market is expressed in a document called *qā'idah* (or *qawā'id*) *al-sūq*, which shaykhs from the protecting tribe or tribes sign as 'guarantors of the market' (*ḍumanā' al-sūq*).[12] Any breach of the market-peace (that is, any offence within the market's bounds on the day of the market, and often a day each side of that) is an insult to the guarantors for which they are due amends.

The scale of amends varies from case to case. Documents relating to Sūq al-'Inān, in Dhū Muḥammad's territory at Jabal Baraṭ, specify that any offence whatever is to be fined eleven-fold; a wound worth YR 100 at YR 1,100, damage worth YR 50 at YR 550, and so on. More usually, amends are due of the same amount as the damage done or the wound inflicted ('shame-money is like blood-money', *al-dhamm mithla l-dam*), and often a fine called *hajar al-sūq* is due for a breach of the peace even where no wound or damage occurs. For al-Ḥarf in Sufyān, for example, this is set at 100 silver thalers, and for the 'new sūq' of Bayt Harāsh in Khārif at YR 1,000. Such payments are generally accompanied by slaughter-beasts of about the same value.

Payment is made to the market guarantors, or divided between them and the victim of the offence. It is the guarantors' prerogative to apprehend anyone who offends against the market, and no one else may do so without insulting them. However, unless exchanges with another tribe are formally severed (which must be done by a public 'announcement' or *ẓāhirah* in the market on market day), the market is 'secure and guaranteed' (*āmin ḍāmin*) for all comers.[13] Anyone who attends the market is 'on the honour' of the guarantors (*fī wajīh-hum*), and an offence by him or against him is the guarantors' concern. For example, Bayt Harāsh is in Khārif's territory (part of Ḥāshid) and under Khārif's protection, but the Tuesday market there routinely attracts buyers from the neighbouring tribes of 'Iyāl Yazīd and 'Iyāl Surayḥ, both of which are part of Bakīl. Firewood is sold there by men from Sufyān and from Dhū Ḥusayn (again, both Bakīl tribes); in season men come from as far away as Ṣa'dah to sell grapes; and others sometimes come from

Bājil in the Tihāmah to sell tomatoes. The guarantors of the market, however, are all from Khārif. Upholding the market-peace is their particular responsibility, right, and prerogative.

Patterns of trade linking different markets are not congruent with patterns of guaranty or with tribal structure. For example, two circuits of weekly markets, one based on ʿAmrān and the other on Khamir, overlap one another and neither is limited to Ḥāshid or to Bakīl (Tutwiler and Carapico 1981: 80). These circuits are more complex than at first appears. Khamir, for instance, supplies the Monday market at Khayār, the Raydah and Bayt Harāsh markets on Tuesday, Banī Qays on Wednesday, and so on (ibid. 81), but Khayār and Banī Qays also form part of a cycle that includes Ḥūth on Friday and Wādaʿah's Tuesday market (Kopp 1977: 39). Bayt Harāsh also forms part of a cycle that includes the Thursday market in northern Arḥab. These circuits, however, are those followed by the petty traders, and until recently all such traders were weak, non-tribal *bayyāʿ*.

Patterns of attendance at markets depend upon more than the market's commercial vitality. Indeed, the commercial fortunes of a market are at least as vulnerable to other upsets in tribal politics as those politics are affected by considerations of trade, and the sense to be made of changes is hard to assess in the absence of documentation. For example, Khayār seemed in 1979–80 to have set up their market, which they did in 1978, in order to avoid sharing a market with Banī Qays, with whom they were at odds (Tutwiler and Carapico 1981: 86). These two sections of Banī Ṣuraym had been intermittently at odds over land on their common border since about 1970. In fact the market which was spoken of in 1980 as belonging to Banī Qays, Sūq al-Ghayl, was established by the two sections together in 1831 (Dresch forthcoming *a*), although it falls just inside Banī Qays's border, and it continued to be used by both sections unless conflict was going on at the time. Khayār's new market was as much a commercial venture as a response to conflict with Banī Qays. Being on the main road, it prospered fairly well, but the involvement in building shops and the like was not limited to men from Khayār. Mention was made earlier of a Wādaʿī buying land there. Men from Banī Qays also have a stake in the venture.

Again, Bayt Harāsh was set up as a market by Khārif, also in 1978, in part to avoid using Raydah, which lies just within ʿIyāl Surayḥ's territory (Tutwiler and Carapico 1981: 86; Schweizer

1985: 114). It was also intended as a commercial venture and as a centre of local administration, but by 1980 men from each tribe were routinely using the other tribe's market as they saw fit. Just before Khārif severed relations with Raydah in 1978, it was said by men from Khārif that Raydah had 'always' been *hijrah* from both Khārif and 'Iyāl Surayḥ; that is, the market-peace had been the responsibility of both tribes *min zamān* ('from long ago'). It transpires that, in fact, Khārif were encouraged or obliged to use Raydah by Imam Yaḥyā in the 1930s, where before their chief market had been in their own territory at Hijrat Khārif (also known as Hijrat al-Ṣayad). By 1979 the general view was that Raydah had 'never' been *hijrah* from both tribes.

False certainty about the past on the part of those involved can distract one from the genuine continuities and repetitions often shown by weekly markets. In Ruhm, for example, which is one of the two major sections of Sufyān, a Wednesday market was held near Birkān until about forty years ago, when it closed after a killing there. Ruhm then used the market at al-Ḥarf, in the territory of Sufyān's other major section, Ṣubārah. In 1980 a small market was re-established in Ruhm, again near Birkān and again held on a Wednesday. Sūq al-Ghayl, by the border between Banī Qays and Khayār in Banī Ṣuraym, is also a Wednesday market. It was established as a Wednesday market 150 years ago. Whether this is a continuity or a repetition we have no sure means of knowing.

The closure of a market by a serious offence being committed there results, in effect, from disagreement among the market's guarantors (Schweizer 1985: 117–18). If, let us say, a market is *hijrah* from a whole tribe, and a man from Section A of that tribe kills someone from Section B in the market, the guarantor who 'gave his face' on behalf of A when the *hijrah* agreement was made is honour bound to rally his section against the culprit. He may fail to do so. The other sections, and particularly section B, then have a claim against A for a breach of the market-peace and for the murder. The structure of guaranty may collapse as the tribe's other sections become aligned with the sections at odds; and when the guaranty collapses so too does the market, which ceases to be 'secure and guaranteed'. Each section defends its own honour against others, and the honour of the whole tribe, which was committed to the defence of their market-peace, ceases to have binding force on the men at odds.

This is not an inevitable outcome. The structure of guaranty is often complex, much as was sketched in Chapter 3. Each set of guarantors is usually made answerable to another specific set of guarantors, so that if A's guarantors fail to act, then they insult B and C, or if B fail to act, they insult C and A. A web of particular, binding commitments is built up between individual signatories.[14] The 'guarantors' (*ḍumanā'*) from the tribe whose market it is are often also supported and overseen by 'secondary guarantors' (*rudamā'*) from elsewhere. For example, the guarantors of the market in Al 'Ammār are supplemented by secondary guarantors from Wāda'ah (in Hamdān al-Shām), Sufyān, Dhū Ḥusayn, and Wā'ilah. The preservation of the market-peace is the object of quite elaborate precautions against one set or other of guarantors seceding.

The guaranty of the market involves the suspension of segmentary loyalties. The agreement between Ruhm and Ṣubārah, the two halves of Sufyān, to uphold the peace at al-Ḥarf is, in this respect, typical.

> Whoever is present if someone is killed [in the market], whether he is from Ruhm or Ṣubārah, must avenge the man killed. If the killer is [then] himself killed, that is an end of it (*qad waṣal,* i.e. parity is reached and no further right to revenge is admitted), whether he is from Ruhm or Ṣubārah. Whoever kills [in the market] no longer has his brotherhood [in the tribe], and no one can shelter him. Whoever shelters him commits '*ayb* [i.e. owes the guarantors amends].[15]

The culprit or defaulter cannot call on his fellows in one section for support against others in the tribe. The market is *hijrah* from the tribe as a whole, and it is as members of Sufyān as a whole that men must act in connection with the market. The peace they are committed to uphold is closely delimited, applying to a given space (at al-Ḥarf about a square kilometre) and for a given time (in this case from Wednesday to Friday). Throughout the week people from other tribes are safe within the market's bounds. Within these bounds, on three days of the week Sufyānīs are also safe from each other, and all claims to revenge are suspended. Outside the bounds at any time, or within them from Saturday to Tuesday, conflict between men from Sufyān can be pursued as they see fit.

Some markets are the joint responsibility of two or more tribes, as Raydah was for a time. The Sunday market north of Ẓulaymah is a case in point. One side of the shallow wash running through the market site is Ẓulaymī and the other Ahnūmī, but on market day the market site as a whole is under joint guaranty of the two tribes. Much more usually, a given market is the responsibility of only one tribe. The defence of the market-peace can then come to have a high value placed on it as a focus of the tribe's cohesion, and attempts to form a tribe into a cohesive unit generally centre on a 'market guaranty' (*ḍamān al-sūq*). The rules governing Sufyān's market at al-Ḥarf, which were quoted above, form part of an agreement drawn up at the end of the civil war when Ruhm and Ṣubārah were faced with potential attack by both royalists and republicans (more will be said of this in Chapters 7 and 9). The shaykhs tried to pull the sections of the tribe together, to make them one unit 'like the upper arm and the lower arm', and the market provided an obvious focus for the attempt.

Older documents from Dhū Muḥammad, which comprise a general agreement between the tribe's sections on the details of customary law, declare that 'offences against the market [at al-'Inān] or on the roads to it, whether from within the tribe or without, are one'; in other words, the tribe will act as one unit against whomever breaks the peace there. It used to be that each 'fifth' of Dhū Muḥammad was responsible for upholding the market-peace for a month in turn. The importance of the market as a focus of unity is made clear in the rules about *jidhns* (a *jidhn*, it will be remembered, is a scarecrow placed in public to shame a man into discharging some obligation). A Muḥammadī who has a claim against someone from another tribe can 'place the blame' in Dhū Muḥammad's market. He cannot, though, 'place the blame' there against a fellow Muḥammadī.

> If one of them vilifies his fellow in the market [i.e. places a *jidhn*], he insults the guarantors; the guarantors of this agreement and the guarantors of the market. He must pay eleven-fold for placing the *jidhn* against his fellow in the market, half going to the guarantors of the market rules [from the fifth responsible] in the month when the blame was placed, and half to the man vilified. The signatories of this agreement can claim dues and amends for the insult/disgrace according to their judgment, in addition to what is [here] mentioned.[16]

The price of a 'mistaken *jidhn*' is specified elsewhere in the same document as 110 silver thalers. Eleven times that is therefore more than one and a half times the cost of full blood-money (the *diyah* was 800 thalers), a very large fine indeed. A *jidhn* is an insult of such magnitude as might easily lead to war. Were one member of Dhū Muḥammad to 'place the blame' against another in the tribe's market, the structure of guaranty would be threatened, and with it the focus of Dhū Muḥammad's identity as any more than the opposite of other tribes.

In Āl' Ammār, in 1983, a *jidhn* was placed at market by a group of Sufyānīs to shame other men from Sufyān. A group of guarantors from Āl 'Ammār then placed a *jidhn* to shame their fellows in Āl 'Ammār who had allowed Sufyān to 'place the blame' in the first place, but this second *jidhn* was placed outside the market. The rule was said to be that the blame must be placed in front of one's own house for two weeks before it could be placed in the market. If the guarantors then allowed it to be placed in the market, they could take forty-four rifles from those who set up the *jidhn*, in token of the fact that the case for which the *jidhn* was placed was now for the guarantors to judge.[17] In the present case the rules had been broken. The amends being talked of for this and for the wrongs which led to it were of the order of YR 3 million (about $600,000 at the time), which suggests how important the market-peace can be.

The importance of the market, be it noted, is given by its place among the tribes and in purely tribal terms. There is no reference to other than tribal values. Within the *hijrah* (the protected space that exists for a given time at a given place) non-tribal elements, such as the 'weak' market-folk, may pursue their own interests and lead their own lives, but the establishment of the protected space makes no reference to them. Nor is there any reference to respected, non-tribal arbitrators or to men with a non-tribal message. Once established, the market guaranty takes its value in part from its contrast with the run of tribal life, where violence is an admitted possibility, and in part, perhaps, from the very difficulty of its preservation. Once established, the guaranty is of comparable importance to a tribe's borders and land, which we have touched on already as being marked elements.

A tribesman may be denied access to another tribe's market if exchanges are 'severed' (*ḥaṣal qaṭā'*) between that tribe and his own, or he may be denied access to market in his own tribe if he commits some disgrace and fails to make amends to his fellow tribesmen. This denial of access to market in a man's own tribe is not primarily an economic sanction (one can always go elsewhere for one's tea and cigarettes).[18] It is a denial of access to a public space or event that the tribe as such shares in. A serious demand on an outside tribe would usually be publicly made there; an outsider who wished to join the tribe would slaughter a bull in the market on market day; an announcement affecting the whole tribe would be made in the market. A man denied access to the market for failing to make amends in a serious case to a fellow tribesman, or more usually to the guarantors, will hear of such events that involve his whole tribe but cannot take part in them.

TOWNS IN TRIBAL TERRITORY

The non-tribal people whom tribesmen persist in referring to as *bayyā'* or even as *mazāyinah* now tend to refer to themselves as *madaniyyīn*; 'townsfolk' or 'civilians', in contrast to the rural and martial tribes. Towns in the tribal areas of Upper Yemen are indeed generally associated with non-tribal people—with the 'traders' (*bayyā'* or market folk, *ahl al-sūq*) and with men of religion—but the safety of most such towns depended historically upon their position among the tribes, rather than on a defence organized by their own inhabitants. Ṣan'ā', Ṣa'dah, and 'Amrān, which were all centres of government or administration, were all walled towns (there is admittedly some doubt how long 'Amrān has occupied its present site). But Ḥūth was not walled, nor al-Ḥarf in Sufyān, nor the towns of the east such as al-Zāhir in the Upper Jawf or al-'Inān at Baraṭ. Khamir's walls were pulled down by the Imam al-Manṣūr in 1398, and in recent centuries no walls have been built there.[19]

Khamir also provides an extreme example of what has happened to many small Yemeni towns in recent decades. A small permanent market has existed in Khamir for as long as anyone knows, and a weekly market held on Sundays attracts tribesmen from throughout the surrounding area. The scale of the market has become far greater over the last decade or two, and the size of the town has increased enormously. Its population of two thousand or so in the late 1960s (Chelhod 1970: 72) must have all but doubled by about 1980 as the town became an important breakdown point for goods trucked in from Saudi Arabia. With the rise of a cash economy, the old town became surrounded with a belt of new houses, groceries, builders' stores, welding shops, repair shops, and warehouses. The place of the town among the tribes shows certain continuities despite this. Most importantly, Khamir is still spoken of as *hijrah* from Ḥāshid, which is to say that violence is forbidden there and the place is in theory protected by all of the Ḥāshid tribes. The confederation's paramount shaykh, who is also himself *hijrah*, lived in Khamir for many years. He still maintains a large house there, and, were he forced to leave Ṣan'ā', he would probably take up residence there again. Khamir would be the natural place to convene a meeting of all Ḥāshid, and the town may sensibly be spoken of as Ḥāshid's 'capital'.

In the old town, the divisions of society as they were just before the boom have not yet been obliterated. Khamir is associated with the qadi ('judge') family of Bayt Ḥanash, who themselves are *hijrah* from Ḥāshid and thus protected by the tribes. Because of this status Bayt Ḥanash are not subject to *ghurm wa-jurm*, the collective levies which apply to the rest of the town's inhabitants just as they do to the members of a tribe or section. Apart from Bayt Ḥanash, the town comprised five groups called *aḥbāl* (pl. of *ḥabl*), which are named as follows: Al-Fuqahā', Bayt 'Imrān, al-Juzzur, al-Afrād, and Bayt Ḥūṭah. As Chelhod (1970: 74) suggests, each of these occupied a fairly discrete quarter of the old town around what was once the main market. The original Fuqahā' ('learned men' or scribes) were Bayt al-Lawandī, but the *ḥabl* they form part of now also contains five other families, of tribal descent, as are Bayt al-Lawandī, but without any tradition of literacy.[20] Bayt 'Imrān provide the shaykhs of Khamir and also of part of al-Ẓāhir in Banī Ṣuraym,[21] the tribe in whose territory Khamir falls.

The other *aḥbāl* are all 'weak', non-tribal people under Banī Ṣuraym's protection. Al-Juzzur, despite their name, are not all butchers, although one of the families who practice this trade are conspicuous as owning one of the largest houses in the old town. Most of the *ḥabl* are traders. All of them are said to be *naqā'il* or 'incomers' from elsewhere, but the details have long been forgotten. The second *ḥabl* of weak people, al-Afrād, are more clearly all incomers to Khamir, and until the mid-1970s any trader or craftsman who moved to the town from elsewhere was assimilated to them. The last *ḥabl*, Bayt Ḥūtah, claim, by contrast, to be the town's original inhabitants. They comprise two named subgroups

(Ḥūṭah itself and Zanjabīlah), and claim that a third part of the *ḥabl* was once made by Hizām, who are tribesmen and form part of the al-Ẓāhir section of Banī Ṣuraym. The weak people of Ḥūṭah and al-Zanjabīlah say that they themselves were once tribesmen too, although long, long ago, and that Hizām have somehow become 'retribalized'. There is no link between Bayt Ḥūṭah and Hizām in such matters as levying collective payments, and Hizām deny there was ever a connection of any sort.

Al-Juzzur, al-Afrād, and Bayt Ḥūṭah are all *bayyā'* or 'market people', and until recently all wore their daggers to the left: most still do so. They are all, though, in their own eyes, quite different from the *mazāyinah*. There is one family of actual *mazāyinah* in Khamir, who work as butchers, barbers, and drummers. They serve all of the old town's other inhabitants. Al-Afrād and Bayt Ḥūṭah seem never to have intermarried with them in either direction. Al-Juzzur did, but al-Afrād and Bayt Ḥūṭah none the less intermarried with al-Juzzur. This scale of distinctions is probably an instance of a more general distinction within market society between lowly servitors and potentially prosperous traders. So far as the tribesmen are concerned, though, these distinctions, which to the market people are important, are entirely irrelevant: the traders are all simply 'weak', 'lacking origins', and therefore protected 'neighbours'.[22]

Until the mid-1960s no one, whether a tribesman or a weak person, could settle in Khamir without killing a bull for the town, just as one would when one joined a tribe. However, in the course of the civil war (1962–70), several Ḥāshid shaykhs who supported the republic moved into the town from the countryside and brought with them numerous tribesmen. The first spate of building outside the old town dates from that period. Between 1975 and 1978, in the course of a tiff with the central government (see Stookey 1978: 278–80), several Ḥāshid shaykhs again based themselves in Khamir. From 1975 onward the boom in Yemen's cash economy, fuelled by emigrants' remittances, was reflected in a building boom on the south side of town. More recently, beginning in the early 1980s, a massive set of government buildings has appeared, with the shaykhs' agreement and staffed by those whom the shaykhs approve. The fort overlooking the town, built by the Imam in the 1920s and named al-Mahalhal, is garrisoned by tribesmen in the pay of the paramount shaykh, and the town itself remains *hijrah*: that is, under Ḥāshid's protection.

The effects of the cash economy on the place of the weak non-tribesmen is hard to judge on short acquaintance. For example, in 1970 Chelhod found that of three *dawāshīn* or 'heralds', who had previously lived in tents, two had recently acquired houses and taken to cultivation, though they had not altogether given up 'the tiny profits their first calling brings them' (Chelhod 1970: 80). A 'traditional' system seemed to be ending. Ten years later the *dawāshīn*'s profits were no longer so tiny. An announcement at market in 1980 cost at least YR 50, and if one did not want the *dawshān* to solicit one's guests at a wedding for contributions one had to pay him to the order of YR 500. The *dawshān*'s subsidiary trade of decorating dagger-sheaths now brought him some YR 300 a sheath (about $65), which represents one day's work. The urge to employ *dawāshīn* in all of these capacities became more marked, not less so.[23] Those who continued to work as *mazāyinah* (barbers and butchers) came more generally to wear 'traditional' dress; the long-sleeved *qamīs* with the sleeves tied back, the overskirt or *maqdab*, and the *sabīghah* or black woollen head-cloth which tribesmen and weak people all wore until soon before the revolution. What 'traditional' means here by comparison with actual past practice and attitudes would be hard to be sure of.

The entry of tribesmen into commerce is more clear cut. Most tribesmen in the area around Khamir no longer see anything shameful about buying and selling at market, and entrepreneurs of tribal birth are found next to those whose fathers were weak 'traders'. Some, perhaps, felt themselves uprooted. A few were attracted to the teachings of a fundamentalist 'institute' which, with the encouragement of the paramount shaykh and with funds that might be hard to trace fully, was established in Khamir in the 1970s. Most tribesmen, however, keep their distance from such things. Their interest is in the pressure or opportunities which arise from relations between tribes or sections and in those which arise from the patronage that central government, and sometimes outsiders, disperse very largely through certain shaykhs. Their religion and loyalties they feel are their own business.[24] Their disputes, which now might arise from the supply of truck-parts as much as from the division of grazing rights, are dealt with by the means sketched out in the preceding chapter. In the small towns of the north, a tribesman who works as a welder or trucker is usually no less a tribesman for doing so, and few sever connections with their villages and land.

In that it has always contained tribesmen and weak people together, Khamir is more like a large village than it is like other towns of its own size elsewhere in the north. Ḥarf Sufyān, for example, seems to have contained only non-tribal weak people until the Imam posted a few learned men there in the 1930s. Some tribesmen have now also moved in to set up truck repair shops and the like, but most of them retain houses outside the town. At al-ʻInān (Jabal Baraṭ) there are still no tribesmen at all. There were only market-people and the qadis of Bayt al-ʻAnsī until the late nineteenth century when a few sayyids (descendants of the Prophet) also settled there.[25] The tribesmen of Dhū Muḥammad still reckon it ʻ*ayb* or 'disgrace' to live there.

Such distinctions are not always plain to the eye. At al-Ḥarf the tribal villages are close to the town, and at al-ʻInān there is no clear spatial divide between them at all. The houses where the *jīrān* or weak protégés live are no different in kind from those which the tribesmen live in; but the 'market' (*sūq*) and the 'countryside' (*bādiyah*) are none the less clearly opposed in the minds of those who inhabit each. Nor does the tribesman's conviction of superiority depend on economic dominance or prosperity. In the east of Yemen it is not uncommon to find the ignoble market-folk living in fine mud houses while their noble protectors, who consider themselves immeasurably superior, live in rude shelters of woven sticks or in tents.[26] Market people often own land which tribesmen work as share-croppers (Bayt al-Qayfī of al-Afrād in Khamir, for example, for a long time owned a great deal). A tribesman may be entirely indigent, but as a 'strong' and 'honourable' man who can bear a rifle he considers himself above his 'weak' protégés. It is not so much the town as such that he despises but the 'market', and al-Ḥarf or al-ʻInān still carry the stain, in the eyes of their tribal neighbours, that marks the 'market-rats'.

Ḥūth is a town of a rather different character, being populated largely by men of religion. The sayyids there distinguish themselves as Ḥusaynīs or Ḥasanīs, according to which of the sons of ʻAlī b. Abī Ṭālib they trace their descent through. The thirteen families of the first group all claim descent from the Imam al-Mu'ayyad Yaḥyā b. Ḥamzah (d. 1349). The second group consists of the descendants of the Imam al-Mutawakkil Muḥsin b. Aḥmad (d. 1878 and buried at Ḥūth; Zabārah 1957: 180), together with a number of families all claiming descent from Amīr al-Dīn b. ʿAbdullāh b. Nahshaf (d. 1620 and also buried there; al-Shawkānī 1929: i. 159; Zabārah 1957: 98). The qadis nearly all claim descent from the founder of Bayt al-Raṣāṣ, who is widely credited with having established or renewed the pursuit of Islamic learning in the town. Apart from these men of religion, Ḥūth until recently contained only weak market people. The tribesmen who protected the town (and Ḥūth itself is always spoken of as *hijrah*) all lived in the surrounding countryside.

Before the revolution Ḥūth was a famous educational centre, but the teaching of Islamic sciences there is now moribund. Those who would have been the best students now go to the university in Ṣanʿāʾ, and a rabble of less able young men have gravitated to the fundamentalists in Khamir. The town itself remains fairly prosperous, being on the main road, but the scholars there are now left to pursue their studies by themselves; many depend for their livelihood on landholdings elsewhere or on relatives with government jobs. Shahārah, which is miles from a main road and perched on top of a 2,500-metre mountain, has suffered far worse. Perhaps 80 per cent of its inhabitants have left since the start of the civil war, and the place itself, which was a fortress town more central to the sayyids' concerns than to those of the plateau tribes, now has a rather forlorn air, not much lightened by tourists who come there in summer. The decay of learning and the rise of a cash economy have between them had results which are not surprising. Shahārah has all but died, while Ḥūth survives on the trade passing through it from Ṣaʿdah to Ṣanʿāʾ.[27]

Among the learned men of Ḥūth a way of life was pursued, and with less vigour still is, that was distinct from that of the surrounding tribes, being based on, or coloured by, reference to a literate Islamic orthodoxy. That self-conscious distinction is in part maintained. For example, the bride-price (*sharṭ*) rose among the surrounding tribes (more particularly in Banī Ṣuraym, but also in Upper al-ʿUṣaymāt) until by 1983 a payment of YR 150,000 was not unusual. The men of religion in Ḥūth clung to their old practice of giving only a 'gift' (*mahr*) to the bride of 100 silver thalers and dresses worth about YR 5,000, until about 1982 when the rot set in with surreptitious payments up to about YR 50,000. The men of religion condemned all this as un-Islamic. They continued a vigorous campaign against it, which had its effect on their fellows but little on the tribesmen, whom the men of religion condemned as incorrigibly 'ignorant' (*jāhil*) and as poor Muslims. The safety of the town, though, has always depended on these 'ignorant' tribesmen, whose shaykhs recognize it as protected or *hijrah*.

Such protected status is accorded to many towns, not least Ṣan'ā' itself, which is said to be *hijrah* from the seven tribes around it. Yet Ṣan'ā' has been sacked by the tribes on a number of occasions, most recently in 1948. The protection of towns is not, then, an invariably reliable mechanism that might tempt an analyst to find some functional tie between towns and tribes, but instead is part of a set of ideas which may be actualized quite exactly in practice or not at all; and that set of ideas, which revolves in large part around the tribesmen's own self-definition—in particular, the preservation of moral autonomy—embraces much more than the particular place of towns. Certain towns are *hijrah* ('set aside', 'protected'). Some of them are associated with markets; and markets, as we have seen, are themselves *hijrah*, whether held in the towns or in otherwise empty country. Some towns are associated with the men of religion, and such people are often *hijrah* ('protected') in their own right, quite apart from where they cluster together on the scale that they do in Ḥūth.

QADIS: FAMILIES OF JUDGES

The men of religion comprise two separate estates: the qadis (who in theory are distinguished from the tribesmen only by learning) and the sayyids (who are distinguished from both by their descent from the Prophet). The sayyids and qadis together are distinguished by their dress. The tribesmen and their shaykhs wear a kilt (*fūṭah*), or a long Saudi-style *thawb*, and a loose head-cloth or turban. The men of religion wear a long *qamīṣ*, the hem of which reaches to about mid-calf and the sleeves of which would reach the hem were they not tied together behind the shoulders. Instead of a turban they wear a straw pill-box hat called a *qāwiq*, wrapped around with white cloth to form the '*imāmah* or head-dress of learned men. They wear their daggers obliquely to the right, with the distinctive sheath in a belt far wider than that which most tribesmen wear.[28]

In theory any tribesman can become a *qāḍī* (pl. *quḍāh*) by the study of Islamic law. In practice the status is largely hereditary, and certain great qadi families have for centuries played a conspicuous part in Yemen's history. Since the revolution, many of them have held high rank in republican governments: 'Abd al-Raḥmān al-Iryānī, for example, was the first post-war President, and his kinsman, 'Abd al-Karīm, who was educated in America, has more recently held several government offices because of his administrative expertise. The core of such families maintains a tradition of learning. The lesser branches of these families and separate families of lesser standing do not always do so, but often they retain the title of qadi without the abilities to which that title refers ideally. Someone whom the tribesmen in the countryside address as *yā qāḍī* may in fact be completely illiterate. However, those families of qadis who are recognized as *hijrah* are usually those who retain at least the rudiments of Islamic learning.[29]

A given branch of a qadi family is usually *hijrah* from only one tribe (that is, only one tribe makes itself responsible for their protection), and the place where they live is generally protected too. For example, Bayt al-Raḍī are *hijrah* only from Khārif. Their seat was at Hijrat Khārif or Hijrat al-Ṣayad, around which were the tribe's old market sites. On the other hand, a learned family may have branches elsewhere. For example, Bayt Ḥanash are found not only in Khamir, but other branches of the family live in Ṣan'ā', at Dhībīn, and at Shāṭib in Sufyān where they were once great landowners. The family as a whole claim to have come from al-Ḥadā, south of Ṣan'ā', and to have been sultans in the time of the Imam 'Abdullāh b. Ḥamzah (d. 1217).[30] Some moved to 'Abdullāh's seat at Ẓafār Dhībīn and from there, perhaps three hundred years ago, some moved to Khamir. Again, Bayt al-'Ulufī, whose main seat is at Hijrat al-Quhāl in 'Iyāl Surayḥ, claim to be 'Umayyads' who moved to Wādī al-'Alāf, near Ṣa'dah, in 'Abbāsid times (ninth century AD) and spread south into Yemen from there. They were powerful under the Imam al-Mahdī 'Abbās (d. 1775) and acquired large tracts of land in Qā' al-Bawn, the intermontane plain where al-Quhāl and Raydah both lie. Separate branches of the family are also found in Khārif (in al-Kalbiyyīn and al-Ṣayad), in Arḥab, in Lower Yemen near Ibb, and in Ṣan'ā'. Some of them are now government functionaries. Some are still men of learning in the tribes where they live. One branch, at Jawb in 'Iyāl Yazīd, have lost their *hijrah* status, though many tribesmen still call them qadi, and for three generations at least have made their living as tailors.[31] Status is by no means immutable.

In north-eastern Yemen a number of related qadi families, all descended from al-Qāsim al-ʿAnsī (d. 1636 and buried at al-ʿInān), were important for centuries.[32] The major families are shown in Fig. 4.1. Bayt al-Sharaʿī are dispersed among Dhū Muḥammad and Dhū Ḥusayn. Bayt al-Ṭawīl and Bayt al-ʿAnsī are concentrated in Dhū Muḥammad. Bayt ʿIzz al-Dīn are found more in the east, around Khabb and in Banī Nawf, with some branches at Marqab al-Marāshī. Most of Āl al-ʿUkām are also at al-Marqab, with some others in central Sufyān. A comparatively recent *hijrah* document belonging to the last of these branches will serve to show the place of such families among the tribes.

In the name of God, these are the laws/decision (*shurūʿ*) of those undertaking the *hijrah* of the qadis of Āl al-ʿUkām, who are to be an honoured, respected *hijrah*, protected themselves and able to give others protection (*āminīn wa-muʾamminīn*) among all those who are making them *hijrah*. Whoever comes to their houses, or wanders with them, or travels with them, or takes refuge with them shall be secure in the security of God, be He praised, and in the security of those undertaking this *hijrah*. This applies to him who fears and to him who makes fearful (*al-khāʾif wa-l-mukhīf*, i.e. those fearing revenge and those seeking revenge), to those who have killed and to those who have [had someone] killed, to those who commit an ʿ*ayb* and to those who have suffered an ʿ*ayb*.[33]

The qadis given this status could thus provide refuge for tribesmen from other tribesmen. They are said explicitly to be granted this general ability to 'intervene', which is recognized among all those

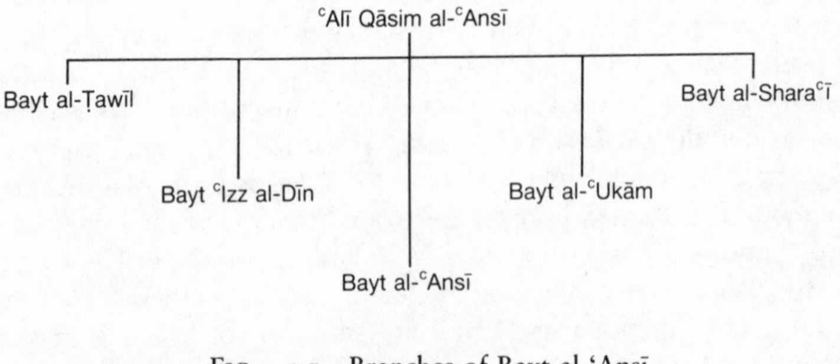

FIG. 4.1 Branches of Bayt al-ʿAnsī

who make them *hijrah (sār al-'arḍ la-hum bayna l-muhajjirah)*. At the same time, they themselves are under the tribesmen's protection, and if they are wronged it is the tribesmen's responsibility to extract amends from the culprit or to take revenge *(al-mathār bi-thār wa-l-'arḍ 'alā al-quḍāh min al-muhajjirah)*.

If some small thing befalls the aforementioned qadis, then whoever committed the offence . . . [against them] . . . must pay eleven-fold. If some large thing befalls the qadis, then those making them *hijrah* are obliged together, each guarantor taking [multiple?] revenge (*yashill 'ūd al-naqā'*). The qadis are trusted witnesses [regarding] their *hijrah*, their meetings and their obligations and what shames them [i.e. their women, etc.] without [the necessity of] oath. These are the laws/decision of those making them *hijrah*, and their past and their progeny . . . (Dated Muḥarram 1321/April 1903)

The status of those made *hijrah* is thus singular, and they themselves are in some measure respected. They were called on to draw up documents in disputes between tribes, in deciding inheritance, in contracts of marriage, and so on. Until recently the tribesmen were nearly illiterate, and what scraps of literacy the qadis could muster were no doubt found impressive. The qadis might also be called on to arbitrate in disputes between tribesmen, but there was no guarantee of this and it is not mentioned explicitly in any of the local *hijrah* documents I have seen.

Qadis made *hijrah* were accorded the tribesmen's own ability to take others into their peace and to provide protection. At the same time they were not subject to collective levies on the tribe (*ghurm wa-jurm*) and were protected by the tribesmen. In tribal terms their status was thus certainly privileged. They were not, however, granted authority, any more than is a notable shaykh who receives *hijrah* status, and the extent to which they could dispense Islamic law, or indeed any form of justice, to the tribesmen around them must have depended largely on personal standing and ability.

The list of signatories to Āl al-'Ukām's document (see App. 4/2) deserves note. A total of fifty-three shaykhs put their names to the agreement as guarantors, of whom twenty-four were Sufyānīs, eleven from Dhū Ḥusayn, eight from Dhū Muḥammad, four from al-'Uṣaymāt, and three from each of Āl Sālim and Āl 'Ammār. The seat of Āl al-'Ukām was at Marqab al-Marāshī. This village lies in the territory of al-Marānāt, a section or tribe who claim to be part of Sufyān but who are separated from the rest of that tribe and surrounded by Dhū Muḥammad and Dhū Ḥusayn. The pattern of responsibility for upholding the *hijrah* sprawls somewhat irregularly over the tribal map. The four signatories from al-ʿUṣaymāt are of course from Ḥāshid. The others are from Bakīl, but there are Bakīl tribes, such as Arḥab, no further from Marqab al-Marāshī than these, which are not involved in the guaranty. One cannot, then, say that the qadis of Āl al-ʿUkām are simply attached to one tribe or to some set of tribes defined by the tribal structure. This is true of a great many qadi *hijrahs*. Although they are embedded in the tribal world, the *hijrahs* have a history and logic of their own. So too do the learned families who have this status. Āl al-ʿUkām, for example, themselves spread as far afield as Dhamār (about 70 kilometres south of Ṣanʿāʾ), from where many of their famous members came.

SAYYIDS: THE PROPHET'S DESCENDANTS

The sayyids dress as do the qadis (both wear the dress of Islamic learning), and the sayyids also are often reckoned *hijrah*. A *sayyid*, though (pl. *sādah*), claims descent from the Prophet. The Zaydi Imam was of necessity a sayyid (in the early days he was sometimes from outside Yemen), and it was the Imam who could appoint qadis his ministers, not a qadi who could appoint sayyids to high ranks of state. Where the two lived together in a protected place, as at Ḥūth, it was the sayyids who were referred to in documents as 'the *hijrah*', while the qadis was referred to as the sayyids' *shīʿah*; their 'party', as in the 'the party of ʿAlī b. Abī Ṭālib' (see e.g. Dresch forthcoming *a*).

The fall of the Imamate in the 1960s dealt a blow to the standing of sayyids generally. In central government the qadis now overshadow them, and in the countryside they are identified by many with 'reaction' or backwardness. Some have relinquished their *hijrah* status, saying tribal protection no longer works (as indeed have some qadis), and have 'become brother' to tribes (*yukhāwī*); that is, they have made themselves tribesmen. Throughout much of the Islamic period, however, the great sayyid houses made up 'a mosaic of theocracies' (Serjeant 1969: 297), each being associated with particular tribes or a particular area. The *hijrah* of Bayt al-Wazīr, for example, was at Wādī al-Sirr in Banī Ḥushaysh (Zabārah 1958: 169). The sayyids of al-Kibs have for centuries been associated with Khawlān al-Ṭiyāl (Khawlān al-ʿĀliyah), east of Ṣanʿāʾ, where the village of al-Kibs itself is. Bayt al-Mutawakkil, Bayt al-Muʾayyad, and Bayt al-Muṭahhar (all branches of descent from the Imam al-Qāsim) have links with Shahārah. Bayt Sharaf al-Dīn were for a long time lords of what Niebuhr (1792: 490), following local usage of the time, refers to as 'the principality of Kawkabān'.

As with the qadis, so with the sayyids, the conspicuous actors in the histories are the scions of a few great houses, but their relatives less close to the core of the family's power, and sayyids from other families, did not occupy any fixed place in political structures or in relations of production. Some taught, some farmed, and some, at particular junctures, governed, although intermittently. They cannot safely be spoken of *en bloc* as having been a ruling class.

The sayyids are, however, all linked in their own view; their identity is given by their lineage and, as might be expected, they preserve detailed genealogies. Noted qadi families are not ignorant of their own ancestry, but for them it seems almost a matter of antiquarian interest; the sayyids, for whom descent is more vital, can often recite strings of ancestors from memory in a way that no tribesman can and few qadis. Not all are word perfect. The difficulty of keeping track of the sayyids' ancestry is increased by the prevalence of certain names, taken by different, unrelated Imams and now used by their descendants. There are, for example, a number of families named al-Mutawakkil: that of Shahārah descends from al-Mutawakkil Ismaʿīl b. al-Imām al-Qāsim (d. 1676); that of Ṣanʿāʾ from al-Mutawakkil al-Qāsim b. al-Ḥusayn b. al-Imām al-Mahdī Aḥmad (d. 1727); that of al-Sūdah and Ḥūth from al-Mutawakkil Muḥsin b. Aḥmad (d. 1878); and so on.[34] The identification of such families by place is only very approximate, since men were posted elsewhere by Imams as judges or governors, moved elsewhere to study with noted scholars, or moved in pursuit of power themselves as claimants to the Imamate. Not everyone is always clear quite who is related to whom. To the expert, however (and in most sayyid families there is someone, at least, who updates their whole genealogy), these lines of descent, together with the equally complex lines of who studied with whom and taught whom in turn, provide the lineaments of a world quite different from that of tribalism (we shall look at this in Chapter 5).

The place of the sayyids among the tribes was and is very variable. But as an example of a *hijrah* agreement between prominent sayyids and important tribes (almost an ideal from the former's point of view) let us take the case of Bayt al-Mu'ayyad and Ḥāshid.

We who place our seals, signatures, and names to this document, blessed God willing by the hands of our noble *sayyids* [lords], the learned Sīdī 'Izz al-Islām Muḥammad b. Yaḥyā b. Aḥmad al-Imām al-Hādī and his son the learned Sīdī Yaḥyā Muḥammad [b. al-Imām], their brothers, descendants and relatives who come after them, the sons of the Imam al-Mu'ayyad billāh Muḥammad b. al-Imām al-Qāsim, peace be on them, who live in al-Madāyir, Ḥabūr, al-Madān, Hanūm [i.e. al-Ahnūm], Shahārah, Wāda'ah, and elsewhere; we state that we are again recognizing them as [or making them] *hijrah* in accordance with [documents] held by our forefathers and theirs, a *tahjīr* by all the men of Ḥāshid for the descendants of [the sayyids'] noble ancestors, the descendants of the lord of mankind [i.e. Muḥammad, the Prophet], God bless him and his family and grant them peace.

The detailed genealogical reference is worth noting. The various sayyids, scattered in towns or villages from Banī Ṣuraym to west of Jabal Shahārah, are together the descendants of the Imam al-Mu'ayyad. His father, al-Qāsim, rose against the Turks in the early seventeenth century. He himself ruled much of Yemen from 1620 to 1644. The document we are quoting from is dated 1918. A postscript signed by the paramount shaykh of Ḥāshid and dated 1977 confirms that the agreement still holds.

The written agreement, which itself is referred to as a renewal of one earlier, has survived for some seventy years. In the course of that time the political relations between the sayyids and tribesmen in question have altered enormously. At the time the document was drawn up, Imam Yaḥyā (whose own family, Bayt Ḥamīd al-Dīn, claimed descent from al-Qāsim, as Bayt al-Mu'ayyad does) had partitioned Yemen between himself and the Turks but could not claim to rule Ḥāshid effectively. The agreement with Bayt al-Mu'ayyad may well have been a move by Ḥāshid to distance themselves from him.[35] In the 1920s and 1930s the Imam established his rule over Ḥāshid firmly. The tribes and the sayyids alike were subject to the state, and the sayyids were given positions of power by the Imam. In the civil war of the 1960s most of Hāshid rallied to the republic against not only the Imam of the time, who was Yaḥyā's grandson, but against what many of them saw as the rule of sayyids generally, and what power the sayyids had over them was broken. Throughout all of this the agreement between Ḥāshid and Bayt al-Mu'ayyad existed. For part of that time it was surely no more than 'a scrap of paper' except in one circumstance; that is, if 'our' sayyids were wronged by some other tribe in the course of explicitly tribal conflict. The defence of the sayyids against outsiders is always of potential importance, whether the sayyids themselves are obeyed and revered, disobeyed and despised, or simply ignored by the tribes around them.

As with the now far less prominent Āl al-'Ukām, the descendants of al-Mu'ayyad are said to be 'in the security of God . . . and of those making the agreement' (*fī amān allāh . . . wa-amān al-muhajjirīn*). Whoever commits a wrong or disgrace against the sayyids, against their property, or against 'those connected with them as brother, soldier, servant, slave, neighbour, or protégé (*labīth*)' is reckoned to have insulted the guarantors from Ḥāshid.

> They [the sayyids] are under the protection of the tribesmen (*fī ẓuhūr-hum*) in supporting them, following them and acting completely with them (*al-qiyām al-tām ma'a-hum*), even to the death. Our territory is open to them to live in where they wish, and we shall protect them (*namna' 'an-hum*) even as we protect ourselves and our children, our women and dwellings and all which might shame us (*jamī' mā ya'ūr-nā*, i.e. that on which our honour depends). Whoever marches by their side shall be safe and secure. Those who associate with them shall have the benefit of the *sharī'ah* [Islamic law] dispensed by a righteous judge, who cannot be accused [of bias, etc.] and is not under the authority of any state. They are not liable to collective responsibility (*'arḍ*) or rights of companionship (*rafaq*) or neighbour-right (*jiwār*) [i.e. they are not liable to the obligations of tribal law] but instead shall be glorified and honoured.

The reference to judgment by Islamic law 'not under the authority of any state' *(lā taḥt sulṭān dawlah)* is worth noting, since the sayyids produced the Imams. A successful claimant to the Imamate would himself be *sulṭān dawlah*, and would claim his authority, in so far as he abided by the laws of Islam, to be absolute. The transition from 'arbitration' to 'rule' (both *ḥukm* in Arabic) and from rule to mere arbitration, is problematic. Around it revolves the whole history of tribes and Imams. In the document under consideration, the tribes simply make the descendants of al-Mu'ayyad *hijrah*. The sayyids may judge by Islamic law, but there is no promise that tribesmen will ask them to do so, or that, if they did, they would abide by the decision. The sayyids are praised as a source of justice, but an optional source, on the tribesmen's sufferance. What is not open to question is their claim to protection. The agreement is binding on the tribesmen and their descendants (*dhurriyyat-hum*), to be handed on to the next generation (*wārith li-mawrūth*), and God is the best of witnesses.

One is often told by tribesmen that all sayyids are *hijrah* or once were, but the reality is less tidy. The village of al-Qāsim in Wāda'ah, for example, is *hijrah* and so are the sayyids living there, but elsewhere in Banī Ṣuraym (in Banī Qays and Banī Mālik, for instance) one finds sayyids who have never had this protected status.[36] Ghayl Maqdaf, near Khamir, is a village cluster populated almost solely by sayyids, but neither they nor the place are *hijrah*. They are simply part of the tribe, although no one disputes their descent from the Prophet.

Even those who are *hijrah* may be little more than scribes, and the status of *hijrah* can itself be ambiguous. A sayyid who is *hijrah* has *'arḍ* like a tribesman; that is, he can intervene in tribal affairs by taking others into his peace and protecting them. He can bear arms like a tribesman, though few *hijrah* people now do so. He is exempt from collective levies on the tribe and is under the tribesmen's protection, in theory if not in practice. However, in most *hijrah* documents (and always in explanations of what these entail, whichever side of the agreement one's informant comes from) one also finds somewhere the phrase *mā la-hum 'alay-him*, meaning 'what they are due is due from them'; any offence by a sayyid against his tribal protectors is to be fined with the same severity as an offence by them against him. The status of *hijrah* is singular. It is not one of unequivocal superiority.

Whatever the vagaries in the respect given sayyids by tribesmen, and thus in the sayyids' own influence, this singularity of their position among the tribes remains. In 1980, for example, a young sayyid from al-Kibs was accused of abducting two girls from Banī Ḍabyān in Khawlān al-Ṭiyāl. Banī Ḍabyān attacked al-Kibs, which is *hijrah* from all Khawlān, and the rest of Khawlān attacked Banī Ḍabyān. A delegation which included nearly every important shaykh in Ḥāshid and Bakīl then imposed a cease-fire. Part at least of the decision they came to was that the sayyids of al-Kibs should pay Banī Ḍabyān four times what the girls' bride-price would have otherwise been and eleven '*ayb*s of a bull and 110 silver thalers each. The settlement was never, I think, concluded. What was noteworthy was the importance attached to these events by the opposed tribes of Khawlān and the importance of the delegation who intervened. There were larger political quarrels in the background to this, but the *hijrah* was the nominal focus of what threatened to be a serious war, although everyone agreed that tribes' care for their *hijrahs* was not what it had been. Whatever the sayyids' own status, their *hijrah* can provide a focus, in the same way a market can, around which the protecting tribe may cohere or fragment.

The sayyids, however, have their own views, and in the past had their own ambitions. As Zaydis they held that the ruler must be one of their number, from 'the people of the House' (*ahl al-bayt*, the Prophet's descendants), and the rule he imposed should be based on God's book and the Prophet's usage: that rule then applied ideally not to this tribe or that tribe, and far less within minor limits of time or space such as those of a single *hijrah*, but instead uniformly to all who acknowledged the sayyids' mission and all whom the 'holy war' brought under Zaydi control. The *hijrah*, from the sayyids' point of view, was a space in the tribal world of which much might be made or little. And the reader will have noticed how, when one comes to discuss men of learning, the citations of indigenous written sources, of names, and of detailed dates begin to thicken—how ethnography in effect starts to read like history. The following chapter will discuss in more detail the historical relations of tribes and sayyids, but we should first pause and take stock of what *hijrah* might mean from the tribes' point of view.

SINGULARITY AND SACROSANCTITY

The term *hijrah* we have now seen applied to prominent shaykhs, to certain towns, to markets, to certain men of religion whom the tribes protect, and to the places where such men live. Related terms, it will be remembered (Chapters 2 and 3), occur in connection with a breach of the house-peace or the peace which exists within a tribe's borders. The idea underlying these terms is of general importance. But the sayyids who live under tribal protection also fit a particular model of the 'holy family' and its associated 'sacred enclave' which has been applied to the history of early Islam and linked with pre-Islamic institutions of South Arabia. In early Islam the *hijrah* was, of course, the Prophet's removal from Mecca to Medina. In ancient Yemen the term *h-j-r* referred to a sanctuary in which was usually placed the pantheon of the protecting commune or tribe-like group. The association of *h-j-r* with the early Islamic *hijrah* is tempting, though no historical link can yet be demonstrated, and the association of both with the latter-day *hijrah* in Upper Yemen is more tempting still.[37]

It is worth stressing, therefore, that ethnographically the 'sacred' enclave is only one still-point in the tribal world among many. Al-Shamāḥī's explanation of *hijrah* as itself meaning 'holy', *muqaddas* (al-Shamāḥī 1972: 240), is thus problematic. The reaction to a breach of *hijrah* (that is, to a breach of inviolability) is in terms of honour. The notion of inviolability may itself, however, be bound up with other ideas, and it is hard to know where certain lines are to be drawn. The analytical point at issue can be shown most conveniently by looking at the semantically rather similar root, *ḥ-r-m*.

The *ḥarīm* is sacrosanct, by which must be first of all understood that it is singular, set aside from the run of potential conflict. An offence against the *ḥarīm* (against a man's womenfolk, for instance) is a disgrace and an insult in a way that an attack on a tribesman is not. The word *ḥarīm* is related to *ḥaram,* which means, in effect, an inviolable space. The 'two *ḥarams*' of Mecca and Medina are perhaps the best known case. In a document from the late 1950s one finds a mention of two tribesmen having fought in Mecca when they were on the pilgrimage (Dresch forthcoming *c*). The man who started the fight was fined 88 silver thalers and a bull, as he might have been for an offence in some country market, but in this case the amends were described as *li-hajar al-ḥaram wa-l-iḥrām*, which freely translated is 'to restore the status of the (sacred) enclave and of the (inviolable) pilgrimage'. The parallels with *hajar al-bayt* or *hajar al-sūq* (the house and the market respectively) need no stressing. Every mosque has or is a *ḥaram*, an inviolable space which, even in Upper Yemen, is often also called a *ḥawṭah*. The bounds of a market too define a *ḥaram*. Around most fields is a *ḥaram*, a space of a metre or two within which sheep must not stray when crops are growing. *Ḥurmat al-waṭan* (from the same root, *ḥ-r-m),* meaning 'inviolability of a tribe's territory', has been mentioned already.

Al-Shamāḥī's gloss of *hijrah* as 'holy', which he makes quite reasonably in connection with a notable sayyid claiming tribal support, contains an assumption that might allow one to gloss all the instances of *ḥaram* just touched on above as 'sacred'. 'Marked' and 'unmarked' seem the less loaded terms to bear in mind. The underlying idea can take very different forms, and the associations apt for one case do not necessarily fit another. One might see the space around fields to keep sheep out as in some way derived from the provisions that govern the ritual centre of the whole Muslim world, or (no more satisfactory) trace the link in the other direction. But to treat the sayyids' *hijrah* as a 'sacred enclave' (which is how the sayyids themselves may present matters) is to be faced with just this problem. On one's understanding of what the term means can depend one's view of the history of Upper Yemen for the last thousand years and one's feeling for what happens next. It is therefore worth adding a few more instances of the idea to the list that we have so far.

Some protected still-points in the tribal world are permanent in the same way as *hijrah*s where sayyids live, but are not associated with a respected non-tribal group any more than are markets (see Puin 1984). Ṣirwāḥ Arḥab, for example, is spoken of as *hijrah*. It falls on the border of Madar (part of al-Khamīs in Zuhayr) and of Mashamī (part of Banī Sulaymān, in Dhaybān), and thus falls on the border between the two halves of Arḥab. It falls within neither and is under the protection of both. The site contains only a cistern (*barīk*) and some Ḥimyarite ruins. No one lives there. It has definite borders, though, and it is said to be at all times 'secure for those fearing and for those causing fear' (*āmin li-l-khā'if wa-li-l-mukhīf*), for those fearing blood revenge and for those seeking blood revenge. Violence is forbidden and the place is, in theory, a sanctuary. The same is said to be true of al-Turbat al-Ḥamrā' in the Jawf, where again there is no settlement, although there is a well there which the nomads used. Ṣirwāḥ Khawlān has this status, although the village there is of no special standing. All are spoken or by tribesmen as permanent *hijrah*s.

Amends may also be judged due as *tahjīr* ('making or restoring inviolable status') even where the status in question had not been formally agreed before being violated. To take an extreme case, in a dispute where a government 'customs' post was attacked, *tahjīr al-jamārik* was paid in the form of slaughter-beasts (we shall touch on the case further in Chapter 8). More usually we are dealing with a status formally agreed between all concerned; however, that agreement can be reached from scratch where there was none before and where no non-tribal object is at issue. For example, in the course of a dispute in the late 1970s between al-Ahnūm and 'Idhar, a village called Bayt al-Wāṣil, on the border between them, was referred to as *hijrah*. There are no learned men there and no market. The tribesmen who live there are too few, or perhaps too exposed, to hold their own against either side. They have opted out, and their neighbours have let them do so. All violence against them or by them within the village is now forbidden. Again, a dispute occurred between Dhū Muḥammad and Dhū Ḥusayn over a wadi in the far east of Yemen which had until then been grazed by both tribes. Water was found and each claimed the area was theirs to farm. When the dispute reached violent deadlock, one of the suggestions made was that the place be 'made *hijrah*', meaning no one from either side could encroach on it without incurring a penalty. A still-point was to be formed and upheld until agreement could be reached on what to do with the disputed area and its resources.

A meeting between tribes, whether or not it is held at a place like Ṣirwāḥ, is also a protected still-point, often spoken of explicitly as *tahjīr*. The procedure is worth describing at length as one of the few large-scale formal actions among the tribes that bears description as in any way ritual. If the meeting is held at an established 'meeting place' *(malqā)*, the tribe which has called the meeting assembles there first. As the others approach, the first tribe draw themselves up in a wide arc to face those arriving, who march in column towards the meeting point, with their *mazāyinah* drumming in front of them, and the tribesmen, perhaps dancing with their daggers aloft, chanting *zawāmil* or 'collective ditties' (pl. of *zāmil*). These *zawāmil* are doggerel poems of the sort quoted in earlier chapters. As the incomers close with the other tribe they spread out to form a crescent or arc in front of them. They may perhaps fire in the air (this firing of volleys is called *ta'shīrah)*, and those first to arrive return the salute by firing in the air over them.

The two groups halt about a hundred metres apart. The *dawshān*s or heralds run between them and shout the praises of the two sides.

ḥayyākum allāh yā rijāl Bakīl.	God grant you life, men of Bakīl.
ḥayyākum yā uṣūl,	Grant you life, you with origins [nobility],
yā zābinīn al-ḥudūd,	You who guard your borders,
yā qahum,	You [who fight] heedless of danger,
yā maḍādah al-matāris . . .	You who attack [another's] breastworks . . .

The *dawāshīn* are not tribesmen, although they all attach to particular tribes: they are neutral figures, who here fill the neutral space. They declaim their stock phrases in a characteristic strained shout as the crescents form opposite each other, then the tribesmen all fire in the air. The firing dies down as a shaykh or group of shaykhs from the first group step forward. They greet those arriving. A formal exchange of *'ilm wa-khabar* ('information and news') then follows. A shaykh of the first group begins this with:

ḥayyā allāh yā waṣālah,	God grant you life, you who arrive here,
wa-narḥab bi-'ilma-kum.	And we welcome your news.
dābī 'ilma-kum,	Give your news,
yā ṭayyibīn al-'ilm.	You whose news is good.

A shaykh from the group just arrived then answers *wājib bi-salāmat-kum* ('We are bound to your welfare'). He then states their reason for coming and ends his oration with *wa-intu, 'ilma-kum?* ('And you, what is your news?'). The shaykh of the first group replies with:

wājib bi-salāmat-kum ahlan wa-sahlan.	Bound to your welfare. Welcome.
wa-aḥnā quddāma-kum,	We stand before you,
munāẓirīn la-kum.	Watching out for you.
wa-llāh yaṣlaḥ al-sha'n,	God settle the matter,
sha'n-nā wa-sha'n-kum.	Our matter and yours.[38]

He steps back a pace or two to his own group, and the two arcs of men then move forward to close the circle. Once the circle is closed, the shaykhs from both sides, or those of them deputed to speak for their men, meet as a group at the circle's centre and, having greeted each other personally, begin discussing whatever the cause may be for the meeting being held. The form is always the same and the wording differs little.

Once the circle is closed, all violence is forbidden. The document from Dhū Muḥammad quoted earlier sets out the rules in terms almost exactly parallel to those used of guaranteeing the market: 'At meetings of Dhū Muḥammad . . . [and sections affiliated with them] . . . where two or more sections (*laḥmatayn wa-ṭāli'*) meet, if someone from one of the sections offers violence to someone at the meeting, he shall have no rights and no relation to those at the meeting [to call on]. Instead an escort will see him to his house.' He shall have no rights anywhere in the tribe's territory, even at market in al-'Inān, but must remain at home until he pays amends to the person he set on and to those who convened the meeting. His standing as a tribesman is forfeit until he does so.[39]

As always with matters of honour, the meaning of rules is exemplified clearly only by their dramatic breach. At any meeting, however, the possibility of that breach is, as it were, acted out. The tribes or sections attending the meeting each march in as if to war. They halt at a distance from each other. The neutral and inviolable figures of the 'heralds' or *dawāshīn* fill the space between them until the shaykhs from each side exchange the 'news' formally, and the circle then closes. The opposition between tribes and the temporary status of binding truce are successively marked on the ground by the tribesmen's movements; a moment, perhaps, 'when the society and its members take emotional stock of themselves and their situation as regards others' (Mauss 1970: 77–8).

The importance of *tahjīr* (making *hijrah*) is in essence the same whether the still-point created is intended to be permanent or to last only an hour, and whether it contains a market or men of religion or simply a group of tribesmen who for the moment are at truce with each other. A breach of the peace requires heavy amends. In the ordinary way of things there is no formal peace between tribesmen, but each man defends his own against others and each group of men against other men; if a man is killed, then the blood-money is paid or revenge is sought, one man of theirs for ours. Where a point is set up that is *hijrah*, by contrast, violence is not any longer ordinary but is paid for by heavy amends; the blood-money might have to be paid not just once but eleven-fold. The protected space has its own value, almost regardless of what one happens to place there. The reversal of values at the boundary of this singularity is as marked as at the boundary of a single man's peace, but there are two distinct aspects to a still-point that is formed collectively: it is protected against outsiders and to that extent shows just the moral seriality stressed in Chapters 2 and 3; yet for those who protect it, the still-point is not identified with particular persons or factions, and what occurs there is not for one faction to support or censure. To that extent it provides an exception of the tribes' own making to the rule of autonomy and seriality whereby right and wrong are always questions of us and them: it provides an opposite and a complement to the dominant values of tribalism by which it is formed and within which it has its sense.

NOTES

1. There have been several attempts to rank or explain these divisions (see e.g. Chelhod 1970; Gerholm 1977; Stevenson 1985), sometimes invoking a division of labour, sometimes the idea of 'status groups', sometimes attachments to institutions, but usually touching on the comparison with Indian castes and leaving a certain residue of confusion.

   I am therefore going to use the word 'estate' here in its early medieval sense (see Jolliffe 1961: 434), where there would seem to have been a indefinite number of such units, each with its rights and duties, but no single structure that would specify their bounds and relations. Indian castes, by contrast, do fall within a single scheme (see Dumont 1970), but the scheme is not identified with temporal power and hence no decision is reached on rival claims to ranking. The idea of three clearly ranked estates, and hence of something like 'status groups', in European history seems to follow the appearance of just such a temporal power in the form of an explicitly centralized monarchy that could claim to be the fount of honour. Similarly in India, clear rankings of caste would seem to derive from rulers, whether petty kings or the colonial British.
2. The Ṣan'ānī Jews were particularly involved in running the mint, and claimants to the Imamate sometimes bought from them the die-stamps (see e.g. al-Sayāghī 1978: 92; al-Ḥibshī 1980: 265). The rural Jews are less conspicuous in the histories, though it is noteworthy how often Jewish millennial outbreaks involved the tribes (e.g. al-Sayāghī 1978: 95–6). Normally the Jews carried no arms. Around Baraṭ, however, late in the last century they were as wild and martial as the tribesmen (Goitein 1941: 54, 63). I am indebted to Andrew Shryock for the information that, as of 1986, Jews around Ma'rib were still, or are again, carrying arms.
3. Gerholm 1977: 133 reports that in the west the Jews too are spoken of as 'deficient'. I have never heard this on the plateau. Various 'just so' stories, by contrast, are told to explain the *muzayyin*s' position (Glaser 1885: 205), and many tribesmen say that they are so different from the rest of us that they have an extra pair of teeth (or alternatively a pair less; cf. Stevenson 1985: 175 n. 6), which I have not heard said of the Jews. A Jew who apostasized could become a tribesman, which a *muzayyin* in theory never could. None the less, in most areas on the

plateau, the Jews and the *mazāyinah* alike are said to take part in a tribe's *ghurm wa-jurm*, the distribution and levying of collective payments.

4. For lists and accounts of these occupations see Rossi 1939: 142–3; Chelhod 1970: 74–5; Stevenson 1985: 95–102.
5. Professed disdain for the market is, of course, common among tribal Middle Eastern societies. 'The village/market dichotomy is no doubt a means of preventing the impersonal exchanges of the market from obtruding the dispositions of calculation into the world of reciprocity relations' (Bourdieu 1977: 186). Given a broad enough interpretation of reciprocity (to include reciprocal violence, which to start with can be highly impersonal) there is a measure of truth to this.

   The Algerian and Yemeni cases differ in several important ways, but the most satisfactory general formulation seems to me to turn on the loss of autonomy required by direct exchange of goods and the fixed moral hierarchy required by trade: the very equality of buyer and seller could only be maintained by a set of values that neither controlled. To introduce *Homo œconomicus,* let alone such loaded terms as 'capital of trust' (ibid. 185), seems to me a severe imposition. Individualism, calculation, and the market are mutually dependent in the logic of our own ideology (Dumont 1977), but the relation of individualism to hierarchy (in as broad a sense as Dumont likes to use those terms) may be differently constructed in the case at hand: at least we must leave room for the possibility.
6. A particularly 'hereditary' ascription may, of course, be rewritten. This does not happen because tribesmen and traders act alike in some market town, but because someone of ambiguous *bayyāʿ* status leaves the field of petty commerce and acts conspicuously as a tribesman. Bayt Kāmil of Khārif, for instance, are said to have been looked on by many people as *bayyāʿ* before the revolution. They are now referred to by most as tribesmen, if not shaykhs. ʿAbduh Kāmil was a hero of the revolution, running messages between disaffected shaykhs in the years before the coup and fighting in the early battles of the civil war, where he was finally killed. For the moment, the possibility of redefinition is still fixed in the affairs of the tribal countryside, not in those of centres of commerce.
7. Unfortunately one must reject Chelhod's appealing suggestion (1970: 79) that the *dawshān*'s place as 'a man of everywhere and nowhere' is expressed in the name of his tent, *khidr*, 'which applies, in classical Arabic, to the curtain behind which a young girl must shelter herself to avoid the gaze of strangers'. Any black tent in Yemen can be a *khidr* (see e.g. Zabārah 1956: i. 2/165). The screen behind which girls are secluded would be spoken of simply as *sitārah*. There is none the less a certain separation. For further notes on the *dawāshīn* see app. 4/1.
8. The two families are Bayt Ṣanāʿanah and Bayt al-Quṭlān. The former now seem to part-own a large well-drilling and machinery import business based at al-ʿInān (Baraṭ).
9. See also al-Hamdānī 1948: 75; *ḥayyā-kum ullāh wa-ḥayyā shākirā /*

qawman yughaddūn al-dakhīl bākirā / wa-yu'aththirūn al-ḍayf wa-l-mujāwirā. As Serjeant says in a slightly different context (1978: 14), a tribesman is *manī'*, *qawī*, *sharīf*, which in reverse order is 'noble, strong, and able to protect'. The attributes are inseparable, and they here apply as much to the tribe as to the particular man.

10. It is worth stressing again this positional quality, which accounts for more than does caste-like purity of occupations. Butchers are all of low status, beasts killed in apology or to impose on other men are hocked by *mazāyinah*, but a tribesman preparing lunch for himself and his guests will happily slaughter and cut up a beast. Nor are there any caste-like constraints on tribesmen eating with, or of course praying with, *mazāyinah* or *dawāshīn*.
11. For historical cases see e.g. al-Ḥibshī 1980: 412; Nubdhah 357; Yaḥyā b. al-Ḥusayn 1968: 212.
12. An example of such an agreement, and some further detail on tribal markets, is given in Dresch forthcoming *a*. For a very useful overview of weekly markets in Yemen see Schweizer 1985.
13. For a dispute where this was precisely one of the points at issue see Dresch 1987*a*: 52. Comparative work on markets remains to be done, but for a rather different system in 'Asīr see al-Zulfa 1982; for Morocco see Fogg 1938. In the Upper Yemeni case the security of the market is established solely by guaranty, whereas in 'Asīr the market may be protected by a fortified tower. Certain of the Moroccan markets, whose protected status is identified with that of a tomb or a holy family, are described as 'explosive' because of tensions between those who attend them (Benet 1970), but in Upper Yemen the strain falls solely upon the structure of guaranty.
14. It should be noted that market guarantors on the plateau take no fees from the traders nor from those attending market, which guarantors in the western mountains seem to do routinely. On the plateau there is no reason why a guarantor should not also invest in land or property in the market, but the guaranty itself must be purely a matter of 'face'.
15. For a full transliteration of this passage see Dresch forthcoming *a*.
16. This rotation of responsibility among the 'fifths' or *akhmās* of the tribe is, so far as I know, unique in Upper Yemen. Usually the guarantors are responsible as an undifferentiated group, none ceding the guaranty temporarily to others or carrying for them temporary responsibility.
17. A full account in Dresch 1987*b* makes the point that the market is one of the few fixed points of moral reference and this role of the guarantors as obligatory arbitrators is common.
18. Very often men will do their routine shopping at the market nearest them, which is not always in their own tribe. The 'Uṣaymī village of 'Unqān, for example, is in clear view of Sufyān's market at al-Ḥarf (almost within extreme rifle range, I would think), but a long way (a hard half-day's walk across the mountains) from al-'Uṣaymāt's major market at Ḥūth. Routine purchases are made in al-Ḥarf. Being excluded from one's own tribe's market is none the less important. Not only is one excluded from collective functions, but one is rendered

in a way invisible. Truce agreements, for example, sometimes contain a condition set by the victims that the aggressors must not enter the market in the hours of daylight, and thus cannot claim acknowledgement as fully part of the tribe.

19. For the destruction of the walls and many houses at Khamir, 'except for some old Ḥimyarite foundations which were too strong to knock down', see Yaḥyā b. al-Ḥusayn 1968: 553. The walls around 'Amrān seem only to have been built in the early eighteenth century (Zabārah 1958: 357). The gates of 'Amrān are said to have been guarded by men from the lowest estate, who were paid out of taxes (Stevenson 1985: 102), a noteworthy contrast with, say, Rembrandt's 'Night Watch'.

20. The other families in the *laḥmah* are Bayt Mahdī, Bayt al-Qumaḍī, al-Ḥajar, Bayt 'Utayfah, and Bayt al-Qurs. They are not related genealogically to Bayt al-Lawandī, who used to be the *umanā'* ('trusted scribes') of Banī Ṣuraym.

21. The shaykhs of Banī 'Imrān seem in fact to be of some antiquity, being mentioned in connection with the fighting against the Turks *c.*1600 (Nubdhah: 123, 131, 214). Quite what the continuity consists in is impossible to say from the sources so far available. Apart from Banī 'Imrān, the *laḥmah* of that name contains Bayt al-Raḥīmī, Bayt al-Mufārrah, and Bayt al-Washshaḥ. All five families claim common ancestry.

22. Considerable support for the idea of a scale of differences within market society comes from Stevenson's essentially 'trader's eye view' of 'Amrān (see particularly Stevenson 1985: 101, 129). Gerholm's excellent sketch of the rather different western Yemeni system is also relevant: there the townsmen are referred to as '*arab*, they claim often to have been tribesmen and seem to be recognized as quite separate from those who entirely lack honour or origins (see esp. Gerholm 1977: 141–3).

23. Throughout the period I worked in Yemen (1978–83) there appeared to be an increase in such 'traditional' marks of status. Some came and went, such as the fashion for expensive woven caps *(kūfī)* made, I think, from palm or cane fibre. Others grew steadily, such as the interest in old daggers and the practice of employing *dawāshīn*. Many tribal families with new money to spend were, perhaps, playing at being great shaykhs.

24. This may sound unduly dismissive of the fundamentalists, who in this case were aligned mainly with Egyptian 'Brothers' and veered wildly in their views on the Saudis. As Eickelman 1987 points out, a consciously 'universalizing' view of religion (of which this fundamentalism is a variety) is apt to a context where one is routinely exposed to non-local questions. This has hardly happened at all among the tribes. With the spread of general education it may do so, and we shall comment on this in ch. 10. For the moment, the attraction of an anti-intellectual insistence on simple answers to the problems of politics is limited to students in Ṣan'ā' and to certain army officers. Among the tribes, groups espousing these ideas (some pro-Iran, some pro-Saudi, some

pro-Brotherhood) have had passing importance, but mainly as a source of guns and money.

25. Until Bayt al-Ḥūthī and the Imam al-Mahdī (d. 1901) settled there, al-'Inān had no resident sayyids. There are still none outside al-'Inān among the tribes. How long the area had been without sayyids is not at all clear (they are frequently mentioned there in the eighteenth century), but the sayyid presence is in fact very thin among many tribes. It could be argued that at many periods of Yemeni history the centre of gravity for the sayyids' own affairs was in the western mountains and their presence among the tribes was a matter largely of more isolated outposts.

26. Even toward the plateau, where the tribesmen themselves nearly all dwell in houses, the imbalance can be marked: al-Darb, for instance, at Wādī Sufyān on the road from the plateau to Baraṭ, is by far the largest village for a considerable distance, and by far the best provided with good farmland, but its inhabitants seem all to be *jīrān*.

27. For notes on Ḥūth and Shahārah prior to the republican period and the cash economy see Zabārah 1941: 12–14, 428. The status of such places as educational centres is dealt with in al-Akwa' 1980.

28. The upright dagger sheath won by most tribesmen is called *'asīb*. The dagger sheath worn by learned men is, by contrast, called *thūmah*, which oddly is also given as meaning the daïs on which the Imam sat to dispense justice (Goitein 1941: 41). Right-hand, oblique sheaths, albeit of a less elaborate form, are often worn by the tribesmen in the east and north-east, particularly on campaign. East of Baraṭ the upright sheath one might think typically 'tribal' may in fact be a dress version, worn when the possibility of violent action is remote.

29. Bayt al-Akwa' (Hijrat al-Ku'ān) at al-Malāḥ in Murhibah provide a case in point. When all the real *'ulamā'* left for Ṣan'ā', their less learned relatives and the place where they lived lost *hijrah* status. The market at 'Arām (a purely 'secular' institution) became the tribe's *hijrah* until that too lost its status in a squabble *c.*1978–9.

The al-Akwa's, who for a long time had branches in Dhamār, Ṣan'ā', and al-Ahnūm, are ascribed a genealogy that goes back to Murhibah or Ḥimyar (Zabārah 1941: 3–4 and 1957: 210–211). Present members of the family grace their book covers with the title al-Akwa' al-Ḥawālī, thus claiming pre-Islamic Yemeni ancestors.

30. For notes on the history and distribution of Bayt Ḥanash see Zabārah 1929: i. 348–52, 1941: 192, and 1952: 220; al-Shawkānī 1929: i. 472.

31. For accounts of Bayt al-'Ulufī see al-Ānisī 1978: 265–6 n. 1; Zabārah 1929: i. 69, 342 and 1958: 160. In the biographical literature it is often suggested that the family takes its name from the protected village of 'Ulafah in al-Kalbiyyīn of Khārif (al-Shawkānī 1929: i. 409; Zabārah 1941: 254). Those members of the family I have known well all claim that the village in Khārif takes its name from them and they take their name from the wadi near Ṣa'dah.

32. The date of al-'Ansī's death is taken from the tombstone in Masjid

al-Raḍmah at al-ʻInān, and the connection of the different qadi houses to him is taken from the view of these houses' members nowadays. The history may well be more complex. The name certainly appears in very early sources (e.g. al-Laḥjī MS I: 107, 110 and *passim*). According to some, Bayt al-ʻAnsī and Bayt al-Ānisī may have a common ancestor (Zabārah 1958: 835). Al-Aswad al-ʻAnsī, the false prophet in the wars of apostasy, is supposed to have been based at Khabb (Zabārah 1956: i. 1/24–6), and a surprising number of the present day qadi family are willing to trace kinship to him.

33. This document was copied in Sufyān from a version held by a very minor member of the family. For comparison, apart from the further documents quoted below, the reader might wish to look at the *tahjīr* of Ẓafār Dhībīn printed by Sālim (1982: 209–22) and translated by Puin (1984). The qadi family of Āl al-ʻUkām are to be distinguished from the shaykhly family named ʻUkkām (with a *tashdīd*) in al-ʻUṣaymāt.
34. By far the most convenient outline of these major sayyid houses is Zabārah 1957.
35. One of the Imam al-Manṣūr Muḥammad Ḥamīd al-Dīn's greatest achievements (*c.*1900) is said to be that he put an end to fiefs controlled by Shahārah sayyid families (Zabārah 1956: i. 2/204), which was not done without creating resentment. Earlier in his career Bayt al-Mu'ayyad and Bayt al-Mutawakkil had been intractably at odds (ibid. i. 2/221). For the signatories to the present document see app. 4/2. Some of the history of the period will be touched on in ch. 6.
36. For an account of al-Qāsim see Kopp 1977, although he unfortunately seems not to have realized that the village was *hijrah*. In the nineteenth century the sayyids there received at least a small tax on oil-sellers at a nearby tribal market (Dresch forthcoming *a*). Sayyids lacking *hijrah* status are in fact quite common. The only sayyids I know of in Khārif, for instance, are Bayt al-Ḥamzī at Kāniṭ, who are simply part of the tribe. Ḥamal, in the south of Banī Maṭar, provides another case. There is no season why someone who happens to be a sayyid should not also be a shaykh (see e.g. Zabārah 1956: ii. 101), although this is unusual.
37. For discussion of the 'sacred enclave' and its relevance to the beginnings of Islam see Serjeant 1962, 1969, 1977, 1978, which between them have quietly revolutionized discussion of the subject. For the pre-Islamic *h-j-r* see Beeston 1971 and Robin 1978, 1982. Of particular interest in the pre-Islamic material are inscriptions recording sacrifices to allow an errant tribesman to rejoin the group (see Ryckmans 1983: 19), which is much what happens at a modern *hijrah*. But Madelung (forthcoming) argues that the resemblance is a purely medieval product, a point to which we shall come back briefly in ch. 5.
38. *Munāẓirīn* carries the meaning of 'watching over' or 'watching out for'. It can also mean simply 'waiting' (*muntaẓirīn*, see al-Ḥibshī 1980: 519) or specifically 'waiting for an enemy' (al-Lahjī MS I: 100), which catches nicely the value of opposition so evident here. A 'meeting' (*liqā'*) carries the same ambiguity of friendship and hostility. In doggerel poetry the otherwise pompous literary phrase, *ilā l-liqā'*

('until we meet') is often used with the double meaning of courteous regards and challenge: 'until we meet [in battle]', 'until I see you [over open sights]'.

39. *Wa-ba'd mā yuwaṣṣil-hu bayt-hu fa-mā la-hu malzam wa-lā 'alqah* . . . The term *malzam* here is roughly synonomous with *'arḍ*, the ability to take on commitments as a tribesman.

5 Sayyid History and Historiography

> If history is the movement whereby a society reveals itself for what it is, there are in a sense as many qualitatively different histories as there are societies . . .
>
> Louis Dumont, *Homo Hierarchicus*

Each enclave of learned families is contained within a local protection pact. But the Zaydi tradition reproduced in protected enclaves used once to extend far beyond the borders of any one tribe, or even group of tribes, and was sustained for several centuries uninterruptedly. This tradition made tribal concerns subordinate to learned interests. It produced, from the learned viewpoint, a reversal of the moral order one sees in field-work, and the tribesmen, too, accepted the value of formalized Islamic learning, for all that they were often at odds with its proponents. The tribes, in short, formed part of a larger whole. This was centred on the Zaydi Imams, who themselves were sayyids.

The last Imam was expelled from Yemen less than twenty-five years ago, and an older image of government has thus been lost only very recently. The first Imam had claimed the tribes' support about a thousand years earlier. A history of the Imamate through the centuries in between is beyond the scope of this study. What demands our attention instead is the form of the relation between sayyids and tribes from which such history emerged, and the fact that the accounts we have are largely written by sayyids or by those who supported them. In the process of its own reproduction, Zaydi tradition left tribesmen at the margin of Islamic government, where they still remain nowadays.

SAYYIDS, IMAMS, AND TRIBES

Al-Qāsim al-'Iyānī was a Zaydi Imam who died in 1003. His tomb at 'Iyān is still tended, and the village is inhabited largely by his descendants. The mosque there is the only large mosque in Sufyān and its minaret, standing out from low trees by the wadi, is visible for miles. The white northern wall of the mosque's interior is decorated with wavy bands of bright primary colours, much as are house interiors in the area, and the tomb, in an adjoining room on the south side, takes the form of a raised wooden catafalque littered with spent joss sticks. The memorial stone, which is not the original, now reads as follows:

In the name of God, the Compassionate and Merciful. Those close to God need not fear, nor do they grieve. This is the tomb of the worthy Imam who gave himself to God, the abstinent and vigorous, the most learned of Imams, crusher of rebels and of the wicked, witherer of tyrants and the stubborn's injustice, warrior for God in the holy war, the guiding star of the Prophet's house (*farqad al-'itrat al-nabawiyyah*). Surpassing them all in his discernment and learning, he was so famous in this community (*ummah*) for his abundant learning that it was said he had sufficient for seven Imams—our master al-Manṣūr billāh, Commander of the Faithful, Abū Muḥammad al-Qāsim. . . . Who wishes to rest in the highest reaches of Paradise, come visit the holy tomb at 'Iyān.

Al-Qāsim thus still has his place in Yemen, but that place is not very grand: his descendants have not even kept up the tradition of learning that sayyids as a group tend to claim, and Imams in the present century sent sayyids from Ḥūth to 'Iyān because those living there were judged unable to lead prayers or provide religious instruction. 'Iyān, however, is still reckoned *hijrah*.

The village lies close to the border between Sufyān's two main divisions, within Ruhm's territory but adjoining Ṣubārah, and is 'set aside' from Sufyān as a whole. Apart from 'the sons of al-Qāsim', the only inhabitants are four families of 'weak' non-tribesmen and two small families of sayyids (from Bayt Ashqas and Bayt Sārī) who were posted there by the Imams forty and thirty years ago respectively. No tribesmen are permitted to live in 'Iyān. If they were, say the sayyids, they would involve the *hijrah* in their own disputes and thus compromise its protected status. The sayyids seem to live in a space whose value is almost purely tribal. Yet this point in the tribal world is defined with reference to an Imam who for a brief time was a ruler. The past and present are linked by a sayyid descent line, and the dispatch of new learned families is enough to suggest how 'Iyān formed a point of insertion for values which applied far beyond the protected village.

Local protection pacts themselves often spanned tribal boundaries. For example, we find that the sayyids of 'Iyān a century and a half ago were protected not only by Sufyān but also by parts of Ḥāshid. The list of signatories to this agreement numbers some forty shaykhs from al-'Uṣaymāt, 'Idhar, and the north of Banī Ṣuraym.[1] At the head of the list is Shaykh Nāṣir b. 'Alī al-Aḥmar, and the document, apparently drawn up at a meeting at Ḥūth, is dated Rabī' Awwal AH 1245 (September 1829). To judge the history of such local ties is extremely difficult. We cannot be sure how long (and whether always or intermittently) 'Iyān, for example, has been under even Sufyān's protection. In the late seventeenth century it lay in ruins, having been razed by the Imam in about 1616 for favouring the Turks. Both Sufyān and Dahm complained of this (Yaḥyā b. al-Ḥusayn 1968: 808–9), which perhaps hints that they considered 'Iyān under their protection at the time, but, if they did, we cannot be sure why: the tribes' proprietary interest in a protected space (Chapter 4) cannot be distinguished from their attachment to the religious principles of those who live there. But religious principles, not tribal allegiances, are what the sources document, drawing in equal manner on all centuries since the Prophet's time, and in doing so they preserve the possibility of transcending any one tribe's interests.

In literary sources (composed by men of religion) the term *hijrah* is discussed theoretically not at all in the meaning of 'protection', but in that of 'flight' from irreligious oppression or to the true Imam of the day. What to tribesmen is local and particular is to the learned, therefore, only an instance of concerns that in no way are limited as to time or place. A good example is provided by an exchange between two early nineteenth-century *'ulamā'*, Luṭf b. Aḥmad Jaḥḥāf and al-Ḥusayn al-Kibsī (Zabārah 1929: i. 361–3). The former asks whether *hijrah* (glossed by Zabārah precisely as 'flight', *firār*, for religion's sake) is a duty or something optional. The reply states that it is not incumbent on whomever can discharge in his own country those religious duties one does in one's heart, and can employ God's prescriptions and study the Islamic sciences. It is if religious life is impossible where one is that one must 'emigrate' (*yuhājir*), a term also used of going elsewhere to pursue one's religious studies or, of course, of seeking refuge in tribal territory.

Maintaining the conditions for this religious life was precisely the Imamate's business, or more accurately the business of successive Imams. The Imam had himself to be a sayyid (a descendant of 'Alī and Fāṭimah). He had to be whole in mind and body, capable of leading the *jihād* or 'holy war' in person, and, by most readings, had to be a *mujtahid*; capable, that is, of forming new law by extrapolation from scripture, a skill which only the learned can judge.[2] In practice he was usually recognized by respected *'ulamā'* (thus binding sayyids and qadis to him) before he could extract the *bay'ah* or oath of allegiance from the tribes who would form his army and provide him the means to enforce religion.

The instability of the process was increased by the theory that 'the Imamate becomes legally valid through the formal "call" to allegiance (*da'wā*) and "rising" (*khurūj*) [i.e. against oppression], not through election (*ikhtiyār*) and contract (*'aqd*)' (Madelung 1971: 1166). No system was recognized for deciding between claimants. Although in theory there should always be an Imam, and the recognition of two at once is exceptional (ibid.), in practice there were long interregna and very frequent rivalries between claimants. Although there are numerous examples of peaceful succession to, and even concession of, the Imamate, there was a tendency for leadership to be wrested by force. Nor did Zaydism recognize any standing divisions of allegiance or territory, 'since . . . evil is not divisible and nor is the obligation to combat it' (al-Wazīr 1971: 69), and the call to moral unity could be directed alike against tribes who had supported the Imamate already or against outsiders with some separate religious claim: the rhetoric applied equally to both.

An attempt by an Imam to discipline one tribe with forces drawn from another could lapse into tribal forms of conflict and settlement, as it often did from the tenth century to the twentieth. To pursue the many detailed examples would be unrewarding (they are highly repetitive), but the presence of an external enemy repeatedly turned the conflict outward, whether toward the Ismā'īlīs in medieval times, the Rasūlids in Lower Yemen in the thirteenth and fourteenth centuries, the Turks in the sixteenth and early seventeenth centuries, or the Turks again in the nineteenth century (Serjeant 1969: 293–4). Apart from the rewards inhering in the settlement of their own disputes, the tribes then had the benefit of warfare against others;[3] and the Imam and his fellow sayyids claimed the canonical fifth of plunder from such *jihād*, allowing them to draw upon further support and acquire perhaps further gains.

When a source of revenue was then seized in Lower Yemen or the west, the Imam gained the means to pay tribes more lavishly and to consolidate his own position, giving groups of his supporters fiefs (*quṭa*ʿ), 'in other words, granting them the proceeds from the area's taxes' (al-Wāsiʿī 1928: 203). We shall come on to this in the following chapter. But note that the rhetoric of Zaydi justice made no reference at all to these practicalities, only to the righteous Imam and scriptural law. In doing so, it presented (both to tribesmen and to learned families) the possibility of unified action (the 'making one word' touched on earlier), and this rhetoric was applied to local affairs also.

The degree of support offered locally to men of religion varies greatly (probably it always did so), but most small *hijrah*s at present are not well endowed. In most tribal territory, *waqf*, which is property 'stopped' from inheritance for pious ends, is not extensive. Such property may, for example, be stopped by a tribesman for the use of a specific learned family to support *darīs* ('study', but also 'recitation' of Qur'ānic verses for the dead). Charitable bequests are also made to mosques and administered by the mosque's custodian (*wakīl*), a position which often runs in a family for generations. Many sayyid families still have, or are linked to, a portfolio of such holdings, besides what personal property their members own. The sayyids of ʿIyān in Sufyān, for instance, had moderately extensive lands (whether property or *waqf* is debated) in the wadis near their *hijrah*, most of which has now been taken by tribesmen. Again, a fairly typical learned family at Ḥūth (about twenty grown men and their dependants) still have between them some 800 *libnah* (about 5.3 hectares) of 'family *waqf*' in the lowlands toward Shahārah, which, were they living solely from agricultural income, would meet about half their needs. Few have much more.

On the other hand, when one looks from Shahārah eastward across the lowlands of al-Baṭanah toward Ḥūth, one's sayyid hosts will claim that nearly everything in view belongs somehow to the learned families of Shahārah. Men of religion will also claim that most of what one sees from Ẓafār Dhībīn is *waqf* land, but that much of it since the 1962 revolution has been taken by tribesmen. Most of this large area at issue probably did once form part of the famous *amwāl manṣūriyyah* (Sālim 1982: 209), the pious bequest established in the early thirteenth century by the Imam ʿAbdullāh b.

Ḥamzah, who also built much of the fortress complex whose ruins still lour over Wādī Dhībīn. These large holdings, very different from those of most local *hijrah*s, are the trace of power and not just of piety.

The link of piety between men of religion and the tribes is nowadays usually not striking; nor do I think it can simply have evaporated in the twenty years since the Imamate's fall. The Zaydi tradition itself placed its stress on learning (always given the restriction of the Imamate itself to the Prophet's kin) and discouraged veneration or the attribution of unnatural powers. This is not to deny that the history is full of sorcerers, false prophets, and writers of talismans. Nor is it to dismiss the importance of such concepts as *barakah* (holy 'luck' or 'blessing'). We hear, for instance, of the sayyid at Wādī Amlaḥ, north of Baraṭ, from whom local people constantly sought blessings (*yatabarrakū*) until he died by falling from a roof in 1708 (Zabārah 1958: 683). At the same time, *barakah* is apparent in the rain and crops, and on occasion it was 'lifted' from the food by God, leaving people to die of weakness (al-Ḥibshī 1980: 61; al-Wāsiʿī 1928: 92). But the idea of *barakah* as a substance which certain persons transmit between heaven and earth is at most periods little stressed, and all types of mediation (*wāsiṭah*) between man and God (as for instance by saints) are frowned on by learned persons.[4] Organized gatherings of tribes around tombs are almost unknown in Upper Yemen, although everyone is well aware that 'pilgrimages' are common elsewhere in the country.[5]

Orthodoxy and heterodoxy were perhaps too tightly linked at most periods for such practices to become general, and Zaydism on the whole retained the standard of a scripturalist Islam whereby rights (*ḥuqūq*) and limitations or punishments (*ḥudūd*) left no place for the spiritual dependence of some men on others. Such at least was the aim. The cultural capital of religious figures (from their point of view and from the tribesmen's) was knowledge of the Law, and the law, unlike 'holiness', requires elaborate ties of referral and education.

As in most traditions of Islam, these latter connections are recorded in biographical dictionaries, arranged alphabetically, and in books of *ṭabaqāt* ('generations', 'classes'). Even an introductory sketch of the sects of Yemen (Sharaf al-Dīn 1968: 224, 233, 293) immediately brings to notice three of these in the Zaydi tradition:

Nāṣir b. Ḥusayn's late seventeenth-century 'classes', then Yaḥyā b. al-Ḥusayn's *Mustaṭāb,* which is known as the 'small *ṭabaqāt*', the 'big *ṭabaqāt*' being that of Ibrāhīm b. al-Qāsim, d. *c.*1740, whose own work is said to run to over three thousand biographical entries.[6] Rather similar works will be cited for other purposes when we come to look at post-medieval history in Chapter 6; but the purpose of the works themselves was to document the tradition of learning. These ties by which knowledge was transmitted were knit together with those of descent by the travels of particular men in pursuit of knowledge,[7] and the comparatively unified tradition that resulted, whether the Imamate at the time was almost crushed by other forces or was ruling the country, was as material a reality as, say, 'invisible colleges' in modern Europe or America. The connections recorded in Zaydi literature formed a large part of the 'programme' (Ardener 1971*c*: 450–1) from which events were generated, and could equally generate what seem sometimes contradictory accounts.

The role of the sayyids as intermediaries, which is apparent not only now but at all periods of history since the first Imam arrived in the late ninth century, perhaps invites comparison with cases better known in anthropology (the Cyrenaican *marabtīn* or the Berber *igurramen*, for example), and, as Meeker says (1979: 212), a standard interpretation has grown up of such non-tribal figures as 'grease in the wheels of a segmentary system'. There is an element of truth in the idea. For example, the case of the murdered Jew late in the last century, mentioned in Chapters 2 and 4, resulted in a confrontation between tribes whom the *hijrah* then separated; but 'the chiefs of the four mightiest tribes of Yemen were appointed arbitrators' (Goitein 1941: 40). Much the same occurred in a battle I saw between tribes in 1978. In this role, the Prophet's descendants are little different from the *dawāshīn* or weak 'heralds'.

Serjeant, on the basis of wide reading in the sources of many periods and wide experience also, offers a grander development of the sayyids' place from effectively the same starting point.

> The true source of political power lies with the tribal leaders who will accept no control from their peers. The solution to this impasse was worked out even prior to Islam by the evolution of the organization centred upon the sacred enclave, managed by an hereditary religious aristocracy respected and protected by the tribes. (Serjeant 1977: 244)

The aristocracy in the case at hand were the sayyids. One could develop a progression through Serjeant's own image of the *hijrah*s as a 'mosaic of theocracies' to an image of the Imams as capable of enforcing even the death penalty on tribesmen, since Imams, as we have seen, were also 'crushers of rebels and of the wicked, witherers of tyrants and the stubborn's injustice . . .': in short, they were portrayed as rulers. In the correspondence from recent Imams which one finds still rolled up in people's personal documents, the tribes are referred to, not as allies, protectors, or even supporters, but as 'our servants (*khuddām-nā*) Ḥāshid and Bakīl'.

All such accounts would be partly true. The explanation of their difference is of course 'historical' (much depended upon Imams' control of taxes), but the temptation to oppose history to anthropology in dealing with this is best resisted. The Eskimo may well have had a different 'social morphology' in summer and winter (Mauss 1979), or the Nuer have appeared sometimes as members of large sets of people and sometimes as small sets (Evans-Pritchard 1940), but the analysis consists in showing the principles that account for both states. More recent attempts to break the 'ethnographic mould' by appeal to 'historical perspectives' (Rosaldo 1980) also often reveal in fact a fairly constant set of ideas that generate, as it were, plus and minus states of the system. In the Yemeni case, for a great many centuries, the *hijrah* provided the point around which both states of the world turned: strong Imams and weak. It could do so because it meant different things to different people. It formed part of two different 'institutional' developments, one learned and the other tribal, one historical and the other more contemporaneous.

Throughout the tribal north, from medieval times onward, were dotted learned enclaves whose numbers ran always into scores. From a local, ethnographic viewpoint at any one time, each seems separate from the others. In a historical view, which was that of the learned, all were connected and were thus merely points of insertion for values applicable at all times everywhere. The learned tradition defined itself and was organized by its own record. Zaydi historiography therefore made history, every bit as much as passing events provided matter one might simply record. The reduced condition of many sayyid enclaves nowadays would seem, were that historiography valid still, less irreversible than in fact it does; and learned writing, by its adherence to principle, obscured all local ambiguities or contradictions. Not least of these is the question of precedence.

The possibility of disputes over precedence is apparent in modern *hijrah* documents, where, it will be remembered, the sayyids are not only *āminīn* ('protected') but also *mu'amminīn* ('themselves able to protect others'). Disputes over who protects whom cut both ways. Tribes may be set at odds by sayyids and even by sayyids who are dead, as in 1076 when Dhū al-Sharafayn brought the bodies of his brother and Sharīf al-Qāsim b. Ibrāhīm to the highlands and a fight broke out among the tribesmen over where to bury them. 'Everyone wanted them buried in his area for the *barakah* they would bring' (Yaḥyā b. al-Ḥusayn 1968: 268). But sayyids may themselves be set at odds by tribes. In 1198, for example, al-Manṣūr 'Abdullāh sent his brother with a group from Ḥajjah called the Banī Baṭīn who were at odds with the Banī Barām, and he was briefly drawn into a fight with another sayyid line when the Banī Barām went instead to the son of the ex-Imam, Aḥmad b. Sulaymān. 'They asked him for help (*istajārū*) and he took them under his protection (*jāra-hum*)' (ibid. 342).

A great sayyid, like a great shaykh, or indeed a tribesman, could take men into his peace and thereby gain honour. The difference lies not in micro-politics but in the sense made of him doing so. An Imam's own standing might be impugned by the breach of his peace (his promise of security, *amān*) just as the honour of a shaykh would be by an offence against someone 'in his face', but the Imam's response is often 'holy war' (see e.g. al-Jirāfī 1951: 168), not the recovery of simply 'good-name'. There is a constant imbalance in the rhetoric, and only that of the learned is recorded for us, so that tribesmen appear as 'warriors in the cause of God', where they support an Imam, or as 'tyrants' and 'evil ones', where they oppose him; only the latter case is dealt with as specifically 'tribal', picking out whatever practice and custom happens not to coincide with the learned vision.

One cannot, therefore, safely find an 'elective affinity' between Zaydism and the tribes, because the relation between them was in large part defined by Zaydism itself. There is no coherent tribal voice that might be raised in contradiction, but only the possibility of turning to an Imam more truly righteous or to some other 'religious' figure of a similar kind. The appearance, correspondingly, is of an all but constant moral relation between sayyids, Imams, and 'ignorant' or 'rebellious' tribes. Indeed, the last point at which we have two autonomous but competing views, that of tribalism and that of Imams, is at about the time the first Imam came to Yemen: the end of the ninth century and beginning of the tenth century AD.

THE BEGINNINGS OF ZAYDI HISTORY

> We have heard of the glory of the Spear-Danes
> in the old days, the kings of tribes—
> how noble princes showed great courage
>
> *Beowulf*, trans. H. D. Chickering

Yaḥyā b. al-Ḥusayn al-Rassī, a sayyid living in the Ḥijāz, was invited by certain Yemeni tribes to intervene in their affairs as an arbitrator in 893. His first attempt failed (with Nihm) but he returned to mediate between the Khawlān tribes around Ṣa'dah after the Prophet appeared to him in a dream (Van Arendonk 1960: 132). The fighting stopped even before he arrived, which his biographer attributes to his *barakah*; he then had those at odds swear on the Qur'ān that they would live in peace, he arranged a truce where the Yu'firid state with 'thousands' of troops had failed, it rained again, the land turned green with crops, and failing livestock revived (ibid. 134–6). Having called men to the *jihād* (the 'holy war' or struggle against ungodliness), Yaḥyā b. al-Ḥusayn then appointed governors to collect those taxes prescribed by religion. He announced himself Commander of the Faithful and Imam, and took the name al-Hādī ilā l-ḥaqq al-mubīn, 'the guide to the manifest truth'. From 897 until his death in 911 he campaigned intermittently in support of these claims against rival powers.

The 'Abbāsid empire's hold on Yemen had already slipped by al-Hādī's time. The Tihāmah was held by the Banī Ziyād; part of the highlands was controlled by the Yu'firid dynasty (based on Ṣan'ā' and Shibām), and the west and south saw the rise of powerful Ismā'īlī or Fāṭimid forces (the people Zaydi history calls 'Qarmatians').[8] Upper Yemen was already at that date tribal, and two great families acquired particular prominence: the Āl al-Du'ām of Bakīl (already powerful when al-Hādī arrived) and the Āl al-Ḍaḥḥāk of Ḥāshid, whose influence spread in the years following. The pair of great families has gone, but the pair of confederations was named then as it now is a millennium and more later and occupied very much the same area. What changes there have been we can look at in a later chapter.

Al-Ḥasan al-Hamdānī (d. 945) has left an extensive account of Yemen at the time, concentrating precisely on the northern tribes, and two of his extant works are of particular interest: his 'geography' (*Ṣifat jazīrat al-'arab*) and the tenth volume of *al-Iklīl*, a genealogical compendium of Ḥāshid and Bakīl (al-Hamdānī 1968, 1948).[9] Taken with the *Sīrah* or 'life' of the first Imam, which was written by one of al-Hādī's own close adherents (al-'Alawī 1972), they provide a fairly full picture of Upper Yemen in the early tenth century. The *Sīrah* and the works of al-Hamdānī are both (for want of a better term) stylized, but the styles are entirely different. The *Sīrah* is concerned with the Imam's claims to uphold true religion, with his piety and his *barakah*; his opponents are the opponents of Islam, and his actions exemplify Islam's prescriptions. Al-Hamdānī's account, by contrast, turns on *furūsiyyah* ('chivalry', 'skill at arms') and every tribe has its great men, both contemporaries and forebears, who are praised as *fursān* ('knights', 'horsemen'). The concordance with some at least of tribesmen's 'heroic' style nowadays is striking.

In a heroic world of single combat, al-Hādī was himself a hero, as his biographer makes amply clear.

> Then Yaḥyā b. al-Ḥusayn told them how to fight, how to thrust with the lance and stab with the sword. Then he took a lance and showed them what he had described. I heard a Hamdānī, Muḥammad b. Bihār, a man well known for his skill at arms and courage say: 'I never saw the like of Abū Ḥusayn [i.e. al-Hādī] . . .', and Aḥmad b. 'Abād al-Ukaylī, also a man known for his skill at arms, answered him: 'no one has the strength to wield a lance like Abū Ḥusayn'. And so it was. (al-'Alawī 1972: 67; cf. Van Arendonk 1960: 251)

But this martial prowess was directed to other ends than that of al-Du'ām or al-Ḍaḥḥāk. In the case at hand, the Imam arrived at Najrān and 'dismounted beneath a tamarisk tree outside the village, where he called Hamdān and Banī al-Ḥārith to him. He had them sit around him and preached them a powerful sermon' (al-'Alawī 1972: 68). They swore to live at peace and to obey al-Hādī, to uphold 'the ordering of what is right and prohibition of what is wrong' (*al-amr bi-l-ma'rūf wa-l-nahy 'an al-munkar*), and the Imam moved on with a greater following to the next village where he preached the Friday sermon. 'When he had finished his prayers they flocked to him to swear allegiance and did not finish doing so until the time of the afternoon prayer' (ibid.).

Al-Hamdānī, by contrast, records heroic deeds and looks for no result from them except renown.

> Muḥammad b. al-Ḍaḥḥāk [of Ḥāshid] begat Aḥmad Abū Ja'far who was lord of Hamdān in his time and fought in many fights and battles. His bosom friend al-Hamdānī praises him and records his battles. He saw one hundred and six fights of which most were between his party and Yaḥyā b. al-Ḥusayn al-'Alawī. (al-Hamdānī 1948: 67)

In other words, against the Imam. In the *Sīrah* this same Ibn al-Ḍaḥḥāk is dismissed at one point as 'a weak and foolish youth' (al-'Alawī 1972: 145). If this were all, it would only be a matter of conflicting allegiances. But while al-Hamdānī's account (to which we can return a little later) is both the first and the last extant work to deal with tribes in terms of 'chivalry', the biography of al-Hādī is only the beginning of a long tradition of historiography in which the tribes hardly appear except as they oppose or support a succession of Imams.

One can only guess, therefore, at the extent to which Zaydism at any particular time (from the tenth century to the twentieth) was an intimate compulsion in the lives of tribesmen. That the claims of the 'holy house' did receive some general recognition in due course is evident from the fact that, for example, the terms *sayyid* and *sharīf*, which al-Hamdānī used of men we would now call shaykhs, came to be used exclusively of the Prophet's descendants.[10] The tribes, though, did not simply submit to the Imams (either in the tenth century or later), nor did al-Hādī's successors act always as successful arbitrators.

Al-Hādī's son, al-Nāṣir Aḥmad, campaigned in the east against the sons of the Bakīl chief, al-Du'ām, who had dissented from their father and aligned themselves with the Ismā'īlī leader, 'Alī b. al-Faḍl. He also fought the Ismā'īlīs in the west, where he was allied with Abū Ja'far al-Ḍaḥḥāk of Ḥāshid, and the Ḥāshid shaykh's power seems to have grown considerably in the process (cf. Wilson 1981: 100): the power and standing of tribal leaders, as we shall see in Chapter 6, was later closely bound up with control of such non-tribal areas and with the Imamate's fortunes. Al-Nāṣir, however, fell foul in the end of tribal leaders at war with each other. Certain of the Khawlān chiefs around Ṣa'dah turned on the Imam, who died of wounds received in a battle with them, and for a time the sayyids were driven out of Ṣa'dah.[11]

Disorders attendant on conflicting claims to the Imamate in the next generation need not detain us, but two later claimants, al-Qāsim al-'Iyānī (999–1003) and his son al-Mahdī al-Ḥusayn (1010–1013) deserve brief mention. They were not descended from al-Hādī (see Fig. 5.1), but reflected the increased interest of Yemen for sayyid houses outside the country and broadened the field of competition for leadership beyond al-Hādi's own kin. Al-Qāsim al-'Iyāni's tomb in Sufyān, as we have seen, is still the centre of a minor *hijrah*.

Even before he came to Yemen from 'Asīr, al-Qāsim had been sent taxes by the tribes around al-Bawn and in the east. His

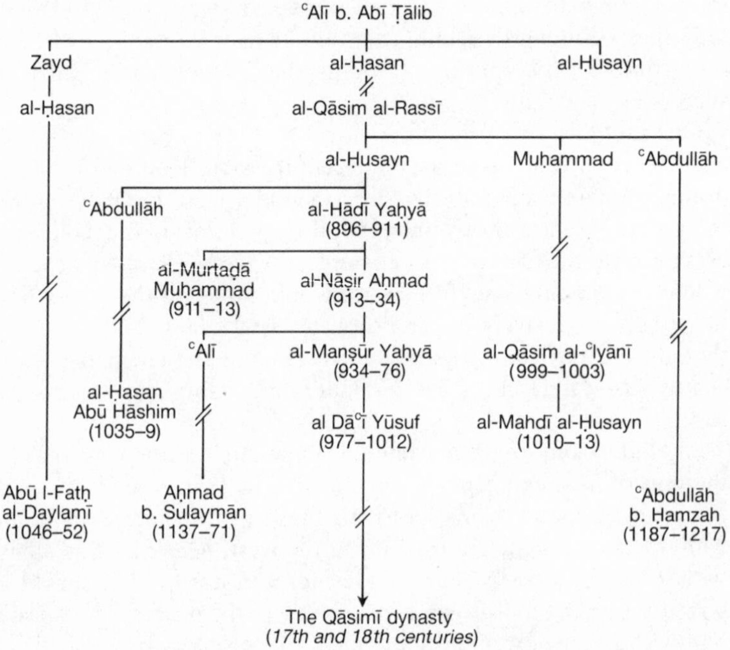

FIG. 5.1 Genealogy of the early Imams

following among the tribes grew considerably, especially in the west where Ja'far al-Ḍaḥḥāk of Ḥāshid was allied with him, and only when his own governor of Ṣan'ā' betrayed him did he give up and retire to 'Iyān, the village in Sufyān where he died and is buried (Yaḥyā b. al-Ḥusayn 1968: 227–34; Zabārah 1952: 74–81). His son, al-Mahdī Ḥusayn, a prodigy of youthful scholarship, claimed the Imamate some years later and gained a following in his turn, but then fell foul of al-Ḍaḥḥāk b. Ja'far al-Ḍaḥḥāk (who had seized Ṣan'ā') and of the kin of al-Qāsim's late governor. His support among the tribes collapsed. Having been driven out of Dhībīn to the Jawf by Ibn al-Ḍaḥḥāk in 1013, he returned and was killed in battle near Raydah: 'On that day he was not quite thirty. Among his ignorant supporters were those who said he still lived and was the Awaited Mahdi . . .' (Yaḥyā b. al-Ḥusayn 1968: 239; Zabārah 1952: 85).

The belief that Ḥusayn was the Awaited Mahdi (a notion quite at odds with the sober Zaydism of al-Hādī's time or more recently) apparently took hold, and for generations afterwards reports were spread of the 'dead' Ḥusayn being seen in company with Jesus, the pair of them even floating together down the slopes of Shahārah (Gochenour 1984: 182, 231 n. 143).[12] This wild heterodoxy has been largely expunged from the histories. Rather as occurs with the early history of Islam itself (Crone 1980: 15), we are left instead with only the respectable outlines of politics, which at the period show tribal leaders in explicit control of at least as wide areas as were the Prophet's descendants (see Yaḥyā b. al-Ḥusayn 1968: 241–2).

Numerous sayyid families, however, were now spreading through Yemen,[13] and their disputes (increasingly phrased in doctrinal terms) gathered in the tribes. Al-Qāsim al-'Iyānī's descendants gained particular prominence, providing (from about 1022) a succession of powerful 'princes' who exploited the belief in Ḥusayn's occultation (Strothman 1934; Madelung 1965: 201); but the next important Imam according to most standard lists was Abū l-Fatḥ al-Daylamī, a Persian who came to Yemen in 1046 having launched his 'summons' in his homeland some seven years earlier. At about the same time, a new Fāṭimid dynasty, the Ṣulayḥids, rose to power and took Ṣan'ā'. In 1052 they cornered al-Daylamī near Radā', and the latest in the hesitant line of Zaydi leaders ended with his head on a pole. No important Imam then appeared until Aḥmad

b. Sulaymān in 1137. In the interim, resistance was offered the Ṣulayḥids primarily by the 'princes' of al-Qāsim al-'Iyāni's house, one of whom founded the sayyid fortress at Shahārah, and (more doctrinally than through force) by the Muṭarrifiyyah.[14]

This latter school or sect, which emerged at the very start of the eleventh century, was composed largely of non-sayyid Zaydi partisans, some of them 'weak' people and some of them tribesmen. Their most distinctive feature was that they proselytized by dispersing among the tribes to live in *hijrah*s (Madelung 1972: 77). It is after their rise that this term appears widely in the general histories with its modern meaning, though not at all restricted in its application to the Muṭarrifīs themselves.[15] Aḥmad b. Sulaymān, for example, is mentioned in 1151 as returning to his *hijrah* at 'Amrān Khārid, in the Jawf, and there receiving the 'sultans' of Āl al-Du'ām (Yaḥyā b. al-Ḥusayn 1968: 306; Zabārah 1952: 100). The same Imam Aḥmad in fact charged the Muṭarrifīs with heresy, and the charge was taken up by his successor, al-Manṣūr 'Abdullāh b. Ḥamzah (1187–1217), who, with tribal support, suppressed them vigorously (ibid. 132–6).

The heretics appear in later Zaydi sources as agreeing with the deviant views of the Jews, Christians, idolaters, and evil Qarmatians. It is only recently that they have been shown to have thought they espoused the views of the Imam al-Hādī (as orthodox as could be) and to have been condemned by these later Imams in terms of new Zaydi doctrine brought in from Persia (Madelung 1972: 79). The histories have covered their tracks. Such recuperation (or indeed invention) of orthodoxy, as with the Muṭarrifīs or with al-Qāsim al-'Iyānī's family, is to be expected (it is the very stuff of Islamic history), but where the Yemeni case perhaps differs from others is in the way this tradition was then reproduced. Rather than the history being formed in urban centres, with its (perhaps minimal) relevance to the countryside subsumed in the opposition between town and country (Gellner 1981), it was often reproduced, from medieval times onward, in small outposts among the tribes. The tribes themselves, one might note, shifted slowly and intermittently. The fortunes of particular sayyid families changed much more rapidly, while certain families of tribal leaders, such as Āl al-Daḥḥāk, disappeared entirely.

The combination of dispersed learning with separate tribal protection pacts was no doubt resilient, but the Imamate's political fortunes depended still upon trial by arms and success in extracting taxes. In his entry for 559/1164, for example, Yaḥyā b. al-Ḥusayn (1968: 316) depicts the Imamate as controlling only the far north, and not a great deal of that, while most of the country was held by non-Zaydi dynasties. Things continued like this, says the chronicler, until the Ayyūbids came to Yemen in 1174. The Ayyūbids (the first of whom was brother of the 'Saladin' of the Crusades) based themselves in Lower Yemen, and the distinction between the country's two poles was greatly strengthened;[16] but they repeatedly struck into Upper Yemen, sometimes as far north as Ṣa'dah, and allotted as fiefs to their allies precisely those areas that had been the Imamate's power-base. In 1229 power in Lower Yemen passed to the Rasūlids, a family that had been in Ayyūbid service, and they in turn were succeeded by the Ṭāhirids of Aden. Upper Yemen was increasingly left to its own devices; Stookey (1978: 125–6) rightly stresses its internal unsettlement.

Only the Turkish invasions of the sixteenth century broke the muddled pattern, and the Zaydi riposte then resulted in Imams and tribes taking Lower Yemen under their own control (we shall look at this in Chapter 6). By then tribal leaders, although seldom 'ruled' by Imams or great sayyids, had long ceased claiming for themselves in their own names dominion over as wide swathes of territory as Imams and other 'state-like' claimants.[17] They were sultans at best, merely secular rulers, usually claiming approval from elsewhere. It had become obvious for shaykhs to look around for claimants unlike themselves. What we must turn to next, therefore, is the way in which learned Zaydis, through their literate accomplishments, formed the continuity of their own tradition and obscured in the process the autonomy of the tribes among whom they lived. Al-Hamdānī's style of representation had been lost at the very outset. Nothing ever replaced it. The loss of this 'tribal' literature reproduces what one sees quite widely in early Islamic history, and it makes of the tribes a 'half-world' residual to Islamic learning.

THE FORMS OF HISTORIOGRAPHY

> Certain structures live on for so long that they become stable elements for an indefinite number of generations . . .; they act as

> limitations ('envelopes' in the mathematical sense) from which man and his experience can never escape.
>
> Braudel, 'History and the Social Sciences'

The Zaydi history of Yemen begins with the first Imam's *Life*. There are then several 'lives' of his noted successors,[18] and a modern author wishing to get on quickly to recent events simply lists the Imams, with short biographies, to connect the Prophet's time and the nineteenth century, thus producing a summary chronicle (e.g. al-Wāsiʿī 1928). In the longer biographies, or as one approaches the present in the case of contemporary matter, one can in any case break into annual chronology ('then came (*dakhalat*) the year so-and-so . . . then came the year after'), and it is common to combine biographical notices with chronicle matter in one proportion or another. At one extreme of this scale is the explicit chronicle, the best known of which for Upper Yemen is *Ghāyat al-amānī fī akhbār al-quṭr al-yamānī* (Yaḥyā b. al-Ḥusayn 1968). This constructs a history from the birth of Muḥammad down to AH 1045 (AD 1635), and, as the title suggests, concerns itself with Yemen almost exclusively.

Dating and naming specific chronicles, however, leaves aside a fact of almost equal importance. Quite unlike the historical record we are used to ourselves, Zaydi literature shows rather little change of style or language over centuries at a time. Apart from the names and the dates within each it would be hard to date the chronicles themselves, and what variations the language shows over time are often small by comparison with those at all times which depend on the author's level of education. One can illustrate the same points with examples drawn equally from medieval times or from the present century: indeed, some of the best 'traditional' historiography was published as late as the 1950s.

Usually natural and social events (if that distinction is the one appropriate) are presented in parallel without further comment. For example:

> The year 1262 [approximately AD 1845].
>
> In the month of Rabīʿ I a large star fell from west to east, bathing the earth in light stronger than the moon, beams of it being red and beams white. It crashed into the ground toward the east in about the time it takes to read the *sūrah* of Fidelity. As it went over there was a powerful noise like thunder. After this, in those same months, there were heavy rains and

fearful strikes of lightning which destroyed many people. There were big hailstorms, each hailstone like an ostrich egg, which smashed houses and ripped through the roofs to destroy everyone inside except those whom God wished to spare.

In the month of Rajab in this year, one of the Sharīfs of Mecca, whose name was Sayyid Ismā'il, set off toward Lower Yemen, always calling on people to support the *jihād* and to expel the Franks from Aden. A mass of people answered him. Then he arrived near Aden, about a *farsakh* away, and besieged the place until he was poisoned and died. Those warriors in God's cause who were in his company dispersed. (al-Wāsi'ī 1928: 68–9)

In a fortunate year, by contrast, the rains were plentiful and thus also the *barakah*, the crops were good and the *sharī'ah* (God's law) was established (al-Ḥibshī 1980: 309). Or when the Imam al-Mutawakkil took power, the saying gained currency that 'since Muḥsin came, the lentils got better' (ibid. 244).[19] Sometimes an explicit link of causation is supplied, as when sickness and locusts took a massive toll 'because the *sharī'ah* was ignored' (al-Sayāghī 1978:100), or the roads were secured and the rain was plentiful 'because the *sharī'ah* was established' (al-Ḥibshī 1980: 131). On occasion the relation is one of sad irony as in 1831/2, when the rains were excellent 'but the afflictions were many, as if the good were conjoined with disorder' (ibid. 43). But always 'rare and far-reaching events' are recorded year by year; the plagues, severe cold spells, droughts, and famines that concern all the Yemeni Muslims, all of them being equally in the hand of God.

Mere sequence of this kind is often falsely obvious, as if it required no explanation. It is very much to Hayden White's credit, therefore, to have asked, at least in general terms, how the annals form works. Yemeni matter does sometimes put one in mind of the earlier entries of the sparser medieval European text he addresses, the *Annals of Saint Gall*, where it seems that 'all of the events are extreme, and the implicit criterion for their selection is their liminal nature' (White 1980: 11). There is no 'plot' in the offing. The calendrical sequence 'has no high points or low points . . . the list of times is full, even if the list of events is not' (ibid. 12),[20] and the unsettling dead-pan quality of the annal (its lack of narrative form and closure)[21] seems to derive from a refusal 'to rank events with respect to their significance for the culture or group that is writing its own history'.[22]

The annal, one might argue, is in fact as centred as the tale of a dynasty; but the unitary chronology and the refusal to take stories out of sequence refer one to the shared experience of conjoined individual persons, rather than to the exploits of a state. In certain genres of European experience over the past several centuries the state has been 'the legal subject which can serve as the agent . . . and subject of historical narrative' (ibid. 15). It produces something very like collective biography, legitimating its existence by the 'inclusion' of past institutions and events, as if the value of the culture itself depended on its past; and our own narrative accounts of other cultures' pasts, so soon as history and ethnography are disjoined and opposed, are liable to suggest that something of the kind is at issue everywhere. What Zaydi experience did, by contrast, was to locate the actions of specific Imams (not the Imamate, which was in no sense a collective entity) against relatively fixed criteria of law. The appearance of fixity was itself carefully reproduced. Instead of a collective agent, a narrative subject in the active sense, one has only the implicit subject of narrative, a group of individual persons who share what befalls them.

The same type of identity should, at first sight, be achieved through genealogy, or rather by co-ordinating separate genealogies to which *akhbār* or self-contained 'tales' attach. Something like this was attempted in the northern Arab lands under the early empire: at about the same time that collections were formed of Prophetic traditions from the different provinces (*c.* AD 700–50), so tribal tales were widely gathered and genealogies sought that extended far beyond one tribe (Duri 1962: 47–8). By the third century of the Muslim era (roughly AD 815–915), the field of knowledge about tales, genealogies, and dates was fairly wide and uniform. But the process then took a distinctive turn.

> This established the concept of the unity of Islamic history, which was probably given a strict chronological sequence in al-Haytham b. 'Adī's work *Kitāb al-ta'rīkh 'alā sinīn* ['the book of history year by year']. They developed the genealogical line into a historical line as in the *Nasab quraysh* of Zubayrī (233–6/844–50) and more clearly in scope and plan in the *Ta'rīkh al-ashrāf al-kabīr* of al-Haytham b. 'Adī. (ibid. 52)[23]

The establishment of a unified vision of Islamic history thus coincided with the development of 'the genealogical line into a historical line'. So soon as all the genealogies and their attendant tales could be seen as one history, they were aligned with each other by picking out one of them (in this case, the Prophet's tribe). But throughout the Arabic-speaking Islamic world, compositions of al-Hamdānī's kind then died away, as too did this assimilation of descent to chronology. It is as if the alignment of separate tribal pasts in a single scheme were irreducibly a contradiction, as indeed it is.

Al-Hamdānī was writing the *Iklīl* perhaps around AD 930–40 (quite late by the standards of most Islamic countries), and there the 'historical line' is not followed. One might explain the uneven development of historiographies by reference to the different times at which the 'Abbāsid grip on different regions lapsed and the way it did so. But the principles of conceiving time and unity are what demand attention. The modes of conceiving time are those of conceiving society, and a logic can be found that relates one such mode to another.[24]

The mode in which the tribes define themselves, though largely obscured meanwhile by the dominance of Zaydi literature, is equally apparent in al-Hamdānī's writing and in what one sees now. The 'history of events' in this tribal mode is dateless and is divided out between equals. The point can easily be made by reference to the passage leading up to that quoted earlier, the passage dealing with the chiefs of Ḥāshid.

> Al-'Abbās begat al-Ḍaḥḥāk, Rizām, and Sa'īd al-Ḥawālī, all of whom fought in the war with Bakīl. Rizām was killed by Abū 'Ayaynah al-'Abdī, the lord of Arḥab. Al-Ḍaḥḥāk begat Muḥammad, who was also chief and was assassinated by Ibn Mas'ūd the slave of Abū Yu'fir on the latter's orders. Hamdān were angered at this. Ḥāshid and Bakīl rose with al-Du'ām b. Ibrāhīm b. Ya's al-'Abdī, the lord of Bakīl, and overturned the Yu'firid kingdom. Muḥammad b. al-Ḍaḥḥāk begat Aḥmad Abū Ja'far . . . (al-Hamdānī 1948: 67)

This particular story can be told quite fully, but many of the details are found elsewhere in the book, attached to the Bakīl chief al-Du'ām b. Ibrāhīm, 'lord of Ḥamdān in his time and greater than all his predecessors, whether real or imagined, in his strength and his skill at arms . . .' (ibid. 179). We know from other accounts of the Yu'firids that Abū Yu'fir Ibrāhīm killed his father in about AD 882, and al-Hamdānī tells us that al-Du'ām visited him immediately afterwards. But al-Hamdānī does not himself give us a date either here or elsewhere.[25] The al-ʿAbdī lords of Arḥab are shown as first killing someone of the Ḥāshid Āl al-Ḍaḥḥāk and then avenging another in the face of outside aggression, illustrating perhaps the segmentary alternation one expects of tribes, but again there are no dates; and 'the war with Bakīl' is not dated either. The prescriptive equality of Bakīl and Ḥāshid depends on their actions being not commensurable, not reducible to a single story.

Tribes and sections share the terms of a moral world, but that world itself they divide between them and experience is conspicuously not shared. There will always be at least two versions of whatever happens (as a field-worker soon discovers), and the ranking of events by chronological sequence or parallel is foreign to the tribal view. It is perfectly apt that, for example, the 'story' of the tribes attacking the Yuʿfirid state should be split by al-Hamdānī between accounts of Ḥāshid's leading family and Bakīl's. It is only the opposition between tribes that gives most events their value. Such opposition can be expressed or exemplified but it cannot be explained, and accounts of conflict do not warp the symmetry of honour by showing change and subordination: so the wars between Ḥāshid and Bakīl, Hamdān and Khawlān, or Hamdān and Murād, for instance, (al-Hamdānī 1948; 55, 67, 86, 112, 162, 214, 251 and *passim*) are none of them dated and none of them won or lost.

By the same rationale, each line of descent in al-Hamdānī's account is potentially the equal of each other line, none coming first and none second. Nawf b. Hamdān b. Mālik, for example, had 'numbers and power/renown' (*al-ʿadad wa-l-ʿizz*) but Nawf's brother ʿAmr had equally 'honour and dominion' (*sharaf wa-mulk*; al-Hamdānī 1948: 11); Āl Abī Ḥātim, Banī Ṭarīf, Banī Ṣuraym, Āl al-Faraj of al-Ḥujayrāt, Jadhīmah of Shākir, and many others had all of them men who were 'knights' (*fursān*) of Hamdān, of Yemen, or indeed of Islam (ibid. 24, 51, 84, 225, 241, and *passim*); group after group boast men who were 'lords' and possessed the martial virtues (ibid. 65, 86, 98, 159, 179 and *passim*), some of them lord of Ḥāshid, Bakīl, or Hamdān 'in their time' (*fī ʿaṣri-hi*), and the times not being set in order to produce any settled ranking.

The linear sequence of events that would produce a ranking (so the lord of Ḥāshid, for example, controls more at present than the lord of Bakīl in the last generation) is avoided, and accounts of the events themselves (*akhbār*) are preserved as fragments attaching to potentially equivalent descent lines. Co-ordination, and thus commensurability, is not constructed. Each line has noble ancestors, and how far back one might have to go to establish equivalence between them is not registered; there is only the simultaneity of the various 'battle days' which indefinitely different men or groups on each side can cite in asserting their own worth. A great deal happens, therefore, but little is conceived to change. Inequality is not elaborated as rank, which is perhaps one further reason 'why one can write a history of Central Asia, but only about 'events' in pre-Islamic Arabia' (Crone 1980: 221 n. 163), or indeed about those aspects of Arabia later that are peripheral to Islamic literature.

A past had to be constructed to produce a coherent tradition, from which a coherent polity might then arise. The tribes of their nature cannot produce such coherence on either count, although tribesmen may of course be involved with these other modes of defining themselves and the world around them, as well as with identities of territory and collective honour. The learned tradition leaves this aside. In doing so it establishes only certain things as 'tribal' and makes them a residue of the attempt to promote Islamic order. Correspondingly, the tribal system, as we saw with al-Hamdānī's works, does not register inequality; and for tribesmen themselves to generalize a concern for order (to conceive, for instance, of 'good' periods and 'bad') requires they turn to the history of a dynasty or tradition. The chronology of the learned tradition is that of Muslims generally. It establishes a sequential history to which tribal identities of their nature (being non-sequential) are peripheral, regardless of their ethnographic importance at any given time.

What tribesmen were doing is not always invisible. For example, in accounts of al-Qāsim's great war against the Turks at the start of the seventeenth century one finds details of shaming support from the tribes by slaughtering beasts (*al-'ārah wa-l-ghūth*), of disputes over escort and guaranty, of claiming '*ayb*s for lack of promised support, and much else that is familiar nowadays (Nubdhah: 170, 218, 239, 301 and *passim*; cf. Chapters 2, 3, and 4 above). But the tribes are in effect the terrain which the Imams and the Turks cross in their battles, the mass of people whom they intimidate or appeal to for help, not a world with its own coherence. The actions of al-Qāsim and his opponents are chronicled in sequence (see also particularly *Rawḥ al-rūḥ*, 'Īsā b. Luṭfallāh 1981), but what changes the tribes underwent are not. The coherence of the world, in the learned view, attaches to a different set of connections.

For a Muslim chronicler (as indeed for his Christian counterpart), what might otherwise seem mere chronology and pointless 'rare but far-reaching events' (Ibn Farighūn, cited Rosenthal 1952: 33) are the evidence of unity. To say the same thing more drily, this care for chronology, for what appears mere succession, is what constitutes the uniformity that in turn allows synchronicity: if one cut across worldly events like a plant stem, there really would be a pattern; the Muslims or Yemenis really would share an experience that in sum, at a given time, had sense.[26] Accounts of events, in the chronicles, suppose a complementary literature which demonstrates precisely this, and both depend upon careful dating.

Besides the rigorously sequential writing of chronicles one finds a large literature of *tarājim* or collected biographies arranged in dictionaries. As elsewhere in the Arabic-speaking Islamic world, this does not at all follow the public course of events

> nor are political figures and events given special attention. On the contrary (and here in marked contrast to the Chinese tradition), political history is entirely incidental to the main structure of the works. Thus it is clear that the conception that underlies the oldest biographical dictionaries is that the history of the Islamic Community is essentially the contribution of individual men and women to the building up and transmission of its specific culture . . . (Gibb 1962: 54)

The recording of these personal connections first attained prominence with the organized study of the Prophet's traditions and the reliability of their transmission (ibid; Makdisi 1986: 174–5); indeed, the very notion of 'dating' (*ta'rīkh*, the word for all kinds of 'history') attaches to this same concern for transmission of lore from teacher to student (ibid. 178 ff.) But personal transmission remained essential. Al-'Amrī explains it extremely well in the case of the nineteenth-century Yemeni scholar al-Shawkānī.

> Usually the [teachers] give their distinguished students or disciples the authority (*ijāzah*, literally 'licence') to teach or relate a *ḥadīth* [a tradition of the Prophet] or a book on any subject. . . . In the *Muqaddimah* of Ibn al-Ṣalāḥ (577–643/1181–1242) the science of *Ḥadīth* reaches its zenith. But some later scholars found it necessary to explain and comment on the *Muqaddimah* as well. Among them, and probably one of the best, was Sirāj al-Dīn al-Bulqīnī (724–805/1324–1401). . . .

Four centuries later, in al-Shawkānī's time, the *ijāzah* method had not changed, but the number of authorities in its *isnād* (chain of authorities) . . . from generation to generation had doubled. . . . Al-Shawkānī . . . followed the steps of the famous ulema and scholars who wrote their own *asānīd* . . . like . . . that of . . . Abū Bakr b. Khayr (502–75/1108–79), to whom were ascribed more than one thousand and forty five books. (Al-'Amrī 1985: 107–8)

One is dealing with a tradition whose appearance is more intimidating than that of most western catalogues (there are fewer epitomes or introductions) and before which one is likely to be paralysed, not knowing where to begin any more than did Flaubert's Bouvard and Pécuchet with the knowledge of Europe.[27]

Beside these complex lines of learning embodied in a massive literature, any other kind of knowledge exists only as disconnected fragments. For instance, Nājī 'Abd al-Wahhāb al-Shāyif of Dhū Ḥusayn died in 1896, and we are told that 'he had knowledge of history and the science of astronomy' (Zabārah 1956: i. 2/204).[28] But he is mentioned only because he fought for the Imam as a warrior in God's cause against the Turks, rather as did his opposite number from Dhū Muḥammad, 'Abdullāh Nājī al-Dumaynī, who died in 1894 and, as he died, bequeathed his weapons and horses to the Muslims' treasury (ibid. 147). Such tribal figures may be knowledgeable in their own right, and may be pious, but they are marginal to formal learning and thus to righteous government.

Zaydism required there be a distinction between what, for the present purpose, we can call 'tradition' and 'custom'. The tribal world presents the claim that the tribes have always been as they are and that usage (*sinnah*, *'urf*) is unchanging, not reproduced by any formal system and not subordinate to any hierarchy of learning; the operative principle in customary judgment, correspondingly, is that settlement agree with *'urf al-jihah*, the custom of the plaintiff's group, and that truth as well as power be fragmented. Islamic learning, by contrast, is constructed explicitly in time and so is capable of forming a single story; its transmission, understanding, and application to circumstance is a matter of particular ties between mortal men, and, as with the original collecting of *ḥadīth* matter, some ties are worth more than others. The ordering of learned tradition is thus hierarchical and can apportion value to purely local knowledge or to those who possess such.

Everywhere there were *fuqahā'* (pl. of *faqīh*), who were scribes, writers of talismans, or merely men with a taste for books. But the *faqīh* in the Zaydi view (cf. Zabārah 1958: 483), which is to say 'properly speaking', was the person skilled in classical jurisprudence, who might judge the rectitude of these local claims[29] by drawing on a learned tradition which was validated by its careful production and was applicable to all localities. Some answers are demonstrably more correct than others, and beneath the right answer other questions should fall in place, so that certain details of local custom are not only *fiqh*'s opposite but can also be defined within it as ignorance or error. On the other hand, whatever of '*urf* or 'custom' is not judged wrong is included in the scope of what otherwise is its rhetorical opposite, *fiqh* ('jurisprudence') and *sharī'ah* ('Islamic law'). It was in this connection that Zaydism played hierarchy to the tribes' equality. Political dominance was only an 'expression' of this, which came and went, often rather rapidly, without deeply affecting the tradition's own reproduction.

The particularity of both chronicles and biographies in the Zaydi scheme is also striking. There is no denial of political events or of the passage of years (indeed, without the years the scheme would lose its validity), but there is no admitted change in the values by which people and events are judged. As elsewhere in pre-nationalist Islam, the 'system started from the idea that there is some principle which stands above the state and society . . . it found this principle in the teachings of a revealed region . . .' (Hourani 1981: 179). Indeed, the state, in the more precise sense this term has had in our own tradition since the Renaissance (the sense used by White, above; a collective agent) was correspondingly absent, and society itself was not conceived of explicitly as a whole that might act or be acted on. Everything was a matter of discrete connections.

The individual person, in the learned scheme, for instance, was important primarily on account of his relations with others. Biographies do not dwell on a personal 'life of the mind' or encapsulate personal experience: 'knowledge, as Locke conceives it, is part of the life history of the individual' (Alexander, quoted Barker 1947: xxiii), but it is not in the Zaydi scheme. Nor is society, or even learned tradition, 'individualized' in this way by the encapsulation of its past.[30] Events and people's actions in the past have lessons to teach, as few historians fail to mention in very standardized terms at the start of their works. But no collective individual is constructed, no 'state' as 'legal subject' (White 1980: 15), which would identify a cumulation of events or individual actions with the values in terms of which those actions are judged. The inconclusive particularity of the chronicles is, in that sense, not illusory. The history could indeed repeat almost endlessly and reproduce the imbalance between tradition and mere custom without the substance or illusion of collective change.

THE IMAMATE'S CONDEMNATION OF TRIBAL CUSTOM

> *Scire debes creatorem tuum dixisse: ego sum veritas non autem usus vel consuetudo.*
> (You are bound to know that your creator said: 'I am Truth', not just 'usage' or 'custom'.)
>
> St Cyprian, quoted by Pope Gregory

The order which Imams claimed to establish, and sayyids with their qadi adherents always claimed to promote (as many still do), was synonymous with the rule of Islamic law or *sharīʿah*.

> Basically *sharīʿah* is the law of the Prophet and his house, the Sayyids and Ashrāf, and they attempt to introduce it everywhere. Yet the tribes and other social groups, whose custom is sometimes at variance with *sharīʿah*, do not always willingly accept the latter. (Serjeant 1977: 242)

Certainly the sayyids might often have claimed so. In fact both Islamic law and tribal law are flexible in practice, and the number of points at which they are wholly incompatible is small. In such matters as blood-money, for instance, an assessment of damages is often sought from a scholar of Islamic law in the process of a settlement by custom. On the other hand, where those at odds have submitted to judgment by Islamic law, the forms of evidence, the structure of guaranty, and even the type of compensation are often not very different from tribal custom (see Dresch forthcoming *a*, *c*). One is usually dealing with something more like sovereignty or jurisdiction than like orthodoxy and heresy.

The sayyids themselves often differed from their neighbours not so much in their detailed practice as in the moral focus to which they referred their doubts. For example, a tribesman's interest in the tomb of a learned man may seem to an educated sayyid to be bound up with ignorant superstition (*khurāfah*), yet sayyids are the ones most prone to such visits; all depends upon intention (*niyah*), and the tribesmen's intention is distrusted. Again, in the histories or at present, a sayyid will not only throw down his turban to demand support (e.g. Nubdhah: 271), but will slaughter beasts for the tribes (ibid. 115, 434) and even demand from them beasts in apology (al-Sayāghī 1978: 56; Zabārah 1956: i. 2/387; cf. Chapter 2, above). Yet the tribesmen's killing beasts in this way arouses suspicion of *shirk* (associating other things with God by sacrificing both to God and to a person), and in the histories the practice is sometimes spoken of as 'their law' or 'their custom', as if something utterly foreign (e.g. al-Ḥibshī 1980: 148). The same worry must presumably rise from the standard phrase of protection pacts, 'in the security of God and of those who uphold the *hijrah*'. All such concerns can be referred to God's Book and to the Prophet's usage, as explained and applied by the learned tradition, but the failure to seek such reference raises fears that God's law is breached.

Tribal custom (*'urf*) and practice is often condemned in the Zaydi histories as *ṭāghūt*, a term from the Qur'ān that is sometimes translated (or mistranslated) 'idol' or even 'devil'.[31]

> Say: Shall I tell you who receives a worse recompense from God than those he has cursed, on whom his wrath has fallen and whom he has turned into apes and swine? The servants of the *ṭāghūt* have a worse place and stray further from the right path. (Qur'ān 5: 60)

> We have sent every nation a prophet to say: Serve God and spurn the *ṭāghūt*'. (Qur'ān 16: 36)

The 'rule of the *ṭāghūt*' recurs frequently in the histories as a phrase describing the fact that some tribal shaykh or another wields power, and the impression sometimes gained from the literature, or from talking to men of learning nowadays, is that *ṭāghūt* forms an organized code at odds with Islamic law (see Rathjens 1951; Serjeant 1977; Dresch 1984*b*). The reality, as we have seen, is less simple.

The Zaydi reading of Islamic law must itself have recognized much that would elsewhere be ignored or condemned—the very notion of tribal territory, after all, is problematic in the light of the Prophet's dictum that 'pasture, water, and fire' cannot be subject to restriction—but unfortunately the sources so far available provide little information on how such questions were resolved. One late eighteenth-century document discusses the problem in terms not so much of the letter of the law as of maintaining the public welfare (*maṣlaḥah*), a concept which gives tremendous latitude to the practice of Islamic law and which allows precisely the 'encompassment' of custom touched on earlier.[32]

In 1781 the Imam of the day (al-Manṣūr 'Alī b. al-Mahdī) asked Sayyid Aḥmad Ḥasan Isḥāq for an opinion on a border dispute between Banī al-Ḥārith and Banī Ḥushaysh, just outside Ṣan'ā', which had first flared up in the time of al-Mahdī Aḥmad (1676–81). The disputed grazing had been partitioned between the two tribes. A fresh round of disputes had later been judged by Ḥusayn Muḥammad 'Uthmān, who had reversed the previous decision and declared the disputed area free for all to use (*intahā amru-hu ilā ibāḥati-hi*). The case had then come to the Imam's *dīwān* and part of the disputed area had again been allotted to one of the two sides, but fighting had broken out with each side claiming to have a sound *sharī'ah* judgment in their favour. Which decision was correct?

The *fatwā* turns on the paramount importance of *ṣulḥ*, a term which in tribal contexts means simply truce (syn. *hudnah*), but which in self-consciously religious discourse associates naturally with the idea of a general peace and of godliness: 'that which is known as necessary according to the *sharī'ah* and the life of the Prophet is that one look to the good of [God's] servants and remove the causes of complaint between them.' The point at issue is that of equality or equity. Upholding this and setting people's affairs to rights is the particular responsibility of the Commander of the Faithful (the Imam) and of the judges, with the proviso (*mashrūṭan*) that this concern for the general good not impinge on personal or particular rights: preventing particular injustice is the first priority. In the present case, drawing limits for and granting rights to each side (*taḥdīd wa-takhṣīṣ kulli ṭā'ifah bi-ba'ḍ*) offered a reasonable way out of the problem (*manfadh al-shiqāq*), promoting precisely the 'union and brotherhood in God on high' that is looked for. The general principle is indeed that 'pasture, water, and fire' are not subject to private ownership, which accounts for the recognition of areas for wood-gathering, grazing, or collecting grass as held in common by the village. But the legality of each village claiming such areas as its own at the expense of other villages is upheld by the tradition of the Caliph 'Umar's treatment of restricted grazing (*ḥimā*) at Medina.[33] The important thing is to settle as the disputing parties wish and on a basis they will continue to observe (*taqrīr mā alafū-hu wa-istamarrū* '*alay-hi*). It is first of all incumbent on Imams and on Muslim judges to prevent further aggression, to settle matters fairly (to restore equality, *musāwāh*), and lift the hand of the tyrant from those he would oppress.

What perhaps is surprising is that no standard answer to the problem existed and that the Imam therefore felt the need to request an opinion. Where Yemeni tribalism is of its nature territorial and the Imamate recognized no such limits, the question must have recurred constantly; yet the Zaydi tradition gave tribalism no theoretical status. Its law, like Western law, was not a sociology. Nor yet was it any expression of sovereignty, although something very like sovereignty was at issue in its application. And one might note how long the case at hand lasted, not being solved definitively but transposed repeatedly into learned language over generations. Yet if individuals, reproducing social facts of the tribal world, appealed to other means of justice than Islamic law courts, they sinned by supporting 'the rule of *ṭāghūt*'.

A standard attribute of such wickedness is that women are denied the inheritance due them in Islamic law.[34] The ambiguities of that claim are revealed by Mundy (1979). Women may indeed be swindled by their menfolk, or they may receive their patrimony as cash and be excluded from the division of farmland (where Islamic law forbids the restriction of types of property by sex), and certainly their rights of inheritance through marriage may not be met explicitly; but the rules appealed to by villagers themselves are often thought to be those of Islam, and the division of property by an Islamic law expert may not be what that law envisages (ibid. 161, 167, 174, 178). The implication of many Zaydi sources that there is a distinct customary code at odds with Islam is scarcely borne out. Agreements quite contrary to the spirit of Islamic law did exist.[35] Usually, however, one is dealing with ambiguous complexities that the rhetorical opposition of '*urf* to *sharī'ah* only obscures. Indeed, a number of inheritance documents I have copied (and a great many I have seen) show strict Islamic form producing just the result for which custom is so often condemned, as with this case from Banī Ṣuraym at the turn of the present century.

There came to us the good-wife Fāṭimah bint Aḥmad in a sound state and chose lawful division of her property. She acknowledged that her marriage payment *(mahr)* accounted fully for the inheritance of her husband, and her debts and all her claims after his death. . . . She retains no rights, no claims, and no demands whatever against the living or the dead . . . except her patrimony.

In other words, her rights to inheritance from her husband are waived, and the holdings of her paternal and marital kin (both male defined) are thus kept separate. The point seems to be less where the inheritance ends up than the means by which it gets there; whether by informal arrangement or through the agency of an Islamic law clerk who would take payment for the trouble.

Again, the constant disputes between Imams and tribes over passage on the roads produced different outcomes according to the respective strength of those involved, but their significance in the histories is always the same and perhaps cumulative. Stookey (1978: 142) takes such disputes to show a 'loose authority pattern' (the sociological jargon does not obscure the fact that no pattern as such existed) and goes on to say: 'The tribes reserved the right of sanctioning passage through their territory not simply as a matter of local autonomy, but also as a way of accounting for the security of travellers, a task clearly beyond the capability of the Imam's own personnel' (ibid.). In fact the tribes might equally be called to account by the Imam or by other tribes, and the 'Imam's personnel' would in any case be tribesmen. Strong Imams did call them to account, and there is no more typical epithet for a successful Imam than that he had a 'white hand' in making roads secure (see e.g. Zabārah 1929: 155). But the significance of these forays goes beyond the very changeable minutiae of power. In the tribes' own usage, roads are 'secure and guaranteed', but the guaranty is provided by the tribe through whose territory a road runs and it is their right to 'cut' the roads as they 'cut off' relations with other tribes in the course of dispute. The prominent part played by trucks and road-blocks at the present day is consistent with the emphasis on roads in accounts of tribal Yemen at all periods.

Separate territories are the expression of separate peaces, each defined in opposition to others. From the point of view of an Imam (or indeed of the present state), however, interference with free passage is tantamount to secession; and in Islamic law 'cutting the road' is one of that limited number of offences for which there is a scripturally prescribed punishment or *ḥadd*.[36] Like the 'King's peace' and the 'King's highway' at certain junctures of English history, public order on the roads is the image of security under a single ruler, not a label for political facts.

Accusations of 'denying inheritance' and 'cutting the roads' apply to phenomena of very different scale. Yet the logic is the same in both. The concern of Zaydism is to deny the validity, and indeed the necessity, of action undertaken in terms of units larger than the single family or in any terms other than resort to public settlement between equal, individual Muslims. Egalitarian justice pervades the whole system, as it does the tribal scheme also; but the history of Upper Yemen turns for several centuries on whether the complex of separate concerns outlined earlier (Chapters 2, 3, and 4) should fall within a man's peace, a tribe's peace, or the peace of God. It may do so again, although sayyids are most unlikely to be those who take the question up. At every level in the tribal scheme, and in the most varied settings, there recurs a wish for unitary truth that would resolve all doubts and ensure for all time that men are indeed to be treated justly.

For the moment, there is only the inheritance of a long tradition which sets tribes at the moral margin. What is constantly clear to any literate person is the condemnation of tribal custom, and of tribesmen who dissent from Islamic law rulings (which is often to say from the Imam of the time), in terms tantamount to idolatry. The most various matters are thus conflated. Al-Hādī himself had been told that al-'Uṣaymāt offered a form of sexual hospitality to their visitors, and he said that such people stood in greater need of *jihād* than the Rūmī Byzantines (al-'Alawī 1972: 125). The same practice is condemned by a chronicler of the seventeenth century (Tritton 1925: 85), and the accusation persists even today (al-Iryānī 1968). Such things would certainly be the 'rule of *ṭāghūt*'. So would wine-drinking, which frequently gets historical mention. But so too would 'forbidding inheritance', with all its ambiguity, and so too would 'cutting the roads'. A nineteenth-century Ṣan'ānī chronicle gives the flavour: the city was cut off by the tribes, food ran short, and the townsfolk clamoured for help until the emissary of an Imam arrived; then 'the people became calm and the roads were secured and the power of the *ṭāghūt* was effaced' (al-Sayāghī 1978: 74). What from our point of view would be sin and mere disorder are run together in blanket condemnation, to the point where the tribes are rhetorically opposed by others to the religion they themselves espouse: 'God comforted the Muslims and the tribes ran away' (al-Ḥibshī 1980: 24).

NOTES

1. The text is sufficiently similar to those cited in the previous chapter that there seems no need to reproduce it. The list of signatories is given in app. 4/2.
2. The widely accepted list of fourteen 'conditions' an Imam must meet is given by Strothman (1934, also Sharaf al-Dīn 1968: 160–1). At one period or another there was quite widespread disagreement on the nature of the Imamate, which even went so far as questioning the degree to which eligibility was restricted within the Prophet's kin (see Madelung 1971: 1166; Sharaf al-Dīn 1968: 158–9). At some periods, also, the Imam was looked to less as a paragon of learning in his own right than as a necessary peace-maker of the kind one more usually associates with Sunni theories: see particularly al-Shawkānī's biography (1929: i. 376) of al-Mahdī 'Abdullāh, who was far more a warrior than a scholar but whose claim to the Imamate in 1816 al-Shawkānī none the less supported. Cf. Zabārah 1929: ii. 64 and al-Shawkānī's own comments (1929: i. 487) on al-Manṣūr 'Alī's claim to the Imamate in 1390.
3. Again and again one finds Imams making peace between two tribes and then turning them together against an external enemy, as if relief at their new-found truce took the form of hostility toward outsiders (see e.g. Yaḥyā b. al-Ḥusayn 1968: 208 ff.; al-Laḥjī MS 1: 87). Where this did not happen, the Imam's attempts to punish or constrain members of a tribe sometimes set against him the whole tribe whose prerogatives or inviolability had been usurped (see e.g. al-'Alawī 1972: 332; Yaḥyā b. al-Ḥusayn 1968: 298).
4. To examine conceptions of the link between heaven and earth would be a work in itself, but it is worth stressing the Zaydi unwillingness to countenance direct mediation, if only because North African material carries such weight in anthropology and the present case is very different. I have never heard a tribesman speak seriously of *barakah* as something that could be acquired from other persons.

   Certainly some people were treated this way, as for example, when a tribesman was cured of sickness by eating the seal from one of al-Hādī's letters (al-'Alawī 1972: 139), and, as Serjeant suggests (1979: 119 n. 44), Imams were often associated with the 'mercy' of rainfall. However, in the lives of the later Imams their *karāmāt* (a word which in other traditions might well translate as 'miracles') are usually rather sober: winning battles, leaving benefactions, and treating people generously.

   Again, Eickelman (1977: 50) explains that, in rural Morocco, *bekri* ('early times') 'refers to an atemporal horizon in which uncanny events occur and certain persons, marabouts, are attributed . . . the ability to perform acts which have no parallel in ordinary social life . . .' The nearest equivalent in Upper Yemen would be temporal, in so far as it is pre-Islamic, and would refer, not to men of religion, but to tribesmen's own predecessors: the 'first people' (*awwalīn*) are sometimes spoken of, for instance, as having moved huge rocks or carried all the soil up to mountain terraces from a valley floor.

5. As Gochenour points out (1984: 132), there is in fact a major yearly gathering of tribes around the tomb of al-Mahdī Ḥusayn b. al-Qāsim al-'Iyānī near Raydah, which seems to him similar to the gathering of the tribes around al-Qāsim himself in the early eleventh century (ibid. 146 n. 151). I would go a step further and hazard the suggestion that the particular villages involved (as opposed to the crowds who attend at the periphery) are very probably those implicated in the death of al-Ḥusayn in 1013. From an ethnographic point of view, however, what is interesting is that the tribesmen involved have not a clue who al-Ḥusayn is, very few even enter the tomb, and this utterly North African looking event, with the crowds set around the little white-washed cupola, has, as it were, a hollow centre. So far as the tribesmen are concerned, it might almost as well take place around a hole in the ground, although the gathering itself (the *tahjīr*) is important to them.
6. The pure *ṭabaqāt* form goes back to the early centuries of Islam when, for example, Ibn Sa'd (d. 845) connected his own time to that of the Prophet through several generations. In a Yemeni context a medieval writer, Musallim al-Laḥjī (d. *c.*1165–70), connected the first Zaydi Imam to himself and his teachers through five such *ṭabaqāt*; but as he says himself (MS IV: 294) in introducing the fifth of these, 'some of them come earlier in time and some later'. The generational format is unwieldy. It tends to give way either to the biographical dictionary or to the linear chronicle.
7. To take just one example, 'Abd al-Qādir al-Kawkabānī travelled to, among other places, Shahārah (al-Ahnūm), al-Kibs (Khawlān), and Dhībīn (Khārif) (Zabārah 1929: 45). One has to plot only a few such itineraries to cover Yemen with a dense web of ties. When tribesmen, by contrast, move on anything but brief visits they change tribes, and their point of reference is then their present identity, not the list of their previous contacts. The political significance of learned connections is touched on in Dresch forthcoming *d*.
8. The Zaydi use of 'Qarmatian' to describe their enemies should be treated cautiously. So far as I know, there is no historical connection established with the actual Qarāmiṭah. The term itself has been revived in recent times, however, to condemn the communists in South Yemen (see al-Shahārī's refutation, 1972: 196 ff.). For accounts of Yemen just before and during the beginning of the Zaydi enterprise see Van Arendonk 1960 ch. 2: 107–26 and Gochenour 1984, ch. 2.

'The coming of the Zaydi Imams probably meant the beginning of the real Islamization of the north . . .' (Serjeant 1969: 291), and there are certainly intriguing hints of conservatism at a much later date than this; for instance, the tribes of Khawlān in al-Laḥjī's time MS IV: 337) would not use the name of God but only the epithet 'al-Raḥmān', which puts one in mind of the last pre-Islamic inscriptions from the area. However, the suggestion that, for instance, there were Jewish tribes in al-Bawn, or that the Āl Dhū La'wah of Raydah 'may well have been Jewish' (Gochenour 1984: 57 n. 23, 286 n. 87), is more adventurous than the evidence warrants. The *Sīrah* of the first Imam would hardly have missed mentioning such things had they been true. The presence of mosques and of learned men, and not least al-Hamdānī's own fascination with 'Alī's battles in the early years of Islam, are enough to suggest Islam's importance for the tribesmen. What form Islam took in the area is another question. There is an intriguing mention, for instance, of tribesmen demanding 'by the *ḥaqq* of 'Alī b. Abī Ṭalib' that the Imam's application of *ḥadd* be revoked (al-'Alawī 1972: 120).

9. For the present purpose, al-Hamdānī's other extant works can be left aside. It deserves to be stressed, however, how many contemporary practices of his time seem to correspond with what one sees now: for instance, multiple blood-money was paid (1977: 66–7), weapons were exchanged as pledges (1966: 304), territory could be closed to other tribes (1948: 103), and refuge given to men at odds with their own people (ibid. 215). Despite these familiar features, Upper Yemen may well have been in a state of transition from a quasi-feudal system to the tribal one (Gochenour 1984: 36 ff.; Dresch forthcoming *b*).
10. The early Zaydi sources also characterize tribal chiefs as *sādah* (e.g. al-'Alawī 1972: 128). Discussing events of the eleventh century AD al-Laḥjī (MS IV: 31) seems still to use *ashrāf* as a tribal title. Quite when these terms became restricted to the Prophet's descendants is unclear.
11. The Imam had imprisoned the poet and genealogist al-Hamdānī, whose 'proto-nationalist' differences with the Zaydi sayyids are again a live issue in our own time: see the references provided in Serjeant 1979: 116, al-Shāmī 1979, and now the extremely interesting work of Zayd 1981, to which al-Maqāliḥ 1982 is in the nature of an 'official' reply. In medieval times (twelfth century AD), Nashwān al-Ḥimyarī revived the 'pro-Yemeni' position and enjoyed a brief career as the country's self-proclaimed saviour before recanting and supporting the Zaydis (see the editors' introduction to al-Ḥimyarī 1957).
12. It deserves to be said that where, as Gochenour mentions, Ḥusayn and Jesus were seen together, they were usually accompanied by Khiḍr (al-Laḥjī MS IV: 260, 291, 336). Khiḍr occupies a curious position in Islamic folklore. He is not conspicuous in the Qur'ān (his identification with the figure who encounters Moses is apocryphal), and references to any interest in him are very sparse in the literature; but in Yemen, as elsewhere, Khiḍr is the subject of innumerable tales told to children at their mother's knee. We shall encounter Khiḍr again very briefly in ch. 6.
13. This spread of sayyid families from the north into Yemen is admirably documented by Gochenour (1984: 150–66), whose work is extremely helpful on the sociology of the period.
14. For an account of the last major Qāsimī princes (late eleventh century), who legitimized themselves as waiting for their 'hidden

Imam', see Madelung 1979. Ḥamzah b. Abī Hāshim claimed the Zaydi leadership in 1060 but only as an Imam *muḥtasib* (Zabārah 1952: 93–4), one lacking the conditions to be full Imam and thus restricted, for instance, to defensive war. He too was killed by the Ṣulayḥids.

15. It is Madelung's contention (forthcoming) that the term *hijrah* before this had only its Zaydi meaning of 'emigration' (whether to the righteous Imam or away from oppression) and was quite distinct from the indigenous term *hajar*. The latter is explained by Nashwān al-Ḥimyarī, writing in the mid-twelfth century, as follows: 'The *hajar* of a tribal group (*qawm*) is the place of its power/repute (*'izz*) and is where they assemble' (1916: 108), which is much what one might say of a tribal *hijrah* nowadays. I hope it is clear from the present chapter and the last that a conception of 'setting apart' is common to the modern term's several instances. One can entirely agree with Madelung's position on the medieval history of the specifically Zaydi terms and still stress the structural resemblance of the ideas behind them and the local usage.

16. The distinction between Upper and Lower Yemen can be traced back almost as far as one wishes, to the distinction between Saba' and Ḥimyar, and then again in al-Hamdānī's work where chiefs in Upper Yemen are sayyids and those in Lower Yemen are *mulūk* (Wilson 1980: 39 n. 38). The Ṣulayḥid state (late eleventh century) had removed to Lower Yemen, and there is a famous passage in which Queen Arwā contrasts the armed and belligerent northerners with the prosperously bucolic southerners (Yaḥyā b. al-Ḥusayn 1968: 271; Kay 1892: 63, cited Stookey 1978: 68–9; Gochenour 1984: 19). Under the Ayyūbids and Rasūlids, Lower Yemen was organized, administered, and taxed by an elaborate state apparatus quite different from anything found north of Ṣan'ā'; see Stookey 1978 ch. 5.

17. The extent to which the Imamate was at one period or another 'state-like' in the view of its adherents remains moot. The language of the early centuries was of a *da'wā* or 'summons' against ungodly oppression. In modern times, chroniclers (e.g. al-Sayāghī 1978: 77; al-Ḥibshī 1980: 309) write unselfconsciously of the *daywalah*, an Imam 'taking power' very much as a king might, and the same perception may well have been shared by non-sayyids from the outset. The tribes who had supported al-Hādī, for example, supported al-Nāṣir against the Ismā'īlīs in the following terms: 'Up stood the Mālikī leader, whose name was Muḥammad b. Ibrāhīm, one of the leading men of the tribe and the greatest speaker among them . . . "O clans (*ma'ashar*) of Hamdān, you know of this honourable state/dynasty (*dawlah*), blessed by God . . . We swore to support the Prophet's kin, . . . our sons and our sons' sons to the end of time"' (al-Laḥjī MS I: 100).

A *da'wā* may itself be a highly organized apparatus of state, as it was with the Ismā'īlīs in Yemen (see Hamdānī 1976), but the Zaydi system was in essence sparse. An Imam *muḥtasib* (one who lacked the full range of conditions, usually those of learning) could not carry out the legal punishments, nor collect alms and taxes (Madelung

1971: 1166): in other words, he was denied the basic sinews of statecraft.

18. This is not the place for a bibliographical excursus (details on available sources are provided in Sayyid 1974 and al-Ḥibshī 1983), but the history of Upper Yemen in the relevant period really begins with three 'lives': that of al-Hādī (published as al-'Alawī 1972), that of al-Nāṣir (quoted extensively in al-Laḥjī MS 1, and the events are well covered in Yaḥyā b. al-Ḥusayn 1968, but the work itself is not available), and that of al-Qāsim al-'Iyānī (unpublished MS). From then on, although little has been published and it remains unclear how much is extant, such lives are a salient part of the historiography right down to our own time.

19. One has to be wary here of adding one's own link of causality and making such statements more quasi-magical than they ever were. For instance, many Yemenis who were greatly attached to President Ibrāhīm al-Ḥamdī (assassinated in 1977) said years later that, 'In Ibrāhīm's time it rained.' The judgement was parallel to that we often make ourselves about politicians and the state of the economy, which, were we taxed with it, we might be hard put to explain in detail.

20. See e.g. Yaḥyā b. al-Ḥusayn 1968: 414, 415, 427: 'Nothing occurred in this year [620/1223] that requires recording'; 'No peculiar story occurred in this year [622/1225]'; 'Nothing occurred in this year [693/ 1245–6) or those following that requires mention'. The intervening entries are, by contrast, rather full.

21. An example from the very last of the chroniclers (Zabārah 1956: iii. 76–7) should be enough to show what is at issue: 'On the morning of Wednesday, 7th Sha'bān in this year [5 April 1922] the Imam left Ṣan'ā' accompanied by . . . [there are ten names given, including 'him who is writing down these words'] . . . with the intention of enforcing a truce between Ḥāshid and Bākil to end the dissension that had arisen between the people of al-Ẓāhir in Ḥāshid and 'Iyāl Surayḥ and 'Iyāl Yazīd . . . That night the Imam stayed in the village of al-Mu'ammar in Hamdān, and the second night in the town of 'Amrān. On the morning of Friday the 9th of that month he moved from there to Raydah in al-Bawn, where he said Friday prayers . . .' There then follows an account of where exactly everyone went on each day until they arrived back in Ṣan'ā' 'on Tuesday 28 Sha'bān in this year'. What the dispute was about, whether it was successfully resolved, why all these particular people went and not others is nowhere mentioned. The author simply moves on to the next event of that year, which was the arrival of Amīn Rihānī and his friend in Ṣan'ā'.

22. As Waldman 1981 suggests, White's attempt rests too heavily on European presumptions (modern ones at that) to sit quite easily with Islamic material. Indeed, chronicles are characterized throughout in negative terms (e.g. 'refusal of narrative'), which, although apt for White's purpose, is not a strategy open to anthropologists. Nonetheless, Waldman's article and White's together provoke one to think about the cultural value of linear historiography. Anthropologists' interests

have so far been focused on non-linear, and therefore more obviously exotic, forms.

A tenth-century writer characterizes history itself in the sort of terms that caught White's attention: '(1) History (*'ilm al-ta'rīkhāt*) is based upon rare events of far-reaching significance, such as a deluge, an earthquake, an epidemic, or a famine. (2) It is necessary to know the succession of dynasties, and the rulers . . .' (Ibn Farighūn cited and translated, Rosenthal 1952: 33). And so on to item (10) 'the history of persons of noble birth, scholars, secretaries, poets . . .' The order of these items can be reversed (see al-Sakhāwī cited ibid. 204–5; Gibb 1962: 55; Makdisi 1986: 179), but what White sees as 'liminal' events seem always associated with this location of persons with respect to others.

23. Al-Haytham died *c.*AD 821/2 (Rosenthal 1952: 65; Makdisi 1986: 184). Monographs of *akhbār* and genealogies were being written decades later (Duri 1962: 62), but this 'History year by year' (no longer extant) is one of the earliest cited annals, and the author himself was known as a collector of *akhbār* or 'tales'. He serves to mark a transition. In the wider Arab world, historians in the eighth and ninth centuries AD were usually also genealogists; but after the ninth century the genealogical idea recedes everywhere but the Muslim far west (Rosenthal 1952: 84–5).

24. Gellner 1964: 1 says that 'the way in which time and its horizons are conceived is generally connected with the way [a] society understands and justifies itself'. I am inclined to state the case more strongly. A society is itself defined by continuity, if not stability, by comparison with which its component people and groups might be identified with contingency or with duration (Pocock 1967). Without society it is hard to imagine what time amounts to, although a society may of course define itself without generalizing a concept of time (Evans-Pritchard 1940; Bohannan 1967; Peters 1977). Nor need individuals be given explicit value in opposition to collective time schemes (Geertz 1966). The layering of different constructions of continuity in complex societies is itself equivalent to the layering of different social identities, as Eickelman suggests in his discussion of modern Morocco (1977).

25. The only conspicuous date in the tenth volume of the *Iklīl* is 290/903, which concerns the extinction of a line closely collateral to al-Hamdānī's own (al-Hamdānī 1948: 200). So long as a line existed, its exchanges of violence and renown with others remained open-ended and the kind of final or interim 'tally' implied by dating was not constructed. Al-Hamdānī is not shy of providing chronological parallels elsewhere, particularly with the early battles of Islam, and the lack of a chronology of his own is to be seen as reflecting the concerns that inform his work, not a lack of sources.

26. The Saussurean idea of synchronicity has lost favour in anthropology. But something very like it is constructed by any unified historiography. When Althusser attacks the similar idea of an 'essential section' which he finds in Hegel (Althusser and Balibar 1970: 93–103), he invites one

correspondingly to think about what the 'homogeneous continuity' of such ideological time in fact does. The resemblance of Muslim historiography and early Christian European works is of interest here. Apart from such obvious cases as *The Anglo-Saxon Chronicle*, one might, for instance, look at Bede. The parallel is not exact (there is no Islamic church and no canon law as such), but when one compares Bede's drama of the timing of Easter as an expression of moral unity (1968: 101, 137, 147, 186, 323, 329) with the concern for synchronicity explained in Makdisi's brilliant article on Islamic biography (1986: 176–7), the common-sensical notion of time as something one might simply 'perceive' (Bloch 1977) has to be dropped.

27. The major part of Bouvard and Pécuchet's problem was that all subjects seemed of equivalent worth to them, a haunting and ridiculous version of that denial of hierarchy which Dumont (1986: 236–7 and *passim*) associates with individualism. In learned Islam, subjects were very definitely not equivalent (for a clear explanation of Sunni Mecca see Hurgronje 1970: 157 ff.). Al-'Amrī (1985: 111–14) provides a very useful account of what al-Shawkānī saw involved in this intellectual pursuit of a unified truth, and al-Shawkānī's own *Adab al-ṭalab* repays attention.

28. What history al-Shāyif knew (the Imam's poem on him mentions 'origins' or 'genealogy', *ansāb*; ibid. 205) was not a commentary on earlier work, nor was it commented on itself by students later. It appears and disappears without issue. Such interests were not suppressed, and we find, for example, a learned man of the late middle ages described also as *'āliman bi-l-'arabiyyah wa-akhbāri l-'arab yurwā 'an-hu ḥubbu l-mufākharah li-l-qabā'il bi-qawmi-hi* (al-Laḥjī MS IV: 334). But such things are irrelevant to *ta'rīkh*.

29. Uneducated tribesmen could interpret such learned hierarchies in their own terms. In the Jawf one finds the term *fuqahā'* used of educated *qarār* or *jīrān*, 'protected weak people', who often are mosque custodians (so a job that might elsewhere be holy is instead that of lowly people), and they are reckoned quite different from qadis. On the plateau one finds *fuqahā'* used of tribesmen and others (such as ex-Jews) who have acquired learning, but again they are reckoned different from the qadis, of whom one often hears it said that all of them are 'Umayyads' pre-dating the sayyids. In some areas (e.g. Sufyān) one comes across *jīrān* who are referred to as *mutafaqqahīn* but even so remain *jīrān*. A great many of the distinctions that the educated associate with learning are recuperated by the tribesmen in terms of birth.

30. 'Encapsulation', of course, is from Collingwood (1961), and the mention of individuals is intended to suggest Dumont (1986). The point at issue will, I hope, be the subject of a separate paper; but readers interested in the question may care to look for themselves at Collingwood's account of historical individuals (be they single persons or collectivities) as constituted by the 'inclusion' of their past

(Collingwood: 1961: 162). Suffice it to say here that the mode of individuation in this Western scheme is common to persons and to collectivities such as states, and the hierarchy of value which Dumont supposes to be missing in the West in fact inheres in the language of history. In the classical Indian system it may well be that hierarchy, quite differently constructed, discounts the individual person and event alike. Islamic Yemen offers an interesting *tertium quid*.

31. The term *ṭāghūt* was also used of course by the Wahhābīs and has gained a certain renown from Khomeini's use of it to describe America. In early times it may have included the sense of 'customary law' (Serjeant 1962: 42). If one looks in Ibn Isḥāq's *Sīrah* of the Prophet (Guillaume 1955: 735, under Ibn Hishām's n. 320), one finds a discussion of what it might denote, and the implication seems to be that the precise meaning had been lost very early in the northern lands of Islam, although the term was no less emotive for that.

32. The same invocation of *maṣlaḥah* occurs in a much later document I have translated elsewhere (Dresch forthcoming *c*). The document discussed here is to be found in *Majmū‘* 35 (27–8) in the Western Library of the Great Mosque, Ṣan‘ā'.

33. 'I swear by God they shall never see themselves wronged by me. It is their land which they fought over in the *jāhiliyyah* and on which they live peacefully / as Muslims in the time of Islam. By Him who holds my life in his hand, even on that land which I hold in God's cause I shall not forbid them [use of] even a foot of their own territory' (see al-Bukhārī's *Ṣaḥīḥ*).

34. The anthropological literature on marriage and inheritance in the Middle East is enormous. It used once to be argued, however (see e.g. Patai 1965), that endogamy kept property in the family. But the learned accusation that women are denied inheritance (so endogamy, on the old argument, would not be an issue) is in fact quite generally accompanied by the accusation that endogamy is enforced, that women are made to marry their close agnatic relatives. Causal arguments about 'corporate groups' are usually beside the point; more important is that both inheritance and endogamy provide expressions of a concern with moral autonomy (ch. 2, above; see also Keyser 1974), on which tribesmen and the learned had different views.

35. For example, at about the turn of the century there seems to have been a formal agreement between Banī Ṣuraym and al-‘Uṣaymāt that marriages between the two tribes would involve no transfer of rights to land. This would certainly have aroused the wrath of the Imams, for whom the same result could be achieved legally only by each woman's formal 'dropping' (*isqāṭ*) of her personal claim. In many tribesmen's view good families would in any case drop claims to land that arose from marrying one's daughters or sisters. It would be a poor set of affines who pressed their claim and then sold the woman's property to outsiders or retained it themselves to everyone's inconvenience. The letter of Islamic law, of course, says nothing about such local estimations of moral worth.

36. Al-Hādī himself acted against those who 'cut the road' (al-'Alawī 1972: 82), so did al-Nāṣir (al-Laḥjī MS I: 78), the theme continues through early modern times (e.g. al-Jirāfī 1951: 164) and down through the nineteenth century (e.g. al-Wāsi'ī 1928: 60, 72). The important point for the present purpose is the fixity of the rhetoric: it does not so much report a succession of like events as define a relation between Imams and tribes.

6 History from the Qāsimīs to the Ḥamīd al-Dīn (*c.*1600–1950)

The Imam of Sana, and the Sheriffe of Mecca, entertain each several regiments of those highlanders. . . . They must have officers of their own nation; and the Schiechs usually . . . raise the regiments. . . . When they go to war with the sovereign of Sana, their countrymen in his service desert and join them.

Niebuhr, *Travels through Arabia*

The apparatus of formal learning set tribes at the margin of Islamic government, but tribesmen were at all times involved with Zaydi history. In the present chapter we shall follow the history through from the Zaydi expansion of the seventeenth century to the disasters of the nineteenth, the Turkish occupation before the First World War, and the rise of the dynasty of powerful Imams who held North Yemen until the 1960s. Certain features of the tribal world are indeed almost timeless. Others cannot be understood without reference to the rest of Yemen, to events linking Yemen to the wider world, and, in short, to the course of regional history. In particular, the fortunes of tribal leaders were bound up with those of successive Imams.

THE QĀSIMĪ EXPANSION: THE SEVENTEENTH AND EIGHTEENTH CENTURIES

In response to growing Portuguese strength in the Indian Ocean, a Circassian Mameluke army was sent to Yemen from Egypt in 1515. The Mamelukes destroyed the Ṭāhirid state that ruled Lower Yemen at the time but were prevented from tackling the Zaydi Imam in his turn by the Ottoman invasion of Egypt (1517), and, when they withdrew, the Imam Sharaf al-Dīn extended his own influence down to Aden; but in 1538 the Ottomans themselves dispatched an army and within ten years conquered Upper Yemen, beginning a century of often fiercely resisted occupation. Al-Qāsim

b. Muḥammad claimed the Imamate in 1597 and fought the Turks for slightly more than two decades.[1] When he died in 1620, his son al-Mu'ayyad Muḥammad took the Imamate and renewed the war, but it was not until 1636 that the Turks were all driven out and the Zaydis came to hold all Yemen.

The armies which expelled the Turks were drawn largely from the northern tribes, and the tribesmen spread with the conquest. This was not the first time they had come west and south (nor was it to be the last), but the Qāsimī expansion was certainly a major episode of this kind, and many families of northern descent who are shaykhs (often considerable landowners) in Lower Yemen or the western mountains trace their migration to approximately this period (Messick 1978: 50; Tutwiler 1987). Shaykhs who remained in the north also gained control of land beyond their own territory. Elsewhere in the country there emerged what were almost distinct traditions, some of them highly unorthodox.[2] But the tribal shaykhs and successive Imams, whether in alliance or competition, always regained control and reserved the great struggles of the time to themselves.

Under al-Qāsim, in the early seventeenth century, areas had been apportioned to the control of sayyids, but the leadership of armies had often devolved on shaykhs; and shaykhs had, for example, controlled strategic western forts well outside their own territory (see e.g. Nubdhah: 106, 121, 131, 172). Some of them may have been associated with such areas for as much a century already, much as shaykhs had held western forts in Rasūlid times.[3] But they now held them for the Imam and were under his eye. They were becoming part of a larger and more prosperous political whole.

At times of truce, al-Qāsim had acted against some of the tribes' own practices: for example, he put a stop to pilgrimages and sacrifices at a tree near Wādī Mawr and flogged men from al-Ahnūm for drinking (ibid. 338); his appointee even wheedled out of the tribes their 'books of *ṭāghūt*' and duly burned them (ibid. 435). Under al-Qāsim's successors, however, the tribes were treated carefully. Al-Mu'ayyad (1620–44), for example, seems not to have pressed the point of Islamic inheritance law and to have left the taxation of Baraṭ in the hands of Bayt al-'Ansī, while his successor, al-Mutawakkil (1644–76), paid the tribes of Baraṭ to support his campaign against Ḥaḍramawt (Serjeant 1983: 79–82). Aden and Laḥj, which had already seceded, were retaken; a decade later al-

Bayḍā' and Yāfi' were subdued; Ḥaḍramawt was invaded; and the Zaydi arms were carried at one point to the borders of Dhufār in what is now Oman. The Qāsimīs also became involved in, though they did not conquer, areas north of Najrān and 'Asīr: 'the conquests spread with the support of the Hamdān tribes and the leadership of the Qāsimī family' (al-Shamāḥī 1972: 145), and al-Mutawakkil moved his capital from Shahārah to Ḍawrān, south of Ṣan'ā'. The state (now called a *dawlah* by its own chroniclers) had to link the north, where armed force still lay, to the richer tax base of Lower Yemen.

Besides the wealth to be extracted from the southern peasantry, the Imams of the period also had available, if they could retain control, taxes from a burgeoning coffee trade. The rise and fall of the Yemeni coffee trade with Europe matches almost exactly the trajectory of the Imamate's wealth (see Boxhall 1974; Niebuhr 1792). The English and Dutch established factories at Mocha in 1618; the trade was probably at its height around 1730; and the world price of coffee finally crashed at the start of the nineteenth century, at which point one gets mention of Imams debasing the currency (al-'Amrī 1985: 59). This wealth, however, had always to be fought for; the rulers became wealthier and more powerful than hitherto, but still were liable to dispute among themselves.

The state the Qāsimīs formed in the midst of this was none the less impressive (for the rulers' genealogy see Fig. 6.1). Al-Qāsim himself, who early in his fight against the Turks had wept over his children starving at Baraṭ, was wealthy when the truce was signed. He built the mosque at Shahārah, then built houses for himself and his followers, planted coffee in al-Ahnūm, and amassed more land than the public treasury (Nubdhah: 258, 334–6). The court expanded with the southern conquests. Al-Mutawakkil received an embassy from Ethiopia and exchanged gifts of fine horses with Aurangzib of India (Serjeant 1983: 80–1), while his relatives expressed concern about his monthly demands for funds from Lower Yemen. Further criticism of his taxation policy came from Muḥammad al-Ghurbānī at Baraṭ, but in 1675 the levies on Lower Yemen were redoubled (ibid. 82). Under Muḥammad Aḥmad, 'He of al-Mawāhib'[4] (1687–1718), the exactions became more severe still, in support of a grandiose court and a large standing army complete with slave soldiers (ibid., Zabārah 1958: 451, 457; al-Shawkānī 1929: ii. 98).

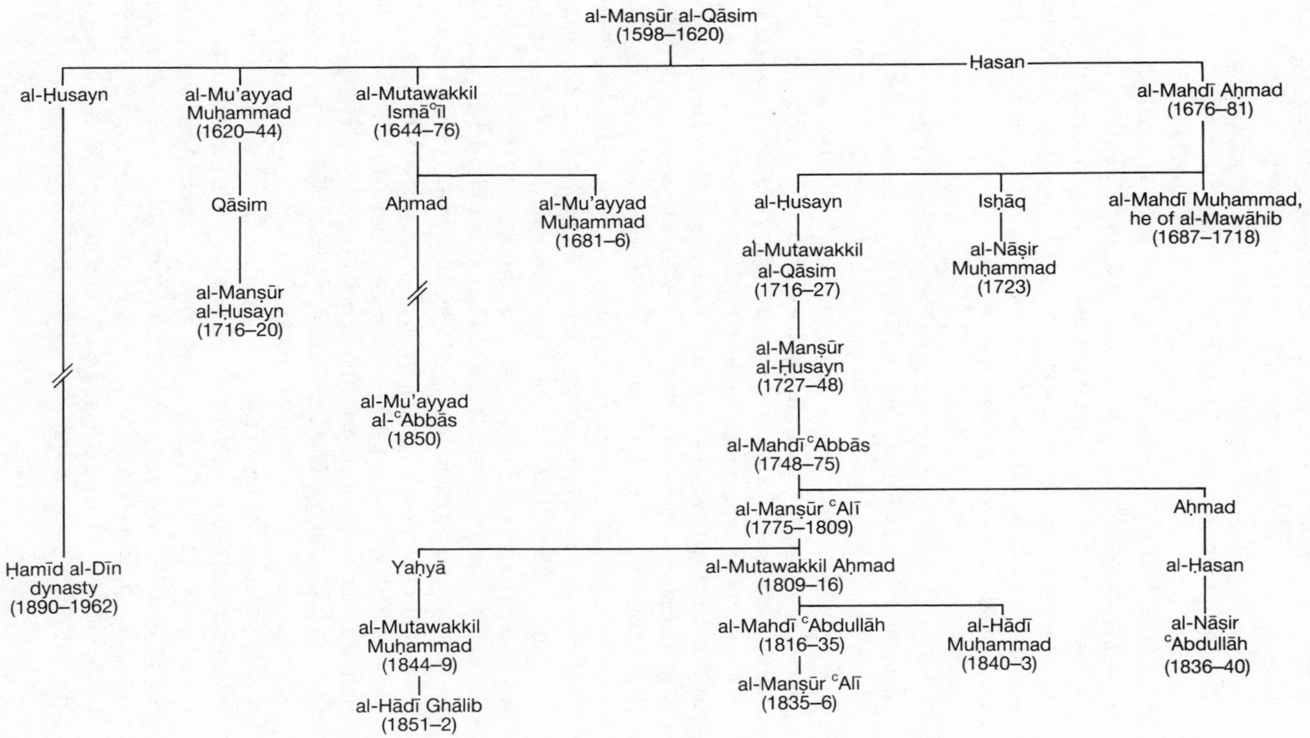

FIG. 6.1 Summary of the Qāsimīs (1598–1852)

At precisely this period, and in the space of a decade, the names of several great shaykhly families important nowadays all appear for the first time: al-Aḥmar of Ḥāshid, for instance, Juzaylān of Dhū Muḥammad, and Ḥubaysh of Sufyān. Some of the lesser shaykhly houses, such as al-Ziyādī, al-Rammāḥ, ʿImrān, al-Ghashmī, and al-Barawī, are attested as much as a century earlier (see e.g. Nubdhah: 111, 121, 123, 175, 453). Many of the tribal divisions familiar nowadays had been present far longer, as readers will have gathered from Chapter 5, but the leading families now identified with them appear only at this later date. They were associated with the state and with events elsewhere than in tribal territory.

Ṣāliḥ Ḥubaysh of Sufyān is first mentioned in 1698 as putting down a revolt of Raymah and Waṣāb (south-west of Ṣanʿāʾ) against al-Mawāhib's governor: women's earrings taken by his men were sold in Ṣanʿāʾ with fragments of ear still attached, provoking certain *ʿulamāʾ* to preach against Ḥubaysh's cruelty (Zabārah 1958: 670). Then, after a disastrous attempt on Yāfiʿ (in what is nowadays South Yemen), which resulted in Ibb being lost to the tribes of the eastern desert, al-Mawāhib called to account the northern tribes who had failed him. In 1702 he sent his nephew to deal with 'Hamdān and their chief Ibn Ḥubaysh', but a truce was made instead (ibid. 428; Zabārah 1941: 297). Five years later, after another failure in Yāfiʿ, al-Mawāhib sent al-Qāsim b. al-Ḥusayn and Ṣāliḥ Ḥubaysh to Khamir to deal with Ḥāshid, where the two fell out. In 1709 Ḥubaysh was again sent to Khamir by al-Mawāhib, this time to deal with al-Qāsim, but Ḥubaysh was finally tricked and killed there (ibid. 778–80; Zabārah 1958: 357).

In the intervening period he had been placed in charge of an army to fight the tribes of the east and Yāfiʿ. Al-Mawāhib had ordered his minister to strike a balance between Ḥubaysh and Bin Juzaylān of Dhū Muḥammad (again, this is the earliest clear reference to this famous family), but the governor's own aim was to balance the pair of them with the eastern tribes whom the Imam wanted conquered. The result of his intrigue was that the two Bakīl chiefs opposed each other and the easterners won (ibid. 875; Zabārah 1941: 773). Soon after this Ḥubaysh was sent with al-Qāsim b. al-Ḥusayn to Ḥūth, and the Imam's men razed a house nearby which belonged to Muḥammad ʿAlī al-Gharībī of Ḥāshid (ibid. 778–80; id. 1958: 684; al-Shawkānī 1929: ii. 46), who, as we shall see, is probably Bayt al-Aḥmar's immediate forebear.

A few years later, in 1713, al-Ḥusayn b. al-Qāsim declared himself Imam in opposition to al-Mawāhib, and 'Alī Hādī Ḥubaysh (probably Ṣāliḥ's brother) supported him (Zabārah 1941: 601–9). 'Alī al-Aḥmar of al-'Uṣaymāt was sent by al-Mawāhib to oppose him (again, this is the first mention of the family by name), but the tribes preferred the new claimant (ibid. 356, 607). The country was at one point divided among several of these rival Imams—although, significantly, none of them claimed control of the major tribes (ibid. 616)—and the struggle between the different Qāsimīs dragged on, with the shaykhs holding the balance, until al-Mawāhib died in 1718.

Al-Mutawakkil al-Qāsim then took the Imamate (Serjeant 1983: 84), and at this stage al-Aḥmar was apparently on good terms with al-Ḥusayn, the new Imam's son (Zabārah 1941: 539); but when al-Nāṣir Muḥammad made a rival claim in 1723 al-Aḥmar and many other shaykhs went over to him. The leading sayyids were meanwhile divided among themselves over the perennial problem of taxation (ibid. 289). In 1726 the Dhaybān section of Arḥab cut the roads, and a group of them made trouble in Ṣan'ā' itself (Zabārah 1958: 359). The Imam had them hunted through the streets, in response to which

> Arḥab tribesmen invited Ḥāshid and Bakīl to join them in taking revenge and wiping out the dishonour they had sustained. The tribes responded. 'Alī b. Qāsim al-Aḥmar, Paramount Shaykh of Ḥāshid, and Nāṣir b. Juzaylān, Paramount Shaykh of Bakīl, proceeded to 'Amrān where they met al-Ḥusayn, the Imam's son, whom they persuaded to join them . . . (al-Jirāfī 1951: 181, trans. Stookey 1978: 151–2).

As Stookey points out, al-Ḥusayn's combination with the tribes against his father availed him little since when his father died, in the following year, and he claimed the Imamate himself under the title al-Manṣūr, they supported his cousin, al-Nāṣir Muḥammad.

But al-Jirāfī goes on, more importantly, to relate that al-Aḥmar wrote al-Manṣūr al-Ḥusayn a brusque letter demanding a meeting. The Imam feared an attempt at assassination; so he assassinated al-Aḥmar first, stuck his head on a lance, and galloped off with it through a hail of bullets from the shaykh's enraged tribesmen (al-Jirāfī 1951: 182). In fact, al-Aḥmar, accompanied by Bin Juzaylān of Dhū Muḥammad and by Aḥmad Muḥammad Ḥubaysh of Sufyān, seems to have come to ʿAṣir, just outside Ṣanʿāʾ, to seek a settlement (Zabārah 1941: 539 and 1958: 486). The details are probably lost forever, and we are told only that al-Aḥmar 'had wished to make independent his own rule of part of the country' (ibid.), which he very well may have done; but al-Manṣūr al-Ḥusayn's view of the matter, as recorded in the histories, has all the vigorous clarity of the Zaydi tradition. The taunt to the tribesmen at the time was, typically, that they were no better than polytheists: he brandished al-Aḥmar's head on his spear and cried 'this is the head of your idol'.

THE ORIGINS OF TODAY'S GREAT SHAYKHLY FAMILIES

> To understand history the reader must always remember how small is the proportion of what is recorded to what actually took place.
>
> Churchill, *Marlborough*

Modern historians, writing under the Imams of the present century, mention only al-Aḥmar's death (al-Jirāfī 1951: 182). His 'life' appears as a brief appendix to that of the Imam who murdered him, and the details it provides are only of the murder (Zabārah 1941: 539). However, ʿAlī Qāsim al-Aḥmar's house near al-Khamrī, just north of Ḥūth, is still standing (it was still inhabited until the 1982 earthquake), and beside it is a small mosque. Beside the mosque is a ruined mausoleum, hardly more than a shelter, with a rough, irregular tombstone on which is crudely scratched his epitaph.[5] After the pious preamble, it reads as follows:

Those killed in the cause of God are not reckoned dead but as living with their Lord. The pool of fate is not only for the feeble but for all people, everywhere. For all the turns they take, death is ordained for humankind. This is the tomb of the exalted and noble shaykh, the mighty warrior chief, Jamāl al-Dīn ʿAlī Qāsim al-Aḥmar al-Gharībī. God have mercy on him. The mercy of God on high and His pardon be shown him. [God] is the Merciful and Forgiving. He died on Wednesday, 10 Muḥarram in the year 1140 [27 August 1727], a treacherous killing under safe conduct, firm pledges and guaranty. This mixed day with night. [Despite] the guaranty, there happened what there did and it drove the people to fury over his death in every place (*alzam-hu al-nās waḥshah bi-qatli-hi ilā kulli makān*). Then, after all that, came an eclipse of the sun, and day turned to darkness. This was on Monday 29 Muḥarram, a span of 19 days from his murder. For those with eyes to see it was a remembrance of him (*fa-kāna tadhkiratan li-ulī l-abṣār*).

The phrasing of the text is of some interest, as applied to a man whom the Imamic tradition depicts as the enemy of religion. The few people in the area with a taste for history preserve the story that al-Aḥmar was in fact a *shaykh 'ilm* (a man of religious learning) as well as shaykh of his tribe.[6] However, almost no one outside the immediate area knows the tomb is there and it does not form part of any wider tradition in the way that tombs of sayyids always did, and perhaps to an extent still do at present.

Of at least as much interest as the inscription are the lines scratched on the outside wall of the mausoleum.

There is no god but God, Muḥammad is God's Prophet, and 'Alī is God's regent (*wakīl*). This is the tomb of the noble shaykh, 'Alī Qāsim al-Aḥmar, who for twenty years ruled the country from this point (*al-ma'rūḍ*) to Ḥufāsh and Milḥān, its castles and lands . . .

Unfortunately there is no date or indication of authorship. The claim, though, is striking: that al-Aḥmar controlled the area from just north of Ḥūth to the fertile mountains near al-Maḥwīt, 120 kilometres away (almost due west of Ṣan'ā'), quite apart from his influence among the tribes of the plateau. The claim receives strong support from details given in the biographies of sayyids and qadis, but these details are scattered and no story is made of them.

'Alī al-Aḥmar is mentioned by name in connection with events in 1713, trading his support between rival Imams. His tombstone, and the local tradition that no doubt incorporates what is written there, gives al-Aḥmar the further name of al-Gharībī, and Muḥammad 'Alī al-Gharībī, as we have seen, is mentioned as a great shaykh based near Ḥūth in 1709. Before that we know nothing of the family or of what they were called.[7] But after al-Manṣūr al-Ḥusayn declared himself Imam, in 1727, he bought a strategic fort near al-Ahnūm from Qāsim al-Aḥmar for one thousand riyals and razed it (Zabārah 1941: 55). When al-Manṣūr was succeeded by al-Mahdī in 1748, al-Aḥmar went down to Ḥabūr, took the area and rebuilt the fort. In the interim, in 1729–30, the Najrān tribe of Yām had attacked the Tihāmah and the west, after Ḥāshid had opened the route to them through Dhībīn. Bayt al-Aḥmar are mentioned specifically as taking (and very probably retaking) areas of Ḥufāsh and Milḥān, and then sending part of the spoil to the Imam as if to legitimate their position (Zabārah 1958: 890–2). No details are given of how extensive their possessions were.

In 1751, however, a millenarian rising broke out in the western mountains, led by Abū 'Alāmah, a black 'magician' who preached a puritanical renewal of Islam. Accounts of the rising mention several forts in the west being taken from Bayt al-Aḥmar: al-Qāhirah at al-Maḥābishah was lost, then Qarāḍah and al-Gharnūq at Najrah, just south of Ḥajjah, then Ṣabrah, and finally the fort near al-Madāyir that al-Manṣūr had bought several years earlier (Zabārah 1941: 53–5). During the forty years since al-Manṣūr al-Ḥusayn b. al-Qāsim (a rival of al-Mawāhib) came to power in 1712, says a contemporary witness, the state had counted for little:

> The rule of 'Alī al-Aḥmar and his sons after him and of other tribesmen from Ḥāshid remained over-great and excessive until God destroyed what they had built and extinguished their flame, proclaiming their weakness and perdition by the appearance of this dervish. (Quoted ibid. 54)

Whatever setbacks they suffered, however, Bayt al-Aḥmar were not displaced permanently. In the year after Abū 'Alāmah's rising, when the Sharīf of Abū 'Arīsh and a rival claimant to the Imamate were active in the north-west, they were again a power to be reckoned with.[8] Certainly they collected taxes as well as rents in the nineteenth century, and local memory credits them with taking revenue even from coastal towns in the north Tihāmah. They retain considerable lands in the west to the present day.

Nor were Bayt al-Aḥmar of Ḥāshid the only shaykhly family in the area: Nāṣir Juzaylān of Dhū Muḥammad lost forts to Abū 'Alāmah at al-Masūḥ, and a garrison from Dhū Ḥusayn were chased out of al-Shā'iq in Banī 'Awām (again near Ḥajjah), but the shaykhly families of Baraṭ retained or re-established a hold there. Āl al-Shāyif of Dhū Ḥusayn, for example, still own land in Ḥajjah province, and Bayt Ḥubaysh of Sufyān have considerable holdings near al-Maḥwīt (Tutwiler 1987). The picture which emerges between the lines of eighteenth-century histories and *tarājim* is of myriad forts in the western mountains, each garrisoned by twenty or thirty tribal soldiers and controlling an area for some shaykh of the northern plateau. As the eighteenth century wears on, so the same pattern comes more clearly to light in Lower Yemen too: in his entry for 1752, for example, al-Jirāfī records for the first time what will punctuate his history thereafter, Baraṭ tribesmen at odds with the Imam south of Ṣan'ā' (al-Jirāfī 1951: 183). They continued to appear there into the present century, leaving behind great numbers of tribal families and large shaykhly holdings of land outside tribal territory.

Tribal possessions in the west and Lower Yemen show up in the histories only as reefs that sometimes break the surface of events, but they are of obvious importance. They are the only substantial source of agricultural surplus. The territory of the tribes themselves, by contrast, is semi-arid and may just produce enough to live on (we shall say more of this in Chapter 8), but would seldom produce much more. To take an obvious example, until the last decade or so, tribesmen on the plateau used often to buy in draft oxen or milch cows from the west once a year and resell them at a serious loss for lack of fodder to support them until the following harvest. Even grain is often scarce on the arid plateau. The men who could provide much wealth beyond this were the tribal leaders who in the histories appear as war-lords.

'Alī Qāsim al-Aḥmar, at the time of his demise, was accompanied by Aḥmad Muḥammad Ḥubaysh, who seems to have lived to a riper age: his tombstone at al-Madaqqah in Sufyān dates his death to Sha'bān 1179/February 1766 and describes him as 'supporter of the Imams'. Again, like al-Aḥmar's grave, this forms part of no wide tradition, and few people outside al-Madaqqah know it even exists. A few yards away is the grave of Aḥmad Muḥammad's close relative and contemporary, Hādī b. 'Alī Ḥubaysh (d. Dhū l-Qa'dah 1174/June 1761), whose rather handsomely carved tombstone gives some clue as to how these men might have seen themselves.

The noble and generous leader, blameless in his efforts for the sayyids and Arabs [i.e. tribesmen]; he was a safe refuge for the protected person (*kāna li-l-jāri ḥiṣnan*) . . . in times of famine he was never unforthcoming or found wanting (*fi l-majā'āt lam yabkhul wa-lam yahinī*—sic); he it was whom battles saw always at the forefront, amid fear and destruction; the great and splendid leader and chief, great in power and influence (*rafī' al-qadr wa-l-majāl*), supporter of kings (*nāṣir al-mulūk*), merciful to the poor and the destitute (*rāḥim al-faqīr wa-l-ṣu'lūk*) . . .

The means for such generosity, particularly 'in times of famine', can scarcely have been drawn from his own tribal territory; they must have come from personal holdings in the west or south and from the state, which itself held these richer areas precisely with the aid of such men as Ḥubaysh.

The structure of payments was that of the state itself. From the time of the Turks (1636) to that of al-Mahdī of al-Mawāhib (1687) Yemen supposedly 'was spared hunger and strife, and that wealth was taken which the law permits'. (As we have seen, this is too rosy a view; but the perception is what concerns us.) 'When this man [al-Mawāhib] arose he took what wealth is permitted and what is not permitted. His state grew strong, his prestige became great, his power expanded, the number of his troops increased, and he became more like a king than a caliph' (al-Shawkānī 1929: ii. 298). Yet the control of such wealth from taxation was surely vital where the country's agricultural base was so vulnerable; as in 1723–4, for instance, when

> a drought struck San'ā' and most of the mountains of Yemen. Most people (sic. *akthar al-nās*) died of hunger and the villages were emptied of their inhabitants . . . People ate even carrion. The price of all grains rose and a *qadaḥ* reached eight [silver] riyals. Prosperous people gave what they had as alms. Al-Mutawakkil Qāsim b. al-Ḥusayn gave out all that was edible from his store-houses . . . and it was distributed among the poor in the alleyways of Ṣan'ā'. Then there was abundance at the start of the next year [i.e. from the end of summer 1724], which went on until prices reached four *qadaḥ*s of wheat for only one riyal, or six of sorghum, or eight of barley. Praise God, then, the Lord of the worlds. (Zabārah 1941: 588)

The role of the Imams' public store-houses in smoothing such fluctuations would be an interesting subject. But what is important for the present purpose is the concept of generosity at work here.

Looking back from the early twentieth century to the great days of the Qāsimīs, an anonymous chronicler paints a picture of righteous patronage (al-Ḥibshī 1980: 300–4):

> The times smiled on the people of that age, and the reason was that all of Yemen was in the hand of the state: its ports, [Lower] Yemen, Raymah, 'Utmah, and everywhere, so fodder even grew in the lands beyond Baraṭ . . . The first thing was that the Imam followed the pure *sharī'ah*, even as it affected himself and what he owned. Then the Shaykh al-Islām was reverenced for executing affairs in accordance with God's Book and His Prophet's usage, and no-one accused him of taking even a pip or a pip-skin from the parties to a case. The reason for that was that he had a fief . . . which paid not less than about 1,000 *qadaḥ* . . . and still had al-Ḥaymah

which paid about 100 silver pieces a month. And everyone he knew or was close to ate with him [i.e. lived off him], and he himself saved nothing of what he got. After him came the sayyids of the Imam's family . . . After them came the ministers, five or six of them . . . every one of whom had limitless people living with him [i.e. off his largesse] . . .

And so on through the ranks (all of them *ad hoc*; Zaydi theory says not a word of this organization), down through the servants of servants all claiming their bread, clothes, and money from someone above them, to the lists of the great's benefactions for poor people at the several festivals. A cataract of pious largesse; and the other half of the cycle (the question of income to support this expenditure) is nowhere addressed in detail.

So far as the tribes are concerned, this need not surprise us. The complement of segmentary equality is very often the gift *min allāh*, from God, which therefore does not require reciprocity; indeed, the position of wealthy leaders in an egalitarian system is scarcely possible without this.[9] But here the ethic of largesse permeated the whole functioning of the state, applying equally to townsfolk and traders, peasants and tribesmen, to everyone who wished for wealth. The lines of payment all ran normal to the axis of precise reciprocity which defines tribes or sections against their neighbours, and each line thus ran parallel to the others; their arrangement in an ordered series ('all of Yemen was in the hand of the state') depended solely on the Imam's 'prestige' (*haybah*). With or without such subordination, however, local lines of subsidy to this tribe or that persisted, and in practice this was a period at which a distinction was made clear which one finds still in documents very close to our own time: that between tribesmen (*qabā'il*) and peasants (*ra'iyyah*), 'subjects', people who pay tax.[10] It was prominent shaykhs who formed the link between the two.

These shaykhs are not the subject of Imamic history. Although the Imamate could not have functioned as it did without them, and although the granting of 'fiefs' to them went on for centuries, the details of their financial and administrative position are nowhere written up. Nor has local documentation come to light. Until it does, we must form what estimate we can by looking at the great shaykhly houses nowadays.

Bayt al-Shāyif, 'the Shawwāf' of Dhū Ḥusayn, whose original territory is Rajūzah of Jabal Baraṭ, comprise nowadays three main *laḥām*: Āl Muḥammad, Āl 'Alī, and Āl 'Ā'iḍ (see Fig. 6.2). A few members of the first group live among the Banī ‘Awām of Ḥajjah but most are at Baraṭ. Of the second group, none lives at Barat, one head of family lives near Ḥajjah, and the rest are at Ba‘dān in Lower Yemen or al-Shi‘r near Yarīm. A few of Āl ‘Ā’iḍ live near Ibb, but most are based at Baraṭ. Between them this last group, from which all three of the tribe's most recent shaykhs came, muster about a hundred grown men in seven *laḥām*, all but two of which own land elsewhere in Yemen. One of these seven *laḥām*, comprising twenty-four men and their dependants, owns about 30,000 *libnah* (about 200 hectares) near Ḥajjah, all of which is held in common: the income is divided between the separate families, but the land is not, and part of the income has been used to expand the holding. At Baraṭ, by contrast, each family of the *laḥmah* holds its own land without reference to the others.

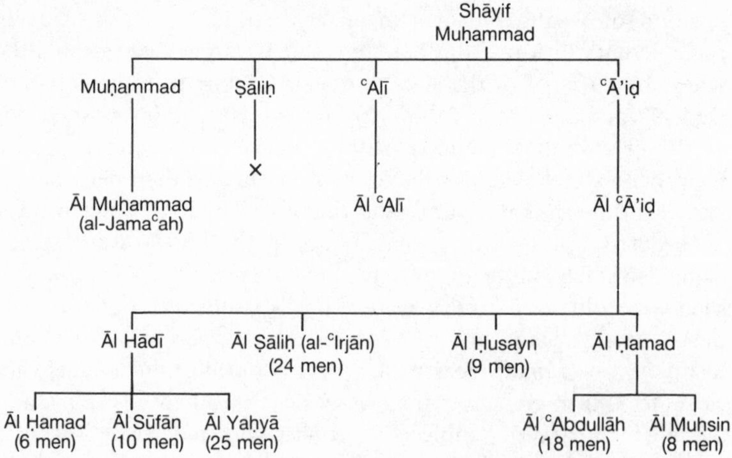

Note: Āl Ḥamad b. Hādī and Āl Sūfān b. Hādī are the only *laḥām* which do *not* own land elsewhere than in tribal territory. Āl Yaḥyā b. Hādī and Āl Muḥsin b. Ḥamad own land in the west but not in Lower Yemen. The last three shaykhs of Dhū Ḥusayn have come from Āl Yaḥyā b. Hādī, Āl Ṣāliḥ b. ᶜĀ'id, and Āl Muḥsin b. Ḥamad, in that order.

FIG. 6.2 Divisions of the shaykhly family of Bayt al-Shāyif

Bayt Ḥubaysh of Sufyān are rather similar. They comprise four *laḥām*: Dhū Khammāsh, Dhū Ṣāliḥ b. ‘Alī, Dhū Rājiḥ, and al-Jubayrī. The last of these now all live around Kuḥlān, to the west of ‘Amrān. Dhū Rājiḥ all live near al-Maḥwīt. Dhū Khammāsh have branches both at al-Maḥwīt and at al-Madaqqah, in Sufyān's territory just outside al-Ḥarf, and their Maḥwītī holdings between them are said to be of the order of 50,000 *libnah*. The shaykh of Sufyān in the last generation was from this latter section and received some 1,000 *qadaḥ* a year from these western lands, although he and other members of Dhū Khammāsh owned no more or less than their neighbours in Sufyān itself. A survey of land within tribal territory would show only bland equality. The present shaykh, 'Abduh, is from Dhū Ṣāliḥ. Apart from his land in Sufyān, he owns only a few hundred *libnah* near Kuḥlān.

To be sure of what we are dealing with, let us return very briefly to Bayt al-Aḥmar. The Ḥumrān at present, it will be remembered, comprise four non-shaykhly *laḥām* and four *laḥām* or Bayt al-Aḥmar itself. Of the former sections, none owns land anywhere than in their tribal territory. Of the four parts of Bayt al-Aḥmar, though, all have holdings elsewhere. At Ḥabūr and in the lowlands just east of Shahārah there is an inalienable family holding (*waqf li-dhurriyyat al-bayt*) of perhaps 20,000 *libnah*, supposedly established by 'Alī Qāsim and to be used for the support of people from all Bayt al-Aḥmar's branches. Each of the main branches of the family is said to have additional *waqf* land of its own, the administration of which is private business. Separate families within a given branch may have similar joint, inalienable land. Individual families and men also have their own property in the west that may be bought, sold, or passed on by inheritance.

Whatever detailed changes there have been at different times, such blocks of wealth outside tribal territory have existed from at least the early eighteenth century right down to our own day (Dresch 1984b: 156). Were there space, we might pursue the holdings of several lesser shaykhly families from the plateau tribes, such as Bayt Radmān of Arḥab (see Dresch forthcoming *d*). The members of shaykhly families now based in the west will sometimes call on the tribes for men to support them. The tribe, however, does not count the western emigrés in the *ghurm wa-jurm* (the levy for collective payments), although the shaykhly house in particular may seek financial aid from their western or southern kin.[11] In a great many cases, also, as with the three great families we discussed in detail, one finds part at least of the western land held as 'family *waqf*' (in other words, a collective holding), while the holdings on the plateau, in tribal territory, are as fragmented as those of any tribal family. The suspicion must be that this contributes to the relative stability of the family's precedence among the plateau tribesmen, though not always to the precedence of a particular descent line. This in turn keys the tribes directly into the affairs of all Yemen, so that order and disorder in the tribal north coincide to a great degree with control by a 'state' of the non-tribal west and south.

'THE TIME OF CORRUPTION': DISORDERS OF THE NINETEENTH CENTURY

> The authority of the king is the keystone which closeth up the arch of order and government, which, once shaken, all the frame falls together in a confused heap of foundation and battlement.
>
> Thomas Wentworth, Earl of Strafford

Al-Mahdī al-'Abbās (1748–75) was very much a Ṣan'ānī Imam, being based on the city throughout his reign. Among learned Ṣan'ānīs he retained a high reputation (al-Shawkānī 1929: 310–12; Serjeant 1983: 85 ff.), but it is plain that all was not well elsewhere. Abū 'Alāmah's 1751 rising in the north-west has already been mentioned. Two years earlier a campaign had been fought in Lower Yemen against a 'sorcerer' who promised his followers immunity against sword wounds and gun shots.[12] In the year before that, Ḥasan al-'Ukām, of the qadi family from Baraṭ and the north-east, was leading tribesmen at odds with the new Imam in Lower Yemen (Zabārah 1958: 684).[13] In both the west and the south, the incursion of tribesmen over the preceding generation had not been quietly absorbed, and the affairs of the Baraṭ tribes in particular (Dhū Muḥammad and Dhū Ḥusayn) became involved with those of the Imam's capital at Ṣan'ā'.

The connections of learning which were often important in an Imam's rise to power (Ch. 5) could also readily generalize a threat to that power if one emerged; and the language of equality, justice, and religious probity linked the learned with the tribesmen also. In 1768, for instance, the *'ulamā'* of Baraṭ (particularly Bayt al-'Ansī) wrote to Zaydi centres such as Ḥūth and Dhamār, calling for the expulsion of al-Mahdī al-'Abbās and his Qāsimī relatives on doctrinal grounds (al-Jirāfī 1951: 187; Zabārah 1958: 521–2; al-

Shawkānī 1929: ii. 134–5), though the Baraṭ tribes' incursions in preceding years suggest that doctrinal detail was not the main motive force (see e.g. Zabārah 1958: 13).

The Qāsimīs were accused of 'innovations' (*bida*'). Zaydism had always recognized *ijtihād* (the formation of new law by extrapolation from scripture), but in the mid-eighteenth century a pronounced movement of criticism was under way. Ibn al-Amīr, for instance, a Zaydi scholar who kept his political distance from the Imamate, blurred the distinction between his own school and the Shāfi'ī,[14] with the result that conspicuous details, such as postures of prayer, became matters of contention among those less learned than he. The Baraṭ qadis blamed the Qāsimīs for supporting him. On at least one occasion, an intestine squabble among Ṣan'ānī *'ulamā'* over mosque appointments, phrased in these terms, led one faction to demand arbitration from al-'Ansī, 'the qadi of Ḥāshid and Bakīl' (Zabārah 1941: 617), rather than from their Qāsimī rulers.

Ḥasan al-'Ansī and the Baraṭ tribes appeared outside Ṣan'ā' in 1770. They were successfully driven off, which provoked some vainglorious poetry from the victors (Serjeant 1983: 86; cf. al-Shawkānī 1929: i. 459), but elsewhere al-Shawkānī suggests (ibid. ii. 136) how this was achieved: an addition to the tribesmen's stipend of 20,000 riyals per annum, the implication being that they already received regular payment. These incursions and payments continued for several decades,[15] and the Baraṭ tribes remained active in Lower Yemen until the Turks took the area in the late nineteenth century. Writing in the 1830s, al-Shawkānī complains that

> it is one of the trials of this world that these evil ones come into Ṣan'ā' for their stipends every year, gathering in their thousands. If they see someone practice *ijtihād* in prayer, by lifting his hands or joining them on his chest or [tucking his feet beneath] his thighs, they condemn him for it, and violence has occurred on account of this. They get together and go to the mosques where one of the *'ulamā'* is reading the books of Tradition and start fights there. (ibid.)

This, he says, is the fault of *shayṭān*s among the learned men, who encourage factionalism.[16] 'As for these brutish Arabs, most of them don't pray or fast or perform any of the duties of Islam . . .' (ibid.). This almost patrician disdain combines a particular Islamic rectitude with the conceptual geography of Yemen sketched in Chapter 1; al-'Amrī paraphrases al-Shawkānī's view as follows:

First there are those subjects (*ra'āyā*) who come under the absolute control of the authority (*dawlah*) and submit to its orders. The majority of them cannot pray, or pray incorrectly. . . . He who does not practice prayer properly is a mere infidel . . .

The second group consists of those of the far north and east (*bilād al-qiblah wa-l-mashriq*) who have not come under the control of the *dawlah*. They are . . . even worse, since they cannot read or write and they submit to the customary laws of their predecessors (*aḥkām al-ṭāghūt*), instead of to the *sharī'ah*. . . . Those who do so . . . are unbelievers.

The third group consists of the townspeople . . . As a result of their ignorance and indulgence, they neglect many of their duties towards God. However, they are quick and readier than others to learn and receive education, if resolved to do so. (al-'Amrī 1985: 122)

The northern tribes are thus the wolves beyond the walls (cf. Gellner 1981), the lack and the antithesis of a civilization whose centre is Ṣan'ā'. In slightly later Ṣan'ānī chronicles (al-Sayāghī 1978; al-Ḥibshī 1980) one is treated to a chorus of invective against these tribes—these 'followers of the *ṭāghūt*', 'dogs', murderers—who swirl around and sometimes plunder 'Ṣan'ā' the protected of God' with no explicit reason but the Imamate's weakness and what seems their own inherent wickedness. The Imamate's weakness we might want to explain in more detailed terms.

Al-Manṣūr 'Alī b. al-Mahdī (1775–1809) was, like his father, a Ṣan'ānī Imam, and from the city's point of view was at first a considerable success (Serjeant 1983: 86–7; al-Shawkānī 1929: i. 359 ff.). But at the state's periphery, Sharīf Ḥamūd of Abū Arīsh was forced south by the Nejd Wahhābīs into territory the Imamate had held or at least had part access to. The resulting loss of port revenue was almost certainly serious.[17] From now on, the Imams' ability to buy off the tribes declined sharply.

At the centre, al-Manṣūr's grip on affairs failed when his sons fell out with each other, and the qadis of Bayt al-'Ulufī fell out with those of Bayt al-'Ansī, in part over stipends to the tribes (al-Jirāfī 1951: 192; al-'Amrī 1985: 52–64; al-Ḥibshī 1980: 4; Zabārah 1929: i. 343–4). In 1818, in the time of the Imam al-Mahdī, a large body of tribesmen from Baraṭ arrived at the capital in search of pay to fight in the Tihāmah (al-Ḥibshī 1980: 18). The Imam, having collected support of his own from Khawlān and Nihm, had 'Alī 'Abdullāh al-Shāyif of Dhū Ḥusayn beheaded and the body strung up for three days, then thrown in the rubbish ditch outside Bāb

Sha'ūb (ibid. 20–1; Zabārah 1929: ii. 66). But Bayt al-Shāyif's call for support to avenge this was answered by Wā'ilah, Ḥāshid, al-'Amālisah, Sufyān, and Arḥab, among others; in short, by tribes from as far away as what is now the Saudi border. They looted the city's outskirts and carried off enough plunder 'to suffice the son's son' (ibid. 23–4; al-'Amrī 1985: 88–91).

In 1823 a severe drought in the east forced a meeting of tribes at Jabal Baraṭ, where they decided to seek aid from the Imam. When he refused and they turned on Lower Yemen, he seems to have been able to do nothing but warn others they were coming. 'When they reached Samārah [the pass that is sometimes taken to define Lower Yemen's border; see Chapter 1], each put down his pledge on a place, and they divided it all up as if their father had left them the land as inheritance' (al-Ḥibshī 1980: 34). It is quite possible, of course, that many had indeed been left inheritance there, either property or presumed rights to 'fiefs' (*quṭa'*): they had been involved with the area for the best part of a century. From 1823 onwards, though, they are said to have held the area unopposed: 'they took control of it by force and coercion, then settled there, married there, and forgot the east until the Faqīh Sa'īd threw them out in [1840]' (ibid.).[18] Even that was not sufficient, and when a further drought struck in 1835, Dhū Ḥusayn, under Muḥsin 'Alī al-Shāyif, began raiding the north-west, while their women and children moved westwards by themselves in great numbers (ibid. 60–2). The Tihāmah had meanwhile fallen to the Egyptians.

At the centre, in Ṣan'ā', the Imamate under al-Manṣūr 'Alī b. al-Mahdī 'Abdullāh lost not only its resources but its moral vigour: 'drunkenness was the prevailing vice among the higher orders, and . . . the corpses of men, women and children lay about the streets, no one taking the trouble to bury them . . .' (Playfair 1859: 145). Al-Manṣūr squabbled with one of his relatives, who fled to Ta'izz and handed it over to the Egyptians. Al-Nāṣir 'Abdullāh Aḥsan was then raised to the Imamate by the soldiers in Ṣan'ā', only to be assassinated at Wādī Ḍahr in 1840.[19] Al-Hādī Muḥammad took the throne and succeeded briefly in regaining Mocha and Ta'izz, but when the Egyptians withdrew—under indirect pressure from Britain (Baldry 1976: 161)—the Tihāmah fell under the control of Sharīf Ḥusayn.

The geographical pattern of power had now changed beyond recognition. Ḥāshid (led in part by the qadis of Bayt Ḥanash), were in Raymah, as well as further north in the western mountains, Dhū Muḥammad and Dhū Ḥusayn were in the south, as well as in the Tihāmah, and all were involved with Yām, whose homeland in Najrān had usually been outside the field of Yemeni events but whose presence in Ḥarāz and the Tihāmah was nothing new. The land of Ḥāshid and Bakīl, on the northern plateau, was itself a dead centre to the whirl of events involving tribesmen elsewhere. Sharīf Ḥusayn's movements in 1845 make the point: starting from the north-west, in the Tihāmah, he moved to the south, around Ta'izz, then to Baraṭ, in the extreme north-east (al-Ḥibshī 1980: 120–31). The Imamate, at Ṣan'ā', retained a mere rump of territory.

There was violence enough in the north itself, particularly in times of drought (see e.g. ibid. 306); but the tribal divisions, one should note, changed very little, and then rather in a *longue durée* than in the order of events recorded year by year. As we shall see in Chapter 9, the geographical detail even of sections within tribes changes hardly at all from al-Qāsim's time (early seventeenth century) to our own, and where change occurs it does so by recognizable quanta. Inequality and movement alike are registered in other terms. The prominence of major shaykhs, for instance, whom the tribesmen followed much as they did Imams, derived from wealth in the west and in Lower Yemen, and this is also where the great non-quantum shifts in territorial control resulted from tribesmen fighting each other. Inequality, power, and geographical change all attach, not to tribal self-definition, but to the history of successive Imams, to the history of a tradition or of a dynasty; and the dynasty had, by this point, collapsed because it had lost control of non-tribal land.

The Imams' attempts to regain the south met with little success. Aḥmad Ṣāliḥ Thawābah of Dhū Muḥammad, who had controlled a large swathe of Lower Yemen, was defeated by al-Mutawakkil Muḥammad and finally executed in 1848, to the delight of the Imam's supporters (Dresch 1987*b*). Within three years, however, his sons were formally granted land in much the same area (al-Ḥibshī 1980: 166). In the interim the Imam had been forced to send Dhū Muḥammad horses as slaughter-beasts (*'aqā'ir*), which they took but did not have killed, and then pay them to fight again in the south (ibid. 146).[20] Dhū Muḥammad, Dhū Ḥusayn, Arḥab, Khawlān, and Ḥāshid were also all fighting in the west, on the Imam's side, the Sharīf's, or both; but the Ottoman Turks now seized the Tihāmah. Ḥufāsh, near al-Maḥwīt, and al-Ḥaymah were both contested, and several rival claimants to the Imamate appeared at once.

In despair al-Mutawakkil asked the Turks to intervene in the highlands. They arrived at Ṣan'ā' in 1849 with 1,200 foot and 500 horse, but a riot ensued and they withdrew after only three weeks (Zabārah 1929: ii. 346 ff.; al-Sayāghī 1978: 25–7). Al-Mutawakkil was killed by his rivals. One of the Ashrāf of the northern Tihāmah, supported by a large following from Ḥāshid, was then bought off with a gift of 2,000 riyals, robes of honour, and a horse (al-Sayāghī 1978: 31). The combination of a Tihāmah Sharīf and Ḥāshid at the gates of Ṣan'ā' is symptomatic enough of the Imamate's weakness.

From the summary histories one forms an impression of steadily increasing disorder through the next twenty years, until 'the people of Ṣan'ā' and others' invited the Turks again to take the city 'after they had tired of the chaos which prevailed there, the dominion of men from the tribes, the cutting of the roads, and the lack of any ordered security' (al-Jirāfī 1951: 205–6). A more recently available, and more detailed, source gives a different impression (al-Ḥibshī 1980: 296 ff.). But the Turks seem in any case to have had designs on the highlands: they had increased their forces on the coast 'until stores were coming ashore with Ṣan'ā' printed on every load' (ibid. 315), and when they finally arrived, in 1872, they demanded the tax registers which would reveal to them the administration and resources of the whole country (al-Wāsi'ī 1928: 110). They were to remain in highland Yemen until 1918.

For much of the eighteenth and nineteenth centuries, then, Yemen had been plagued by disputes between rival Imams and by tribal disorder. The Imamate had taken the form of an elaborate dynastic state, yet failed to secure the means to support itself or to transmit authority without dispute. Al-Shamāḥī credits the Qāsimī *dawlah* with surviving until the middle of the nineteenth century. In name it did. He rationalizes the great decline of its power by saying that al-Mu'ayyad Muḥammad (d. 1686) was the last of the Qāsimīs to possess all the qualities needed of an Imam, and that the rulers after him were more like kings (al-Shamāḥī 1972: 144–6). Similarly, al-Wazīr (1971: 50) attributes the collapse of the state to the appearance of 'evil Imams'. Authors writing nearer the time each choose some point at which the real decline starts, always simply by reference to the actions or fate of a particular Imam (e.g. al-Ḥibshī 1980: 193).

While the tradition of the state may be saved by the appearance of a 'good' Imam, however, the standing of the tribes as savage hordes, in the view of townsfolk and learned men, could only be confirmed. It is the tribes who are held responsible.

It is clear from what has come before that these events were basically in accordance with the wishes of the tribal shaykhs and that they supported Imams [only] as a means to plunder, pillage, kill, and so on. They raised up for themselves an Imam in each area so as to attain their ends in his name. (al-Sayāghī 1978: 125)

Or again, 'these people are sons of dirhams and dinars, and have no religion . . . The man in the right so far as they are concerned is the one with great wealth who is open-handed' (al-Ḥibshī 1980: 54). But the specific image of the period is that of movement, of the tribes overrunning the rest of Yemen.

Depraved people spread throughout the land. Dhū Muḥammad and Dhū Ḥusayn, families like al-Juzaylān and Banī Shāyif, took much of Lā'ah and Lower Yemen; families like Abū Ra's, Āl Ṣalāḥ, Baḥūr, and many others became virtual kings. The tribesmen of Khawlān al-'Āliyah, Murhibah, and Nihm took some areas . . . Ḥāshid, the Ḥumrān [i.e. Bayt al-Aḥmar], Banī Nāshir, and others from Khārif, Ṣuraym, or al-'Uṣaymāt took much of Ḥajjah and Lā'ah. Men from Arḥab took parts of the same area. Excesses spread and turmoil increased, with people raiding and pillaging others, and the worst of the corrupt were from the tribes. (al-Sayāghī 1978: 125–6)

In fact the tribes and families mentioned here had been involved with the west and south long before the catastrophes of the nineteenth century. Some at least of them remained attached to these areas throughout the Turkish occupation afterwards. Certainly there were great movements of people, but the land being divided, redivided, and fought over had been in tribal spheres of influence well before 1800; it was not simply that tribesmen spread out to escape famine or to gather loot, but that the country's governance as a whole collapsed. Yet it is the tribes who again and again are condemned as 'corrupt' and 'wicked', 'dogs and sons of dogs'.

THE SECOND TURKISH OCCUPATION: 1872–1918

Enough battles and fights to fill books and to empty ink-wells . . .

al-Wāsi'ī, *Ta'rīkh al-Yaman*

With the Turkish occupation (1872–1918), the dramatic events that historians record shift in part from the west and south into the tribes' own territory. The political reality was complex, and at most points up to 1918 the Turks found support from Yemenis, not least from certain northern shaykhs whose fortunes were bound up with the Turkish presence.[21] The clerk of the Ṣan'ā' court learned Turkish. Many of the '*ulamā*' supported the Turks even when the Imam's fight against them was at its height, and the ambiguities of resisting the Turkish Sultan, who himself was seen to be beset by Christendom, were usually marked. None the less there was sustained resistance in the north. Tribes and Imams fought the Turks repeatedly, and the dynasty of Imams emerged that was to rule Yemen until the 1960s.

When the Turks arrived at Ṣan'ā' in 1872, the Imam al-Mutawakkil Muḥsin slipped away, first to Banī 'Alī in northern Arḥab and then to Ḥāshid, moving between Ḥūth, al-Khamrī, and al-Qaflah (al-Ḥibshī 1980: 335). Al-Khamrī, of course, is Bayt al-Aḥmar's home area. The al-Aḥmars and Ḥāshid acquired a very prominent place in relations between the Turks and the Imam, which they retained under al-Mutawakkil's successors (ibid. 336, 354, and *passim*). By comparison, the Baraṭ Bakīl tribes, who had been so conspicuous in the mid-nineteenth century, played a somewhat subdued role. A little later, in 1882, Muḥammad al-Ḥūthī declared himself Imam at Baraṭ and took the name al-Mahdī. He persisted in the claim until his death in 1901, but he was quite overshadowed by the Imams al-Hādī Sharaf al-Dīn (1879–90) and al-Manṣūr Muḥammad (1890–1904), both of whom were concerned with great events on the plateau north of Ṣan'ā'. His own career at Baraṭ was a *vita umbratilis*, and even to Glaser in the Jawf (1903: 82) he was little more than a rumour. Dhū Muḥammad and Dhū Ḥusayn are mentioned both in the north and in Lower Yemen (e.g. al-Ḥibshī 1980: 519, 554, 558)—a little later, in 1908, we find a mention of Nājī Abū Ra's of Dhū Muḥammad as a Turkish '*āmil* in Raydah (Zabārah 1956: ii. 126)—but the great axis of dispute between the south and the far north-east collapsed:[22] it was the leaders of the more central northern tribes who now came to the fore. The great tribal families of today had appeared at the start of the eighteenth century; but what one sees at the start of the present century is the establishment of their present differences in wealth and power.

Al-Hādī Sharaf al-Dīn died in 1890. Al-Manṣūr Muḥammad Ḥamīd al-Dīn, who was in Ṣan'ā' at the time, was called on to take the Imamate and had little option but to leave the city.[23] The sayyids of the Ṣa'dah area took time to organize themselves around him (al-Mahdī Muḥammad was still active at Baraṭ), and meanwhile some hundreds of Ḥāshid chiefs came into Ṣan'ā', returning still in receipt of large Turkish stipends (al-Ḥibshī 1980: 393–9). But the rains then failed, and fighting broke out between the tribes just north-east of Ṣan'ā'. The sorghum crop was ruined in the summer by locusts and the Turks applied severe pressure to the shaykhs of Ḥajjah, among other areas, presumably to extract taxes (ibid. 403, 411, 412).

It was around Ḥajjah that the most serious results ensued. The Turkish governor attacked Mabkhūt al-Aḥmar's property and provoked a counter-attack. The Imam had already promoted an attack on the Turks in January 1891, but serious fighting only now broke out in May, and in June Ẓafīr Ḥajjah was taken by a force which Mabkhūt al-Aḥmar led (ibid. 422; Zabārah 1956: 1. 2/18–20). Arḥab, 'Iyāl Surayḥ, and Hamdān all rose and attacked the areas around Ṣan'ā', although the Turks sought advice from Bin Sinān 'the '*āmil* of Arḥab' (al-Hibshī 1980: 424). Parts of Khawlān sent hostages to the Imam, the Turks sealed the city off, and fires began to appear at night on the surrounding mountains. Many of the outlying Turkish garrisons were withdrawn or overrun, and Ṣan'ā' itself was besieged (ibid. 425–37; Zabārah 1956: i. 2/20–44).

The siege was lifted only in October. Perhaps as many as thirty thousand troops were transferred to Yemen (Zabārah 1956: i. 2/50), and the Mufti of Ḥamāh arrived in Ṣan'ā' on the Sultan's orders to attempt negotiations with Imam al-Manṣūr, but the talks foundered. In May 1892 Fayḍī Pāsha began moving north. Banī 'Abd, on the mountains north of Raydah, put up stiff resistance, but parts of Banī Ṣuraym submitted in return for stipends. The Imam almost despaired. But, as one of his advisors pointed out, he could not afford to dispense with Ḥāshid, and without Ḥāshid he had no security at all (ibid. i. 2/79–80). In June Fayḍī reached al-Qaflah, destroyed the houses of the Imam's supporters there and promptly withdrew. Four months later, when Ḥāshid reaffirmed their support for the Imam at Ḥūth, they could only express their regret at having let Fayḍī in (al-Ḥibshī 1980: 500).

In the west the Imam suffered further setbacks. From the start of the rising certain northern shaykhs were conspicuous in the area, probably fighting around their own landholdings: Nāṣir Mabkhūt al-Aḥmar of al-'Uṣaymāt and Muḥsin al-Qāyifī of Khārif around Ḥajjah, for instance, and Aḥmad Ḥubaysh of Sufyān around al-Maḥwīt (Zabārah 1956: i. 2/47, 51–2, 68; al-Ḥibshī 1980: 495, 520, 549). Ẓafīr Ḥajjah was finally surrendered after having been held by the Imam's supporters for a full year.[24] Nāṣir al-Aḥmar admitted that although the water tanks were running dry and his men were exhausted, the surrender itself involved 'a sum of money' (*shay' min al-māl*). 'Alī al-Iryānī reckoned it at 11,000 riyals (Zabārah 1956: i. 2/81–2), an enormous sum by the standards of the time.

Fayḍī Pāsha, at Khamir, had meanwhile been trying to regain his prisoners, whom the Imam had sent to Baraṭ. He had been negotiating with Abū Fāri' of al-'Uṣaymāt, Jibrān al-Ghashmī of Hamdān, and al-Thamthamī of Sufyān, all of whom were mediating secretly with the Baraṭ shaykhs. He now moved up to Sufyān and met Nājī Abū Ra's and Āl Juzaylān of Dhū Muḥammad, 'the great landowners of Lā'ah and Lower Yemen' (ibid. 82), whom he alternately threatened with confiscation of their property and cajoled with promises of payment, while they themselves had one eye on their promises to the Imam. In the midst of these tangled talks, Fayḍī let out that he was moving on Ṣa'dah. He turned aside and took Baraṭ by surprise (one of the best-remembered episodes of the war), then on his return march picked up Ḥasan Yaḥyā al-Shāyif of Dhū Ḥusayn on the road past 'Amrān and brought him to Ṣan'ā' in chains. Yemeni opinion, though, remained divided as to who was in the right.[25]

Al-Manṣūr suffered a stroke, and in September 1904 he died (ibid. 393–403). His son Yaḥyā took the Imamate, which he was to hold until his death in 1948. As a number of authors have noted (Sālim 1971: 72 n. 1; Serjeant 1983: 94), the success of his claim was very probably due to the support of Nāṣir Mabkhūt al-Aḥmar, who had (at least most of the time) supported al-Manṣūr. With al-Aḥmar's backing, Yaḥyā took binding agreements (*qawā'id wa-ḍawābit*) from the shaykhs about the conduct of the *jihād*, stipulating that the weak be protected, looting be controlled, and any artillery captured be surrendered to the public treasury (Zabārah 1956: ii. 8). Almost immediately after his accession he dispatched forces to the west and south, the outlying Turkish garrisons fell, and Ṣan'ā' was again besieged (Sālim 1971: 74; Baldry 1977: 45 ff.). In the midst of an atrocious famine the Turkish garrison withdrew under safe conduct in April 1905. 'Ṣan'ā' after the surrender was a ruin. Its markets were destroyed, its houses empty, and only a few of its inhabitants were left,' but when the tribes saw the victory that had been won 'every tribe wanted to control some province or another of Yemen as a fief . . .' (al-Wāsi'ī 1928: 203).

The Porte again pursued negotiations and again sent reinforcements, this time landing some 42,000 fresh troops at al-Ḥudaydah by June 1905 (Baldry 1977: 50). At the beginning of September, Fayḍī reoccupied Ṣan'ā' and then moved north, again being let pass by Banī Ṣuraym. Ten battalions were committed to besiege the Imam at Shahārah. The sheer cliffs there are imposing at any time, with birds of prey always circling above them; even rifle fire at weddings echoes off the mountains like thunder. A veritable war, with small arms and artillery, was fought there for more than a month (Zabārah 1956: ii. 28–31) until the Turks gave up and withdrew with heavy losses. A battalion detached to 'Iyāl Yazīd was annihilated, and a thousand troops surprised by the tribesmen near Khamir were wiped out to the last man (Baldry 1977: 58). There was nothing to show for it. At Shahārah now there is still a pair of field-guns, engraved in ornate Ottoman script at the breech with 'Frederick Krupp, Essen': an oddly specific remnant from the period of dreadnoughts and diplomacy elsewhere. The pattern of events, though, was much as it had been in the first Turkish wars three hundred years earlier in the time of the Mamelukes.

In 1910 Yaḥyā sent emissaries to Jabal Baraṭ to organize a renewal of the fighting against the Turks (Zabārah 1956: ii. 174–80) and Ṣan'ā' was again besieged: with huge numbers of fresh troops the Turks again reconquered the areas south of Ṣan'ā' and reached the city itself in April 1911. But this time, mindful of the empire's commitments elsewhere (the Italians had just invaded

Tripoli), they did not pursue the Imam northwards. Instead negotiations were begun at once. In October 1911 the Turks and the Imam met at Da‘‘ān, on Jabal ‘Iyāl Yazīd, and signed a truce that, although not ratified by imperial firman until two years later, was upheld by both sides thereafter. Upper Yemen was ceded to the Imam's control.

With the treaty of Da‘‘ān the Imam became a Turkish ally. The Idrīsī of ‘Asīr, who had risen to prominence in the Tihāmah some years before and fought the Turks much as Yaḥyā did, became the enemy of both. The great tribal shaykhs had alternately supported the Imam and exploited the possibility of playing off the Turks against him, and certain of them had been present at Da‘‘ān when the truce was signed: Nāṣir al-Aḥmar, for instance, Ḥamīd Shariyān of Dhū Ḥusayn, and Jibrān al-Ghashmī of Hamdān (Zabārah 1956: ii. 208–9). As the polarity between the Imam and the Idrīsī intensified, however, so shaykhs and tribes again found themselves between two competing powers. In 1912 fighting broke out between the Imam's men and the Idrīsī's in Ḥajūr, Khawlān, and Jabal Rāziḥ, west of Ṣa‘dah (al-Jirāfi 1951: 223; al-Wāsi‘ī 1928: 226; Zabārah 1956: ii. 253; see also Wyman Bury 1915: 40). Some of the Ḥāshid shaykhs, not least of them Bayt al-Aḥmar, went so far as to swear the Idrīsī allegiance and send him hostages (Sālim 1971: 162; al-Wishalī 1982: 123), which might remind us how careful we should be about thinking of them always as ‘Zaydis’,

At this point let us give some consideration also to how events are remembered. Even now, men will take one over the ground and point out in detail where the tribesmen stood and where the Turks. But they rarely place events in sequence. Indeed, it is usually impossible to co-ordinate different local accounts without the help of history books (in other words, the learned version), although the histories usually confirm as accurate the conjunction of names and geographical detail contained in each local tale.

The tribal divisions, from which the sense of most stories derives, are taken as geographically fixed, and neither personal histories nor divisions of the past into reigns and periods are connected with them. The names and events brought together in tales attach primarily to place, and, as Cunnison (1951: 39) says of a very different style of local history, place itself may be equivalent to perpetual relationships. Whether the events of a story took place in ‘the Imam's time’, ‘the time of the Turks’, or ‘the time of the first

Turks' is given by the names in the tale if it is given at all, while families who have moved from tribe to tribe retain only the fact of movement, not a detailed tradition of what causes led to this. To place local tales in particular sequence reflects the fortunes of particular people, not the identity of the tribes themselves, while the summary of such tales together (such as one finds in a chronicle) refers to 'good' Imams and 'bad'. The 'collective memory', in so far as one can use the phrase at all, is remarkably vivid and remarkably fragmented also.[26]

As we shall see in Chapter 10, this may perhaps be changing with the spread of mass education, and a unified narrative of the country's history may well become the site of arguments over present concerns: for the moment, however, each locality in Upper Yemen has its own fund of personalized stories that overlap, without challenging, those of other localities. Even great shaykhly families are the subject of fragmented tales about particular shaykhs, not of cumulative sequence that explains these families' present status, although the material to conceive the past in terms of factions or of social class is abundantly to hand.

THE RISE OF THE ḤAMĪD AL-DĪN: 1918 ONWARDS

By the terms of the European armistice at the end of the First World War, the Turks were obliged to abandon Yemen. The Imam filled their place. Even before he entered Ṣan'ā' in 1918, Imam Yaḥyā sent a force of tribesmen under Sayyid 'Alī al-Wazīr to take Ḥarāz from the Ismā'īlīs (al-Jirāfī 1951: 225), some of whom turned for help to the Idrīsī; and as the Turks withdrew, the Imam also turned his attention southward. The tribes were directed against the Shāfi'ī areas of Lower Yemen, much as they had been by the Qāsimīs, in a *jihād*. 'The tribesman who enrolled under the Imam's standard and came from north of Ṣan'ā' to the lowlands of the Tihāmah, to Ibb, to Ta'izz, and al-Bayḍā' was not referred to as a soldier but as a warrior in the cause of the God' (Nu'mān 1965: 27). Not all of Nu'mān's writing is intended as sober history, but the nature of these campaigns is not in doubt and they occurred of course well within living memory.[27]

The armies that conquered these southern areas were made up of northern tribesmen. But those who in Lower Yemen were *anṣār al-*

ḥaqq or *mujāhidīn* ('supporters of the truth', 'warriors in the cause of God'), were in their own territory still most often cast as 'evil ones' (*ashrār*), 'tyrants' (*bughāh*), and unbelievers. They were most conspicuous in the west, where the Tihāmah was in the hands of the Idrīsī and the coastal towns were occupied for some years by the British who supported him. At the same time as their fellows were supporting the Imam's southern conquests, 'greedily ambitious people from Ḥāshid and Bakīl' appeared with the Idrīsī in the Tihāmah (Zabārah 1956: iii. 28). Three thousand tribesmen were sent to oppose them, and in one of the battles Naqīb Ṣāliḥ Radmān of Arḥab was 'martyred' for the Imam. On the Idrīsī's side was 'Alī Daḥḥān al-Aḥmar of Ḥāshid.

The Imam then arrested his own appointee in Ḥajjah, Yaḥyā Shaybān, probably over a discrepancy in the accounts, and Muḥsin Shaybān announced an insurrection. A recent (republican) author asserts that 'Shaykh Nāṣir al-Aḥmar had no choice but to send a force from Ḥāshid under the command of his son, Shaykh Ḥusayn' (al-Shamāḥī 1972: 172), which is probably to collapse into one episode a struggle that went on for years.[28] Certainly, however, Muḥammad Ghālib al-Qudaymī of Khārif was present in support of Shaybān (ibid. and Zabārah 1956: iii. 27), and when the insurrection failed Shaybān fled to Ḥāshid (almost certainly to Khārif), which was beyond the Imam's control. Just after this, Ḥāshid tribesmen again appeared with the Idrīsī, further west.

In April 1922 the Imam intervened in a dispute between Ḥāshid and the two Bakīl tribes of 'Iyāl Yazīd and 'Iyāl Surayḥ, staying the night at Hijrat al-Ṣayad (part of Khārif in Ḥāshid), where he was evidently welcome enough as arbitrator (Zabārah 1956: iii. 76). In January 1924, however, the troubles around Ḥajjah again flared up. The Imam's son, Sayf al-Islām Aḥmad, seems to have pursued an attempt of his own to 'trim the claws' of the al-Aḥmars and built three forts at Najrah (ibid. iii. 89), precisely the area the al-Aḥmars had held since at least the mid-eighteenth century. 'In those days Ḥajjah governorate was controlled by two factions: the local shaykhs or families and shaykhs from Ḥāshid and Bakīl such as Āl al-Aḥmar, Āl Juzaylān, Āl Harāsh, Āl Mu'ammarī, Āl al-Dumaynī, al-Zarqah, Abū Ra's, Shamsān, Āl al-Shāyif, and others, (al-Shamāḥī 1972: 173). Sayf al-Islām Aḥmad attacked this control systematically, while the Imam exploited divisions within the tribes to establish his own control nearer Ḥāshid's 'capital'. This is worth a brief account, since it illustrates so clearly the combination of force and alliance that was typical of Imamate politics.

Men from Hamdān had fired on Ṣan'ā' at about the same time as a dispute flared up within 'Iyāl Surayḥ between 'Alī Farāṣ al-Dhayfānī and Shaykh Rājiḥ b. Sa'd al-Maymūnī. Farāṣ sought help from those in Ḥāshid and Arḥab 'with whom he had made ties of brotherhood' (*man kāna qad māla ilā makhwati-him*): in other words, those he had gone to for help in the manner described in Chapter 3. Some of al-Aḥmar's people turned out to support him. So did men from Hamdān. The Imam had gathered a considerable force to be sent to Ḥajjah (eight companies of regular infantry and 2,500 tribesmen), but he now sent them to attack Hamdān, who were forced to hand over not only those who had fired on Ṣan'ā' but also another 200 prisoners and hostages. A large contingent from Hamdān was then attached to the regular army and sent against Farāṣ in 'Iyāl Surayḥ (ibid. iii. 101–2).

Men from Khawlān al-'Āliyah were then sent to join the rest of the Imam's forces and to move against al-Ṣarabāt, in 'Iyāl Yazīd, where again there were 'depraved fools from Ḥāshid' (ibid. iii. 112). Reading between the lines would suggest what one is told now: that people from 'Iyāl Yazīd had invited these Ḥāshidīs in as allies. The Ḥāshidīs withdrew to al-Matrad in 'Iyāl Surayḥ, near the border with Banī Ṣuraym, which is still well remembered as the subject of a dispute over 'brotherhood'. The dispute itself had arisen over the question of paying for hostages whom the Imam held.[29] The history tells us nothing of this, but only of the battles by which the Ḥāshidīs were pushed out and Khamir taken. After the arrival of further reinforcements, hostages were extracted from Banī Ṣuraym, Khārif, and Arḥab, and '*āmil*s were appointed by the Imam to run these separate areas. Khārif was split administratively between Dhībīn and Raydah (ibid. iii. 113–14).

In 1925 Ḥāshid, as well as 'Iyāl Yazīd, contributed men to the Imam's campaigns against the Tihāmah (Zabārah 1956: iii. 119). But in 1928, al-Aḥmar's own tribe of al-'Uṣaymāt was finally invaded (see al-Jirāfī 1951: 237). These long campaigns were evidently well remembered in the 1930s, when Rossi heard *zawāmil* from the Imam's soldiers warning 'Ḥajj Nāṣir' of Ḥāshid that 'we'll flatten al-Khamrī and build on his land' (Rossi 1939: 118). The most detailed of the general histories, however, refers to this simply as a 'punitive campaign' and explains it as an isolated incident,

1. Argument

2. ʿAlī Zāyid arbitrating in Murhibah

3. Lunch for guests

4. Mujāhid trying to 'gather the word of all'

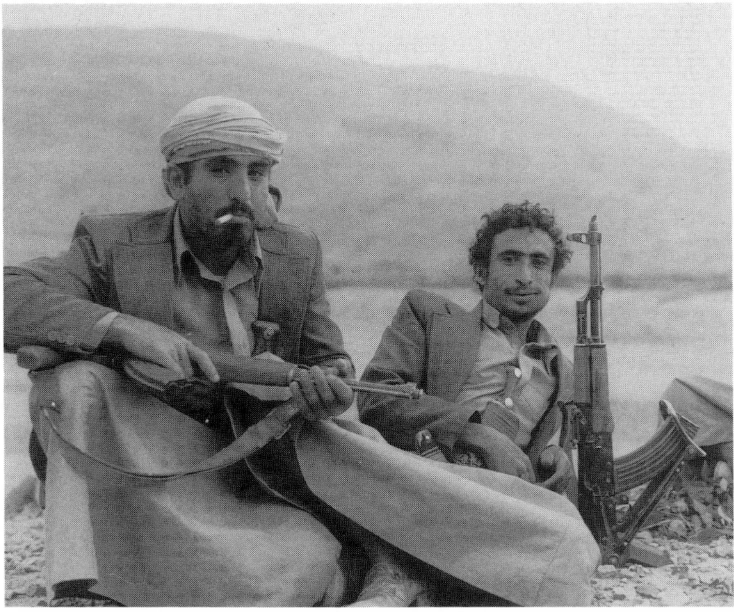

5. Tribesmen by the road (both men are chewing *qāt*)

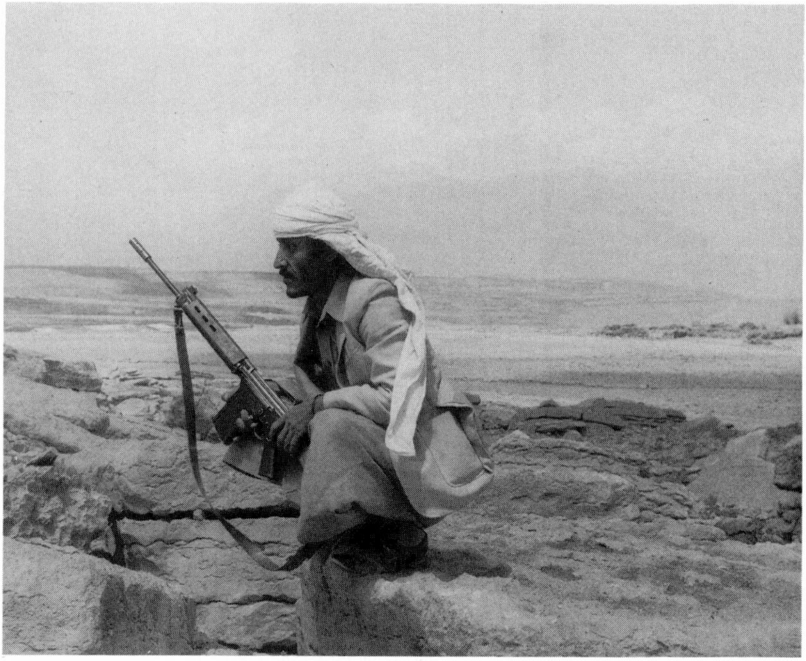

6. On the plateau edge near Khamir

7. *Muzayyin* drummer at a wedding

8. Gun-truck at a tribal meeting

9. One of the Khamir market people (note the dagger worn as was previously the right of learned men)

10. Tribal meeting east of Jabal Baraṭ

11. Houses at Jabal Baraṭ

12. Dancing with daggers (Khārif)

13. Ploughing for winter barley

14. Smugglers breaking down goods in the far north-east

using the standard terms of Zaydi rhetoric. 'When trouble from them increased and judgment by the *ṭāghūt*, rulings [at the expense of] the plain and tolerant *sharīʿah*, and the denial of inheritance to women, the Imam—God strengthen him—ordered Sayf al-Islām Aḥmad to be sent to discipline the tribes of Ḥāshid' (Zabārah 1956: iii. 197). In fact, as we have seen, this was the culmination of a long struggle. Even now the results were limited. Any colonial power worth that dubious name might well have hung half Bayt al-Aḥmar and exiled the rest, but the Imam made terms after Nāṣir b. Nāṣir fled to 'Asīr and his brother Ḥusayn took his place as chief of Ḥāshid.

Throughout the 1920s the Imam and his sons involved themselves in the affairs of the tribes to Ḥāshid's north and east more as arbitrators than as rulers (see Zabārah 1956: iii. 125, 149, 188). Late in 1932, however, Sayf al-Islām Aḥmad began preparations to subjugate the east directly. He

> marched with a great force to Ḥarf Sufyān . . . There soon came to him the Ashrāf of the Jawf, the chiefs of Dhū Ḥusayn, and others. He informed them that the aim and intention of his coming was simply to reform the people of the area, to make the roads secure, and to establish the pure *sharīʿah*. He demanded from them chosen hostages and they obeyed. (al-Jirāfī 1951: 241)

Dhū Muḥammad, though, did not obey (Zabārah 1956: iii. 313), and Jabal Baraṭ was taken by force. A delegation came to Aḥmad even from Banī Nawf, 'the wild beasts of the empty spaces who have no work but raiding the eastern tribes . . .' (ibid.), and the *ʿāmil* appointed to al-ʿInān took some three hundred hostages from them, Dhū Muḥammad, and Dhū Ḥusayn. He was then sent to establish the rule of law among Wā'ilah, who rebelled in mid-1933 and sought aid from Yām. The Imam's army pursued the latter well into Najrān (ibid. iii. 314) where the Saudis, advancing from the north at the time, also had their claims. The breakdown of the talks resulted in the Saudi–Yemeni war of 1934.

The resulting loss of 'Asīr and Najrān is often taken to have provoked the beginnings of a 'modernist' opposition to the Imams, which grew until the Imamate's overthrow thirty years later (we shall come back to this in Ch. 7). But for the moment the tribes' independence had been lost—none of them had territory beyond the Imam's influence—and from the mid-1930s to the 1960s the tribes, who had alternately supported and resisted the Imams, were all under the Imams' strict control. We should briefly look at what their position was.

The first thing to be said is that no attempt was made to abolish tribalism as such. Where tribal practice was equated so readily with ignorance, and thus with irreligion, this might seem surprising, but it is as if the phenomenon were God-given; as much part of the intractable world and God's will as the mountains or the weather.[30] Indeed, there were only 'tribes', not tribal*ism,* and the radical ambition of rebuilding humanity to some human design (a 'sociological' ambition, of its nature) is more a feature of our own time. Nor did the Imamate command the means to root out institutions on any large scale. The Ḥamīd al-Dīn Imams, Yaḥyā (1904–48) and Aḥmad (1948–62), did not reproduce the elaborate courts and armies of the early Qāsimīs but were rather frugal men who personally supervised even small, local matters and ran their administrations with the forms of power available to them (see e.g. Rihani 1930: 220 ff.; Scott 1942: 174–5). Over the following decades they gradually built an army, whose officers in the end were to be part of the Imamate's undoing, but the tribes remained the stronger force, always carefully fragmented by their rulers' policy.

The aim was that 'the pure *sharī'ah* be established', which (as in most pre-bureaucratic Islamic states) meant first of all that the *zakāt*, or canonical tax, be collected and a modicum of order retained. 'Broadly speaking, the tribal Zaydi north was governed by indirect rule with subsidies provided for the chiefs. The Shāfi'ī south was less fortunate in being under direct rule by government officials working in concert with local headmen' (Serjeant 1979: 92). In both areas the 'headmen' received a cut of the tax which it was their responsibility to collect. One is sometimes told now that this was a quarter of the total for northerners and a tenth for the Shāfi'ī south (Messick 1978: 170), but the details in the north were in fact irregular. Bayt al-Aḥmar, for example, are said to have received a quarter as the *rājiʿ* or 'return' on al-'Uṣaymāt's taxes until Imam Yaḥyā's death in 1948, but only a tenth after that. The shaykhs of al-Ghūlah, on the other hand, had been among the first in 'Iyāl Surayḥ to send Yaḥyā hostages; but they were allotted a *rājiʿ* of only a tenth, while those who resisted longer got a quarter. Their own stipend rose to a quarter only in Imam Aḥmad's time.

To enforce this system, many tribesmen were posted elsewhere in Yemen, to the west or south, and stationed in groups of three or four with the local *'āmil* or district governor. A form of petty corruption grew up which has not altogether vanished nowadays. When these tribesmen were sent out on *tanāfīdh* ('executive duties'), to bring someone to court or to the presence of the Imam's officials, they would charge their prisoners a riyal a head for their trouble. The practice of 'selling orders' (*mabī' al-awāmir*) became widespread. The official would sell to the tribesman the job of bringing someone in, and the tribesman would turn a profit by charging the prisoner. Northern tribesmen began to attach themselves to officials in the west and south without any appointment by the state but as *khābiṭīs*, freelance policemen and bailiffs. Numerous men from the north drifted to the south and west in this way and stayed there permanently.

In the north itself the rhetoric of Islamic law against tribal custom (*sharī'ah* against *ṭāghūt*) was vigorously sustained: in Imam Yaḥyā's time, it was said, 'merely to possess a book of *ṭāghūt* would be punished by death' (Serjeant 1969: 297). Practice was often much more ambiguous, with tribal institutions such as guaranty being used to sustain Zaydi administration (Dresch forthcoming *a* and *c*); but large-scale, independent actions by tribal groups were suppressed almost entirely. The suppression was worked precisely through the tribal leaders, and the imbalance between their several families was in large part maintained by the Imams' use of them (ibid.). The ranking of their powers seems almost the same at the end of the period as at the start. But Aḥmad required that the more important of them stay as 'guests' in his capital at Ta'izz. Ḥusayn al-Aḥmar, for example, maintained open house at Ta'izz and was given 50 or 60 Maria Theresa (silver) thalers a week by the Imam to support this, in addition to his monthly stipend of some hundreds of thalers. He and the other great shaykhs were closely under Aḥmad's eye. Hostages from their families were held in great numbers, either where the Imam was in Ṣan'ā' or in fortresses remote from their own territory.

The resulting security is remembered by everyone who knew the period, and in effect became proverbial: 'the roads were secure to the point where the traveller from the Jawf to Ma'rib needed only one escort (*rafīq*), though the distance is about six days and previously one could not cross it except in large groups' (Zabārah

1956: iii. 313). Before or after this period a government could only bring in dissidents or collect taxes from such areas by sending a strong column of troops, but the Imam could send a solitary soldier 'with a *bashlī* [an old Italian rifle] on his shoulder and a couple of cartridges' to bring in whom he wished. The soldier had only to remind them that 'behind me is Aḥmad'. The affairs of the tribes were, in effect, frozen for more than a generation, and those of Yemen with them: there are few tales told of the period at all by tribesmen, except those that concern the Imam's own judicial cunning.

NOTES

1. Al-Qāsim's career is the subject of several published works. See 'Īsā b. Luṭfallāh 1981; Nubdhah; Yaḥyā b. al-Ḥusayn 1968; Sālim 1974; al-Nahrawālī 1968; Tritton 1925; and al-Madāḥ 1982, which despite the unnecessarily poor maps is very useful.
2. One Muḥammad al-Sawdī was implicated in a millenial outbreak in the western mountains in 1644. His student or acolyte, Ibrāhīm al-Maḥaṭwarī, later launched a rising of his own in al-Sharaf in 1699. He assumed the Imamic parasol, declared himself the Awaited Mahdi, banned the use of tobacco, and massacred a great many Jews and Baniyān (Hindu traders). For three months or so his following may have been as large as 20,000, a great many of them tribesmen. Half a century later in 1751, and in just the same area, one Abū 'Alāmah led a similar movement, which we shall touch on below. Again he drew in many tribesmen (Zabārah 1941: 40–57).
3. The evidence for the long-term presence of northern shaykhs in the west is thin: 'Īsā b. Luṭfallāh (1981: 41) mentions a shaykh named al-Ghaylānī holding western forts in 1527, as does Zabārah (1952: 405). The name presumably connects with Dhū Ghaylān, the collective name of Dhū Muḥammad and Dhū Ḥusayn, although the earliest clear reference I know of to these tribes themselves is not until almost seventy years later. For tribal involvement with western forts in Rasūlid times, when the Imam al-Mahdī Aḥmad was at odds with the Ḥamzah Ashrāf, see ibid. 159.
4. Al-Mahdī Muḥammad b. al-Mahdī Aḥmad was called 'he of al-Mawāhib' after the fortified town he built for himself near Dhamār. For convenience I shall refer to him as 'al-Mawāhib'. For a sketch of his career see Serjeant 1983: 82–3.
5. 'Alī Qāsim's house in fact stands on the ridge at Kharāsh, overlooking al-Khamrī and Wādī Ḥumrān. Beside it is the ruined base of a large stone round-tower which is said to have belonged to his father. The tombstone is an irregular slab only 35 millimetres or so high, with a

single line scratched around it as a margin: it contrasts very much with the beautifully carved stones of Ṣa'dah workmanship that adorn most of the few graves in Upper Yemen which have tombstones at all.

6. Qāsim b. 'Alī is remembered as, among other things, a fine copyist of the Qur'ān. His father, 'Alī Qāsim (the one killed by al-Manṣūr), is the subject of a very curious story. He is said to have been coming up from al-Baṭanah with a camel-train of grain, when he encountered a leper, whom he treated kindly and indeed carried over the last stretch of trail to the highlands. When he set him down, the leper had changed to a handsome, richly dressed man who said, 'God bless you and all your descendants, *yā aḥmar ibn al-aḥmar*.' No one can attach any meaning to the phrase, but they say this is where the name came from. The poor stranger was perhaps Nabī Khiḍr, who still wanders the world since before the Prophet's time, and from him came 'Alī Qāsim's *barakah*, wealth, and power. The story is curious because one simply does not hear tales of this sort on the plateau: it really is exceptional, and it is not at all widely known. It was told to me by one of the poorer members of the family at al-Khamrī.
7. Serjeant was told that Bayt al-Aḥmar were once *fuqahā'* and came originally from Ḥabūr (Serjeant 1977: 228–9 and 1983: 97). Most of the family members I have known have suggested their spread was in the other direction, to Ḥabūr from al-Khamrī just north of Ḥūth. From the late sixteenth century onward there are mentions of a group called al-Ḥamrā' or Banī Ḥamrah and of a place called Najd Banī Ḥamrah, which would seem to have been between Ḥabūr and Shahārah (Yaḥyā b. al-Ḥusayn 1968: 763, 783; Nubdhah: 223, 287, 360, 365, 474; Īsā b. Luṭfallāh 1981: 17). No connection can yet be demonstrated. One should remember that family names are not always given by descent or origin: Bayt Ḥamīd al-Dīn, for instance, the last dynasty of Imams, acquired their family name through marriage (see Zabārah 1957: 117). It might well be that certain shaykhly names (e.g. Ḥubaysh, Radmān) are connected with areas outside tribal territory with which the family became associated (cf. Goitein 1941: 52 n. 29).
8. 'At the end of Shawwāl, Bakīl and Ḥāshid gathered and descended on the west to regain their fiefs. War broke out between them and a group of peasants (*al-ra'iyyah*, people who paid taxes) in the villages of Ḥajjah. In Shawwāl, Sharīf Aḥmad Muḥammad of Abū 'Arīsh emerged with a faction of Yām, intending war with the ruler of al-Sharaf' (Zabārah 1941: 56).
9. It was the weakness of an earlier anthropology, perhaps, to deal with Middle Eastern tribes in isolation. But looking over the literature one finds everywhere this theme of generosity as a tribal virtue, the mark of a man who is given God's bounty and whom one might honourably follow, while the means to practice such virtue comes only from outside the tribes' own moral world. See particularly the apparently contradictory accounts of the Rwala by Musil (1928) and Lancaster (1981), and the information to resolve the contradiction (Khoury 1982)—grants from the Ottomans of agricultural land. Again, all

along the northern edge of Arabia one finds petty tribal states rising and falling as one tribal leader or another gains control of an oasis town (Rosenfeld 1965). Lancaster's own paper (1979) 'The Development and Function of the Shaykh in Nomad/Settler Symbiosis' could as well have been entitled 'The Function of Nomad/Settler Symbiosis in the Development of Shaykhs': here we have the same phenomenon played out in a very different ecological setting.

10. In the *tahjīr* of Bayt al-Mu'ayyad quoted in ch. 4 we find a reference to offences *min ahl 'arḍi-him aw ṣaḥbi-him aw min ghayr-hum dawlah aw ra'iyyah aw qabīlah* . . . The tribes themselves were certainly taxed (until Imamic tax registers come to light we cannot say much of the detail), but the *ra'iyyah* or *ra'āyā* would seem to have been the subjects of tax-farming, which the tribes were not to anything like the same degree.

11. In the former respect the shaykhs are just like the tribesmen: emigrés are partly lost to the tribal world, and often they are lost entirely. The one exception to this rule are Dhū Muḥammad, whose shaykhs and tribesmen in Lower Yemen maintain very strong ties with Baraṭ over the generations. Their neighbours in Dhū Ḥusayn do not. In many tribes, however, there are shaykhs who grew up with relatives in Lower Yemen and have, for instance, learned from childhood the Shāfi'ī form of prayer.

12. These followers, interestingly, are said to have included numerous *akhdām* or lowly 'servitors' (Zabārah 1941: 240). *Akhdām*, more strictly speaking, are blacks, associated by many Yemenis with the Tihāmah, who work nowadays often as beggars and itinerant musicians. It used to be that they came up into the highlands as migratory workers at harvest time. Unlike the various estates of 'weak' people touched on in ch. 4, they do not have any particular place in tribal custom; they are more truly 'outsiders' than anyone.

13. Al-'Ukām and the Baraṭ tribes had already been involved in the long disputes in Lower Yemen between al-Manṣūr al-Ḥusayn (1727–48), his brother Aḥmad, and the newly independent 'Abdalī Sultan of Laḥj (see Zabārah 1941: 215). By the time of al-Mahdī al-'Abbās (1748), these disputes over local power had become engrossed in the more general crisis of legitimacy in taxation. Zabārah (1929: i. 237–8) relates the story of Ḥasan al-Ẓafrī, who was sent to Lower Yemen as a governor and insisted on taking only the legitimate amount from the peasantry. To al-Mahdī's great surprise (much dwelt on in the story to point the contrast with the usual state of things), the income from the area of Jiblah and Ibb shot up from almost nothing to 45,000 *qadaḥ* per year. Although al-Mahdī amassed enormous wealth in Ṣan'ā', and 'everyone agreed on his honesty and the goodness of his life' (al-Wāsi'ī 1928: 59; not true in fact), the provinces already suffered unproductive oppression.

14. To speak in terms of the distinction between Zaydi and Shāfi'ī is in fact to adopt the view of the mob. Ibn al-Amīr's position, and that of al-Shawkānī after him, would seem to have been that a *mujtahid*,

rejecting false 'imitation', draws on the best sources available and thus transcends 'sectarianism'. It is this which accounts for the influence of such writers among reformers elsewhere in the Muslim world (see Ṣubḥī 1980: 729 ff.). With the burgeoning of interest among Western scholars in Egyptian, Syrian, and Indian *salafīs* of the nineteenth century, the study of these Yemeni thinkers now cries out for attention.

15. The next Baraṭ leader, 'Abdullāh b. Ḥasan al-'Ansī, opposed the next Imam, al-Manṣūr 'Alī b. al-Mahdī in 1782 (Zabārah 1941: 198). In this particular engagement Ṣalāḥ Radmān of Arḥab was killed on the Imam's side, which might remind us that the shaykhly adherents of an Imam, as much as his shaykhly opponents, were drawing on the state's resources in these constant battles. In 1784 alone, al-'Ansī led four attacks on Ṣan'ā' before turning on Lower Yemen; in 1786 there was trouble from his followers inside Ṣan'ā'; in 1793 Ḥusayn b. Ḥasan al-'Ansī was bought off, but two years later he cut the Samārah pass in Lower Yemen with a following of Baraṭ tribesmen (al-'Amrī 1985: 44). Again in 1807–8 they besieged the capital (ibid. 59–60; al-Jirāfī 1951: 192).
16. The precise bone of contention here—the movements of prayer—is the subject of differing views even within Zaydism. For a brief account of the question see Sharaf al-Dīn 1968: 216–21. It is not an issue nowadays, and usually was not. The reasons for the disturbances were not doctrinal.
17. Discussing a Turco-Egyptian proposal to return part of the northern Tihāmah to the Imam in return for fixed tribute, *c.*1818–19, Zabārah (1929: ii. 421) says no income had derived from the area since the start of the Qāsimī period and all it would provide was a little coffee for the Sultan's kitchen and bakshish for the troops. Yet elsewhere (ibid. i. 73) he says that in 1782 it had been cause for the Imam's anger that the revenue of al-Ḥudaydah (not the greatest port) had fallen to 3,000 riyals a month. In early Qāsimī times it had been much greater. The income mentioned in connection with Sharīf Ḥamūd's conquests is very large (ibid. i. 410), and al-'Amrī's reading among other historians, such as Jaḥḥāf, leaves no doubt of the importance of coastal revenues, especially those of the great coffee port at Mocha (see al-'Amrī 1985: 30, 66, 92). In the 1730s the 'Abdalī sultans of Laḥj near Aden (who originally are from 'Iyāl 'Abdillāh in Arḥab, not from Yāfi' *pace* Serjeant 1983: 84) had seceded from the Imams, depriving the north of vital revenues from Aden.
18. For brief accounts of al-Faqīh Sa'īd b. Ṣāliḥ al-'Ansī (*sic*) see Messick 1978: 56, Serjeant 1983: 89, and al-Kibsī n.d. 305 ff.
19. Stookey 1978: 152–3 selects events after al-Nāṣir's assassination to illustrate 'the complex relations among the war-like tribes'. The Imam had been murdered by pro-Ismā'īlī elements of Yām and Hamdān, both of which claim descent from Ḥāshid. So 'the punitive forces', says Stookey, 'could not, obviously, come from Ḥāshid'. In fact the source he is quoting (al-Jirāfī 1951: 197) goes on to say clearly that the punitive force from Arḥab (Bakīl) was combined with 'a gathering

from Khawlān, Nihm, and Ḥāshid'. Tribes were not solidary blocs in those days, any more than before or since. The same point might be made with reference to Imam Aḥmad's campaigns against Bayt al-Aḥmar in the 1920s, where the paramount shaykh of Ḥāshid was attacked with a force including men from Banī Ṣuraym (see ibid. 237).

20. Similarly, when Sharīf Ḥusayn was captured in the Tihāmah his daughter offered horses for slaughter to the tribes of Najrān (Serjeant 1983: 89). The use of horses should emphasize the point that we are not dealing with any kind of sacrificial 'communion' in a commensal meal, but with the imposition of an obligation by a gift between conceptual equals. At the same time there is an axis of largesse, of gifts that do not elicit any response but an expectation of further gifts: e.g. when an Imam gave robes of honour and the recipient returned to demand a turban and slippers (Zabārah 1929: ii. 158), very much as one sees happen nowadays.

21. Yaḥyā b. Hādī Abū Fāri' of al-'Uṣaymāt, for instance, arranged for the return of a field-piece that other tribes of Ḥāshid had captured, and later arranged for two of the sons of al-Mutawakkil Muḥsin to come into Ṣan'ā', where they were lavishly welcomed, dressed as Turks, and given salaries. Their salaries were later paid to them at al-Khamrī (see Zabārah 1956: i. 2/98). In the 1880s al-Dulā'ī, a shaykh of 'Iyāl Surayḥ who wore his moustaches in the Turkish manner and was known as 'Abdullāh Pāsha, frequently mediated between the Turks and the Imams. His family seem already to have acquired great wealth and influence as officers of al-Mahdī al-'Abbās (Zabārah 1929: ii. 100–1), but their power was later broken by the Turks. 'Abdullāh Pāsha's successor, Rājiḥ b. Sa'd al-Maymūnī, took his furnishings, weapons, slaves, and horses, then went over to the Imam. In the ensuing confusion, Ḥāshid, who had been quiet for five years, were again drawn into fighting the Turks (al-Ḥibshī 1980: 347–50; Zabārah 1956: i. 2/96; al-Wāsi'ī 1928: 122–5).

22. The tribes of the far north and east, such as Sufyān and Dhū Ghaylān, had been weakened by successive droughts in their homelands, and the Turkish grip on Lower Yemen was too firm for them to operate there as they had in the mid-nineteenth century. As so often, the detailed pattern of events in the tribal north depends on considerations elsewhere in the country. For a discussion see al-Ḥibshī 1980: 245–6. For a brief account of al-Mahdī Muḥammad see Zabārah 1956: i. 2/353–9. The only account in which he is a conspicuous figure is that written by one of his relatives, Majd al-Dīn (n.d.).

23. Al-Manṣūr's departure for the north was made, or at least recorded, with tidy symbolism. He left Ṣan'ā' by one gate, having entrusted his library to the care of friends as would any man of learning. His son, by another gate, brought him his dagger, his sword, and his copy of *Sharḥ al-Azhār,* the standard reference work of Zaydi jurisprudence with which he struck off northward to 'enforce the right' (Zabārah 1956: i. 2/9).

24. Accounts of what happened differ, but Banī Ṣuraym are agreed to have left the garrison first: it may be that Fayḍī had gained hostages from

their fellows around Khamir, and he is said to have given them two hundred cattle, two hundred sheep, and two hundred *qaḍah* of grain. (But see also Baldry 1976: 168–9.) The triple form of the alleged payment is worth noting. In the previous century Dhū Muḥammad had been bought off by an Imam for 3,000 riyals, three horses, and three lengths of cloth (al-ʿAmrī 1985: 37). A very similar pattern is evident in the Baraṭ *qawāʿid* quoted in earlier chapters, in payments for offences against women (ch. 2), and indeed rather generally.

25. Two poems relating to this period are provided in app. 6/1.

26. Much of Rosaldo's fascinating account of the Ilongot (1980) turns on his own co-ordination of different sequential tales. Cunnison (1951) suggests that one could do something similar in the Luapula case, although the Luapula clans, conspicuously, never do so themselves. Perhaps the most striking contribution of Cunnison's excellent article is the connection it establishes between the past and geographical space (1951: 3, 10, 35–8). The second component of the Luapula scheme—the impersonal or general account of successive cultural stages in the area, from Pygmies to farmers to a world with chiefs (ibid. 24–5, 28, 40)—has less close an equivalent in the Yemeni scheme. The third and most striking component has no real parallel at all in Upper Yemen: the 'personal' clan and lineage histories told by headmen, always stopping at the point where present identities are established, the length of which is correlated to the rank of their 'owners' (ibid. 3–9, 31–3). The reason is clear enough: that in the Yemeni system individual and collective identities are not connected by any equivalent of office or of rank.

27. Within the first two years after the Turkish withdrawal we hear of tribesmen from Ḥāshid and Bakīl being sent to Raymah, Waṣāb, al-Makhādir in Lower Yemen, al-Maḥwīt, al-Ḥaymah, al-Maqāṭirah, Qaʿṭabah, and as far south as Yāfiʿ territory in what is now the People's Democratic Republic of Yemen (Zabārah 1956: iii. 5, 7, 12, 26, 31–2, 54). For further notes on campaigns in the south see Nājī 1977: 79.

28. The troubles around Ḥajjah had begun as early as 1919, in the time of Nāṣir b. Mabkhūt al-Aḥmar, and they continued into the 1920s under his son, Nāṣir b. Nāṣir. The disputes were far longer lasting than Shaybān's particular revolt. Shaybān himself seems to have controlled part of the area under the Turks and to have opposed the Imam in 1909 or so, at a point when the Imam was aided by, among others, Muḥammad Radmān of Arḥab (see Baldry 1976: 183).

29. The original dispute was within Maktab Ḥamadah (part of 'Iyāl Surayḥ) over payment for hostages from the shaykhly family of Bayt al-Qufayhī. With the Imam's encouragement, al-Qufayhī seized two boys from al-Matrad at Ḥamadah's market. Al-Matrad and al-Ṣarabāt then went and slaughtered beasts for Ḥāshid. Again, for two poems from approximately this period see app. 6/1.

30. Cf. al-Wāsiʿī 1928: 147–8, where he attributes the ruination of al-Rawḍah to floods, bats, and tribesmen; compare also the discussion of historiography in ch. 5, above.

7 The September Revolution and the Post-War Republic

Now tell us all about the war
And what they fought each other for.
Southey 'After Blenheim'

It was not purely internal factors that spelled the end of the Imamate and of the tribes' subjection to the last Imams. Nor was it external 'causality' in the form, say, of trade or conquest, all of which Yemen had seen before. Such considerations are important. But more important still is that certain Yemenis acquired a different view than previously of the country's place among other countries, which in turn had implications for the tribes within it.

Much has carried through intact to the present from before the 1962 coup which established the republic. But one suspects the same is true of tribalism in Yemen as of the religious practices Peters wrote of in pre- and post-revolutionary Libya: 'Since the language in which beliefs are expressed remains the same, the temptation is to marvel at their persistence; but . . . the differences in the historical contexts make the beliefs themselves fundamentally different' (Peters 1976: 13). From the perspective of the present it is hard to judge. But there is no doubt that 'contexts' have changed, not least in that the tribes, and for the first time tribal*ism*, now form part of an explicitly national whole. We can best start, therefore, with the rise of nationalist political language. The bulk of the chapter will deal with the civil war of the 1960s. The post-war republic will be briefly sketched at the end. In later chapters we can then better judge, I hope, the relation between the obvious fracture with the past which the republic constitutes and the equally obvious continuity of tribal forms within it.

LIBERAL OPPOSITION TO THE LAST IMAMS

Imam Yaḥyā (1904–48) was a figure whose strong points and weak points alike could be measured in the terms applicable to his distant ancestors. By those standards he was a man to respect. The world around him, however, changed out of recognition. When the Turks withdrew he did perhaps have a chance to make some mark in the wider Arab world (al-Wazīr 1971: 52), but he adopted an isolationist policy which set Yemen aside from much that was happening elsewhere, and contradictions were bound to appear in the following decades, not least in the country's cultural life.[1] While concern for a general Arab identity rose throughout the region, Yemen seemed to turn the other way. Though not an accurate report on how things were, it is none the less an important statement when older men tell one nowadays, 'We thought the sun rose in Ma'rib and set in al-Ḥudaydah.'

Signs of a different perspective on Yemen's position are noticeable quite early. Al-Wāsi'ī's chronicle, for instance, written in the 1920s and in some ways a classicizing work, suddenly makes mention in the entry for 1314/1896 of newspaper reports from elsewhere, of a landslip in America and of the death of twenty thousand children from disease in France (al-Wāsi'ī 1928: 163). In the entry for 1909 we are given an account of a letter from the Imam to the Ottoman Turks that was printed in an Egyptian newspaper, then several more items on Yemen from the world press, and a report on Yemen in a Turkish paper (ibid. 221–5). Decades later, Zabārah cited for the same period a number of foreign press reports, articles by Rāshid Riḍā, and letters to the Imam from Muslims in the Far East (Zabārah 1956: ii. 129, 192, 260). The country's self-estimation (or that of its thinkers) had become bound up with its estimation by others, to produce the effect of endless mirror reflections that is common to national identities everywhere.

It is from within that set of reflections, and only within it, that comparative ideas of 'modernity', 'progress', or 'backwardness' make sense; and these ideas define the modern era. It was to be some time before the particular image of tribes as backward or archaic became persuasive. But Yemen itself was felt by many to be 'backward', and this was discussed at an early date by educated men.

The emergence of the 'modernist' opposition is often dated to 1935, immediately after the war with Saudi Arabia, when Sayyid Aḥmad al-Muṭā' is said to have founded *hay'at al-niḍāl*, 'the group for struggle'.[2] The more generally emerging desire among young, educated men for progress and reform became allied, however, to disputes over who should succeed Imam Yaḥyā; and Yaḥyā himself (almost inevitably, given the system of national borders that appeared in the area after the First World War) had become 'King of Yemen' as well as Imam. Prince Aḥmad b. Yaḥyā has already been mentioned as leading several campaigns against the tribes. Quite early (see Rossi 1939: 118) he acquired the nickname al-Baḥḥūt, 'the terrible', but the enmities he acquired on his own count were supplemented when his candidacy as crown prince was promoted at the expense of his immediate relatives and of other sayyid families, particularly Bayt al-Wazīr, who had supplied Imam Yaḥyā with noted army commanders. Yahyā finally extracted a formal *bay'ah* or oath of allegiance for Aḥmad in 1937.

It was at about this period that Muḥammad al-Zubayrī, now 'the hero of Yemen Arab Republic ideology' (Serjeant 1979: 87), went to study in Cairo. When he returned to Yemen in 1941, he was imprisoned a while for seditious talk, but after his release he joined a coterie of intellectuals whom Crown Prince Aḥmad had gathered around himself in Ta'izz.[3] The spell there was broken only when Aḥmad, presumably in a fit of temper, burst out with, 'I ask God that I do not die before I have coloured my sword here with the blood of modernists' (al-Shamāḥī 1972: 191; cf. Stookey 1978: 218). Several 'modernists' fled to British-occupied Aden, where al-Zubayrī and Aḥmad Nu'mān soon came to head the Free Yemeni Party (*ḥizb al-aḥrār*).

The liberal reformers adhered to 'Abdullāh al-Wazīr in 1948 when Yaḥyā was murdered and al-Wazīr proclaimed himself Imam. A leftist writer (al-Shahārī 1972: 75) dismisses the coup as no more than a 'palace revolution' of the sort that had always occurred among 'feudal princes', but it took place under a unique mix of rhetoric: al-Wazīr sought the *bay'ah* much as Imams had always done, but at the same time there was issued a 'sacred national charter' (*al-mīthāq al-waṭanī al-muqaddas*) which ruled that the oath be given by 'representatives of the Yemeni people' and that government be 'by consultation and constitution' (*shūriyyan dustūriyyan*). The whole episode forms a striking link between two concepts of how a state might be organized. But the planning was tragically inadequate.[4] Aḥmad reached Ḥajjah, where he rallied a tribal army, and three weeks after his father's death he had Ṣan'ā' surrounded. The tribesmen he had gathered were sent in to sack the city, the ring-leaders of the coup were executed, many others were imprisoned, and Aḥmad established himself as Imam, which he was to remain until 1962.

It had been most conspicuously a coup of learned men, and the reaction against them was indiscriminate (see al-Shāmī 1975: 46). However, the tribes also had been implicated in more than the sack of Ṣan'ā', and Aḥmad's victims included, for example, Muḥammad and 'Abdullāh Abū Ra's (Dhū Muḥammad) and Aḥsan Ṣāliḥ al-Shāyif (Dhū Ḥusayn). Several other tribal figures were arrested. The prisoners not only exchanged and refined their own ideas, but set about extricating themselves by appealing via friends to the Imam, by petitioning Aḥmad himself (in verse), and not least by cultivating Aḥmad's son, al-Badr Muḥammad. Several of the imprisoned liberals were in correspondence with al-Badr as early as 1951, and he soon came to occupy an ambiguous position as 'Imam of the liberals and of the future'; indeed, the liberal reformers at home and in exile may have been as influential as anyone in suggesting to Aḥmad that al-Badr be named crown prince (see al-'Aynī 1957: 72).

A number of those involved look back at 1955, when there was an abortive coup against Aḥmad and al-Badr stood by his father, as the time when the idea of the republic, and thus an end to the Imamate in any form, began to take hold (Markaz 1981: 137, 138, 142, 144). Yet, at the same time, al-Badr had risen somewhat in his father's estimation, and was also still the focus of many liberal hopes. On his father's behalf he visited several countries during the 1950s, including Egypt,[5] but at home he tended to remain in Ṣan'ā' (Imam Aḥmad after the 1948 revolt had based himself in Ta'izz), and men from Ḥāshid remember al-Badr associating closely with Ḥamīd b. Ḥusayn al-Aḥmar: indeed, he raised something very like an *'ukfah* (Imamic bodyguard) of his own, with Ḥamīd as one of its leaders.[6]

In the outside world the tide of republicanism was rising with the encouragement of Nāṣir's Egypt, and the exiled liberal movement began to stress opposition not only to the Imam, but to the Imamate, a line that at last gave some place to the tribes and to their leaders.

On our soil democratic humanism, consultation (*shūrā*), and popular government were known for the first time in human history. Did not the bountiful Qur'ān say, in the words of Bilqīs, Queen of Sheba, 'O chiefs, advise me on my affairs. . . . I have never issued an order before you expressed your views' . . . Was she [simply] a queen? Was the system of government in Yemen monarchist? Certainly not. . . . It was republican. (al-ʿAynī 1957: 60)

The ruler, al-ʿAynī argues (ibid. 143), should derive his authority from the tribes and from other parts of the nation. The image used to argue this is distinctive of nationalism and quite different from anything available in older Zaydi language: rather than a sequence of discrete connections specifying the place of named persons in a tradition and in a history of particularities, 'the people' (*al-shaʿb*) is defined collectively by an identity of its future with the distant past.[7] The tribes unavoidably form part of this.

Within Yemen a tribally based plot to remove Aḥmad was apparently undertaken in early 1957 by a group that included Qāsim Abū Ra's (Dhū Muḥammad), ʿAlī Abū Laḥūm (Nihm), and Ḥusayn al-Aḥmar (al-ʿUṣaymāt, Ḥāshid), as well as Qadi ʿAbd al-Raḥmān al-Iryānī (Markaz 1981: 280–1). Evidently, little came of it. Quite how early such tribally based resistance took cohesive form is not clear. There is some doubt, for example, whether Ḥamīd and Ḥusayn al-Aḥmar began to organize in 1959 or in the year preceding (ibid. 42, 52); but it deserves noting that, although they nowadays make no connection of it with political action, many minor shaykhs remember being forced by bad harvests to sell their small western landholdings at about this time (1958 or early 1959). In Taʿizz, disaffected army officers were meanwhile spreading pamphlets denouncing the Imam.

In April 1959 Aḥmad left for Rome in search of medical treatment; affairs now devolved on al-Badr. The period remains one of the most obscure in recent Yemeni history, but there is no doubt that a great many tribesmen streamed into Ṣanʿā', and that certain of the younger shaykhs were as insistent on reform as were their contemporaries in the army, 'especially those who had been released from the prisons in Taʿizz and Ḥajjah, such as Ḥamīd b. Ḥusayn al-Aḥmar and Sinān Abū Laḥūm [who] tried to force al-Badr to form a new, free government' (al-Shamāḥī 1972: 307). Al-Badr probably required little forcing. He himself had spoken out for reforms on several occasions. He and Ḥamīd al-Aḥmar had been closely associated for some time, as we have seen, and the story cannot be discounted that a plan existed for the pair of them to form a government.[8]

Aḥmad returned in August 1959, much to the surprise of many of his opponents, who had assumed he would die abroad, and when he landed at al-Ḥudaydah he broadcast a poem threatening retribution (for the text see Serjeant 1982: 47–8). Many of those at odds with him panicked, and whatever plans were half-formed to oppose him fell apart. Ḥamīd al-Aḥmar seems first to have gone to al-'Ashshah in search of support from his own tribe, al-'Uṣaymāt, and then to have come south toward Ṣan'ā' with a group including Dāris, 'Awfān, and Abū Sabā of Dhū Muḥammad, Muḥsin Shūkhī of Banī Ṣuraym, and others. When they reached Ḍaḥyān, north of Raydah, they found that no one would let them into the villages, far less support them. Shūkhī went to Sufyān, where he had relatives. The others moved out to the Jawf, where Dāris, 'Awfān, and Abū Sabā turned toward their homes at Baraṭ.

An attempt was made by Sinān Abū Laḥūm and Aḥmad al-Zāyidī to raise Khawlān (al-Shamāḥī 1972: 310), and a plot was laid by shaykhs from Ḥāshid, Dhū Muḥammad, Murād, and elsewhere to assassinate the Imam at Sukhnah (Markaz 1981: 282). But Aḥmad's mere presence in the country seems to have been sufficient to paralyse resistance. 'Imam Aḥmad finished splintering Ḥāshid's front from within, as he had done before. He also completed his preparations to advance on Ḥāshid, then Baraṭ, the Jawf, Nihm, and Khawlān, for which the disintegration of Ḥāshid's unity paved the way' (al-Shamāḥī 1972: 312). 'Abd al-Laṭīf b. Qāyid al-Rājiḥ (Khawlān) was captured after a brief battle at al-'Awd in Lower Yemen. Nājī b. 'Alī al-Shāyif (Dhū Ḥusayn) was captured after being wounded near al-Ḥazm in the Jawf. By the time Ḥamīd al-Aḥmar was taken, in the same area, he had no one with him but a boy from al-Ashmūr named Muḥammad al-Duqaymī. Ḥusayn al-Aḥmar, by most accounts, did not know that his son had been captured. He had gathered together a large force of tribesmen near Ḥūth, at the same time as the Imam's governor there was collecting forces of his own (ibid.), but he left them, against his followers' advice, and went to Ṣan'ā' by himself on the promise of safe conduct from Imam Aḥmad. On the Imam's orders Ḥamīd and Ḥusayn al-Aḥmar and 'Abd al-Laṭīf Rājiḥ were beheaded at Ḥajjah. Many lesser shaykhs fled to Aden.[9]

It was only at this late stage, and in his last major prose work, that al-Zubayrī, in exile, turned to the tribes. Although they had indeed crushed al-Wazīr's revolt a decade earlier, the defeat of the 1948 revolution was the strange but effective means by which the idea of revolution spread to a wider circle. It filtered down from the upper, ruling levels to the popular base just as Islam did among the Tartars, who smashed the Islamic empire only to suffer a spiritual collapse of their tyranny. They thus embraced Islam and became its greatest power. (al-Zubayrī 1961: 63)

The Tartars in the case at hand are precisely 'greater Hamdān, to which belong Ḥāshid and Bakīl, the two mightiest tribes in our country, our history, and indeed in the history of Arabism and Islam' (ibid. 148). Quite how far such ideas had 'filtered down' in practice is hard to say, but this placement of the tribes at the moral centre of reformist thought is striking.

Zubayrī's *Tragedy of wāq al-wāq* is a literary work much more than a political manifesto, and the plot or mechanism turns on a kind of 'night journey' in which the author's double goes to paradise to meet, among others, 'Alī b. Abī Ṭālib, As'ad al-Kāmil the Ḥimyarite king, the martyrs of Āl Abī Dunyā, al-Hamdānī, al-Shawkānī, and the first Zaydi Imam in Yemen, al-Hādī.[10] In the dream world of the book, the same pre-Islamic imagery is used as by al-'Aynī a few years earlier: 'All the tribes agreed on the rule of law: that things must be in the future as they were in the days of Ma'īn, Qatabān, Saba' and Ḥimyar, where there was a special council in which all were represented and took part in government' (ibid. 264). The future will recover the golden age, and the period of later Imamic rule will be revealed as a mistaken 'tragedy'. The tribes in particular now appear as the repository of the people's will: 'And in their vanguard Ḥusayn b. Nāṣir al-Aḥmar and 'Abd al-Laṭīf Rājiḥ, who represent the honour of all Hamdān, both Ḥāshid and Bakīl, and represent behind them the whole of the people' (ibid. 244). The back cover of the original edition carries a photograph of Ḥamīd al-Aḥmar (the present shaykh's older brother) over the title, the martyr of Ḥāshid's Karbalā': in other words, the contemporary expression of a doomed quest for justice pursued by Ḥusayn b. 'Alī over twelve hundred years ago. The book does not, however, provide any detailed suggestions on how the contemporary tyrant might be overthrown. Changes in the relation of 'the tribes' to 'the people' were in fact to come only in the course of a long civil war.

THE OUTBREAK OF THE CIVIL WAR

Imam Aḥmad died on 19 September 1962 and was succeeded by his son, al-Badr, who was driven out of Ṣan'ā' within the week. In the period before Aḥmad's death a group of Yemeni army officers had been in contact not only with the liberals in exile but with the Egyptian government (al-Juzaylān 1977: 89–90).[11] The circles of conspiracy were so tangled, and the coup is now of such importance in the definition of the republic, that the details may perhaps never become clear; but late on the night of 26 September 1962 tanks began to shell the Dār al-Bashā'ir palace in Ṣan'ā', where al-Badr had held a meeting. The 'siege' went on all night, but the Imam slipped away from Ṣan'ā' to Hamdān, stopped briefly at Ḍula', and pushed on with only ten or a dozen men to 'Amrān. Pursued by small groups of republicans, he found his way north to the border with Saudi Arabia, while Ṣan'ā' and Cairo radio persisted in the claim he was dead.

In Ṣan'ā' the shaykhs most implacably opposed to the Imam (or at least to Bayt Ḥamīd al-Dīn) were armed with what weapons were available and sent in pursuit or to occupy outlying areas. The few coherent army units were deployed around Ṣan'ā' itself. By the end of October the shaykhs and the army officers were opposed in the countryside by the princes of the royal house. Al-Badr's uncle Ḥasan crossed from Saudi Arabia to Yemen with his followers near Ṣa'dah; they left part of their number to reduce the fort at al-Sinnārah, and advanced toward the south, only to be met and turned back by a motley force of republicans under Amīn Abū Ra's of Dhū Muḥammad ('Abd al Ilāh 1964: 71). Al-Badr himself recrossed the border in the northern Tihāmah. Other princes moved into the western mountains, the Jawf, and the territory of such eastern tribes as Nihm, Arḥab, and Khawlān.

The republicans in Ṣan'ā' were rapidly, although largely unwillingly, brought under the control of their Egyptian allies, who had landed troops within forty-eight hours of the coup. 'Abdullāh al-Sallāl (the ex-chief of staff to Imam al-Badr) had been pronounced president of the revolutionary council on 28 September. But the Egyptians then produced their list of approved persons, and 'Abd al-Raḥmān al-Bayḍānī arrived from Cairo on the fourth day after the coup as minister of economics. He was quickly named deputy president (after al-Sallāl), deputy commander of the armed forces, and foreign minister as well, making it clear that Egyptian aid depended on his wishes being followed ('Abd al-Ilāh 1964: 30).[12] Within a week of the coup there were at least three thousand Egyptian soldiers in Yemen with supporting arms (Nājī 1977: 221), and their numbers rapidly increased. The Shāfi'ī areas south of Ṣan'ā' and in the Tihāmah nearly all accepted the change of government at once. The western mountains, by contrast, largely fell to the Ḥamīd al-Dīn princes. The war was very much the tribesmen's affair, with the north and east (i.e. tribal territory) divided between the different camps.

At the outset each side attempted to forestall the other, and the results of these attempts in many cases drew lines across which the war then went on for years. In the first few weeks, for example, the republicans sent three columns to the east ('Abd al-Ilāh 1964: 75). One of these, under Amīn Nu'mān, was intended to move past Dhībīn to the Jawf and was hurried on its way by news that the princes were already gathering support around al-Ḥazm. The republicans reached the fort at Sinwān, in the northernmost part of Arḥab and very close to Sufyān, where, as 'Abd al-Ilāh tells the story, they failed to picket the surrounding hills and were set upon by night. Most fled, while a few firmer spirits stayed to destroy the stores and were themselves killed or captured (ibid. 80).

But the events which the author presents as happening in an instant are remembered by those involved as having spread over several weeks. The first mixed force of republicans, mainly from Ḥāshid, 'Iyāl Surayḥ, and 'Iyāl Yazīd, arrived some ten days after the coup, at about the same time as letters from Prince 'Abdullāh Ḥusayn reached Murhibah, Arḥab, and Sufyān. These latter tribes were not at first committed as wholes to either side, but men from each of them joined the royalist force moving in from the Jawf. The republicans pushed the royalists back to Harān before themselves retiring to Sinwān. Some weeks later a larger royalist force, joined by men from Murhibah, Sufyān, and other tribes of the area, came in from the Jawf and laid siege to Sinwān. The siege was raised by republican reinforcements from Ṣan'ā' (probably under Sinān Abū Laḥūm of Nihm), some of whom went on to loot livestock from Sufyānī territory. Resistance stiffened.

Men from 'Iyāl Yazīd and 'Iyāl Surayḥ who had come with the first republican group began to drift back to their own homes, where the conflict between republicans and royalists was also starting to set in. Men from Murhibah, southern Sufyān, and northern Arḥab were now receiving royalist pay and were increasingly inclined to fight the republican garrison, who themselves had begun to resemble a purely Ḥāshidī force. When the royalists finally fell on Sinwān in great numbers the remaining republicans fled in disorder, not stopping to regroup until they reached Raydah. The royalists stopped short at Dhībīn. They were later driven back to Harān by the Egyptians, who themselves fought several bloody actions over just the same ground (see Schmidt 1968: 134).

Much the same was occurring on the plateau to the north and west. In the first days after the coup some of the Ḥāshid shaykhs had gone from Ṣan'ā' to the area between Ḥūth and Shahārah, and 'Abduh Kāmil of Khārif had chased the Imam's governor out of Ḥūth itself. Shahārah, a town populated largely by sayyids, was occupied briefly; but the town's inhabitants threw out the republican garrison in a matter of days, and Shahārah remained royalist thereafter. So did al-Ahnūm, whose relations with Shahārah and with Bayt Ḥamīd al-Dīn were close. 'Abdullāh al-Aḥmar of Ḥāshid spent almost two weeks in Khamir, gathering and organizing his forces, while his cousin, Ghālib b. Nāṣir, held the fort of al-Maqalqal at Ḥarf Sufyān. With a few exceptions, such as Nāshir b. Ṭāli' of al-Ḥayrah (killed by the royalists a few years later), most of Sufyān went over to the royalists as soon as letters reached them from the princes.

Neither military nor purely tribal considerations, nor the political histories of individual figures, explain all the alignments; but from the outset the rhetorics of national politics and tribalism were entangled, with the latter showing remarkable resilience. Dhū Muḥammad and Dhū Ḥusayn, for example, arrived at a series of local agreements despite the deep, and even bitter, differences between them (Dhū Muḥammad was largely pro-republican, Dhū Ḥusayn largely pro-royalist). So did Arḥab (royalist) and Khārif (republican). Ḥāshid had similar agreements with 'Iyāl Yazīd and with 'Iyāl Surayḥ. Al-Ahnūm's *qāt* trade with the plateau went on throughout most of the war, under agreements guaranteed in common by men who on other grounds were at daggers drawn, and at several points Sufyān and Ḥāshid also arrived at truces, containing on more than one occasion the provision that roads through (royalist) Sufyān to Ṣa'dah and Baraṭ be secure and guaranteed (*āmin ḍāmin*) even for the Egyptians. None of this should be taken to show the war was not serious. A reasonable guess would be that close to 200,000 people died in the war (Halliday 1974: 106), and many of these were tribesmen. But the war was fought by curious rules. Some three or four months after the coup, for instance, Khārif, Banī Ṣuraym, and al-'Uṣaymāt met at Khamir to confirm 'Abdullāh al-Aḥmar's *hijrah* status as the paramount shaykh of Ḥāshid. Soon afterwards Sanḥān and Hamdān demanded to join in the agreement, although by then these latter two tribes were largely anti-republican, if not actually royalist, because of heavy-handed Egyptian action against them.

The opposition between royalists and republicans cannot be dismissed as secondary and, despite the reservations each side soon came to have about its leaders, this opposition did by itself account for much of the fighting between tribes. The rhetoric on each side was often straight-forward, as two pairs of verses from the early years of the war make clear:

Royalists:
By God Jamāl, we'll not go republican.
The people have risen and want to fight,
Even if the sun rose in the west
And the heavens fell to earth.

Republicans:
You've had your say, now listen.
With Jamāl it will be over in an hour.
He'll give us machine guns and artillery
And the rebels will be forced to obey.[13]

Jamāl here, of course, is Jamāl 'Abd al-Nāṣir, with whom the republican shaykhs had an ambiguous relation from the earliest days of the revolution but who was none the less the symbol of republicanism for both sides. He is referred to again in the republicans' answer to a second royalist ditty, and again the republicans refer to the military strength of their allies:

Royalists:
The high cliffs called and every notable in Yemen answered;
We'll never go republican, not if we are wiped off the earth,
Not if yesterday returns today and the sun rises in Aden,
Not if the earth catches fire and the sky rains lead.

Republicans:
The Egyptian leader rules Yemen with his forces.
Migs and Ilyushins seek out your foxholes.
Bullets from M.1s and Lee-Enfields won't stop mortars.
Nājī, tell Ḥasan and al-Badr that maybe their silver is only brass.[14]

Nājī is Nājī b. 'Alī al-Ghādir of Khawlān, a noted royalist shaykh;[15] al-Badr is the Imam; and Ḥasan his uncle. The reference to silver is a typical republican taunt that the royalist tribes had simply been bought by Saudi money and the standard answer to the accusation that they themselves were tools of the Egyptians. Beneath the uncompromising rhetoric, however, confrontations between tribes, as always, involved as much negotiation as fighting. The fact that the two sides could meet and exchange threats was itself important.

ATTEMPTS AT SETTLEMENT

Which is the side that I must go withal?
I am with both: each army hath a hand;
And in their rage, I having hold of both,
They whirl asunder and dismember me

Shakespeare, *King John* III.

By the beginning of 1963 there were probably 15,000 Egyptian soldiers in Yemen, and over the next six months their numbers rose to 35,000 or 40,000 (Nājī 1977: 223, 226; 'Abd al-Ilāh 1964: 88). A year or two after that there may have been as many as 60,000. The regular army on the republican side remained small and the Egyptians did not encourage its development, but instead used their own troops and those tribesmen who were rallied to the republic by their shaykhs. Apart from armour and artillery, the Egyptians also had air power and bombed their opponents almost indiscriminately, on occasion with mustard gas. On the royalist side there was at first no regular force except the Imam's small 'bodyguard' (*al-'ukfah*) and even later in the war the great majority of their troops were simply tribesmen who were rallied for each campaign (Schmidt 1968: 66). Supplies reached them from Saudi Arabia by way of Wā'ilah and Dhū Ḥusayn in the north-east, from

Bayḥān in South Yemen where the British soon came to offer support, and later by way of the mountains between Ḥaraḍ and Jabal Rāziḥ in the north-west. Guns and money were handed out by both sides, however, and the power of certain shaykhs increased, since it was they who gathered the fighting men and it was through them largesse was given.

The sheer scale of foreign support dwarfed the older complex of pious endowments, possession of extra-tribal land, taxes, and division of booty. The *hijrahs*, or protected enclaves, remained important, and one hears several stories about pro-royalist sayyids taking refuge there and support for them then forming in response to republican attacks on the *hijrah* which their refuge provoked. But the resources to be fought for were from foreign governments. Nor was the particularity of the sayyids' old position maintained. They were not any longer only 'our' learned men or 'theirs' but began to seem to many a 'class' whose relevance might be judged by the standards of other countries. The factions were not defined in solely Yemeni terms, and the war forced comparison and generalization on almost everyone: the fact that the Imam's supporters were willing to call themselves 'royalists' (not 'supporters of the truth', for instance) is enough to suggest what was happening. The point of such comparison and generalization was greatly sharpened by the presence within the country of a new social group: Yemeni workers who had returned from abroad soon after the coup and, based in the cities, now pinned their hopes for a better life on Arab nationalism and the promise of socialism. From their point of view, shaykhs and tribesmen, whether royalist or republican, seemed a throw-back to the 'feudal' age, though it was tribesmen who were fighting to decide the republic's fate.

Where a shaykh and his section or tribe chose opposite sides, it seems more often to have been the case that the shaykh adhered to the republic: for example, Bayt al-Maṭarī of Banī Maṭar, Bayt al-'Idharī and Bayt al-Mahdī of Arḥab, Bayt al-Quhālī of 'Iyāl Surayḥ, and Bayt Abū Laḥūm of Nihm. Even from Khawlān, which was to lead a prosperously independent existence under Nājī al-Ghādir, families such as al-Ruwayshān and Āl Duwaydī gravitated to the republican side, as did shaykhs from certain other tribes, who often owned land in (republican) Lower Yemen. It is harder to think of royalist shaykhs from republican tribes; and on the republican side the major shaykhs soon played a role of a kind quite different from that of their fellows with the royalists in that they acquired formal government posts.

Very early in the war an important faction within the republican camp, including these tribal figures, realized that their problems were less military than political; and a group of liberal politicians, revolutionary officers, and republican shaykhs drew up a provisional constitution which they submitted to al-Sallāl. He announced its terms on 13 April 1963. These were that the President should promulgate only those laws agreed upon by a 'presidential council' (*majlis al-ri'āsah*), that an 'executive council' (*majlis tanfīdhī*) of ministers be formed to oversee the workings of government, and that a council of shaykhs be formed to express the wishes of the major tribes. Al-Sallāl and his patrons responded by sending the leaders of this group off to the contested areas away from Ṣan'ā' ('Abd al-Ilāh 1964: 130–1).

In September 1963, substantially the same group as had drawn up the April constitution made a fresh attempt to gain a measure of control, this time basing themselves at 'Amrān. A meeting was convened by certain republican shaykhs, notably al-Aḥmar and Abū Ra's, which attracted delegates from avowedly royalist areas and was 'chaired' by Muḥammad al-Zubayrī. Among the royalist tribes who came were 'Iyāl Yazīd, who walked out of the meeting over the question of the Egyptian presence in Yemen. When they were brought back they demanded that a delegation be sent (two shaykhs from Ḥāshid and two from Bakīl) to demand an account from Nāṣir of his role in Yemen. It is an indication of the way in which tribal forms persisted that among those who brought them back to the meeting were shaykhs from 'Iyāl Surayḥ who by then had their own quarrel to pursue with Ḥāshid and with the latter's republican allies.

The meeting passed twenty-eight resolutions, among them to establish a popular army; to return the members of the presidential council to their posts; to establish a committee of shaykhs to resolve inter-tribal disputes, to alter the council of shaykhs to a 'consultative council'; and to establish a further committee of shaykhs to ensure by military measures that foreign intervention in tribal affairs be ended ('Abd al-Ilāh 1964: 152–3). Some of the tribes who had been most seriously at odds with Ṣan'ā' demanded from the conference sworn guarantees of their autonomy but refused to deal with the republican government.[16] Al-Zubayrī returned to Ṣan'ā' with these various demands and with a new proposal for a constitution. The tribally based attempt at a national settlement broke down when it was taken to the national government.

One is tempted to find a reversal here of the older urban and learned view. The tribes that before this had been known primarily for their violence, and had been at the periphery of moral order, now found themselves on occasion at the centre of attempts at settlement, while the source of disorder was supposedly 'foreign intervention' at the country's borders. At the same time, the context of tribesmen's self-estimation was changing. Radio news of the wider world had become a commonplace (both sides poured out transmissions to the Arab world, as did other governments), and this wider world, which for the first time became an intimate part of everyone's imagination, was not one in which tribes were prominent. As sayyids began to look to some like a 'class', so there began to be visible an idea of 'tribal*ism*', not just this tribe and that. The immediate importance of the tribes in politics was accompanied by the new idea that one day there might no longer be tribes, and countries such as Egypt might somehow be more 'advanced' for not having tribes at all.

At the crux of this potential contradiction were the major shaykhs, whom urban nationalists (primarily, the young men who returned to Yemen just after the 1962 coup) increasingly saw as a single interest group (see Halliday 1974). The major shaykhs, for their part, had little time for these *awlād shawāri*' ('riff-raff', 'street people') who lacked tribal standing and who preached the equivalent of permanent revolution. Republican shaykhs, in contrast to the urban nationalists, adhered to an older style of claim to justice: in particular, they drew closer to al-Zubayrī, while their tribesmen in the northern countryside continued fighting for and against what was still an ill-defined republic.

In February 1965 al-Zubayrī left Ṣan'ā' to work for a settlement among the tribes, as he had done on occasion earlier, travelling by mule with his four bodyguards. He concentrated his efforts in the eastern areas that were predominantly pro-royalist or anti-Egyptian (Serjeant 1982: 28; Schmidt 1968: 226). His announcement of a 'party of God' (*ḥizb allāh*), to pursue national reconciliation, built on the result of a great many meetings within and between tribes over the past eighteen months; but elements in both the republican and royalist camps saw his efforts as a major threat. On 1 April 1965 he was murdered just outside Rajūzah in Dhū Ḥusayn's territory, having been at al-'Inān in Dhū Muḥammad.[17] Under threat of massive tribal secession, al-Sallāl asked al-Zubayrī's colleague, Nu'mān, to form a government.

'Abdullāh al-Aḥmar of Ḥāshid had been minister of the interior under the previous government and in the same capacity under Nu'mān he convened a meeting at Khamir. The dissatisfaction in the republican camp was such that Amīn Abū Ra's, for example, attended only under pressure. The leading royalist shaykhs refused to attend at all, but Sayyid Ibrāhīm al-Wazīr's 'Union of Popular Forces', which had come to be spoken of in the foreign press at least as the 'Third Force', did take part.[18] The conference met from 1 May to 5 May 1965 under the chairmanship of al-Iryānī and passed a number of resolutions: to contact other Arab states; to form a popular army; to conclude the war; to establish a committee for the resolution of problems between tribes, and so on. Many of the leading figures who organized the meeting had played a part in convening the conference at 'Amrān in September 1963, and the proposals they made were largely the same. A new constitution was again drawn up, this time providing for a 'republican council' to be chosen by a 'consultative council' which was itself to contain ninety-nine members. The President was to promulgate only those laws agreed to by both councils.[19]

Al-Sallāl and his patrons were no more willing to countenance these decisions than those reached at 'Amrān. Although a delegation left in May to contact other Arab states, al-Sallāl declared in June that a 'supreme council of the armed forces' had been formed. Nu'mān resigned and flew to Cairo on 1 June, soon to be followed by nineteen members of the Khamir conference committee and then by another twelve shaykhs and ministers including 'Abd al-Salām Ṣabrah (al-Wazīr 1965: 19). Most of them were simply detained by the Egyptian government, and al-Sallāl went on to appoint new ministers despite them. In Yemen a new wave of arrests began, and the remaining shaykhs who had supported the Khamir conference met near Ṣan'ā'. A further delegation whom the government sent to talk them round joined them instead, and they decided in July to take matters into their own hands by going to South Yemen.[20]

The course of the rivalry between Nāṣir and King Fayṣal during this period is perhaps more complex than that between various groups of Yemenis (Kerr 1971: 108 ff.). After violent bouts of rhetoric and threats of outright war from Nāṣir's side, they met at Jiddah in August 1965 and announced an agreement to disengage from Yemen. Al-Sallāl was ordered to withdraw his condemnation of the Khamir conference, all but eight of the thirty-seven shaykhs who had left in July came back, and the Yemenis were told to meet at Ḥaraḍ and resolve their differences. They had not been included in the talks at Jiddah, and at this late date it is difficult to guess at the precise grounds of difference between the various factions or between them and the two Arab leaders.[21] But the conference failed.

At the time of the Ḥaraḍ conference the Egyptians may well have intended, as they claimed, to leave Yemen. However, in February 1966 the British government announced they would withdraw completely from Aden by 1968, and the Egyptians decided to retain their own position in North Yemen with a view to future possibilities in the South, where they already had a stake in the nationalist movement. They began a 'strategy of the long breath' by which their hold on the Ta'izz–al-Ḥudaydah–Ṣan'ā' triangle was consolidated and their army reinforced, but the tribal areas of the north and east were abandoned.

A month after an abortive meeting between the Saudis and the Egyptians in Kuwait, however, al-Sallāl was again returned to Yemen, this time after an absence of almost nine months. In Ṣan'ā' a veritable purge was carried out; thousands were arrested amid shrill accusations of imperialist plotting. As had happened before, many republican politicians fled to the north and more particularly to Ḥāshid, where by the end of the year attempts were being made to form something very like a government in exile under 'Abdullāh al-Aḥmar's protection at Ḥūth. In Ṣan'ā' a 'court for state security' was set up, and the Egyptians again began heavy bombing of the north and east, straying across the border on occasion to hit targets inside Saudi Arabia. The cycle of events was only broken when Nāṣir's dependence on intransigent bluster led him into war with Israel.

When the war broke out, in June 1967, the republican shaykhs, who had been largely isolated from the Ṣan'ā' government for the best part of a year, came into the capital with an enormous following of tribesmen to declare their support for Egypt. No doubt they did so with genuine feeling.[22] Most probably they also realized that their position might be greatly improved. By mid-October 1967 the last Egyptian soldiers had been withdrawn. On 5 November al-Sallāl was deposed in favour of a Presidential Council composed of al-Iryānī, Nuʿmān, and Muḥammad ʿAlī ʿUthmān. On 23 November Nuʿmān resigned, complaining that no real effort was being made to end the war, and at the beginning of December the royalists cut all the roads to Ṣanʿāʾ in a final attempt to overthrow the republic now that Egyptian support for it had disappeared. Events in and around Ṣanʿāʾ were particularly important, not only militarily but also because divisions emerged within the republican camp there which were to replace those between republican and royalist (we shall touch on this at the end of the chapter). Fighting also went on, however, in Arḥab, on the border between Sufyān and Ḥāshid at Jabal Aswad, in ʿIyāl Surayḥ and Hamdān, and between al-Ḥudaydah and Ṣanʿāʾ, most notably in Banī Maṭar and al-Ḥaymatayn. Nor was the encirclement quite complete. Some of the republican tribes continued to receive supplies from the capital even though Ṣanʿāʾ itself was supposedly cut off.

The siege was finally raised by a column from al-Ḥudaydah which broke through by a combination of force and persuasion; and the campaign ended with the collapse of royalist resistance around al-Matanah in Banī Maṭar when the royalist pay-chest was ambushed and the funds carried off. The royalist forces around Ṣanʿāʾ melted away and the tribesmen went back to their particular territories. Despite this, fighting continued sporadically through 1968: in May there was fighting in the Jawf; in September the republicans took Ṣaʿdah after Prince ʿAbdullāh b. Ḥasan had been assassinated there; in December they took the area around Ḥajjah, and at the end of the year the territory of Sanḥān, just south of Ṣanʿāʾ, was bombed to drive out ʿroyalistsʾ. Quite what the latter term meant by then is hard to be sure of. The Saudis had long before cut off serious aid to Bayt Ḥamīd al-Dīn and the restoration of the Imamate was no longer a plausible possibility.

TRIBAL CONUNDRUMS AND TRANSPOSITIONS

The great events of political history are usually phrased in terms far removed from the experience of ordinary people, and we should therefore settle for a while on smaller-scale events. The first case in point concerns ʿAlī Zāyid ʿAbdullāh, shaykh of ʿIyāl Dāʿir, which is one of Murhibah's 'tenths'.[23] Murhibah was royalist, and the document recording the case concerns a disagreement in 1966 between the shaykh and several of his own men over how payment from the princes had been divided. Much of it turns on the protocols explained in Chapter 2. It begins with ʿAlī Zāyid's plaint:

When I arrived from the east [i.e. from the lower Jawf where royalist headquarters were] they came to me and demanded from me the wages due them. I agreed to pay them along with [members of the other] tenths of Murhibah. Some of them accepted this and were satisfied, others refused. People from al-Taḥḍah [part of ʿIyāl Dāʿir] and Shaykh Muḥammad Ẓāhir then came to me. I offered them judgment *(badhalt la-hum ṣawāb)* and a rifle [in token of this] and [accepted] guaranty. . . .

Some time has gone by with me offering judgment [i.e. they still hold the rifle and so a formal truce exists] but during this past month ʿIyāl Dāʿir have attacked me in my house, demanding that I give a rifle [directly] to them and pay what they themselves judge [they are owed]. I asked them to be patient and gave them a Bashlī [an old Italian rifle used by Imam Aḥmad's army] as they asked. We decided to abide by the decision of two chosen trustworthy persons from Murhibah. We agreed to meet at ʿArām [the tribe's market and *hijrah* at the time] to choose trusted persons for myself and them. After that the dispute between me and them erupted because we went to al-Ḥarf.

Al-Ḥarf is in Sufyān's territory. It is just north of Jabal Aswad and Jabal Aḥmar, a mountain ridge that for much of its length marks the border between al-ʿUṣaymāt and Sufyān, between Ḥāshid and Bakīl, and for most of the war between republican and royalist. ʿAlī Zāyid now went there to join a muster of royalist forces.

When he returned he wrote to the other shaykhs of Murhibah, asking them to come to ʿArām and intervene in the dispute between himself and his tribesmen. The shaykhs duly came. None of ʿAlī Zāyid's opponents did. ʿAlī Zāyid therefore demanded payment for the expense he incurred in putting up these other shaykhs, first at ʿArām and then for three days in his house at al-Taḥḍah. Aḥmad Ṣāliḥ ʿAzīz replied that men came to him demanding a 'rifle of right', but they gave the impression that the demand was from ʿAlī Zāyid, so he refused; he was not going to hand over a rifle to his antagonist, but would hand one over to intermediaries only at Murhibah's *hijrah* (i.e. ʿArām) or at a meeting of the whole tribe or as part of a settlement by Islamic law. If they did not believe him, he would be their hostage. But his claim, he said, stood.

> 'Alī Zāyid had received subventions (*mīzāniyyah*) from the sons of the Imam, cash for weapons and wages [paid to Murhibah] as part of Bakīl. . . . He received the ammunition due to us for [fighting at] Harān, 'Ashsh, the Jawf, and Jabal Aḥmar. We deny receiving anything from him, no stores, cash, or ammunition. Seven of our men went with him and got nothing at all.

'Alī Zāyid entered a counter-claim of his own that Aḥmad Ṣāliḥ owed him two years' wages for the fighting at 'Aqabat al-Miftāḥ, an area miles away in the western mountains.

As is usual with intractable disputes, this one attracts to itself a string of separate claims: a dagger has been taken for judgment at some point and never returned; some previous structure of guaranty persists from an attempt to settle a dispute over grazing, and the guarantors are now summoned; the grazing dispute itself is revived, with 'Alī Zāyid claiming that certain of his fields are traditionally off-limits to others grazing their sheep there (*muḥājarah mamnū' 'an al-ra'y bi-l-ghanam*), but some of Aḥmad Ṣāliḥ's followers have been trespassing there and have even chased his womenfolk off at gun-point. Not a bit of it, say the other side; the restricted grazing area is for the use of all 'Iyāl Dā'ir, and the accusation that they threatened a woman there is quite false.

The complex, lengthy document (some 2.5 metres or so of tangled prose in appalling script) might almost be set as a test-piece for a student of *'urf*. Much of the argument turns upon points of procedure, such as the circumstances in which one is obliged to give a 'rifle of right'. The first judgment recorded at the end of the document requires that 'Alī Zāyid pay Aḥmad Ṣāliḥ a bull worth 55 Maria Theresas and cash to the same amount for shooting at his house without good reason, while Aḥmad Ṣāliḥ is to pay 'Alī Zāyid a bull worth 30 Maria Theresas and 25 Maria Theresas in cash for firing back. The totals of 110 Maria Theresas and 55 Maria Theresas are explained as being two-thirds and one-third of the *hajar* or fine for breach of the village's inviolability, presumably agreed to in existing documents. Aḥmad Ṣāliḥ is also required to pay a half *'ayb* of a beast worth 44 Maria Theresas to the shaykhs whose mediation he refused. A fine of a bull and 50 Maria Theresas is to be paid for disrespect of the market guaranty, two-thirds from 'Alī Zāyid and one-third from Aḥmad Ṣāliḥ.

But throughout the document run the related themes of the shaykhdom and the royalist money. At a number of points the former issue is referred to as 'the position of shaykh with the [royalist] government and with the tribe' (*al-mashīkh 'ind al-ḥukūmah wa-'ind al-qabīlah*), and this mediating function was evidently the crux of the matter, as it was with many tribes at the time. Both 'Alī Zāyid and Aḥmad Ṣāliḥ claim that their forebears were shaykhs. Both claim that their tribe, or at least their particular section, has chosen them; and the arbitrators agree that the tribe has the right to choose (*al-ḥaqq li-l-qabīlah*). But it is not clear whether the 'tribe' here is 'Iyāl Dā'ir by itself or Murhibah, and 'Alī Zāyid is judged to retain his position almost by default: 'He remains as he was unless he commits some grave fault (*badar min-hu ay mushaqqah*) against Murhibah or the government, in which case he would be deposed in accordance with the documents/agreements [which exist] between [the sections of] Murhibah.' Aḥmad Ṣāliḥ's attempt to promote himself from 'headman' (*'āqil*) to shaykh was beaten off. However, the rights and duties of the shaykh are nowhere laid down; no general rules are set out to govern the division of payments within the tribe and thus prevent the problem recurring.

The details of these payments are immensely complex. The princes had alloted three silver riyals to whomever came to Hāyir al-'Ashsh (a remote place amid the wadis and basalt crags of the east) and seven riyals to those who attended the muster in Sufyān's territory, together with a grant of 3,500 Maria Theresas to be divided as the leaders saw fit between those of Murhibah who had come to Sufyān and those who remained in the Jawf, whether at Harān or further out toward Ma'rib. Rifles were also handed out, some fifty 'jarmals' (Second World War Mausers) for a campaign at Harān and then another forty for the fighting near al-Ḥarf. These too were given to the shaykhs.

Harān is near Murhibah's own territory. Men from Murhibah had fought there at the very start of the war and repeatedly since then, but after the latest campaign most had gone home and only about fifty were left: hence the fifty rifles. However, these fifty rifles were not simply issued to the men who were present: if a man who was actually present did receive one, then he received it on behalf of his village or his extended family. Each of the ten sections of Murhibah received five rifles (to be exact, 'Iyāl Dā'ir received three for tribal families and two for the *fuqahā'* or men of religion attached to them), but even at this level there was plainly no systematic co-operation. There are several references in the document to men claiming 'half a rifle'. And the same ambiguities attach to the money paid for each man who served in the Jawf. At every level, from the tribe to the household, payment was being received in the name of a group but by individuals whose relation to their group was evidently quite undefined: a shifting system of personal patronage was being played out in a rhetoric of collective endeavour.

Another seven riyals per man was paid from the Jawf for the campaign at Jabal Aḥmar in Sufyān by another royalist prince, and another forty rifles for Murhibah; or four rifles to each shaykh of a 'tenth', or a rifle to each man who was present at the muster, depending on whose point of view one adopts. One of the plaintiffs objected that he was owed a rifle because he was at a royalist camp in Najrān for five months around the time of the Jabal Aḥmar muster and received no extra weapon while he was there. 'Alī Zāyid's claim for payment for campaigns in the western mountains contained a rather similar explanation, that he was away in the Empty Quarter at the time and thus missed the issue of weapons. In neither case was the claimant present for the particular campaign, but he still felt himself due something.

Ten men from each 'tenth' had also had their names entered for the *'ukfah*, the Imam's bodyguard, which was intended to be a standing force. Did their regular payment preclude payment as part of Murhibah's levy at particular musters? Were their rifles part of the tribe's allotment? If they had been issued weapons already, could their kinsmen claim a share of more general handouts? A group of them mention in passing that they had gone to Prince Muḥammad Ḥusayn and Prince Muḥammad Muḥsin, as well as to the Imam himself, in the course of their own disputes over payment in what was supposed to be the royalist bodyguard. To do this they must, in the midst of the war, have crossed and recrossed the breadth of Yemen. And the fact that weapons were admittedly convertible to cash allowed the complexity of claims to flourish in tangled detail.

Perhaps most interesting of all is what happened immediately before the intervention of Murhibah's shaykhs and the round of arbitration which the document records. 'Alī Zāyid had 'fled from Murhibah's judgment'. Finally, they judged that I should return to the tribe of Murhibah and they judged that I should pay slaughter-beasts (*baqarī wa-ghanamī*), and my fine was raised to 500 riyals. I returned to the brotherhood of Murhibah. I announced at Sūq ʻArām that I was one of Murhibah and that Murhibah accepted my return and restored me to the ranks of Murhibah's shaykhs. . . . I only remained a month. Aḥmad Ṣāliḥ kept attacking me. . . . I and Muḥsin ʻAwāḍ and Manṣūr al-Najjār went and slaughtered beasts for Banī Ṣuraym, and protection was extended to me and those with me (*qāmat aʻrāḍ ʻalayyā wa-man maʻī*). We chose shaykhs from Ḥāshid, and Murhibah chose shaykhs from the tribes of Sufyān for summons, reply, and dispute over judgments (*daʻwā wa-ijābah wa-munāqishah fi l-aḥkām*, i.e. for legal process). The two groups of Ḥāshid and Bakīl decided on our return to our brotherhood in Murhibah . . .

Banī Ṣuraym was stoutly republican. Elsewhere in the document it appears that ʻAlī Zāyid went in fact to Khamir, which is in Banī Ṣuraym's territory but is also, as was said earlier, Ḥāshid's 'capital', and throughout the war was the 'capital' of the republican tribes. Sufyān, by contrast, was very largely royalist; indeed, were one to search for an example of a determinedly royalist tribe, it would be hard to find one better. Murhibah's internal disputes, then, which threatened to unseat one of the shaykhs and which turned upon problems in the royalist logistical system, were mediated by a combination of opposed outsiders, republican and royalist.

In purely tribal terms there is nothing to be surprised at in this. Tribes as such do not overrun each other, and there is no reason to refuse help in settling a dispute within or between tribes; indeed, if someone claims your protection, then honour demands that you respond. From the point of view of political leaders outside this system, whether royalist or republican, tribalism itself may have appeared as nothing more than codified treachery. But for men involved in the fighting no contradiction was seen between tribalism and a close adherence to one side or other in the national struggle—any more than a Westerner who accepted the necessity of 'total war' need accept along with it that he should murder his prisoners or abuse their families.[24]

Agreements within and between tribes were made intermittently throughout the war, preserving the tribesmen's own forms of action amidst claims from the royalist and republican camps. The document from Sufyān quoted in Chapter 4 is a case in point, where the tribe's two halves, Ruhm and Ṣubārah, came together around a market guaranty. This was drawn up in November 1968. The royalists at that point were advancing into northern Sufyān (they had reached al-Madarraj in Ruhm's territory), the republicans were dug in at al-Ḥarf (in Ṣubārah's territory), the sections of the tribe were divided against each other, and everyone, to put it bluntly, was playing the ends against the middle.

The provisions to deal with the threats of civil war are not distinguished in the document from those that deal with other problems. For example, the signatories agree that whoever takes in a foreign refugee (*qaṭīr ajnabī*) is responsible for the refugee's actions, 'whether he is a nomad or settled person' *(sawā badawī aw qarawī)*: that by itself subsumes all other questions one might ask about whether this incomer was a royalist or a republican, uniformed or otherwise, foreign in the sense of non-Yemeni or just in the sense of coming from another tribe. So long as he is a refugee, the old rules apply (*ḥasab al-ʻurf min al-sābiq*). But 'as for the foreigner whom it is now for Ṣubārah to decide about, whether he is in the fort [outside al-Ḥarf] or elsewhere in our territory, after Ṣubārah had heard these decisions and agreed to them . . . they answered that . . . the Muḥammadī should be expelled from their territory altogether.' The Muḥammadī in question was Aḥmad Fāḍil of al-Dumaynah (part of Dhū Muḥammad at Baraṭ), who was republican commander at al-Ḥarf. Most of his troops were from elsewhere in Yemen, some were from Dhū Muḥammad, and throughout the civil war (as indeed for many years before it) Dhū Muḥammad had a border dispute with Sufyān that owed little or nothing to the war itself. The possible lines of argument about the presence of a Muḥammadī shaykh in Sufyān's territory at the time are numerous and endlessly diverse.

What is of interest for the present purpose is that Ṣubārah were asked by Ruhm to make up their minds about outsiders in Ṣubārah's part of Sufyān. Ṣubārah had been largely royalist at the outset. By this stage of the war many of them were nominally republican, since republican posts controlled much of their territory. Most of Ruhm, on the other hand, remained nominally royalist, with such notable exceptions as ʻAbdullāh Dhaybān of Dhū Rabḍān. The royalists were moving into Ruhm's territory. Ṣubārah's position was unenviable. If they decided to leave the Muḥammadīs be in al-Ḥarf, then they incurred the wrath of the advancing royalists; and if they tried to expel the Muḥammadīs, then the republic was in a position to do them considerable damage. Rather than lose the support of Ruhm, they decided to expel the Muḥammadīs. The die was cast. Ruhm then suggested that, as the two parts of the tribe were 'brothers',

> they should appoint representatives from both parties to go to the [republican] government and ask that [the post] be removed and [the Muḥammadīs] expelled from the territories of them both. If the government help them, then they will remove [the Muḥammadīs] from the territory. If not, then all of them [i.e. Ruhm and Ṣubārah] are brothers and throwing out [the Muḥammadīs] is incumbent on all of them, even if they dislike it. After that they must [together] defend all the [tribe's] territory. All of them, Ṣubārī and Ruhmī, agreed to this.

Largely royalist Ruhm, with republican Dhū Rabḍān in their midst, were here hedging their own bets while not reducing by much Ṣubārah's discomfort. Each party could claim to its backers (if any) that it was pursuing their aims, but necessarily having to disguise these to carry with them other sections of the tribe. Ṣubārah had been pushed to a clear declaration of policy, though they could still claim to the republicans that tribal considerations forced them to it.

The one point of general agreement would seem to be that the tribe stand together against attack by outsiders and defend its territory as a whole. But even that is by no means a simple statement. Each section has village territories of its own within that of Sufyān, and the document contains lengthy passages exempting these particular territories from the agreement governing the whole. All that everyone agrees on is that the market be a general responsibility, that rights of escort be upheld by the tribe at large, and that all should stand together against outsiders who might attack their shared borders with other tribes; nor can the concern for setting aside one's trees and grazing rights be distinguished from a concern to avoid a commitment to one side or the other in national politics.

Largely republican Dhū Rabḍān and their predominantly royalist neighbours in Dhū Ja'rān (their villages are in places adjacent) then add a final caveat, apparently accepted by all the parties: 'If a man should be away and the royalists come when he is not at home, then the tribes must guard his house, his family and possessions. If the republicans should come when he is away, then the same applies.' The tribe's territory is set aside as in effect a refuge for Sufyānīs of either allegiance, providing that they do not choose to stand and fight. However, there is nothing to say that royalist or republican forces cannot enter Sufyānī territory at the invitation of one or other of the tribe's sections. Disputes between tribesmen or between sections are in no way forbidden, although they might derive in part from national politics. Nor does the tribe resolve to prevent royalists and republicans fighting in the tribe's territory. What the document does, as so many have done before and since, is to transpose the course of dispute and settlement into language that the tribesmen command.

THE POST-WAR WORLD

In the wake of Egypt's defeat by Israel in 1967 Field Marshal 'Āmir, who aided Nāṣir throughout his career and particularly promoted Nāṣir's policy in Yemen, was required to commit suicide and leave an exculpation. On Yemen he is supposed to have said: 'We did not bother to study the local, Arab and international implications or the political or military questions involved. After years of experience we realized that it was a war between the tribes and that we entered it without knowing the nature of their land, their traditions and their ideas' (quoted O'Ballance 1971: 89). This was true as far as it went. However, the 'war between tribes' had changed the tribes' position: although they had often been strong (in fighting the Turks, for instance; al-Wazīr 1971: 150–1), they had not before been represented in government as they now were. The involvement of shaykhs in government during the war itself had been far more a feature of the republican camp than of the royalist, but important shaykhs from both sides were now brought into first the National Assembly (1969) and then the Consultative Council (1971), both of which were headed by Ḥāshid's paramount shaykh. Al-Baraddūnī (1983) distinguishes the period from al-Sallāl's time as the 'second republic'.

Under al-Iryānī's long presidency (1967–74), the shaykhs were prominent, and in particular, as al-Baraddūnī argues (1983: 579 ff.), those who had stood by the republic and yet been close to al-Zubayrī's attempt at mediation, such as 'Abdullāh al-Aḥmar, Sinān Abū Laḥūm, and Aḥmad 'Alī al-Maṭarī. Somewhat less central, though still important, were those who had adhered to the 'third force', most notably Amīn Abū Ra's of Dhū Muḥammad who became 'a near perpetual Minister of State' (Peterson 1982: 110) until his death in May 1978. The involvement of lesser shaykhs in different capacities was quite extensive. Shaykhs were unlikely to disappear, not least because the government, like the tribes, deals with people for preference through 'guaranty', not only in Upper Yemen but in Lower Yemen too (cf. Messick 1978: 206–9). Their more obvious importance for many years, however, derived yet again from their position between conflicting powers: their place between the Imam and the Turks or the Idrīsī, and then between royalists and republicans, was now replicated in terms of right and left.

Already by the end of the war a division had appeared within the republican camp between, on the one hand, older 'liberal' politicians and republican shaykhs, and, on the other, certain Lower Yemeni army units, Shāfi'ī politicians, and activists from South Yemen. The British had left Aden in November 1967, and a South Yemeni contingent joined the republican garrison at the siege of Ṣan'ā'; but disagreements during and after the siege resulted in the dominance of older 'liberals', certain northern shaykhs, and army officers from Upper Yemen.[25] The government of South Yemen adopted a progressively more radical rhetoric over the next several years. Saudi Arabia moved the other way, interfering as it did so in the composition of North Yemen's governments. A border war between the two Yemens broke out in the summer of 1972 and ended with North and South declaring their intention to unite as a single country, which they did not and have not done since.

The North's opposing neighbours continued trying to win over tribes and shaykhs, so large subventions were made by the Saudis and weapons given out by the South. For all this, the land of Ḥāshid and Bakīl remained comparatively quiet. The shaykhs who benefited most from subsidies were those who had been republican in the war, and a core of these was from Ḥāshid; those who benefited least had been royalist, and the key figures here were from Bakīl tribes such as Khawlān, Sufyān, and Arḥab. This latter group swung around the older republican axis, so that many of those who supposedly had been 'royalist' were supposedly now 'leftist' (Dresch 1984*b*: 170).[26] But their enthusiasm had been cut short when Nājī al-Ghādir and some sixty other shaykhs were murdered by South Yemen in February 1972. In the border war that summer, most of them simply stood to one side. They continued doing so for several years, while, from 1973–4 onward, uncentralized wealth in the form of migrant remittances began reaching tribesmen everywhere.

Al-Iryānī's government was deposed by the 'corrective move' of June 1974, and a government formed instead by Ibrāhīm al-Ḥamdī, an army officer from Upper Yemen. Al-Baraddūnī (1983: 593) distinguishes the corrective move as the beginning of the 'third republic', and this was briefly the period when 'colonel–shaykhs' were at their most conspicuous: 'members of important shaykhly families who have been given military training . . . and sought to expand their power base not within the tribe but via the army' (Peterson 1982: 128). But the alliance fell apart. Many of the Ḥāshid shaykhs withdrew to Khamir (indeed, there came to be a border between their territory and that of the government), so that those who previously had been most closely involved with Ṣan'ā' were now opposed to it diametrically. Al-Ḥamdī received no help with the rivalry between North Yemen's neighbours. Union with the South (*waḥdat al-shaṭrayn*, union of the country's 'two parts') became a major theme of his political rhetoric, but little progress was made before al-Ḥamdī's murder in 1977 and his replacement by Aḥmad al-Ghashmī. The results of this will be described in Chapter 10. For the moment it is enough to say that tribal disputes became greatly exacerbated.

Yet it was now, as it had been for some years, a matter of one republican faction against another: the idea of the republic was accepted by nearly everyone, and with it certain implications for the conceived position of men against each other within the national whole and in comparison with adjoining nations.[27] It is an oddity of the nation-state that, quite unlike the Imamate, it includes the whole population. For all that one may squabble with the government *(ḥukūmah)*, one is part of the people *(sha'b)*, and the state or *dawlah* now claims to be both at once, defined both by a single history and by contradistinction to the states around it.

A double relation of tribes to state in the post-war world (identity and at the same time contrariety; Dumont 1986: 227) was apparent, as it is quite widely, in scraps of poetry that were circulating late in 1977, after al-Ḥamdī's death. The first poem was of the nature of a semi-official eulogy on al-Ḥamdī and on his brother who was murdered with him:

Peace, you two horns sweeping up from one head.
If you shook the mountain you would leave it destroyed.
He [al-Ḥamdī] was as open-handed as Ḥātim Ṭayy,
And like Abū Zayd al-Hilālī the way he struck.[28]

There is an old folk-tale that the world rests on the horns of an ox which when it moves makes earthquakes, and it is this the poem suggests in its image of the two murdered brothers. Ḥātim Ṭayy and Abū Zayd are heroes of pre-Islamic chivalry. The reply to this, when al-Ghashmī took control of the government, shifts the imagery slightly:

The two stars have set, and the mountains obscured them,
Who brought reinforcements and stores and weapons.
This 'unity of the country' made each notable hate them,
And al-Ghashmī's much better, a righteous person.[29]

The 'summons and riposte' (*daʿwā wa-ijābah*) are of a kind one might find elsewhere than tribal Yemen, although the particular style is familiar among the tribes. The argument is only about who better leads the nation of which we all form part: both sides in the argument are identified with the national state. A second answer, however, composed by a tribesman, is highly distinctive and could hardly have come from anywhere else:

Two after two they come leaping forward.
If they were struck still, so would the whole hive be.
One's son of Yaḥyā, one's son of Ḥusayn,
Who grappled those horns and their lawless rule.
We mean the two mountain goats who in Ḥāshid are lords.
If *they* leaped the mountain they'd leave it destroyed.[30]

The mountain goat, *waʿl*, can be specifically the oryx, a symbol whose use goes back to pre-Islamic times; and the thrust of the poem is that these two really do shake the earth, where al-Ḥamdī and his brother did not. The two in question (son of Yaḥyā and son of Ḥusayn) are Mujāhid Abū Shawārib and ʿAbdullāh al-Aḥmar, whose contemporary prominence has been touched on in earlier chapters.

The theme of 'two after two', however, produced a deeper resonance in those who heard it at the time: not only do the two lords of Ḥāshid come after the two al-Ḥamdī brothers, but the two before them are most obviously Ḥamīd and Ḥusayn al-Aḥmar, murdered by Imam Aḥmad back in 1959, before the revolution.[31] Al-Ḥamdī and his brother are aligned with the last Imams as if it were a matter of Ḥāshid against an undifferentiated government, or Ḥāshid *contra mundum*, without regard for the changes of political history. Similar themes could be drawn from Bakīl, or indeed from particular tribes within either confederation, and the effect is of endless, fragmented oppositions each of which is in effect as timeless as those offered by al-Hamdānī a thousand years ago. These tribesmen, however, are now also 'citizens' (*muwāṭinīn*); the 'lords' of Ḥāshid have held government rank; and the legitimacy of the government itself is defined by the progression which the poem ignores, the overthrow of the Imams and the series of republican adjustments since then. The complement to tribal opposition is no longer what it was before the revolution. The authority of the state is now supposed to extend in Weberian fashion uniformly everywhere and to guarantee the rights of its citizens by comparison with the states adjoining.

Equal and unconnected 'citizens' can be conceived of as such only as members of a single body, the nation state; and their equality before the law must be upheld by the state, just as is the equality of the nation against its neighbours. Indeed, these two demands are inextricably linked. To maintain the equality of the citizens as a bloc against outsiders, as well as singly against each other, is one of the state's prime functions. Dissension is provoked by anger at inequality, and in the Arab world takes primarily the form of factions, many of which, such as those of the Ba'th party, recur across the boundaries of different states and within the state do not correspond to tribes. One of the striking features of the post-war period has been the way in which tribal forms can in fact contain these: adherents of different factions can reside in different territorial spaces, and no decision between them is ever sought. Judgment, as so often, is in effect suspended. But that is not, of course, the language of modern government or of adherents to political factions in the tribal countryside.

Unity is the catchword of governments, and has been particularly since the demise of al-Iryānī (1974). The idea of the military answers to this most directly (though the military more than most institutions also refracts rival concepts of uniformity; it is very prone to factionalism itself), and since 1974 it has become natural to assume that the military will hold power. Technical expertise and pious learning are now separate questions from that of political order. The older association between power and knowledge has been severed, and far more so that between power and birth. 'Alī 'Abdullāh Ṣāliḥ, the President since 1978, seems himself to illustrate a process of levelling, being a man of very ordinary birth, a tribesman as it happens, but certainly not a man whose rise to prominence depended on a tribal career. As al-Ḥamdī is supposed to have said of him, he was the *tays al-ḍubbāt*, the lead ram of the officers, the one who would butt his way through to prominence; having done so, he has ruled Yemen quite successfully. Others might do so, regardless of tribal affiliation or of coming from a non-tribal group. The army has become immensely important and grows in size and cohesion almost constantly. The Central Office of National Security has for many years been a power, at least within the cities, and in the 1980s a separate Presidential Security Unit has blossomed to ensure more fully the safety of the head of state. The state itself (which of its nature demands its name be hypostasized) has been growing rapidly, and comparison of its achievements with those of states around it seems to sharpen almost year by year.

In the absence of other traditions, a 'colonel–president' seems the modern *wāzi'* (Ibn Khaldūn 1967), the one who 'constrains' other factions of society to prevent disorder. Beneath such a figure the experts of various kinds (the planners and economists, for instance) can operate in their own terms, and each element of society can exist in safety. But the modern emphasis on development (from which the legitimacy of particular governments largely derives now) exacts also a price: 'the government is apt to regard the individual as a statistical unit and all forms of private association as obstacles to its plans. In an age of planning, there is a danger that the state will come to control everything' (Hourani 1981: 191). Centralization would not be quite the right term to describe this; but unity and uniformity already form a prominent part of political language, and the 'forms of private association' which appear as obstacles of course include the tribes. It should be said at once and clearly that Yemen's experience has so far been fairly happy. That of countries which Yemenis might look to as models has often been less so, and these models (such as Syria, Iraq, and Egypt, lately Libya and even Iran) are now important. A generation ago, for most people, they were only a rumour, but radio and television now make of them, and have done for almost twenty years, the subject of daily experience in every village and almost every household. The great change came with the civil war.

What has changed most markedly since the Imam's time is the toplogy of self-definition. It used to be that a succession of Imams was the moral centre of the Zaydi scheme, and the scheme itself was of linear transmission from student to teacher without reference to the opinion of outsiders. The tribes were left at the margin, and the rest of the world at the far periphery. The tribes are still marginal to the language of government. But the importance of government itself and of the state now lies in its relation with the world beyond, and for many citizens what was once the periphery is now the main point of reference—other Arab states primarily, and other Islamic states beyond them (cf. Peters 1976: 10). Emulation, both within and between states, is a prime concern. The tribes, identified with the country's past, are an element within, not outside, the community defined as 'the people'; and in the opinion of many they are a 'backward' element, which may hold the whole country back in its emulation of others. The assumption is that all these nations are on the same trajectory of 'development' and 'progress', an external sequence not of Yemen's own making.

The nationalist language developed before the revolution by such writers as al-'Aynī, al-Zubayrī, and Nu'mān is now a commonplace, and the unspoken comparison with other nations such language implies has come more to the fore. But the world is no longer that in which al-Zubayrī wrote thirty years ago. The nationalist projects of the 1950s and 1960s, when it seemed to the young that only imperialism stood between them and success, have elsewhere often soured into brute impositions of uniformity; and new 'Islamic' language offered as an alternative to existing states and governments is as little given to restraint and compromise. Older tribesmen who lived through the Nāṣirist period, when power, uniformity, and progress were first so solidly knit together in the region, now speak of tribal practice not only in terms of strength or prowess but also in terms of a civility they fear may one day be lost. An element of nostalgia is apparent in what they say, a noticeable complement to the language of repute and opposition still apt to encounters between tribe and tribe. A story of the civil war, for instance, was told by Nu'mān b. Qāyid al-Rājiḥ of Khawlān as follows:

People from Jahm of Khawlān were held up. It doesn't matter if they were royalist or republican. What matters is that they were on the road through there (*al-ṭarīq al-ʿābirah*) and only convoys which carried weapons could be held up. As for commerce, there was commerce through the republican areas and commerce through the royalist areas, and that was because it's tribal custom (*ʿurf*). That's how it was, do you see (*samaʿt*, do you hear)? Roads were secure and guaranteed.

But they fired on them although all that was in the trucks was goods, things for their houses. They stopped their trucks and shouted, 'Who is this? Who are you, shooting at us?' The idiots who had shot at them ran away. They got back in their trucks and went; left it behind, left it behind them until they reached the village. And they said, 'You in the village are the ones to intervene (*mudarrikīn*), because the culprits came here.'

Then some of them went to their own territory and called on their people for support (*nakkafū ʿalā aṣḥāb-hum*), and their people marched to the village in ʿAbīdah where this happened. When the people there saw they were a fighting group (*qawm*) they asked them for a respite (*mahl*) until al-Muʿaylī came. When al-Muʿaylī came he gave them rifles for patience. He was a big shaykh or headman of that part of ʿAbīdah, this al-Muʿaylī.

He gave them ten rifles for patience and said to them, 'Peace be on you.' They said nothing back to him. They refused to return the *salām* because the *salām* is considered a pact (*ʿahd*, i.e. of truce). He said to them then, 'The rifles I give you are rifles of judgment, you men' [i.e. you have the right to judge for yourselves the amends due you], and they then said, 'On you be peace, and the mercy of God' [i.e. they returned the *salām*]. Then they said, 'We accept right of judgment, and we will choose whatever you choose to judge.' And this Ibn al-Muʿaylī judged. He judged the blood-money due where no damage is done (*diyat al-salāmah*) for the truck and also for [each of] the four men in it. The *diyat al-salāmah* is half the [real] blood-money, do you see? So this was a lot.

They drew up an agreement, *bismillāhi l-raḥmāni l-raḥīm* and so forth, and he said, 'These rifles which come back to me for judgment [i.e. the ten rifles he had offered in the first place] now go back to Āl Jahm as a pledge of good faith (*ʿirbūn al-wifāʾ*), for a period of a month [i.e. to delay actual payment]. Do you accept this, you men?' They said, 'Yes, we accept it; but the *diyat al-salāmah* is more than just. The *diyat al-salāmah* for the truck and what's in it we take, but as for the men, where's there no damage done, there's no fine to pay (*lā fī salāmah gharāmah*). Then he said, al-Muʿaylī, 'I give you the rifles and you are guests today, but the period of respite I now say is ten days [instead of the usual three].' And that was the end of the matter. That was how it was.

NOTES

1. The point is well made (al-Baraddūnī 1983: 364), that Zabārah, whose work was quoted often in chs. 5 and 6 and who died in the

early 1960s, continued to write the lives of his contemporaries in a style appropriate to any earlier century of Zaydi history; while at the same time Yemenis were belatedly reading modern Arabic authors, absorbing ideas that were distinctive of their own period, and evolving styles of their own that aligned them with much that was happening elsewhere than Yemen. Yet Zabārah himself was one of the first to take a sustained interest in the foreign Arabic press and the possibility of reform (see Peterson 1982: 77). A separate paper is needed to assess his works, informed as they were by the belief that no one was writing sound *tarājim* any more. One might note in passing, however, the way his life of Imam Yaḥyā (1956: vol. iii) tails off into lists of *ḥadd* punishments and little else: the suggestion would seem to be that the Imamate itself had, by the end of Yaḥyā's time, become a hollow shell.

2. The group grew to include Qadi 'Abd al-Raḥmān al-Iryānī and 'Abd al-Salām Ṣabrah (al-Shamāḥī 1972: 179–80), both of whom later played major roles in the republic. This was a loose coterie of like-minded men, however, not an organized party, and even al-Shamāḥī's attribution to them of the title *hay'at al-niḍāl* may well be anachronistic. The modernist and later 'liberal' opposition can be touched on only briefly here. The best available work on the subject so far is that of the late Leigh Douglas (1984, 1987). Stookey's chapters on the period (1978, chs. 7 and 8) are also extremely helpful.

3. Aḥmad was a man of many parts and is not to be dismissed lightly. However, in a world to be dominated by nationalism he was a worrying anomaly, with his bristly beard and alarming, protruding eyes that were widely believed to have been deliberately cultivated. There is a particularly fine photograph of him in his later years attending an execution (Serjeant 1983: 105). He must have been a most intimidating character to meet.

4. 'Ḥamzah, an Egyptian journalist who visited Ṣan'ā' during the coup, spoke of how some Yemenis were trained to sing the anthem of the Arab League: how more than five ministers in the new government were sitting the whole day beside Jewish craftsmen who were working on the furniture to be prepared for the delegation of the Arab League; and how al-Wartilānī [the emissary of the Muslim Brotherhood], occupied himself preparing a long list of spoons, forks, plates and tinned food to be brought from Aden for the honourable visitors' (al-Abdin 1975: 82).

Serjeant 1979: 91 characterizes the Imam's assassin, 'Alī Nāṣir al-Qarda'ī of Murād, as 'a notorious tribal malcontent'. In fact al-Qarda'ī seems to have been displaced from his paramountcy in Murād and was sent by the Imam on an abortive expedition to prise Shabwah from the British: his relatives presumed he was meant not to return, and certainly he had reason to be malcontented.

The 1948 coup has become of particular interest in recent years, and part of its rhetoric (most notably the 'national charter') has been taken up by the present President, 'Alī 'Abdullāh Ṣāliḥ. For accounts of the coup see Markaz 1982, al-Saidi 1981 and al-Baraddūnī 1983, pt. 6. The text of the charter is given by al-Shamāḥi 1972: 210–19.

5. In Egypt al-Badr met al-Zubayrī and other liberals in exile and is said to have fallen very much under the sway of Nāṣir. At home al-Badr was subject to almost routinized humiliation by his father, who in public would refer to him as 'the handkerchief' and as 'Alī Maqla': a *maqla'* is a stone pot, and the implication was that al-Badr was good only for loafing around and gorging himself, not for any serious work. This rejection of a son is not unusual. One sees it with certain of the great shaykhs and their children nowadays, and although some of the young men in question are genuine wastrels, there are others who very plainly are going to play Henry IV parts 1 and 2.
6. Opposition to Aḥmad had spread, and ties were now firmly established between prominent liberals and several families of shaykhs. Qadi 'Abd al-Salām Ṣabrah provided the link, the *hamzat al-waṣl*, between these circles of resistance (Markaz 1981: 143, 148, 163). It should not be forgotten that many of the young shaykhs were in fact educated by captive liberals. The most striking example is that of the young Shaykh 'Abdullāh, who seems to have been taught at different times by both al-Iryānī and Nu'mān. A number of shaykhs of this older generation are highly cultivated persons, and their education was nearly all acquired in their time as hostages. Just as important was the spread of the transistor radio, which as much as anything was the downfall of colonial powers and of monarchies throughout the region. The idea that shaykhs were cut off from all knowledge of the outside world is quite wrong; and these associations in the 1950s were politically important.
7. Compare Hourani's comments on nationalist rhetoric (1981: 1–2): 'At some time or other the Arabs have appealed against the Ottomans to early Islamic history, the Egyptians to the Pharaohs, the Lebanese Christians to the Phoenicians, the Turks themselves . . . to the Hittites . . . the romantic cult of a distant past [is] blended with the revolutionary idea that man is free to break and remould his social world.' See also Anderson 1983.
8. One hears it said that there was a plan for al-Badr to be President and Ḥamīd prime minister, which is not implausible. It is also said that Ḥamīd had accompanied the Yemeni delegation to the 1956 Jiddah conference with Egypt and Saudi Arabia, where he met exiled liberals attached to the Egyptian delegation. Whatever their plans and motives may have been, al-Badr and Ḥamīd were closely associated. Certain other shaykhs, such as al-Ghādir and al-Zāyidī of Khawlān, claimed to support al-Badr but in reality were heavily involved with those who favoured al-Badr's uncle Ḥasan.
9. Among the shaykhs who fled to Aden were 'Alī and Muḥammad Ruwayshān, 'Alī al-Zāyidī and Aḥmad al-Miṣrī of Khawlān; Sha'lān al-Ghubaysī of Khārif; 'Abdullāh Dhaybān of Sufyān; 'Alī Shawīṭ of Banī Ṣuraym; Muḥsin Radmān, 'Abd al-Ilāh Abū Dijānah, and Muḥammad al-Ḥabbārī of Arḥab; Sinān Abū Laḥūm of Nihm and

Mahdī al-Qudaysh of al-'Uṣaymāt. They and several others took refuge with the exiled liberals in the South. Most drifted back on parole during the following year.

10. For a description of al-Zubayrī's earlier works see Serjeant 1979. Until the end of the 1950s, as al-Saqqāf points out (1977: 23), the liberals had been inclined to follow the broader Arab politics of the time. *Wāq al-wāq* (1961) represents a return to purely Yemeni concerns, connected, one might think, with the experience of those who spent their exile in Egypt.

11. Not only was al-Badr threatened by conspiracies which the Egyptians promoted, but his position was insecure even with conservative elements in Yemen, many of whom favoured his uncle Ḥasan. In the week after Aḥmad's death several plots were pursued, and Schmidt's suggestion (1968: 22) that only al-Badr and the Egyptian chargé d'affaires knew of all of them might well be correct. Al-Juzaylān's 1977 account of the coup is useful but tends to give its author a rather inflated importance. The account by a 'committee of liberal officers' (Ḍubbāt 1978) was published as a corrective. See also al-Baraddūnī 1983: 409 ff.

12. 'Abd al-Ilāh's work remains one of the best on the first year of the revolution, animated as it is by such spluttering anger that the Arabic all but collapses at points. Not quite all the details are reliable, but those who were involved in the events he describes give very similar accounts. For accounts of the various battles and conferences later in the war see Schmidt 1968 and O'Ballance 1971. A full account remains to be written.

13. *Jamāl wa-llāh mā ba-najambar shay' / al-sha'b thār wa-rawwam al-qar'ah*
law tashriq al-shams min al-maghrib / wa-lā samā'-hā tasquṭ al-qā'ah
yā bādī' bi-l-qawl ba-tasma' / ma'a jamāl yadmur-hā fī sā' ah
ya'ṭī li-nā rashāsh wa-l-madfa' / wa-yuqarrib al-'āsi(n) l-iṭā'ah.

14. *Al-ḥayd al-ṭiyāl a'lan wa-jāb-hu kull shāmikh fi l-yaman / mā ba-najambar qaṭṭ law nafnā min al-dunyā khalāṣ*
law yarja' ams al-yawm wa-lā al-shams tashriq min 'adan / wa-l-arḍ tush'il nār wa-amzān al-samā' tushbil al-raṣāṣ
al-qā'id al-miṣrī bi-qūwāt-hi taḥakkam fi l-yaman / wa-l-mīgh wa-l-yūshin 'alā dīrah qiyās
mā yaqra' al-hawn raṣāṣ al-shuraf wa-l-mīmwan / qul li-l-ḥasan wa-l-badr yā nājī qad al-fiḍḍah nuḥās.
Al-mīgh, *al-yūshin*, and *al-mīmwan* are self explanatory; *yuqāyis* is 'to look for' or 'seek out' (syn. *yudawwir)*; *dīrah* is here a breastwork or sangar (syn. *matras*), though in other contexts it can mean a tight spot; *shuraf* is the plural of *sharfah*, the Mk. III Lee–Enfield; the Mk. IV is *al-kanadā*, being made in Canada by the Ross company, and large quantities of both sorts were provided from Pakistani stocks.

15. Nājī b. 'Alī al-Ghādir of Khawlān had at first come to Ṣan'ā' in support of the revolution but made it clear, as had many shaykhs, that he was not willing to support al-Sallāl (al-Juzaylān 1977: 135). He

had returned to Khawlān, accepted royalist funds, and played a leading part in the fighting against the republicans and the Egyptians alike around Ṣirwāḥ. Early in 1963 he came to an agreement with the republican government, accepted funds from them, and was hailed by them as a supporter, but they arrested him in March of that year for trafficking with the royalists. He was released on promises of renewed co-operation, accepted more funds from the princes, and from late 1963 on was constantly opposed to the republic. By his own efforts he came to be paramount shaykh of Khawlān, and then paramount shaykh of most of Bakīl, but his experiences were those of many shaykhs writ large.

Al-Ghādir became known to a wider public through his interviews with Eric Rouleau (*Le Monde*, 12 May 1967). His dislike, and the dislike of many other shaykhs, for al-Sallāl is attributed by authors of very different inclinations (Halliday 1974: 101; Serjeant 1977: 230) to the fact that al-Sallāl's father was of lowly birth. My own feeling is that had al-Sallāl shown more grip on affairs a suitable lineage would have somehow been found him, as has happened with several figures before and since.

16. 'Abd al-Ilāh's suggestion (1964: 153) that al-Ahnūm and 'Iyāl Yazīd might have come over to the republic at this stage is probably not well founded. Al-Ahnūm had nearly all turned to the royalists at the very start of the war and remained with them thereafter. It is worth noting that these areas where the great sayyid families were most prominent were among those most closely attached to the royalists, and an explanation of the war in terms of spontaneous class struggle against land-holders or the like would here be hard to sustain: Lower Yemen is another matter.

On the other hand one cannot accurately describe the royalists' opponents as 'tribal leaders who supported the Republic for traditional reasons, knowing that patronizing the central government could advance their position . . .' (Halliday 1974: 105). Shaykh 'Abdullāh and others in fact pursued a consistent line through several governmental changes: one may approve or disapprove their politics, but they and certain older liberals were in effect an axis around which other factions swung with much less consistency.

17. Both the killers were apparently from Baraṭ, and one of them was seen at Egyptian headquarters in Ṣan'ā' a day or two before the murder. On the other hand, a few months earlier in Arḥab Prince Muḥammad Ḥusayn had offered large sums of money to have al-Zubayrī killed; and certain shaykhs claim to have seen orders from the royalists to have him murdered at Baraṭ. There were plenty of people on both sides who wanted al-Zubayrī dead.

18. The term 'third force' invites confusion. Halliday, for example, at one point describes it as comprising 'free Yemenis and Shāfi'ī merchants' (1974: 105) and at another as comprising 'tribal leaders' (ibid. 114). The core of the third force was in fact Ibrāhīm b. 'Alī al-Wazīr's group, whose rhetoric was of a constitutional 'Islamic state': they

continued receiving Saudi support throughout al-Iryānī's post-war presidency (1967–74), and as late as 1980 al-Wazīr ran an office in Jiddah that gave hand-outs to disaffected Yemeni shaykhs.

19. For an account of the proceedings see al-Thawr 1968: 154 ff. and al-Wazīr 1965, the latter of which is as interesting for its omissions as for its content. 'Abdullāh al-Aḥmar, who was in effect host of the conference, receives no mention at all except in a quotation from the proceedings. Amīn Abū Ra's, on the other hand, a supporter of al-Wazīr's own Union of Popular Forces, receives extensive coverage. It is said that al-Wazīr's mother was from Āl Abū Ra's, although that does not by itself account for the alliance.

20. According to some accounts, the delegation was led by 'Abdullāh al-Aḥmar (O'Ballance 1971: 148). Certainly it included Nu'mān b. Qāyid al-Rājiḥ, Sinān Abū Laḥūm, and Aḥmad 'Alī al-Maṭarī, among others (al-Wazīr 1965: 109).

21. Many non-tribal republicans distrusted the Ḥaraḍ conference from the start and feared they would be sold out. The Popular Organization of Nationalist Forces (*al-tanẓīm al-sha'bī li-l-qūwāt al-waṭaniyyah*), very strong among returned Yemenis in the towns, began registering names of those willing to fight, if the need arose, for what they saw as the true republic.

It is an indication of continuing dissatisfaction within the older republican camp that Sinān Abū Laḥūm, who had been minister of defence in an earlier government and was to re-emerge as one of the most important republican shaykhs, actually attended the Ḥaraḍ conference as part of the royalist delegation. The inclusion of the 'third force' representatives (Abū Laḥūm, al-Wazīr, and Nu'mān al-Rājiḥ sat together) in the royalist delegation is also an indication that Saudi support for Bayt Ḥamīd al-Dīn was not total. For a list of delegates to the conference see Schmidt 1968: 307–8 and al-Ḥasanī 1966: 35–8.

22. One might note that more than 60 years earlier, the news that the Italians had invaded Libya produced similar tribal declarations of support for the Turks (Zabārah 1956: ii. 211–12). There must surely, however, have been an immense qualitative difference between rumour in the first case and constant radio coverage in the second. Cf. Peters' comments (1976: 10–11) on the broadening of conceptual horizons in Libya.

23. 'Iyāl Yaḥyā and 'Iyāl Dā'ir together make up the village cluster of al-Taḥḍah, which itself counts as two 'tenths'. 'Arām also counts as two tenths, having four discrete settlements associated with it, each of which has a single shaykh of guaranty. The other tenths of Murhibah are Kuḥl, al-Kassād, Kharfān, Dabbal, Dithān, and al-Khaysayn. Each is a discrete village cluster and would seem to have two main shaykhly families, each identified with a formally distinct 'half' of the cluster in question.

24. Notoriously, what decencies are flimsily preserved in modern war depend too often on recognizing one's opponents as moral equals: so

soon as racism and the like enter into it, men often act like brutes. The same was true in the present case. Schmidt 1968: 117 mentions royalist poems threatening to cut off the noses of Egyptian soldiers, and I have heard such myself. 'Decapitation of enemy soldiers' is not 'an old Yemeni custom' (ibid. 59), but Saudi money was offered for Egyptian heads at a couple of points in the war. Beheading and mutilation were used by Imams in the past as a means of degradation (Dresch 1987*b*), but in tribal custom they are a disgrace: the Egyptians often fell outside the pale of shared morality, as indeed certain enemies of the tribes in Lower Yemen have even in our day.

25. Halliday 1974: 122 ff. depicts these events as a 'Thermidor' in which the reactionary tribes were brought in to make a counter-revolution. Stookey 1978: 253 depicts the victors as the 'moderates'. Neither description is satisfactory, but it does deserve pointing out that the coalition which emerged in control of the situation was very much that which had made the 1962 revolution in the first place. It also deserves noting (contra Halliday 1974: 119) that the South Yemeni contingent in Ṣan'ā' were largely from FLOSY, the Nāṣirist wing of the southern resistance, not from the NLF who were installing the self-proclaimed Marxist regime in Aden.

One of the leaders of the Shāfi'ī left, 'Abd al-Raqīb Wahhāb, who was exiled in August, returned to North Yemen in December, and was shot dead in Ṣan'ā'. One of his supporters at the time was Amīn Abū Ra's of Dhū Muḥammad, who had urged Bakīl to support 'Abd al-Raqīb in the August 1968 fighting by cutting the road into Ṣan'ā'. 'Abd al-Raqīb had a considerable following among young men in Lower Yemen who originally were from Baraṭ, and to divide up the personalities involved into 'right' and 'left' does little justice to what was happening there (see also al-Wazīr 1971: 143–8).

26. Interest in supposedly revolutionary South Yemen on the part of ex-royalist shaykhs began very early. Al-Wazīr (ibid. 135 n. 1) mentions Qāsim Munaṣṣar of Khawlān approaching the South for aid against Ṣan'ā' almost before the civil was was over.

The subsidies being paid were very large. Aḥmad Nu'mān resigned as prime minister in July 1971 and complained publicly about the extent of the subsidies paid by or through Ṣan'ā'. YR 50 million per annum is a figure I was often quoted. Stookey (1978: 262) estimates the Ṣan'ā' government's total income from *zakāt* at less than YR 11 million and the expenditure on tribal leaders at almost YR 40 million. These were not the only payments. The Saudis' major payment to Ḥāshid at the time (not by way of Ṣan'ā') is said to have been some SR 7 million a month, and it was only one of several.

27. There are no surviving pockets of royalism worth mention, although there are old men here and there who, having forgotten what it was like, will praise the 'system' and 'security' imposed by Imam Aḥmad. Even at the period of my field-work one heard that this shaykh or that was in touch with Prince Muḥammad Ḥusayn, but this was flummery: not only is there no organized royalist party, but one would have to

educate the population in a forgotten language before the royalist claim would even make sense to them.

28. *Salām yā qarnayn min ra's istawayn / lā hazhazayn al-ḥayd khallayn-hu ṭayāḥ*
yushbih li-ḥātim ṭayy mabsūṭ al-yadayn / wa-mithl abā zayd al-hilālī li-l-naṭāḥ

29. *Qad ghābat al-najmayn wa-l-shamm a'dharayn / wa-jābat al-najdah wa-l-dhakhīr wa-l-salāḥ*
min waḥdat al-shaṭrayn shannat-hum kull 'ayn / wa-l-ghashmī abṭal min-hum yā abū ṣalāḥ

30. *Ithnayn ba'd ithnayn hunn ba-yaṭla'ayn / idha qad ishtalayn fa-ishtall al-jibāḥ*
wāḥid walad yaḥyā wāḥid bin ḥusayn / dhī ḥāzat al-qarnayn wa-l-ḥukm al-mubāḥ
ba-naqṣud al-wa'layn fī ḥāshid rabbayn / ba-yaqfizayn al-ḥayd khallayn-hu ṭayāḥ.

31. There is always a 'near' and a 'distant' meaning, as Yemenis put it, but this resonance with the past was caught even by a young educated sayyid friend from Lower Yemen. Before the 1959 debacle there was a verse in circulation that included the lines: '*imām-nā al-nāṣir wa-min ba'd-hu ḥamīd / subḥāna man radd al-'awāyid li-ahli-hā*'—'Our Imam is Nāṣir' (or, in front of us is al-Nāṣir, i.e. Imam Aḥmad), 'and after him Ḥamīd' (i.e. al-Aḥmar, but the line is ambiguous as to whether Ḥamīd is loyally following the Imam or hoping to succeed him). 'Praise to him who returns benefits to their owners' (or those who do good to others). When Ḥamīd was brought to al-Sukhnah in chains, Aḥmad is meant to have asked him what 'benefits' he had brought, before he ordered him off to his death at Ḥajjah. The first line of the present poem brought this almost instantly to mind with a number of people to whom I showed it.

8 Village Life and Means of Livelihood

> With the single qualification that settlements, to a certain extent, permeate one another, we can say that each of them constitutes a fixed and defined social unit which contrasts with the changing aspect of the tribes . . .
>
> Mauss, *Seasonal Variations of the Eskimo*

A generation has now grown up for whom the last Imams are not even a memory. A great deal has changed, not least that emigrant labour and imported grain mean that few people under middle age can imagine famine. The old adage in Upper Yemen was 'no one who stays put gets bread, except he who turns the soil or goes to fight at the breastworks' (*mā quraṣ ya'tī li-jālis illa man qallab al-ṭīn aw 'amad fi l-matāris*);[1] but one need not now stay put, and the cash economy has opened up several possibilities other than farming and warfare. Despite this, the majority of tribesmen inhabit the same type of settlement as they did before; it is worth, I think, pausing for a single chapter to document what wealth they have there.

Throughout the period we know anything of (which extends back to pre-Islamic times), the population of Upper Yemen has lived mainly in villages and has depended in large part on agriculture. These villages now each contain of the order of two or three hundred people. Some villages are larger, some smaller, and none can fairly be presented as typical, but a sketch of a single village will at least give an idea of these units which underpin the whole tribal system. The village to be used for this purpose lies on the plateau between Ṣan'ā' and al-Ḥarf. Let us call it Bayt Ḥusayn. Where its characteristics differ markedly from the average I shall say so, but the reader should be aware that villages do in fact differ a great deal from one to the next.

Bayt Ḥusayn forms a discrete cluster of about forty houses set on a rocky outcrop.[2] The nearest other village is little more than a kilometre away to the south, and there are further villages two or three kilometres off to the north and west. Around Bayt Ḥusayn itself are expanses of bare rock where little grows but some sparse scrub and a little grass in the cracks of the rocky substrate. On the slopes and in the hollows of this bare landscape are the fields, most of which are arranged in short series of shallow terraces.[3] Between Bayt Ḥusayn and the neighbouring villages are known borders, which in some places are precisely marked by circles scratched on the rock, and within these borders the waste-land (*faysh*, pl. *fuyūsh*), used for grazing and for gathering fuel, is open to all Bayt Ḥusayn's members. Outsiders can use it only with explicit permission. The grazing might be said to be held in common by the village. Arable land ('wealth', *māl*, pl. *amwāl*), by contrast, is all privately owned; some is held in common by brothers whose father has died, but none is held by large patronymic groups, far less by the village as a whole.

Bayt Ḥusayn is large by tribal standards. Of the 147 adult tribesmen who now live there or are still closely enough linked with the village to be spoken of by others as village members,[4] more than half claim descent from Ḥusayn himself. The others belong to quite unrelated families. There were also, until the mid-1970s, about twenty Jews in the village, but all of these, with the exception of a few old people, now live in a nearby market town. They are still attached to the village for purposes of collective payments (*ghurm wa-jurm*) and of protection. A small family of *mazāyinah*, two grown men and their dependants, still live in the village. The tribesmen themselves comprise the families or *buyūt* (pl. of *bayt*) shown in Fig. 8.1.

No distinction of rights or obligations is made between Awlād Muthannā as a whole and the other tribal families, but Muthannā's descendants are the 'original house' and it is from them the shaykh is chosen. The village shaykh is also shaykh of the section that contains Bayt Ḥusayn and a half-dozen other settlements. Muthannā himself we know to have died at the end of the last century, but how far back his line goes to the eponymous Ḥusayn is not known

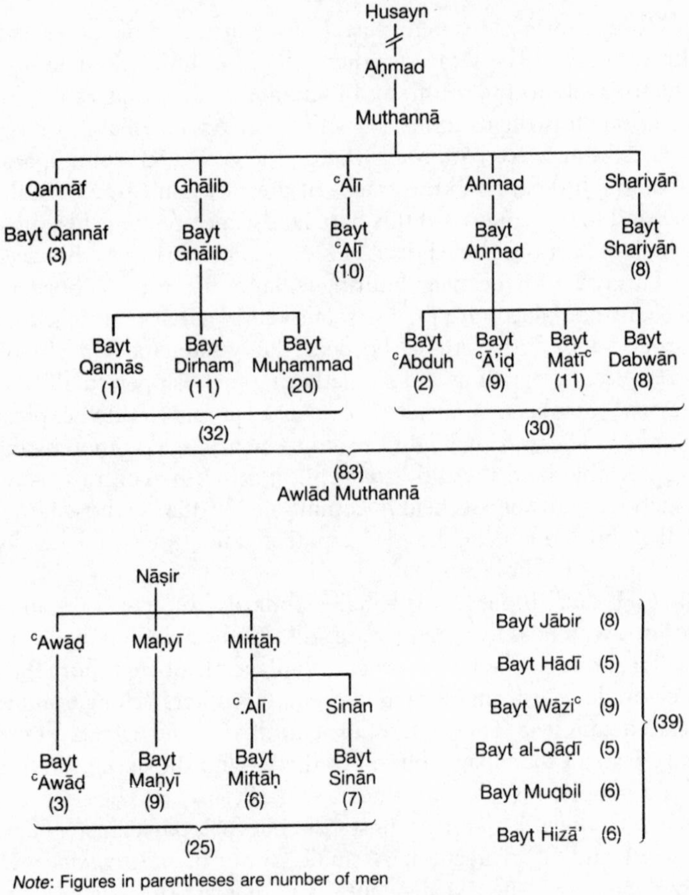

FIG. 8.1 Families making up the village of Bayt Ḥusayn

to the villagers. Ḥusayn is said to have founded the village 'some hundreds of years ago' in concert with the ancestor of the Jews who lived there, and the other families are, by comparison, reckoned 'incomers' or *naqā'il*, although no one claims to know quite where they came from or when.

The shaykh has no rights over other men's land. The present shaykh controls quite a large holding by village standards (not the largest by any means), but the previous shaykh, 'Abd al-Raḥmān, is not conspicuously well off in this regard, and nor was the one

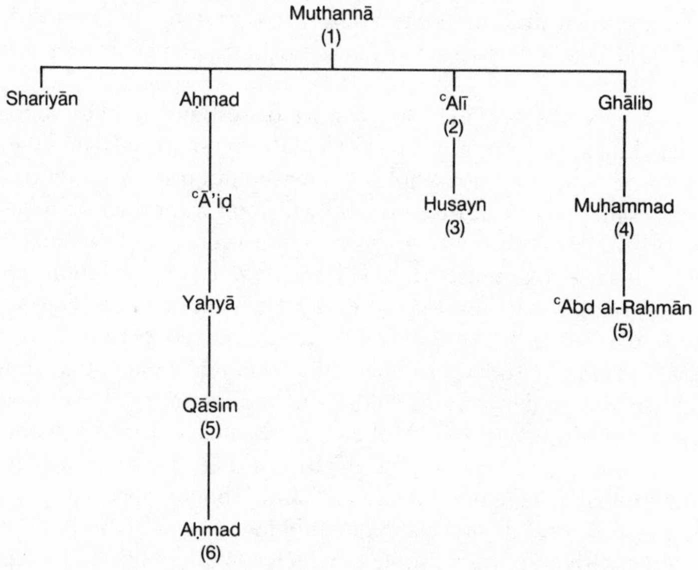

(ᶜAbd al-Raḥmān and Qāsim were, for a time, shaykhs concurrently.)

FIG. 8.2 Skeleton genealogy showing succession of shaykhs

before (see Fig. 8.2). The particular families which have held the position (or, to be more exact, the particular men who have been the shaykhs or their fathers and grandfathers) had small holdings of land near Ḥajjah of a few hundred *libnah* each, but all this had been sold by about 1960.[5]

Land, as we said, is not held in common by large patronymic groups such as Bayt Aḥmad Muthannā or Bayt Ghālib Muthannā. The groups of agnates who do hold their land in common are very small, as can be seen from many of the family diagrams (e.g. Figs. 8.3–8.5).[6] The size of the holdings varies. Some are held in common by brothers whose father is dead, some belong to men whose sons are now grown, and it is therefore as well to tabulate the amount of land held per head, dividing each holding by the number of grown men who share in it (see Fig. 8.6). However one breaks down the figures, the distribution of land is not inequitable by comparison with the western mountains or with Lower Yemen, where most land is owned by great landlords and many people therefore own little or nothing (cf. Tutwiler and Carapico 1981: 58, 65). None the less, a significant number of men are by no means well off.

As a very rough guide (the vagaries of soil and rainfall, among other things, rule out any exact calculation), one needs about 150 *libnah* to support a household. A great many men, even ignoring the presence of immature sons who will soon want their own land, are on the borderline of agricultural subsistence, and historically Bayt Ḥusayn, like most tribal villages, exported population. One family, Bayt Wāzi', has done so on a large scale recently (Fig. 8.7); those marked with an asterisk have all moved permanently to Lower Yemen. Aḥmad Daḥḥān and Daḥḥān Muḥammad both went to the Ba'dān area as soldiers of the Imam and have stayed there ever since, Daḥḥān Muḥammad having married a woman from there and Aḥmad Daḥḥān having married Daḥḥān Muḥammad's daughter. Whatever land Aḥmad once had is no longer spoken of as his. Daḥḥān Muḥammad and his son are still credited with 300 *libnah*, some of which is worked by Muḥammad 'Alī and by 'Alī Daḥḥān, but the owners never claim any share of the produce. Muḥammad 'Askar and his sons, with their miserable holding of 20 *libnah*, have pursued one of the modern equivalents of soldiering for the Imam: all three sons have government jobs in Ṣan'ā', and the father lives off their earnings. The men marked with crosses all work on occasion as emigrant labourers in Saudi Arabia, which we shall say something more of later.

The total area of arable land which members of the village own within the village borders is some 42,000 *libnah* (about 3,000 *libnah* within the borders belong to outsiders), and the average per man is thus about 285 *libnah*. But if the members of Bayt Wāzi' (above) are on the whole poorly off for land, the members of, for instance, Bayt 'Ā'iḍ Aḥmad are between them quite prosperous (see Fig. 8.3). Let us stress once again that even a group such as Bayt 'Ā'iḍ Aḥmad, only nine grown men, does not hold property jointly. The landholders are small groups (usually brothers) or individual grown men and their dependants. It also needs stressing that averages of land held per head can mean almost nothing in the course of village history where so much depends on demography: 'Ā'iḍ Aḥmad, for instance, had only two sons to claim his

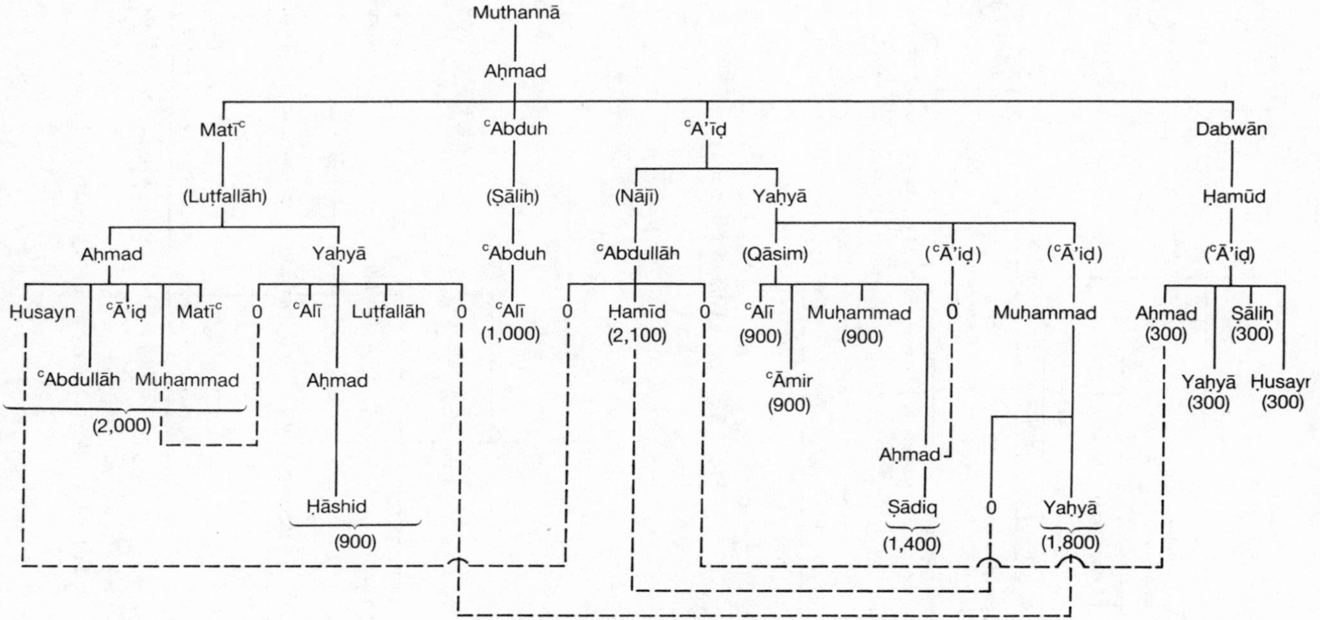

Note: Figures in parentheses here and in the following tables are land-holdings in *libnah* (150 *libnah*=approx 1 hectare)

FIG. 8.3 Bayt Aḥmad Muthannā (with selected close-range marriages)

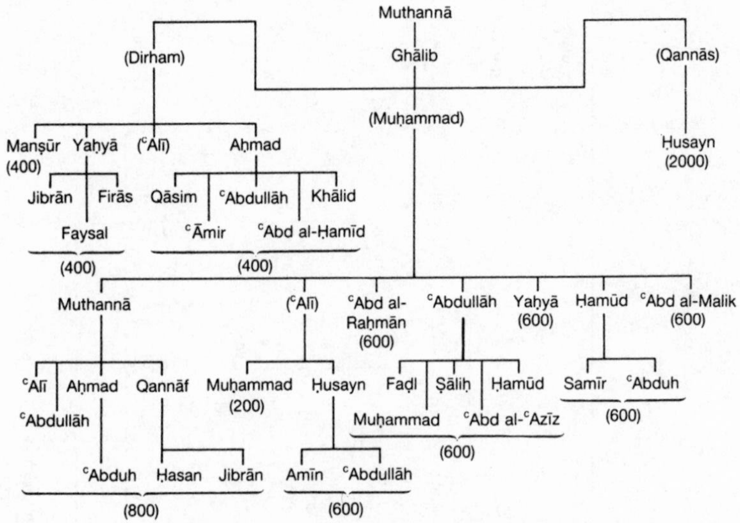

FIG. 8.4 Bayt Ghālib Muthannā

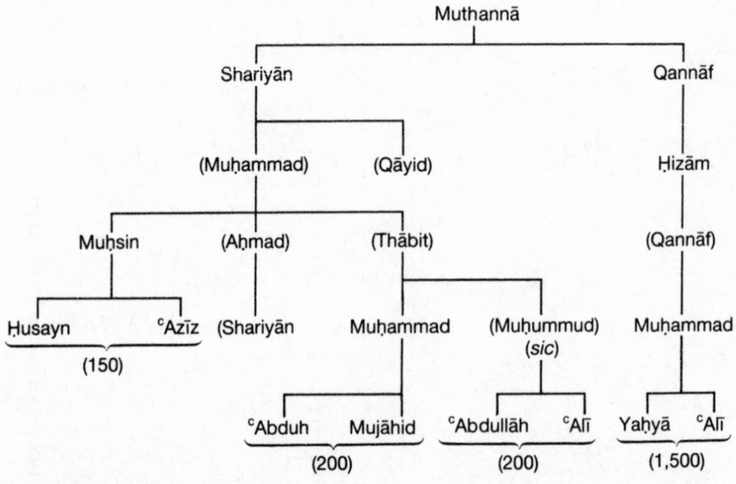

FIG. 8.5 Bayts Shariyān and Qannāf Muthannā

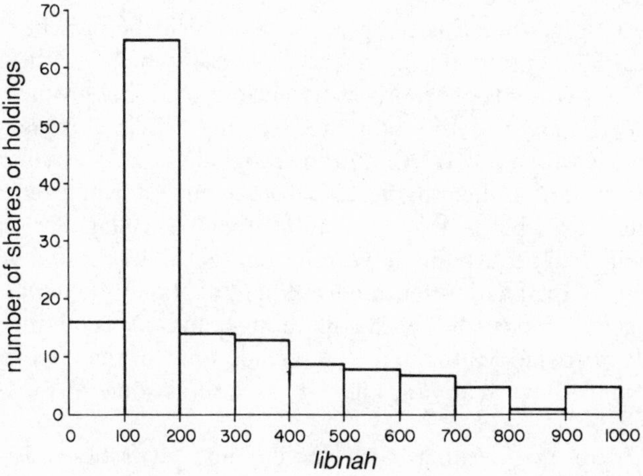

FIG. 8.6 Distribution of holdings and shares, by size

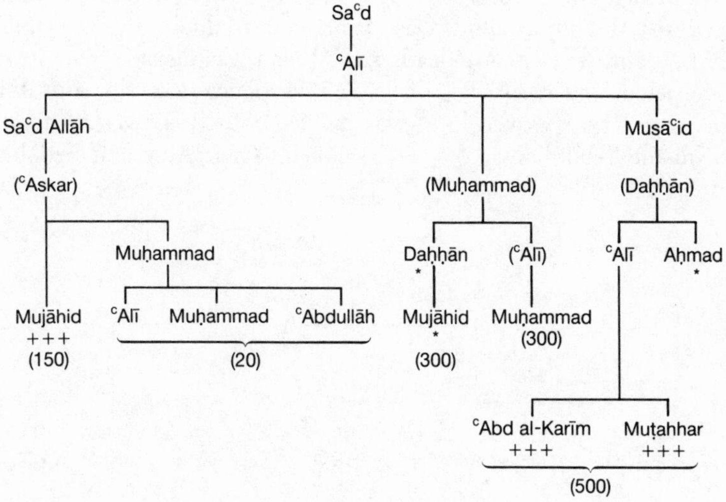

FIG. 8.7 Bayt Wāzi‘

inheritance while Muḥammad Ghālib (Fig. 8.4) had seven. Still, the disparities deserve noting.

Bayt 'Ā'iḍ Aḥmad is the group from which the present shaykh comes. He himself controls 1,400 *libnah*, of which 500 belong to his wife (we shall say more of this below), and his brothers have 900 each. He and they inherited equally. Their closest agnatic kinsmen (Muḥammad 'Alī and his son Yaḥyā) hold about 1,800. Those related to them by descent from an ancestor one generation further back (that is, from Aḥmad Muthannā; see Fig. 8.3) include not only Ḥamīd 'Abdullāh, with his undivided 2,100 *libnah*, but a number of men with respectable holdings of about 300 *libnah* each. One generation further back still, though, and one is talking of the whole of Awlād Muthannā, who include some of the families with least land (Bayt Shariyān; Fig. 8.5) as well as some of those with most.

We are not dealing with landholding dynasties, nor with collective holdings (whether formally divided or undivided) that a few men of a large patronymic group might in some way control for their own ends.[7] Most land is inherited, divided, and reinherited. The course of inheritance is sometimes complex, as can be seen from the distribution of land among the men of Bayt Hādī (Fig. 8.8). Sa'd willed one-third of his land (as one is allowed to do by Islamic law) to 'Alī and Mujāhid: Qāsim and Sa'd 'Abdullāh were not then born, Ṣāliḥ was already dead, and Aḥmad was his sole male heir. The remaining two-thirds of Sa'd's inheritance (less a portion for his wife who survived him) was divided equally between Aḥmad Ṣāliḥ and 'Abdullāh Sa'd when Sa'd died. When 'Abdullāh died, his

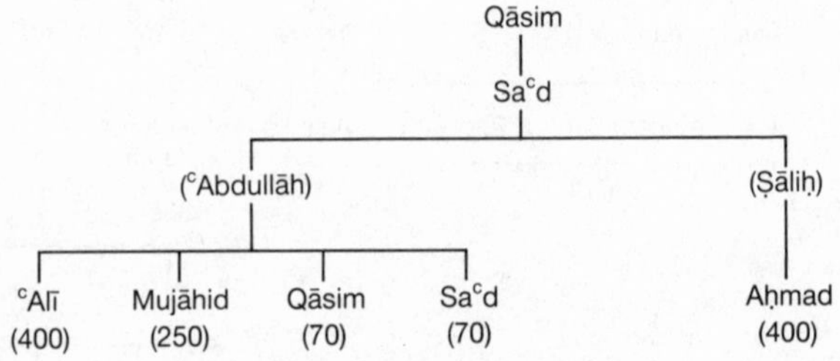

FIG. 8.8 Bayt Hādī

portion (less a portion for his two daughters) was divided among his four sons.

The amount a man inherits thus depends not only on the timeless prescriptions of Islamic law, or even on the way that the law is understood locally, but also on when he was born, when his father dies, and when his other close relatives died or were born. Younger sons, for example, often suffer in that their older brothers gain control of the better land (and often of more land) before they themselves can contest matters.

Such considerations of timing are more important still in the case of women's inheritance. As Mundy explains, a woman traditionally required male labour to exploit even land that she clearly owned, and required male representatives to state or maintain her claims against others. If she were due a portion of land, she would rarely receive it early in her marital career. Her brothers would usually work it for her until well after her father's death. Only when her own sons were grown up could she effectively press a claim to separate her portion from those of her brothers, at the same time as her sons were pressing for land from their father (Mundy 1979: 163–9). She risked losing all claim to land if her father died when she was very young, a circumstance in which male heirs are also badly placed; on the other hand, she was likely to exert explicit control over land if she had no brothers to obscure or contest her claims (ibid.). This latter case is that of the shaykh's wife (or one of his two wives) in Bayt Ḥusayn. She is his *bint 'amm* (FBD). She had no brothers and brought 500 *libnah* to add to the 900 that the shaykh himself inherited.

Women's property in land appears on all tables and charts in the present chapter under the names of men. That is how men always speak of things (it would be an invasion of privacy to do otherwise) and how women themselves speak of things unless the control of their property is at issue, which usually means their husband's and father's kin are placed somehow at odds. The particular woman may be pulling the strings, or may be utterly powerless. The control of property by or through women is hard to assess overall (one gets the details only of particular cases where one knows those involved), and most transfers of land by women are apparent only in the imbalance of amounts that related men hold or control. On that basis, it would seem that marriage often produces no significant land transfer. The division of land, once a few known sales and purchases are deducted, can very often be explained by the division of inheritance solely among men. Women are due inheritance (as the villagers see it, as well as in Islamic law), but their rights may be waived explicitly, their share of land may be bought out for cash, or their share in the estate as a whole may all be given in cash and movables so that land forms no part of it; but much more usually they own at least some land, though under the public stewardship of men.[8]

Most fields are divided into several plots, owned or controlled by different people, some of the plots having recently been divided through inheritance, some being held by more distant relations through descent or marriage, some having been bought or exchanged for others. If adjacent plots are offered for sale or exchange, one may have recognized rights of pre-emption (*shuf'ah*, *juwārah*), and if land is to be apportioned by inheritance, one might wish to gain control of certain plots in preference to others. Some dispersal of landholdings is desirable because fields on one side of the village are best for winter wheat, on another side for spring lentils, and on another still for sorghum in summer. Where rainfall is thin and scattered, it is in any case best not to hold all one's land in one block. Yet a measure of consolidation is needed too if one is not to spend much of the day tramping from one tiny plot to another, and holding all the land on a series of terraces allows one to declare it *maḥjūr*, 'off limits', to others so they cannot graze their flocks on the stubble.[9] Who owns what plots of which fields, and what they do with these, is a matter of constant interest.

LINKS OF MARRIAGE

The tendency to marry in is not, perhaps, as marked as some literature on the Middle East might lead one to expect, and links by marriage outside the village are numerous. Of the 147 grown men, 22 were still unmarried, 1 had 4 wives, and 7 had 2. There were thus 135 wives in the village or closely tied to it (at most times only 5 or 6 would be absent), and their places of origin were as shown in Table 8.1. The broad category of 'outside the tribe' includes marriages to women not only from nearby villages that happen to lie across a tribal border but also from as far away as Lower Yemen. Indeed, there is one Egyptian lady in the village whose

TABLE 8.1 *Origin of Wives in Bayt Ḥusayn*

FBD	Others in the *bayt*	Other *bayts* in the village	Other villages in the tribe	Outside the tribe	
7	6	63	26	33	No.
5	4.5	46	19	24.5	%

Within *bayt*	13=9.5%
Within the village	76=56%
Within the tribe	102=75.5%
Total	135

parents met her husband on the Mecca pilgrimage. It was not possible to draw up a complete list of where Bayt Ḥusayn's daughters married to, but there is every reason to suppose that the village is neither a net importer nor a net exporter of women to any significant extent.

What is plainly significant, even without complete figures, is the way in which marriages at a distance tend to cluster and repeat. Of the 19 wives of Bayt Muḥammad Ghālib, for instance, all but 3 were from outside the village: 4 were from one nearby village, 4 more from a second, 3 from another, and 2 from another still. In the present generation a similar number of brides passed the other way along the same axes. In the last generation the same was true. Recent marriages of this sort were spoken of as being simply to the *bint khāl* (MBD), but the precise personal relation was often through an aunt, or a cousin's aunt, or a woman related to some distant agnate of one's own and to an equally distant agnate of the woman one married in the other village. To pin her identity down as a FFBS–W–BFBSD, or whatever it may be, is not very helpful. The important thing is that one is marrying into a group already linked to, and known to, one's own. The honour of each is less exposed than it might be, and the interests of each are more manageable. Each of the groups in question, one might note, is a particular *bayt* within each village, and it is not the case that villages as wholes are thought of as allied by affinal ties.[10]

Personal interests and the interests of small groups of relatives are pursued in part on the basis of kin-ties. A few repeated marriages between families make these ties very complex. As is common in Middle Eastern societies, one finds that not only is one linked to a number of people, but one is linked to them in a number of ways and can define one's relation to a given person by tracing the link through a number of different paths.[11] The skein becomes closely tangled. The bases on which one might make or receive claims, and in general conduct one's affairs, mount up very quickly.

The same is true (but to a greater extent) when one marries within the village. The skein of relations is that much more tangled. Awlād Muthannā (those who descend from the founding stock) are in this respect somewhat differently placed from their neighbours in that, quite apart from particular marriages, they have that many more degrees of agnatic ties to count. One does not just marry inside the *bayt* or out, but inside what we could call a primary, secondary, or tertiary *bayt*; Bayt Dabwān Aḥmad, for instance, Bayt Aḥmad Muthannā, or Bayt Muthannā itself (see Table 8.2).[12]

TABLE 8.2 *Origin of Wives in Awlād Muthannā*

FBD	Others in primary *bayt*	Secondary *bayt*	Tertiary *bayt*	Other *bayts* in village	Elsewhere	
5	1	3	14	13	31	No.
7·5	1·5	4·5	21	19.5	46	%
9%			25.5%			
Within *bayt* 23=34.5%						
Within village			36=54%			
Total				67		

The denser web of ties that results from this gives a man that many more options to exploit, and perhaps gives a successful man a greater chance to arrange, for example, the outcome of inheritance to suit him. However, belonging to a wide range of *'iyāl 'amm* (agnates, father's brother's offspring) does not guarantee success: see Bayt Shariyān (Fig. 8.5). Nor is success precluded by a lack of agnates: see Bayt 'Awāḍ (Fig. 8.1), who have no known agnatic links (the relationships among the parts of Bayt Nāṣir are indeterminate) but whose three adult men share an undivided 1,600 *libnah*.

The village is by no means an isolated unit. Though it is spatially quite distinct from others like it, set apart from them by fields and by bare rock, it is connected to some of them and to points further off by marriage. If we were to mark ties of marriage by lines on a map, many lines would run parallel, either to nearby villages or to places elsewhere in Yemen. A few would project on their own to some family in which a villager had made a personal friend he could trust as kinsman. The village would be at the centre of an irregular star burst. The village itself, if scale allowed us to depict it properly, would be densely cross-hatched with ties within or between the *bayts*, and the same irregular star-bursts would show up with each *bayt* as their focus.

It is along these lines that the women's own aims are promoted, and the influence of women is at its greatest where such lines converge, near the centres of the webs that spread out from each house. The mere mapping of lines, however, would obscure the point that the rhetoric of agnation is public, while affinal ties are personal and can be declared suspended in times of collective conflict. The rhetoric of agnation itself usually carries weight only when men are more or less co-resident—*jār-uk al-qarīb wa-lā akhūk al-ba'īd* ('your close neighbour, not your distant brother') is a proverb one hears often quoted—and the language of male ancestry may in any case apply to men not linked by actual descent (so all the men of the village are 'sons of Ḥusayn', as against the village next door). It would be more accurate to see the public identity of the family as an instance of the more general scheme of collectivities than to see tribes and the like as the family writ large. But there is always an arbitrary line drawn. When collective identity is invoked, personal ties become problematic.

The imagery of tribal identity is itself, as we have seen, agnatic: fellow tribesmen are 'sons' of their collective eponym, although no personal ties of descent are elaborated. The men of a family are actual co-descendants, but the language of agnatic identity applies to them in just the same way. Personal kin ties of other types are also stressed and denoted by terminology, so a man is supposed to be close to his *ibn 'amm* (FBS) but scarcely less close to his *bazī* (ZS, a descendant, as it were, on the distaff side). The *man'* or *nasīb* (WB) is important and is chosen with care—a 'golden' affine (*nasīb dhahīb*) is highly valued—and one's wife's kinsmen in general (one's *manū'* or *ansāb*) should be granted help if they demand it.

One's wife's father is addressed by the same term (*yā 'amm*) as one's father's brothers.[13] One's wife's father's sons and brothers, however, are conspicuously not one's *'iyāl 'amm*, and the latter phrase is explained as meaning those who stand together as a group (*al-jam'*).

The rules one elicits do not, of course, predict who will stand with whom on each occasion, but the existence of certain types of rules is by itself significant: a particularly elaborate 'rule' is a theoretical reflection on principles, not an accompaniment to practice (cf. Dumont 1970: 82). In Upper al-'Uṣaymāt, for instance, one hears the 'rule' that the mother's brother and his sons must be supported to the cost of precisely seven camels (which few people own any more), and that if this proves insufficient he has right of refuge as a *labīth* for precisely three years. What in fact happens in serious cases is that, if his own tribe provide him no satisfaction, the affine takes refuge with your tribe as a *qaṭīr* and in the end becomes part of your tribe, part therefore of the group of *'iyāl 'amm* (father's brother's children). The contradiction between individual ties and collective identities, if pursued to a conclusion, results in the individual switching identity from one collectivity to another; the identity of the village and its place among others cannot be reduced to a summary of ties between people living there.

In the area where Bayt Ḥusayn lies, the territory of each village is closed for grazing to the villages next door; and the village territories together exhaust the territory of a section, while the territories of the sections, in turn, exhaust that of the tribe.[14] Territory is in this sense exclusive. Arable land, by contrast, although the amount is not in practice all that large here, can be owned by outsiders, just as members of Bayt Ḥusayn own a few thousand *libnah* in the territories of other villages: *al-ḥadd mā yadkhul al-maḥdūd*, 'borders do not enter into questions of private property'. Along the border lines, indeed, fields are intermingled. In the busy spring season of ground-breaking and ploughing, men from different villages are at some points crossing and recrossing each other's paths, men from Bayt Ḥusayn working their land in the territory next door, and men from next door working land within the territory of Bayt Ḥusayn.

The borders, despite this, are very clear. At some points, as we have seen, they are marked by scratched circles on the rocks, at others by natural features such as the edge of a shallow wash, at still others by a line of sight between features further off, such as a mountain ridge or outcrops of rock. These borders are said never to move. But people may do. Where a man's rights are not upheld, he can move to another village; and when, if he stays where he is, his ties with outsiders conflict with collective self-definition, these personal ties are for a time suspended, which occurs most often in the 'cutting' or closing of borders. A man who owns land in another village may, therefore, if his people are at odds with the village, be denied access to his own arable. It is for him to decide in the end where his identity lies. Those who cannot sustain the contradiction are excluded from the system (they move out or sell up), just as are those who cannot sustain a household and move off to the west or to Lower Yemen. The geographical shell survives them, and so too does the collective identity.

CROP PRODUCTION

The types of crops and the precise time at which they are sown can vary in a given year from field to field around a single village. The differences between large areas are enormous. In general, a distinction is drawn between sorghum (*dhurah*) and other grains (called *nadhāyah*, and supposedly 'hot'), which is also applied to the fields where one category or other of crop does best and to whole geographical areas: Sufyān's territory and the lowlands west of Ḥūth, for example, are sorghum country, while Arḥab, Khārif, Banī Ṣuraym, and 'Iyāl Yazīd are grain country (*bilād al-nadhāyah*), relying more on their wheat and barley. Bayt Ḥusayn lies in this latter type of area.

In both types of area it is sorghum which provides a fixed point of reference in the agricultural calendar. Around Ḥūth the sorghum is sown in the last week of May (during the star period *ṭulū' kāmah*, 20 May–1 June). In Wādī Ḥumrān, just north of Ḥūth but much warmer and less wind-swept, the sorghum is sown a week earlier. Khaywān sows about three weeks ahead of Wādī Ḥumrān, and al-Baṭanah (in the lowlands between Ḥūth and Shahārah) begins sowing some two weeks ahead of Khaywān. In the colder, more exposed areas of Banī Ṣuraym, just south of Ḥūth, the sorghum is sown about one week later than around Ḥūth itself. The dates in a particular place are said to be fixed,[15] and the timing probably does need to be fairly close: either the crop will be exposed to stem-borers, if planted too early, or the plants' vegetative phase will miss the August rains, if planted too late. On the plateau the growing season lasts about five months, from the end of May until early November.

The ground for sorghum must be prepared. 'The sorghum summer, you ignoramus, [depends on] its winter' (*ṣayf al-dhurah yā 'ayy fī shitā-hā*), and if no intermediate winter or spring crop is planned, then the preparation of sorghum plots can start as soon as last year's sorghum is cut. This strategy of growing sorghum where sorghum was grown last year, with no intervening crop, is often pursued in areas such as Wādī Ḥumrān. Success depends upon 'turning' the soil very thoroughly and on getting good rains at the start of the growing season. In certain other areas the strategy of leaving plots empty for more than half the year is not practicable; but even where sorghum does not have the prominence given it in Wādī Ḥumrān, the ground where it is grown is prepared very thoroughly.

The dry surface is first broken up with a *makhrash* or *mashabbar*, a heavy, toothed board which is dragged behind a donkey or bull, and the soil is then ploughed. The plough (*ḥarāthah*), fitted with an iron 'tooth' or *ḥalī* often made from an axle spring, furrows the dirt rather than turning it.[16] The more often one ploughs, so it is said, the better the result. In the star periods immediately before planting time (*ghurūb kāmah*, 24 April–6 May, and *ghurūb al-thawr*, 7 May–19 May), the landscape is alive with men riding *mashabbars* behind their beasts or guiding their ploughs back and forth. Once the ground has been broken and ploughed, one then 'levels' (*yakumm*) the soil with the reverse side of the *mashabbar* or with a flat board called *maḥarr*.

Seed is either spread along ploughed furrows (*ḥallāl*) or planted in clusters every cubit or so (*zajdah*). Procedures vary from place to place, but the shoots are everywhere thinned out about twenty days after they show at the surface (assuming they do show), and again twenty days after that.[17] Two months after planting, the crop in sorghum country should already be more than 2 metres high. About three and a half months after planting (some time during September, during the star periods *khāmis* and *sādis 'allān*) the lower leaves start to yellow and should be removed, to be followed a month or so later by the leaves from the plant's upper half.[18] Once all but a small spray of leaves at the very top are removed, one has ten days or so to harvest the crop before the grain starts spoiling. The stalks are cut near the bottom, leaving a foot or so standing. The heads are then severed and the grain is threshed off them. It is stored and will last for years if sealed up properly, while the stalks, 2 metres or even 3 metres long in sorghum country, are stacked in bundles to be used for building and, along with the leaves, for winter fodder. The root system (*jarza*ʿ) is sometimes dug up and used for fuel.

In the warmer areas, a crop of broad-leaved bean plants (*tujrah*) is often sown among the sorghum in alternate rows and is harvested about a month before the sorghum is cut. In the cooler areas *qillah* (the broad bean known as *fūl* to most Arabic speakers) is grown by the same means and over the same period as is *tujrah* elsewhere. In most plateau areas *qillah* also appears as a winter crop. In some places (as in Banī Ṣuraym) *qillah* grows in winter and *tujrah* is grown among the sorghum in summer. Both before and after the sorghum harvest there are also harvests of non-sorghum grains, the importance of which varies from place to place.

The sorghum on the plateau south of Ḥūth is in any case shorter than that in the warmer areas (grain yields can be high despite this), but when in Sufyān or Wādī Ḥumrān the sorghum, two months or more after planting, is already a rustling jungle well above a man's height, in Banī Ṣuraym, Arḥab, or Khārif it is often a feeble ruin, not more than a metre tall, on which good heads of grain are not going to form.[19] Much of it might by then already have been despaired of and ploughed under. If rain failed to come at the time to plant sorghum but fell just a little later, one could immediately sow wheat or barley (that is, in the star period *ṭulūʿ kāmah*, 20 May–1 June). The timing of these other crops is not so fixed as that of sorghum. In the next two star periods (*ṭulūʿ al-thawr* and *ṭulūʿ al-ḍilm*, which between them cover June) little of anything is sown in most plateau areas for fear of insect pests. During *ṭulūʿ al-ṣilm* (28 June–11 July), on the other hand, it is said that practically any crop other than sorghum can be sown, if there is rain to sow at all, with fair hopes of success: *man ṣullam mā ẓulam*, 'he who sows in this period will suffer no harm'. In, for example, the northern parts of Banī Ṣuraym this *ṣilmī* crop can include lentils (*bilsan*, *ʿadas*), wheat, barley, peas (*ʿatar*), and fenugreek (*ḥalbah*).

In many plateau grain areas (the north of Banī Ṣuraym, for instance), it is reckoned that nothing but barley can usefully be sown from the end of *ṭulūʿ al-ṣilm* until *khāmis ʿallān*; that is, from mid-July until early September. In other areas, barley sown in late July should be ready to harvest by early October. But September is a critical period. It is usually then that the prevailing wind backs from south-west to north-east. If rain comes in time, and falls where one needs it, this north wind ripens the late barley, but if the rain fails to come, then the wind parches the crop and leaves only withered wreckage. In some areas, wheat as well as barley is reckoned a possible crop to sow in July and August.[20] And in parts of sorghum country (in Wādī Ḥumrān, for instance), the constraints are almost the opposite of those noted for the north of Banī Ṣuraym: late July is precisely the point at which crops other than barley become a possibility, particularly wheat and lentils, which in Banī Ṣuraym give way to barley at about the same date.

Whenever they are planted, most summer crops take about two and a half months before they can be harvested. But the timing of planting depends primarily on the rain, and the rain is irregular: even in fields around a single village, and far more so between distant villages, a given crop will not all be in phase, but one field will be a week or two ahead of the next, and another a week behind.

The overall amount of rain and its precise timing vary considerably from year to year (see Figs. 8.9 and 8.10). The geographical distribution of rain at any given time is hard to summarize, but there is no doubt from the endless talk that its distribution is most irregular. When one adds to this the differences imposed by yearly shifts in timing of rain (the effect of those shifts itself differs with local climate), the differences of strategy appropriate to separate areas, and the differences in timing sorghum (around which much else turns; preparation of plots is more elaborate and the growing period longer than for other grains) one is faced with an extraordinarily fragmented system.[21] The effect of these different constraints overlapping irregularly is perhaps more marked in grain country than in sorghum country, but usually, whether at village level or at that of whole tribes, what cycles emerge are to be thought of as statistical summaries. They do not correspond to the ordered activity of discrete groups of persons, the inhabitants of this village or that tribal section, throughout the farming year.

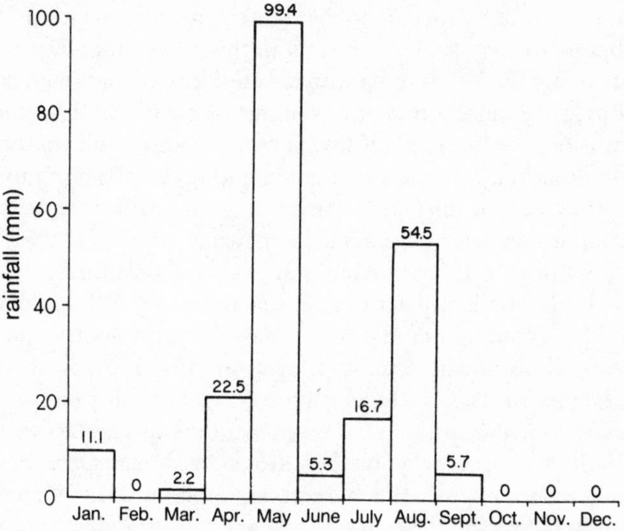

FIG. 8.9 Monthly rainfall in 1979 at al-Bawn

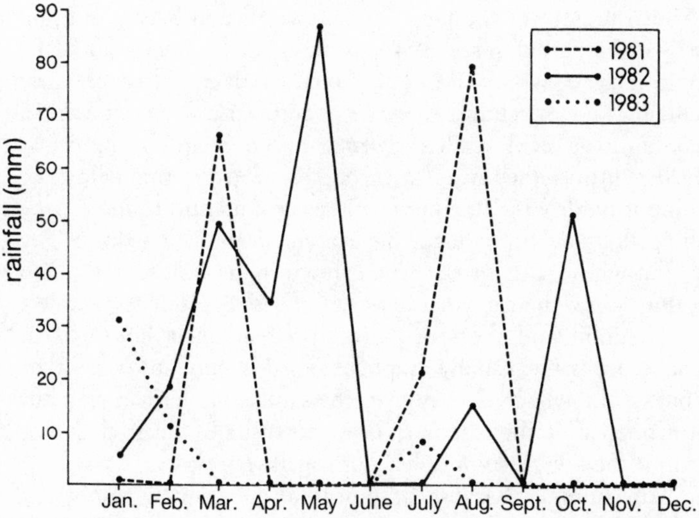

FIG. 8.10 Fluctuations in rainfall, 1981–1983, Ṣan'ā'

In sorghum country it is sorghum which takes the work; 'the sorghum summer depends on its winter', and preparation begins long before the season, but throughout the season thinning the crop and stripping the leaves to be stored as fodder demands a great deal of effort. In grain country 'the summer is two summers, and the winner is he who hunts it' *(al-ṣayf ṣayfayn wa-l-fattāḥ man ṣād-hu)*, meaning that one is always ploughing and reploughing in an effort to grow two crops during a span of time that in fact starts before the sorghum season and extends somewhat after it. The focus of attention is rather different from that in sorghum country, and with it perhaps the rhythm of activity. The summer wheat or barley in an area such as Wādī Ḥumrān is a stop-gap and is given little space. In an area such as northern Banī Ṣuraym, by contrast, it is of central importance and may be the best crop people get all year.[22]

Most summer crops, planted whenever the rains allow one to do so from June to around September, are referred to as *ṣarbī* (they are intended to ripen before the 'harvest' of sorghum, *ṣurāb*). The term is vague and refers to the crops, not to any specific dates. In practice it overlaps with *'allānī*, a term which refers to crops sown or harvested in the period 2 September – 10 October, typically wheat and barley. As a rule of thumb, *ṣarbī* are those summer crops that are harvested before the sorghum and *'allānī* are those that come after. But the bulk of the late summer wheat and barley in grain country is harvested just before or in the two weeks after the sorghum harvest, which itself falls for most plateau areas in early November. Like sorghum, the wheat and barley are cut with a curved knife or sickle called *sharīm*. Everyone in the family is involved, cutting the crop, carrying it in from the fields, or threshing it by driving a team of donkeys round and round on the threshing floor. Many villages have a single threshing floor. The work, though, is organized primarily by households, with help from other kin if their harvest does not coincide exactly with one's own. The grain and the straw are stored in one's house or in personal caches. It usually happens at this time of year that everyone in the village is busy over the same couple of weeks, but the coincidence of their activity does not usually mean close co-operation: they work in parallel, not together.

The late summer harvest of wheat and barley is important in grain country, but rain is often short at sowing time. Even in August (the height of the wet season) rainfall is fickle, but in

September and early October, when one might want to sow *'allānī* grain and could do so only if rain fell, the skies are usually completely clear except for columns of swirling dust. From the end of September to early January rain is particularly scarce on average, and at this time of year the temperature drops, often to below freezing in December and January; but in grain country precisely these months are an essential crop season. Indeed, on high ground, crops are often planted, if rain comes at all, immediately after the November harvest. In the higher parts of Khārif, for example, wheat and barley are put in if possible, and this crop is referred to as *qiyāḍ*, as are crops sown as late as the end of January. Barley sown in Banī Ṣuraym during the same period is referred to as *rabī'*, presumably meaning that it is intended to ripen in 'spring'.[23]

The rate at which grain germinates and matures when sown in winter varies enormously, with the result that crops in different fields or different villages seldom grow quite in phase or in tidy succession. Barley sown in December may be harvested in mid-February, if the frost does not ruin it. Wheat planted at the same time may grow with similar rapidity or may not be ripe until as late as June, presumably lying dormant in the cold. Some fields are always colder than others, but overall fluctuations of temperature and rainfall alike add to the irregularity of yields and timing.

During the winter season (*qiyāḍ* or *rabī'*), not only are barley and wheat sown, but also lentils (*bilsan* or *'adas*) and beans (*qillah* or *fūl*). Most such crops, unless stopped by the cold, require about three months to ripen and are harvested in February or March. Throughout the high plateau areas these winter crops, which are sown wherever the scarce rainfall allows, are reckoned crucial; but they are scattered, vulnerable, and unreliable. *Qiyāḍ* is followed by *dithā'*, a term applied to crops sown from mid-February or so onward on land where no earlier crop was planted, or where an early *qiyāḍ* crop has just been harvested, or (quite frequently) where a later *qiyāḍ* crop has been despaired of and ploughed under. *Dithā'* is the crop which should catch the spring rains.[24] On the higher parts of the plateau, this is the season when one can reasonably hope to start getting some steady return on one's efforts, if only the rains come; and in Khārif, lower Banī Ṣuraym, Arḥab, and 'Iyāl Yazīd the fields are often at their greenest in March. Wheat, barley, lentils, beans, *ḥalbah* (fenugreek), and peas are all sown as the rain allows, but already, as early as February, one has an eye on the 'sorghum summer' and on the problem of rotating crops.[25]

A late *qiyāḍ* crop may run right through the late winter or early spring season and not be harvested until just before time to sow sorghum. At Kāniṭ (in northern Khārif near the border with Arḥab), for instance, wheat sown in early January was not cut until mid-May (so the *dithā'* season was entirely lost), and the fields were then immediately broken, ploughed, and levelled for sorghum. In adjacent fields early *dithā'* crops of wheat, barley, beans, and lentils sown in mid-February ripened at about the same time. Some rain fell in mid-March and a late *dithā'* crop of barley and peas was put in, which in this cold area was not ready to harvest until early July;[26] in other words, after the time when one might plant sorghum. These March rains had come too late to plant beans (they would have died of thirst with the onset of the *jaḥr* or hot, dry season) and the chance of rotating the crops was lost by a week or two: instead the fields where winter barley had been were left empty for about two months to put sorghum there when the time came. When the time did come, the rains were poor and the sorghum grew very poorly.

The timing of the spring rains often presents the farmer with a gamble: to leave his plots empty for sorghum, which may very well fail, or to plant what he can when it rains in the knowledge that he will thereby lose the chance to put sorghum there and so lose the chance of a heavier grain yield and a yield of essential fodder. The sorghum stalks wrapped in alfalfa as bundles (*'asā'ib*) are the staple support for cows, of which most households have at least one for milk, and for oxen, which are commonly used for ploughing. The price of a 'bull', so called, YR 4,000 or 5,000 most of the time, would go as high as YR 7,000 in the early summer ploughing season. A bull can plough 50 or 60 *libnah* in a day, where a donkey at best can do half that; but without fodder one would have to buy and sell yearly at a major loss.

The sorghum which takes 5 months to grow in most plateau areas takes 6 months at al-Baṭanah, 7 further west, and as long as 9 around Maswar in the western mountains where 'the woman, her cow, and the crops', as they say, are all the same. In the east the season may be only four months. Low-lying parts of the desert east are in any case out of phase with the plateau, sometimes harvesting their sorghum only a month or so after the plateau tribes have sown theirs. But, roughly speaking, the longer the season, the greater the yield: a scale of productivity, most apparent in production of fodder, spans the country from west to east, the west being very much more productive. This was always important, but the pattern remains apparent nowadays and has major effects on decisions about which crops to grow.

The planting and harvesting of crops, with the preparation of ground that immediately precedes planting, is not all that needs to be done. Each plot must be 'turned' (*qallāb*) every three or four years. There are three techniques used. The first, *qalūd*, involves digging over the whole field to a depth of about a metre with the *mufris* or short-handled pick. The second, *qalūb*, involves ploughing a furrow three times or more in the same place, tipping the soil to the next furrow, and furrowing that in turn, from one side of the field to the other. The third, *khays*, involves repeatedly ploughing a strip about two metres wide and at every turn shifting the soil to the previous strip with a drag-shovel called *masabb*, one man digging in the flat wooden blade and two others then hauling on ropes, until all the soil has been upped and moved. In recent years tractors have increasingly been used to dig and invert the soil, but there remain a great many terraced plots that are too small for machinery to work, and in the past all the land had to be 'turned' with no more help than that provided by draft animals.

The turning of the soil and the fact that fields collect runoff, and therefore nutrients, from rock slopes, from wadis, or from higher terraces, must together account for the frequent occurrence of successive crops with little or no rotation. Tribesmen are well aware that sorghum does better on plots where the crop was beans or lentils than on plots where the last crop was wheat or barley.[27] Lentils and barley, for instance, are alternated, perhaps as *qiyāḍ* and *dithā'*, where a farmer can do so. Plots where alfalfa has been harvested after two years' growth are retained for sorghum if a good crop of fodder is needed. However, the timing of most crops, except sorghum (fixed date), alfalfa (not seasonal), and *qāt* (long term), is determined by just when in the year the rain comes. There is often no option but to plant barley twice in a row or to squeeze in a crop of wheat where one wants to put sorghum later; beans or lentils would have been better, but the rains came too late to plant them. One plants what one can when one can.

A *libnah* of rain-fed land in any of the areas discussed will yield about half a *qadaḥ* of barley in a reasonable year, which represents a return of about 10 : 1 on what one sows. A similar return can be expected on beans, wheat, and lentils, although wheat usually takes more space and is more prone to failure. In a bad year one may get nothing back. In the best possible conditions, rain-fed barley and wheat will hardly yield more than 20 : 1 (about one *qadaḥ* per *libnah* with barley), which is what these grains give in most places under any conditions with pump irrigation. Sorghum yields more than other grains almost everywhere (80 : 1 is not unusual in an area like Wādī Ḥumrān), and it covers more ground per unit weight of sowing (often ten times what other grains cover). Again, though, yields can be low in a poor year, and pumped water makes a huge difference. A rain-fed plot in Wādī Ḥumrān, for example, that yielded about one-fifth of a *qadaḥ* per *libnah* one year (between a third and a half a *qadaḥ* per *libnah* was what they hoped for) had a pump-fed plot next to it that gave slightly over one and a half *qadaḥ* per *libnah*: in other words, seven times as much. But if one has pumped water, one would not often use it on sorghum, but rather for cash crops such as *qāt,* alfalfa (for animal feed), or tomatoes.

The number of areas where wells can be usefully drilled for farming is small. Even those that have drilled wells have encountered problems, as in Qāʿ al-Bawn where good money has been made from growing watered crops but where the water-table, in some places at over a hundred metres to start with, fell by some twelve metres in the space of about four years.[28] Even if pump-fed farms in al-Bawn prosper (most probably they will not for long), the number of other areas that can exploit drilled water in the tribal north is small. Nor can existing yields be much improved where farming remains rain-fed. If other parts of the country attain greater agriculture yields and establish themselves in the cash-based production of staple foods, then the north is very likely to be marginalized further still.

Given the unpredictable patchiness of rain-fall, such that one field may prosper and another produce very little in a given year, one might expect some social response; some system whereby the households in a village or the villages in a tribal section could be relied on to assist one another in times of trouble. What one finds instead is 'dog eat dog', or 'fish eat fish' as Yemenis have it. There is, for example, no tradition of village grain stores. Enquiries about times of drought and scarcity turn up stories of how one family with a small surplus took advantage of another who suffered a shortfall and bought part of their land at low prices. Similar stories emerge of how land was lost through debt to people in towns (usually the 'weak' people spoken of in Chapter 4) or to the Imam's officials.

The lack of co-operation in practice is perhaps not as marked as in stories told of the past, but it is still marked enough. Neighbours occupying adjoining houses or working adjoining plots may help one another gratuitously in time of trouble, usually, as Doughty put it, 'betwixt free will and their private advantage'; one would work to repair someone else's terrace if one's own terrace might be placed in some danger, for example, but hardly for long otherwise. Yet Bayt Ḥusayn is a comfortable place for those who live there, and what ease men enjoy in their relations with others they attribute very largely to the village shaykh. Ties between households are seldom raised to a formal principle or a collective representation of the village itself as a connected whole: the system of raising *ghurm wa-jurm* (collective mulcts), for instance, does not quite coincide with patronymic sets, and the ceremonies in which villagers come together refer not to village identity but nearly always to personal rites of passage—so one's relatives from elsewhere may take part in these, and some of one's neighbours perhaps may not.[29] But the border-line with adjoining villages is in no doubt at all.

In the case at hand it happens that the line on one side of Bayt Ḥusayn is not only the village's border, but that of the section in which the village falls, of the tribe to which the section belongs, and of one confederation with the other. Much of the villagers' time and interest is taken up with concerns that attach directly to these larger identities. While the discrete village settlements are the site of most decisions to do with farming, with marriage, and with investment in the cash economy, the position of each village in the tribal system is what inserts it in patterns of dispute and settlement and in questions of national politics, all of which shift more rapidly than the constraints on raising crops and livestock.

THE PRESENT-DAY ECONOMY AT VILLAGE LEVEL

Economically villages were once largely self-sufficient (or rather their insufficiencies were made up by exporting people), but few families now depend only on what they produce. The employment pattern for men in Bayt Ḥusayn as of late 1983 was as shown in Table 8.3. In many families, the father or the older men work as farmers and the young men work elsewhere.[30] There is little doubt that the number of non-farmers has increased over recent years, but one must be wary of assuming that generational differences at a given time are all the result of catching the society at a point of transition: probably there were always a number of absent young men. Previously, though, there was little employment available outside the village except as a soldier for the Imam. Now there is a wide range of choice.

TABLE 8.3 *Male Employment in Bayt Ḥusayn*

	No.	%
Agriculture	65	44
Military	20	14
Government	10	7
Private employment	18	12
Total employed in Yemen	(113)	(77)
Emigrants	27	18
Students	7	5
Total	147	100

Many families in Bayt Ḥusayn have something of a tradition of schooling (this is most unusual in itself), and of the twenty village men in the army all but two are officers. In most tribal villages the proportion of officers to other ranks would be reversed, but the proportion of men in the army to the total population is often high. By the army here is meant the regular army, not the 'popular army' or tribal levy from which men in many northern areas draw stipends. Even the regular army is not as time-consuming as might be supposed, at least not for northerners. Some come home at weekends. Others turn up when there is agricultural work to be done. Still others enjoy extended leaves of absence whereby they collect their pay from the army once a month, but otherwise stay at home. A few are posted elsewhere for lengthy periods, but all of them are reckoned residents (*sākinīn al-qaryah*), their families are in the village, a large part of their pay passes through the village, and they themselves are very much part of Bayt Ḥusayn.

The same may be said of others who spend part of their time elsewhere: the non-military employees of government, the private wage-earners working in Yemen, the emigrant workers, and the students. The first of these categories is something new. Administrative posts were in any case few in the Imam's day, and those that existed were the prerogative largely of qadis and sayyids. The bureaucracy in Ṣan'ā' has blossomed since the early 1970s. But it is still unusual to find tribesmen in office work (most are illiterate), and non-military government jobs of other sorts are comparatively rare. The civil organizations present in the countryside (new health centres, schools, and so forth) have been staffed largely by foreigners, and the Yemenis now moving into such work tend to come from the cities or Lower Yemen. Those northerners who are educated, as several are in the village at hand, have so far tended to cash in their skills for more immediate influence by passing through officer's school.

The proportion of emigrants (18 per cent of Bayt Ḥusayn's adult men as of late 1983) is striking, but in fact is much lower than in some northern tribal areas.[31] The emigrant workers, all of whom were in Saudi Arabia, are not drawn by any means equally from all the families or larger patronymic sets. Of the 38 men in Bayt Aḥmad Muthannā, for example, only 2 work as emigrant labourers, and of the 32 men in Bayt Ghālib Muthannā only 1 does. On the other hand, 5 out of 13 men from Bayt Miftāḥ work outside the country and, to take the extreme case, all 5 adult men of Bayt Hādī do so whose inheritance we touched on earlier. Their land is worked by their sons and womenfolk.

Traditionally, agricultural work is divided between the sexes: women are responsible for livestock and usually cut fodder, thin the crops where necessary, and sort the grain, while men do the ploughing and digging. But, as Tutwiler and Carapico very rightly remark (1981: 17), 'no man would allow a cow to go unmilked, nor [a] woman let a field go unplowed if the other were unexpectedly sick or unavailable'. With more men absent, women in many families took on part at least of what used to be men's work, thus doing regularly what they used in any case to do on occasion. Control of land is still attributed to the men in all public contexts, and it is in terms of men that arrangements to work land are discussed.

These arrangements are extremely varied, but the fragmented forms of co-operation deserve note. They are probably not only the result of emigration.[32] Most men in Bayt Jābir, for instance, are farmers (see Fig. 8.11). Ḥusayn Ṣāliḥ and 'Alī Yaḥyā (at the bottom left of the diagram) are both full-time farmers, working their land in common and contributing to a joint household. Ḥusayn Aḥmad and his father (at the diagram's centre) share a house. 'Abdullāh is an army officer based in Ṣan'ā', but contributes to the common purse and works on the common land when free to do so. Aḥmad, Ṣāliḥ and Ḥusayn (the sons of Qāyid), however, have divided their already small patrimony. Ṣāliḥ and Ḥusayn married women from other villages. Intermittently they co-operate with each other, but they maintain separate kitchens and purses. Aḥmad co-operates with neither of them, nor does any of them co-operate with their relatives by marriage, Ḥusayn Aḥmad and his kin. Aḥmad Qāyid is married to a woman from Bayt Shariyān. He runs a 'chicken factory' (fattening chicks under lamps) in partnership with someone

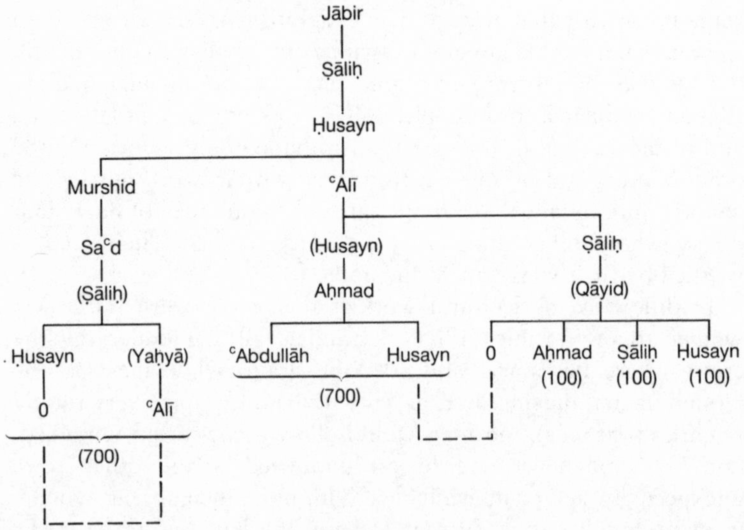

FIG. 8.11 Bayt Jābir

quite unrelated to any of them, from Bayt Muḥammad Ghālib, and also runs the only shop in the village.

Until the late 1960s it would have been reckoned a disgrace for a tribesman to run a shop, but since then there have been a great many changes. Bayt Maḥyī, for example, collect most of their earnings in cash, not kind (see Fig. 8.12). Aḥmad Aḥmad farms for his own consumption. Sirḥān, though, grows little but *qāt*, which he sells to the other villagers. Muḥammad and Ṣāliḥ Qāsim, retaining their patrimony undivided, have also gone into the *qāt* business, as well as producing grain for their joint household. Ḥusayn ʿAbdullāh earns a living driving a mechanical digger, while his father keeps their land in production. Qāyid, Alī and Ṣāliḥ have divided their patrimony and each heads a separate household, but in practice Qāyid farms all their land for their common benefit. The other two are drivers and part-owners of diggers.

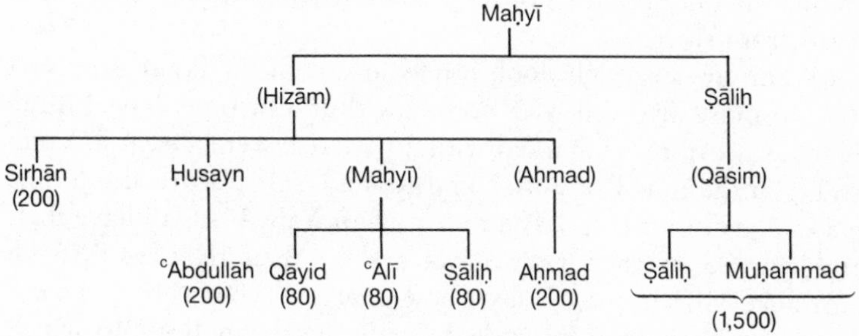

FIG. 8.12 Bayt Maḥyī

Sets of agnatic kin do not react to opportunities as cohesive wholes. Bayt ʿAlī Muthannā, from which two successive shaykhs came early this century, exhibits every one of the options we have looked at (see Fig. 8.13), but there is no common purse or common interest above the level of each family household. ʿAbdullāh Ṣāliḥ (at the left of the diagram) is a farmer. So are Muḥsin Ḥusayn and one of his sons, while the other is an army officer. ʿAlī Ḥusayn farms too. One son is a driver and the other an emigrant. The sons of ʿAlī Ṣāliḥ (at the right of the diagram) number two drivers and a farmer. Near the centre of the diagram are two sons of Ḥusayn marked with asterisks: Mishlī moved permanently to Saudi Arabia

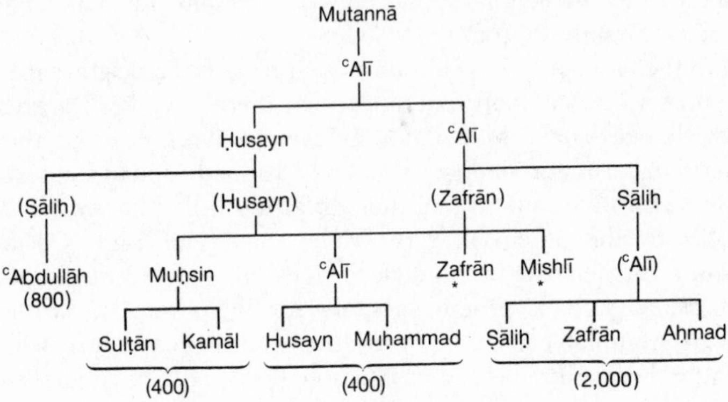

FIG. 8.13 Bayt ʿAlī Muthannā

and gave up his land, but Zafrān has disappeared entirely—he simply left one day for no one knows where and has never been heard from since.

To sum up, we might look briefly at one of the families in Bayt Ḥusayn most involved with non-agricultural income, Bayt Miftāḥ (Fig. 8.14). All those marked with an asterisk were absent in Saudi Arabia at the time I enquired, and Aḥmad Yaḥyā worked full time in Ṣanʿāʾ as a carpenter. The four sons of Yaḥyā ʿAlī all have their land worked by their womenfolk and by their relatives through marriage: Miftāḥ and Ḥusayn both married women from Lower Yemen, so their land is worked by the local families into which their sisters married; Muḥammad and Aḥmad both married locally (one to a woman from the village, the other to a woman from a nearby village that belongs to another tribe), so their land is worked by the families from which their wives came. When the emigrants return from their spell in Saudi Arabia they work the land of these various relatives, which allows the relatives in turn to work as emigrant labourers. What is not happening in any of these cases is the subjection of one set of men to another within the village as labourers or sharecroppers. The inequalities of wealth and opportunity reach beyond the village and indeed outside the tribal system, as in different ways they always did.

The place of the village remains important. It is here that most of the partnershps to buy and operate trucks and machinery are made. It is here that a great deal of money ends up in the building of houses, the chewing of *qāt*, and the pursuit of one aspect at least of what is seen as the good life: even those men who spend a great deal of time in Ṣan'ā' like to come home (where their mothers and wives often are) to admire their patrimony. Village life is perhaps on an edge. It is not hard to visualize tribesmen moving into the capital on a permanent basis and retaining their villages only as the locus of quite imaginary values they no longer pursue. The forces that would promote such a process or reverse it utterly are largely beyond Yemeni control (let alone the control of tribesmen), and to guess at what happens next is frivolous.

The options at present are kept open. Land is kept in production wherever possible (it is still reckoned 'untribal' not to do so), although the labour required makes no sense in terms of the cash economy; one could, for example, buy imported wheat cheaply, but the produce of one's own land is reckoned 'better'. Production is by the members of a household for household consumption, and what surplus there may be is passed on to one's relatives in Ṣan'ā' or elsewhere, not taken to market unless otherwise it would go to waste (cf. Tutwiler and Carapico 1981: 57). Imported grain was by the late 1970s a staple for a great many tribesmen;[33] yet the surprising thing was not how much land had gone out of production but how very little (cf. Steffen 1978: ii. 75). More generally, as Varisco and Adra (1981) argue in a rather different Yemeni case from this one, economic change by itself is not

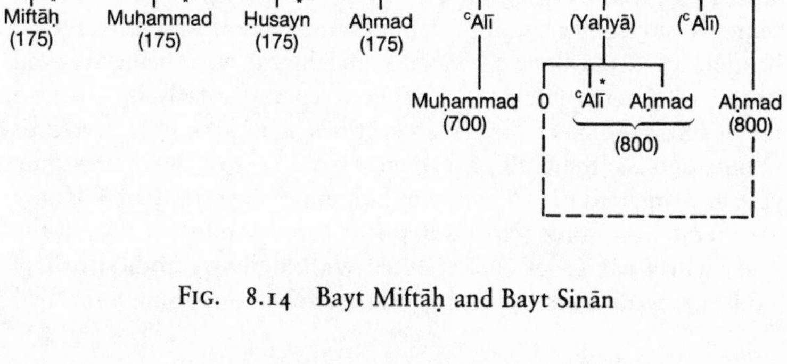

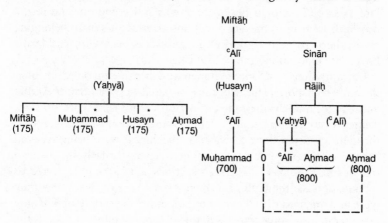

FIG. 8.14 Bayt Miftāḥ and Bayt Sinān

sufficient to wipe out what men think of as tribal values. Even massive investment in non-agricultural options makes little difference to tribal forms so long as the village remains men's base, but the scale of investment is still striking.

By late 1983, for instance, the members of Bayt Ḥusayn had amassed an extraordinary total of three dump-trucks, five mechanical diggers, and six bulldozers in Yemen, with another five bulldozers and a digger working for them in Saudi Arabia. Each piece of plant in Yemen was owned by three or four villagers together, one of whom operated it for wages or for a greater share of the profits (most of the units in Saudi Arabia were part-owned by Saudis). Some of the co-owners were relatives by descent, some by marriage, others were simply friends. A bulldozer cost about YR 220,000. Most were bought with a down-payment of between a quarter and a half of the total price, the balance being paid off in a year or two, but the sums involved were very large. Some of the capital was raised by working as a labourer in Saudi Arabia. Some came from other sources: for instance, a spell as a customs officer on the Saudi border. The repayment of credit to city-based importers of plant was not worked out in much detail at the start, and the schedule of payments was in practice flexible.[34] A digger or bulldozer rented for about YR 250 an hour in 1983, and in the countryside there were constantly unpaved roads to be built or repaired. But much of the work that would pay for such plant was found in Ṣan'ā'. As of late 1983 the building boom there was still going on, and in the northern suburbs of the city one found contractor's plant belonging to northern tribesmen, parked in ranks for hire, with each tribe having its place along the half-finished streets.

Certain villages in Upper Yemen also became involved in long-distance transport. The tribes are situated between Saudi Arabia and Ṣan'ā', and throughout the period of my field-work most of Yemen's consumer goods (from tinned food and cigarettes, through imported flour to washing machines) were being trucked across tribal territory. Banī Ṣuraym were particularly involved in this business. Some of the tribe's sections were jokingly referred to by outsiders as 'the Gulf of Yemen' on account of the money they were making, and the village of al-Sinnatayn (just south of Khamir) was credited by some with as many as three hundred trucks; four- or six-wheel Mercedes chassis fitted with high box bodies for dry goods or with tanks to transport petrol.[35] Al-Ghūlah in 'Iyāl

Surayḥ also owned a large fleet. The petrol trade deserves extended mention as an extreme case of income derived from outside the village and from non-governmental sources.

Until about 1974 there was little traffic in the north, and what petrol there was to run trucks was brought in by the barrel. Some people used to buy it off the Chinese road crews. In about 1976 a few tribesmen began to buy tankers and to truck petrol in from Saudi Arabia through Wā'ilah's territory, north and east of Ṣa'dah. By mid-1980 there were some 250 tankers plying back and forth. A 30,000-litre load (the size of a tank fitted to a standard six-wheeler Mercedes diesel) cost SR 8,000 in Saudi Arabia and sold in Yemen for YR 27,000. The customs dues on a load that size came to about YR 1,300. The tankers, which were owned by Yemeni tribesmen, were all fitted with Saudi licence plates and provided with bogus papers to show they belonged to Saudi citizens so no tax was payable on the vehicles themselves. No one bothered with driving licenses. The profits were handsome.

Wā'ilah then cut the road against Ḥāshid for five months, and Ḥāshid cut the road against Wā'ilah (we shall touch on this again in Chapter 10). The government told the Ḥāshid truckers who complained about it that they could go to Saudi Arabia by the coast road through Ḥaraḍ, but driving permits and vehicle taxes would have to be in order (Ḥaraḍ, in the north Tihāmah, is not tribal territory). The Ḥāshidī truckers (mainly from Banī Ṣuraym) were furious. At dawn one morning they parked a truck outside the military high command in Ṣan'ā', and the driver ran off, taking his keys with him. Another truck was parked nose to tail with the first, another behind that, and so on all the way out to Ḥasabah in the suburbs. The road remained blocked as a public reproach to the President. Certain prominent shaykhs intervened and a deal was done whereby the vehicles were taxed, but at about one-third of the legal rate, and the government issued the relevant papers to those tribesmen who wanted them.

A law was then promulgated that all petrol be sold through the Yemen Oil and Minerals Corporation (YOMINCO, a government agency). They bought at YR 300 a barrel and sold at about YR 370. The tribesmen–truckers preferred to sell direct to their customers at YR 350, which the government could do little about in tribal areas, and a period ensued when, elsewhere in Yemen, roadblocks were circumvented, subverted, or (on not a few occasions) run flat. By now the price of a 30,000-litre load in Saudi Arabia had risen to SR 14,000, but one could still, so they say, clear a profit of almost YR 20,000 a trip. Tribesmen started buying tankers in large numbers. When the asphalt road through Ḥaraḍ was finished, articulated tankers appeared which could carry 60,000 litres and clear a profit of YR 50,000 a trip. The customs dues on petrol, levied at the border, slowly rose to about YR 5,000 per 30,000 litres.

In 1981 the government attempted to tighten their control. Not only were the customs dues on petrol raised from YR 5,000 to YR 12,000 per load, but checks on all other sorts of goods were increased, so that a truck coming in from Saudi Arabia might be searched at or near the border (usually at Qudam in Hamdān al-Shām), again at al-Jabal al-Aswad (in Sufyān's territory), and yet again at customs headquarters in Ṣan'ā'. A crowd of tribesmen–truckers, mainly from Bakīl, marched from the customs all the way across town to military high command, where they slaughtered two bulls. On the way, in the best tribal manner, they chanted *zawāmil*: 'Let us rely on God, and leave the customs to themselves. Since the soldiers took power we've never met with justice.'[36] For this fit of *lèse majesté* the shaykh of al-Ghūlah ('Iyāl Surayḥ) and some others spent three days in jail. A few personal waivers were granted, but the system as a whole was not shaken. On the border itself, events took a more dramatic turn.

Faced with a demand for YR 12,000 for a load of petrol, a number of truckers refused to pay. Two tankers successfully crashed through the barriers at Ḥaraḍ customs and escaped. Eight were stopped. A minor Ḥāshidī shaykh then arrived with his tanker-load from Saudi Arabia and appointed himself, with two others, as representative of the truckers. Rash words were spoken on one side or the other and three officers were assaulted and deprived of their weapons, after which the truckers retired to where their vehicles were parked and the officers repaired to Ḥajjah. The governor of Ḥajjah at the time was *khāl* (MB) of one of the insulted officers.

By the next morning about fifty tankers and other trucks were at Ḥaraḍ, prevented from going further into Yemen by a strong force of soldiers brought up from 'Abs. The governor of Ḥajjah demanded that those who had assaulted his nephew and the other officers be handed over. A delegation of truckers, four from Banī

Ṣuraym and one from 'Iyāl Surayḥ, went to Ḥajjah for talks, but when they claimed not to know who the particular culprits were they were thrown into prison. Further troops were dispatched. Two weeks after the initial incident there were about 200 trucks in a laager (non-inflammable loads on the outside) surrounded by about 1,000 soldiers and 60 gun-trucks. About 400 tribesmen from the truckers' tribes had accumulated, some inside the laager, some outside, and the truckers themselves were increasingly well armed. About 30 soldiers of tribal background went over to the truckers.

The truckers' representatives gave the governor of Ḥajjah right of judgment, but the governor, who was from a noted shaykhly family himself and should have known better, demanded compensation for the insulted customs officers forty-four fold (*bi-l-marbū' bi-l-muḥaddash*). A delegation went to see him. The delegation was headed by the *'āmil* of 'Abs, who was himself from a shaykhly family of 'Iyāl Surayḥ (a tribe with a great many truckers), and the members of the delegation were mainly shaykhs from the Ḥajjah area, mobilized, it seems, by the shaykhs of the plateau tribes, who themselves were intervening with the President in Ṣan'ā'. The delegation were offered 'surety' or *'adl* by the truckers in the form of the keys to a six-wheeled Mercedes, rather than the more usual rifles. Finally, they prevailed on the governor ('to honour those present') to accept from the truckers the dagger, the pistol, and rifle which had been taken from the officers, plus three more of each. Three bulls were slaughtered for the officers, and two more *li-tahjīr al-jamārik* ('to restore the inviolable status of the customs post'), each bull being accompanied by a pair of sheep.[37] The cost of these amends was shared among all the truckers present (256 of them by the end), and the traffic started moving again.

For months afterwards, the truckers from the tribes that had been involved in this episode paid even less tax than previously. They often intimidated the soldiers into passing petrol (down again to YR 5,000 tax per load) as kerosene (YR 700 tax per load). The magic, as it were, wore off only in the summer of 1983 when the import of kerosene and diesel fuel across the border was banned altogether, the tax on a 30,000-litre load of petrol was set at YR 8,000, and the government made an organized effort to collect it. At the time these new arrangements were made there were more than a thousand tankers owned by men from the northern tribes. There was a similar number of large Mercedes trucks for transporting other goods. Smuggling of petrol and other imports was extensive, especially in the east of Yemen; campaigns against this were repeatedly started and abandoned according to central government's own fiscal problems, the balance of interests within the government, and the balance that government as a whole needs to strike with other elements, some of whom are attached to foreign governments. In the long term the tribes' position as truckers and middlemen is plainly vulnerable. An extension of port facilities at al-Ḥudaydah would cut their business from under them. In the late 1970s and early 1980s, however, they were thriving.

As men were drawn into such interests as transporting goods or hiring out bulldozers, they were involved with the broad tribal structure more fully, not less so. To be sure of access to contracting work for one's plant in Ṣan'ā', let alone to take part in escapades such as that at Ḥaraḍ, one needs mediation with central government. The mediators are certain great shaykhs. Mediation and patronage on a broadly tribal basis are nothing new, although their extent and intensity perhaps have become more marked, but when conflicts of interest that in Ṣan'ā' might be played out within an office building are instead played over large geographic areas then the appearance is of all other concerns being reduced to tribalism. Road-blocks are put up (*qaṭā'*), access to territory is denied by men 'guarding the borders' (*zābinīn al-ḥudūd*), delegations are formed to provide 'mediation' (*wāsiṭah*), rifles are proffered, guarantors appointed, and arbitration pursued by the same means as were used before the new economy came to Yemen. Between such episodes, which are frequent, men are 'at home' (*fi l-bayt*) in their villages, where they chew over what is happening and till their fields as the rains allow.

NOTES

1. Varisco and Adra 1981: 134 quote a variant, attributed to the legendary 'Alī b. Zāyid, that says: 'No wealth comes to the one who sits, unless it is a merchant or a learned man' (*ahl al-dakākīn wa-man qara' fi l-madāris*). The distinction between this variant and the one quoted quite widely on the plateau seems apt: neither trade nor learning were options for most tribesmen.
2. Readers should be aware that certain names of patronymic sets and the like have been changed to disguise Bayt Ḥusayn's identity. The size of the village, the composition of the families, the distribution of land, and so forth are, by contrast, reproduced as exactly as I am able.

3. All the fields would seem to have names, whether or not they are divided into plots owned by different people. Some examples are al-Ma'arad, Jirbat Masāḥat, al-Mutazirah, Maḥiyyah, Saddāl, and Khuraysah. To judge from a rather slight knowledge of the inheritance documents, these field names are fairly stable. The fields themselves may be divided and redivided as several strips of property.
4. There is an arbitrary decision to be made here about who is still a member of the village and who is not. However, there was practically no disagreement among the villagers, nor were there any squabbles on the subject in the five years or so over which I knew them.
5. A *libnah* is about 64 square metres; 1·50 *libnah* is approximately equal to one hectare. The usual dry measure for grain is the *qadaḥ*, equal to about 36 litres, or somewhere between an American and an Imperial bushel.
6. Village studies make such various uses of genealogies, figures for landholdings, and the like that it seems best to include as much as one can without boring the reader thoroughly. I have therefore tried to cover all the families in the village, giving landholdings for each, and to provide at least representative examples of such things as employment patterns. To that end, the family diagrams all use the following conventions: where a name is placed in brackets, the man is dead, and so are those above him in a descent line, unless another figure higher up is bracketed also, in which case the intermediate figure is alive still; numbers below names refer to landholdings in *libnah*, and horizontal brackets indicate joint holdings. Dotted lines denote marriages.
7. Comparative work remains to be done, and one looks forward to Mundy's publication of her very detailed data from a better-watered area of the plateau than Bayt Ḥusayn. One's impression of the preliminary suggestions in Mundy 1979 is that far larger landholding groups, co-resident units, and cohesive patrilineal structures are to be found there than in the case at hand. All the land in Bayt Ḥusayn is rain-fed.
8. Within the village at hand, there seem to be very few cases where a woman is entirely bought out by her agnates. What tends to happen is that, by the time she separates for herself a part of the patrimony, her male kin have acquired control of an equivalent amount from elsewhere by purchase or marriage. The particular plots are swapped off to leave her paternal kin much where they were. Where outright purchase or waiving of land rights is common is, as one would expect, where the woman marries outside the village, but again there seem rather few cases where women own no arable land at all.
9. The usual form in such areas is that other people's livestock are kept off one's fields while crops are growing and for a brief period after they are harvested: one day in the case of barley, and three in the case of sorghum. These latter periods begin when one's own sheep or goats are first let into the stubble. If the owner keeps his own livestock off his fields for a couple of weeks, say, no one else may graze the stubble until he lets them.

In these densely farmed areas fields are only permanently *maḥjūr* (as opposed to *maḥjūr* for the growing season and the few stubble days) if all the fields of a terrace system are owned together: not only are the fields then *maḥjūr*, but so is the area from which they take runoff. There are a few exceptions to this rule, where an area of fields has 'always' been *maḥjūr* and remains so despite the fact that its ownership is now mixed. Customs differ considerably elsewhere in the north. The total number of sheep and goats in Bayt Ḥusayn is of the order of 200.

The term *khashr* or 'refusing' to others (cf. *khāshir*, Tutwiler and Carapico 1981: 186) is in fact used mainly of shared runoff, and not of shared grazing or of arable land held in common as perhaps it may be further west.

10. Peters's 1967 account of camel-herding groups in Cyrenaica stresses the importance of affinal ties between whole sections, although it remains slightly unclear whom the ties bind: whole tertiary or secondary or whatever grade of section, or smaller groups within these. Even in the drier, more pastorally oriented parts of Upper Yemen this seems not to be the pattern. The case is far closer to that depicted in pre-war Palestine by Granquist 1931, and the marriage maps one might draw would look very much like hers. The overall rates of endogamy of different degrees are rather similar to Granquist's also.

11. Cf. Peters 1963, Granquist 1931, and Lancaster 1981. Where the rhetoric of endogamy and exogamy is related to resources primarily as a metaphor (Keyser 1974), rather than as a causal summary of individual interests, the importance of these connections is less their overall pattern than which type of connection is invoked on which occasions.

For an interesting review of literature on endogamous marriage see Holy 1985. Holy complains that 'few anthropologists have paid attention . . . to the fact that the ratio of close agnatic marriages is uneven among different agnatic groups . . . or that it differs over time' (ibid. 104). On the second point I was unable to gather reliable information. On the first point let me simply stress that 'agnatic groups' comparable, say, to Palestinian *ḥamūlahs* (Cohen 1965) are not a feature of the case at hand. A full break-down of the figures shows no clear correlation between wealth and endogamy, and the units brought always to the fore in discussions of land are in any case the individual families.

12. Genealogies are often, in effect, forms of power (cf. Peters 1963). We should therefore be clear that no one by himself commands a village genealogy or even the genealogy of his own *bayt* apart from his close relatives. The overall presentation here is that of the ethnographer, and was put together with the help of a great many people. The villagers, including the shaykhly house, are more like Peters's 'peasants' than like his 'learned families'.

13. One's wife's brothers and the like are referred to or addressed in public as simply *yā Aḥmad* or whatever it may be. The phrase *yā 'amm*

Aḥmad or *yā'ammī* (O, my uncle') is used with respected strangers older than oneself. The same form used to one's wife's father would make heads turn: one should say instead, *yā 'amm*, without either the possessive suffix or the man's name. He is owed respect because one's wife is his daughter and his link to her is far weightier than one's own. The husband has his wife only in trust, as it were.

14. If a neighbouring village want temporary access to grazing in the territory of Bayt Ḥusayn, perhaps in time of drought, then one of them will come to a kinsman there (perhaps a mother's brother or sister's husband) and put the request to him. He in turn puts the request to his fellow villagers. On the two occasions I have seen this done, the request was made at the mosque after Friday prayers. Villages as wholes are not represented as allied by marriage.

15. In the areas I knew well, the timing was primarily by local marks (e.g. the shadow thrown by a nail in the wall) and by reference to the Islamic calendar. Few people could provide a system in the abstract. For example, the Islamic calendar is lunar and shifts by about eleven days a year against the solar calendar—*yā ghabbī al-zamān zayyad thalāth wa-thamān*; 'you who don't know the time, add three and eight'—but people constantly misquoted even this, often forgetting the three.

    There has been a great deal of work on South Arabian star calendars (see Varisco's excellent article, 1985, and the references given there), but very few tribesmen could reproduce much of it. The star periods I give are those reproduced in *al-jayl al-jadīd* bookshop's calendars, which is what tribesmen in fact refer to most often. In Wādī Ḥumrān there are four sorghum planting periods, each 14 days after the other, but the first is best. On colder ground there is one period only. Readers may wish to compare the system in Lower Yemen (Messick 1978: 440 ff.) or in the west (Varisco 1982*b*: 113 ff.).

16. Al-Laḥjī (MS IV: 279) gives *ḥalī* as the wood in which the 'tooth' is fitted. As late as 1978 one came across *mashabbar*s with flints for the teeth, but by 1983 iron was being used even by the poorest farmers.

17. The initial thinning is called *thamm* (al-'Uṣaymāt), *thamūm*, or *thamām* (Banī Ṣuraym and Murhibah). The second thinning is *faqūḥ*. In most areas the space between the lines of sorghum is ploughed to heap up soil around the plants. This is often referred to as *ḥajn* or *ḥajūn*, although the term is sometimes used more specifically of heaping soil with a pick. The ploughing technique is then called *tashwīl* (or *mashwal*, Upper 'Usaymāt; *mashqal*, al-Baṭanah and the west; *mathmar*, around Ḥajjah; and so on). Working with the pick and one's hands, one builds a hollow around the stalks to keep weeds away and to trap water. This is more common in mountainous areas, where it is sometimes also called *qazūl*.

18. Again local vocabulary varies. Stripping the lower leaves is called *shariyāf* (al-'Uṣaymāt), *falūṭ* (al-Ahnūm), *sharnāf* (Banī Ṣuraym), or *ṣawwām* (Ḥajjah). In stripping the upper leaves one usually says simply *ba-nu'allī*, 'we're doing the top bit'.

19. Yields on sorghum in a hypothetical good year are often quoted at about 30 : 1 or 40 : 1 in grain country. In sorghum country such estimates can run as high as 100 : 1, and they are not gross exaggerations. None of these areas, however, can compete with al-Baṭanah where the harvest in October lasts a whole month, comprising not only several varieties of sorghum, but also millet (*dukhn*). Millet is grown in the warm areas of the plateau too, such as Sufyān and Shawābah. But in none of these areas can one do with it what is done around Ḥajjah, which is to cut the heads and leaves off and get a second crop of leaves for fodder with the next rain. Rūmī, Shāmī, or Hindi sorghum (a quite different plant) is sown even in a few parts of Banī Ṣuraym, but it needs more rain than it usually gets. Further west it comprises a major winter crop, again used largely for fodder. In many plateau areas it will not grow at all.
20. In parts at least of Qā‘ al-Bawn (the plain on which Raydah stands) such crops sown after rain in August seem to ripen successfully without further rainfall, presumably drawing on soil moisture. In most areas, though, rain is required not only to allow planting and germination but also to support the growing crop.
21. To all of this must be added the range of varieties of each crop. Even to list the names and characteristics of those in a single area would take pages (there are three main types of 'white *dhurah*' in Lower al-‘Uṣaymāt, four quite different ones in Upper al-‘Uṣaymāt; four major types of barley in northern Khārif, three next door in neighbouring Murhibah), but each farmer keeps the best grain of one year to sow next year, thus acting as a sort of village Mendel. The genetic diversity must be immense and the effect on timing considerable.
22. A holding of 700 *libnah* at Bayt Ḥusayn (which is very much grain country) was disposed as follows in early October: 150 was under *qāt* (not a seasonal crop), 50 was left idle, 60 was under sorghum (in very poor shape), 150 was under ripe wheat about to be harvested, 40 was under alfalfa (*qadhb* or *barsīm*, not a seasonal crop), 50 under lentils, and 200 was being prepared for wheat to be sown in November. At the same stage of the year in Wādī Ḥumrān nearly all the land was under sorghum, with a very few plots of barley and lentils.
23. *Qīyāḍ* in Khārif and *rabī‘* in northern Banī Ṣuraym are thus roughly interchangeable; but *qīyāḍ* in Banī Ṣuraym, as in Murhibah, is used of a late summer period. Following the progression of crops in their different areas is straightforward. The naming system, although the main terms are widely shared, is more fragmented and farmers do not ask 'Is it *qīyāḍ* yet?'; they ask 'When did you plant your barley? Do you have any wheat ripe?'
24. In general Tutwiler and Carapico's summary of the agricultural system as two great halves, summer and winter (1981: 56 and *passim*), is in most northern areas better replaced by a three-part scheme: the 'sorghum summer' and two periods of activity with non-sorghum grains.
25. A family at Bayt Ḥusayn, for example, with only 150 *libnah*, left 40 of

these empty for later sorghum when they sowed in February: they sowed 40 *libnah* of lentils where there had been *qiyāḍ* wheat and 40 of wheat where there had been barley previously, 15 were put under alfalfa (*qadhb*), and 15 under barley where an earlier barley crop had been ruined by frost and ploughed in.

26. Note again the local use of vocabulary here. The crop harvested at Kāniṭ in early July was referred to as *ṣilmī* (from the name of the star period 28 June–11 July). The same term was used some miles north in Banī Ṣuraym of crops planted in this period and harvested in late summer.

27. Sorghum can be planted in rather dry ground. Ideally one wants rain a couple of weeks beforehand, after the soil has been thoroughly ploughed and levelled; but sorghum will germinate with rather little stimulus. Other grains will not, nor will seed simply wait in dry ground for the rain to come. On the other hand ground must be prepared in advance even for barley, and one cannot plough soil directly after rain as it is too heavy. The constraints that prevent the desired crop rotation are quite severe in most years. The word used of 'changing' or rotating crops is *yakhluf*, the same term as is sometimes used of 'begetting children'.

28. Having a well drilled cost of the order of YR 2,000 per metre, depending on the type of rock encountered. A 100-metre well is a massive investment, but they are not by any means rare.

29. There are not, for instance, the equivalent of harvest festivals. Peters 1963 found a similar gap in a Lebanese village, which he attributed to something very like class divisions. But the same gap was found among most Middle Eastern pastoralists (Peters 1984), which he attributed to the lack of any cohesive society one might celebrate in this Durkheimian manner. Here we have a further example in yet another setting. The mode of village identity in the present case, and the importance of ceremonies at births, marriages, and deaths, will I hope be the subject of a separate paper.

Such material is of its nature quite rich, but readers should be supplied, perhaps, with two isolated points here. First, the one collective occasion that refers directly to the village land as a whole occurs only *in extremis*: the rain prayers said in time of drought. Second, the occasion when village identity is most directly displayed, at weddings (when the bridal party is greeted with rifle volleys at the village edge), is also the one occasion on which men routinely confess to a concern for magic. The groom is reckoned to be at risk. The collective event reveals a shadow of individual vulnerability which perhaps is quite often thrown by the explicit forms of *droit et morale.*

30. The extreme case in the village at hand is that of Bayt al-Qāḍī. The father farms their undivided 800 *libnah* full time. Two of the sons work in Saudi Arabia and the other two drive trucks; and all help with the farming when they can.

31. See for example Steffen 1978: ii. 74; almost 50 per cent of 'Iyāl Yazīd's adult men worked in Saudi Arabia at the time of the census. It is the

smaller families in Bayt Ḥusayn (those not part of the larger patronymic sets) who seem most heavily involved. Bayt Hizā', for instance, comprises two pairs of brothers. The first pair, who own 400 *libnah* each, take turns farming and working abroad. The other pair of brothers (cousins to the first) also own 400 *libnah* but both have grown sons who work abroad, while the fathers farm. Bayt Muqbil are rather similar: one man farms his 300 *libnah* and his sons both drive diggers; two brothers with 30 *libnah* between them both work abroad while their womenfolk work the land; and the last man, having no grown sons yet, works his 300 *libnah* by himself.

Unfortunately, the amounts of money brought in by emigrant labourers proved impossible to estimate reliably. They are plainly large. The same goes for army pay and for stipends from the 'popular army'. It should be said, though, that the distribution of these funds is highly irregular and some men do far better from them than others; but in no case is a patronymic set larger than a family the beneficiary of money either from the government or from emigrant labour.

32. Inheritance documents (though I stress that I was not able to survey them systematically) suggest that landholdings were always fragmented. Forms of co-operation one may guess to have been similar. There is no memory or tradition of, for instance, collective work for rebuilding terraces or cleaning water cisterns such as is rather common further west.

33. In the early 1980s American wheat sold for about YR 70 per hundred lb. sack (about YR 55 per *qadaḥ*, as most tribesmen reckoned it). It went up as high as YR 110 per 100 lb. in 1983 and then settled at around YR 100. Yemeni sorghum, by contrast, was YR 140 per *qadaḥ* for the yellow variety and YR 120 for the white (see Tutwiler and Carapico 1981: 95 for figures a few years earlier). In Bayt Ḥusayn some land was being worked far less intensively than before but only about 200 *libnah* in the whole village could properly be said to be out of production.

34. I can hardly imagine myself making a commitment of this magnitude without working out the debt schedule in reassuring detail. Tribesmen I knew well enough to know how they were doing this would put up YR 50,000 or more without a single real calculation. Partly this may be due to the difficulty their creditors in Ṣan'ā' would have in bringing extreme pressure on them, but their own attitude to the future is very far from timid. Indeed the *Flucht nach vorn* seems a common mode.

35. The figure quoted for al-Sinnatayn can hardly be accurate (there would be as many trucks as grown men), but the area's involvement in trucking was certainly very heavy. The section in which the village falls may well have had at least shares in that many vehicles. Before the 1962 revolution they were heavily involved in camel transport to Ṣan'ā'. They were among the first to buy into the transport boom of the 1970s.

36. *Aḥnā tawakkalnā 'alā allāh / nukhallī al-jumrūk li-ḥāl-hu / min ḥayth tawallū l-'asākir / mā zudd laqaynā fī 'adālah.*

37. Typically, one of the raconteurs of this tale added the detail that they had intended to kill four bulls but one died, 'so we gave it to the *'abīd* (the black servile stratum)'. This is not only a dig at the Tihāmīs (eating carrion is an appalling breach of religious law), but also a boast of the tribesmen's own devil-may-care attitude. Having been forced to make amends, they imply, they came up with slaughter-beasts that could hardly totter to the meeting.

9 The Morphology of Tribal Self-Definition

Morphology is not only a study of material things and the forms of material things, but has its dynamical aspect.

D'Arcy Thompson, *On Growth and Form*

A society, like a mind, is woven of perpetual interaction.

Bloch, *Feudal Society*

Villages are often long lasting and occupy the same physical sites for many centuries at a time, which American and European readers, with an eye on their own societies, will almost expect of a culture involved with plough-land. The continuity of tribes and of the tribal system is a separate question. There were tribes before the first Imam arrived in Yemen (he came, indeed, to arbitrate in their disputes), and there are still tribes now the last Imam has gone and Yemen has become a republic. The names Ḥāshid and Bakīl are pre-Islamic. Some of the constituent tribes of each are themselves very old, and there has been occasion to mention them already in connection with events as long as a thousand years ago. In the present chapter we shall try to summarize what sort of entity tribes are that they survive demographic and political change over such long periods.

THE FORMS OF CHANGE IN HISTORICAL GEOGRAPHY

Imagine a vast sheet of paper on which straight lines, triangles, squares . . . and other figures . . . move freely about, on or in the surface, but without the power of rising above or sinking below it, very much like shadows—only hard and with luminous edges.

E. A. Abbott, *Flatland*

The historical geography of Upper Yemen might stand as a subject by itself and deserves specialist study, but certain continuities are striking. Moreover, the forms of change (where change has occurred) demand our attention as providing major lineaments of tribalism itself and as a corrective to the easy view of change as either random or non-existent. As a base-line we can take the detailed (though very uneven) account of al-Hamdānī, who died in about 945 and whose works we touched on in Chapter 5. The possibility must be borne in mind that the tribal system was still taking shape in his day. Some of the changes since then may in fact have occurred only a century or two after his death.[1] But for the present purpose, the dates and details are less important than the general pattern. What one finds is a system of territorial redefinition that encompasses change but registers neither growth or decay.

One of the most salient geographical continuities between al-Hamdānī's time and our own is that of Sufyān's territory. In the *Ṣifah* it is said to extend from Khaywān, which is still Sufyān's border with Ḥāshid at present, to the borders of Ṣa'dah (al-Hamdānī 1968: 110), which means, in effect, to the borders of Khawlān.[2] In the south-east, around Shawābah and Harān, Sufyān bordered Dhaybān b. 'Aliyyān of Arḥab very much where Sufyān and Arḥab abut nowadays (al-Hamdānī 1948: 234). The border in the north-east was with Banī 'Abd. b. 'Aliyyān of Arḥab at al-Marāshī (al-Hamdānī 1968: 110). Arḥab no longer extends so far north. Around al-Marāshī, though, is still the outlying Sufyānī tribe or section of al-Marānāt, separated from the rest of Sufyān by a narrow strip held by Dhū Muḥammad. East of Khaywān, but north of Shawābah and south-west of al-Marāshī, the border ran between Sufyān and Wāda'ah (ibid. 112) very much where it now runs between Sufyān and Banī Ṣuraym. Some of the continuities may be older still. Brief mention was made in Chapter 7, for instance, of a border dispute between Sufyān and Dhū Muḥammad at the time of the civil war. It is still going on. The line under dispute, however, is only a matter of kilometres from that on which Sufyān supposedly fought Qays of 'Adnān in pre-Islamic times (al-Hamdānī 1948: 222–3 and 1968: 110, 112). Such continuities are all the more striking when one remembers that perhaps a fifth of Sufyān's people are semi-nomadic, grazing sheep and goats in large numbers quite far from their villages.

Not only is Sufyān mentioned by al-Hamdānī but so are its two major sections of the present day, Ruhm and Ṣubārah. The latter eponym is described as a 'son' of Sufyān, and the section is ascribed territory in the north-east and south-east of Sufyān (ibid: 112; al-

Hamdānī 1948: 218–35). It is also ascribed several 'brothers', some of which were the major section names of al-Hamdānī's time but are not, so far as I know, extant nowadays. No clue is given as to their precise geography. Ruhm, which is at present Ṣubārah's complement, was given a curious status by al-Hamdānī (ibid. 228) as one of the *hujan* or 'imperfect ones' whose female ancestors were apparently from elsewhere, but it had extensive territory in the south of Sufyān at the present border with Banī Ṣuraym (al-Hamdānī 1968: 112).

In the more detailed account of the *Iklīl*, Ruhm is associated with 'Amīrah, which in turn was part of Mu'āwiyah b. Sufyān (al-Hamdānī 1948: 218) as shown in Fig. 9.1. Salmān b. Mu'āwiyah we hear of at a number of points as being 'part of Arḥab', occupying the central parts of Sufyān's present territory around 'Iyān and Birkān (al-Hamdānī 1968: 244; al-Alawī 1972: 127). Sufyān was 'genealogically' a descendant of Arḥab but, as Gochenour (1984: 327) rightly says, Arḥab and Sufyān were probably separate tribes at that time as they are now. That Salmān was Sufyānī is in little doubt.

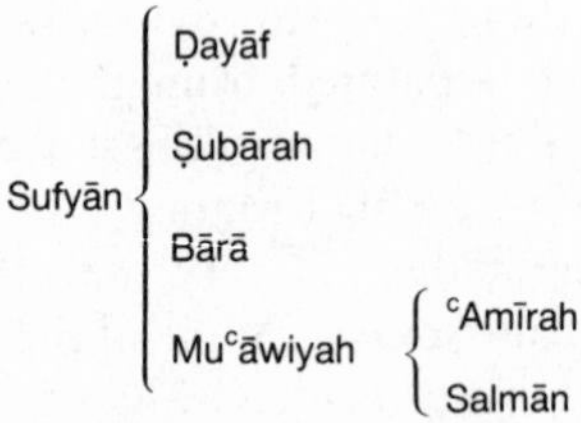

FIG. 9.1 Main divisions of tenth-century Sufyān

None of the small subsections of present day Sufyān is listed by al-Hamdānī (I shall list them later); most of the major section names within the Sufyān of his day have disappeared; part of 'Amīrah b. Mu'āwiyah extended further into the Jawf than Sufyān now does (al-Hamdānī 1948: 226); and there has been a change of territory west of Khaywān. But Sufyān as a whole is where it was. For all the internal changes, Sufyān as such forms a geographical category of quite remarkable stability and, to within a few kilometres, we can be sure that its borders at some points, such as Warwar and Khaywān, have not moved in a thousand years.

Khārif occupies at least as prominent a place in the genealogies of the *Iklīl* as does Sufyān (ibid. 53–6), and at the present day is as important a tribe. But neither of al-Hamdānī's accounts (nor the two combined) allows one to attribute Khārif a territory. The places or groups claiming the name in their ancestry were widely scattered.[3] Two of Khārif's present-day divisions, al-Kalbiyyīn and Banī Jubar, are conspicuous by their absence from al-Hamdānī's version. Nor do the names of Khārif's twelve sons (ibid. 53) survive as major tribal or section names. Al-Ṣayad, though, (one-third of the present-day tribe) would seem to pre-date the larger geographical unit.[4] It was then very much where it now is, between Raydah and Warwar (al-Hamdānī 1968: 111). Its borders extend further south than they then did, to ʻAraqat al-Qudaymī and al-Manjidah, where they are now also Khārif's borders with Arḥab and ʻIyāl Surayḥ. Part of what was al-Ṣayad's territory in the north currently attaches to al-Ṣayad's 'brothers', al-Kalbiyyīn and Banī Jubar; but the line which the latter set has inherited as its border with Sufyān at Warwar, near Dhībīn, is precisely the line which separated Ḥāshid and Sufyān in al-Hamdānī's day. The continuity of al-Ṣayad is itself striking, but even the changes around this are far from random.

By no means all the elements of the present day tribal scheme are as old as these. The geography of tribal divisions in al-Bawn, for example, is irregular in al-Hamdānī's account (see Wilson 1981: 98), and perhaps no clear borders existed. Al-Hamdānī knew this particular area well but his account makes no mention of the two prominent present-day tribes of ʻIyāl Yazīd and ʻIyāl Surayḥ. Jabal ʻIyāl Yazīd seems not to be mentioned until 1391–2 (Wilson 1980: 493; Yaḥyā b. al-Ḥusayn 1968: 547). ʻIyāl Surayḥ is apparently attested where it now is by about 1150 (Gochenour 1984: 328, but unfortunately the source is not cited). The names, both of which, of course, are common personal names, can be found in al-Hamdānī's genealogies associated with the relevant areas, but whether they were taken up locally or introduced from elsewhere we have no way of being certain. All we can say is that the Zaydi histories, to which al-Bawn is usually of central concern, record no invasion or displacement of one tribe by another. The change of nomenclature is likely to have been a mutation *in situ*.

The one clear case of movement which al-Hamdānī gives is that of ʿIdhar (al-Hamdānī 1948: 90 and 1968: 113; cf. Dresch 1984*a*: 47). Part of ʿIdhar's territory is said once to have been at Maṭirah, north-east of Ṣanʿāʾ, and some indeterminately long time before al-Hamdānī was writing there was a migration to the lowlands near Shahārah to establish ʿIdhar Shaʿb, which corresponds to modern ʿIdhar. The old ʿIdhar Maṭirah would seem to have remained in existence some centuries later (see al-Laḥjī MS IV: 338, MS I: 85), but even the new ʿIdhar of the lowland north-west assimilated part of the older order, rather than entirely destroying or displacing it.

> Shaʿb . . . was in the west before ʿIdhar. Then ʿIdhar retreated from Barāqish and settled beside Muqaṣṣaṣ and Banū Salāmān at Maṭirah, which before that had belonged to Yām. The rest of ʿIdhar descended on Shaʿb and conquered their territory. Those who remained there entered [i.e. became part of] ʿIdhar. (al-Hamdānī 1948: 90–1)

The name here moves with a group of people, and the people of Shaʿb are included in the category that name denotes.[5] From then on, however, and throughout the plateau area, the process seems always to be the opposite: even if people move, they are included in the category that attached already to the area they enter. Tribal categories, in other words, are not geographically displaced, although they may, as we said, be reordered *in situ*, and people, as mentioned in Chapter 3, may themselves move from tribe to tribe.

In the north-east we find an important gap in al-Hamdānī's account by comparison with the present. Dhū Muḥammad and Dhū Ḥusayn, who are so conspicuous in accounts of the nineteenth century (Chapter 6), are not mentioned, and their collective eponym, Ghaylān, appears most prominently as a place name to the west of Ṣaʿdah (al-Hamdānī 1968: 69, 125).[6] The earliest reference I know of to Dhū Muḥammad in Zaydi sources concerns events around 1600 (Nubdhah 237, 254, 256), but the sources are seldom good on Baraṭ, and at Baraṭ itself there is a local tradition of invasion. The tribesmen (quite unlike those of all the plateau areas) claim not to be the region's original inhabitants.[7] Even in the far north-east, however, where movement is an admitted possibility, the toponomy is in some respects highly stable.

Dhū Ghaylān's present neighbours and classificatory relatives, Wāʾilah, were a millenium ago much where they now are (see e.g. al-Hamdānī 1948: 237–43 and 1968: 111, 168, 169; al-ʿAlawī

1972: 244, 250, 308). The higher-order set to which Dhū Ghaylān belong but Wā'ilah do not (that is, Duhmah or Dahm) is also recorded as filling roughly the area it now does (al-Hamdānī 1948: 243 and 1968: 167, 194; al-'Alawī 1972: 83). Whatever may have happened on the ground, therefore, the tribal categories at one level have been filled and refilled rather than shifted on the map or destroyed.

The case of Banī Ṣuraym is more complex but illustrates the process of recombination in some detail. At present the tribe occupies most of the high plateau from south of Khamir to just south of Ḥūth and comprises nine named sections. Not only the tribe, but many of these sections appear in accounts of al-Qāsim's struggle against the Turks *c.*1600: Khayār, Banī Mālik, Banī Qays, Banī Ghuthaymah, al-Ghashm, Āl Abī l-Ḥusayn (or Bā al-Ḥusayn), and Wāda'ah, for example are all mentioned (see Nubdhah 108, 140, 182, 214, 267, 270, 397, 399, 436). The only disparity between the details at present and 350 years ago is that Banī Mālik might perhaps have been reckoned part of Wāda'ah (ibid. 475), but this isolated phrase is hardly evidence. The tribe's main divisions and the location of each have scarcely changed since al-Qāsim's day, despite the constant flux through the area of armies and of tribal warfare.

Our sources for the centuries immediately before al-Qāsim's time are not good, but in al-Hamdānī's account we find a certain reversal of the scheme: at that time (early tenth century) 'the crest of the highlands' *(sanām al-ẓāhir)* was the territory of Wāda'ah b. 'Amr b. 'Āmir . . . b. Ḥāshid (al-Hamdānī 1968: 112). The contiguous block of territory now occupied by Banī Ṣuraym was largely occupied by Wāda'ah (now the name of one of Banī Ṣuraym's sections), and Banī Ṣuraym was itself a section of Wāda'ah. Parts of the tribe were among the Imam al-Hādī's most constant supporters, and from accounts of his battles the scheme shown in Fig. 9.2 comes out clearly. The geographical information in both the *Ṣifah* and al-Hādī's *Sīrah* is scanty but Banī Ṣuraym would seem to have been furthest south, Banī Rabī'ah just north of it, around Ḥūth, and Banī Mu'mir in the area near Khaywān (al-'Alawī 1972: 93, 99, 105, 222; al-Hamdānī 1968: 59, 82, 244).

Al-Hamdānī's genealogies of Wāda'ah reveal further divisions (see Figs. 9.3 and 9.4). The most salient is that of Mu'mir's

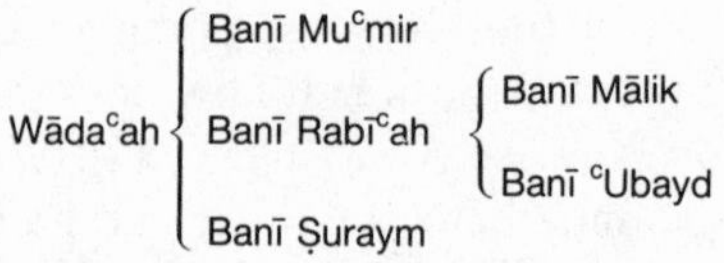

FIG. 9.2 Main divisions of tenth-century Wāda‘ah

relatives, Banī Ḥarb, who held Ḥūth and the neighbouring mountain of Ramīḍ (ibid. 82). They are the larger set that contained both Rabī‘ah and Ṣuraym, and are probably to be identified with the Banī Ḥarb of Nashwān al-Ḥimyarī's famous lines on Ḥūth (al-Ḥimyarī 1916: 29). Banī Mu‘mir themselves, whom we know to have occupied the area near Khaywān (al-‘Alawī 1972: 134), are probably to be identified with the present day al-Ma‘āmirah in much the same area. But al-Ma‘āmirah are now part of al-‘Uṣaymāt. Again, Khamir is now in Banī Ṣuraym's territory and is Ḥāshid's 'capital' but was then part of Bakīl, as was the area just south and west of the town (al-Hamdānī 1968: 112 and 1948: 103, 108).

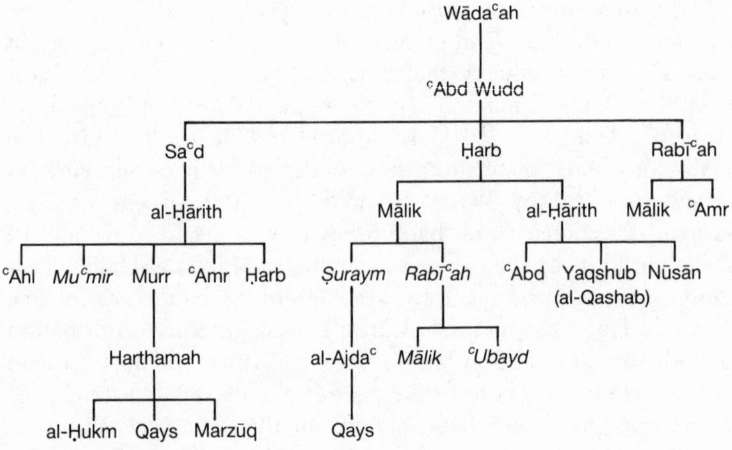

Note: Italicized names correspond to those in Fig. 9.2.

FIG. 9.3 Subdivisions of tenth-century Wāda‘ah

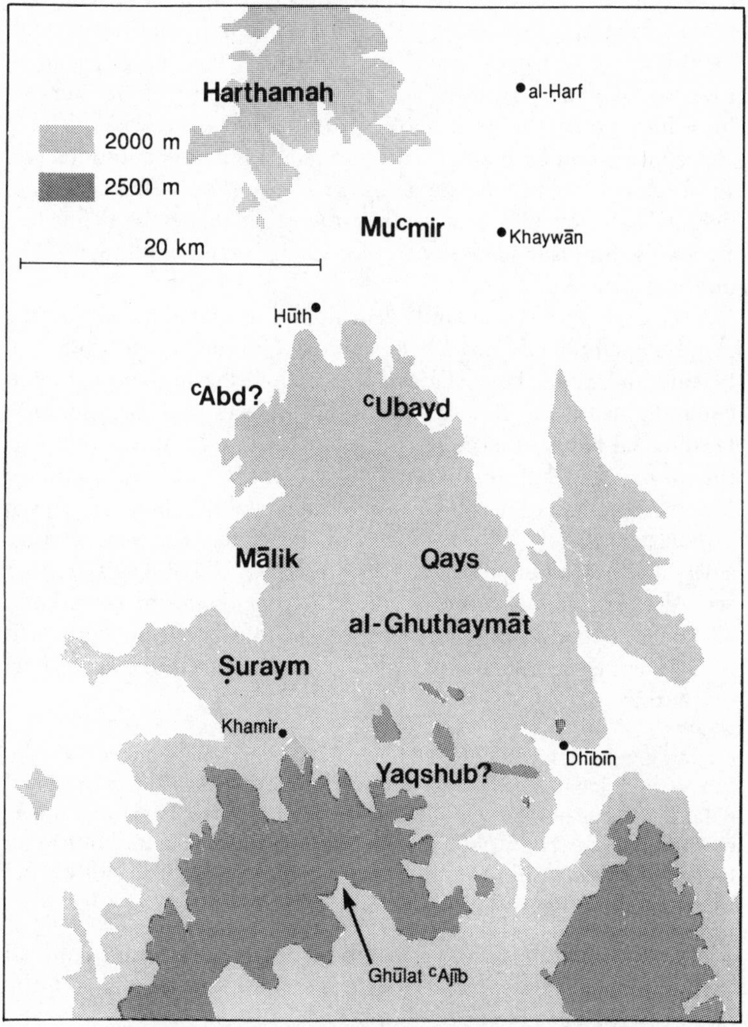

FIG. 9.4 Geography of tenth-century Wāda'ah

The changes of border lines to make tenth-century Wāda'ah into modern Banī Ṣuraym would seem to be largely the exclusion and inclusion of pre-existing named units. If Mu'mir has been lost to al-'Uṣaymāt by redefinition rather than by physical movement, certain other names which are those of Ṣuraymī sections nowadays were already in their present position and needed only to be redefined as parts of the larger unit: for example, Qays and Ghuthaymah (al-Hamdānī 1948: 193–5, 216; al-'Alawī 1972: 105, 126). The main reversal of order, from Wāda'ah including Ṣuraym to Ṣuraym including Wāda'ah, itself took place within a remarkably fixed space and could be made by the same means as the additions and subtractions at the borders. Ṣuraym need only be separated definitionally from Wāda'ah, then the other names be defined as Ṣuraym's subsets, and Wāda'ah then join Ṣuraym. Nothing need be physically moved.[8]

Very early in al-Hamdānī's genealogies of Hamdān we find the process exemplified: Zayd b. Jusham b. Ḥubrān was a brother of Ḥāshid and Bakīl, but 'Āl Zayd [the people sharing that eponym] entered Ḥāshid and they then said that he was Zayd b. Jusham b. Ḥāshid' (al-Hamdānī 1948: 28). Again, after a local war that was fought not long before al-Hamdānī wrote, the Āl Dhū Raḍwān of Khaywān, who had been Ḥāshidī, 'became Bakīlī' (ibid. 56; Dresch 1986: 323). They did not move but they did, as it were, change sides; and having done so, were as much part of Bakīl as any other set. Al-Hamdānī's account is littered with cases of the same kind. The lines are constantly redrawn, not to abolish units outright or to move them elsewhere but to redefine an element of one set as part of another.

> Kahlān divided into Madhḥij and Hamdān. From Madhḥij came Murād, 'Ans, Zabīd, Janab, and Sanḥān. From Hamdān came Kindah, Ḥāshid, and Bakīl. . . . Some of the tribes merged with others or combined with others by brotherhood (*mu'ākhah*) as Ānis and Banī al-Ḥārith are brothers to Hamdān, Khawlān al-'Āliyah are brothers to Bakīl, Bilād al-Rūs and Sanḥān are brothers to Ḥāshid. (Ṣabrah 1972: 121)

A system of redefinition thus combines geographical and political units in new patterns, but it does not identify those units with the fate of particular groups of people.

At a given time, people's actions and passions take their sense from the scheme of collective identities: not only do such matters as escort and refuge depend on one's position in the tribal scheme, but so do one's liability to be attacked and the possibility of finding allies for an attack oneself. Whatever the detailed outcome of such events, they are assimilated to the 'balance' between tribes; and memorable events are assimilated to collective honour, which itself is informed by the contradistinction of one tribe to another. But this relation of event to structure is not reversed, at least not explicitly; in other words, a tribe or section is never defined by a particular action or set of actions, whether done by a person or by a group within the larger set.[9] Instead the categories are reshuffled to maintain their equivalence. The modern period, one might say, is defined by the language of national progress. The Imamic period was defined by that of Zaydi law and scripture. The far longer tribal period, which contains them both, is defined by the specific way in which a structure of collective equivalence is transformed through time and shifts only in the *longue durée.*[10]

'BROTHERHOOD' AND OTHER FORMS OF CHANGE

The practice of forming alliances or changing tribal identity by 'brotherhood' is plainly old. For the details of the procedure, however, we must rely on modern cases, which illustrate more clearly the types of event that are likely or possible. What we find is the effect of broader politics on the details of tribal classification, while the process of classification none the less recuperates or contains these effects in such a way as to restore moral 'balance', not necessarily between individual men or families but between the main units of the moral geography.

Al-Dawā'ir and Bayt Tha'īl are two villages which used to be part of Arḥab; the first belonged to Banī 'Alī and the second to 'Iyāl 'Abdillāh. Both are near the border with Khārif. When the Ṣan'ā' government was at odds with South Yemen in the late 1970s, Arḥab was divided over whom to support and Banī 'Alī was on the route by which arms were smuggled in from the Jawf. Al-Dawā'ir tried to stop this. The shaykhs of Banī 'Alī dissuaded them, arguing not in terms of national politics but that the road was *āmin ḍāmin* (secure and guaranteed) for all comers. Al-Dawā'ir disregarded this and held up an arms shipment on a truck that belonged to Banī Nawf, a tribe whose territory lies a long way further east near al-Ḥazm. In retaliation, Banī Nawf, Dhū Ḥusayn, and Nihm combined to impound trucks from Banī 'Alī in the Jawf, and Banī 'Alī's shaykhs (or rather the shaykhs of all the section's other villages) demanded that al-Dawā'ir give back what they had taken, so as to reopen the road. Al-Dawā'ir's refusal led to a fight with the rest of Banī 'Alī. The arms were recovered, and in disgust al-Dawā'ir joined Khārif, whose shaykhs at the time favoured the government in Ṣan'ā'.

Bayt Tha'īl of 'Iyāl 'Abdillāh had complaints of their own that they were receiving no development aid from Ṣan'ā', perhaps because all Arḥab was suspect in government eyes. When they saw what al-Dawā'ir had done, they followed suit. They 'became brother' to Khārif and, in a separate agreement, also became brother specifically to al-Dawā'ir. The leading shaykh of Khārif arranged for the two villages, now part of his tribe, to receive a school and gave them arms lest they be attacked.

Political influence, then, at a number of levels, made membership of Khārif desirable in the circumstances. The result was redefinition. The villages slaughtered bulls at Khārif's weekly market, and with the spilling of blood became part of the tribe. A document was then signed by them, which read as follows:

The Ḥāshid tribe of Khārif attended, represented by those mentioned [i.e. the document's signatories], together with their brothers (*makhwat-hum*) al-Dawā'ir and Bayt Tha'īl who are changing by brotherhood (*mu'ākhiyyīn*) from Arḥab to the Ḥāshid tribe of Khārif and who are represented by those mentioned at the bottom of this [document]. All of those mentioned were present [to agree] that they are brothers to each other (*ba'ḍ-hum al-ba'ḍ*) and what gathers them all (*tajammu' al-jamī'*) is the name of Khārif.

They agreed that they are one in small matters and great. They agreed that their right of escort (*masīrat-hum*) is one, that their aims (*ittijāh*) are one, their borders and roads, their gathering (*tajammu'*, i.e. for collective action), and their union of brotherhood are one.

In passing, one might note that the diacritica of identity are very much those touched on in earlier chapters: borders, roads, and rights of escort. It is on that basis that men can declare themselves a single unit.

All gather together for better and for worse (*li-khayr wa-sharr*), and blood will be judged by blood [i.e. we shall act as a single vengeance unit]. Our honour (*'arḍ*), borders, and territory are one, from the furthermost border (*aqṣā ḥadd*) of al-Dawā'ir and Bayt Tha'īl to the furthermost border of the tribe of Khārif. They agreed that counsels and judgment (*al-shuwar wa-l-ra'y*) unite all of them as Khārif [i.e. they would sue and be sued together]; that they are brothers who exchange views and take counsel of each other. Their collective levies (*ghurm wa-jurm*, i.e. for mulcts on or paid to the tribe) and their direction will be one for better and for worse. No difference of ancestry shall divide them (*lā yufarriq-hum mafraq khalf 'an al-aslāf*). This is by agreement of them all, by common consent and concurrence (*bi-riḍā' al-jamī' bi-ijāb wa-qabūlan*), a sincere pact of brotherhood. God grants success and is the best of witnesses. Dated 22 Jumād Awwal 1400 (8 April 1980).

What has changed is an identity: an element of one set becomes part of another, although the sets are still defined in the same terms of territory, of honour, and of contradistinction as before. Solidarity is a separate question.

The new school was placed near the border between al-Dawā'ir and Bayt Tha'īl, but just within the former's territory, and the two villages went to war within a matter of months over what it should be called. They repudiated the agreement between them. Both were still formally part of Khārif, but 'Iyāl 'Abdillāh of Arḥab now supported Bayt Tha'īl and Banī 'Alī of Arḥab supported al-Dawā'ir. A dispute between what were supposed to be two parts of Khārif produced a dispute between the two parts of Arḥab they used to fall in. Banī 'Alī and 'Iyāl 'Abdillāh then made a truce between themselves after two days of fighting and drove the two villages to arbitration by the Khārif shaykhs. Another school was built, this time just within Bayt Tha'īl. The two villages remain part of Khārif.

A bloodier case of broadly the same kind occurred on Khārif's south-eastern border about a year later. Two men of 'Usām in Arḥab fell out, and one of them, who failed to win support from his fellows in this local squabble, left the village to 'become brother' to Bayt Marrān, which also is part of Arḥab. Bayt Marrān took up the case and two of them were killed in pursuing it (a dispute between two men from one village, one might note, had set two villages at odds); but the rest of Arḥab then arranged a truce between Marrān and 'Usām. When the truce expired, Marrān ambushed an 'Usāmī truck at Khubbah—a quite separate third location, but also Arḥabī—and killed eight people. The government arrested ten men from Bayt Marrān and ten from Khubbah, the latter on the principle that a section or tribe is responsible for what happens in its territory. Khubbah appealed to the rest of Arḥab for help in retrieving their prisoners, but no help was forthcoming; so they went in the end to Khārif, slaughtered bulls at the market, and redefined their village as Khārifī. A dispute between two parts of Arḥab had involved a third part, and the third part had switched tribes in consequence.

This example raises a distinction which is important in grasping historical geography and which is probably worth underlining. When the man in 'Usām fell out with his fellow, and his kinsmen or neighbours failed to support the claim, he moved to another village. As explained in Chapter 3, men do not do this lightly. As it happened, his original fellows in 'Usām did not reclaim him by 'lifting the blood with blood'; so he moved with his immediate family and took his name with him, just as men do, for this or other reasons, between tribe and tribe. On the other hand, when the village of Khubbah failed to receive support and became brother with Ḥāshid, so the borders were redefined (Khārif, if you like, became bigger), it was precisely because no one at all moved. Khubbah, as it were, stood their ground and the line between tribes was redrawn. Territorial fixity is definitive of collective identities, while families and particular men can move and take their names with them.

Both possibilities derive from the formal equality of opposition between man and man, section and section, or tribe and tribe. When the contradictions of a man's position, or that of a group of men, become unmanageable (that is, when moral subordination is unavoidably implied), they are resolved by reordering one's place in the system of categories, whether that involves physical movement or redefinition *in situ* (cf. Dresch 1986: 320–1). As was suggested in the previous section, redefinition can take place at any level of the classification: al-Ahnūm, for example, were a Ḥāshid tribe in al-Hamdānī's time (al-Hamdānī 1948: 107–8) but they are now (*pace* Chelhod 1970: 84–5) very plainly a Bakīl tribe (see also Dresch 1987*a*: 69). But always the territory of a unit redefined in this way remains as and where it was, much as we saw in Chapter 8 that village borders are said to remain fixed, and a geographical shell thus outlasts the transactions and exclusions of particular villagers.

To the empirical eye, the village, set apart as it usually is by a physical space from its neighbours, may appear more 'real' than do larger divisions of the classification, and we should therefore insert a word of caution. Certainly a tribal section comprises several villages, and most villages belong clearly to one section or another, which in turn forms part of a specific tribe. But occasionally a single settlement is split arbitrarily by a border. Al-Hamdānī devotes a separate section of the *Ṣifah* to villages 'whose inhabitants form two opposed parts' (*allātī yakūna ahla-hā juz'ayn mutaḍāddayn*;

al-Hamdānī 1968: 123), by which he means that half were from one tribe or such-like group and half from another.[11] The phenomenon is not unknown nowadays. To take a particularly clear example, there is a settlement on the borders of Khārif, Arḥab, and 'Iyāl Surayḥ which, having come to it from the Khārif side, I knew as Bayt Bādī; but this turned out to be the name only of the Khārifīs there, and Arḥab knew the place as Bayt Jā'il, the name of the Arḥabīs there, while 'Iyāl Surayḥ referred to it as Bayt Ziyād. It is none the less a discrete settlement. The rate of intermarriage among its inhabitants is reportedly high. They speak of the place themselves as one village and they act as such in, for instance, weddings and funerals. In the event of fighting between their tribes, they say, if they could not each separately opt out, they would certainly fight; but they would do so elsewhere along the relevant border, not from house to house in their close-knit settlement.

Even where two distinct villages are recognized, that distinction may not be obvious to the eye. Bayt Sāyil and Bayt Najjād, for instance, at the northern end of Qā' al-Bawn, seem two complementary parts of a single settlement through which runs a small wash or wadi; but the first belongs to 'Iyāl Surayḥ and the second to al-Kalbiyyīn of Khārif. More generally, one could not safely guess at the location of borders by drawing lines through the blank spaces on a map of villages. A village is a political unit, not just a geographic fact, because it has a specific place in the broader scheme of territory and of tribal identity; and if a village changes tribes, then the territory of the village is reallocated as a unit, not broadened, removed, or shrunk.

The only circumstance in which territory is explicitly ceded by the smallest unit to which it belongs is the settlement of blood-debts. A section that owes blood-wealth to an adjacent section, or a village to the village next door, may transfer part of its common grazing land (*faysh*). For this to happen the debt would have to be clearly collective; it would have to have been incurred on a 'white day' of general warfare or in a case where the particular killer could not be identified. If a corpse is found in a section's territory, for instance, and the killer is not known, then responsibility devolves on the section as such or on the particular village. Compensation would be paid by the section's members in cash unless the victim were from the section adjacent, when a shift of the border line may be made instead.

The village of al-Taḥḍah in Murhibah offers two circumstances of a more complex sort which illustrate the same principle. Wādī Ẓulam, which runs down from Murhibah's territory to Wādī Dhībīn, was once shared grazing between Murhibah and Banī Jubar of Khārif. All of it is uncultivable rock. A man from elsewhere in Khārif was killed there long ago, so the story runs, and Banī Jubar accused Murhibah, who denied the charge. Since the border line was unclear, so too was the responsibility. Murhibah finally paid the blood-money in return for a definite line being recognized that included all the wadi in al-Taḥḍah's territory. On the other side of the village is grazing that belongs to al-Taḥḍah although it is closer to a village called Bayt Malīḥ and is on Bayt Malīḥ's side of a small watershed from al-Taḥḍah. The story goes that a man from Jabal Baraṭ was killed there when it belonged to Bayt Malīḥ. Bayt Malīḥ either could not or would not pay the *diyah*. Al-Taḥḍah paid on Murhibah's behalf, and the land was transferred to them. The essential link is between territory and joint responsibility. If a section or tribe can be held answerable, the territory must be theirs; if the territory is theirs they must be answerable.[12]

At any one point in time (such as an ethnographer usually sees), these divisions of the tribal classification appear fixed: one is fortunate to catch a change by brotherhood as it occurs, and it deserves to be stressed that these changes are comparatively rare. Groups of men and their actions take their value, not simply from their relation to other actions and groups, but from their position (or the position claimed for them) in the tribal scheme. And individuals claim their debts against others, not simply as anonymous persons, but always as tribesmen or through tribesmen: that is, as men who derive their standing and rights from their membership in particular tribes. The validity of these identities derives precisely from their fixity. Were tribal sets admittedly as changeable as the groups which form and unform in their names, the language of ancestry and of territory would have no sense and the concept of 'balance' between sets would be meaningless.

The opposition of such units is the condition for a certain type of history whereby past and present are assimilated in the language of 'ancestral' honour (cf. Meeker 1976); but the history of these units themselves, the sequence and form of their changes, exhibits just the principle of moral equilibrium which men claim to derive from their fixity. The changes that occur in the formal alignment or definition of tribes turn out to occur in the same terms as disputes between them. The opposition between tribes is what allows a single man or a family to change from one tribe to another, seeking refuge within a moral space that is equal yet opposite to the one in which his own claim to equality was unsuccessful. And a section changes tribe because its members conceive that it has been wronged, and the debt of that wrong has not been paid: the fixed equality of opposition is then that between two tribes or between the two confederations. Obscured by the great events of Imamic history and by the claims of party politics now, there is a structural logic which may be taken to characterize the tribal order.

None of this means an insurance of political order for those involved (Dresch 1984*b*: 160). The upheavals of the nineteenth century, touched on earlier, are enough to suggest how often people were driven from their houses by hunger or violence and how often men were killed in disputes. A great deal is excluded from the tribal system altogether by, for instance, the movement of failed tribal farmers to the west or to Lower Yemen; but within the system's boundaries a constant reshuffling of persons and categories excludes much that would otherwise imply moral hierarchy and temporal supersession. No ranking is ever built.

Both changes in territorial extent, as a result of blood-debt, and changes of definition, whereby a given territorial unit switches identity by brotherhood, are explicit. A date can, in principle, be set to them by documents. Tacit changes are by their nature invisible to a history of events, but they are a possibility that deserves mention. The fear of them is presumably what motivates many disputes over grazing and the like, and certainly their possibility seems implied in much that tribesmen do. The possibility of such claims is carefully watched for. They might, for instance, arise from the purchase of land in the territory of another tribe if the purchase were on a sufficient scale.

The border between Khārif and Sufyān, for example, is fairly clear, since Ẓafār Dhībīn stands between the two tribes and a mountain spur runs out into the wadi. On the Sufyān side of the border, at Warwar, however, one of the shaykhs of Khārif has purchased all the land to establish a model farm (cf. Tutwiler and Carapico 1981: 174–5). It was here the shooting incident occurred which was touched on in Chapter 3. The drainage on the slopes around the farmland remains Sufyānī, but the bed of the wadi is all under cultivation and men of Sufyān therefore have no right of access. In a situation like this, where a holding forms a contiguous block and no personal rights to use it are held by men from the other tribe, the area's identity with a definitional unit (what Evans-Pritchard 1949: 55 very vaguely called 'residual rights')[13] might be forgotten over time.

For this to be a possibility there must be a particular relation between tribal territory and private ownership or rights of use. If a tribe were simply an aggregate of people exploiting a given valley or mountain to the exclusion of other people (Marx 1977: 344), there would be no ambiguity. But for the analyst to define a tribe in this way means ignoring people's own account of the tribes they in fact belong to (ibid. 348, 358), which may count as geography or ecology but is surely not anthropology. On the other hand, if by definition all land whatever within the borders 'belonged' to a tribe in the same way as their kitchen belongs to an urban family in modern housing, then again no possibility of dispute or ambiguity could arise. In reality, the relations of collective identity to people's rights of use, rights of access, and responsibility are complex. Here, as in much else, the tribes are neither solidary blocks nor legal persons, and the system in any case varies from place to place.

SCHEMES OF TERRITORIALITY

> Je ne dis point que le climat n'ait produit, en grande partie, les lois, les mœurs et les manières de cette nation; mais je dis que les mœurs et les manières . . . devroient avoir un grand rapport à ses lois.
>
> Montesquieu, *L'Esprit des lois*

Ecological determinism continues to haunt discussions of Middle Eastern tribalism, and it is as well to be clear that in the Yemeni case tribal borders are often arbitrary with respect to natural features. Borders are seldom where one expects them. The line between Banī Ṣuraym and Sufyān, for example, follows a mountain ridge; but the border is at the base, not the crest, so the slopes belong to Sufyān and the runoff from them to Banī Ṣuraym. The border between Sufyān and Āl 'Ammār, on the other hand, follows the watershed. Again, the line between Sufyān and Arḥab (rather poorly defined, as we shall see) runs along the wadi north of Dhībīn out towards the Jawf. Between these two Bakīl tribes and the Ḥāshid tribe of Khārif, though, the line runs across the wadi so that upstream is Ḥāshidī and downstream is Bakīlī. The same is true of Khārif's eastern border with Arḥab: both Nā'iṭ and Kāniṭ are Ḥāshidī but the lower reaches of the wadis that run down from them to the east, to Ḥaḍar and Rajaw, are Bakīlī.

The result is that drainage systems are not shared by tribes, with the branches of wadis corresponding to those of a segmentary tree. Section 1 of tribe A may share a wadi system with section 3 of tribe B, while section 2 of tribe A shares another drainage block with tribe C, and sections 1, 2, and 4 of tribe B share the drainage to a wadi held by tribe D. Even in the north-east, where intensive settlement is all but limited to a few wadis, one does not find much vertical integration of water systems: Wādī Amlaḥ, for instance, to the north of Baraṭ and itself running out to the east and north-east, is said to be held by Āl Sālim at the top, Wā'ilah in the middle, and al-'Amālisah lower down, all of which tribes have extensive territory that embraces quite separate drainage. On the more densely populated plateau, particular rights to grazing, fuel, or pre-emptive purchase will be explained by the direction of runoff (*ittijāh al-mā'*); but the argument is suspended at arbitrary section borders that may run through a single group of fields.

Nor do ecological constraints determine collective actions in any simple way. For example, in the late 1970s, drought restricted the grazing in Dhū Fāri' of al-'Uṣaymāt and part of Ṣubārah in Sufyān. The first is part of Ḥāshid and the second part of Bakīl. They are immediate neighbours. The Sufyānīs took their flocks down to pasture with 'Idhar (part of Ḥāshid), and the 'Uṣaymīs moved their own flocks by truck down to 'Iyāl Surayḥ (part of Bakīl). In other words, the Ḥāshidīs went to Bakīl and the Bakīlīs to Ḥāshid. Such arrangements are made not simply on the basis of shared tribal membership but through personal claims; in the present case they were entangled with broader questions of politics. The tribes and confederations are not in any simple way means to allot shared resources.

A priori arguments in terms of adaptation fall usually foul of tribalism's own logic: what one might see as men's best interests are thwarted by enmity between men from different tribes. Sufyān and

Dhū Muḥammad, for example, as mentioned earlier, have for years had a dispute over borders. At al-ʿĀdī, west of Wādī Madhāb, there was a government outpost in the Imam's day, which kept the peace and allowed extensive cultivation by the wadi; but now the tribes disagree on whose territory it is and the fields all lie abandoned, although (indeed, because) arable land in the area is very much at a premium.[14] A large market used to be held nearby at Darb Banī Jaysh; that too has been abandoned, leaving a wide area of ruined stone booths to suggest its former prosperity. Such scenes of desolation are not uncommon in the east.

Economic rationality explains little, therefore, or rather one cannot predict which unit's benefit will be accepted as a common goal and which will be opposed in terms of tribal rivalry. Ecology, by contrast, has its place in the different forms that territoriality assumes from one tribe to the next, and a gradient of territorial systems runs from the areas of comparatively high rainfall (200–300 millimetres per annum) to those with less.

In the more densely farmed and populated areas such as that in which Bayt Ḥusayn lies (Chapter 8), territory attaches to villages. The territory of Khārif, for example, is the sum of the territories of al-Ṣayad, al-Kalbiyyīn, and Banī Jubar; the territory of al-Ṣayad, in turn, is the sum of the territories of that section's 'fifths', and the territory of each 'fifth' is exhausted by those of its constituent villages; there are no blank spaces that belong only to al-Ṣayad as such or to Khārif as such.[15] The same pattern occurs in southern Arḥab, southern Banī Ṣuraym, and in several tribes close to Ṣanʿā'. Within the territory of a given village, members of another village may own arable land but the grazing is held in common by the members of the village whose territory it is, and outsiders cannot bring their sheep there without permission.

The same rights and restrictions, whereby outsiders can acquire arable land but not use common grazing, apply in some areas to units of the next order above villages: that is, to minor sections. Banī ʿAlī of northern Arḥab, for instance, comprise eight 'eighths', and each eighth contains some half-dozen villages. There is no grazing land attaching only to Banī ʿAlī as a whole, but on the other hand there is none attaching to the individual villages; instead each 'eighth' holds its grazing in common. Members of the eighth can graze anywhere within the borders of the eighth as a whole, except on arable land (*māl*), which is personally owned and is set aside (*maḥjūr*) for the owners alone to graze sheep or goats on the stubble.[16] The same pattern is found in Khayār of Banī Ṣuraym, where grazing attaches to each of the section's 'sixths' but none to Khayār as a whole and none to the constituent villages. In the neighbouring Ṣuraymī section of Wāda'ah, however, there do seem to be areas of grazing land (*faysh*, *fuyūsh*) that attach to Wāda'ah as such and which are open to all Wāda'ah's members. Most of this is probably in the comparatively empty spaces adjoining al-'Uṣaymāt to the west.

When we move a little north, either from Banī Ṣuraym or from Arḥab, to Sufyān we find most of the tribe's territory attaching to one or other of the two major sections, Ruhm or Ṣubārah. In the south-east of Sufyān's territory, adjoining Arḥab around Shawābah, there are settlements of Ruhm and of Ṣubārah mixed in together. North of Khaywān, however, the north-west of Sufyān's territory is Ruhmī and the south-east Ṣubārī, with a line running between the two, on one side of which nearly all the non-arable land (*faysh*) is open for all Ruhm's members to graze and on the other side of which all Ṣubārah's members are free to graze their flocks.

All of this is flat, dry land. The major wadis, which are shallow washes not conspicuous from a distance, run roughly from north-west to south-east; that is, normal to the border dividing the two main sections.[17] Each of these major sections subdivides extensively, as shown in Fig. 9.5. The villages of each subdivision tend to cluster together along the wadis, but the subdivisions themselves are not territorial entities: there are no borders (*ḥudūd*) that define the territory of al-Shumaylāt or Āl Khurays or Āl Ṣāliḥ. When people speak of '*ḥudūd* Āl Ṣāliḥ' they refer to borders of a village or village cluster that itself belongs to Āl Ṣāliḥ, not to borders that define Al Ṣāliḥ as such.

Each settled and farmed area (*ḥayy*) belongs to a particular *laḥmah*; that is, to a unit of the order of Dhū Aḥmad or Dhū Ja'rān in Bal'ak. These settled areas may abut one another along a wadi. Around each settlement are *muqaṣṣarāt*, areas which include both arable land and grazing which is off-limits to all but the members of that settlement. Such off-limits areas are not large, rarely more than two or three kilometres across: the slopes of the hills running down to the wadi at Wāsit (north of al-Ḥarf), for instance, are off-limits to all except those who live there, but the far slopes of the hills are not. In a few cases one finds shared restricted grazing; for example,

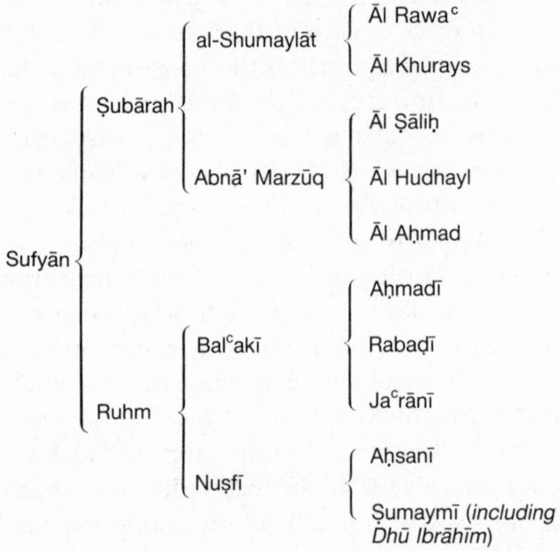

FIG. 9.5 Divisions of modern Sufyān

between Wāsiṭ and Ḥibāshah where some five kilometres or so are *muqaṣṣarāt li*-Aḥmadī and Rubaḍī together. Between these small restricted areas, however, all the territory of Sufyān attaches either to Ruhm or Ṣubārah and is open to grazing by all the members of one or other of these two major sections.

Perhaps as many as a fifth of Sufyān's people are, as we said, at least semi-nomadic. Nearly all of them have houses and land in the settled areas along the wadis, and part of the family is often minding the farmland while another part minds the flocks in the wasteland many miles away. Even those families who are wholly settled own significant numbers of livestock: a mixed herd of about forty sheep and goats per household is not unusual. The major crop is sorghum, which depends more on runoff down the shallow wadis than on direct rainfall, and rainfall in the area is sparse.

Moving eastward from Sufyān to Dhū Muḥammad and Dhū Ḥusayn, we find the rainfall more patchy still: as of late 1983 there had not been enough rain for five years to plant crops at Baraṭ, although the grazing survived and most wells still held water. Here we find most of the territory belonging to the whole tribe as such, little or none to major sections, and only very small restricted areas abutting arable land around the villages.[18] Dhū Husayn, for example, comprise eight 'eighths', as shown in Fig. 9.6 (cf. Steffen 1978: ii. 180). The territory of Dhū Ḥusayn is enormous: from the border line with adjoining villages of Dhū Muḥammad at Baraṭ it stretches to the southern edge of Wādī Jawf and an indeterminate distance eastward into the Empty Quarter. Villages belonging to the different eighths are scattered at wadis and oases throughout this vast area. Despite their geographical scatter, the eighths of Dhū Ḥusayn are politically important. If a fight breaks out between eighth A and eighth B at a given place where both have houses, then other members of A and B may go to the scene of the fighting to join in. They do not automatically start fighting wherever they may be. However, if a debt of blood arises between A and B, then fighting may indeed break out wherever A and B are neighbours, as members of one seek revenge from the other. A mulct on the whole tribe by some other tribe should in theory be raised by the eighths equally.

Only at Rajūzah (Jabal Baraṭ) are all the eighths found together. Each also had a fortified tower *(nūbah)* at al-ʿUqdah in the Upper Jawf, but now only four or five of the eighths are represented there. The villages of each eighth do not cluster together, and the eighths

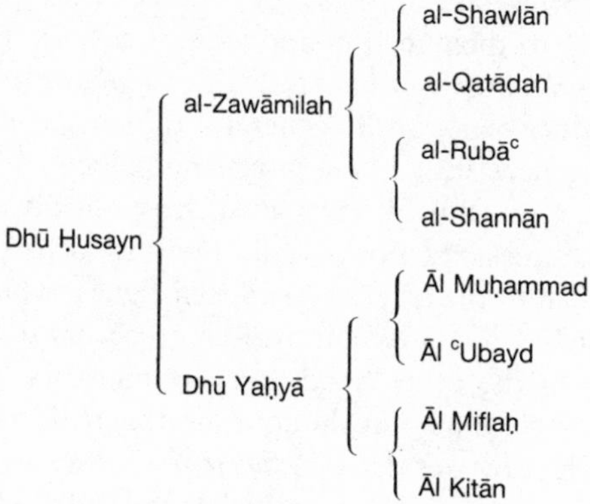

FIG. 9.6 Divisions of Dhū Ḥusayn

as such have no borders whatever. Nearly all Dhū Ḥusayn's territory attaches to Dhū Ḥusayn as such, not to the tribe's constituent parts, and the tribe counts a significant number of camel-herding nomads.

Around the settled areas at Baraṭ the restrictions on the use of natural resources are complex. On Dhū Muḥammad's side, for instance, are several areas of restricted grazing (*ḥijrah* or *maḥjūr*) which are off-limits to other people twice a year. One such area attaches to Āl Ṣalāḥ, another is split between Āl Dumaynah and al-Ma'āṭirah, another belongs to a single house of Dhū Mūsā, still another belongs jointly to a single house of Dhū Mūsā and a single family of Āl Aḥmad b. Kawl.[19] No new off-limits area can be declared. They are said all to have been as and where they are since the distant past. Apart from the territory of the tribe as such and these seemingly arbitrary shared *maḥājir*, there is only private property: *mā ḥuwwar wa-duwwar*, 'what has been ploughed and built on'. The restrictions here (among both Dhū Ḥusayn and Dhū Muḥammad) are quite the opposite of those found in the more agricultural areas of, say, Khārif, Arḥab, or Banī Ṣuraym. There *al-ḥadd mā yadhukl al-maḥdūd*, 'borders do not enter into questions of private property', and a man from one village, section, or tribe could own land in another's territory, but could not graze flocks there. In the north-east, by contrast, grazing is fairly free, and one routinely comes across herders from one tribe in the wasteland (*fuyūsh* or *sha'rā'*) of another tribe's territory. Men cannot, though, own land, or bring land into use, or sink wells except in the small areas attaching to their section and village; that is, in the *maqāṣīr* (pl. of *maqṣūr*, cf. Sufyān's *muqaṣṣarāt*) or *maḥājir* (pl. of *maḥjūr*). If one sinks a new well in the general scrubland, it is reckoned *li-sabīl*, for the general use, like a pious endowment.[20]

The territory of Dhū Ḥusayn as such is not an expression of control of resources: the ecologically limiting factors (arable land and wells) attach to the local parts of each eighth, while the grazing area that attaches to the whole tribe is freely used by men from other tribes. On the other hand, borders mark the extent of the tribe's peace, on which the honour of the tribe depends. Dhū Ḥusayn as such is answerable to other tribes for what happens in its territory, at Baraṭ, for instance, or the Upper Jawf, and has the right to deny access to its territory by 'cutting off' exchanges with outsiders.

In this respect territory has always the same significance. Whether on the more southerly parts of the northern plateau (where each element of tribal classification is identified with territory, and the territory of a higher-order element is exhausted by those of its constituent parts) or in the north-east (where only parts of the tribal classification correspond to geographical boundaries), borders always define an area of answerability. To uphold the peace there is the right, responsibility, and prerogative of the unit in question. Moreover, whether the land in question is the exclusive grazing of the plateau village or the area in which wells and arable would be exclusive in the desert north-east, the association of land with vulnerable honour (*'arḍ*) is the same; and the appeal for help from one's tribal fellows to defend that land is always made in the same terms, regardless of the different rights to use of land that unite or divide these fellow tribesmen and the man attacked. The ecological constraints vary greatly from place to place. The specific territorial systems vary with them from tribe to tribe. A single conceptual and rhetorical system contains all of them, however, and gives merely geographical facts their social value.

To the north and east of Baraṭ the territorial scheme seems finally to give way to a system of identity and land-use more resembling that of, say, inland Oman or North Arabia. Information on the area remains sparse, but there is little doubt that territory ceases to be contiguous.[21] What one finds instead are scattered 'territories' (tribesmen speak of them in terms of borders, *ḥudūd*) that coincide with wadis and seem to represent exclusive areas of potential arable land (very little is sown but occasional sorghum planted straight in the sand) and exclusive areas of grazing (though formal permission to use others' territory is said to be granted readily). In a few places there are houses, but mostly one sees tent-dwellers. Between and around the fragments of territory (see Fig. 9.7) would seem to be no man's land, or rather land that is spoken of in terms of habitual but not exclusive grazing zones reminiscent of North Arabian *dīrah*s.

One might argue that, from the densely farmed plateau zone near Ṣan'ā' all the way to this area of transition on the edge of the Empty Quarter, territory and exclusive use rights are built around whatever in the particular case is the ecologically limiting factor (cf. Johnson 1969; Wilkinson 1983): grazing on the arable plateau, and arable in the more pastoral east. At some points these limits have

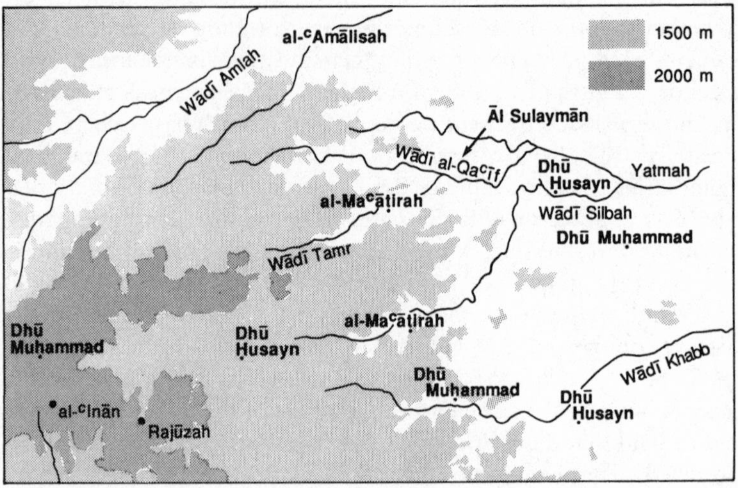

FIG. 9.7 Fragmentation of territory east of Baraṭ

changed with new technology. In the following section we shall look at an example from the north-east, but here we should look briefly at a case nearer the plateau centre to see what is at issue.

Arḥab and Sufyān share a border at Shawābah along Wādī Dhībīn on the route from Qāʿ al-Bawn to the Jawf. Serious problems began there in the early 1970s with the advent of machinery and the rise of land prices, but the scene had been set some thirty years earlier: Ibn al-Subayʿī of Sufyān had owned some land further east along the wadi in Nihm's territory, but sold it after a dispute with Nihm and bought land at Shawābah within Arḥab's borders, about 1,000 *libnah*. One Ibn Shārān of Arḥab had bought about 700 *libnah* close by, but just within Sufyān's borders. In those days, well before the revolution, the exact position of the border line at all points had not been an issue. The arable land on each side was separated from that opposite by two or three kilometres of sand and rock which everyone grazed without cause for dispute, and at only a few points were there border marks where some dispute over blood-debt had occurred in the past.

Nor was grazing a major problem for men who owned land within the territory of the other tribe. People had, in any case, often to take their sheep and goats all the way to Sinwān or Warwar to water them (a half-day's round journey), which severely limited the number of animals worth keeping. Since then, new diesel pumps have allowed people to start thinking of establishing arable land in the old grazing area of the wadi bed, and wells have been sunk further back among the arable land on each side of the wadi. These wells are used also to water flocks. The number of animals one can keep has shot up. Al-Subay'ī, for example, the Sufyānī who owns land in Arḥab, increased his flock from fifty or so to about four hundred. The grazing rights in Arḥab suddenly became of major importance. So too did rights to gather fuel.

Starting in about 1974–5, men throughout this area began gathering dead wood on a commercial basis and trucking it down to Raydah, 'Amrān, or even Ṣan'ā' to sell as firewood. Banī Shārān of Arḥab told al-Subay'ī of Sufyān that he could no longer either graze his flocks or gather wood in their territory, and shooting broke out. Shaykhs from the immediate area of Arḥab and Sufyān intervened, and those at odds then agreed to judgment by Bin Sinān and Bin Ḥubaysh, the leading shaykhs of Arḥab and Sufyān respectively.

The judgment, very reasonably, was that al-Subay'ī could have sufficient grazing and water for his personal needs (even the sheep could all stay, providing they were kept off other people's private property), but he could not sell wood or water from Arḥab's *faysh*. Al-Subay'ī refused the judgment. A succession of truces was sustained for four years, until Bin Sinān and Bin Ḥubaysh 'drove' those at odds to a *sharī'ah* judge, al-Marwānī of Ḥayfah in Arḥab. He confirmed the judgment. Al-Subay'ī again refused it, and a further set of truces was imposed. They then all went to Mujāhid Abū Shawārib of Khārif, late in 1980, and he too confirmed the judgment. The atmosphere at the time was somewhat fraught because of troubles in national politics, and serious fighting soon broke out between larger sections of Sufyān and Arḥab, which was stopped by Dhū Ḥusayn, Nihm, Murhibah, Khārif, and 'Iyāl Surayḥ. A delegation including Yaḥyā al-Ghūlī ('Iyāl Surayḥ), Aḥsan Nufaysh (Khārif), Manṣūr Radmān (Arḥab), and 'Abd al-Walī al-Shāyif (Dhū Ḥusayn) together forced a truce and attempted arbitration. Nājī al-Shāyif then tried to take the process over. Finally they all went back to Abū Shawārib. The dispute was contained yet again, but the basis of the problem remains unsolved: al-Subay'ī's flocks are restricted to his own property in Arḥab's territory and to grazing in Sufyān, but the tribesmen's intention to establish new arable land on what was wasteland (*arḍ bayḍā'*, 'white land', as they called it) is entirely blocked. It remains wasteland, and one can no longer even graze there.

The old categories of land-use, therefore, are in some areas causing new problems. But disputes over land are mentioned quite frequently in the histories and are not themselves a new phenomenon (see e.g. al-Wāsi'ī 1928: 244–5). To the planner they are simply irrational. The 'grey literature' on, for example, range management grows yearly and has little effect but to point up how different are the assumptions of those writing it from those who raise the flocks and crops. One might conclude indeed, as Wilkinson does in the Omani case, that 'the tribal system is . . . fundamentally unsuited to the needs of the land' (Wilkinson 1977: 228); yet for those involved, of course, the land as a whole has no needs, only people do, and people with identities dependent on a broader scheme. Claims may be made, however, in different structural terms, for instance individually or in terms of a section or tribe. And in the short term these different claims and counter-claims give a distinctive rhythm to people's lives, much as do the fragmented contraints of farming outlined in Chapter 8.

ALLIANCE, COHESION, AND FIXED IDENTITIES

Within a tribe the relation between sections is usually that purely of opposition, each section guarding its own against others. The whole tribe in turn is opposed to other tribes, but in times of conflict part of the tribe may stand aside, and in time of calm little stress can be put on the sections' common identity: it becomes scarcely relevant. To make of tribal identity some more solid construction that maintains men's alignments from one event to the next requires conscious effort and application: to cease being at the mercy of events and to take them in hand requires binding agreement.

The different forms of agreement and obligation vary greatly. To summarize them without lapsing too far into generalities it is easiest to take first the case of the north-eastern tribes, who are unique in recognizing an explicit alignment of 'ancestry' between one tribe and another (see Fig. 9.8).[22] In spring 1976 Dhū Muḥammad tried

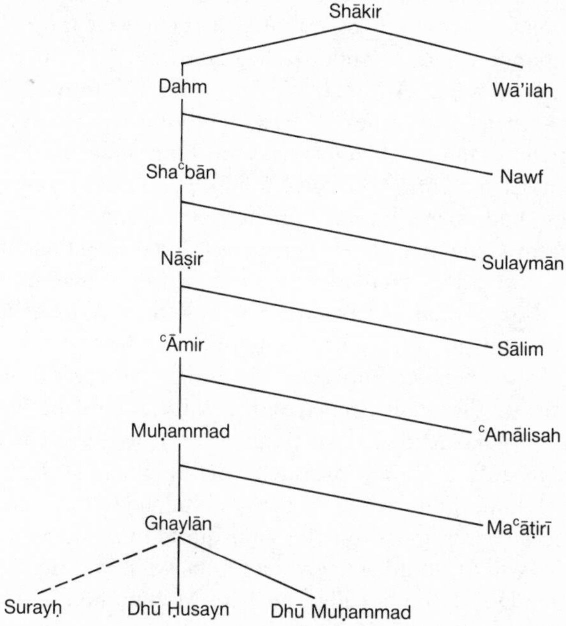

FIG. 9.8 Related tribes of the far north-east

Source: After Steffen 1978: ii. 119

to unite all of Dahm against Wā'ilah. In fact most of the tribes, and particularly Dhū Ḥusayn, refused to have anything to do with this, but an alliance (*ḥilf*) was formed between Dhū Muḥammad, al-'Amālisah, and Āl Sulaymān. This alliance was solely for the defence of al-'Aqīq, an area that was once part of Wā'ilah but had become brother to Dahm perhaps a century ago and now controlled the road to the border post of Buq'. The reasons for Dhū Muḥammad's intitiative were to be found in national politics, where tension was increasing between al-Ḥamdī and the Saudis. The agreement to combine against Wā'ilah was revived in June 1981.

In the interim (around 1977–8), Dhū Ḥusayn found themselves at odds with Āl Sulaymān over previously barren wadis north-east of Baraṭ, particularly the lower reaches of Wādī al-Qa'īf (see Fig. 9.7), that both now wanted to cultivate with the aid of drilled wells and diesel pumps. Āl Sulaymān also fell out, for the same reason, with al-Maʿāṭirah, who are so closely associated with Dhū Muḥammad as often to be counted a section of the tribe. Dhū Muḥammad refused to support al-Maʿāṭirah, but intervened as mediators between Āl Sulaymān and Dhū Ḥusayn. By most accounts their intervention was temporarily successful, but Muḥammadīs later claimed it was at this point that they found Dhū Ḥusayn asserting control of all Wādī Silbah. Dhū Ḥusayn claimed that they had farmed areas further out along the wadi, past Yatmah, for some time. They were simply extending their activities. Dhū Muḥammad claimed ancestral rights of their own in the area.

In 1978–9 Wā'ilah cut the road against the Saudis. Alignments were now shifting somewhat in national politics, and the shift around Baraṭ was accentuated by a dispute (again over new cultivation of the wadis, particularly Wādī Silbah) between Dhū Ḥusayn and Dhū Muḥammad. Four arbitrators were chosen, two from each side, but they produced no judgment.[23] Beasts were exchanged in both directions to demand judgment or truce, but the two sides later disagreed on the vital question of quite when this happened, which would entirely determine what was meant, and at some stage Dhū Ḥusayn called on Dhū Muḥammad to accept the sworn testimony of five Ḥusaynī witnesses.

Al-Maʿāṭirah refused to support Dhū Muḥammad, who themselves turned, as the dispute developed, to support Āl Sulaymān against Dhū Ḥusayn. Dhū Ḥusayn resumed building and fencing in Wādī Silbah, and Dhū Muḥammad raided the area, destroying several vehicles. Dhū Ḥusayn summonsed the culprits at market, but agreed to let the matter rest until the whole question of Silbah was resolved, which it never was. Dhū Muḥammad then resumed their dispute with Wā'ilah and called again for support from al-ʿAmālisah and Āl Sulaymān. The 1976–81 pact was renewed, and in 1983 was extended from mere alliance (*ḥilf*) to full brotherhood (*ikhā'*) between Dhū Muḥammad and Āl Sulaymān. This was a political initiative undertaken by activists in Dhū Muḥammad, who for months lobbied for signatures to the document, wheeling and dealing much as one might in a quite different system of politics.

One feature of the pact (the *ḥilf* becoming *ikhā'*) deserves particular note. Besides the usual formula that 'the roads are one and the borders are one' was a specific and complex provision that rifles which clear one (*banādiq al-ṣafw*) would be accepted from outsiders but not permitted from parties to the agreement: in other words, if we are at odds with another tribe and part of that tribe wishes to opt out of the confrontation, we shall allow them to do so; but no one of our confederate tribe is allowed to opt out, and we must act as one unit. The purpose of the asymmetry is obvious.[24]

In July 1983 Dhū Muḥammad appeared at Silbah in strength, and intermittent fighting started. In September a large delegation of Bakīl shaykhs arrived, from Arḥab, ʻIyāl Surayḥ, ʻIyāl Yazīd, Banī al-Ḥārith, Khawlān al-ʻĀliyah, and Sufyān. Al-ʻAmālisah forced a truce between Dhū Muḥammad and Dhū Ḥusayn, soon broken by fighting on the border at Baraṭ. A detachment of paratroops from Ma'rib tried to force a settlement. Aḥmad ʻAlī al-Maṭarī, now governor of Ṣanʻā' province, also made an attempt. None of these was successful.

Dhū Muḥammad wanted land that they could newly cultivate, and they said that whatever they gained would be split between the tribe's 'fifths'; Dhū Ḥusayn said among themselves that they might divide new space for arable land according to their own 'eighths',[25] but they were badly divided by rivalry over the shaykhdom of their tribe. They tried, but failed, to coalesce around the 'setting aside' of a single leader and by means of 'brotherhood' between their different sections. A settlement with Dhū Muḥammad was blocked precisely by the success of such manœuvres on the other side: when Dhū Ḥusayn insisted on a separate truce with Āl Sulaymān, Dhū Muḥammad said that only one truce was acceptable, with themselves and Āl Sulaymān together, who were now their 'brothers' so 'their borders were one, their collective honour (*ʻarḍ*), and all that might shame them'. The Muḥammadīs had taken the initiative and held it throughout.

Throughout this long dispute there has not been only automatist cohesion and fragmentation. There has certainly been a great deal of unthinking response, but the course of the dispute has been both marked and determined by explicit pacts duly signed and witnessed. Such arrangements might almost be expected in cases of alliance (*ḥilf*) or of redefinition by brotherhood (*ikhā'*, *mu'ākhah*). What is perhaps more surprising is that a pact of 'brotherhood' may be formed between units which already are brothers and always have been, as the eighths of Dhū Ḥusayn hoped to do among themselves. There is no change of definitions. The existing definition is merely affirmed and made binding.

The document drawn up by Sufyān that was mentioned earlier (Chapters 4 and 7) provides an example of this kind from nearer the central plateau. Most of the major tribes are said to have made such internal agreements at one time or another in the indefinitely distant past, but this one must serve by itself for illustration.

The tribe of Sufyān met, its shaykhs and men and notables, and they decided upon what follows: First, that they form a pact of brotherhood and of fellowship (*ṣaḥb*), honour bright (*sharīf naẓīf*). No quittance shall make a man quit [of the agreement] henceforth. They are brothers who shall [together] follow up [any offence] from inside [the tribe] or outside (*akhwah mutatābi'ah 'alā min 'aẓm-hum wa-khārij*), whether they gain from it or lose from it (*buqshah tukhsar wa-buqshah tafyud*). In all the losses that occur in killing and revenge concerning their territory and what shames them (*mu'awwarāt-hum* i.e. women, dependants, etc.), their honour is one. Their right is recognized in all their territory (*al-'arḍ māḍī fī kulli l-bilād*, i.e. any tribesman can act as escort or protector in the name of all), and their territory outside the *muqaṣṣarāt* is one.

The off-limits areas attaching to villages thus remain the responsibility of those who hold them, and no one else in the tribe may interfere with what happens there. Apart from that, the inviolability of Sufyān's territory is affirmed to be in the care of Sufyān as a whole: no part can leave another to defend itself.

They will all pursue together [the claim] of one who suffers a loss. Whoever kills makes quit and whoever is killed is avenged (*man qatal aṣal wa-man qutil nuṣṣab* i.e. we shall kill and be killed as one vengeance unit, recognizing any one of ourselves as exchangeable for any other). . . . The man distant can call for help and the man near must care for him. Whoever delays after the call for help is due a *jidhn* without further claim [for the *jidhn* see Chapters 3 and 4], and their costs/losses will be borne by him.

The document then states that all this is what Ṣubārah have decided (it was they who took the initiative) and that Ruhm adhere to the agreement. The two halves of Sufyān, who are brothers already by virtue of their shared 'ancestor', now declare a pact of brotherhood with regard to 'borders, territory, the market, the countryside, what might shame them, their rights (e.g. of escort), matters of killing and revenge (*qatl wa-tanṣīb*) . . . and collective payments (*ghurm*)'.

The obligations and rights which in the abstract might be claimed always to derive from shared tribal identity are here affirmed as binding in a concrete agreement (cf. Dresch 1987*b*). The different sections of the tribe are each represented by shaykhly guarantors (*ḍumanā'*), and these in turn are overseen and supported by secondary guarantors (*rudamā'*, 'guarantors of the covering') from Āl 'Ammār and from Dhū Ḥusayn. To form a tribe into a cohesive unit, it seems, nothing will suffice but commitments from other tribes. The attempt, as was mentioned in Chapter 4, centres upon guaranty of the market at al-Ḥarf. Provisions for this guaranty take up much of the document. But built around this is a general agreement for the defence of borders and tribal territory, and the elaborate structure of guaranty which is common in the case of markets applies to the whole agreement: if any party secedes from the pact of tribal solidarity, then he insults the guarantors and owes them amends.

The practical weakness of this particular pact is evident in the number of special conditions and exceptions made by different sections. Dhū Ṣumaym, for example, insist that they are brothers to the other sections only 'with regard to the tribe's outer borders with the other tribes facing them' (*'alā l-ḥudūd wa-l-wathīn 'alā irbā' al-bilād*). As for matters within Sufyān's territory, they say, the agreement does not cover them. Parts of al-Shumaylāt are concerned to stress that the agreement does not affect their restricted areas: at Maḥḍyān and Sanām (in the east of Sufyān), for example, where there are 'farmland and *'ulb* trees owned by particular subsections' (*māl wa-'ulūb mamlūkah li-laḥām makhṣūṣah*). But they also insist that 'whoever of the tribe responds to a call [for assistance from some other section] and owes the tribe a blood-debt shall be safe [from attempts at revenge] until he returns to his house. Any action against him is an insult to the signatories and the secondary guarantors.'[26] In other words, internal disputes are to be suspended in the face of external aggression; but the only way to ensure this is by reference to the guarantors, some of whom themselves stand outside the tribe.

Sufyān's pact of fellowship was formed in difficult circumstances toward the end of the civil war. It was signed in November 1968, but within a few years had lost its force; Sufyān nowadays is notorious as a tribe that fragments very easily, each part going its own way. None the less the pact illustrates very well the way in which the abstract identity of shared tribal membership is conjured as a binding agreement. The possibility of a section opting out of a general confrontation with outsiders is forsworn. Instead a written undertaking is given that each part will always support the other and that anyone who secedes insults personally each of the signatories. Not only are internal disputes to be suspended in case of external confrontations, but an attempt is made to set the guarantors as a body over all disputes between different sections. That attempt, always centred on protection of a neutral space, seldom meets with much long-term success. The market or learned family may be protected reliably, but beyond that the sections pursue their squabbles, without which their own identity might perhaps lose its sense.

Dhū Muḥammad's agreement, which was quoted in Chapters 3 and 4, provides an impressively (indeed, uniquely) long-lived example of a pact built around protection. It has been renewed repeatedly, and perhaps developed, since the early eighteenth century, and is still often referred to nowadays, though not always enforced in full detail. At many points it draws a distinction between what is permissible among the tribe's own sections and what is permissible against other tribes. For example, 'if one of the tribesmen rustles livestock from his fellow (*jall sāḥib-hu*) on grazing land belonging to the tribesmen, then he insults the guarantors and he has no companionship [i.e. no one to call on for support]. Rustling between the tribesmen [as opposed to outsiders] is to be fined four-fold, whether much or little.' This begs the whole question of enforcement, and no doubt the extent to which the guarantors acted as a unit (rather than each just supporting his section) has varied greatly from time to time. In principle, however, there is not only a law agreed on by all concerned, but something like an Austinian sovereign; not the tribe hypostasized, but the several guarantors together.

The segmentary internal organization of the tribe is sometimes suspended (as with protecting the market; cf. Ch. 4), but sometimes it is formally included in the general agreement and thus made subordinate to an idea of unity. 'If one of the tribesmen offends against a protégé who is under the protection of a section or two sections or more then [the victim's] neighbours/protectors cannot take revenge until after the neighbours from the culprit's own section have failed to do so. If [the latter] fail to do so, then the culprit may be set upon by any of the tribe's sections.' A political system here does not simply emerge from a series of misunderstood conflicts, as many readings of the 'principle of contradiction' would insist, but is consciously elaborated by those involved. The general preamble to Dhū Muḥammad's rules makes the point clearly. The men of the tribe

> set themselves to establish the customs of their forefathers, to clarify/correct these and to clarify their rules, their brotherhood, their commitments, and who are their guarantors. . . . Their customs and commitments are established for now and forever, and what is recorded is their renewal and clarification from this date on. These were the customs of our fathers and forefathers, and are the means of settlement for whomever has a dispute with his fellow.

An agreement of this kind is a veritable constitution. At a given date men organize themselves by invoking a tribal identity and agreeing on specific laws, all of which are themselves supposed to be indefinitely old. The parallel with certain episodes of English constitutional history needs no stressing.[27]

The identity invoked is that of the tribe, the shared 'ancestor' in terms of which men are already brothers. That ancestor is opposed to others. Some impulse to uphold an internal agreement may be given by our place under others' watchful eyes (perhaps reinforced by involving some of them as secondary guarantors), but the strongest impulsion remains that of constantly facing others in circumstances of potential hostility: Dhū Muḥammad's own position, cramped into half of Jabal Baraṭ by Dhū Ḥusayn, deserves noting. Even so a form of internal cohesion can be set up, and a form that in this case is acephalous in so far as no one shaykh is in charge. But much the same means can be used to place a head to a tribal confederation.

The 'renewal' in May 1959 of *hijrah* status for Ḥusayn and Ḥamīd al-Aḥmar (the father and brother of the present shaykh of Ḥāshid) provides an example of coalition around a powerful family: 'All of Ḥāshid came according to its sections, Ṣuraymī, Khārifī, 'Idharī, 'Uṣaymī, Hamdānī, 'Amrānī, Shamūrī [i.e. al-Ashmūr], Bilād al-Rūs, al-Ḥadā, Ḥajūr, Ẓulaymah, al-Sharafayn, al-Ahnūm, and Banī Ḥadīlah of Ḥajjah, [answering to] the summons of Ḥāshid.' The reader will notice that some of these may not be Ḥāshidī at all. The agreement sweeps in elements beyond those of the set in whose name the agreement is made, and the name of the core tribe gets loosely used of the penumbra too.

They placed their signs to this document and agreed to its drafting/promulgation (*taḥrīr*) that they are brothers to each other in affairs both of tribe and state. Whoever suffers a harm that demands collective action, such as to his *mu'awwarāt* and so forth, they shall each and together answer the one who calls them. . . . Who gathers the word of all of them (*jāmi' shaml kalimat al-jamī'*) is Shaykh Ḥusayn b. Nāṣir b. Mabkhūt al-Aḥmar and his son Shaykh Ḥamīd b. Ḥusayn. In all that is done by them or befalls them, whether it raises or lowers their lot, [the tribesmen] shall do to them good and protect them from evil so far as they are able. . . . This is a renewal of preceding pacts of brotherhood . . . and renewal also of previous [agreements] giving *hijrah* status and precedence (*al-tahjīr wa-l-taqdīm*) to the honoured shaykh . . .

Brotherhood and gathering (*shaml*) around the paramount shaykh are here one and the same thing. The renewal of the shaykh's *hijrah* itself provides the articles of confederation for the tribes who recognize themselves as his protectors, much as they might do for a man of religion or for a market site. How well the confederation holds together always remains to be seen. Only months after this document was drawn up, as we saw in Chapter 7, the Imam killed Ḥusayn and Ḥamīd while the tribes' support for them was far less than total.

To dwell on the failures of agreements (whether Ḥāshid's or Sufyān's) is to risk missing the point. We are in the habit of equating power and identity; as if, for example, state and nation were the same, or as if, more generally, a collective identity, like that of a person, only is what it does. The present status of a social unit would be defined by a singular past, distinct and quite separate from that of similar units. The tribes are not conceived like this. They are instead defined against their equals, as are sections against sections, villages against villages, and even men against men. Agreements within tribes are the lineaments of power, and power adds to the honourable repute of the tribe among whom it rises, as well as adding on occasion to the security of the tribe's own members; but power is elaborated on the basis of tribal identity, and that identity far outlives power's demise, retaining the memory and repute when the substance has gone. Power does not threaten the tribe as such (tribes are not overrun or destroyed by others), and the identity of men as tribesmen derives from the more stable definitions of the units they fall in, not simply from the actions of their contemporaries. Their achievements and sufferings are made sense of in terms grounded in collective identities, but the order of event and structure is not reversed. What inequalities there may be between men have so far been registered as part of the history of states and of Imams, not of tribal identity, and disorder has not been directly tied to collective self-definition.

Formations of power rise and fall in the tribal system without changing much part of tribal classification. Tribes seldom, if ever, win or lose definitively. The course of power is of vital concern to understanding events in the short term and guessing who will support whom at present. But *sub specie aeternitatis* it does not matter, and in the comparatively long run of a thousand years it is best distinguished from the slow shift of those categories which at any one time allow power to be made sense of.

It may be that power will in future be seen by the Yemenis themselves, and even by tribesmen, *sub specie saeculorum*. The questions raised would be entirely new. But if the tribal system (to hypostasize it crudely for brevity) is to be seen as a source of problems for modern politics, it has also been capable of absorbing and indeed containing an extraordinary range of conflicts imposed on it from elsewhere in the course of the last thousand years. Its resilience has, in its own way, been as great as that of, say, the great religions and philosophies whose combinations of a few clear principles with an indefinitely wide range of practice gives the illusion of unchanging permanence. It has reduced most interventions to the terms already known to tribesmen, and for the moment it continues doing so.

NOTES

1. For a slightly fuller discussion see Dresch forthcoming *b*, from which the information in the present section is drawn. As there, I should record the considerable debt owed to Wilson's 1980 gazetteer of place-names in Upper Yemen. From a purely anthropological point of view, the historical record of Yemeni tribes, like that of Oman (see Wilkinson 1977, 1987), obliges one to rethink several assumptions. It seems fair to say that Peters's 1967 article on Cyrenaica, for instance, debunked an anthropological model of equilibrium only to transfer it to the local people, as if they were deluding themselves about an unknowable past. In the present case presumptions of equilibrium or disequilibrium are equally inapplicable (Dresch 1984*a*: 32–3).
2. This would seem to o̱mit the strip of territory along Sufyān's northern

border now held by Āl ʿammar̄, whose establishment in the area I have not been able to date. Their territory extends east and west. Between Sufyān and Khawlān b. ʿĀmir (i.e. north to south) they now set a gap of about 20 kilometres.

3. See al-Hamdānī 1968: 111–13. At least one mention (ibid. 242) associates Khārif with roughly its present location, but the others are scattered throughout the north and north-west. Khārif does, however, appear in the list of delegations from Yemen who went to the Prophet three centuries earlier (Guillaume 1955: 787; Ibn Saʿd 1905: i. 2/73; vi. 162). In the intervening period the tribe had been involved in al-Mukhtār's revolt in the Islamic borderlands of Khurāsān (al-Ḥimyarī 1916: 32; al-Ṭabarī 1968: vi. 83), and it is by no means unlikely that the name, perhaps available in Yemeni tradition, gained prominence outside Yemen before it came to designate a particular tribe on the plateau in Yemen itself.

4. Al-Ṣayad extended from Raydah to Warwar and held part of the high ground at the north end of al-Bawn which now attaches to al-Kalbiyyīn. The genealogy given al-Ṣayad in the *Iklīl* (1948: 96) is conspicuously separate from that of the main Ḥāshid tribes, but its status as part of Ḥāshid was none the less clear (see also Wilson 1980: 337). For some centuries afterwards, al-Ṣayad continues to be mentioned as an independent unit in contexts where one would nowadays expect a reference to Khārif (e.g. al-Laḥjī MS IV: 189, 250, 332). Gochenour 1984: 328–9 lists Khārif as a tribe of the early period but unfortunately gives no reference, and certainly one would need to say it is conspicuous by its absence in a great many early contexts.

5. Al-ʿUṣaymāt, who nowadays are ʿIdhar's neighbours in these lowland areas, were themselves reckoned part of ʿIdhar or as ʿIdhar's descendants (al-Hamdānī 1948: 60). It is unclear from the early sources how far their territory extended. ʿIdhar Maṭirah, to the north-east of Ṣanʿāʾ, seems not to be represented by any modern place or section name unless by that of the shaykhly family of Bayt al-ʿIdharī, which Arḥabīs tend to associate with present-day ʿIdhar. ʿIdhar Maṭirah would seem, however, to have survived in its old location until at least the twelfth century (see al-Laḥjī MS IV: 338).

6. Perhaps more plausibly, the name Ghaylān appears also in the genealogies of Murhibah and Sufyān (al-Hamdānī 1948: 139, 234). It is hard to construct a sequence that would place the name where it now is, although there is said to be a range of hills named Raḥāwā Ghaylān west of Baraṭ between al-ʿAmālisah and Āl ʿAmmār. The history of the name remains a mystery.

7. Dhū Muḥammad recognize a category of persons called *manūʿ* who attach to the 'fifths' of the tribe, may fight among themselves or for their fifth or for the tribe against outsiders, but cannot provide escort in Dhū Muḥammad's name or provide refuge for one Muḥammadi against another. They are tribesmen, but of somewhat subordinate status. The assumption is that these people were the original

inhabitants and were conquered by Dhū Muḥammad. A rather similar stratum is comprised by the *qabā'il al-wasaṭ* among Dhū Ḥusayn, and I am told (though I cannot confirm it) that such people are also to be found among the neighbouring tribes of Āl Sālim and al-'Amālisah. There is no equivalent stratum among the plateau tribes.

8. To propose a detailed sequence at this stage would be premature. For some suggestive intermediate mentions of Wāda'ah/Ṣuraym and its components, however, see e.g. al-Laḥjī MS IV:63, 211, 260 (where Khamir would seem to be Ṣuraymī), 262, 284, 293, 312; Zabārah 1952: 77, 106, 119 (where Wāda'ah and Banī Ṣuraym seem separate), 210. In an earlier publication (Dresch forthcoming *b*) I was tentative about equating Mu'mir with al-Ma'āmarah; but the small print of another document (Dresch forthcoming *a*) in fact shows the section being referred to as Mu'mir in the present century also. Khayār, in present Banī Ṣuraym, is said by its more learned members to derive from 'Ubayd b. Rabī'ah and to have once been known as Wāda'ah al-Sharq. It acquired its present name, they say, when the Imam 'Abdullāh b. Ḥamzah sent to the area for picked troops and all those selected were from this section; hence 'Khayār al-Qawm', the pick of the army.

9. The contrast might be drawn here with many African societies where collective identity is defined precisely by reference to the actions of individual persons or particular groups. Quite apart from origin myths, one has very sober sequential histories which employ this mode, as do those in Luapula valley (Cunnison 1951). Again, many African kingdoms (the Barotse, say, or the Zulu) were defined with reference to individual groups and persons, be they kings or royal clans: a singular event, such as conquest or migration, quite commonly forms the reference point of a hierarchical structure (apparent often in cosmology) which defines the collectivity itself. This seems not to occur at all widely with tribes in the Arabic Middle East: the Rwala (Musil 1928) are not defined by reference to the history, genealogy, or cosmological centrality of the Sha'lān princes, any more than Ḥāshid are defined by reference to Bayt al-Aḥmar. Tribes in the Iranic Middle East may be a different matter. One might also want to compare the apparent growth of tribes around sections in Oman (Wilkinson 1987:103 ff.), which is rather different from what one finds on the Yemeni plateau although comparable to the much smaller-scale phenomenon of shaykhs as the 'original family' of sections.

10. To confirm the point, were there space, one could look at what came before the present tribal system: that is, at the system of self-definition apparent in pre-Islamic inscriptions. There the names of noble families were given to the units they controlled. The contrast between the two systems is discussed in Dresch forthcoming *b*, but for accounts of pre-Islamic 'communes' see particularly Beeston 1972: 258 and 1976: 3; Robin 1977: 101 and 1978: 52.

11. The addition of 'such-like group' is needed because one of al-Hamdānī's examples is Ṣan'ā', which was divided between the

Shihābiyyīn and the Abnā', the descendants of the Persians who had occupied Yemen before Islam.

12. This was the point at issue in a dispute between Sufyān and Dhū Muḥammad some years ago. Just within Sufyān's territory (by most estimates) is an area known as *diyat al-sab'ah*, 'the seven men's blood-wealth'. Presumably it had been transferred as compensation some time in the indeterminately distant past. A further killing took place there and Sufyān denied responsibility. Dhū Muḥammad then applied the obvious fork: either the place is Sufyān's, in which case they owe us blood-money; or they do not owe the blood-money, in which case the place is not theirs and must presumably be ours.

13. I do not suggest that Evans-Pritchard was the first to be so vague on the question, but the phrase 'residual rights' falls squarely in a continuing tradition. To put the matter bluntly, there seem to be two separate literatures on Middle Eastern tribes, particularly on pastoral nomads: one describes the formal definition of collective sets, and the other describes the way groups use resources. The essential link would be an explicit consideration of concepts of territoriality, which is rarely made. An exception is Wilkinson 1983, which still relies analytically on Latin terminology. Wilkinson's summary of modes of territoriality and their relation to political history in Oman (1987: 116 ff., 128 ff.) is excellent. However, detailed study of local terminology and, most importantly, the way it is used remains oddly undeveloped throughout the literature. The result, whichever side one starts with, is an unrewarding problematic of 'rules' and 'exceptions'. I hope to make territoriality in tribal Yemen the subject of a separate paper.

14. Sufyān claim that their territory runs to within six or seven kilometres of al-Marāshī so that Wādī Madhāb and Wādī Sufyān are theirs, which is roughly how al-Hamdānī 1948: 221–3 depicted it. Dhū Muḥammad claim the border is at Jabal Asḥar and have done so for some time (this is where their eighteenth-century *qawā'id* place it in discussing security of roads to market). The upper reaches of Wādī Madhāb are now held by Āl 'Ammār, and the lower reaches are grazed only by Dhū Muḥammad. The upper reaches of Wādī Sufyān (east of Madhāb) are Āl Sālim's, the lower reaches are Muḥammadī, and in the middle is a Sufyānī area cut off from the rest of Sufyān. Plainly Dhū Muḥammad have moved in.

15. In this particular case there seem to be two small exceptions: Jabal Dhanayn is shared grazing for al-Ẓubr, al-Lajān, Hajar, Sāk, Bayt al-Jirbah, and al-Maḥam; Jabal 'Ajīb is shared grazing for Daḥyan, Bayt al-Yatīm, Shaybarah, Jalādī, and Maḥam al-Kalbiyyīn. In both cases the lists include villages from different fifths. In neither case are the borders unclear, however, and the different village borders can be traced quite readily, although the grazing rights are combined in these two places.

16. The rules here are much as those outlined for Bayt Ḥusayn (ch. 8). Fields are off-limits while crops are growing there, as is a *ḥaram* of ten

metres or so around them. The owners have first use of the stubble, and then their neighbours have access too after a few days.

17. The major wadis in Sufyān, from north to south, are: Wāsiṭ, Jūfān, Birkān, al-Ḥayrah, Saḥbal, Shabārik, al-Jayrah (which is a border with Ḥāshid, west of al-Ḥarf), Jazzāh, and ʿUnqān. All of these run roughly north-west to south-east and all are used by more than one *laḥmah* of Sufyān.
18. As is to be expected, this affects the distribution of shared responsibility: there is little option but for the whole tribe to share rights of escort and the like everywhere except immediately around their villages. The Baraṭ *qawāʿid*, which apply to Dhū Muḥammad and al-Maʿāṭirah but not Dhū Ḥusayn, specify that an outsider seeking refuge must be taken to 'the nearest settlement' (*aqrab ḥayy*) and rights of escort and refuge be begun from there.
19. The major units mentioned here are all, except al-Maʿāṭirah, 'fifths' of Dhū Muḥammad. Jabal Āl Ṣalāḥ would seem to be restricted grazing for the whole fifth of that name, but the others would seem in practice to be only for particular villagers who belong to the relevant fifth and actually live at the place in question.
20. To bring new land into production or sink a new well requires permission from all those who are connected to the site by shared runoff, which in settled areas means no permission is forthcoming. A well sunk on 'white land', where there is no settlement, can be accompanied by a dwelling, in which case property rights accrue but new settlement must be spaced out: the houses as far apart as they are high, and the wells as far apart as they are deep.
21. What follows here is tentative. Fighting in the area made detailed enquiries difficult. For further information on the far north-east see Steffen 1978: ii. 119 ff.
22. The connection with ʿIyāl Surayh, suggested by the diagram, might perhaps derive from a local reading of the *Ṣifah* (al-Hamdānī 1968: 111), where areas now in ʿIyāl Surayḥ are associated with Shākir. Few people know of it, and it is not politically significant. I spent ten days with a Surayḥī delegation who were mediating between Dhū Muḥammad and Dhū Ḥusayn east of Baraṭ and never once heard the connection suggested by any of them.
23. The arbitrators from Dhū Muḥammad were ʿAskar Abū Ḥarb al-Juzaylān (Dhū Mūsā) and ʿAbduh ʿIsmāʿīl Aḥmar al-Shaʿr (Āl Ṣalāḥ); those from Dhū Ḥusayn were Turkī b. Khursān (Āl Muḥammad) and ʿAlī Muḥammad al-ʿUkaymī (al-Shawlān). One might note that this is an arbitrator from each of the two main classificatory divisions of each tribe.
24. One might compare the provisions that established the original Islamic community at Medina (Serjeant 1978). Those involved in promoting the alliance themselves drew the parallel quite spontaneously with the Prophet's manœuvres, but not with any particularly 'religious' colouring.

25. The fifths and eighths become relevant when a fixed resource needs dividing. Just the same was true of Lancaster's Rwala (1981: 13) when they acquired a new farming village.

26. *Man faza' min al-qabīlah ka-mā bi-hi ṣawt wa-'alayhi dam li-l-qabīlah fa-inna-hu āmin li-ḥattā yarja' bayt-hu wa-mā waqa' fī-hī fa-'ayyab al-wajīh wa-l-rudamā'.*

27. At this point one might ask why the tribes do not produce states, or at least 'semi-states' (Runciman 1982). In part perhaps they did, as with the Banī Ḥātim or Zuray' in medieval times, and certainly with the 'Abdalī Sultans of Laḥj (Dresch forthcoming *d*). But the state is an idea as much as an organization, and in the north the idea has been usurped, as it were, by non-tribal interests, most notably the Zaydi Imamate. One should also note that cohesion turns on 'setting aside' a person or space from the run of tribal interaction, not subordinating such interaction to anything that continues throughout the generations as does a dynasty. Tribal documents put one often in mind of early English documents such as the *Dooms of Aethelberht* or the *Dooms of Wihtread*, but the extension of the King's peace to embrace all others, which one finds beginning in the later *Dooms of Alfred* or *Dooms of Edward*, has no real parallel. Only Imams and great sayyids did that, extending their peace and the writ of Islamic law from the bounds of the *hijrah* to the roads leading to it on market day, to the territories of the protecting tribes, and so on (see Puin 1984; Sālim 1982: 209 ff.; Dresch forthcoming *a*).

10 Tribes and Events in the Modern World

> As for discontentments, they are in the body politic like to humours in the natural, which are apt to gather a preternatural heat and to inflame. And let no prince measure the danger of them by this . . . whether the griefs upon which they rise be in fact great or small . . .
>
> Francis Bacon, 'Of Seditions and Troubles'

> Essentially, hierarchy is the encompassing of the contrary.
>
> Dumont, *Essays on Individualism*

In the years around 1980 the tribes were often as little subject to direct governmental control as they had been in, say, the mid-nineteenth century. Much of what happened in the short term was connected with an intense rivalry between North Yemen's neighbours, South Yemen and Saudi Arabia. Not all of it need concern us. But to ignore the wider political context would be to discount the genuine problems the North had to face and which on the whole it faced successfully. Nor would events among the tribes, such as those on which we drew in the opening chapters of the present book, make anything but a mythical sense.

Yet in the midst of this the tribesmen were passing through what one can guess is a transition. More importantly, and more exactly, the idea of transition has become relevant to Yemenis, not least to tribesmen, as it has to the people of 'developing countries' everywhere. They live, by their own estimation, in a new era.[1] The deposing of the last Imam, 'the glorious (or immortal, *khālidah*) revolution of 26 September 1962', is taken as a break with the past; and the future is ordered to such concepts as development and progress. It is here as much as in the measurable aspects of a cash economy that the difference is to be found between the Imam's time and our own.

FROM THE END OF THE CIVIL WAR TO THE TROUBLES AT JABAL ASWAD (1978)

If one sees, as one can quite reasonably, the recent political history of North Yemen as a sequence of short stages—as al-Barradūnī (1983), for instance, writes of a 'first republic', 'second republic', and 'third republic'—then al-Iryānī's government, which lasted from 1969 to 1974, appears in retrospect transitional: a stoutly republican coalition that retained none the less a great deal of the administrative style of the old regime (see Stookey 1974). It was replaced by a government with a different style,[2] and a style that has since then been developed, not forgotten or revoked.

When al-Ḥamdī took power, the first appearance to many foreign observers was that 'traditional shaykhs' were being ousted by 'progressive army officers';[3] but there is no reason in fact why shaykhs should be more traditional than other people or officers more progressive (in Yemen, the two sets of people are often from the same families), and the composition of the 'command council' set up by the 'corrective movement of 13 June (1974)' had a large tribal component. Mujāhid Abū Shawārib, for example, was a very prominent member of the council and, as we have seen, is a prominent shaykh of Khārif; two members of Bayt Abū Laḥūm were included, officers in the regular army but none the less from the shaykhly family of Nihm; so too was Aḥmad al-Ghashmī, an army officer whose brother was shaykh of Hamdān Ṣan'ā'. Lower down in the government list was Amīn Abū Ra's of Dhū Muḥammad as a minister of state, just as he had been under al-Iryānī. Ibrāhīm al-Ḥamdī himself, the President of the Command Council and thus in effect of the republic, was an army officer from a qadi family of 'Iyāl Surayḥ.

Five days after the 'corrective move' a large meeting of tribes was convened, primarily by Shaykh 'Abdullāh, at al-Mu'ammar in Hamdān Ṣan'ā' to approve and support 'the men of the new era of 13 June'. Rather oddly, this meeting gave rise to a printed pamphlet titled 'Conference of the Tribes of Yemen: On the Path of Progress'.[4] The men who attended came from a far wider area than is normally considered 'tribal', even from the Tihāmah and Lower Yemen. Shaykh 'Abdullāh's opening speech was followed by an address from Aḥmad 'Alī al-Maṭarī, then addresses from certain others, and the proceedings closed with a statement from Amīn Abū Ra's.

The detailed provisions for establishing a 'permanent conference of tribes' and its subcommittees are prefaced with a long historical passage, quite unexceptionable to the modern eye but highly indicative of how different the conceptual background of the modern world is from that outlined in Chapters 5 and 6.

> Whereas our people had lived for long centuries in the shadow of eras of oppression and darkness, during which there sat on the throne of government persons who kept fighting among themselves . . .
>
> This people (*sha'b*) was stamped with the mark of infighting as if God had created them and their sons to fight each other and to struggle among themselves . . .
>
> Our people continued even through the ages of darkness to seize every opportunity to show its true face and to express its aspiration for stability, peace, prosperity, affection, and good. . . .

Attached to a strong invocation of Yemen's Islamic identity and its adherence to God's law, this theme of the break with the past is then developed in an account of successive struggles against the last Imams. In the vanguard of this movement, says the pamphlet, were the tribes, and the passage culminates in an invocation of the prosperous future.

> In order to put an end to all aspects of backwardness (*takhalluf*) and to resolve all obscurities and tribal differences, to settle all contradictions between tribes by organized, peaceful means . . .
>
> To establish a society ruled by justice, equity, love, brotherhood, and the good of all, the men of the Yemeni tribes resolve . . .

These are the major shaykhs speaking, situated as they are in the midst of the 'tribal differences' to which they refer and from which comes much of their own importance. The rhetoric of progress in the contemporary period is not anyone's particular property, and if the rhetoric of an older orthodoxy did much to constitute the world in a particular way (Chapter 5), so too will this.

It is the very obviousness of such concerns that indicates their power. The cynic and the empiricist equally will point to what has not changed in relations of dominance or competition since Imamic times (this amounts, it is true, to a great deal); but the more subtle shift in what such relations mean is at least as important, and one might quote several local tribal agreements from the following years which unselfconsciously use the same language. The phrases quoted are only illustrations of ideas that in fact define the modern era. The collapse of al-Ḥamdī's particular government is therefore less striking in the focus of an anthropologist than in that of, say, a political scientist.

Al-Ḥamdī was trapped between the demands of North Yemen's neighbours. As much to win himself space for manœuvre, one might think, as for any other reason, he successively dismissed or made marginal a great many of his colleagues: some of the members of Bayt Abū Laḥūm were squeezed out of government as early as October 1974; Mujāhid Abū Shawārib was dismissed in June 1975 while he was on an official visit to China; the Consultative Assembly was finally suspended in October (its head, Shaykh ʿAbdullāh, withdrew to Khamir; Abū Ra's of Dhū Muḥammad remained a minister of state); and there emerged in due course what was in effect a border between the government and those tribes whose leaders had before been most closely involved with Ṣanʿāʾ (see Stookey 1978: 278–80).[5] Some of the Bakīl tribes who had been royalist in the civil war, by contrast, came to think of themselves as al-Ḥamdī's allies.

Al-Ḥamdī himself was gradually engrossed by a populist style, stressing his connection with the local 'co-operatives' (*taʿāwuniyyāt*), establishing a Supreme Corrective Committee to attack corruption, and travelling extensively where he could to meet local people. Especially in later years, he often set aside his military uniform in favour of a short-sleeved sun suit, which may itself have been Egyptian tailoring but contributed to a much more widely recognizable image of popular reform. His career became little short of tragic. Even in Lower Yemen, where the rhetoric of reform had a widespread attraction, sadly little was achieved. In Upper Yemen, his disputes with one set of men (a great many of whom were sympathetic to his general aims) involved his alliance with a second set no different in type than the first. The rhetoric of reform at the centre, disconnected from any concrete programme, left a moral vacuum across which tribes might dispute as pointlessly as they did in Umayyad Syria. In October 1977, 'Ibrāhīm' was murdered. Aḥmad al-Ghashmī took power, trying in his turn to strike a balance; but problems between tribes now multiplied to an extent not seen since the civil war. This is roughly the point at which the field-work started on which the present book is based.

Even before reaction to al-Ḥamdī's murder began in Lower Yemen, a meeting of tribesmen was convened in 'Iyāl Surayḥ by an army officer named Mujāhid al-Quhālī and then, only a week after al-Ḥamdī's death, another meeting was held near 'Amrān, to which several Bakīl shaykhs came. A delegation of them went into Ṣan'ā' demanding to know who the murderers were. When they returned with no proper answer, al-Quhālī sought allies from the immediate area (he sent forty rifles to Muḥammad Badr al-Dīn of 'Iyāl Yazīd, for instance, who promptly sent them back) and then called on tribes much further away, such as Sufyān and Wā'ilah, sending cases of weapons from the stores at 'Amrān and Thulā. In early 1978 there was an attempt to start a general war between Ḥāshid and Bakīl as the first move in toppling al-Ghashmī's government.

Men from Sufyān tried to provide a convincing *casus belli* by burning one of their own vehicles near al-Jirāf in the territory of Banī Ṣuraym, and a close relative of Abū Shawārib (Khārif) and his truck taken from him in Sufyān's territory. As the tension increased, certain of the Ḥāshid shaykhs, still based at Khamir as they had been in al-Ḥamdī's time, called out their tribesmen and posted them near Ḥāshid's borders, to the south facing 'Iyāl Yazīd and 'Iyāl Surayh, to the north facing Sufyān. There was no secret at all about the guns being issued to Bakīl, and at a meeting of Bakīl where several disaffected army officers from 'Amrān were present (most of them paratroops) a Sufyānī shaykh finally broke his own dagger sheath and called on the Bakīl tribes for support. Fighting started at Jabal Aswad, on the border between al-'Uṣaymāt (Ḥāshid) and Sufyān (Bakīl).

The causes of the war were all derived from central government politics, and known to be so; but the forms of provocation were eminently tribal, and so too were the forms of settlement. The sayyids and qadis of *hijrah* Ḥūth immediately interposed themselves by slaughtering bulls. The brief cease-fire they imposed collapsed, and sporadic firing broke out again between the two thousand men or so who had gathered on each side, with Bakīl holding the mountain ridge that overlooks Khaywān while Ḥāshid held the wadi below them and some mountain tops west of the road. Both sides were heavily armed. Recoilless artillery on trucks was brought up, together with machine guns and a number of mortars of civil war provenance, and the fighting intensified as more men arrived from outlying tribes.

At the time the fighting started, Aḥmad ʿAlī al-Maṭarī was in Khamir. His tribe, Banī Maṭar, is just west of Ṣanʿāʾ, rather removed from most of the plateau's squabbles, and he himself, since the end of the civil war, has often played a mediating role between conflicting tribes or between tribes and government. He immediately went to Ṣanʿāʾ. The President, al-Ghashmī, was by most accounts unwilling to be found; but al-Maṭarī quickly gathered a *lajnah* or committee of shaykhs and brought them north to intervene. They started to arrive within hours of the first fighting, each accompanied by a group of followers in trucks streaming white truce flags. A truce was finally imposed at the end of the third day. Ḥāshid marched out after dark in a long column, chanting their *zawāmil* and dancing with daggers in the moonlight until they camped at Khaywān. Bakīl withdrew in similar style on the other side of the mountains and camped at Ḥarf Sufyān.

The imposition of the truce was of its nature public. The discussion itself was punctuated with the usual gestures, proferring and returning rifles and daggers, holding out the skirt hem to gain a hearing, plucking twigs of old *qāt* from the floor to be held between thumb and forefinger as one made a point and spelled out one's position. The rhythm of argument was much as would be seen in any local dispute. Guarantors were at last appointed and a hundred rifles collected from the two sides for surety by committees of arbitrators, who themselves no doubt felt some community of interest in national politics but whose role in the proceedings was conceived in purely tribal terms.[6] The containment of the dispute in these terms, as men 'gave their faces', was at the same time the temporary displacement of the terms of party or faction politics.

FROM AL-GHASHMĪ'S DEMISE TO THE MEETING AT BĪR AL-MAHĀSHIMAH (1981)

In the aftermath of these events, al-Quhālī, the disaffected army officer, was exiled to Czechoslovakia, and the National Democratic Front, with South Yemeni help, began to organize a serious struggle in the North against al-Ghashmī's government (Peterson 1982: 122, 124). For a time, ʿAbdullāh ʿAbd al-ʿĀlim, who had been one of the original Command Council in 1974 and remained a member under al-Ghashmī, stayed in Ṣanʿāʾ. He was sympathetic to al-

Quhālī and was commander of the paratroops, a unit recruited in those days almost entirely from Lower Yemen, but he had links with certain Upper Yemeni shaykhs as well; for a time his men held Jabal Samā, near Ṣan'ā' airport, which overlooks southern Arḥab where some at least of the shaykhs were strongly opposed to al-Ghashmī. When the Command Council was dissolved, 'Abd al-'Ālim withdrew to Lower Yemen and then was forced into South Yemen by army units under 'Alī 'Abdullāh Ṣāliḥ. When al-Ghashmī was murdered in June 1978 it was 'Alī 'Abdullāh who took over the Ṣan'ā' government. He still holds power at the time of writing, some ten years later.

The National Democratic Front, backed by the South, had an agenda of land reform and overthrowing shaykhs that won support over the next several years in Lower Yemen and encouraged quite vigorous guerrilla warfare. At times it won support from further afield, particularly from Libya. But it also won support from several shaykhs and tribes in Upper Yemen, whom one can fairly say, despite their radical rhetoric, were at odds with the Ṣan'ā' government because they thought other tribes and shaykhs than themselves were in receipt of the government's favours. The results of this polarity were sometimes farcical. A dispute between different factions of Bayt Sinān over land in their home area of Arḥab, for instance, led to one noted shaykh of this family going not just to Aden for help against his relatives, but all the way to Tripoli. Every minor dispute, within tribes or between them, seemed to threaten recourse to great political factions and indeed to opposed foreign governments. Almost everyone, it seemed, could go to the South and get weapons to fight the supposed reactionaries or to the Saudis and get money to oppose the supposed godless communists; and not a few men, particularly in the east, went to both in turn and made handsome profits.

At the same time, the remittance economy was booming. The tribes were crossed by the routes along which consumer goods came from Saudi Arabia or the Gulf, and as we saw in Chapter 8, men in several tribes had invested in large Mercedes lorries for the business. Some of the trade involved smuggling. The routes on which goods were smuggled (coming in mainly from the north) and those on which arms were smuggled (coming in mainly from the south) crossed and recrossed in the undermarcated east of the country before running up to the northern plateau. Tribal borders, of their nature, can be 'closed' or 'guarded' against one's neighbours, and the period provided a continual object lesson in not reducing social facts to individual motive. The closures and reopenings of borders, whether within or between tribes, went on to form what patterns they did, while the people involved would 'explain' each event in divergent terms of political allegiance, commercial advantage, and indefinitely old blood-debt.

As early as 1978, the introduction of such devices as drilled wells and diesel pumps was also provoking new disputes in several areas, disputes of the kind touched on in Chapter 9. But the forms of dispute were still those of territoriality, mediation, and guaranty. The tide of prosperity did little to undermine these forms (in some respects it strengthened them), and even the absence of large numbers of men as emigrant labourers offered little distraction: indeed, their coming and going brought them up constantly against tribal identities. Within each tribe or section territory, also, men returning with cash savings bought land, built new houses, and chewed more *qāt* of better quality than they had done; but they also looked to see feeder roads put into their area, clinics and, far from least important, schools, all of which things were thought to be the government's gift. The government at the time very probably lacked the means to meet half these expectations, and in any case it was trapped by rivalry between other states into fighting for control of its own territory. To detail the fights within North Yemen would, unfortunately, require naming people whose interests have since changed.

In February 1979 a second border war with the South broke out. The regular army of the North performed poorly, and forces backed by the South made considerable initial gains of territory, but where the anti-Ṣan'ā' forces were halted it was largely by northern tribesmen who were levied for the purpose. In places they pushed their more heavily armed opponents back across the border. Elsewhere they fared less well. Stories were told of their leaders all but weeping with rage at their internal disputes, at their abandonment by regular army units, or, in more than one case, at regular troops deliberately firing on tribal groups with whom they had political differences. But those who fought were paid well. The sudden prominence of Yemen in the world's headlines coincided with the provision of military largesse from outside, and for several days huge American aircraft shuttled tanks and wire-guided missiles into Ṣanʻā', while Saudi aircraft flew in quantities of ammunition.[7] Much of the ammunition ended up in tribal hands.

The war was ended by mediation from other Arab states. Another declaration was made of the Yemens' intention to unify, but in fact little was done and the struggle soon resumed, rather grimly at times in guerrilla fighting in Lower Yemen and quite inconclusively in the endlessly mediated tribal disputes north of Ṣanʻā' which continued intermittently for the next three years. In 1982, due partly to events in the wider Arab world and to South Yemen's near bankruptcy, but due also to the much better organization of North Yemen's regular army, the Front in Lower Yemen was at last suppressed. In 1983, correspondingly, Upper Yemen was surprisingly quiet. The road blocks were far less frequent than they had been. Disputes between tribes were contained more easily. A considerable effort was being made to involve previously dissident tribal elements in the state's system of patronage, and some at least of the northern shaykhs who had been with the Front were now being paid to raise units of the popular army.[8]

Poems were still in circulation from a year or so earlier, and extracts from two of Sufyān's poems will give the flavour.

Greetings from Sufyān, to spread among all the comrades,
From Wā'ilah, al-Buqʻ, ʻAmmār, and Arḥab, Dahm, Surayḥ, al-Ghūlah,
    Banī ʻAbd, and al-Jabal [i.e. ʻIyāl Yazīd].
We raised the sign of war in the central areas,
And we are the ones with our heads held high.
You hirelings, we'll go to our own land but tell you this:
That you've no say in what we do. The army's not much, compared to the
    people.
Say, force doesn't much affect us. Our enemy's still a disgrace to us
If we don't take our due revenge.
The people of Yemen are one, the north and the south and the [eastern]
    sands.[9]

The image of Yemeni unity (i.e. between Ṣanʻā' and Aden) was widely used in such rhetoric. Those shaykhs of Sufyān who were active in the Front (not all were by any means) could hardly have been less wary of the end result of unity with the South than were the shaykhs they were fighting. But the prospect was remote. The more immediate prospect was always of a greater share in the patronage of an unreformed Ṣan'ā' government, and the rhetoric was exciting while it lasted.

The last half of the second poem goes further. Having warned al-Aḥmar of Ḥāshid that 'the unity of the people will pass judgment against him', the poem boasts of fighting at Wādī Banā near the southern border:

> Banā how are you, now that we have gone
> And you remain? Get at them again with a line of fire.
> Tell them, Banā, though we've gone we'll be back.
> We'll always kindle the red revolution.[10]

This sounds very stirring. When one talked with these self-styled red revolutionaries in 1983 they said laughingly that the South had given them guns and money; now they hoped Ṣan'ā' would. The difference with Lower Yemen cannot be stressed too firmly. There the issue of local land-reform was immensely serious, and it remains so now, as it does in the western mountains and in the Tihāmah also. In Upper Yemen, by contrast, inequalities of wealth and power depend on resources outside the area, and reform or development are also felt to depend upon outside aid.

Already in the year or two before the Front's collapse, there had been an attempt, not by the South, but by the Saudis to pull together the disaffected Bakīl tribes. The attempt had centred around Nājī b. 'Abd al-'Azīz al-Shāyif of Dhū Ḥusayn, who was promoted as paramount shaykh.[11] At the end of 1980 he had sent a xeroxed form letter to the shaykhs of Bakīl.

> The gallant Shaykh———. God preserve you. Peace be on you, and the mercy of God and His blessings. You know and we know, as does everyone, what state the affairs of Bakīl have come to. Almost twenty years have gone by without any plan being formulated. . . .
>
> Despite the expenditure (*badhal*) and the contribution ('*aṭā*, gift, donation) [that Bakīl has made] and its ample share (*musāhamah sakhiyyah*) in the course of events . . . we are still looking for a return (*mardūd*) on that great contribution and that excellent share in so many fields. . . .

If fortune has not favoured us with success, says the letter, this can only be due to our lack of unity. The contrast, though not drawn explicitly, is with certain of the Ḥāshid tribes who for some years already had, with exaggeration, spoken of themselves as 'like a unit in the army' (Dresch 1984*a*: 43). Bakīl too must 'make one our word,' says the letter, and its shaykhs must 'tear up the roots of mutual estrangement' when they meet at Bīr al-Mahāshimah. They have responsibilities before this generation and those to come after: the confederation's standing must be again what it once was, and their history (*ta'rīkh*) is 'full of glorious deeds' (*malī' bi-l-mafākhir*). Note again this unselfconscious invocation of history (not 'renewal of custom') which the documents we cited in earlier chapters did not, and no doubt could not, make.

The meeting was held on 11 January 1981 in the wastes east of Baraṭ (there is a blurred video film of the occasion), and a document was issued which again deserves brief quotation.

> Each of the peoples of the earth glories in its own heritage (*turāth*), prides itself on its distinctive attributes (*mumayyizāt*), strives to maintain its own character, and sacrifices what it has in the cause of its beliefs and its dignity (*karāmah*), the unity of its lands, and its self-rule. Neglect of any part of this is considered a betrayal of the nation and a crime against history (*khayānah waṭaniyyah wa-jarīmah ta'rīkhiyyah*). . . .
>
> Our Muslim Yemeni people is at the head of such peoples in its adherence to its origins (*tamassukan bi-aṣālati-hi*), its values, its beliefs, and opinions despite its cultural ambitions and its aspirations toward what is best by comparison with all [previous] periods and ages. . . .

This oration was hurriedly, and not beautifully, composed; the language wanders badly at points; yet it is perfectly natural now that it should turn on the question of 'authenticity' (*aṣālah*), on the crux between past and present, which no pre-revolutionary tribal rhetoric took the slightest note of. The related terms *aṣl* and *aṣīl* referred then, as they still do in most tribal documents, to 'authenticity of descent', to one's standing as a tribesman opposed to others. The complementary issue now, in part, is one of collective identity in a world where one might question what it means to be a tribesman at all and question, with reference to other nations, what it means to be Yemeni and what one's place should be within the national whole.

As was to be expected in the circumstances (there were Saudi observers present), the references to the Law of God are numerous, and the rhetoric of immediate national unity with the South ('these tunes played on *mizmār*s') is opposed strongly.

> Promoting the unity of a people already unified is contradictory to nature (*mukhālif li-l-ṭabī'ah al-mafrūḍah*), and its results have been dissension in

our ranks and gaps (*nawāfidh*) in the structure [of the nation] through which flow the exploitation of others' leanings and desires, and the pursuit [solely] of wealth (*al-mīl ilā l-istithrā'*) . . .

Throughout the post-revolutionary period, they claim, Bakīl have been neglected. In a nationalist style one might encounter in any number of countries, the blame is put on unspecified deceivers who 'climbed the walls of [foreign] embassies' to sell the peoples' birthright in return for nothing but national humiliation. It is they who have set tribe against tribe. It is they who have condemned Bakīl, that vast portion of the one Yemeni family, to isolation and exclusion (*'uzlah wa-ḥirmān*); and Bakīl have now met to escape these narrow straits for the wide expanse where all Yemenis can freely join hands.

The first resolution was that only dependence on God's Book and the Prophet's usage could secure the cohesive brotherhood of all Bakīl; but, with that aim in mind, Nājī b. 'Abd al-'Azīz al-Shāyif of Dhū Ḥusayn must be paramount shaykh. All of them would now pull together to regain their historical place. Clause seven then makes the demand specific.

On account of the need of the community and the nation to build an army capable of protecting the country and defending Yemeni and Arab rights, Bakīl is enjoined to raise 50,000 soldiers and officers, leaving to its other brothers in Yemen [in other words, Ḥāshid, though no one says so] the decision whether to raise a similar number. The men of Bakīl undertake to provide that number of their sons under the supervision of the shaykh of shaykhs, Nājī. . . . Every effort will be made to secure aid for their necessities and expenses.

To call the demand extravagant would be overpolite. In fact the government side-stepped the problem gracefully, finally inviting Nājī into Ṣan'ā', where he built a huge house, providing him no doubt with a generous stipend, and at the same time giving responsibility for popular army units directly to different Bakīl shaykhs, not least of them 'Abdullāh Dāris of Dhū Muḥammad.[12] The conjoined conceptions of national identity, popular progress, and massive state patronage remain none the less salient. To probe their implications we can best look briefly at a more traditional concern of anthropology, the question of 'exchange' and of 'the gift'.

RECIPROCITY, GIFTS, AND THE MORAL BOUNDARY

> Behold the fowls of the air; for they sow not, neither do they reap, nor gather into barns; yet your heavenly Father feedeth them . . .
>
> Matthew 6: 26

> . . . with what judgement ye judge, ye shall be judged, and with what measure ye mete, it shall be measured to you again.
>
> Matthew 7: 2

Tribesmen and shaykhs have always squabbled over wealth and over patronage from rulers ('sons of dirhams and dinars' a hostile witness called them in the nineteenth century), but the setting in which they do so has changed. With the emergence of the cash economy, the payment of wages or crop-shares to peasants elsewhere in Yemen has risen to the point where one can no longer extract great wealth from the west or south; and the shift of the moral boundary to include the whole Yemeni people makes brute exploitation in any case inadmissible. Yet wealth is still sought which must come, as it always did, from elsewhere; if need be, from outside the country. The shift of the moral boundary coincides also with a new set of questions among the tribes themselves which affect rather more than is usually reckoned 'economic'.

Generosity among tribesmen is usually confined within a logic of place. A guest, for example, is due all you can give him precisely because he is in your care; and were you in his care, he would give what he can. When both of you, by contrast, are in your respective places and thus opposed to each other, transactions can only take the form of debt to be repaid, or recuperated if need be by violence. The moral good, as it were, is limited.[13] Where that logic is denied and one is given things in a setting where neither hospitality nor opposition is apt, then the implication seems to be that the donor is giving what is not really his. The more one takes, indeed, the more one expects, since the man who gives is plainly favoured and cannot be drawing on those around him but has gained what he has by good fortune; all of which used once to coincide with the fact that wealth came from outside the tribal system, from the west or from Lower Yemen.

This conjunction of possibilities, rather differently ordered than in our own scheme of obligation, recurs in the minutiae of everyday life and in such extravagant settings as Bakil's claim for government pay.[14] There are two distinct axes of moral transaction: on the one hand, claims to debt of quite niggling exactitude (a matter of refusing subordination by so much as a pennyweight), and, on the other, a seemingly endless stream of largesse that gives its donors little hold upon those receiving it and does not at all imply subordination. Which axis of transaction is applicable is determined not by the particular objects given, nor by the particular men, but by the setting in which the latter act.

Writing about the civil war, Nājī (1977: 221) quite fairly called money and guns 'the two things that make tribesmen's mouths water', and firearms are still a prominent part of the largesse tribesmen seek, whether handed out by shaykhs as a private donation or issued by the army and not returned. Weapons can be bought and sold freely. When they are bought and sold between tribesmen, however, it is through 'weak' (non-tribal) intermediaries. There is nothing more typical of markets in the north than the stall or shop-front where guns, ammunition, and daggers are piled always together with jewellery, silver coins, and paper money, the currency dealer being also the arms dealer and not himself a tribesman.[15] So long as guns are convertible wealth they are treated as separate from the tribesmen who will one day own them, and the tribesmen themselves are kept separate from one another.

When a tribesman owns a weapon it is his. To take it from him by force is usually recognized in custom as a distinct offence called *shaqdh* (Dresch 1987*a*: 84), and it is no imposition to see rifles and daggers as part of the tribesman's person. Correspondingly, the worth of such items is high. And a weapon is always handed back. It is held for a time as a pledge of its owner's good faith or commitment and is then returned to him, not passed on to a third party so as finally to leave the system or so as to return through a circuit of indirect exchange. The token of a person's honour is returned directly. It is a temporary loan, and is usually part only of a direct exchange (that is, back and forth between two parties).

This exchange of weapons shows always the two qualities of publicity and temporality one finds in the Qur'ānic view of contract, which itself is concordant with many latter-day exchanges, whether of tokens, money, or goods.[16]

O you who believe. When you contract a debt for a specified time, write it down. Have a scribe write it down between you fairly. . . . Have two witnesses from your men attest it . . . so that if one of them should be satisfied to err, the other will remind them. . . . And if you barter among yourselves, have witnesses . . . (Qur'ān 2: 282)

The contrast is clear enough with what one might think of as more 'Maussian' societies (see Mauss 1970), where elements of the social order are defined by relations of exchange between them and debts therefore sustained, perhaps indefinitely, without reference to third parties. Here it is only the immediate exchange of merchandise actually present at the transaction (*tijārah ḥāḍirah*) that can properly proceed unwitnessed.

A widely quoted passage from Bourdieu (1977: 171) seems therefore to have part of the matter backwards, in that 'self-interest' is allowed to obscure the part these witnesses ideally play and a common time-scale of the analyst's devising is attributed to tribesmen.

If it is true that the lapse of time interposed is what enables the gift or counter-gift to be seen and experienced as an inaugural act of generosity, without any past or future, i.e. without *calculation*, then it is clear that . . . objectivism destroys the specificity of all practices which, like gift exchange, tend or pretend to put the law of self-interest into abeyance. A rational contract would telescope into an instant a transaction which gift-exchange disguises, by stretching it out in time.[17]

But the gift that appears generous does indeed dispense with a determinate time-frame. Were one to look at great donors as 'buying loyalty', one would have to admit that they are very bad at it: Shaykh Nājī's generosity, for instance, brought him little, and the same might be said of many other figures more successful than he in national politics. Again, the hospitality shown outsiders constitutes part of an 'undifferentiated exchange' (Pitt-Rivers 1977: 100, 104), which of its nature cannot be tallied because the set of men involved in it is in no way bounded.

The set of standard equivalences which Bourdieu would invoke to produce an 'account' of all men's relations is produced by the ideology of economics. Whether or not the men ever meet, the 'market' guarantees their equivalence or ranks them by such means as wages, much as does the uniform sovereignty of a Weberian state. But this general conception is not constructed by the tribes. The meeting of two men or groups is instead a contingency.[18] The supposedly rational mode of instantaneous transaction is common merchant practice;[19] but tribesmen have usually avoided it by the use of 'weak' intermediaries, as they still do to a remarkable extent, and thus avoided the very question of a balance of interest. Even now, when tribesmen buy and sell directly with each other, they do so 'at market', in a context set aside. Moreover, men are not only equal morally but are equally entitled to judge, so in all such settings two claims to valuation are brought together; and the question of balance is instituted precisely by the adoption of some determinate lapse of time (*ajalin musamman*, as the Qur'ān has it), which connects determinate exchange partners whose relation must be witnessed publicly.

To understand the issue a clear distinction is needed between abstract principles and concrete cases of settlement: the first are timeless and the second calendrical. Abstract principles are embodied in language. The lexical equivalence between the disgraceful action of the wrong-doer and the insult suffered by the person wronged has already been noted (both are *'ayb*, and so too is the payment that requites this), but such equivalences in fact are common: *gharāmah*, for example, is the loss inflicted and also the payment that requites it; the same is true of *naqṣ*, *naqā'*, and *ḥashm* in several contexts. Such terms as *gharīm* and *khaṣīm* ('opponent' and 'antagonist') are of course applied symmetrically; but more generally one encounters pairs of phrases such as *ahl al-qatīl* and *ahl al-qātil* ('the victim's people' and 'the killer's people') or *al-khā'if* and *al-mukhīf* ('one fearing', i.e. fearing revenge, and 'one causing fear', seeking revenge) all of which denote couplets linked by moral symmetry.

Concrete settlements are examples of usage and thus not specified fully by the terms deployed, although the tribesmen's presumption is that in fact they must be. The care for exactitude is noteworthy. One of the more common types of document concerning the supposed rules of customary law (usually hidden away, one might note, as if secret and esoteric) is the list of wound prices, such as this fragment from Sufyān which was first written out in 1892 and recopied most recently in 1980:

> As for wounds that are *jā'ifah*, in other words, penetrate the interior of the body, these require one-third of the blood-money; and each tooth a half-tenth [i.e. a twentieth], and every joint of a finger twenty-six and one quarter [silver riyals], except the thumb which is a twentieth of the blood-money. . . . A swelling (*wārimah*, a 'goose egg') of any seriousness is four

less an eighth on the head and half that on the body. . . . A bloody wound of the lesser sort (*dāmiyyah ṣughrā*) from which blood does not freely flow is five [riyals] less a half of one eighth if on the head. . . . A cutting wound (*bādiʿah*) which only splits the flesh is sixteen riyals less one quarter if to the head. . . .

And so on. The elaboration is extraordinary. These lists are in effect long meditations on damage to the body and on the precise recompense which would balance that damage. But the same kind of hair-splitting detail recurs in any dispute over damage to property, sales of land, or unbrokered exchange of goods. The results of actual dispute and arbitration are often as seemingly precise.[20]

The process of 'paying for what has perished' restores balance. But this takes place, as we saw in an earlier chapter, within a structure of containment. It is here that the movement is made from abstract to concrete, from general to particular, and back, the difference being marked by the terms used. The abstract relation between men or tribes that the anthropologist discerns is not registered or named by tribesmen (it remains unthought as the presupposition of what is said and done); the relation formed by an unpaid debt and expressed in conflict, however, is called *ʿalāqah*, and it is this which must be 'cut' in settlement; the cutting is made by forming a different kind of tie, called *ʿalqah*, between the particular men at odds and particular others now made answerable for their conduct and safety. The resumption of balance is then made by a timed set of payments. The ties of guaranty are only severed when these payments are completed and those at odds are again quite separate, when, as Yemenis say, 'there is nothing between them' (*mā bayna-hum shay*'):[21] the question of equality is then no longer at issue, and the prescriptive equivalence of moral units can be taken again as given.

What happens, therefore, is this. The moral equivalence between men and between their respective tribes or sections can only be displaced temporarily, that is, 'for a time'. The proceedings at arbitration are carefully dated, witnessed, and signed to specify not only the precise point at issue, but the time for which connections last. The settlement is snipped out, as it were, from the equivalence of opposed units, which itself is timeless. It has the status of a transient event that takes its sense from the apparently unchanging order of tribal classification (how that order itself in fact shifts was shown in Chapter 9); and arbitration is individual in the very broad sense used by Pocock (1971: 102, 109, and *passim*), that is, as something separable from the collective and the unremarked. By contrast with many ethnographies, however, the collective and unremarked is not a representation of a bounded moral unit, but instead is the lack of 'relations' between autonomous men (Dresch 1987*b*).[22] It is autonomy that 'for a time' is surrendered along with one's rifle of right or judgment. On neither side of that process may equivalence be summed on a common time-scale.

The assumption of nationalist language, such as that in the documents from al-Muʿammar or from Bīr al-Mahāshimah, is of course quite different. A ranking between units is at issue always, in that all are now part of a common history and lead a parallel existence within the national whole, and this sensibility recurs at every level of identity from the family through tribes to the two whole confederations. The nation or people (*shaʿb*) is itself now an individual, related to others like it by problems of equivalence ('Each of the peoples of the earth . . . its own heritage . . . its distinctive attributes') and related to its members by an identity grounded in a single past ('long centuries in the shadow of oppression' . . . 'its adherence to its origins' . . . 'its aspirations toward what is best . . .'). Within this larger whole the relation of particular event to collective order (apparent equally until now in dispute and donation) would, were the implications of the rhetoric pursued, be collapsed and entirely rebuilt. The old presumption of equality (where no measurement was ever made) would have to be realized politically in so far as the separate fortunes of indefinitely fragmented tribal units were all subject to one valuation. A society 'ruled by justice, equity . . . and the good of all', as the meeting at al-Muʿammar put it some years ago, would need to be built by a single authority. The tribes would become mere factions, and their conflicts would require explaining in terms other than collective debt; or the tribal identities which, in effect, are timeless, would cease to be of major relevance as men adhered to factions and to patronage of a different kind.

To break apart this eminently modern 'total social fact' is perhaps not useful. In particular cases it may appear that 'economics' produces the effects in question: the rise of a cash economy and of wage-labour. In others it may seem that 'politics' is the major issue: the spread of a state in which all men are equal before the law and the law is defined by national sovereignty. In Western history, one suspects, the 'individualism' of the state more often preceded that of the market than the other way around; but here the mere idea of either is enough to suggest revaluation of one's place in the world by reference to other countries and to people far beyond one's own. 'Religion' has the same effect, in that a universalizing view of Islam becomes compelling in modern contexts. The 'traditional' concerns of exchange and of self-definition are simply a point at which a very general conception is refracted clearly.

Bakīl's meeting at Bīr Mahāshimah, it will be remembered, sought a 'return' on their 'expenditure' and 'share' or 'participation' (*musāhamah*) in national life. This latter term, 'participation', or any equivalent for it, is conspicuously absent from older tribal documents, where the concern is with apportioning debts and responsibilities, not at all with 'taking part' in some larger whole. Bakīl, however, are now presented as a unit symmetrically related to the nation (expenditure and return; *badhal* and *mardūd*), precisely as they claim to be part of 'the one united Yemeni family' whose prosperity is in God's gift; the resolution of the contradiction by blaming 'deceivers' linked to foreign powers seems almost inevitable.

Unity seems the key to success. The same questions are now posed in Yemen, within tribes or between them, that recur elsewhere in the tribal parts of the Middle East: questions of particularism and of universalism (Peters 1976: 10, 13; Eickelman 1977: 53 and 1987: 47) which are sharpened by travel abroad, by radio and television news, and by increasing literacy, but are not the products solely of any one of these. 'Participation' in the nation and the course of progress is now the form of rural as well as urban modernity. This raises new questions in turn, primarily questions of what difference signifies. To set these out, without lapsing too far into abstractions, we should next look at disputes between Ḥāshid tribes who, in Bakīl's estimation, had established some measure of unity already.

INSOLUBLE PROBLEMS AND HIDDEN HANDS

Several years ago, perhaps around 1970, a dispute began between Dhū Jaktām (part of Sallāb in al-'Uṣaymāt) and al-'Aqīdah (part of

Dhū Qāsim in ʻIdhar). The squabble was pursued near the border of the two tribes close to Sūq Maḥnūsh in the lowlands between Ḥūth and Shahārah, and some half-dozen men were killed; but the two tribes, ʻIdhar and al-ʻUṣaymāt, were not involved as wholes. A minor section of one was left to dispute with just as minor a section of the other. It is quite typical of such disputes that no one can now point definitively to how it began—the equality of opposition between tribes in the present means that the past is an indefinite series of replies to some presumed provocation. Certainly there were fights over grazing. An attempt by a family of al-ʻUṣaymāt to build a house that overlooked ʻIdhar's borders is also widely cited. But the troubles then broadened in disputes over al-Ḥayjah, an area of lightly wooded grazing on the borders between al-ʻUṣaymāt and ʻIdhar near the airstrip at al-Qaflah.

Somewhere in this general area were large tracts of land that had once belonged to the deposed royal family, and particularly to Prince Ḥasan who owned a tract of several thousand orange trees now defunct. Shaykh ʻAbdullāh of Ḥāshid is said to have acquired much of this land. His close partisans say the claim is ridiculous because all the royal land reverted to the republican government; those less attached to him say this only makes it worse, that the land which should be the government's has been purloined by the shaykh; and the possibility of a harmlessly legal purchase (which no doubt was what it was) seems to have been forgotten by all the factions in their enthusiasm for a simple story. A person is needed to make the story work. There is no public version of the past and no tribunal to define who stands where at present, so the vacuum of knowledge is filled by stories of who must have done what under the table, or 'under the blanket' as Yemenis have it. In the present case it was some time before this logic had its effect.

The disputes around al-Ḥayjah drew in ʻIdhar and al-ʻUṣaymāt as wholes, but as mediators, not combatants. Shaykhs from both sides (Fayshī, Abū Shawṣā, al-Dawḥamī, and others) imposed a six-month truce, the guarantors from both tribes being joined together (*shabkan*) in overseeing those who were particularly at odds. When the truce ended, the fighting broke out on a larger scale. The two tribes, not just a village or two from each, were involved. A flurry of exchanged rifles ensued, with parts of each tribe trying still to stand aside, other parts being pulled together, truces being formed and severed between tribes and within them.

While 'Idhar and al-'Uṣaymāt were at truce with each other (or rather, guaranteeing the peace between elements of each), a squabble broke out between these two tribes (both Ḥāshidī) and al-Ahnūm (Bakīlī). Again, however, the roots of the problem were by no means simple. In this particular case, part of al-Ahnūm had fallen out with part of 'Idhar, having stood guaranty for the 'Idharīs in a dispute with other 'Idharīs. To follow that back would lead us into smaller and smaller histories, each known only to its own protagonists. Part of the story has been published elsewhere (Dresch 1987*a*). For the present purpose it is enough to say that al-Ahnūm, trying to 'chase up' (*yuḥawwirū*) their charges in 'Idhar, seized trucks from both 'Idhar and al-'Usaymāt, and the latter two tribes took trucks from each other and from al-Ahnūm. The roads were cut and recut several times in the area of al-Baṭanah (the lowlands betwen Shahārah and Ḥūth), interfering with al-Ahnūm's great *qāt* trade to the main asphalt road and the major cities. Al-Ahnūm went for help quite outside the area.

Al-Ahnūm went and slaughtered bulls for Wā'ilah, a Bakīl tribe on the border with Saudi Arabia. Wā'ilah duly cut the road against all the Ḥāshid tribes, strangling the important trucking business into Yemen from the north. They had reasons of their own for doing this so promptly, reasons very much bound up with national politics, and the events we are following in fact straddle an attempt to start a civil war among the tribes (early 1978) and an actual border war between the two Yemens (early 1979). Wā'ilah had tribesmen from the South in its territory attempting to produce a border dispute with the Saudis. Suffice it to say that '*qaṭā*' Wa'ilah', the great 'cutting' of the road, was finally ended after the war by a distinguished gathering of shaykhs from both confederations, and of all stripes in national politics, whose efforts were directed largely toward containing the dispute in the lowlands among al-Ahnūm, 'Idhar, and al-'Uṣaymāt.

In July 1979 an attempt was made by 'Alī Shawīṭ of Banī Ṣuraym to resolve definitively the disputes between the three tribes (see Dresch 1987*a*). The lists of claims produced by the various parties were extremely long, including a claim from al-Ahnūm, for example, for forty-five camels they said they had lost in Imam Yaḥyā's day, some time in the 1930s. No overall settlement was reached. But al-Ahnūm were fairly satisfied with the opening of the roads achieved earlier, while 'Idhar and al-'Uṣaymāt , whose truce had survived the events with Wā'ilah, now fell to fighting each other.

A large delegation of shaykhs (including some from as far away as Khawlān al-'Āliyah and Murād) went to the disputed area in early 1981 and 'sat on' the two sides for a week, feasting their followers at the expense of the disputing parties and finally extracting yet another truce (cf. Chelhod 1970: 71). Khārif and Banī Ṣuraym supplied the guarantors. Two *sharī'ah* judges were chosen, and the tribes sent delegations into Ṣan'ā' to resolve their case there; but with the move from the territorial format of the tribal countryside to the more contained format of the city, conspiracy theories began to flourish.

In the countryside no definitive change took place. In the summer of 1982, six hundred men of the 'popular army' (the tribal levy) went to al-Baṭanah with their commander, 'Abdullāh Dāris of Dhū Muḥammad. They imposed yet another truce, but then fell to squabbling among themselves. A Sufyānī (the same man, in fact, who was later shot dead in his own territory, as described in Chapter 3) tried to take a truck from the Dhū Muḥammad contingent, and within a few weeks all but ten of the six hundred tribal soldiers had gone home in disgust, taking with them the cash and weapons. A massive column of regular troops from 'Amrān invaded the area, arrested a few men, and withdrew again.[23] Nothing was settled. The rumours multiplied.

Now that the leading shaykhs were in Ṣan'ā', one heard throughout tribal territory all kinds of wild stories about what was happening. Before this, the stories had been of events in the public domain. Motive had not been an issue, although discussion of presumed rights to property went on in small circles. With the lull in explicit tribal gestures (gatherings on the borders, meetings with *'ilm wa-khabar*, exchanges of rifles and bulls), the gap was filled by talk of implicit causes. What had been a matter of private gossip became the matter instead of public imagery and of general debate.

According to many stories, the paramount shaykh's landholding at al-Ḥayjah was the root of the problem. The squabbles between the two Ḥāshid tribes were insoluble only because some personal advantage to do with this land was being pursued by hidden means. Then, at about the time of the 1979 border war with South Yemen, several men from both tribes had gone to the South to collect pay and weapons. The government of North Yemen had cut off their popular army stipends (quite why or at whose urging was variously guessed at), and these tribesmen had then held up government vehicles to extort their pay. It was the dispute between certain of the major shaykhs and these tribesmen connected with the Front, so the rumours ran, that was supposed to underlie the intractable conflict. According to some, the shaykhs from opposing tribes had a common interest in keeping their tribesmen 'backward' and cut off from the central government.

In the same vein it was argued that certain shaykhs of Banī Ṣuraym (who had been meant to act as guarantors and stop the fighting) were primarily concerned lest these disputes of national politics again result in the roads being cut. Banī Ṣuraym own a great many trucks. These shaykhs, supposed to guarantee the peace, had therefore, so the story ran, supplied guns and money to men in al-'Uṣaymāt to have them fight 'Idhar. So long as 'Idhar and al-'Uṣaymāt were busy killing each other in the area toward Shahārah, al-'Uṣaymāt would not start hostilities with Sufyān, which would at that time (1980–1) have likely involved the rivalry between the Ṣan'ā' government and the Front and again threatened blockage of the main asphalt road to Saudi Arabia (the squabble with Sufyān went back to before the fighting at Jabal Aswad). What relation there might be in all of this between the paramount shaykh (himself from al-'Uṣaymāt), these shaykhs with commercial interests (from Banī Ṣuraym), and those supposed to sympathize with the Front (from 'Idhar) was open to endless debate.

What truth there was to any of the stories one cannot say: not very much, would be the safe guess. What is important is the way the stories blossomed and spread so soon as the explicitly tribal forms of dispute and settlement were in any way supplemented by other forms or, for whatever reasons, not pursued. Conspiracy was as obvious an explanation as it would be in doctrinaire democracies or any polity of Jacobin cast. The telling of these tales did not reproduce at all neatly the tribal identities: the shaykhs of al-'Uṣaymāt were not the villains of 'Idharī stories, for example, and the shaykhs of 'Idhar villains to al-'Uṣaymāt; nor were al-'Uṣaymāt restricted to blaming their own leaders and 'Idhar to blaming theirs. Least of all did those closely involved find compelling the theory that a cabal of shaykhs was somehow in this together at the expense of tribesmen on both sides.[24] That was a view held by those at a distance. But what counts as distance has changed also, in that men are more concerned with their neighbours' lives than hitherto.

The idea of a hidden reality to political events is nothing new, and the histories make quite frequent reference to appearances being one thing and intention another.[25] But tribesmen only rarely do so. The explicit actions and declarations between tribe and tribe or section and section are of far more interest to them, and indeed are of more importance: what people may think or do among themselves scarcely matters until they take up arms and close a border or impound a truck, at which point their actions are assimilated to the language of previous debt, and involvement on either side is established by such public means as the exchange of rifles. When the pursuit of balance is plainly blocked, however, no explanatory principle is available but that of individual action, and in a world where the rhetoric of national unity is now a commonplace the principle takes on a different value: in the absence of a sociology, conspiracy explains disorder. Not to those involved, but to those watching, the struggle in the lowlands near Shahārah begins to look like the action of hidden hands, very much as in the Bīr al-Mahāshimah document disorder is attributed to deceivers who climb the walls of foreign embassies.

It is no part at all of the present work to examine the detail of contemporary politics in Ṣan'ā'. But if one transfers in the imagination the problems of these outlying tribes to the capital (as many modernists would do forthwith, had they the power), then the implication is disturbing. 'From the Qur'ānic assurance that the Muslim community will not agree on an error it ensued logically that when those best qualified to judge are in accord on a principle, disagreement is reprehensible. Truth being indivisible, in politics as in theology or law, partisanship signifies the presence either of error or treachery' (Stookey 1974: ii. 410). This is well put. One need only add that the apparently timeless connection between scripture and Jacobinism is in fact only possible in these times and within a particular view of the political world. Even as late a ruler as Imam Aḥmad (d. 1962) did not have such a concept of politics. And within the tribal system the question of an indivisible truth was always hard so much as to pose, save for non-tribal specialists in the singular space of protected *hijrahs*.

In most tribal practice, the relation of uniformity to particular practice is ordered differently. Throughout the dispute between

'Idhar and al-'Uṣaymāt, for example, rules of refuge and escort were still observed (indeed they were revived and clarified as the dispute went on): one could move through one's antagonists' territory, whether they were from one's own tribe or the other, if someone else would only 'give his face' as protector. In fact a few people moved by brotherhood to the other tribe. None of this is either error or treachery, but a question of 'truth', if one wishes, being thoroughly divisible. The man seeking refuge is, as it were, lost to his antagonists' view by moving under 'cover' of someone else: indeed, as we said much earlier in the book, a verb sometimes used of taking refuge or seeking escort is *taḥajjaba*, from the same root as the standard Arabic term for a woman's veil. More generally, the language of 'covering' permeates the whole ethnography, as does that of moral symmetry. Some of the identities which correspond to this are permanent. Others, quite distinctive of the tribal system, are established by movement or denied by outright avoidance.

The last of these possibilities is typical of small-scale tribal affairs, but is felt by tribesmen themselves to be somehow at odds with modern values and something no longer to be spoken of in educated company. We can take as an example a document drawn up between sections of Sufyān and Āl 'Ammār, who at the time were also heavily involved with the Front and with the rhetoric of imminent revolution.

A man from Sufyān had killed a man from Āl 'Ammār some years before and the case had never been resolved, but a structure of guaranty was renewed repeatedly. The guarantors from both sides swore they were answerable together for actions that might arise from past or from future events (*'afw wa-'āfiyah*), firm and unchanging (*hāmid jāmid*), cold as water (*bārid bard al-mā'*), and no quittance would make a man quit of this (*lā barā wa-lā bā'ir-hu*). They stood guaranty for each group against the other. But not for the particular culprit. He and his family, rather strikingly, remain open, at market or in the countryside, to whomever of their antagonists can 'swallow' them (*zaqamū-hum*). Correspondingly, they are excluded from their own tribe's market on market day, and their antagonists must not enter their village 'in the hours of daylight' (*fi l-nahār*). So long as no one is 'seen' in a shared or public space, there need be no collective conflict; those particularly at odds are enjoined, in effect, to remain socially invisible at the relevant times or places and to pursue their dispute without involving the whole sets of men to whom those spaces attach. Avoidance of a general and collective issue, to which there could only be one general and collective answer, is not only acceptable but is in fact required.

The alternative to this curious civility of violence is a factionalism that is impersonal and constrained by no moral limits. A long dispute between Dhū Muḥammad and Dhū Ḥusayn, for instance, ran parallel to that between ʻIdhar and al-ʻUṣaymāt. A sudden pause to the whole conflict was precipitated when several members of Āl Abū Ra's (Dhū Muḥammad) were killed or injured, not by rifle fire in visible combat with the other side, but by a land-mine planted in a track that led to the disputed area. A mine is of its nature impersonal and indiscriminate, a rather brutal instance of something hidden which in tribal terms should be explicit and thus particular; the avoidance of a general issue by being 'covered' oneself counts for nothing, and hostility is pursued against a 'type' of person, instead of a determinate enemy: this particular person, family, or tribe, all of which definitions are free to shift their relevance. It is striking how seldom such things are used in tribal disputes, how often in disputes pursued in non-tribal terms.

In the case at hand, the assumption was made that the Front was responsible. Extreme supporters of the Front, whether from Dhū Muḥammad, Dhū Ḥusayn, or other tribes in the general area, were spoken of by men from both sides as a single group at odds with tribal custom and with *sinnah*: in other words, with that which is right because accepted. Tribes and political factions were explicitly spoken of as alternatives, one of which had in the end to contain or dominate the other. Something similar occurred among ʻIdhar, al-ʻUṣaymāt, and al-Ahnūm at the period when the leading shaykhs were all away in Ṣanʻā'. Both sets of disputes ran on long after the period of disturbance coinciding with the Front's heyday. Both seemed insoluble problems stirred by hidden hands.

With the assumption now widespread that tribalism will one day disappear, the contrast between the two styles of action becomes pointed. It is not the anthropologist's concern to guess whether that assumption is correct. One simply notes it as part of the contemporary world. But the problems posed by such assumptions are a legitimate concern and deserve attention. Plainly tribes as such are not the major issue here: for many purposes, as we saw in Chapter 9, they are simply names and spaces. Tribal*ism* is now more to the point, and certain rival styles of imagination in which relations between persons are conceived differently.

THE TRIBAL AND NATIONAL IMAGINATIONS

> For perfection is not like light, centred in any one body; but, like the dispersed seminalities of vegetables at the creation, scattered through the whole mass.
>
> Sir Thomas Browne

The world of most tribesmen's imagination (especially that of older tribesmen) extends usually in a single dimension, reaching as far from home as one wishes but formed of persons whose characters are serial: everyone's faults and virtues are potentially the same as everyone else's, and the tales that we tell of them may well be the tales they tell of us. 'Regionalism' is not the mode in which tribesmen conceive their differences.[26] No two views of the world can be quite the same, but wherever one stands or whomever one talks with, an interest is evident in disturbing events that occur beyond one's own home or village. Very often the listener is put in mind of Meeker's comment on Musil's Rwala tales, that 'the concern of the narratives is the possibility of defending a peaceful life within the camp or the tribe, *the precise shape of which remains obscure*' (1979: 94, his emphasis).

What might be added is that the imagination tends to fill all available space with the stuff of such tales. The physical space of the northern plateau and the east of Yemen is indeed exhausted by tribal territory, but men's imaginations, as they are formed in conversation with others, fill it with men like themselves, excluding most other possibilities. The case is very different in Lower Yemen or the west. There one often hears stories, for example, of a parallel reality of *jinn*s, where the ranks of society are replicated in a normally unseen world. Among the tribes no such ranks are admitted. Nor can I say I have ever heard a tale seriously told of the effects of unseen and non-human beings. *Jinn*s exist, of course, in most people's opinion because they are mentioned in the Qur'ān (e.g. 15: 27); but they may as well do so, like Cicero's gods, in the intermundane spaces.[27] What one worries about at night or in places far from roads and villages is the presence of people, unknown and unnamed but in character much like oneself.

Again, in Lower Yemen one comes across inversions of the normal order, as on feast-days, for example, where a carnival figure of authority called the 'qadi' is sometimes portrayed with a sheep's head. In Upper Yemen, by contrast, the tribesmen play only at being tribesmen. Where at weddings, for instance, there is a buffoonery of lewd songs and dancing, including, say, mock copulations, it is 'weak', non-tribal people who act out the entertainment. By contrast, the tribesmen (though others may join in) dance the *bar'ah*, as they do at festivals, at meetings, and indeed at odd moments when a group of them have space to dance. In line abreast, usually at the centre of a circle and with daggers drawn or rifles on their shoulders, they move parallel to each other with a tripping step which they and the *muzayyin* drummers build up in tempo to a kind of effervescence. Tribesmen dance a great deal like this and take pride in doing so: indeed, the word *bar'ah* itself suggests excellence or surpassing skill (Adra 1982: 239).[28]

In the later stages of the dance the circle is cleared for the best performers to work in pairs. Particularly the old men, whom one had thought constrained to a creaking hobble, come out to 'leap like goats', but always with a driving parallel movement as they skip and whirl around each other with daggers drawn. In the group sections, there is tacitly a leader; but this parallel skipping and whirling, this moving in a rapid but unscripted and unconstrained unison, is the dominant motif. The excitement is collusion in a tribal ideal, an expression of what we should be anyway, not an inversion or denial of the usual values.[29] These patterns of entertainment correspond, one might note, with those of dreams of political betterment, which in Upper Yemen are largely still a matter of 'making one word', and in Lower Yemen of a 'world turned upside down'. One suspects that such dreams of the future are becoming everywhere more alike.

The equivalence of individual men, so apparent in the dance, does not entail their identity, and what differentiates men most noticeably from each other is their position in the tribal scheme: a Ṣuraymī can only act as host or escort in the territory of Banī Ṣuraym, for instance, and a Sufyānī in the territory of Sufyān. Either can take refuge in the other's territory and be lost to his antagonists' view. Most relations in fact show the temporal sequence and spatial alternation (Pitt-Rivers 1977: 109) which informs the whole system, the exception being conflict (ibid. 102), which is also, of course, the one 'transaction' that takes place instantaneously (Bourdieu 1977: 109). One begins and ends with separation. In conflict and the dance alike there is a temporary cohesion and parallel action of men who otherwise are portrayed as not interdependent, and Adra (1982: 244) makes the valuable point that the *bar'ah* is supposed to give 'energy' or *nashāṭ*: arranged performances lacking spontaneity, as for instance on television, are not considered by the tribesmen to be real *bar'ah* (ibid. 248). The nationalist imagination, of course, orders the matter differently.

At about the time the Front was defeated, in 1982, a new initiative was launched to reform the country's political system. This same initiative has been pursued, with considerable success, from then until the time of writing, and when the political history of Yemen in the 1980s comes to be written it will surely have a central place. A 'national charter' (*al-mīthāq al-waṭanī*) was issued and very widely distributed throughout the countryside in conjunction with a campaign to establish a 'general popular congress' embracing the whole republic. Drawing on Islamic rhetoric and on a general theme of national democracy, it promises primarily freedom and justice within a national whole.

> No supremacy shall be given on grounds of kinship and wealth, or to an individual, or to a group of people, but all citizens together are one body that draws its life from each member (*bunyah wāḥidah tastamadd ḥayātahā min kulli 'uḍw*). The right of participation in this common activity (*nashāṭ*, also vigour or strength), the right to enjoy all political and civil rights, and the right of candidacy and election [to the popular congress] must be guaranteed to every citizen.

A national identity is already acted out in small ways at rural schools, where children are marched to and fro before lessons to do exercise drills, to salute the flag, and sing the republican anthem. Ethnographically it is important to note that schools are what tribesmen now clamour for, and few providers of schools have missed their importance.[30] But there is more than coincidence to the appearance of the term *nashāṭ* (the same term used of the 'energy' produced in dancing) in the 'national charter'; and the national rituals acted out at schools, as well as broadcast by television, are an alternative that makes older tribal practices seem to some men archaic. Moreover, the parallelism that in the dance is temporary is here constant, and the newly minted citizens are committed in theory to a permanent, collective project whose 'energy' is formed in the comparison with other countries.

In the admirably produced new textbooks that teachers use, a unified view of the national past is developed and tribalism receives passing mention, as in this *Medieval History of Yemen* for the sixth year of primary schools:

> The tribe is a large collection of people who live in one area. Between them are ties of descent, proximity, and shared interests. Islam had called on [people] to give up their differences.
>
> But tribal clannishness (*al-ta'aṣṣub li-l-qabīlah*) was still to be found. Members of the tribe would carry out the orders of their chief and fight under his banner and show distaste for outsiders.
>
> The tribe had some praiseworthy characteristics, such as co-operation, courage (*najdah*, also 'mutual aid'), and generosity. Similarly the upheavals (*intifāḍāt*, rebellions) of the tribes were part of resistance to foreign invasion and to the rule of tyrants in Yemen.
>
> But some tribal chiefs and governors and rulers used to nurture the tribal spirit (*yughadhdhūna al-rūḥ al-qabaliyyah*) and preserve it for their own ends. Tribal clannishness is a blameworthy characteristic which makes the individual pay allegiance to the tribe more than to the state or the country. Islam had forbidden this and the reformers in this nation (*al-muṣliḥūn min hādhā l-sha'bi*) have fought it. The new Yemen, unified Yemen, needs the efforts of all its citizens in the towns, the countryside, and the mountains (*shi'āb*).[31]

The balanced exposition of these elementary texts is on the whole attractive. But the message is clear enough, and the idea of homogeneous time which underlies it is very different from anything to be found in earlier periods. The concept quite unremarkably underlying any modern school-book is of concerted action by a social group whose existence seems natural. To this extent, in Yemen as in Morocco, 'the subuniverse of meaning that is constituted by "bookish" conceptions of history is increasingly creating a "shock" with commonsense notions of the past' (Eickelman 1977: 53). The old 'pluralism' (ibid.) is perhaps breaking down. Invocation of the *sha'b* or 'people' suggests a serial quality whereby equivalence and identity are themselves equated: men are 'sons of the people' and as such share a single past and a promised future, as well as a collective life at present. Our advancement or backwardness will be established as a unit against other national units like ours, and tribal identities, where not mischievous, might be found irrelevant.

The people become a social 'mass' and the political stakes are raised accordingly. When the world is apprehended as a whole and is seen to be radically flawed, then 'what was individual and understressed in the normal rhythm of society now becomes,' as Pocock (1971: 112) suggests in the case of more spectacular quandaries, 'social and overstressed at the expense of forms which no longer render experience meaningful'. What is individual and usually understressed in the case at hand would be precisely the 'peaceful life' which is always defended but whose shape 'remains obscure' (Meeker 1979: 94). Puritanical reformers, whose influence among the tribes has been quite minor in recent times, are nothing new. From the time of the Imam al-Hādī onwards one finds intermittent calls in times of crisis for public enforcement of rules about domestic morality—the banning of music and the veiling of women are conspicuous features of such calls to date[32]—all of which may be one day repeated in a very different modern context. But for the moment the nationalist project is still compelling, and with it the language of progress and development. The future still seems for most rural people to lie with the *shabāb* or educated young.

It is in that perspective, drawn as much from the common sense of other countries as from indigenous thought and perhaps in the long term fragile, that tribes appear as a 'survival' from some earlier stage of history. It seems obvious that the future belongs to something other than tribalism. It has seemed obvious at least since the civil war, when the tribes in fact were those fighting to decide the issue, and it continues to seem obvious now. It is not in any simple way a report on the contemporary world—the tribes had never been stronger than in, say, 1980—but a pervasive judgment of value which a great many tribesmen share in.

We should therefore note clearly that precisely the material with which we have been dealing ourselves is suddenly of interest to a small group of Yemeni authors (e.g. Abū Ghānim 1985; al-'Ulaymī 1986), who at the time of writing are also concerned with custom, tribal structure, the position of shaykhs, and customary law. To turn the present enterprise inside out and write instead about their ethnography, with the tribes as part specifically of their conceptual world, is properly a subject for a separate work. But the broad shape of their problematic is suggested by the title of an earlier work by Ḥamūd al-ʻŪdī (1980): *The Popular Heritage and its Relation to Development* . . . For these writers there are no neutral facts. The past cannot be lost entirely without losing one's identity ('Each of the peoples of the earth', . . . 'its distinctive attributes'), and yet the products of the past must be turned to the ends of national progress. The range of views developing in this type of literature is broad. But those already highly educated in the modern mode find only some things exotic and noteworthy: so the Baraṭ *qawāʻid*, for example, from which I have quoted quite often, become a 'text' worth publishing (see e.g. al-ʻUlaymī 1986: 117 ff.), while the documents to buy a truck would not be.

To search out what is definitively tribal, indeed to do field-work among 'the tribes', is therefore to participate in a certain representation of what is happening. The tribes were a 'half-world' defined by the Imamate tradition, and they remain one now, so only part of what tribesmen do counts as 'tribal' and attracts comment. The question of vengeance and refuge is a case in point.

> The first matter is the law of killing. Whoever kills to clear his good name ('*alā maḥḍ al-naqā*', i.e. in defence of honour) has the right of first intervention (*la-hu awwal darak*) offered him or his tribesmen [i.e. whoever intervenes to protect him, the killer can accept such protection from his antagonists]. Whoever [of the tribe] is present can intervene [like this] and such intervention is good for fifteen days . . .

This particular fragment is again from Sufyān. The people who wrote it were precisely those who in another context were singing of Yemeni unity and the red revolution. But the 'traditional' provisions appear to the modernist as archaic and as inextricably tied up with the 'tribal clannishness' condemned in school-books. There is a certain reticence among the tribesmen themselves in admitting such things occur, and a great many men presume that it must one day all disappear as their own supposed 'ignorance' gives way to education.

Again, a special supplement in the police magazine, *al-Ḥarās* (No. 20, May 1984), deals with 'vengeance' as a 'custom of the age of ignorance' ('*ādah jāhiliyyah*), and then includes separate sections on 'the crime of vengeance in Ma'rib governorate' and 'the crime of vengeance in Jawf governorate'. The articles in fact make clear that it is not limited to these places. But the conceptual geography at work is little different from that before the revolution; and, as before the revolution, the tribes do not oppose to this an explicit alternative model, and do not wish to. Among the articles by intellectuals and journalists[33] is an interview with Shaykh 'Abdullāh, who himself says:

> The fact is that this is an evil and criminal phenomenon. It is actually very old, particularly in the eastern and northern areas, but it disappears or diminishes when the authority of the state is present there and appears when state authority is weak or absent. Were the state present and doing what it should when the tribes flared up and perpetrated this sort of crime—because the state's duty is to seize the perpetrator and imprison him . . .—then they would not have recourse to vengeance on innocent people so long as the culprits were in the hand of justice.

In particular places, therefore, the state does not provide the security one might hope for; and this aspect of tribal practice, as so many others, is equated with the lack of state authority.

Yet the state is very much the interest of the man whom the journalists chose to represent the tribes: 'an interview with the paramount shaykh of Ḥāshid', and, though they do not say so, with a man who has also been speaker of the country's parliament. In an interview more recently (*al-'Arab*, 7 December 1987) he stated his intention of running for the newly revived Consultative Assembly, as no doubt did many shaykhs.[34] But it is symptomatic that an interviewer would label him in one way or the other. The language of tribalism is not that of the state, any more than it was in Imamic times, and a man who is fluent in both, as are several great political figures, must portion his competence out according to place and circumstance.

This portioning out by place and context becomes more pressing an issue as travel, radio and television news, and the cash economy pull the citizens of the country more closely into each others' lives. Either the languages of tribes and state must be integrated explicitly, making one admittedly subordinate to the other, or their separation takes the form of nothing less than secession (as happened, indeed, in al-Ḥamdī's time); or the language of tribes is abandoned altogether, as many modernists assume will happen. But the language of the state and the nation must itself evolve in any case. It cannot, of its nature, stand still. In Chapter 5 we touched on a pre-modern conception that the principles which govern righteous action stand above society. As elsewhere, so in Yemen, 'men's minds have moved . . .' (not all of them by any means, but far more than enough to be important here) 'to the idea that society is its own judge and master . . .' (Hourani 1981: 179). Nationalism remains the organizing concept: the energy generated by nationalist songs and expressions remains entirely genuine. But, as Hourani says in more general terms, 'nationalism is not by itself a system of principles by which a state or a society can be organized; for that it must depend on the other ideas it can attract and absorb' (ibid. 189). The alternative is that power becomes the only value.

To go forward with much prospect of success now seems to demand considerable thought about what the past counts for. Some of Yemen's sociologists have been mentioned already. Among the historians one might mention 'Alī Muḥammad Zayd's work (see particularly Zayd 1981) as an example of a new historiography: one that does not any longer set events against a line of dates and a purportedly unchanging set of values, but questions the past, as it were, from the present's viewpoint and examines in the process what the values of the present are. Zayd himself writes on the past of learned, Zaydi tradition. Those interested in the tribes (e.g. Abū Ghānim 1985; al-'Ulaymī 1986) write much more on the present. But the two sets of interests will no doubt come together in deciding what the *turāth* or national 'heritage' amounts to: that is, in resolving the paradox of tribal practice affecting contemporary affairs quite deeply and yet belonging, in the view of many, to a previous age.

Fifteen years ago and more, as was mentioned in Chapter 1, 'Alī Ṣabrah could already write on 'Tribal society and its characteristics' and express severe concerns about tribalism's place in the country's history. But he found himself drawn despite this to accept the suggestion that tribal councils were the root of an indigenous Arab democracy, albeit for rather Hobbesian reasons:

> the egotistical individualist attitude of the badu, the equality of manners among all the tribe's members, their love of violence and their pride in it set a limit to individual influence in so far as things became as our popular proverb says: 'everyone is the other's nose ring', because, as we say, 'nothing can break a stone but its sister'. (Ṣabrah 1972: 114)

The reality, as we have seen, is a great deal more complex. Avoidance and indirection are at least as important as conflict, and the course of conflict turns on several unstated assumptions quite foreign to 'a war of everyone against everyone'. Nonetheless, the generalized image of 'tribal society' (*al-mujtama' al-qabalī*) provides, from this point of view, a potential complement to that of the unitary state and not simply a residue or a dangerous antithesis. It makes of the tribes not just a problem, as they may well have been before, but a question of some relevance to everyone. A more sophisticated history and sociology than Ṣabrah used are now developing, which might provide a realistic answer. But even were the tribes not still practically important, even had they disappeared by now, they would not form an alternative to what is happening around them, a 'world we have lost' or a timeless pastoral one could plausibly oppose to 'the modern world'.

At no point in the last thousand years have tribes been a bounded, self-sufficient whole, a closed conceptual world that one might speak of as a simple hierarchy—'a place for everything and everything in its place', as carpenters say of tool chests. The famous line from de Tocqueville on the passing of the old regime, 'Aristocracy had made a chain of all the members of the community . . . democracy breaks that chain and severs every link of it' (quoted Dumont 1970: 18), would scarcely apply here: severance of relations was always and explicitly a part of tribesmen's self-conception. The shared values that underpinned that image of autonomy remained largely unstated, and only part of them appears explicitly in the 'heroic' language men associate with tribes most readily. But the anomie and enforced uniformity that seem sometimes the only modern alternative to a stifling conception of rank was scarcely present either. The tribes provide one of the more interesting of several other possibilities. Persons were prescriptively moral equals, as were sections or tribes, but no standing measure of their detailed equality was ever sought, or could be; and the hierarchy that informed men's conceptions of their social world was not of persons, or ranks, or conditions of men, but of contexts and settings whereby men could avoid moral contradiction by avoiding common measurement of their different aims. Autonomy was the prime concern, and in part still is.

That will not serve by itself satisfactorily in the modern world. Its precondition was the exclusion of non-tribal people defined by birth, a conception at odds with the language of modern politics. The individual, whose rights are stressed again and again in such documents as the 'national charter', had to pay too high a price in poverty and the risk of violence. Not least, the older particularism, whereby no overall ranking was ever made between tribe and tribe, is hard to sustain where the nation as a whole is ranked by its members against other nations, all of them being on what seems to their citizens a single trajectory of development and progress. But tribalism did not stand by itself in an older world either. To determine what its worth might now be, if any, falls to history and to sociology as the Yemenis themselves might practise these, however they may be conceived and whoever the practitioners are, whether politicians, planners, intellectuals, or the tribesmen in their villages, who increasingly feel themselves part of an explicit 'society'. Yemeni intellectuals have taken the question up in terms that were unavailable fifty years ago. For the tribesmen themselves, in some measure, their identity is now open to question and reflection as it was not before. The common past, which defines what the nation is, is being rethought to discover what the nation can be. Yet the tribes, which have some of them been where they are for ten centuries, threaten constantly to slip out of time and thus out of the national history.

NOTES

1. There is not occasion to quote them extensively, but two works have certainly influenced my thinking in much of what follows: Gellner 1964 and Anderson 1983.
2. The usual explanation of the timing of the coup is that it forestalled a Ba'thist plot. That this was no simple question is apparent from the number of supposed Ba'thists in the government the coup installed. Nor is a struggle between tribes and army a very likely possibility, as we shall see when we quote the speeches given at a tribal meeting soon afterwards. But for a discussion of the coup see Stookey 1978: 269 ff.
3. See, for example, *Le Monde diplomatique*, October 1974, pp. 37–8, and cf. Stookey 1974, pt. 2, and Peterson 1982: 115–17.
4. Unfortunately the pamphlet, of which I have a copy, carries no indication of where it was published or by whom. It contains portrait photographs of both Ibrāhīm al-Ḥamdī and Shaykh 'Abdullāh.
5. In 1976 there were sporadic bombing campaigns not unconnected with the tribes, and by the end of that year some of the Ḥāshid tribes were more or less in revolt. There was a meeting between leading Ḥāshid shaykhs and al-Ḥamdī in January 1977, but by July of that year road-blocks against government vehicles were frequent. As early as November 1975 there had been a great meeting of disaffected

shaykhs at Khamir and an attempt to establish 'sectors' for resisting the government: this did not prevent, for example, Mujāhid Abū Shawārib remaining governor of Ḥajjah throughout the period in question.

6. The guarantors of this six-month truce were drawn primarily from Khawlān al-'Āliyah and the tribes near Ṣan'ā'. No judgment was ever attempted, but the truce was upheld and by the time it ended those shaykhs who had been concerned to provoke the war (most of them from Sufyān and Āl 'Ammār) had withdrawn to the south-eastern desert on the borders with South Yemen.
7. This was a period when President Carter for domestic reasons was looking around for somewhere to 'stand up to the communists'. It happened to be Yemen. For a sensible account of this farce and of the actual politics of the area at the time see Peterson 1981*a*, 1981*b*.
8. Not all the money paid to the shaykhs got to the tribesmen, and it was an open secret long before this that many tribal leaders had far more men on their books than were ever mustered. Nevertheless, Bakīl tribes were talking enthusiastically of YR 10,000 per village per month as a possible rate of support precisely as western diplomats were calculating that the Ṣan'ā' government had only $3.5 million left, enough for three months ordinary governmental expenditure. The tribes got far less than they hoped. The government was bailed out by the Saudis at the eleventh hour.
9. *Salām min sufyān mutaqassam ilā jam' al-rufaq,*
min wā'ilah wa-l-buq' wa-l-'ammār (sic) wa-arḥab wa-dahm,
wa-surayḥ wa-ghūlī wa-'abdī wa-l-jabal
shallāt-hu narfa' shi'ār al-ḥarb
fi l-wusṭā wa-man fī-hā samad
yā murtaziq wa-arḥal bilādī wa-ḥaddad
mā la-k majāl al-jaysh nādir sha'b
wa-qāl al-'unf mā bī-h majāl 'adū-nā khālid 'alay-nā 'ār
law mā nantaqim sha'b al-yaman wāḥid shimāl wa-janūb-hu wa-l-raml.
10. *Yā salām yartafa' nashwān ka-l-mawaza' / kam qadhā'if dafa' min yad-hu ra's-hu*
qul li-l-aḥmar wa-l-ajdā w-ayn ba-yarja' / waḥdat al-sha'b bi-taqḍī 'alā ra's-hu
yā banā kayf ḥāl-ak ba'd-mā sirnā / wa-ant jālis tuwāṣil-hum bi-khaṭṭ al-nār
qul la-hum yā banā sirnā wa-narja' / nish'al al-thawrat al-ḥamrā bi-l-istimrār.

This poem, which Sufyānī tribesmen quoted as very much a 'tribal' product, was probably composed in fact by non-tribesmen in Lower Yemen during left-wing struggles for land reform in the early 1970s. It seems to have been taken up years later by northerners, probably by those who received guerrilla training in South Yemen. It then came to be thought of as part of the endless 'challenge and riposte' between Bakīl and Ḥāshid.

11. The story of Shaykh Nājī's sudden prominence as paramount shaykh deserves note. Nājī, apparently, is bin 'Abd al-'Azīz b. 'Abdullāh b. Nājī b. Aḥmad b. Ḥamūd b. Ṣāliḥ b. Muḥsin, and Muḥsin had formed a *ḥilf* or pact with the Āl Sa'ūd at the time of the first Wahhābī movement. Nājī, so his relatives say, found the document and took it with him when he visited Saudi royalty, who supported his claim and provided him with generous funds of his own. Before that his stipend came by way of Ḥāshid. Later it was to come through Ṣan'ā'. For a time he had the royal beneficence directly.
12. Dhū Muḥammad was mentioned earlier in connection with the 1968 struggles between left and right (see the notes to ch. 7, above). Before that they had been the only major Bakīl tribe to be anti-royalist throughout the civil war, and their particular political history made them an obvious place to seek allies from Bakīl, quite apart from Dāris's own abilities.
13. Black-Michaud 1980 works with a conception of 'total scarcity', which I would think more applicable, as Sartre suggests, to Western capitalism than to other ethnographies. It is in the situation of opposition that the moral good is limited. To guests one should be 'generous as Ḥātim Ṭayy' regardless of ecological scarcity.
14. It is of some interest that Niebuhr (1792: i. 249–50, 264, 370–2, 385) already felt the uncomfortable mismatch of European and Yemeni styles of gift-giving. I should note that I misunderstood these assumptions myself and at the end of my second period of field-work offered directly all my household possessions at bargain prices to someone I had known well for almost two years. Rarely have I had so strongly that alarming feeling that the world is unravelling. Within the space of 30 minutes we had gone from a very easy friendship to what seemed likely to end in physical violence. What I should have done, of course, was go through the Jewish family who lived next door. At a more elevated level, it is commonly felt by Westerners that the 'gift' of development aid and the like should give them some moral hold over the recipients (very much the sort of view that Mauss so loathed). Tribesmen, however, are likely to respond to the news that country X has given Y dollars to Yemen by complaining that they should be giving a lot more.
15. Convertible and impersonal wealth (grain, for instance, is not impersonal and must be carefully brokered) seems to fall in a single category. The status of weapons as convertible wealth is not new. Zabārah 1941: 795 mentions a minister of al-Mawāhib in Lower Yemen at the start of the 18th cent. who hoarded a vast amount of misappropriated wealth, including some 240 precious daggers. See also ibid. 504 and Zabārah 1958: 766.

    The price of rifles varies suprisingly with the supply (where there are so many extra weapons one might have expected the market to be less sensitive): in 1978 a new FN self-loading rifle could be had in Saudi Arabia for SR 3,000, but after the Mecca incident of 1979 the price shot up and by 1983 had reached YR 12,000; a Korean made AK-47 apparently cost as much as YR 18,000 in the mid-1970s, but by 1979 was down to about YR 10,000 and by 1983 to YR 5,000 or YR 6,000; a 1942-vintage Mauser was of the order of YR 5,000 and a short-barrelled Belgian version in mint condition with the grease still on it cost as much as YR 20,000—very much a status object. Gifts of weapons are quite valuable.

16. One cannot, of course, explain the contemporary world by reference to sacred scripture: several readings are possible, few tribesmen can read at all, and much that people do is simply not related to the Book of God. It is the concordance that is striking. Just as striking is the richness of the text to an anthropologist, but Mauss (1970), while he brackets his argument with Semitic references (to Hebrew *ẓedaqa* and to the Qur'ān), was concerned with an archaeology of Indo-European institutions (cf. Parry 1986) and affords little help. Indeed his reading of a Qur'ānic passage (Mauss 1970: 75–6) seems rather to twist its meaning: far from extolling generosity in the name of sociability it seems to say that one should give without thought of return so as to escape one's fellows and one's kin, 'For surely among your wives and children is an enemy for you' (Qur'ān 64: 14). This is not the place to begin it, but the analysis of such material and its comparison with South Asian and early European gift schemes, among others, is long overdue. So far as I know, not even the pre-Islamic Arabic material has drawn anthropologists' attention.

17. 'Objectivism' in Bordieu's scheme represents the stance of an outside analyst who locates people's practice in (or perhaps reduces it to) a 'totalizing' model. Much of Bourdieu's own analysis (e.g. 1977: 30 ff., 57) has to do the same so as to distinguish one local strategy from another. He also, however, introduces such a model of his own, that of 'symbolic capital', 'rationality', and 'self-interest', such that 'by drawing up a comprehensive balance-sheet of symbolic profits . . . it becomes possible to grasp the economic rationality of conduct which economism dismisses as absurd . . .' (ibid. 181). This is thoroughly illusory. There are no units to quantify 'symbolic profits', and to deduce symbolic profits from the imbalance of material transactions is only to uphold a tautology. How would one ever register an 'imbalance'?

To maintain the individual as a central part of one's model one has to have him always conform to the rational strategy, very much as 'transactionalism' once did. Bourdieu's way of doing this, having rejected such notions as 'structural causality', is to transfer social regularities to the individual as the *habitus* (presumably a concept taken from Panofsky or from Mauss). The individual is thus doomed or fated to be what he is, which is less than enlightening with Middle Eastern material and downright sentimental when applied to French schoolchildren (ibid. 87) or the peasants of Béarn. The 'well-formed utterance' of formal analysis is in effect replaced with the 'well-trained actor' who supposedly cannot do anything but what he has always done (see ibid. 11, 15, 80, 87, and *passim*).

18. The elaborate protocol of greetings between persons and between tribes was touched on earlier (chs. 2 and 4). It might be added that returning a salutation (*radd al-salām*) may be treated as forming a truce in customary law (see Rossi 1948: 23 and the story at the end of ch. 7, above). Certainly I have seen men refuse to return a salutation in the setting of arbitration for fear that it would prejudice their freedom to attack their antagonists if the attempt at arbitration failed. It should also be noted that, especially in the east, one is taught the correct greetings as something much more than a matter of manners: without such competence one is attached to no one and, in the tribesmen's estimation, at considerable risk. There are, as it were, no natural links between strangers.
19. An objection needs to be entered here against Bourdieu's conception of an instantaneous 'contract'. Pollock, of course, described a contract as 'a promise or set of promises which the law will enforce', and the very notion of a promise introduces a time axis which Bourdieu wants somehow to elide. Where the transaction itself is instantaneous, the law of contract reintroduces that axis by appealing to implicit offers and acceptances. Islamic law seems not to be very different in this respect from our own (cf. al-Murtaḍā 1973: ii. 3 ff.), and the role of contract as uniting two moments of time was of course one of the pillars of Mauss's argument (1970: 35). It cannot so easily be conjured away.
20. In a document from the late 1950s, for example, that deals with a dispute between 'Iyāl Surayḥ and Khārif, one finds reference to 'a bullet in Hādī Ḥusayn Ḥamzah al-Ḥā'iṭī which entered above his right kidney and exited at his bottom left rib, [the distance] between the points of entry and exit being a span and two finger widths [which is the equivalent of] two internal wounds and a bone wound' (Dresch forthcoming *c*). Later on, in the list of specific compensation to be paid, the injured man is said to be due 'five hundred and seventy three riyals and a quarter and an eighth and one half of an eighth [of a riyal] and one bull for accepting the wound-money and to placate people' (ibid.). The result has the appearance of precise equivalence. However, the application of general terms to the specific wound suggests a certain indeterminacy in how 'rules' are applied.
21. In English, the phrase 'something between them' can be used of friendship or romantic attachment as well as of enmity. In Upper Yemen it seems only to apply at all naturally to the latter. One might also note that 'severing relations' is almost inevitably a bad thing in Western usage (let alone in that of diplomats), while in tribal usage it is very much a good thing.
22. It is here that the lack of fit is most conspicuous with analyses drawn from ethnographies of a different kind. At least since Durkheim, the assumption has been easily made that representations will be found of societies as whole, and thus of standing relations between parts within them; but here (cf. Peters 1983) such collective imagery seems largely absent. At least since Van Gennep the assumption has been

made in turn that standing relations exist in ordinary time, and correspondingly the exceptions to the normal order (which include the order's periodic affirmation by ritual means) count as 'sacred time', something out of the ordinary. In the case at hand the assumptions are reversed. It is calendar time that is out of the ordinary and connections between men that are counted exceptional, in contrast not only with many pre-modern societies but with part of our own ideology.

23. This intervention by some 30 tanks of the 7th armoured brigade was 'the war of Charles Ward's foot'. Mr Ward was head of the USAID mission to Yemen at the time. On a private trip to Shahārah, he was shot in the foot by an 'Uṣaymī tribesman who tried to take his vehicle on the assumption that it belonged to the Yemeni government. Mr Ward very properly submitted a statement to the court that so far as he was concerned it was an accident and he would as soon see clemency shown. One hopes USAID can find more senior staff of his calibre to send to Yemen.

24. What was happening on the disputed border was on occasion depressing. Bayt Abū Rukab of al-'Uṣaymāt lost about 15 men over the years and had only 7 men left by mid-1983. Bayt Abū Qishaḥ of 'Idhar lost about 11 men and had 4 left. Both were widely seen as being pawns of other people. Certain other characters and groups on both sides had stood apart throughout. Sulṭān Abū Shawṣā and Jābir Ghubayr of al-'Uṣaymāt, for example, had maintained friendly relations with the 'Idharī villages opposite their own, while the war went on along the border each side of them. In 1981 Abū Shawṣā was arrested on a visit to Ṣan'ā'. By the time he got out, six months later, other families in his section had broken the peace with 'Idhar and his section was embroiled in the war. Early in 1983 'Idhar were fired on from Ghubayr's territory, but supposedly not by Ghubayr's own people. A little later, Ghubayr's territory was fired on from the part of 'Idhar directly opposite, but supposedly by men from elsewhere in 'Idhar, and his people too were now embroiled in the fighting.

25. See e.g. al-Ḥibshī 1980: 37, 'The state of the judges of *sharī'ah* was externally excellent and internally very poor . . .' Also ibid. 90, where tribes coalesced 'apparently to avenge the Imam, but in fact . . .'

26. Elsewhere (Dresch 1987*b*) I have noted briefly the difference between this serial imagination and the 'village societies' of North Africa and Southern Europe, where neighbouring villages are each ascribed some specific character. The latter scheme is found also in northern Europe, where diacritica of local identity are often quite elaborate, particularly linguistic oddities that are held to be typical of this area or that. Something of the kind is true of Yemenis' distinctions between Upper Yemen, the west, and Lower Yemen, so 'they say *mā ghult* instead of *mā qult*, and we say *mā gult*'. But these diacritica, although abundantly to hand, are not made much use of in differentiating tribe from tribe. One might relate this also to the difficulty 'the tribes' have in conceptualizing themselves as a bounded subset of greater Yemen or as a whole opposed to the state: European 'ethnicities' (a very recent

word), such as the areas of Southern France on which Bourdieu has written, distinguish themselves by having a supposedly distinct history from that of other areas and of the state; the tribes do not and for the moment perhaps cannot.

27. Travel accounts (e.g. Goitein 1941: 46, 50) leave little doubt that *jinns* were once a common possibility, and the histories and biographical literature mention them fairly often. They are now only rarely mentioned by northern tribesmen, and then by the elderly and indigent. One might note that of the two types of *jinn* reported from tribal South Yemen (Serjeant 1949) one seems to lead only a rather shadowy existence, while the other 'does everything that you do . . . and imitates all your actions. If you fire at it, your bullet will miss it, but it will fire back at you, doubtless with evil consequences.' The *jinn* seems simply to mirror the tribesmen. On the whole, women seem more interested in *jinns* than do men; but it should be mentioned that there are rather marginal-seeming male characters in the north who converse with *jinns* specifically to cure madness. I have so far found out little about these people, but the overall contrast with the west and south is striking.

28. Adra's account of genres of dance provides a very useful approach to understanding the sociology of Upper Yemen. On only one point would I disagree slightly with her analysis: partnering someone is described as *yusāyir* in *bar'ah* as well as in *li'bah* (a more personal type of dance), and the meaning seems to be less 'to get along together' (ibid. 284) than 'to go along with', to move in parallel with. In many other contexts its meaning is close to that of *yatasāyar* ('to go with', 'to travel together'), which was touched on in ch. 2 above.

29. Unlike, for instance, a meeting between tribes, the dance does not mark on the ground the opposition of collective sets to each other. Nor does it realize or express the identity of any single unit: if the men of a village are dancing, there is no reason why others should not also join in. What it exemplifies instead is the temporary combination of equivalent and independent men.

30. See for example, *al-Sharq al-awsaṭ* (22 May 1986) where the governor of Ma'rib is reported as claiming 135 elementary schools opened in his province. The same publication (5 June 1986) reports that the Saudi government pays for the salaries of more than 1,500 teachers in Yemen. Arguments over the curriculum and control of the educational apparatus have for years now gone on almost constantly between different political factions (see Peterson 1982: 120).

31. Unfortunately these text-books provide no place or date of publication. They are available from the Ministry of Education. It deserves to be said in passing that Yemeni identity is not one of those, like that of modern Greece for instance, that had to be 'invented'. At least since al-Hamdānī's time there has been a keen awareness of Yemen as somewhere distinctive. The way in which Yemen is 'imagined' as a nation (Anderson 1983), however, is plainly something new, and the

idea of North and South as a natural unit emerged from a specific conjuncture of political history (see Nājī 1984).

32. Al-Hādī himself had ordered veiling (al-ʻAlawī 1972: 126, 386), but the striking enforcements of domestic morality are those of the 'days of corruption' in the nineteenth century (see e.g. al-Ḥibshī 1980: 69). As one might expect from Meeker's argument (1979: 94–5), such puritan enthusiasms have usually found more favour with townspeople than with country folk. Certain aspects of that difference are being reshaped, not least by the rise of literacy and the presence of mass media. To conceive a unitary answer to the world's problems one must have a unitary conception of the world itself (cf. Eickelman 1987; Anderson 1983).

33. It is a matter for regret that the photographs at the head of the articles are printed too roughly to reproduce here. They form a gallery of contemporary 'types'; the intellectuals and journalists in their sharp-creased suits and wide ties, the dapperly bearded shaykh with a Kashmir shawl flung across his shoulder and another wound up in a turban, the officers in their uniform berets, and the head of the *sharīʻah* college with a beard but a puritanically hairless upper lip and the general air of one who reads Sayyid Quṭb.

34. In the event, Shaykh ʻAbdullāh himself seems not to have run for elective office. Instead, his son Ṣādiq took a seat in the Consultative Assembly, as too did Nājī al-Shāyif's eldest son.

Appendices

APPENDIX 3/1 FORMS OF OATH

The common forms of oath used in formal depositions are these:

b-illāh al-ʿaẓīm qāṭiʿ al-sīb wa-l-nasīb wa-l-dhurriyyah, anā akhruj min ḥawl allāh ilā ḥawl al-shayṭān . . . w-allāh ʿalā mā aqūl shahīd. ('By God almighty who can cut off benefits, descendants, and offspring, I leave the power of God for the power of the devil [if I lie . . .], and God is the witness to what I say.')

w-allāh wa-naʿm tazīl al-ʿawāfī wa-l-niʿam wa-tajlib al-maṣāʾib wa-l-niqam wa-nadam ʿalā raʾs ʿadūw allāh al-fājir fī ʿahd. ('By God indeed, cut off from me boons and grace [if I lie . . .], bring misfortunes and afflictions, remorse on the head of God's enemy, the one who lies on oath.')

Nowadays, either the plantiff or the arbitrator simply takes by the hand the man giving the oath. It used to be, apparently, that the oath-giver stood within the *khaṭṭ allāh*, a line drawn around him in the dust with a dagger point. I once saw a line drawn in this way around a man who had collapsed from a seizure, but I was unable to elicit any rationale for this or for the procedure at oath.

A particularly strong oath can be sworn by the man giving the oath clasping hands with the man demanding it. The Qur'ān is then placed over their linked hands, open at *Sūrah al-barāʾah* (Qur'ān 9, 'Immunity'). One can refuse to accept the offer of an oath from a person one fears will lie, saying, 'I do not want you to swear, on the book, on the circle, or even on water (*wa-law ʿalā mā*).' This last would seem to refer to the badu's practice of scooping up a handful of water and saying, 'I swear by the One who created this . . .' Almost everywhere, tribesmen are reticent about discussing such oaths for fear that their practice in the matter may be somehow unorthodox; and the learned tradition is certainly free in criticizing tribal practice. Several tribesmen believed the oaths they use, such as those reproduced above, are a traditional form called *al-yamīn al-zubayrī*. In fact the latter phrase seems to be used by the learned of oaths that impiously omit mention of God. See e.g. the discussion in *Majmūʿ* 8, Western Library, Great Mosque, Ṣanʿā'.

APPENDIX 3/2 TERMINOLOGY APPLIED TO SHAYKHS

By far the most common term used of tribal leaders or notables is *shaykh*, plural *mashāyikh* (the alternative plural, *shuyūkh*, is never used of them, only of learned men in the capacity of teachers or various lowly figures such as *shuyūkh al-layl*, night watchmen). There are other terms available, but these do not designate different 'ranks'.

The most interesting of these other terms is probably *naqīb*, plural *nuqabā'*. Glaser (1884: 175) concluded that this referred to 'a more distinguished (*vornehmer*) shaykh', but this is not really the case. Bayt al-Aḥmar of Ḥāshid are the most distinguished shaykhs of all, yet they do not now refer to themselves, and are not referred to by others, as *nuqabā'*. In the histories they are occasionally given the title. On the other hand, many of the shaykhs at Baraṭ are still referred to, and refer to themselves, as *nuqabā'*: Aḥmar al-Sha'r, for instance, Abū Ra's, and Juzaylān. Al-Wazīr (1971: 150) suggests that *naqīb* is a Bakīlī term for what in Ḥāshid are called shaykhs or paramount shaykhs, but this is not so either. The following five families of Ḥāshid shaykhs are all *nuqabā'*: Bayt Shawīṭ (Khayār, Banī Ṣuraym), Bayt Nāshir (Khayār, Banī Ṣuraym), Bayt Dāwūd (Banī Qays, Banī Ṣuraym), Bayt Abū Miflah (al-Kalbiyyīn, Khārif), and Āl Dhū Fāri' (al-'Uṣaymāt). Families around them, of similar standing, are simply 'shaykhs', and one can properly refer to the *nuqabā'* themselves as shaykhs also.

The geographical distribution of the title is very uneven. There are few families given it in Ḥāshid, many at Baraṭ, many in Arḥaab, and some in Sufyān (e.g . al-Thamthamī and Ḥubaysh). Most probably the explanation is historical in the coarsest sense of mere contingency. Although Gochenour (1984: 103) lists *naqīb* as an early alternative to shaykh, along with sayyid, it is not in fact at all conspicuous in early Yemeni sources. The term itself is very old indeed (the leaders of the tribes around Yathrib in the Prophet's day were *nuqabā'*), but its widespread use in Yemen seems to come with and after the first Ottoman occupation, and one's suspicion must be that shaykhly families acquired the title as an Ottoman rank. Certainly it was used as a rank in Qāsimī times, and Niebuhr (1792: ii. 89) draws an interesting distinction: 'Nakib is the highest title that the Imam can confer. Schiech is a title that can only come by descent, and is peculiar to sovereign princes and independent lords.'

The term *'āqil* (literally, a 'wise' or 'intelligent' person) can be used of 'headmen' of all sorts, regardless of the extent of their power or prestige. For instance, Qāyid Sinān, the chief of all Arḥab whom the Turks recognized late in the last century, is mentioned in the histories as *'āqil al-ḍamān* (al-Ḥibshī 1980: 367–8). His predecessor as the chief the Turks recognized, 'Abd al-Wahhāb Maraḥ, is referred to as *mudīr* (Zabārah 1956: i. 1/38), the 'director' or 'administrator' of Arḥab. In ordinary usage, however, *'āqil* may also be applied to more minor figures than can shaykh; so, although every shaykh or *naqīb* might properly be called an *'āqil*, not every *'āqil* could be called a shaykh without causing heads to turn.

APPENDIX 4/1 DAWĀSHĪN

These non-tribal 'heralds' have been little studied, and some notes on them may therefore be of help. They seem always to have carried weapons, much as tribesmen do, but their distinctive weapon, as late as the early years of the civil war, was the lance. It is said that when a tribesman died, of whatever cause, a *dawshān* would often break a lance over the grave and be given largesse by the dead man's relatives.

As Chelhod suggests (1970: 79), *dawāshīn* in settled areas often lived in tents. They seem not to have been forbidden to own houses or land but were usually too poor to do so. The present *dawshān* of Khamir, Fāyiḍ Shaddād Sikrān, remembers his father owning a little land in the area before the revolution but being forced by debt to sell it. Another branch of the family had a small plot of land just east of Kharāsh and built on it a *daymah* or stone shelter (the word is the same as that for a kitchen but often used of small permanent shelters, for instance in the lowlands of al-Baṭanah). None the less there is a tendency (not a rule) for *dawāshīn* to be distinguished from tribesmen by their dwellings: where the tribesmen are predominantly settled one finds nomadic *dawāshīn*, and where there are nomadic tribesmen one finds *dawāshīn* in houses.

Each family of *dawāshīn* has a traditional area in which it can seek gifts from tribesmen. These areas do not always correspond to tribal territories. Banī Sikrān, for instance, work not only in Khamir but in all Banī Ṣuraym except the northernmost four 'ninths'. They also work Shawābah, out to the Jawf, Murhibah, and part of Nā'iṭ, though not the rest of Khārif. All of Khārif except Sikrān's part of Nā'iṭ is worked by *dawāshīn* of Bayt Abū Ḥusayn. Until just before the revolution, apparently, they also worked part of al-Taḥḍah in Murhibah. There would seem to have been some kind of 'swap' arrangement between the two families of *dawāshīn*, though no one was able to suggest the reason.

Separate branches of Banī Sikrān work most of Sufyān. However, the *dawāshīn* of Birkān are Bayt Nawbī, and those east of 'Iyān are Bayt Ṭashsh, neither of whom is related directly to Banī Sikrān. The Birkān and 'Iyān *dawāshīn* would seem always to have lived in houses and dealt with messages between the parts of Sufyān and with Sufyānī weddings. The tent-dwelling Sikrān dealt with Sufyān's meetings and markets.

Bayt Yaḥyā 'Abdullāh work all of 'Iyāḥ Surayḥ and half of Jawb, the other half being worked by Bayt Sa'd Allāh of Dhībīn. Jabal 'Iyāl Yazīd seems to be divided among three families of *dawāshīn*: Banī Ḥātim, Bayt Qarāqish, and Bayt 'Alī Muḥammad. Arḥab is mostly served by Bayt al-Hamshah, who seem all to have houses but spend most of their time in tents, wandering among the villages. There is another family of *dawāshīn* in

Arḥab named Bayt ʻAlī Aḥmad, who seem not to use tents at all. The division of labour between the two sets of *dawāshīn* seems to be much like that in Sufyān. Al-ʻUṣaymāt, ʻIdhar, and the northernmost four ninths of Banī Ṣuraym would seem to be the territory of Banī Muzlam. Bayt Maṭar serve Hamdān Ṣanʻā'.

Banī Muzlam appear in areas such as Wādī Ḥumrān twice at the time of the sorghum harvest, once for a contribution of unstripped sorghum heads called *kisb*, once for a contribution of sifted grain called *ḥarīs*. Similar contributions are made at the harvests of other grains also. On the major Islamic feast-days the *dawāshīn* announce that *al-ʻīd ʻind fulān*, 'the feast is with so-and-so', and the tribesman named then gives them cash or sheep, the cost of which is afterwards quietly shared out by the members of his village. Something of the kind would seem to be the case elsewhere too.

The leading *dawshān* of Dhū Muḥammad, Jārullāh b. Ḍayfullāh Dawmān (a man known as 'Tiny', *ṣughāyir*, on account of his huge bulk), says that all of Dhū Muḥammad's *dawāshīn* are from Banī Dawmān. Only one now lives at ʻInān (there used to be more before the revolution), but there are perhaps as many as forty members of this large *dawshān* family at Bayt al-Qayl. All of them live in houses, and they seem never to have counted among them any tent-dwellers as tribal sections around Baraṭ certainly do. The *dawāshīn* seem also to have always carried rifles as well as daggers, which their counterparts on the plateau do not.

In Dhū Ḥusayn the *dawāshīn* seem all to be from Banī Ịd and Banī Ḥawāyij. Again, in this tribe that counts many nomads or semi-nomads, the *dawāshīn* are all settled and have been for as long as anyone knows. There are a great many at Rajūzah and at al-Zāhir. Their homes, like those of qadis in the area, are spoken of as *muhajjar* ('protected', 'set aside'). The *dawāshīn*, however, are only *mu'amminīn* (able to protect) at home and have no right to offer escort since they have no *ʻarḍ*. *Dawāshīn* in both Dhū Muḥammad and Dhū Ḥusayn claim, none the less, to be *hijrah*, 'because we are all *bi-l-muḥaddash* (protected by an eleven-fold fine) like the qadis and sayyids', while their counterparts in al-ʻAmālisah, they say, are 'like *jīrān*, just four-fold'. On the plateau I have not heard either tribesmen or *dawāshīn* suggest such equivalence between 'heralds' and men of religion; but in the east, it should be remembered, men of religion are very thin on the ground, and the ordering of the different estates there may well not correspond to that on the plateau. Compare Ḥayyim Habshūsh's account of the area (Goitein 1941).

APPENDIX 4/2 SIGNATORIES TO DOCUMENTS

If a history of Upper Yemen is ever to be written, the names of signatories to local agreements will be an important resource. I have listed them here for each of three major documents quoted in the text and for the guaranty of the market at Ḥūth (Dresch forthcoming *a*) which I cite but do not quote. In the case of more modern documents those holding them asked that I not reproduce the names. The signatories of the Baraṭ *qawā'id* will, I hope, be given in a separate publication, as too will the signatories to the *tahjīr* of Ḥusayn and Ḥamīd al-Aḥmar.

Tahjīr of Bayt al-'Ukām (Muḥarram AH *1321)*

Dhū Muḥammad: Nājī Muḥsin Abū Ra's, 'Abdullāh Yaḥyā al-Muṭla'ī, Juzaylān b. 'Amr, Aḥmad Muḥsin Farḥān, Hādī Aḥmad, 'Alī Muḥammad 'Awfān, Muḥsin Aḥmad al-Kharāshī, Muqbil Murshid Ya'qūb (al-Ma'āṭirah, but listed with Dhū Muḥammad).

Dhū Ḥusayn: Ṣāliḥ Yaḥyā al-Badawī, 'Ā'iḍ Ḥusayn al-Farjī, 'Arfaj Yaḥyā al-Farjī, Nājī 'Aqlān al-Sha'bī, al-Naqīb Aḥsan Ṣāliḥ, 'Alī Hādī al-Hayyānī, Aḥmad Muḥsin Mulhibah (Banī Nawf but listed with Dhū Ḥusayn), Yaḥyā Muḥammad al-Aswad, 'Abdullāh Shamlān, 'Abdullāh Jazzār, Yaḥyā Hādī Ismā'īl.

Sufyān: Ḥaydar 'Alī 'Aṭiyyah, 'Alī 'Abdullāh Jābir, Yaḥyā Aḥsan al-Waṣmī, Jābir Abū Khurs al-Marānī, Murshid Yaḥyā Hudayyān, Qāyid Muḥammad Abū Jābir al-Marānī, Aḥmad Aḥmad Madḥash, Aḥmad Sālim al-'Usaylī, Aḥmad Mus'ad al-Tawbah, 'Alī Muṭlaq Mughniyyah, 'Alī Munaṣṣar Da'ākam, Aḥsan 'Āmir Abū Shams, Muqbil Hādī Abū Qillah, Yaḥyā 'Āṣī Waqqāz, Muqbil Qāyid Dhaybān, Mahdī Ṣāliḥ Mus'ad, Muḥammad Ḥusayn, Hādī Dā'il Qabūl, Sa'd 'Ā'iḍ Shintar, Aḥmad al-Thamthamī, Hādī Ṣāliḥ Ḥubaysh, Swaydān Muḥammad Farthān, Muḥammad Shamlān al-Marānī, 'Ā'iḍ Yaḥyā al-Marānī.

Āl Sālim: Ḥasan Nājī Mu'ayl al-Sālimī, Yaḥyā Ṣāliḥ Rabī'ī, Ḥusayn Qāyid Qumlān.

Āl 'Ammār: Dallāq Ṣāliḥ Habjah, Aḥmad Muṭlaq 'Andal, Nāṣir Aḥmad Khaḍrān.

al-'Uṣaymāt: Aḥmad Qāyid, Aḥmad Yaḥyā Fāri', Ṣāliḥ Nāṣir Fāri', Muḥammad Fāri'.

Tahjīr of Bayt al-Mu'ayyad (Shawwal AH *1336)*

The names only are roughly grouped by tribe on the original document. I have grouped for myself all the others that can be identified reliably.

al-'Uṣaymāt: Aḥmad 'Alī Abū Sa'īd, Ṣāliḥ 'Ā'iḍ Abū Sa'īd, Ḥusayn Munaṣṣar Fayshī, Qāyid Sa'ūd al-Ṣawlānī, 'Abdullāh 'Alī al-Ṣawlānī, Muḥammad 'Alī Bajjāsh, Hādī Ṣāliḥ al-Gharībī, Jābir Muḥammad Abū

Shawṣā, Ṣāliḥ 'Alī al-Muṭarī, Zāyid 'Awwāsh, Ḥasan Mus'ad Rawā'ī, Aḥmad Qāsim Rawā'ī, Munaṣṣar 'Alī al-Aḥmar, Ḥusayn Muḥammad Shāwish al-'Īdī, Ṣāliḥ Ḥusayn Abū Dāwūd al-Gharībī, Ḥusayn Qāsim al-Gharībī, Aḥmad 'Alī al-Aznam Fāri', Aḥmad Yaḥyā Fāri', Nāṣir Mabkhūt al-Aḥmar, Yaḥyā Ḥizām al-'Unāshī, Ṣāliḥ Ṣāliḥ Manīf.

Banī Ṣuraym: Ḥusayn 'Ā'iḍ Radmān al-Khayārī, Muḥmmad Hādī al-'Arjalī, Nājī Nāṣir al-'Arjalī, Sinān Sinān al-Jirāfī, Ḥusayn Aḥmad Sinān al-Jirāfī, Ṣāliḥ Muḥsin al-Ṣamūt, Ṣāliḥ 'Abdullāh Ḥashshār, Muḥammad Qāyid Qa'shān, Muqbil Mabkhūt al-Ḥalḥalī, 'Alī Ḥasan al-Ḥalḥalī, Muḥsin Muḥsin 'Imrān, 'Alī 'Alī Sha'lān al-'Uqayli, Ḥizām Ḥizām Shawīṭ.

'Idhar: Nājī Jābir Sabtān, Qāsim Qāyid Maghrabah, Qāyid Shāyi' al-Ghashshāsh.

Khārif: Yaḥyā 'Alī 'Abdullāh, Ḥizām Sa'd Mūdī, Muḥammad Hādī Abū Shawārib.

Hamdān: 'Alī Qāyid al-Ghashmī, Jibrān 'Alī Yaḥyā al-Ghashmī.

Not firmly identified: 'Alī Nāṣir Abū Kuhlān, Nāṣir 'Alī al-Shaḥb, Muqbil Mabkhūt Abū Dhakhīnah, Aḥmad Muḥammad Shāyi' (Dhū 'Īsā at al-Shaṭṭ), Hādī Ḥusayn Abū 'Albān, Muḥammad Hādī Abū Qashshah (Dhū Bāriq and Dhū Munaṣṣar), Murshid Ḥusayn al-Bāriq, Nāṣir Rafīq Shubaylī, Nāṣir Nāṣir Munṭash, Jābir 'Alī al-Najjār, Ḥizām Aḥmad al-Ḥanashī (Dhū Munṭash), Ṣāliḥ Muqbil al-Qushayrī, Nāṣir Ja'mān (Dhū Hadhyān), Ṣāliḥ Jibrān al-Damdamī, Jibrān Hādī al-Hadhyānī, Ṣāliḥ Muḥammad Abū 'Awjah, Muḥammad Jābir Jakhdam, Qāsim Muḥammad Jakhdam, 'Alī Aḥmad Ḥayjān, Nājī Jibrān al-'Aṣabah, Qāsim Khamīs, Jābir Māni' (Dhū Shāyi'ah), Aḥmad Muḥsin Farthān, Ḥusayn Mahdī al-Maḥraf, Nāṣir Hādī al-Zuhayd (Dhū Madhyāb), Nāṣir Muḥsin Saylān, Thābit Qāsim Zimām, Ṣāliḥ Nāṣir Sanḥān, Nāṣir Ḥizām, 'Ā'iḍ Yaḥyā al-Ghāwī, Yaḥyā Ḥizām al-Ṣalīḥ, Ḥusayn Nāṣir Ja'far, 'Alī Aḥmad Ṭayyāsh, Ḥusayn Murshid Ṭawwāf, Muḥammad Sirḥān al-Majānī, Nāṣir Nāṣir al-Shāmī, Muḥammad Ṣāliḥ al-Falaysī, 'Ā'iḍ 'Alī al-'Idharī, Alī Yaḥyā Sālim, Nāṣir 'Alī al-Aqra', Ḥamūd Ḥamūd al-'Armazī, Qāyid Muḥammad, Aḥmad Yaḥyā, Muḥammad Rājiḥ Tamīm.

Tahjīr of 'Iyān (Rabī' Awwal AH *1245)*

The names are not grouped by tribe on the original document, but for convenience I have grouped for myself those that can be identified reliably.

al-'Uṣaymāt: Shaykh Nāṣir 'Alī al-Aḥmar, Nāṣir Muṣliḥ al-Aḥmar, Yaḥyā Hādī Fāri', 'Ali (. . .) Fāri', 'Alī Samḥ Fāri', Yaḥyā Qāsim Fāri', Nāṣir Abū Dāwūd, Muqbil Muṣliḥ Fāri', Muṣliḥ Abū Shawṣā, Munaṣṣar Hādī 'Ukkām.

Banī Ṣuraym: Yaḥyā Hādī Dāwūd, Ḥusayn Nāshir, 'Alī Shams Nāshir, Aḥmad Hādī al-'Arjalī, Qāsim Nāṣir Ja'wān, Muḥammad 'Alī Ja'wān, Munaṣṣar Shawīṭ, 'Abdullāh Yaḥyā al-Ṣamūt, Ḥajj 'Alī al-Būmah, Aḥmad Nāshir al-Ḥashshār, Shaybān al-Jirāfī.

'Idhar: Qāyid Maghrabah, Yaḥyā 'Alī al-Dawḥamī.

Not firmly identified: Ḥusayn Hādī Musallam, Muqbil Aḥsan, Ṣāliḥ 'Alī Shahūf, Aḥmad Munaṣṣar, 'Alī Abū 'Awjah, Muqbil Yaḥyā, 'Alī Yaḥyā (. . .), Sāliḥ Ghālib, Muḥsin Salmah, Hādī Qāsim Zimām, Ṣāliḥ Yaḥyā Zimām, Ṣāliḥ Mismār, Muḥsin Nāshir Madāghish, Nāṣir Ṣāliḥ, Ghālib Qāsim Abū Shawī'ah, Muḥammad Shāwash.

Guaranty of Ḥūth market (Ramaḍān AH *1346)*

al-'Uṣaymāt (guarantors, ḍumanā'): Ḥusayn Nāṣir al-Aḥmar, Yaḥyā Muqbil Fāri', Muḥammad Ḥizām al-Gharībī, Mahdī 'Alī Manīf, Aḥmad 'Alī al-Aznam, Muḥammad 'Alī Aḥmad al-Aḥmar, Sha'lān Muḥammad al-Mu'ammarī, Yaḥyā Ḥizām al-Qaṣṣ.

Banī Ṣuraym (guarantors, ḍumanā'): Ṣāliḥ Mabkhūt Shawīṭ, Qāyid Muḥammad Qa'shān, 'Alī Ḥasan al-Ḥalḥalī, Aḥmad Yaḥyā Dāwūd, Ṣāliḥ 'Ā'iḍ Ṭamās, Yaḥyā Yaḥyā Za'karī.

al-'Uṣaymāt (secondary guarantors, rudamā'): Ḥamūd Ṣāliḥ Muṭarī, Sa'd Nājī al-La'sah, Muḥammad Aḥmad (. . .), Mu'ayḍ Muḥammad 'Awwāsh, Yaḥyā Qāsim Qarnān (. . .), Ḥusayn Khamīs, 'Abdullāh Hādī al-Maḥraq, Nuṣayb Hādī al-Dhīb, 'Alī Murshid al-Naqīb (Dhū Aḥmad 'Alī), 'Alī Munaṣṣar al-Shintarī, Hādī Muḥammad al-Ghulaysī, Ḥusayn Sa'd al-Rubū'ī, Jābir Munaṣṣar Bajjāsh, 'Alī Muḥammad al-Bayḥānī, Nāṣir Ḥamūd Qa'bān, Ḥusayn Munaṣṣar Fayshī, 'Alī Jābir Abū Shawṣā, Muṣliḥ Nāṣir (. . .), Muqbil Aḥmad Ghubays.

Banī Ṣuraym (secondary guarantors, rudamā'): Nāṣir Alī Fatḥ, Ṣāliḥ Ṣāliḥ Fāḍil al-Ghashmī, Ḥusayn Aḥmad al-Shāmī, Muṭlaq Muḥammad al-Sanīnī, Aḥmad Aḥmad Ja'rah, Yaḥyā Sinān al-Jirāfī, Sayyid Muṭarī al-Ghaylī, Muqbil Muqbil al-Dughaynī, 'Azīz Qannāf al-Ḥaydarī, Sinān Muḥammad Rājiḥ, Muḥammad Manṣūr 'Imrān.

al-'Uṣaymāt (bondsmen, ṣawānah): Nājī 'Alī Samḥ, Ṣāliḥ Ṣāliḥ Bathān, Muḥammad Hādī 'Abduh, 'Alī Qāyid al-Ṣuraymī, Muḥsin Yaḥyā Musarraḥ, Ḥamūd Muḥsin al-Aqra' (all of these from Dhū Faḍl); 'Alī Ḥizām Ḥājib, Murshid 'Alī al-Ziyādī, 'Abdullāh Nāṣir al-Barūshī (all of these from Banī Mu'mir); Nājī Mahdī al-Qudaysh, Hādī Nāṣir al-Sannadī, Qāsim Kandash, Aḥmad Murshid Saylah (all of these from Dhū Jabrah).

Banī Ṣuraym (bondsmen, ṣawānah): Aḥmad Ṣāliḥ Abū Fannah, Ṣāliḥ Munaṣṣar (. . .), Mu'ayḍ Ṣāliḥ Mu'ayḍ, Qannāf 'Alī Sha'fūl, Muḥsin

Muḥammad Nāshir, ʿAbdullāh Aḥmad Dhaybān, Yaḥyā ʿAlī al-Ṣamūt, Ṣāliḥ Munaṣṣar al-Muntaṣir, Aḥmad Ṣāliḥ Jaʿwān, Muqbil al-Akhram, Ḥusayn Aḥmad Ḥashshār.

APPENDIX 6/1: COLLOQUIAL POEMS

The poems transcribed and translated below were recited to me by Ḥajj Ḥasan Saʿd Qayfī of Khamir. At points the 'weight' of the lines is faulty (especially in the first pair of poems) and a word or syllable may be missing, which is probably entirely my fault. The sense is not at all in doubt. I have transcribed the poems as I heard them, however, in the hope that someone with a better ear than mine for scansion can restore the true metre. The translation is intentionally fairly free.

The first pair of poems dates from the Turkish period, and the battles referred to will be found in Zabārah's history (1956). The 'challenge' is said to have been composed by Sayyid ʿAbdullāh b. Ibrāhīm and the 'riposte' by Qadi Ḥasan b. Yaḥyā Ḥanash.

adrī al-ḥadīth ʿan al-maqām al-akbarā / wa-alladhī qāda al-juyūsh ilā al-wirā,
sulṭān-nā ʿabd al-ḥamīd la-hu l-bayḍā / mā dāmat al-afkār fī umm al-qurā.
min faḍli-hi akhraj li-nā man fayḍ-hu / fayḍ al-fuyūḍ wa-khayr man jād al-tharā
bi-ʿasākir min fityat al-atrāk / mā lāqū ʿadūw qaṭṭ illā dumirā.
sal bayt ʿadharān wa-sal jadhr fa-sal / yawm al-khamīs fa-sal bi-dhālik tukhbarā
mā ḥāshid mā ḥarf sufyān alladhī / malak al-ʿinān wa-l-asārī qad sarā
ḥattā taffaraq jamʿu-hum wa-tashattatū / lam yaṭlubūn sawā al-amān a-lam tarā
hādha huw al-fatḥ al-mubīn bi-ʿayni-hi / ḥaqqa ka-mā fattaḥa al-rasūl al-aẓharā.

I know the news of the great uprising
And all about him who led his troops backwards.
The right's with our Sultan ʿAbd al-Ḥamīd,
Which is still the opinion in Mecca city.
Out of his goodness he sent us Fayḍī,
A stream overflowing, the best the earth offers.
And with him came soldiers, the youth of the Turks,
Who met with no foe but they left them destroyed.
Just ask ʿAdharān, and just you ask Jadhr,
Ask Yawm al-Khamīs and for that matter tell me
Where's Ḥāshid now, and where's Ḥarf Sufyān?

He took al-'Inān and let out the prisoners
Till the enemy divided and all of them scattered—
Those who didn't surrender. Can you not see
That this is itself the 'manifest victory'
As the Prophet Muḥammad once won so completely?

yā qā'il qad qult zawar wa-munkarī / ka-miqlad khanzīr durar wa-jawharī,
thakalat umm-uk ḥayn qultu maqālatan / wa-madaḥt man huw bi-l-ma'āṣī jāhirī,
wa-madaḥt fayḍī al-la'īn wa-qult huw / khayr al-wulāh wa-khayr man jād al-tharā
min dhī ṭaghā wa-baghy 'alā al-islām / min dhī baddal al-aḥkām min dhī ghayrī
hāt al-dalīl min al-kitāb in kuntu / dhī dīn wa-dhī 'aqli raṣīn zākhirī
ammā midḥat ibn al-nabī muḥammad / khayr al-wulāh wa-khayr man jād al-tharā
kam waqa'at min jawā'ib la-hu / wa-shuhūd-hā al-a'dā fī-him atharā
bi-'asākir nabawiyyah zaydiyyah / mā lāqu 'adūw qaṭṭ illā dumirā
qad jā' min qawl al-nabī maqālah / qad qāla-hā qawlan ṣaḥīḥ wa-qararī
man aẓhara l-baghḍā' li-āli muḥammad / min ghayr al-ḥall hal li-dhālik munkirī?

What you have said is all lies and is wicked,
Like a necklace of pearls and jewels on a pig.
When you said what you said you bereaved your own mother.
When you praised a man who proclaims sin openly.
When you praised cursed Fayḍī and went on to say he
Was finest of rulers, the best the earth offers,
A man who's a tyrant, transgresses religion,
Who changes the judgments [of God] for others.
You'd take heed from the Book if you were religious,
If you were of calm and abundant intelligence.
As for praising [as we would] the son of the Prophet,
The finest of rulers, the best the earth offers,
How many answers has he returned him,
As the enemy witness who'll tell you about it,
With Zaydi soldiers, troops of the Prophet,
Who met with no foe but they left them destroyed?
There comes from the Prophet a noteworthy saying.
What he said was quite true and not open to question.
Who offers hate to the clan of Muḥammad
Is in the wrong. Or can you deny that?

The second pair of poems dates from the late 1920s. The 'challenge' is said to have been composed by Sayyid Yaḥyā Dhārī and the 'riposte' again by Ḥasan Ḥanash.

alā ablighū (li-nā?) anṣāra āli muḥammadin / wa-asyāfu fī-hā li-bāghī wa-mu'tadī.
fa-yā qawm-nā man sāri' al-ḥaqq inna-hu / sarī' wa-ḥizbu allāh hizban mu'ayyadī.
fa-lā tahdamū fī 'izzi-kum shāmikh al-dhurā / wa-mā qad banaytum min fukhārin wa-su'dadī.
nasaḥnā-kum an tuqbilū nasīḥat-hu / ka-mā al-nasḥu wājibun ka-marwā li-aḥmadī.

Listen, tell the supporters of the clan of Muḥammad,
Whose swords are now given to traitorous aggression,
O army of ours: who throws down the truth
Is himself thrown down. God's party's the chosen one.
Don't because of your pride threaten mighty achievements,
Nor what you have built up of power and of glory.
We advise you to heed the advice that he's given you,
For advice is a duty, as the Prophet has told us.

alā (qul la-hum?) ahlan wa-sahlan bi-mā atā / min al-sayyid al-nadb al-karīm al-mumajjadī.
'amād al-hudā wa-l-dīn yaḥyā alladhī la-hu / al-makārimu lā tuḥṣā 'alā kulli mashhadī.
taqaddam 'alay-nā bi-l-nuẓāmi ka-anna-nā / naṣāra wa-man min-nā baghiyyun wa-mu'tadī.
wa-lā bayna-nā fī l-dīni maylun wa-inna-nā / 'alā dīni khayri l-mursalīna muḥammadī.
fa-qātal-na wa-nāṣar-nā al-ā'immah dā'iman / fa-kam min qatīlin ṣāra fi l-qabri mulḥadī.
wa-ālāti ḥarbin qad akhadh-nā wa-mawnatan / fa-raddat 'alay-nā inta yā rabbi mushhadī
alā fa-nẓarū mā al-aṣlu fi l-fitnati llātī / buli-nā bi-hā yā bn al-nabiyyi muḥammadī.
wa-lā miṣra shallay-nā wa-lā arḍa bābilin / fa-kam dhī l-taḥarrī fi tawallī [?] al-matradi.
'adim-nā ḥayātin an raḍī-nā bi-dhillatin / fa-ḥāshā wa-lā yabqā 'alā l-arḍi ḥāshidī.

Well, welcome indeed to what's just arrived
From the noble and excellent sayyid who's deputized
By Yaḥyā, that pillar of guidance and piety
Who's won numberless victories on all fields of battle.
You send us this poem as if we're all Christians

And all of our people are traitorous aggressors.
There's no one among us religiously deviant.
Our religion's Muḥammad's, the finest of messengers.
We've fought for Imams and always supported them,
And how many dead have been buried to prove it?
We took weapons of war and the stores to go with them,
Which rebound now against us, as you, Lord, are witness.
So look what the cause was of all this disorder
We wore ourselves out in, you son of the Prophet.
We didn't take Egypt, we didn't take Babylon;
And what's the account for you taking al-Matrad?
Should we give up our lives to accept that we're humbled?
No, never, until the land's left with no Ḥāshidīs.

Arabic References Cited

References are entered in the order of the Roman alphabet, ignoring the definite article (al-) and diacritical marks.

'Abd al-Ilāh b. 'Abdullāh, 1964. ('Abd al-Malik al-Ṭayyib) *Naksat al-thawrah fi l-yaman*. (No place of publication indicated; photocopy in my possession.)

Abū Ghānim, Faḍl b. 'Alī, 1985. *al-Bunyat al-qabaliyyah fi l-yaman bayn al-istimrār wa-l-taghyīr*. Damascus: Maṭba'at al-Kātib al-'Arabī.

al-Akwa', Ismā'īl b. 'Alī, 1980. *al-Madāris al-islāmiyyah fi l-yaman*. Ṣan'ā': Ṣan'ā' University (offset print by Dār al-Fikr, Damascus).

—— 1984. *al-Amthāl al-yamāniyyah*, 2 vols. Beirut: Mu'assasat al-Risālah; Ṣan'ā': Maktabat al-Jayl al-Jadīd.

al-'Alawī, 'Alī b. Muḥammad, 1972. *Sīrat al-hādī ilā l-ḥaqq yaḥyā b. al-ḥusayn*, ed. Suhayl Zakkār. Beirut: Dār al-Fikr.

al-Ānisī, 'Abd al-Raḥmān, 1978. *Tarjī' al-aṭyār bi-marqaṣ al-ish'ār*, ed. 'Abd al-Raḥmān al-Iryānī and 'Abdullāh al-A'brī. Beirut: Dār al-'Awdah; Ṣan'ā': Dār al-Kalimah.

al-'Aynī, Muḥsin, 1957. *Ma'ārik wa-mu'āmarāt ḍidd qaḍiyyat al-yaman*. (No place of publication indicated; photocopy in my possession.)

al-Baraddūnī, 'Abdullāh, 1983. *al-Yaman al-jumhūrī*. Damascus: Maṭba'at al-Kātib al-'Arabī.

Ḍubbāt, 1978. *Asrār wa-wathā'iq al-thawrat al-yamaniyyah* (lajnah min al-ḍubbāt al-aḥrār). Beirut: Dār al-'Awdah, Dār al-Kalimah.

al-Ghazzālī, 'Abd al-Ḥafīẓ b. Yaḥyā, 1979. *al-Diyāt wa-l-urūsh fi l-sharī'at al-islāmiyyah*, ed. Ṭaha Aḥmad Abū Zayd. Cairo: Maktabat 'Ālam al-Fikr.

al-Hamdānī, al-Ḥasan b. Aḥmad [1884–91], 1948. *al-Iklīl min akhbār al-yaman wa-insān ḥimyar*, vol. x, ed. Muḥibb al-Dīn al-Khaṭīb. Cairo: al-Maṭba'at al-Salafiyyah.

—— 1966. *al-Iklīl min akhbār al-yaman wa-insān ḥimyar*, vol. ii, ed. Muḥammad 'Alī al-Akwa'. Cairo: Maṭba'at al-Sunnat al-Muḥammadiyyah.

—— 1968. *Ṣifat jazīrat al-'arab: Geographie der Arabischen Halbinsel*, ed. D. H. Müller. Repr. of original Leiden edn. Amsterdam: Oriental Press.

—— 1977. *al-Iklīl min akhbār al-yaman wa-insān ḥimyar*, vol. i, ed. Muḥammad 'Alī al-Akwa'. Baghdad: Dār al-Ḥuriyyah.

al-Ḥasanī, 'Abdullāh, 1966. *Mu'tamar ḥaraḍ: wathā'iq wa-maḥāḍir*. Beirut: Dār al-Kātib al-Jadīd.

al-Ḥibshī, 'Abdullāh b. Muḥammad (ed.), 1980. *Ḥawliyyāt yamāniyyah min sanah 1225 h. ilā sanah 1316 h.* Ṣan'ā': Wizārat al-I'lām wa-l-Thaqāfah.

al-Ḥibshī, 1983. *Maṣādir al-fikr al-ʿarabī al-islāmī fi l-yaman*. Ṣanʿā': Markaz al-Dirāsāt al-Yamaniyyah.

al-Ḥimyarī, Nashwān b. Saʿīd, 1916. *Muntakhabāt fī akhbār al-yaman min kitāb shams al-ʿulūm*, ed. ʿAzīmuddīn Aḥmad. Gibb Memorial Series xxiv. Leiden: E. J. Brill; London: Luzac and Co.

—— 1957. *Mulūk ḥimyar wa-aqyāl al-yaman*, ed. ʿAlī Ismāʿīl al-Mu'ayyad and Ismāʿil Aḥmad al-Jirāfī. Cairo: al-Maṭbaʿat al-Salafiyyah.

Ibn Saʿd, Muḥammad, 1905. *Kitāb al-ṭabaqāt al-kabīr*, 9 vols., ed. E. Sachau *et al.* Leiden: E. J. Brill.

ʿĪsā b. Luṭfallāh, 1981. *Rawḥ al-rūḥ fī-mā jarā baʿd al-mi'at al-tāsiʿah min al-fitan wa-l-futūḥ*. Photoreprint of MS. Ṣanʿā': Wizārat al-Iʿlām wa-l-Thaqāfah.

al-Jirāfī, ʿAbdullāh b. ʿAbd al-Karīm, 1951. *al-Muqtaṭaf min ta'rīkh al-yaman*. Cairo: ʿĪsā al-Bābī al-Ḥalābī.

al-Juzaylān, ʿAbdullāh, 1977. *al-Ta'rīkh al-sirrī li-l-thawrat al-yamaniyyah*. Beirut: Dār al-ʿAwdah.

al-Kibsī, Muḥammad b. Ismāʿīl, n.d. *al-Laṭā'if al-sanniyyah fi akhbār al-mamālik al-yamaniyyah*. Beirut, Maṭbaʿat al-Saʿādah.

al-Laḥjī, Musallam b. Muḥammad. MS I. 'Kitāb fī-hī shay' min akhbār al-zaydiyyah bi-l-yaman'. Ahlwardt 9644; Prussian Staatsbibliothek, Berlin. Mf. 1300, fo. 38*b*–70.

—— MS IV. 'Akhbār al-zaydiyyah bi-l-yaman' vol. iv. MS (photocopy in my possession, kindly procured for me by Muḥammad al-Muṭahhar, Ṣanʿā').

al-Madāḥ, Amīrah bint ʿAlī, 1982. *al-ʿUthmāniyyūn wa-l-imām al-qāsim b. muḥammad b. ʿalī fi l-yaman*. Rasā'il Jāmaʿiyyah, 4. Jeddah: Tihāmah Publications–Dār ʿUkāz li-l-Ṭabāʿah.

Majd al-Dīn b. Muḥammad b. Manṣūr al-Ḥasanī al-Mu'ayyadī, n. d. *al-Tuḥaf sharḥ al-zulaf* (no place of publication indicated).

al-Maqāliḥ, ʿAbd al-ʿAzīz, 1982. *Qirā'ah fī fikr al-zaydiyyah wa-l-muʿtazilah*. Beirut: Dār al-ʿAwdah.

Markaz, 1981. *Thawrah 26 September: dirāsāt wa-shahādāt li-l-ta'rīkh*. Ṣanʿā': Markaz al-Dirāsāt wa-l-Buḥūth al-Yamanī; Beirut: Maktabat al-Jamāhīr.

—— 1982. *Thawrah 1948: al-mīlād wa-l-masīrah wa-l-mu'aththirāt*. Ṣanʿā': Markaz al-Dirāsāt wa-l-Buḥūth al-Yamanī; Beirut, Dār al-ʿAwdah.

—— 1983. *Wathā'iq al-mu'tamar al-shaʿbī: al-ʿām al-awwal*. Ṣanʿā': Markaz al-Dirāsāt wa-l-Buḥūth al-Yamanī.

al-Mujāhid, ʿAbdullāh b. Muḥammad, 1980. *Usus zirāʿah wa-intāj al-maḥāṣil al-ḥaqliyyah fi l-arāḍī al-yamaniyyah*. Cairo: ʿĀlam al-Kutub.

al-Murtaḍā, Aḥmad b. Yaḥyā, 1973. *Sharḥ al-azhār fī fiqh al-ā'immat al-aṭhār*, 4 vols. Ṣanʿā': Maktabat al-Yaman al-Kubrā.

al-Nahrawālī, Quṭb al-Dīn b. Muḥammad, 1968. *al-Barq al-yamānī fī l-fatḥ al-'uthmānī*, ed. Ḥamad al-Jāsir. Nuṣūṣ wa-abḥāth jughrāfiyyah wa-ta'rīkhiyyah 'an jazīrat al-'arab, 6. Riyad: Dār al-Yamāmah.

Nājī, Sulṭān, 1977. *al-Ta'rīkh al-'askarī li-l-yaman 1839–1967*. Aden: publisher unclear.

Nubdhah. *Kitāb al-nubdhat al-mushīrah ilā jumal min 'uyūn al-sīrah fī akhbār . . . al-manṣūr bi-llāh . . . al-qāsim b. muḥammad*. Photo-reproduction of MS. Ṣan'ā': Maktabat al-Yaman al-Kubrā.

Nu'mān, Muḥammad b. Aḥmad, 1965. *al-Aṭrāf al-ma'niyyah fī l-yaman*. Beirut: Mu'assasat al-Ḍabbān.

Ṣabrah, 'Alī b. 'Alī, 1972. *Naḥw idyulūjiyyah 'arabiyyah*. Ta'izz: al-Sharikat al-Yamaniyyah li-l-Ṭabā'ah.

Sālim, al-Sayyid Muṣṭafā, 1971. *Takwīn al-yaman al-ḥadith: al-yaman wa-l-imām yaḥyā 1904–1948*, 2nd edn. Cairo: Ma'had al-Buḥūth wa-l-Dirāsāt al-'Arabiyyah.

—— 1974. *al-Fatḥ al-'uthmānī al-awwal li-l-yaman 1538–1635*, 2nd edn. Cairo: Ma'had al-Baḥūth wa-l-Dirāsāt al-'Arabiyyah.

—— 1982. *Wathā'iq yamaniyyah*. Cairo: al-Maṭba'at al-Fanniyyah.

al-Saqqāf, Abū Bakr, 1977. *'al-Zubayrī shā'iran wa-mufakkiran'*, in *al-Zubayrī: shā'irun wa-munāḍilun*, ed. al-Saqqāf. Beirut: Dār al-'Awdah.

al-Sayāghī, Ḥusayn b. Aḥmad (ed.), 1978. *Ṣafaḥāt majhūlah min ta'rīkh al-yaman*. Ṣan'ā': Markaz al-Dirāsāt al-Yamaniyyah.

Sayyid, Aymān Fu'ād. 1974. *Maṣādir ta'rīkh al-yaman fī l-'aṣr al-islāmī*. Cairo: Institut Français d'Archéologie Orientale.

al-Shahārī, Muḥammad b. 'Alī, 1972. *al-Yaman: al-thawrah fī l-janūb wa-l-intikāsah fī l-shimāl*. Cairo: 'Ālam al-Kutub.

al-Shamāḥī, 'Abdullāh b. 'Abd al-Wahhāb, 1972. *al-Yaman: al-insān wa-l-ḥaḍārah*. Cairo: Dār al-Hunā.

al-Shāmī, Aḥmad, 1979. *Jināyat al-akwa' 'alā dhakhā'ir al-hamdānī* Beirut: Dār al-Nafā'is.

Sharaf al-Dīn, Aḥmad b. Ḥusayn, 1964. *al-Yaman 'abr al-ta'rīkh*, 2nd edn. Cairo: Maṭba'at al-Sunnat al-Muḥammadiyyah.

—— 1968. *Ta'rīkh al-fikr al-islāmī fī l-yaman*. Cairo: Maṭba'at al-Kaylānī.

al-Shawkānī, Muḥammad b. 'Alī, 1929 (AH 1348). *al-Badr al-ṭāli' bi-maḥāsin min ba'd al-qurn al-sābi'*, 2 vols., ed. Muḥammad Zabārah. Photoreprint (n. d.). Beirut: Dār al-Ma'rifah.

Ṣubḥī, Aḥmad b. Maḥmūd, 1980. *al-Zaydiyyah*, pt. 1 of vol. ii of Ṣubḥī's *'Ilm al-kalām*. Alexandria: Munsha'at al-Ma'ārif.

al-Ṭabarī, Abū Ja'far Muḥammad, 1968. *Ta'rīkh al-rusul wa-l-mulūk*, 10 vols, ed. Muḥammad Abū l-Faḍl Ibrāhīm. Dhakhā'ir al-'Arab, 30. Cairo: Dār al-Ma'ārif.

al-Thawr, 'Abdullāh b. Aḥmad, 1968. *Thawrat al-yaman: 1948–1968*. Cairo: Dār al-Hunā.

al-ʿUdī, Ḥamūd, 1980. *al-Turāth al-shaʿbī wa-ʿalāqat-hu bi-tanmiyyah fi l-bilād al-nāmiyyah: dirāsah taṭbīqiyyah ʿan al-mujtamaʿ al-yamanī.* Cairo: ʿĀlam al-Kutub; Ṣanʿāʾ: Markaz al-Dirāsāt al-Yamaniyyah.

al-ʿUlaymī, Rashād, 1986. *al-Qaḍāʾ al-qabalī fi l-mujtamaʿ al-yamanī.* Ṣanʿāʾ(?): Dār al-Wādī li-l-Nashr wa-l-Tawzīʿ.

al-Wāsiʿī, ʿAbd al-Wāsiʿ, 1928. *Taʾrīkh al-yaman.* Cairo: al-Maṭbaʿat al-Salafiyyah.

al-Wazīr, Zayd b. ʿAlī, 1965. *Muʾtamar khamir: nuṣūṣ wa-wathāʾiq.* (No place of publication indicated; copy held by University Library, Cambridge.)

—— 1971. *Muḥāwalah li-fahm al-mushkilat al-yamaniyyah.* Beirut: Muʾassasat al-Risālah.

al-Wishalī, Ismāʿīl b. Muḥammad, 1982. *Nashr al-thanāʾ al-ḥasan al-munbiʾ bi-baʿḍ ḥawādith al-zaman*, ed. Muḥammad al-Shuʿaybī. Ṣanʿāʾ: Maṭābiʿ al-Yaman al-ʿAṣriyyah.

Yaḥyā b. al-Ḥusayn b. al-Manṣūr al-Qāsim, 1968. *Ghāyat al-amānī fī akhbār al-quṭr al-yamānī*, 2 vols., ed. Saʿīd ʿAbd al-Fattāḥ ʿAshur. Cairo: Dār al-Kātib al-ʿArabī.

Zabārah, Muḥammad b. Muḥammad, 1929 (AH 1348). *Nayl al-waṭar min tarājim rijāl al-yaman fi l-qurn al-thālith ʿashar*, 2 vols. bound as one. Photoreprint. Ṣanʿāʾ: Markaz al-Dirāsāt wa-l-Buḥūth al-Yamanī; Beirut: Dār al-ʿAwdah.

—— 1941 (AH 1360). *Nashr al-ʿarf li-nubalāʾ al-yaman baʿd al-alf ilā 1357 hijriyyah* vol. i. Photoreprint. Ṣanʿāʾ: Markaz al-Dirāsāt wa-l-Buḥūth al-Yamanī.

—— 1952 (AH 1372). *Āʾimmat al-yaman: al-juzʾ al-awwal* (From al-Hādī to AH 1000; there is some doubt as to the status of *al-juzʾ al-thānī*). Taʿizz: Maṭbaʿat al-Naṣr al-Nāṣiriyyah.

—— 1956 (AH 1376). *ʾĀʾimmat al-yaman bi-l-qurn al-rābiʿ ʿashar*, 3 vols. (of which the first contains two separately paginated parts). Cairo: al-Maṭbaʿat al-Salafiyyah.

—— 1957 (AH 1376). *al-Anbāʾ ʿan dawlat bilqīs wa-sabaʾ.* Cairo: al-Maṭbaʿat al-Salafiyyah.

—— 1958 (AH 1377). *Nashr al-ʿarf li-nubalāʾ al-yaman baʿd al-alf ilā 1357 hijriyyah* vol. ii. Cairo: al-Maṭbaʿat al-Salafiyyah.

Zayd, ʿAlī b. Muḥammad, 1981. *Muʿtazilat al-yaman: dawlat al-hādī wa-fikr-hu.* Beirut: Dār al-ʿAwdah; Ṣanʿāʾ: Markaz al-Dirāsāt wa-l-Buḥuth al-Yamanī.

al-Zubayrī, Muḥammad, 1961. *Maʾsāh wāq al-wāq.* Cairo. (No publisher indicated; copy in my possession.)

References Cited in European Languages

References are entered alphabetically by author, ignoring the definite article (al-) in the case of Arabic names.

Abu Zahra, N., 1982. *Sidi Ameur: A Tunisian Village*. London: Ithaca Press.

Adra, N., 1982. 'Qabyālah: The Tribal Concept in the Central Highlands of the Yemen Arab Republic', Ph.D. thesis, Temple University.

Abdin, al-Tayyib Zein, al-, 1975. 'Islam and the State (1940–1972, Yemen)', Ph.D. thesis, Cambridge University.

—— 1976. 'The Yemeni Constitution and its Religious Orientation', *Arabian Studies*, 3: 115–25.

'Amri, H. A., al-, 1985. *The Yemen in the Eighteenth and Nineteenth Centuries: A Political and Intellectual History*. London: Ithaca Press.

Althusser, L., and E. Balibar, 1970. *Reading Capital*, trans. Ben Brewster. London: New Left Books.

Anderson, B., 1983. *Imagined Communities: Reflections on the Origin and Spread of Nationalism*. London: Verso Editions and New Left Books.

Ardener, E. W., 1971*a*. 'Introductory Essay', in E. Ardener (ed.), *Social Anthropology and Language*. ASA monograph 10. London: Tavistock.

—— 1971*b*. 'Social Anthropology and the Historicity of Historical Linguistics', ibid.

—— 1971*c*. 'The New Anthropology and Its Critics', *Man* (n.s.), 6/3: 449–67.

Baldry, J., 1976. 'Al-Yaman and the Turkish Occupation, 1849–1914', *Arabica*, 23 fasc. 2: 156–96.

—— 1977. 'Imam Yaḥyā and the Yamanī Uprising of 1904–1907' '*Abr-Nahrain*, 18: 33–73.

Barker, E. (ed.), 1947. *Social Contract: Essays by Locke, Hume, and Rousseau*. World's Classics 511. London: Oxford University Press.

Barnes, J. A., 1971. 'Time Flies Like an Arrow', *Man* (n.s.), 6/4: 537–52.

Bates, D., and A. Rassam, 1983. *Peoples and Cultures of the Middle East*. Englewood Cliffs, NJ: Prentice-Hall.

Bede, the venerable, 1968. *A History of the English Church and People*, trans. Leo Sherley-Price. Harmondsworth, Middx.: Penguin Books.

Beeston, A. F. L., 1971. 'The Functional Significance of the Old South Arabian "Town"', *Proceedings of the Seminar for Arabian Studies*, 2: 26–8.

—— 1972. 'Kingship in Ancient South Arabia', *Journal of Economic and Social History of the Orient*, 15: 256–68.

Beeston, A. F. L., 1976. 'Warfare in Ancient South Arabia: Second to Third Centuries AD', *Qaḥṭān: Studies in Old South Arabian Epigraphy*, fasc. 3. London: Luzac and Co.

Behnstedt, P. 1985. *Die Nordjemenitischen Dialekte*, i. *Atlas*. Jemenstudien 3. Wiesbaden: Reichert.

Benet, F. 1970. 'Explosive Markets: The Berber Highlands', repr. in L. Sweet (ed.), *Peoples and Cultures of the Middle East*, i. Garden City, NY: Natural History Press.

Black-Michaud, J., 1980. *Feuding Societies*, paperback edn. Oxford: Basil Blackwell.

Bloch, M., 1977. 'The Past and the Present in the Present', *Man* (n.s.), 12/2: 278–92.

Bohannan, P., 1967. 'Concepts of Time among the Tiv of Nigeria', repr. in J. Middleton (ed.), *Myth and Cosmos*. American Museum Sourcebooks in Anthropology. Garden City, NY: Natural History Press.

Bourdieu, P., 1965. 'The Sentiment of Honour in Kabyle Society', in J. G. Peristiany (ed.), *Honour and Shame: The Values of Mediterranean Society*. London: Weidenfeld and Nicolson.

—— 1977. *Outline of a Theory of Practice*, trans. Richard Nice. Cambridge: Cambridge University Press.

Boxhall, P., 1974. 'The Diary of a Mocha Coffee Agent', *Arabian Studies*, 1: 102–18.

Braudel, F., 1972. 'History and the Social Sciences', trans. Keith Folca, in P. Burke (ed.), *Economy and Society in Early Modern Europe: Essays from Annales*. London: Routledge and Kegan Paul.

Carapico, S., 1979. 'Local Resources for Development: A Preliminary Socio-economic Profile of Hodeidah and Hajjah Governorates', Ṣan'ā': USAID.

Caton, S. C., 1984. 'Tribal Poetry as Political Rhetoric from Khawlān al-Ṭiyāl, Yemen Arab Republic', Ph.D. thesis, University of Chicago.

—— 1985. 'The Poetic Construction of Self', *Anthropological Quarterly*, 58/4: 141–50.

—— 1986. 'Salām Taḥīyah: Greetings from the Highlands of Yemen', *American Ethnologist*, 13/2: 290–308.

Chapman, M., 1978. *The Gaelic Vision in Scottish Culture*. London: Croom Helm; Montreal: McGill–Queen's University Press.

Chelhod, J., 1979. 'L'Organisation sociale au Yémen', *L'Ethnographie*, 64: 61–86.

—— 1973. 'Les Cérémonies du mariage au Yémen', *Objets et mondes*, 13: 3–34.

—— 1976. 'Le Droit inter-tribal dans les hauts plateaux du Yémen', *al-Bāḥith* (Studia Instituti Anthropos, St Augustin bei Bonn) 28: 49–76.

Cohen, A. 1965. *Arab Border Villages in Israel*. Manchester: Manchester University Press.

Collingwood, R. G., 1926. 'Some Perplexities about Time: With an Attempted Solution', *Proceedings of the Aristotelian Society*, 26/8: 135–50.

—— 1933. *An Essay on Philosophical Method*. London: Oxford University Press.

—— 1961. *The Idea of History*, paperback edn. London: Oxford University Press.

CPO, 1977. *Statistical Yearbook, 1976–1977*. Ṣan'ā': Central Planning Organization, Office of the Prime Minister.

—— 1980. *Statistical Yearbook, 1979–1980*. Ṣan'ā': Central Planning Organization, Office of the Prime Minister.

—— 1982. *Statistical Yearbook, 1981*. Ṣan'ā': Central Planning Organization, Office of the Prime Minister.

—— 1983. *Statistical Yearbook, 1983*. Ṣan'ā': Central Planning Organization, Office of the Prime Minister.

Crone, P., 1980. *Slaves on Horses: The Evolution of the Islamic Polity*. Cambridge: Cambridge University Press.

Cunnison, I. G., 1951. *History on the Luapula*. Rhodes–Livingstone Institute Paper 21. London: Oxford University Press.

Diem, W., 1973. *Skizzen Jemenitischer Dialekte*. Beiruter Texte und Studien 13, Orient-Institut der Deutschen Morgenländischen Gesellschaft. Beirut and Wiesbaden: Franz Steiner Verlag.

Dorsky, S., 1986. *Women of 'Amrān: A Middle Eastern Ethnographic Study*. Salt Lake City: University of Utah Press.

Dostal, W., 1974. 'Sozio-ökonomische Aspekte der Stammesdemokratie in Nordost-Yemen', *Sociologus* (n.s.), 24/1: 1–15.

—— 1983. 'Some Remarks on the Ritual Significance of the Bull in pre-Islamic South Arabia', in R. Bidwell and G. R. Smith (eds.), *Arabian and Islamic Studies Presented to R. B. Serjeant*. London and New York: Longman.

Douglas, J. L., 1984. 'The Free Yemeni Movement: 1935–1962', in B. R. Pridham (ed.), *Contemporary Yemen: Politics and Historical Background*. London: Croom Helm.

—— 1987. *The Free Yemeni Movement: 1935–1962*. Beirut: American University; New York: Syracuse University Press.

Dresch, P. K., 1981. 'The Several Peaces of Yemeni Tribes', *Journal of the Anthropological Society of Oxford*, 12/2: 73–86.

—— 1984*a*. 'The Position of Shaykhs among the Northern Tribes of Yemen', *Man* (n.s.), 19/1: 31–49.

—— 1984*b*. 'Tribal Relations and Political History in Upper Yemen', in B. R. Pridham (ed.), *Contemporary Yemen: Politics and Historical Background*. London: Croom Helm.

—— 1986. 'The Significance of the Course Events take in Segmentary Systems', *American Ethnologist*, 13/2: 309–24.

Dresch, P. K., 1987*a*. 'Episodes in a Dispute between Yemeni Tribes: Text and Translation of a Colloquial Arabic Document', *Der Islam*, 64/1: 68–6.

—— 1987*b*. 'Placing the Blame: A Means of Enforcing Obligations in Upper Yemen', *Anthropos*, 82: 427–43.

—— forthcoming *a*. 'Guaranty of the Market at Ḥūth' (to appear in *Arabian Studies*, 8, Middle East Centre, Cambridge).

—— forthcoming *b*. 'The Tribes of Ḥāshid wa-Bakīl as Historical and Geographical Entities' (to appear in W. Madelung (ed.), *Festschrift for Prof. A. F. L. Beeston*.

—— forthcoming *c*. 'Keeping the Imam's Peace: A Response to Tribal Disorder in the Late 1950s' (to appear in *Peuples mediterranéens*).

—— forthcoming *d*. 'Imams and Tribes: The Writing and Acting of History in Upper Yemen' (to appear in P. S. Khoury and J. Kostiner (eds.), *Tribes and State Formation in the Middle East*).

Dumont, L., 1970. *Homo Hierarchicus: An Essay on the Caste System*, trans. Mark Sainsbury. Chicago: University of Chicago Press.

—— 1977. *From Mandeville to Marx: The Genesis and Triumph of Economic Ideology*. Chicago: University of Chicago Press.

—— 1986. *Essays on Individualism: Modern Ideology in Anthropological Perspective*. Chicago and London: University of Chicago Press.

Duri, A., 1962. 'The Iraq School of History to the Ninth Century: A Sketch', in P. Holt and B. Lewis (eds.), *Historians of the Middle East*. London: Oxford University Press.

Eickelman, D. F., 1977. 'Time in a Complex Society', *Ethnology* 16: 39–55.

—— 1987. 'Ibadism and the Sectarian Perspective', in B. R. Pridham (ed.), *Oman: Economic, Social and Strategic Developments*. London: Croom Helm.

Errington, S., 1979. 'Some Comments on Style in the Meanings of the Past', *Journal of Asian Studies*, 38: 231–44.

Evans-Pritchard, E. E., 1937. *Witchcraft, Oracles and Magic among the Azande*. London: Oxford University Press.

—— 1940. *The Nuer: A Description of the Modes of Livelihood and Political Institutions of a Nilotic People*. London: Oxford University Press.

——. *The Sanusi of Cyrenaica*. London: Oxford University Press.

—— 1956. *Nuer Religion*. London and New York: Oxford University Press.

—— 1973. 'Some Reminiscences and Reflections on Fieldwork', *Journal of the Anthropological Society of Oxford*, 4/2: 1–12.

Fardon, R. (eds.), 1985. *Power and Knowledge: Anthropological and Sociological Approaches*. Edinburgh: Scottish Academic Press.

Fogg, W., 1938. 'A Tribal Market in the Spanish Zone of Morocco', *Africa*, 11/4: 428–58.

Geertz, C., 1966. 'Person, Time and Conduct in Bali: An Essay in Cultural Analysis', Yale South East Asia Program, Cultural Report Series, 14.

Gellner, E., 1964. *Thought and Change.* London: Weidenfeld and Nicolson.

—— 1981. *Muslim Society.* Cambridge Studies in Social Anthropology 32. Cambridge: Cambridge University Press.

Gerholm, T., 1977. *Market, Mosque and Mafraj: Social Inequality in a Yemeni Town.* Stockholm Studies in Anthropology 5. Stockholm: Stockholm University Press.

Gibb, H. A. R., 1962. 'Islamic Biographical Literature', in P. Holt and B. Lewis (eds.), *Historians of the Middle East.* London: Oxford University Press.

Glaser, E., 1884. 'Meine Reise durch Arḥab und Ḥāschid', *Petermanns Mitteilungen*, 30: 170–83, 204–13.

—— 1885. 'Die Kastengliederung im Jemen', *Ausland*, 58: 201–5.

—— 1903. *Eduard Glasers Reise nach Mārib*, ed. D. H. Müller and N. Rhodokanakis. Vienna: Alfred Hölder.

Gochenour, D. T., 1984. 'The Penetration of Zaydi Islam into Early Medieval Yemen', Ph.D. thesis, Harvard University.

Goitein, S. D. (ed.), 1941. *Travels in Yemen: An Account of Joseph Halévy's Journey to Najrān in the Year 1870 Written in San'ani Arabic by his Guide Hayyim Habshush.* Jerusalem: Hebrew University Press.

Granquist, H., 1931. 'Marriage Conditions in a Palestinian Village', *Commentationes Humanarum Litterarum*, 3/8 (Helsingfors: Societas Scientiarum Fennica), contd. in *Commentationes*, 6/8 (1935).

Guillaume, A., 1955. *The Life of Muḥammad: A Translation of Ibn Isḥāq's Sīrat Rasūl Allāh.* Karachi: Oxford University Press.

Halliday, F., 1974. *Arabia Without Sultans.* Harmondsworth, Middx., Penguin.

Hamdani, A., 1976. 'Evolution of the Organisational Structure of the Fāṭimī Da'wah: The Yemeni and Persian Contribution', *Arabian Studies*, 3: 85–114.

Herzfeld, M., 1980. 'Honour and Shame: Problems in the Comparative Analysis of Moral Systems', *Man* (n.s.), 15: 339–51.

—— 1984. 'The Horns of the Mediterraneanist Dilemma', *American Anthropologist*, 11/3: 439–54.

Holy, L., 1985. 'Power, Agnation and Marriage in the Middle East', in R. Fardon (ed.), *Power and Knowledge: Anthropological and Sociological Approaches.* Edinburgh: Scottish Academic Press.

Hourani, A. H., 1981. *The Emergence of the Modern Middle East.* London and Basingstoke: Macmillan.

Hurgronje, C. Snouck, 1970. *Mekka in the Latter Part of the Nineteenth Century*, photoreprint of 1931 edn. Leiden: E. J. Brill.

Ibn Khaldūn, 1967. *The Muqaddimah: An Introduction to History*, 3 vols., trans. Franz Rosenthal. Bollingen Series 43. Princeton: Princeton University Press.

Iryani, K., al-, 1968. 'Un témoignage sur le Yémen: l'Organisation sociale de la tribu des Ḥāshid', *Cahiers de l'orient contemporain*, 70.

James, W., 1979. *'Kwanim Pa: The Making of the Uduk people*. Oxford: Oxford University Press.

Johnson, D. L., 1969. *The Nature of Nomadism*. Department of Geography Research Papers 118. University of Chicago.

Jollife, J. E. A., 1961. *The Constitutional History of Medieval England*, 4th edn. London: Adam and Charles Black.

Kay, H. C., 1892. *Yaman: Its Early Mediaeval History*. London: Edward Arnold.

Kerr, M. H., 1971. *The Arab Cold War*, 3rd edn. New York: Oxford University Press.

Keyser, J., 1974. 'The Middle Eastern Case: Is There a Marriage Rule?', *Ethnology*, 12/3: 293–309.

Khoury, P. S., 1982. 'The Tribal Shaykh, French Tribal Policy and the Nationalist Movement in Syria between Two World Wars', *Middle Eastern Studies*, 18/2: 180–93.

Kopp, H., 1977. *Al-Qāsim: Wirtschafts- und sozialgeographische Strukturen und Entwicklungsprozesse in einem Dorf des jemenitischen Hochlandes*. Wiesbaden: Dr Ludwig Reichart.

—— 1981. *Agrargeographie der Arabischen Republik Yemen*. Erlanger Geographische Arbeiten 11. Erlangen: Vorstand der Fränkischen Geographischen Gesellschaft.

—— 1985. 'Land Usage and its Implications for Yemeni Agriculture', in B. R. Pridham (ed.), *Economy, Society and Culture in Contemporary Yemen*. London: Croom Helm.

Lancaster, W., 1979. 'The Development and Function of the Shaykh in Nomad/Settler Symbiosis', *Arabian Studies*, 6: 195–204.

—— 1981. *The Rwala Bedouin Today*. Changing Cultures series. Cambridge: Cambridge University Press.

Lévi-Strauss, C., 1966. *The Savage Mind*. London: Weidenfeld and Nicolson.

Madelung, W., 1965. *Der Imām al-Qāsim ibn Ibrāhīm und die Glaubenslehre der Zaiditen*. Berlin: Walter de Gruyter.

—— 1971. 'Imāma', in *Encyclopaedia of Islam*, 2nd edn., iii. 1163–9. London: Luzac and Co.; Leiden: E. J. Brill.

—— 1972. 'A Muṭarrifī Manuscript', in *Proceedings of the 6th Congress of Arabic and Islamic Studies*, Historie och Antikvitets Akademien, Filologisk-filosofisk serien 15, 75–83. Stockholm.

—— 1979. 'The *Sīrat al-Amīrayn* . . . as a Historical Source', in A. al-Ansary *et al.* (eds.), *Studies in the History of Arabia: Sources for the History of Arabia*, pt 2. Riyad: Riyad University Press.

—— forthcoming. 'The Origins of the Yemenite *hijrah*', to appear in W. Madelung (ed.) *Festschrift for A. F. L. Beeston.*

Makdisi, G., 1986. 'The Diary in Islamic Historiography: Some Reflections', *History and Theory*, 25/2: 173–85.

Marx, E., 1977. 'The Tribe as a Unit of Subsistence', *American Anthropologist*, 79: 343–63.

Mauss, M., 1970. *The Gift: Forms and Functions of Exchange in Archaic Societies*, trans. Ian Cunnison. London: Cohen and West.

—— (with Henri Beuchat) 1979. *Seasonal Variations of the Eskimo: A Study in Social Morphology*, trans. J. J. Fox. London and Boston: Routledge and Kegan Paul.

Meeker, M. E., 1976. 'Meaning and Society in the Near East: Examples from the Black Sea Turks and the Levantine Arabs', *International Journal of Middle East Studies*, 7: 243–70, 383–422.

—— 1979. *Literature and Violence in North Arabia.* Cambridge Studies in Cultural Systems. Cambridge: Cambridge University Press.

Messick, B. M., 1978. 'Transactions in Ibb: Economy and Society in a Yemeni Highland Town', Ph.D. thesis, Princeton University.

Metcalf, B. D., 1984. *Moral Conduct and Authority: The Place of* adab *in South Asian Islam.* Berkeley, Los Angeles, and London: University of California Press.

Mundy, M., 1979. 'Women's Inheritance of Land in Highland Yemen', *Arabian Studies*, 5: 161–87.

—— 1985. 'Agricultural Development in the Yemeni Tihama: The Past Ten Years', in B. R. Pridham (ed.), *Economy, Society and Culture in Contemporary Yemen*, London: Croom Helm.

Musil, A., 1928. *Manners and Customs of the Rwala Bedouins.* American Geographical Society, Oriental Explorations and Studies, 6. New York: Charles R. Crane.

Naji, S., 1984. 'The Genesis of the Call for Yemeni Unity', in B. R. Pridham (ed.), *Contemporary Yemen: Politics and Historical Background.* London: Croom Helm.

Niebuhr, C., 1792. *Travels through Arabia and other Countries of the East*, 2 vols., trans. Robert Heron. Edinburgh: R. Morison and Son. Photoreprint. Beirut: Librairie du Liban.

O'Ballance, E., 1971. *The War in Yemen.* London: Faber and Faber.

Parry, J., 1986. '*The Gift*, the Indian Gift and the "Indian Gift" ', *Man* (n.s.), 21/3: 453–73.

Patai, R., 1965. 'The Structure of Endogamous Unilineal Descent Groups', *South Western Journal of Anthropology*, 21: 325–50.

Peters, E. L., 1963. 'Aspects of Rank and Status among Muslims in a Lebanese Village', in J. R. Pitt-Rivers (ed.), *Mediterranean Countrymen.* Paris and the Hague: Mouton.

Peters, E. L., 1967. 'Some Structural Aspects of the Feud among the Camel-herding Bedouin of Cyrenaica', *Africa*, 37/2: 261–82.
——1976. 'From Particularism to Universalism in the Religion of the Cyrenaican Bedouin', *Bulletin of the British Society for Middle East Studies*, 3/1: 5–14.
—— 1977. 'Local History in Two Arab Communities', *Bulletin of the British Society for Middle East Studies*, 4/2: 71–81.
—— 1984. 'The Paucity of Ritual among Middle Eastern Pastoralists', in A. S. Ahmed and D. M. Hart (eds.), *Islam in Tribal Societies*. London: Routledge and Kegan Paul.
Peterson, J. E., 1981*a*. 'The Yemen Arab Republic and the Politics of Balance', *Asian Affairs*, 12/3: 254–66.
—— 1981b. 'Conflict in the Yemen and Superpower Involvement.' Center for Contemporary Arab Studies, Georgetown University, Occasional Papers series.
—— 1982. *Yemen: The Search for a Modern State*. London and Canberra: Croom Helm.
Pitt-Rivers, J. R., 1977. *The Fate of Shechem*. Cambridge Studies in Social Anthropology 19. Cambridge: Cambridge University Press.
Playfair, R., 1859. *A History of Arabia Felix or Yemen*. (Bombay Presidency.) Photoreprint. St Leonard's: Ad Orientem; Amsterdam: Philo Press.
Pocock, D. F. 1967. 'The Anthropology of Time-reckoning'. Repr. in J. Middleton (ed.), *Myth and Cosmos: Readings in Mythology and Symbolism*. American Museum Sourcebooks in Anthropology. Garden City, NY: Natural History Press.
—— 1971. *Social Anthropology*, 2nd edn. London: Sheed and Ward.
Puin, G-R., 1984. 'The Yemenite *hijrah* Concept of Tribal Protection', in Tarif Khalidi (ed.), *Land Reform and Social Transformation in the Middle East*. Beirut: American University.
Rathjens, C., 1951. 'Ṭāghūt gegen Scherī'ah: Gewohnheitsrecht und Islamisches Recht bei den Gabilen des jemenitischen Hochlandes', *Jahrbuch des Museums für Ländes- und Völkerkunde*, 172–87. Stuttgart: Linden-Museum.
Rihani, A., 1930. *Arabian Peak and Desert: Travels in al-Yaman*. Boston and New York: Houghton Mifflin and Co.
Robertson Smith, W., 1885. *Kinship and Marriage in Early Arabia*. Cambridge: Cambridge University Press.
Robin, C., 1977. 'Le Pays de Hamdān et Ḫawlan Qudā'a (Nord-Yémen) avant l'Islam', thèse de trosième cycle, Paris. Reworked as *Les Hautes-Terres du Nord-Yémen avant l'Islam*. Leiden: Nederlands Historisch–Archaeologisch Instituut te Istanbul, 1982.
—— 1978. 'Le Problème de Hamdān: Des *qayl*s aux trois tribus', *Proceedings of the Seminar for Arabian Studies*, 8: 46–52.

—— 1982. 'Esquisse d'une histoire de l'organisation tribal en Arabie du sud antique', in P. Bonnenfant (ed.), *La Péninsule arabique d'aujourd'hui*, ii. Paris: Centre d'Etudes et de Recherches sur l'Orient Arabe Contemporain (CNRS).

Rosaldo, R., 1980. *Ilongot Head-hunting: 1883–1974*. Stanford: Stanford University Press.

Rosenfeld, H., 1965. 'The Social Composition of the Military in the Process of State Formation in the Arabian Desert', *Journal of the Royal Anthropological Institute*, 95/1: 75–86 and 95/2: 174–94.

Rosenthal, F., 1952. *A History of Muslim Historiography*. Leiden: E. J. Brill.

—— 1962. 'The Influence of the Biblical tradition on Muslim Historiography', in P. Holt and B. Lewis (eds.), *Historians of the Middle East*. London: Oxford University Press.

Rossie, E., 1939. *L'Arabo parlato a Ṣan'ā'*. Rome: Istituto per l'Oriente.

—— 1948. 'Il Diritto consuetudinario delle tribu Arabe del Yemen', *Rivista degli studi orientali*, 23: 1–36.

Runciman, W., 1982. 'Origins of States: The Case of Archaic Greece', *Comparative Studies in Society and History*, 24: 351–77.

Ryckmans, J., 1983. 'Biblical and Old South Arabian Institutions: Some Parallels', in R. Bidwell and G. R. Smith (eds.), *Arabian and Islamic Studies Presented to R. B. Serjeant*. London and New York: Longman.

Sahlins, M., 1981. *Historical Metaphors and Mythical Realities: Structure and History in the Early History of the Sandwich Islands*. Ann Arbor: University of Michigan Press.

Saidi, A. K. al-, 1981. *Die Oppositionsbewegung im Jemen zur Zeit Imām Yaḥyās und der Putsch von 1948*. Berlin: Baalbek Verlag.

Saussure, F., de, 1986. *Course in General Linguistics*, trans. Roy Harris. La Salle, Ill.: Open Court Press.

Schmidt, D. A., 1968. *Yemen: The Unknown War*. London: Bodley Head; New York: Holt Rinehart and Winston.

Schweizer, G., 1985. 'Social and Economic Change in the Rural Distribution System: Weekly Markets in the Yemen Arab Republic', in B. R. Pridham (ed.), *Economy, Society and Culture in Contemporary Yemen*. London: Croom Helm.

Scott, H., 1942. *In the High Yemen*. London: John Murray.

Serjeant, R. B., 1949. 'Two Yemenite Djinn'. *Bulletin of the School of Oriental and African Studies*, 13/4: 4–6.

—— 1962. 'Ḥaram and Ḥawṭah: The Sacred Enclave in Arabia', in 'Abd al-Raḥmān al-Badawī (ed.), *Mélanges Taha Husain*, Cairo: Dār al-Ma'ārif.

—— 1969. 'The Zaydis', in A. J. Arberry (ed.), *Religion in the Middle East*, ii. Cambridge: Cambridge University Press.

Serjeant, R. B., 1974. 'The Cultivation of Cereals in Mediaeval Yemen', *Arabian Studies*, 1: 25–74.

—— 1977. 'South Arabia', in C. van Nieuwenhuijza (ed.), *Commoners, Climbers and Notables*. Leiden: E. J. Brill.

—— 1978. 'The *sunnah jāmi'ah*: Pacts with the Yathrib Jews and the *taḥrīm* of Yathrib', *Bulletin of the School of Oriental and African Studies*, 41/1: 1–42.

—— 1979. 'The Yemeni Poet al-Zubayrī and his Polemic against the Zaydi Imams', *Arabian Studies*, 5: 87–130.

—— 1982. 'The Interplay between Tribal Affinities and Religious (Zaydi) Authority in the Yemen', *al-Abḥāth*, 30 (special volume on State and Society in the Arab World, ed. Fuad Khuri), 11–50.

——1983. 'The Post-medieval and Modern History of Ṣan'ā' and the Yemen, *c.*953–1382/1515–1962', in R. B. Serjeant and R. Lewcock (eds.), *Ṣan'ā': An Arabian Islamic City*, London: World of Islam Festival Trust.

Shāmī, A., al-, 1975. 'Yemeni Literature in Ḥajjah Prisons 1367/1948–1374/1955', *Arabian Studies*, 2: 42–59.

Siegel, J., 1979. *Shadow and Sound: The Historical Thought of a Sumatran People.* Chicago and London: University of Chicago Press.

Steffen, H. 1978. *Final Report of the Swiss Airphoto Interpretation Team* (Airphoto Interpretation Project of the Swiss Technical Co-operation Service, Berne). Dept. of Geography, University of Zurich (for CPO, Ṣan'ā').

Stevenson, T. B., 1985. *Social Change in a Yemeni Highlands Town.* Salt Lake City: University of Utah Press.

Stookey, R. W., 1974. 'Social Structure and Politics in the Yemen Arab Republic', *Middle East Journal*, 28/3: 248–60; 28/4: 409–18.

—— 1978. *Yemen: The Politics of the Yemen Arab Republic.* Boulder, Colo.: Westview Press.

Strathern, M., 1985. 'Knowing Power and Being Equivocal: Three Melanesian Contexts', in R. Fardon (ed.), *Power and Knowledge: Anthropological and Sociological Approaches.* Edinburgh: Scottish Academic Press.

Strothman, R., 1934. 'al-Zaidīya', in *Encyclopaedia of Islam*, 1st edn., iv. 1196–8. London: Luzac and Co.; Leiden: E. J. Brill.

Swanson, J., 1985. 'Emigrant Remittances and Local Development Co-operatives in the Yemen Arab Republic', in B. R. Pridham (ed.), *Economy, Society and Culture in Contemporary Yemen.* London: Croom Helm.

Tritton, A. S., 1925. *The Rise of the Imams of Sanaa.* London: Oxford University Press.

Tutwiler, R., 1977. 'General Survey of Social, Economic and Administrative Divisions in Mahweet Province', Ṣan'ā': USAID.

—— 1987. 'Tribe, Tribute and Trade: Social Class Formation in Highland Yemen', Ph.D. thesis, State University of New York, Binghamton, NY.

Tutwiler, R., and S. Carapico, 1981. *Yemeni Agriculture and Economic Change*. Yemen Development Series 1. Ṣan'ā': American Institute for Yemeni Studies.

Van Arendonk, C., 1960. *Les Debuts de l'imamat zaidite au Yémen*, trans. J. Ryckmans. Publications de la Fondation de Goeje 18. Leiden: E. J. Brill.

Varisco, D. M., 1982*a*. 'The *arḍ* in Highland Yemeni Agriculture', *Tools and Tillage*, 4/3: 158–72.

—— 1982*b*. 'The Adaptive Dynamics of Water Allocation in al-Ahjur, Yemen Arab Republic', Ph.D. thesis, University of Pennsylvania.

—— 1985. 'The Production of Sorghum (*dhurah*) in Yemen', *Arabian Studies*, 7: 53–88.

—— 1986. 'On the Meaning of Chewing: The Significance of *qāt* (*Catha edulis*) in the Yemen Arab Republic', *International Journal of Middle East Studies*, 18/1: 1–13.

Varisco, D. M., and N. Adra, 1981,. 'Affluence and the Concept of Tribe', in R. F. Salisbury and E. Tooker (eds.), *Affluence and Cultural Survival*. Proceedings of the American Ethnological Society. Washington, D.C.

Waldman, M. Roberts, 1981. 'The Otherwise Un-noteworthy Year 711', *Critical Inquiry*, 7/4: 784–92.

Weber, M., 1970. 'Politics as a Vocation', in H. H. Gerth and C. Wright Mills (eds.), *From Max Weber: Essays in Sociology* (Paperback edn.). London: Routledge and Kegan Paul. (First published 1919, repr. in *Gesammelte Politische Schriften*, 1921).

Weir, S., 1984. 'Tribe, *hijra* and *medina* in North-west Yemen', paper presented at the Franco-British Symposium on the Comparative Analysis of Arab and Muslim cities, Birbeck College, London.

—— 1985. *Qāt in Yemen: Consumption and Social Change*. London: British Museum Publications.

White, H., 1980. 'The Value of Narrativity in the Representation of Reality', *Critical Inquiry*, 7/1: 5–27.

Wilkinson, J. C., 1977. *Water and Tribal Settlement in South-East Arabia*. Oxford Research Studies in Geography. Oxford: Oxford University Press.

—— 1983. 'Traditional Concepts of Territory in South East Arabia, *The Geographical Journal*, 149/3: 301–15.

—— 1987. *The Imamate Tradition of Oman*, Cambridge Middle East Library. Cambridge: Cambridge University Press.

Wilson, R. T. O. 1980. 'The Investigation, Collection and Evaluation of Geographical Material in Yemeni Texts for the Mapping of Historical North-west Yemen', Ph.D. thesis, Cambridge University.

Wilson, R. T. O., 1981. 'Al-Hamdānı's Description of Ḥāshid and Bakīl, *Preedings of the Seminar for Arabian Studies*, 11: 95–104.

Wyman-Bury, G., 1915. *Arabia Infelix: or, the Turks in Yemen*. London: Macmillan.

Yalman, N., 1969. 'De Tocqueville in India: An Essay on the Caste System', *Man* (n.s.), 4/1: 123–31.

Zulfa, M., al-, 1982. 'Village Communities in Bilād Rufaydah: Their Political and Economic Organisation', *Arabian Studies*, 6: 77–96.

Index